Organization of Behavior in Face-to-Face Interaction

World Anthropology

General Editor

SOL TAX

Patrons

CLAUDE LÉVI-STRAUSS

MARGARET MEAD

LAILA SHUKRY EL HAMAMSY

M. N. SRINIVAS

MOUTON PUBLISHERS · THE HAGUE · PARIS

DISTRIBUTED IN THE USA AND CANADA BY ALDINE, CHICAGO

Organization of Behavior in Face-to-Face Interaction

Editors

ADAM KENDON
RICHARD M. HARRIS
MARY RITCHIE KEY

PHILLIPS MEMORIAL
LIBRARY
PROVIDENCE COLLEGE

MOUTON PUBLISHERS · THE HAGUE · PARIS

DISTRIBUTED IN THE USA AND CANADA BY ALDINE, CHICAGO

BF
637
C45
O73

Copyright © 1975 by Mouton & Co. All rights reserved.
No part of this publication may be reproduced,
stored in a retrieval system, or transmitted,
in any form or by any means, electronic, mechanical,
photocopying, recording or otherwise without the
written permission of Mouton Publishers, The Hague
Distributed in the United States of America and Canada
by Aldine Publishing Company, Chicago, Illinois
ISBN 90-279-7569-8 (Mouton)
0-202-01146-1 (Aldine)
Jacket photo by Cas Oorthuys
Cover and jacket design by Jurriaan Schrofer
Indexes by John Jennings
Printed in the Netherlands

General Editor's Preface

In order to understand species similarities and differences of all kinds — biological, psychological, social, cultural, linguistic — anthropology has always been interdisciplinary, calling upon whoever appeared to have knowledge relevant to a problem. The present book, which catches the human sciences at a moment of discovery, is an excellent example. It reaches back to a primordial problem in human relations — the behavior of people when facing one another in small groups — to ask how we can discover which regularities might turn out to be universal in the species, and why. It is authored by practitioners of psychology, sociology, anthropology, ethnology, linguistics, and mathematics and is a prelude to the discovery, from scratch, of cultural differences which modify human behavior. This requires as well the broadest worldwide participation. Hence the occasion — and atmosphere — of an international Congress.

Like most contemporary sciences, anthropology is a product of the European tradition. Some argue that it is a product of colonialism, with one small and self-interested part of the species dominating the study of the whole. If we are to understand the species, our science needs substantial input from scholars who represent a variety of the world's cultures. It was a deliberate purpose of the IXth International Congress of Anthropological and Ethnological Sciences to provide impetus in this direction. The *World Anthropology* volumes, therefore, offer a first glimpse of a human science in which members from all societies have played an active role. Each of the books is designed to be self-contained; each is an attempt to update its particular sector of scientific knowledge and is written by specialists from all parts of the world.

Each volume should be read and reviewed individually as a separate volume on its own given subject. The set as a whole will indicate what changes are in store for anthropology as scholars from the developing countries join in studying the species of which we are all a part.

The IXth Congress was planned from the beginning not only to include as many of the scholars from every part of the world as possible, but also with a view toward the eventual publication of the papers in high-quality volumes. At previous Congresses scholars were invited to bring papers which were then read out loud. They were necessarily limited in length; many were only summarized; there was little time for discussion; and the sparse discussion could only be in one language. The IXth Congress was an experiment aimed at changing this. Papers were written with the intention of exchanging them before the Congress, particularly in extensive pre-Congress sessions; they were not intended to be read at the Congress, that time being devoted to discussions — discussions which were simultaneously and professionally translated into five languages. The method for eliciting the papers was structured to make as representative a sample as was allowable when scholarly creativity — hence self-selection — was critically important. Scholars were asked both to propose papers of their own and to suggest topics for sessions of the Congress which they might edit into volumes. All were then informed of the suggestions and encouraged to re-think their own papers and the topics. The process, therefore, was a continuous one of feedback and exchange and it has continued to be so even after the Congress. The some two thousand papers comprising *World Anthropology* certainly then offer a substantial sample of world anthropology. It has been said that anthropology is at a turning point; if this is so, these volumes will be the historical direction-markers.

As might have been foreseen in the first post-colonial generation, the large majority of the Congress papers (82 percent) are the work of scholars identified with the industrialized world which fathered our traditional discipline and the institution of the Congress itself: Eastern Europe (15 percent); Western Europe (16 percent); North America (47 percent); Japan, South Africa, Australia, and New Zealand (4 percent). Only 18 percent of the papers are from developing areas: Africa (4 percent); Asia-Oceania (9 percent); Latin America (5 percent). Aside from the substantial representation from the U.S.S.R. and the nations of Eastern Europe, a significant difference between this corpus of written material and that of other Congresses is the addition of the large proportion of contributions from Africa, Asia, and Latin America. "Only 18 percent" is two to four times as great a proportion as that of other Congresses;

moreover, 18 percent of 2,000 papers is 360 papers, 10 times the number of "Third World" papers presented at previous Congresses. In fact, these 360 papers are more than the total of ALL papers published after the last International Congress of Anthropological and Ethnological Sciences which was held in the United States (Philadelphia, 1956).

The significance of the increase is not simply quantitative. The input of scholars from areas which have until recently been no more than subject matter for anthropology represents both feedback and also long-awaited theoretical contributions from the perspectives of very different cultural, social and historical traditions. Many who attended the IXth Congress were convinced that anthropology would not be the same in the future. The fact that the next Congress (India, 1978) will be our first in the "Third World" may be symbolic of the change. Meanwhile, sober consideration of the present set of books will show how much, and just where and how, our discipline is being revolutionized.

Among the other books in this series which will especially interest readers of the present volume are those on language, psychology, primate behavior, ritual education, and social theory.

Chicago, Illinois   SOL TAX
July 14, 1975

Preface

The articles collected in this volume were presented and discussed at a Research Conference held in the Department of Psychology of the University of Chicago. The proceedings of the Conference were reported to a session of the IXth International Congress of Anthropological and Ethnological Sciences in Chicago on September 3. This report serves as the basis for the Introduction.

The Conference was originally thought of by Richard Harris, who did much of the preliminary correspondemce, and who was responsible for getting the conference accepted as part of the program of the IXth Congress. Adam Kendon and Mary Ritchie Key joined forces with Harris to form an Organizing Committee in November of 1972, when Kendon also agreed to act as Chairman. Victor H. Yngve, of the University of Chicago joined the Committee to handle local arrangements. He was given much assistance by Starkey Duncan, and together they took care of the innumerable details of housing and hosting the participants and the conference sessions. We are very grateful indeed to the Department of Psychology of the University of Chicago for allowing us to use a room for the Conference sessions, free of charge, and for a small grant in aid of various running expenses. Without this assistance, the Conference would not have been possible. We should also like to thank Bronx State Hospital, New York, and Temple University, Philadelphia, for bearing some of the costs of postage and telephone calls.

ADAM KENDON   RICHARD M. HARRIS   MARY RITCHIE KEY

Australian National   *Bronx State Hospital*   *University of California*
University, Canberra   *Bronx, New York*   *Irvine, California*

Table of Contents

General Editor's Preface   v
Preface   IX
Introduction   1
   by *Adam Kendon*

PART ONE: THEORETICAL PERSPECTIVES

A Human Ethological Approach to Communication: Ideas in
   Transit Around the Cartesian Impasse   19
   by *Harvey B. Sarles*
Human Linguistics and Face-to-Face Interaction   47
   by *Victor H. Yngve*
Models and Epistemologies in the Study of Interaction   63
   by *Albert E. Scheflen*

PART TWO: METHODOLOGICAL STUDIES

When Infant and Adult Communicate How Do They
   Synchronize Their Behaviors?   95
   by *M. Bullowa*
Tonic Aspects of Behavior in Interaction   127
   by *Siegfried Frey*
Facial Expression Dialect: An Example   151
   by *Henry W. Seaford, Jr.*

PART THREE: ORGANIZATION OF BEHAVIOR IN SOCIAL ENCOUNTERS

Micro-Territories in Human Interaction by *Albert E. Scheflen*	159
One Function of Proxemic Shifts in Face-to-Face Interaction by *Frederick Erickson*	175
Coverbal Behavior Associated with Conversation Turns by *Norman N. Markel*	189
Interaction Units during Speaking Turns in Dyadic, Face-to-Face Conversations by *Starkey Duncan, Jr.*	199
Communicative Functions of Phatic Communion by *John Laver*	215

PART FOUR: BEHAVIOR IN INTERACTION AND LINGUISTIC THEORY

The Correlation of Gestures and Verbalizations in First Language Acquisition by *Walburga von Raffler Engel*	241
Paralanguage, Communication, and Cognition by *Richard M. Harris* and *David Rubinstein*	251
Linguistic and Paralinguistic Interchange by *Philip Lieberman*	277
Cross-Cultural Study of Paralinguistic "Alternants" in Face-to-Face Interaction by *Fernando Poyatos*	285
Face-to-Face Interaction: Signs to Language by *William C. Stokoe, Jr.*	315
Problems and Methods of Psycholinguistics in Face-to-Face Communication by *A. A. Leontiev*	339

PART FIVE: INTERACTION, SOCIAL RELATIONSHIPS, AND SOCIAL STRUCTURE

Territoriality and the Spatial Regulation of Interaction by *Ian Vine*	357
Expressive Interaction and Social Structure: Play and an Emergent Game Form in an Israeli Social Setting by *Don Handelman*	389

Interactions and the Control of Behavior 415
by *Glen McBride*

PART SIX: CULTURAL DIFFERENCES IN COMMUNICATIONAL BEHAVIOR

Communicative Styles in Two Cultures: Japan and the United States 427
by *Dean C. Barnlund*
Culture-Style Factors in Face-to-Face Interaction 457
by *Alan Lomax*

POSTSCRIPTS

Domains of Definition in Interaction: Postscript to Expressive Interaction and Social Structure 477
by *Don Handelman*
Afterthoughts 483
by *Frederick Erickson*

Biographical Notes 487

Index of Names 495

Index of Subjects 501

Introduction

ADAM KENDON

This introduction is based upon a report of the pre-Congress conference on face-to-face interaction that was read to a session of the IXth International Congress of Anthropological and Ethnological Sciences. In this report an attempt was made to characterize the main topics that were dealt with at the conference and to comment upon some of the more important themes that were discussed. It is reproduced here in full, though with some minor changes, but a few paragraphs have been added in order to provide some historical perspective. As we shall see, the approach taken in this conference to the study of interaction is relatively recent. However, as a discussant at the Congress session reminded us, the study of face-to-face interaction is by no means new. Indeed, it has been a focus of attention in social science at least since the beginning of the century.

One of the earliest social scientists to focus upon interaction was Georg Simmel. For him "SOCIETY is merely the name for a number of individuals, connected by interaction" (Coser 1965: 5). He believed that the main concern of sociology should be with the phenomena of face-to-face interaction. He published several essays which were directly concerned with certain forms of behavior in face-to-face situations, such as sociable conversation and coquetry, and in a well-known passage from his *Soziologie*, published in 1908, excerpted by Park and Burgess in their early and influential reader (1924) he deals with the "sociology of the senses," showing how the sensory organs are mobilized in interaction, including such topics as the interactional significance of mutual eye-to-eye gazes.

Simmel had an important influence upon the development of the

Chicago school of descriptive sociology, where a great deal of attention was paid to behavior in face-to-face situations. Paralleling this development, and closely related to it, was the growth of symbolic interactionism. This was developed by Cooley (1902) and later by Mead (1934), who emphasized the importance of understanding interaction for throwing light upon some of the key concepts of social psychology, such as the "self." By the second and third decades of this century, studies were emerging, particularly from industrial settings, which laid great stress on the importance of the "primary group" as the immediate setting for the behavior of individuals. This focused the interest of many upon the interrelations of behavior of people in each other's immediate presence. A parallel development in anthropology, the emergence of "functionalism," likewise led to a focus of interest upon the interrelationships between people and thus a concern with how they actually behaved in each other's presence.

These developments led to the emergence of several different methods of measuring behavior in face-to-face interaction, and in the fourth and fifth decades of this century there was a considerable increase in literature on face-to-face interaction. It is of interest to note that this literature is scarcely referred to by the contributors to this conference. Indeed, the approach represented here appears to be a separate and more recent development.

In the approach taken in this conference the focus of interest is upon the BEHAVIOR of face-to-face interaction and how it functions interactively. In this it contrasts with earlier approaches in which the phenomena of interaction were studied, not for their own sake, but because it was felt that by studying interaction light would be thrown upon the structure of social institutions or on the nature of human relationships. In the present approach the questions of concern have to do with the means by which occasions of interaction per se are brought off. Thus we find great interest in the description of patterns of speech or body motion as they occur in interaction. Linguistics and ethology, in particular, at least insofar as these are descriptive sciences, have had great influence here. We may also observe the influence of communication theory and general systems theory.

One of the earliest attempts to deal with behavior in face-to-face interaction was developed by Eliot Chapple. Here the attempt was made to identify some measurable aspects of behavior in terms of which consistent predictions could be made. Chapple has found, for instance, that individuals show certain characteristics in the way they pattern their periods of activity in time. He identifies a unit of behavior known as an ACTION which, in talking situations, comprises the duration of time an individual spends in active speech or gesture. The frequency and duration of actions may be measured within occasions of interaction, and various quantitative indices of the individual's interactive performance may be extracted. These have been found to be predictive of how the individual may behave in a variety of other interactive situations (Chapple and Lindemann 1942; Chapple and Donald 1947; Matarazzo, Saslow, and Matarazzo 1956; Kendon 1963). Chapple has also proposed that patterns of social organization and the structure of social relationships may be described in terms of the frequency and patterning of interaction (Chapple 1940; Chapple and Coon 1942; Arensberg 1972). It will be seen, however, that Chapple's interest is in finding a single dimension of behavior which can provide a means of assessing individual differences in interaction style, and a means of giving quantitative expression to social relationships and social organization structure. Thus Chapple's focus, though upon behavior, is upon behavior as a means of measuring something else. His approach, though effective in giving a means of assessing the consequences of interaction, and having implications for the nature of that phenomenon, does not focus primarily on behavior in face-to-face interaction in all its complexity.

A rather different and more widely used approach to the analysis of interaction is one in which an attempt is made to devise categories in terms of which the CONTENT of what people communicate to one another could be classified. Here the usual procedure has been for observers to score the behavior in an interacting group in terms of sets of predetermined categories of meaning. The various frequencies with which the different categories are scored then become the data to be analyzed. The first fully systematic category system for the study of interaction was proposed by Bales (1950). His system has been very widely used, and a large number of studies in which it has been used have been published (see Hare, Borgatta, and Bales 1955; Hare 1962). Many other category systems have been developed, based upon a variety of theoretical principles, and aimed at a variety of questions. Many of these have been reviewed by Heyns and Lippitt (1954) and by Weick (1968). I shall not attempt here to comment specifically on any of these. I would like to point out, however, some of the more important features these various systems have in common.

First, the "acts" or units in terms of which the behavior is observed are not units of BEHAVIOR. They are CATEGORIES or PIGEON HOLES into which the observer may fit behavior. However, in classifying the behavior the observer classifies not so much the behavior itself as the intent that is judged to lie behind the behavior. Thus in Bales' system the categories are given labels such as "gives information" or "asks for opinion." Second, the categories are not derived empirically but from some set of theoretical presuppositions. In the case of Bales' category system, for example, the categories were derived from a theory of the interactive process as a problem-solving process. The problem-solving process was analyzed into various phases, the categories being derived from these phases. In the case of another category system, more recently proposed by Longabaugh (1963), the guiding theory was exchange theory — that people in interaction offer, through their acts, rewards and costs to one another. Other category systems have been derived from theories heavily influenced by psychoanalytic concepts.

In short, in all of these systems, behavior is looked upon not so much for its own sake, as for what motivations or intents it is expressing, or for what results follow upon it. It is in terms of these supposed motives or intents or in terms of its supposed results that it is classified.

In addition to these features, it is most important to notice that the use of the category approach involves a reliance upon natural human judgment of motive, intent, or result. This has certain very important consequences. It has meant that all those features of social interaction that we, in our ordinary daily lives, take entirely for granted, are also taken for granted by investigators using the category approach. For example, the investigator must assume, as he sits down behind his one-way mirror, that he knows when the meeting that he is to observe has begun and that all the participants know this too. He must assume that the participants know how to speak, how to maintain themselves as participants in the situation, that they know (and he knows) who is being addressed and who has the next turn at speaking. The whole of what might be termed the machinery of interaction, which we take for granted in our daily lives, is also taken for granted by the investigator using the category approach. Such an investigator, thus, is forever limited in what he can study of the phenomena of interaction.

Since 1960, approximately, there has been a steady increase in the number of investigators who have been interested in the direct measurement of behavior in situations of social interaction. Many of these studies have been reviewed by Weick (1968). For example, a number of studies have appeared in recent years in which particular behavioral variables have been examined, most notably personal space (Evans and Howard 1973), gaze (see, for example, Exline 1972; von Cranach 1971), various aspects of body motion and facial expression (see Davis 1972 for an extensive survey of the literature) and various aspects of vocalization, such as hesitation, and other "paralinguistic" features (see Harris and Rubinstein, this volume, for references to much of this literature). Secondly, and even more recently, studies have begun to appear in which attempts have been made to observe behavior systematically in a way somewhat similar to that followed in descriptive ethology. Studies using such methods are well summarized in Hutt and Hutt (1970), Blurton-Jones (1972), and McGrew (1972).

It is to be noted, however, that in much of this work the primary focus has been not so much on INTERACTION and how it is brought off, as it has been on the significance of the behavior measured for the psychological state of the individual. Much of the work on gaze, for example, has considered variations in amounts of looking in relation to such psychological variables as liking or embarrassment. The work on facial expression is almost wholly confined to investigating it as a symptom of emotional state. Much of the work done under the influence of ethological methods, done for the most part with children, has a predominantly diagnostic interest. That is, it has been concerned with characterizing sex differences in behavior, pathological behavior patterns such as autism, or with characterizing types of children in terms of clusters of behavior patterns.

The approach to interaction and the behavior of interaction represented by the present conference departs in several ways from the approaches referred to above. First of all, the focus is upon systems of behavior rather than upon systems of motivation, intent, or effect. Second, the focus is upon interaction itself rather than upon the behavior of individuals or upon the consequences of interaction for individuals. The starting point of this perspective, thus, is the interdependency of the behavior of individuals that obtains whenever they are in one another's presence. The endeavor, in this perspective, is to understand how OCCASIONS OF INTERACTION are organized. The encounter is taken as a starting point — the conversation, the greeting, the interview — and one seeks to understand how the behavior that participants make use of within such occasions functions in the creation of them. In other words, in this perspective the concern is with the behavior characteristic of occasions of interaction and with its significance for those occasions.

From this perspective, it quickly becomes apparent that the full range of behaviors observable in interaction must be comprehended. An integrated approach to behavior becomes necessary, and we cannot be content with dealing with behavioral variables one at a time. In seeking to set up the pre-Congress conference whose proceedings make up this volume, therefore, we sought participants who had already expressed interest in developing such an integrated point of view.

This conference perhaps may be seen as one of a series. The first within this perspective was the paralinguistic and kinesics conference that was held in Bloomington, Indiana in 1962 which resulted in the volume *Approaches to semiotics* (Sebeok, Hayes, and Bateson 1963). Since then there have been three others: on Long Island in 1968, in Oxford, England in 1969, and in Amsterdam in 1970. The Amsterdam conference, organized by Erving Goffman and T. A. Sebeok, though unpublished, was of particular significance insofar as it was organized explicitly to promote the development of "interaction ethology" — a term Goffman has put forward to label the study of the behavior of interaction from exactly the perspective we are trying to distinguish here (see Goffman 1971: xii).

All of these earlier conferences brought together workers from different disciplines, and the present conference is no exception. In the present conference psychology, linguistics, anthropology, ethology, mathematics, and sociology are all represented. Yet, at this conference at least, in listening to the discussion, one would not so readily recognize these different backgrounds. This would appear to be because each participant recognized that the study of the behavior of face-to-face interaction is not adequately encompassed by any one discipline. Though the diverse skills and knowledge such a diverse range of disciplines can provide are needed, it seems that an adequate discussion of these phenomena demands new terms and new concepts which no existing individual discipline adequately supplies.

Several members of the present conference expressed some surprise at the apparent ease with which representatives of such a diverse range of disciplines were able to have profitable discussions. This ease could be accounted for by the joint recognition that no one existing discipline had an adequate language in which the phenomena could be discussed. It was also suggested that each participant recognized that his interest in face-to-face interaction is not a fully legitimate interest for him to have, insofar as he still claims to be a member of a particular field. Each thus feels somewhat peripheral to his official field, and it is this joint feeling of peripheralness that brought about a sense of commonality among members of the conference.

If there was a good sense of agreement among the participants that there is indeed a coherent field of study, yet one that cannot be contained within any existing discipline, there was also agreement that this field is still in an emergent state. It was generally agreed however that an increasingly common set of approaches is emerging or, perhaps, an increasing degree of recognition of how the different approaches that different investigators follow fit together.

One theme that runs through many of the papers and that ran through much of the discussion which illustrates this general point in a more concrete way is that any current distinctions and definitions are quite unsatisfactory. There was a recognition that current notions of "language" are unusable. It was recognized that when people are in face-to-face interaction all aspects of their behavior and of the setting which they are in are involved in creating the order that may be discerned and that it is a matter of further investigation to establish how the various strands of behavior that may be distinguished — speech, gesture, spacing, posture, facial display — are interrelated and what functions they subserve.

A second theme, obviously closely related to the first, is that we need to re-immerse ourselves in the phenomena. It seemed to be generally recognized that we understand very little about how behavior in face-to-face interaction is organized, so that in order to gain more understanding we must go back and look at it. Sound-film and videotape are thus the primary instruments because these are the only means available by which behavior may be "fixed" and so made into a specimen that can be repeatedly examined.

In sum, then, we may say that the perspective represented in this conference is characterized by an interest in the organization of behavior of face-to-face interaction. It is, therefore, descriptive in outlook, and it demands behavior specimens as material to work from. It does not seek to construct an extensive theoretical framework, but is content with only such local theory as is needed to make systematic descriptions of particular phenomena possible. It finds past distinctions, based upon narrower or less precise examinations of behavior, or based upon theoretical presuppositions more than upon observations, as less than useful.

We may now look at some of the specific topics dealt with at the conference, and comment upon some of the more important issues that were raised. In dealing with these topics, I shall treat them in what appears to me to be a logical order. This is not necessarily the same as the order in which they were considered in the conference. Furthermore, what follows is not intended to be a review of the papers that were presented. It is intended as a personal survey of some of the principal topics and issues suggested in the conference.

Social occasions of all sorts take place in physical space. Indeed, individuals who participate in such occasions require space. However, more particularly, in any social occasion there is always a particular spatial organization and thus the occasion itself has characteristic spatial demands. For example, the spatial demands of an occasion in which one or a few individuals are the focus of attention of a large number of others simultaneously, as in a lecture or a play, are quite different from the spatial demands of an occasion in which a number of individuals all have access to one another at the same time, as in a conversation or conference. This kind of observation can lead one in a number of different directions. It was pointed out that the fixed features of our physical environment have an organization that enshrines some of the most general aspects of spatial organization of social occasions. In this way bounded segments of space, through their shape and size, through the kind of boundary they have — whether merely marked by changes in the ground or floor covering, or by walls — and through the kind of arrangement of furniture that they contain, provide a "frame" which can set limits upon the range of types of occasions of interaction that can occur in them. Thus considerations of space lead us directly to a kind of social ecology. On the other hand, within a given physical setting, the people who together are setting up a social occasion of some sort usually have some degree of freedom to arrange themselves in space in relation to one another. Which kind of spatial arrangement may be adopted sets limits to the way the other behavior of interaction is organized. People in small conversational groups, for example, can relate to one another's behavior in a way that is quite different from people in large gatherings; and so the kind of behavioral organization by which the participants are interrelated will be different. Thus HOW people arrange themselves in space is part of the way people select, as it were, how they are going to relate to one another for the duration of the interactional event in which they will be involved.

The spatial arrangements that we find people to occupy in co-presence are often relatively sustained. We may mark the duration of an "interactional event" by the way a given spatial arrangement is sustained. Alterations — or adjustments — in the spatial arrangement of participants within an established framework are often, it appears, related to changes in topics of conversation or phases or themes of the interaction. The indications are that the sustained spatial framework that the spatial arrangements of people in interaction set up functions as one of the ways in which the "definition of the situation" is established and maintained.

Introduction 9

The concept of the "definition of the situation" is rather ill-defined, and yet it appears that we need to have some such notion, for it is apparent that we cannot account for what happens in an encounter solely in terms of the separate psychologies of the individual participants. It refers to what may be described as the set of rules that prevail in any interaction which govern how conduct in that interaction may be organized, which govern what may and what may not be incorporated as the focus of attention of the participants, and which perhaps may be said to govern what may become possible within a given situation. It should be stressed that the immediate frame or definition of a given encounter is almost always CREATED. It is something that is jointly elaborated by the participants. Yet it is not, of course, by any means INDEPENDENT of the institutional framework of the encounter, of the physical setting within which it takes place, or of the social roles, relative statuses, and so forth, of the participants. The essential point here is twofold: FIRST, that we cannot adequately account for what happens in interaction unless we have some notion like "frame" or "definition of the situation," some notion, that is, that the participants have together committed themselves to some principles of conduct which govern them jointly; SECOND, that this "frame" is, in its particular form, EMERGENT, the special product of a given encounter. That is, you can't account for what happens in interaction by looking merely at physical setting, social role, relative status, and so forth. These elements all enter, of course, but they do so mediated by the interchanges that the participants engage in together, the outcome of which is the negotiation of a "frame" which is special to that encounter and indeed, within a given encounter, subject to further development or change.

In more than one paper in which the micro-structure of interaction was considered, we could see the attempt to describe or formulate the general rules governing behavior in interaction being made. For example, we spent a considerable amount of time on the CONVERSATION. This is in part because such interactional occasions can be recorded relatively easily — at least as far as the speech featured in them is concerned — and also, of course, because all of us are conversationalists we are all aware, if only dimly, that conversation, for all its variety, has an orderliness to it that can be described.

One feature of conversation to which much attention was paid is that in conversation speakers TAKE TURNS. There was some disagreement, in discussion, as to what, exactly, is meant by a "turn" in conversation. That conversationalists do take turns, however, was seen as a major feature of conversation, and more than one paper was devoted to the question of how this ordering of behavior, the taking of turns, is brought about.

One question about turn-taking is: how does the next speaker know that it is his turn? It is supposed that the participants in a conversation must offer one another signals by which they inform one another of whether they are ending a turn, and so providing a turn for someone else; whether they are BEGINNING a turn, and so preempting conversational space for themselves; whether they are continuing; or whether they are continuing as an auditor rather than as a speaker. Without such a set of signals, it is supposed, conversationalists would constantly be colliding; that is, they would be interrupting one another, and the orderly exchange of utterances that quite often occurs in conversation would not be attained.

This question has been tackled by transcribing audiovisual records of conversations and then examining them for the behavioral features that occur at points where turns are exchanged, continued, relinquished or taken up. The behavioral features that are found in an apparently regular fashion are then postulated as the set of turn-taking signals. Whether or not such features are regularly associated with, say, turn exchanges, may then be tested statistically by some measure of goodness of fit. By this means it is hoped to demonstrate what the turn-taking signals are, in terms of particular kinds of behavior, and what the rules are that govern their use.

A rather different approach to the problem is to suppose that participants in a conversation collaboratively develop a solution to the problem of time-sharing which inevitably arises whenever we are dealing with a situation in which simultaneous talking cannot occur. Features of the sequential relationship between utterances are then examined in actual examples of conversation, and rules which the participants appear to be following are then postulated. The rules that are thus put forward are regarded as the solution that was arrived at. Such rules are seen to be applicable, however, in all conversations, and the substantial differences that may appear in the surface structure of different conversations are nevertheless to be seen as but the outcome of different modes of application of these rules. The reason these rules are quite general, it would appear, is not because they are rules that exist "in society" in some sense, and which people learn to follow, but the inherent properties of the behavior that are brought into conversations, properties that conversationalists have because they are human beings.

This last point gave rise to some controversy. It was argued by some that in some cultures conversations were carried on without any turn-taking at all. It was maintained that the very different patterns of conversational organization that are said to occur in different cultures could not be accounted for by some universal set of rules of conversation, that each culture had elaborated its own rules and its own means of structuring events that might be called conversations.

This controversy was not resolved. Furthermore, the discussion of it did not last very long. There are a number of reasons for this, but I suspect that one important reason is that we are so lacking in examples of conversational organization from other than English-speaking societies that everyone realized the futility of further argument in the absence of observations to back up his position.

Another reason why the controversy about the universality of conversational rules could not be resolved, and why the discussion of it could not go further, was because the issue of what a TURN is and what a CONVERSATION is was never really resolved. These terms seem transparent enough when we start to use them, yet as soon as we begin careful discussion we find that they are fraught with ambiguity. Great care in the use of words as we write and talk in this area would seem to be at a premium, for there is as yet no generally acceptable vocabulary.

However, this lack of agreement about what counts as a conversation or what counts as a turn in a conversation refers us to another issue of great importance in this area which, though raised in a number of different papers in the conference, was yet never really discussed. This is the issue of behavior structure, the question of how the flow of behavior may be divided into its various strands and segmented into its various units. To take the disagreement about what counts as a turn once again, it seemed that this disagreement arose because some wanted to use the term in a FUNCTIONAL sense, while others wanted to define the term in terms of some particular behavior, for example a period of continuous speech. Yet even among those who favored a non-functional definition, there was disagreement about just which aspects of behavior the term might be said to point to.

The issue of behavior structure was raised in particular when we were confronted by film or a videotape. During the conference we had two sessions in which we looked at audiovisual records of interaction. In the comments that the various participants made on the material, differences in the way in which behavior can be described and analyzed became sharply apparent. Some people, as they commented on such material, characterized what they saw in dispositional terms: they said they saw DOMINANCE or AVERSION or that particular behavior as a case of someone TAKING A TURN. Others attempted to stick more closely to units of behavior and refrain from giving them functional names in the first instance. Yet even here there was disagreement, for behavior is continuous; it appears to have a multilayered structure; and unless we agree upon a clear notion of this structure, even simple matters, such as whether or not a series of head movements (say) should be grouped into one unit or separated into several parts, cannot be resolved.

Among the participants in the conference one may detect a difference in how they approach the problem of dealing with the records of behavior which constitute their starting point. On the one hand there are those who, recognizing the great importance of being consistent in their identification of units and feeling the need to deal with large amounts of data, spend much time in developing a system of transcription, which they then use to provide the basis of their analyses. On the other hand there are those who do not develop any consistent transcription system, at least not at the outset. They make charts and transcriptions from their original records, but they do this only as a device which helps them shape the formulation of patterns in the data. The formulation itself is done in direct dialogue with the original material. These "direct" workers, as they might be called, would argue in justification for their approach that behavior is too complex to transcribe completely, that any transcription system presupposes the nature of the behavioral structure, and that therefore to use that transcription system as the basis of analysis is to remain constrained by the presuppositions of that transcription system, presuppositions which are almost certainly incorrect in any particular case.

So far issues and topics that deal directly with the phenomena of interaction have been discussed. We have seen that there is a general recognition that when people engage in interaction the behavior that each of them separately produces, as it were, becomes incorporated into SYSTEMS of interrelatedness which can then become an object of study in their own right. From another point of view, however, we can examine the way the performance of individuals in interaction is organized and seek to describe the various systems of behavior that are made use of in such performances, such as speech, gesture, and so on. Several papers were presented from this orientation. Most of them were written from a linguistic point of view and, as will be apparent, they appear to have important consequences for linguistic theory.

The main burden of these papers would appear to be that it is unsatisfactory to approach systems such as speech or gesture in terms of any prior notions about the abstract structure they are supposed to display. If one looks, for example, at how the voice operates in interaction, it quickly becomes obvious that the traditional boundary between language and paralanguage cannot be sustained. Furthermore, if one takes into account how the body moves as a speaker speaks, the boundary between speech and body motion, or kinesics, likewise cannot be simply maintained. Body motion appears to be not merely an accompaniment of speech. It appears as a fully integrated component of a system of behavior that subserves a range of functions in interaction which includes those functions more usually thought of as typically subserved by language. Indeed, in one paper it was documented that linguistic functions, in all their complexity, can perfectly well be carried out in the complete absence of speech or any of its derivatives. It can be done entirely through movements of the hands, face, and body. The example, in this case, was American Sign Language.

This realization that language does not NEED speech, and that in everyday situations among normal people speech does only part of the work it is usually thought to do, obviously has very important consequences for linguistic theory. At the very least, theories of language raised upon a corpus derived from speech alone must henceforth be thought of as but SPECIAL language theories. GENERAL language theories must await the systematic development of a study of communicative behavior which shows how all the different strands of behavior together function linguistically.

More specifically, the recognition that language may be regarded as a FUNCTION of behavior, whether kinesic or vocal, should have consequences for studies of language acquisition, and this also was expressed very clearly by several participants. It appears that if we are ever to understand how the individual human acquires, as he grows up, the capacity to communicate with others in the way that is generally labeled as linguistic, we will have to study the structure of the interactional situations in which the child and adults together engage — for speech it appears is, from the first, fully embedded in interaction, and its operation cannot be understood without systematically dealing with this embeddedness. This point was demonstrated with particular clarity by Bullowa.

Before concluding, one further matter deserves comment. It was notable that the whole issue of cross-cultural comparisons of communicative behavior, in both its theoretical and practical implications, was not discussed, except for the above-mentioned discussion of the universality of conversational structure. Apart from this, only one paper dealt with this question directly. However, the major focus of the participants appeared to be upon the question of the underlying approach, the question of methodology, and upon studies which appeared to raise general questions or which were interpreted as pertaining to general underlying processes. I think the reason for this may be that it is only now, when more than a handful of workers have begun to concern themselves with the phenomena of face-to-face interaction, that the significance and complexity of the field is being fully realized. There is a need to develop theory and methodology and a well articulated approach before attempting to deal with the problem of the variety of ways in which communicative behavior is organized in interaction in different cultures.

It was mentioned at the outset that many of those who are concerned with this field have moved to it FROM some point nearer the center of a more traditional discipline. The study of the organization of behavior in face-to-face interaction is neither linguistics nor anthropology, neither psychology nor ethology. Yet it draws from all of these fields. It could be argued, however, that this field of study is in some ways the most central to all of the various social sciences of man, for it is in systems of behavior as organized into interactional events that human society is ultimately grounded. This, as we saw at the beginning, was Simmel's belief. In the years immediately ahead we may expect that the issues to emerge in this field will be of major theoretical importance. It is my expectation that, if we meet again on this same topic at the next international Congress (and it is my hope that we will), we will be able to record very substantial advances.

REFERENCES

ARENSBERG, C. M.
    1972 Culture as behavior: structure and emergence. *Annual Review of Anthropology* 1:1–26.
BALES, R. F.
    1950 *Interaction process analysis: a method for the study of small groups.* Reading, Massachusetts: Addison-Wesley.
BLURTON-JONES, N., *editor*
    1972 *Ethological studies of child behaviour.* Cambridge University Press.
CHAPPLE, E. D.
    1940 Measuring human relations: an introduction to the study of the interaction of individuals. *Genetic Psychology Monographs* 22:3–147.
CHAPPLE, E. D., C. S. COON
    1942 *Principles of anthropology.* New York: Holt.

CHAPPLE, E. D., G. DONALD, JR.
  1947 An evaluation of department store sales people by the interaction chronograph. *Journal of Marketing* 12:173–185.
CHAPPLE, E. D., E. LINDEMANN
  1942 Clinical implications of measurements on interaction rates in psychiatric interviews. *Applied Anthropology* 1:1–11.
COOLEY, C. H.
  1902 *Human nature and the social order.* New York: Scribner's.
COSER, L. A., *editor*
  1965 *George Simmel.* Englewood Cliffs, New Jersey: Prentice-Hall.
DAVIS, MARTHA
  1972 *Understanding body movement: an annotated bibliography.* New York: Arno Press.
EXLINE, R. V.
  1972 "Visual interaction: the glances of power and preference," in *Nebraska symposium on motivation.* Edited by M. R. Jones. Lincoln, Nebraska: University of Nebraska Press.
EVANS, G. W., R. B. HOWARD
  1973 Personal space. *Psychological Bulletin* 80:334–344.
GOFFMAN, E.
  1971 *Relations in public: microstudies of the social order.* London: Penguin.
HARE, A. P.
  1962 *Handbook of small group research.* New York: The Free Press of Glencoe.
HARE, A. P., E. F. BORGATTA, R. F. BALES, *editors*
  1955 *Small groups: studies in social interaction.* New York: Knopf.
HEYNS, R. W., R. LIPPITT
  1954 "Systematic observational techniques," in *Handbook of social psychology,* volume one. Edited by G. Lindzey. Reading, Massachusetts: Addison-Wesley.
HUTT, S. J., CORINNE HUTT
  1970 *Direct observation and measurement of behavior.* Springfield, Illinois: Charles C. Thomas.
KENDON, A.
  1963 "Temporal aspects of the social performance in dyadic social encounters," Unpublished doctoral dissertation, Oxford University.
LONGABAUGH, R.
  1963 A category system for coding interpersonal behavior as social exchange. *Sociometry* 26:319–344.
MATARAZZO, J. D., G. SASLOW, RUTH G. MATARAZZO
  1956 The interaction chronograph as an instrument for objective measurement of interaction patterns during interviews. *Journal of Psychology* 41:347–367.
MCGREW, W. C.
  1972 *An ethological study of children's behaviour.* London and New York: Academic Press.
MEAD, G. H.
  1934 *Mind, self and society.* Chicago: University of Chicago Press.

PARK, R. E., E. W. BURGESS
  1924 *Introduction to the science of sociology.* Chicago: University of Chicago Press.
SEBEOK, T. A., A. S. HAYES, MARY C. BATESON
  1963 *Approachs to semiotics.* The Hague: Mouton.
VON CRANACH, M.
  1971 "The role of orienting behavior in human interaction," in *Environmental space and behavior.* Edited by A. H. Esser. New York: Plenum Press.
WEICK, K. L.
  1968 "Systematic observational methods," in *Handbook of social psychology* (second edition), volume two. Edited by G. Lindzey and E. Aronson. Reading, Massachusetts: Addison-Wesley.

PART ONE

Theoretical Perspectives

A Human Ethological Approach to Communication: Ideas in Transit Around the Cartesian Impasse

HARVEY B. SARLES

One must either acknowledge that it is beyond one's powers to understand how body and mind are united, how they interact, or, if one claims to have any understanding, attribute it, not to philosophical insight, but to having learnt the lessons of "ordinary life and conversation." This is the Cartesian Impasse... (Vesey 1965:11).

After an appreciable apprenticeship in traditional linguistics, paralinguistics and kinesics,[1] I found that deeper understandings of human interaction and human beingness were not available within these conceptual frameworks. No matter how carefully done, more of the same approaches seemed incapable of producing the sorts of ideas and insights that many of us have felt to be lacking in the behavioral sciences. They seemed to yield excellent descriptions but lacked explanatory power.

The aim of transcending one's (apparent) human experience was not obtainable in these traditions. We needed new vision to become finely tuned critics of our beliefs, to grasp any sense of when and how a circular theory nears its cyclical consummation, to be able to look outside in order to look back at man with new rigor and new reality filters. How else can one begin to observe the obvious: the dynamics of human communication?

It seemed a natural extension of my training (i.e. to think of language as all human languages) to think of how other species might perceive us (Sarles 1969, 1971a, 1972a, 1972b). A search of the literature on

My thanks to Janis Sarles for a careful and critical reading of this paper.

[1] Studying with Smith and Trager (Buffalo) and McQuown (Chicago) in degree studies, and with R. Birdwhistell for more extended periods.

animal communication seemed in order. But the animal behaviorists have looked at animal verbal behavior primarily as deficient human behavior (Busnel 1963). Because one tends to hear even other human languages in terms of one's native language, the biologists' listing of the "calls" of other species in terms of what the human hears appeared anthropomorphic in the extreme and uneducated at best. It seemed that the field of animal communication had not yet established its own subject matter. The inventive conclusions about animal verbalization only served to confirm the beliefs of those who imagine that human "language" is extranatural and intrinsically noncomparable to the so-called speech of other species that occasionally modify and vibrate the air expelled from their lungs (Lancaster 1965). For one who was already secure in his beliefs that humans were indeed as unique as any other species, this seemed defensive beyond proportion. If other features of our being were similar to other species, what made language so super-special? I saw no reason to invoke a new "creationism" merely to maintain man's dignity (an element of being which ought to be striven for in any case) (Bronowski 1965).[2]

But the deeper motive for looking beyond was to look again at assumptions and definitions of why we believe language to BE, and to be what we say it is. It is not that the beliefs were "wrong" in some transient existential sense, but that they were either too simple or too complicated (one cannot easily distinguish between simplicity and complexity from the inside). Besides, the ideas seemed to be very old, deserving an occasional airing but not necessarily true fidelity. And they pointed directly to the individual as the locus of being and believing, rather than as a hub in a social network. Interaction, in this theoretical orientation, was inconsequential to being, developing, or even reproducing. The mind of man appeared disembodied, a behavioral science developed which is far removed from the personified bodies that most of us seem to occupy, if not to be.[3]

In Cartesian tradition, belief in the individual as the locus of knowledge, consciousness, and thought sanctioned the essential neglect of

---

[2] Creationism — in some sense of instant creation of man as opposed to a gradual evolution/change, with adaptation.

[3] In the history of Western thought, the dominance of the mind in the context of a mind-body oppositional dualism has effectively eliminated the body from consideration as being the essential LOCUS of behavior control. Rather, the body has been considered principally as a repository for mind. Most theories of behavior, even of interaction, regard the body as a vehicle for carrying the messages and intent of the mind, not as being in its own sense. This is parallel to theories of language in which sound (= body) is presumed to CARRY messages (language, words, thoughts, mind), but not to be meaningful in and of itself (Spicker 1970; Vesey 1965).

questions of interaction. Interaction remained a problem, not a fact, designated the "problem of other minds" (Ryle 1949). One "knew" that he existed because he thought (had consciousness, language), but it remained unclear that he could or did relate to others' minds. In other words, an intellectual, philosophical basis for the very study of interaction appears to have been lacking.

Whatever their "intellective capacities," however, different species do have different sorts of bodies that move differently in velocity and rhythm. Yet all socially reproducing species "know" others of their own species: what and how do they know? If one considers the possibility that the ability and propensity of "bodies" to interact is interesting, perhaps observation and conceptualization may begin again.

But there is more intellectual baggage borne on the wings of traditional thought. Theories of mind and language became interwoven with a theory of society (Cassirer 1946). Man presumed to be unique as he acquired language; this acquisition was followed in some historical sense by stable social interaction, the achieving of "culture." Individual man became social man via the vehicle of language. And this story, simple to complex, pervades our views not only of human development but also of the ontogenesis of each human. Interaction is considered not as a fact of life but principally as a problem in living.

But actual observation of other species shows that they also live socially, in relative calm and peace. By all modern accounts, society must have predated the emergence of man (Darling 1952). Although each animal appears to be no more or no less individual than are humans, the solitary, nonsocial feral being who evolved to wander in the Edens of the past does not actually occur in the natural world. Evolution did not occur in nonsocial individuals; development does not occur in nonsocial individuals; language does not develop in nonsocial individuals. Why do our language THEORIES not ask about the input of others into the so-called minds of individuals? Of whom or what is language a property? Is language disembodied, or just our theories about language?

Not only has ethology confirmed that society is as natural a condition in man as individuality, it has nudged the evolutionary biologists to grudgingly admit that behavior, like bodies, has continuity and species specificity. Evolution, claims Mayr (1963), has taken place as much or more in terms of behavior as of the "solid," more tangible tissues, soft and hard. In fact, even anatomy has shown recent signs of reconceptualizing the dynamics of bone shaping in terms of social interaction (Enlow 1968). Behavior appears to be "harder" and bones "softer" than the objective scientist had thought them to be. The cliché is that "behavior is heritable" (Lorenz 1965:xiii); its serious consideration has raised to collective consciousness the old questions of nature versus nurture, which many had hoped were permanently interred.

In some mysterious *Zeitgeist* dynamic, similar questions appeared simultaneously in the behavioral sciences, but with a biomorphological twist. Language was said to be heritable because of our natural properties as (normal, individual) human beings (Chomsky 1968). Linguists, whose anti-body orientation made them essentially immune to observing the observable, fought to attribute this ability to the "mind," although a few of us suspected that this attribution was some sort of cover either for a new creationism or for a new biologism in which variation and continuity were to be eliminated from purview. But this era did educate us, intellectually, into the mysteries of idea shifts and into the baser reasons thereof. Every man's law of ideation: most people prefer to have intellectual dressing on their beliefs!

But a more engrossing facet of the issue also appeared — if behavior were to be considered heritable, thus "genetic," would this affect the notion of genetic in any sense (Stebbins 1965)? If "normal" humans have language and reproduce, how do they get to be or remain "normal"? Were they born with some fixed propensities for which interaction and experience could only provide nutrients, or was the concept of normality an emergent interactional dynamic of any sort? Can the study of face-to-face interaction be considered to be BIOLOGICAL, in terms of its contribution to variety, continuity, and evolution? Is there a conceptual pathway along which the biological AND behavioral aspects of man can be seen to be integrated or coterminous?

Consider the human face, that aspect of our being which seems as rich a source of information as our very languages (Sarles 1972b). How is it to be considered — as a surface projection of internal affective states; as a contrastive set of surfaces that highlight the myriad movements of eyes and mouth; as a partial representation of the internal dynamic of linguistic formation; as a place to yawn, smile, grimace, blink, wink, and smirk; as a place to imagine that the real "I" is located; as a map "betraying" entry into our being; as a reactive covering through which other beings are personified and confirmed; as a net and network by which one can feel, image, mimic, project others' feelings, imagings, mimes, and projections of themselves; as a place that tells not only about itself, and oneself in reflection, but about the object-event-time of one's discourse; as an array of territories that one loves to study and remember, and that one can recall in multiple dynamic contexts even after years have transpired between interactions; as the seat, the locus of the continuing moral feelings about ourselves as played out often in imagined, subtle re-creations of family; as the interplay of human surfaces that receive and direct the sounds of interactional speech toward the ears; as the obverse of its internal surfaces, the place that feels tongue movements but refuses to show them to the world; as the prime locus of many so-called senses; as the largest unclothed surface; as the most notably dynamic surface of the body because its hair is so light-reflective; as the region of being by which we tell others about the state of our health, and beseech or refuse help; as our sex and age; as the site of one's external projection as a whole, successful person, or not; as the determinant of whether one "belongs" in a situation or is a "vision"; as a class marker; as a place to cream and color, to call attention to or away from itself; as beauty, stupidity . . . ?

No notation system yet contrived can begin to describe the human face. What has been developed so far is a series of approaches, mostly nondynamic, that tend to obscure problems as much as they illuminate (Eibl-Eibesfeldt 1970; Ekman 1972). If the recent history of linguistics can be taken as any measure, we are susceptible to shortcuts that appear to offer potentially complete insight.

In the context of "behavioral-biology-so-far," there has been a movement to look at faces and language as if their genetic-innate components were fixed in each individual sometime prior to his emergence into the social-experiential world (Eibl-Eibesfeldt 1970). Instead of using a genetic-interactional scheme in which GENETIC refers to a potentially continuous aspect of living, the popular assumption is that NATURE means built-in forever, and NURTURE means modifiable. Some behaviors are caused in essence by built-in features of being; in this theory facial expression is the external mapping, the performance of a fixed, humanoid set of affective states (Ekman 1972). This represents a literal interpretation of the Darwinian exhortation that the face is the site for the EXPRESSION of the emotions (Darwin 1872). And it is a direct equation of biology and inflexibility (as if adaptability were a notion that applies only in the long run).

What happens to the notion of human normality in this view? Is it also a built-in feature of one's being: once abnormal, always abnormal? Simpson once admonished me: "Only normal human beings have language!" (1970). Yet I was taught in human anatomy that each of us has some anomalies; that viability, growth, and reproduction were the major issues; and that there were either fairly wide parameters of being or a variety of pathways.

Who decides which "anomalies" are to be considered within normal limits and which outside the boundaries of acceptable normality? We might respond that "nature" decides. But all of us need social "tender loving care" (TLC) to survive. No human is fit to survive at birth. By this definition of normality we scarcely can be said to exist at all! Biological normality for social species cannot be said to exist solely within the individual. If the individual organism can be said to "decide" anything that is precisely nonsocial, it may be able to decide to abort itself. Otherwise, it does not seem to have any sense of being that can be construed purely as extra-interactional. Continued viability of any individual must be some complex set of quid pro quos between its imaginings of itself and its other-bodied *Umwelt*. If organisms are BODIES, then we must begin to account for their social-intellectual abilities without presuming a "mind," a deus ex machina, as an explanatory mechanism.

By construing the problem of human knowledge within a framework of dualist thought, in which one must impale oneself on one horn or the other or try precariously to ride both, the issues have been obscured. Knowledge is either built-in and learning is chimerical, or experience is the be-all of existence. The notion of life as interaction contains the seeds, I believe, of alternative conceptualizations and paths of study of human behavior.

I think that this will be the basic conceptual contribution of an ethological approach to communication, at least for the foreseeable future, that it will be a most useful exercise to take seriously the empty half of the mind-body antagonism, place it directly into interactional perspective, and see where it takes us.

It will take great perspicacity to avoid the pitfalls of already assuming that which we desire to discover, a mark of essentially all theories that set out to explain man's presumed uniqueness. Most theorists, including behavioral biologists who examine man, tend to invoke psychical explanations to account for behavior BEFORE they move to simpler, mechanical explanations. Questions like "How is man unique?" must be addressed anew, or simply passed by.

Let me submit a number of observations about man, which might be considered as case studies. All are incomplete, but (I hope) suggestive of how we might begin to rethink, particularly in terms of how our bodies might "understand" others' bodies.[4]

---

[4] The observations on music are derived principally from my own self-analytic experience as an amateur violinist, amplified by talking with a few professional musicians; jogging, likewise. Observations on Mongoloid infants were made at the University of Minnesota hospitals and on several home visits.

A. An old anatomical cliché: certain parts of our bodies are highly mimetic (Goss 1954).

Although the notion of mimesis SEEMS quite straightforward, it is essentially the only concession anatomy has ever made to the possibility that bodies are in some sense social. (Actually, anatomy has only recently begun to concede that bodies might be alive!)

Mimesis literally means copying. One body can make itself "look like" another (at least to express emotions, because it is precisely those muscles that anatomists call mimetic). That is, we have the ability to copy others' expressions.

It is the facial surface of another body that one sees — it has or is given depth, shadow, color, contrast, many parts. But one sees external surfaces (Sarles 1974). In order to mimic, to produce on his face the same movements he sees on other faces (does an infant know that faces are faces?), an individual must produce an expression by moving his own muscles. His face must see and analyze another's expression and translate a visual dynamic (or static) into his own facial muscles. I suggest that we have no understanding of the mechanisms for mimesis, but that they are critical for the deeper understanding of interaction and of the individual. Expression seems to be interactional as well as internal or innate.

B. At an early age — three months or so — one can elicit a smile on a baby's face. Upon testing, it was learned that a humanoid figure, principally one with our type of high-contrast EYES, would also elicit apparently the same smile (Spitz and Wolf 1946).

Not only can an infant organism mime, for example, by opening its mouth when its mother opens hers, but the infant apparently can transduce interactional eyes into its own mouth dynamic. Although there seems to be no explanation for this almost universally observed phenomenon, it adds weight to the notion that our bodies can (and want to) respond to and with others' bodies in complex ways. Although some smiles may be due to a release of an internal affective state, others may indeed be related to other bodies.

A neglected question is why a smile should have positive affect. What "feels good" about a facial surface moving superior and laterally to the point where we judge it to be a smile? It might be primarily because its occurrence in infants has such a high positive load for their parents, who interpret it as a confirming sign of normal development and increasing love.

There are children whose attempts at smiling are not completely successful, i.e. though there is oral movement, it seems not to be sufficient to be seen as a smile. Among the children who "do not smile" are the bulk of Down's syndrome (Mongoloid 21–trisomy) children who can be diagnosed at birth by facial inspection (Sarles 1972c). These children do not (cannot?) move their mimetic muscles very well. Deeper muscles, eyes, tongue, sucking seem to work pretty well, but the external ones, including those used for smiling, do not.

Is their inability to smile well a function of a muscular weakness or of a defective brain? Most of them turn out to be retarded, more or less severely. Does this have to do with their inability to properly demonstrate affective expression, to "tune-in" on others completely, and their having a facial map that most of us will label as "stupid"? Or do they have a built-in intellectual defect that remains neurologically undemonstrable? Or both? Mind theories posit defect, as mind theories seem particularly wont to do in "exceptional" cases.

C. Some aspects of our being which have dynamic facial components seem to be "catching" (mimetic behavior?). These include yawning, coughing and dryness of the throat, whispering (I find this really intriguing), and shortness of breath. Many essentially internal aspects of our bodies find themselves interacting with other interactants' bodies. Mimesis is thus not only facial and external but also internal in barely understood senses. What kind of pact is communication that it produces "symptoms" in an observer-interactor's body in an essentially UNCONTROLLABLE way?

D. Although there is no question that humans are rhythmic creatures, how are these rhythms shared and controlled?

Musicians are highly rhythmic creatures, trading on rhythm to make a living. Many musical instruments are held, supported by one or more body parts. Good musicians can and must SUPPRESS the feeling of rhythm in those supportive areas, or their musical output will suffer (ask any amateur musician!). That is, humans can apparently control the organization of rhythm distribution in their bodies.

In ensemble music, a musician must not only "know" about his own internal rhythms, but must be able to tune in on others' with remarkable precision and speed. Human bodies seem to have little or no difficulty tuning in to the rhythms of others' bodies. One can organize his own body, and simultaneously track on and share an interactant's time.

There are certain situations and/or states of relational being in which people (bodies?) seem incapable of interaction. One of these is the jogging state. Joggers have little or no problem in conversing with co-joggers, apparently regardless of how far they have run. But there seems to be no way for a jogger to talk with or relate to (e.g. maintain eye contact with) a person who is in a normal state. On checking common pulse rates, it appeared that the pulse of the jogger was literally "pulled down" during eye contact, a very precarious and certainly a very uncomfortable state.[5]

This suggests that interaction involves shared rhythms, that the heart or pulse rate is also susceptible of being shared, and that eye contact is sufficient to set up shared rhythms. On checking common pulses of people at rest, I found that their pulses jumped together into a kind of momentary synchrony when they came into mutual eye contact or related mutually to the same voice. Quite probably speech is also a rhythmic, synchronizing activity (Sarles 1973a).[6]

E. One way of thinking about speech is as a function of a continuously varying muscular dynamic whose rhythmic features have been considered outstanding. From this perspective, speech can be considered as muscular vibration altering a column of air.[7]

The rhythmic aspects of language may be felt as well as heard. That the listener in any interaction is subvocalizing has long been noted (Gibson 1966). It may well be that some of this activity is rhythmically related to what is being spoken in such a way that the listener then analyzes his own subvocal activity as representing part of the message. This might imply that at least some (linguistic) interaction is primarily a bodily interaction.[8]

Perhaps, then, human bodies as perception devices are the sorts of

---

[5] To check common pulse rates, one person monitors (holds) the wrist pulses of the two interactants simultaneously. I have asked several psychologists about the wisdom or validity of this procedure but remain unenlightened.

[6] It has been suggested that at least some body or circadian rhythms are also social, in some senses. To speculate, it might be suggested that rhythmic changes after air travel are heavily affected by trying to interact with people who are in a phase of daily rhythms quite different from one's own. Anecdotally, I have heard mention that isolated troops of sufficient numbers tend not to suffer body rhythm difficulties on long flights.

[7] IF WE ASSUME and believe that our ears mainly perceive tonal relationships, then we are primarily sound/phoneme analyzers (Helmholtz 1954). The grounds for this assumption are certainly open to question; its reception of continuing loyalty tends toward dogma. It is a clear case of a popular move in the tradition of human behavior study: noting an interesting characteristic of humans, elevating it to central, thus primary status, using it to characterize very incomplete observations as if they were exhaustive, and even attributing it to all other animals. It has certainly obscured as much as it may have illuminated.

[8] To extend this even further, it does seem remotely possible that "face shaping" of any individual may have to do not just with the interactional feedback of others responding to one's expressions, but also with the attempt to hold one's face in ways that mold at least some aspects of sound in interesting and comfortable ways.

things that resonate (in an almost literal sense) to sounds. In mind theories, the ability to understand and create is attributed a priori to mind.

When the deaf men of Gallaudet College used to play football, play was started and stopped by whacking the biggest bass drum imaginable. Evidently this set the earth in motion in ways directly and rapidly perceptible by the deaf players. All of us "feel" bass sounds of trucks and distant stereos. Yet the usual metaphor of speaking-hearing has only to do with the impingement of sound vibrations on internal ear mechanisms. Why, then, do small children find it interesting and necessary to do a lot of face-to-face interaction instead of putting their ears to their parents' mouths? I suggest that the human body, particularly the face, is a major shaper (absorber, censor, amplifier?) of our sound perceptions (and all that this may imply for the study of nonhuman speech!).

F. On observing slow motion movies, it can be easily noted that there is a time lag between mouth opening and vocalization. Consider the possibility that the infant, though he may both hear and see the face, has no way initially of knowing that his mother's (or his) face and voice are related in any direct sense.

Consider the mouth as a purely VISUAL dynamic phenomenon, for the moment. Whatever the precise total relationship between speech and movement, there is no question that the mouth moves with (actually just preceding) speech. On examining the "visual phonetics" of speech (akin to lip reading), the mouth appears simpler, in the sense of having fewer easily differentiable positions or movement dynamics. For example, the mouth of most English speakers is pursed, the upper lips especially everted with essentially the entire class of palatal sounds. Phoneticians have indeed noted that high vowels are preceded or accompanied by relatively closed mouths and low vowels by more open mouths. Bilabial sounds involve mouth closings and openings; back vowels are seen as more rounded lips in English.

These movements are all exaggerated in so-called baby talk — a special dialect used occasionally in many, if not most, languages for directly interacting with infants. Like mimesis, the notion of visual exaggeration is usually internalized but left undescribed. It consists principally of lips being more than usually tense and moving further; it may be slower than ordinary speech, but is certainly more marcato, the movements rapidly occupying the first part of the duration, leaving gaps or spaces in the dynamic. (Here, I can only analogize to the musical idiom.) It also appears that speech is more closely tied in to visible movements, i.e. it lags behind the lips by a smaller interval than usual. It seems to be more evenly rhythmic, the "line" being divided into more even event-moments than in ordinary speech. (To test this, imagine saying "Baa, baa, black sheep" to a young child.)

G. The visual aspects of speech must be very EXCITING to an infant, especially because they occupy so much spatial figuration on the Brobdingnagian ground of the parental mask. It may very well be that this relatively limited silhouette of speech is the one that infants use as their first approximation to language. Recall that the first "words" infants are universally said to speak are bilabials (ba-ba, ma-ma, pa-pa), which have highly visual, vertical mouth movements accompanied by a relaxed tongue and vocalization. Parents interpret this composite as words and speech and presume that the infant does also. It is just as likely, however, that the infant makes no such presumption (so it must be, except in mind theories). At this point in his development, all we can reasonably believe is that he is aware that his external and internal vocalization apparatus are to be considered as part of the same process. (Stated another way, the question might be: "How and when does the infant come to know that his face moves while he vocalizes?")

Why do faces seem to be exciting, not merely interesting, to humans? Granted that faces are potentially rich sources of information about other persons, and about ourselves, why should bodies "care" (Mead 1934)?

One course of thought might be to ask about other visual aspects of being that seem also to be exciting, and to seek out those features to which we respond. Although I hesitate to infer universality from my individual projection, it seems to me that fireworks, rockets, and fire engines come close to being a humanoid "turn-on," as does practically any event that occupies a lot of visual ground rapidly with increased visual intensity and includes a lot of noise. These tend to be episodic events, bounded in space and time.

In the interactional vis-à-vis, the adult face seems to have many exciting features, especially viewed up close: lips moving from a quiescent state to full open to pursed, teeth flashing, tongue darting. A carefully watching infant, drawn to the vast change in observed lips, feeling his own lip muscles vibrating sympathetically, hears and feels a rapidly rising, seething noise, pulsing vaguely in time with the mouth changes. It stops . . . and begins again.

From this point of view, there is no strong reason to assume that the human infant "knows" about language in any direct, pre-wired, innate sense. But it is necessary that he be strongly attracted to the perceived dynamic, and that he "care" about making it his own. He does this presumably by the muscular processes of mimesis, gradually coming to match what he sees, feels, and hears with what he does himself. Whatever the exact details, language learning appears to be a dynamic, muscular, interactional process.

If this is a useful perspective, a number of issues arise. How do "normal" children become and stay normal? How do blind and deaf children learn language? How much "micro-information" is available in the face and speech dynamic; how much of this information do children and/or adults use, regardless of their awareness? How does a perceived dynamic become episodic or evented, and in what senses? Why has this perspective not arisen in a general approach to human behavior?

Within this context, the most exciting event to humans is other humans; through one's knowledge and interaction with other bodies, one gains a sense of oneself and the external world. Does this approach allow us to observe language dynamics as an exciting event?

The amplitude of the voice is probably the most clearly bodily variable in speech. Beginning from silence, the voice can rise slowly or rapidly to greater or lesser amplitude. If either the velocity of rise or the actual amplitude increases beyond some point (empirically discoverable?), most of us experience a severe bodily reaction; we might then interpret the voice to have "scared the hell out of us!" The so-called angry voice proceeds from a great deal of glottal tension and explodes to full amplitude. It is well recognized across species as an alarm call.

In ordinary speech, the amplitude also is in constant variation. Although adults tend not to be aware of the finely tuned control of amplitude (and tone), it is continuous and, in my opinion, both extremely subtle and investigable.[9] Although it has been given a highly restricted role in linguistic theory, or banished to paralinguistics, amplitude variation may be a major variable in interaction and in language learning. What we call clarity may, for example, be a direct

---

[9] I wish to suggest that the stream of sound is as full of variables as the violin. We can hear and distinguish — all simultaneously and often continuously — the personal identifying characteristics of one's voice, age, sex, relationships to interactants in terms of a large number of social-contextual variables; we hear continuity, room size, the "profession" of the speaker as priest, professor, mother, student. Baby talk is one personal dialect among many. And the reasons they have escaped our attention have to do with under- (or over-)estimating their subtlety, and assuming they were idiosyncratic (*parole*), thus uninvestigable.

statement about amplitude control; the same may be true for frequency.

It is possible that the infant has some sort of built-in phoneme or distinctive-feature recognition-analyzing device. But this is surely an adult-centered view. How do we know that a sound is that sound? Or is this even an important question in the context of studying interaction? It was pointed out a decade ago that whole words could be excised, even from out-of-context sentences, with little or no loss in intelligibility (Pollack and Pickett 1964). Are sounds, or some sounds, inconsequential to understanding? What are the senses in which organisms try to understand one another?

How does the child come to know that a particular word is that word, when essentially every repetition of it varies from all others in at least some respects? Presumably the formants remain relatively constant, although the data base for this assertion remains out-of-context for the most part (Flanagan 1965).

Each and every word spoken by humans is not merely or solely that word (Sarles 1967). It literally sounds different if spoken in various parts of sentences than it does "in isolation" (it always occurs in a particular space and all spaces shape the wave form). The difference between males and females saying the "same" word is acoustically great. The amplitude, which is likely to be the most apparent feature to infants, is related very directly to distance between interactants.

But what about the subtleties, the nuances of speech? Mood, person, audience, age, sex, "type of person" (priest, professor, president), telephone, continuity — we hear them all, and must therefore have and use much better acoustical theories than acousticians do.

Sound is the disembodied vehicle for language. Sound keeps words apart; it does not convey directly any information which has to do with language. But these statements cannot illuminate because they are part of the explanatory device that assumes that language is a passive link whereby minds attempt to understand one another. And, I feel certain, these theories lend themselves to by-passing the necessity of life, as easily as they do the necessity to observe bodies as part of the human condition.

In ethological perspective, the question of how a child comes to know that certain constant features of a (shaped) wave form are to be interpreted as a particular word remains an intriguing problem. It forces us, I believe, to a position of much greater respect for the entire human organism than is inherent in a view that sees the body as a circumstantial abode for its mind.

The fact is that we have only the barest glimmerings of how one person understands another — in terms of sound alone — and this fact should not remain obscured by traditional claims of what ears are, or of what sound is and is not.

H. There appears to be no good explanation of how and why our bodies can relate to such exciting happenings as occur in sporting events to the extent that some people find themselves standing and cheering at home, watching sports events on television. And there seems to be little question that the pornographic movies "turn on" a number of observers (or set a scene that people can use to turn themselves on).

These observations suggest that our bodies are highly attuned to others' bodies, perhaps particularly to their rapid movements, and especially to deviations from "normal" (our own?) states. But perhaps this is the sense in which we know what "abnormal" is, i.e. our own bodies find themselves forced to change or alter their images in ways that we label "uncomfortable." (But how does one's body come to its own ongoing homeostasis? Does the hoarse-voiced person "know" about himself, or do we tell him as we respond to him?)

To extend this further into the realm of speculation, how is it that our bodies react to "deviant" bodies in such interesting ways, often causing us to laugh or cry? Do we (involuntarily) try to create their infirmities in our own bodies and respond to our own failures as if loaded with affect?

Perhaps some extreme extrapolation of this bodily propensity might shed some light on why we feel afraid of some species (e.g. snakes). That is, do our bodies find it difficult and troubling to redo themselves into certain shapes? Possibly, the human ability to manage fears is related to our bodies; maybe we can begin to account for our "humanism" by contrasting and comparing fears in different species as related to their bodily organization.

I. Eyes: not only do they focus, but they are the "windows into the soul." Mutual eye gaze has received a good deal of attention with respect, at least, to the total effort of interactional study.

In body perspective, this curious fact may be stated in a slightly different way: eyes "don't like" (?) to spend much time relating to one another. This seems to be true for many species, and those of us who try feel that it is no more difficult to make a dog, cat, or ape blink than another conspecific.

Why is it that eyes find other bodies' eyes so sensitive to mutual eye contact? It is even true of nursing infants: if one moves one's head in front of a (bottle-) nursing infant and "catches" the baby's eyes, the baby will either look away, or stop nursing and usually smile. (It is about as difficult to maintain even momentary eye contact with a hungry baby as with a jogger.)

I suggest that the eyes are in constant motion in the sense of readjusting focus, and that mutual eye contact forces the interactants' eyes into a constant search for the very subtle, dynamically varying focal plane(s) of the others' eyes. If they declare the "staring game," children can stare at one another's eyes for a relatively long while — until it "hurts" from dryness or from trying to balance a focus dynamic. And lovers can stare — perhaps they are busy transfiguring each other's bodies, and the eyes diminish in interactional importance. It may also be that the dilation of female eyes during courting has to do with a "willingness" to relax some of the eye focus movements.

I have noted that the ability to stare does increase with distance. After about fifteen feet, it is a much less uncomfortable thing to do. For example, in the context of teaching, students in the back of the room can stare at the teacher for quite long periods, and it seems to be quite congruent with the situation.

Also in the teaching context, I have noted that even a rapid fixation — a momentary meeting of the eyes of teacher and each individual student — seems to PERSONIFY the lecture. That is, the student seems forced, in some sense, to be more responsible for or to the course because the lecture has been a one-to-one interaction. One or two such moments per class hour per person seems to have a notable effect. In my teaching experience, the rapidity with which I can fixate on an entire array of students has increased gradually to the point where it is very easy to do in classes of up to about thirty, and can be done, with effort, in larger groups. Why this should have a strong apparent effect on the teaching/learning process might lead us to rethink at least some aspects of (human) vision.

J. An uncanny ability of humans is memory of others' faces, keeping them in dynamic completeness, for long periods. Many people seem to visualize others principally as faces. But we do less well in distinguishing those faces with which we have less familiarity, "THEY all look alike to me — and to mine!"

Perhaps we can infer that we attend carefully to the facial features of those around us, but how carefully, with what depth? Is this learned? Do different populations attend to very different aspects of faces?

To my knowledge, we do not yet know. Although most of us can and do distinguish male from female faces, there seems to be no careful accounting for what it is that we attend to. For this most usual and ordinary human ability, there is no adequate description. Why? My guess is that we are extremely bad observers (on purpose) of those aspects of bodies that we use for our ordinary life-taxonomies.

Is the ability to visualize other faces and remember them of any deep importance to the problem of memory? Perhaps memory (and consciousness?) begins, at least, in one's ability to translate how others' faces represent their worlds into one's own body and brain.[10]

K. Imaging? Obviously an individual/mind process? Upon reading Luria's *The mind of a mnemonist* (1968), one is struck with the visual imagery, layer upon layer of how the professional mnemonist concentrated in remembering to remember to remember. Asking students in classes over the past year about what things were like when they were eight or nine years old, one is struck with the very common imagistic accounts of how they "get into" such memories. The most usual picture was associated with either home or school, and they could proceed to remember from there.

Although I have no understanding of what this might mean, one striking factor in imagistic memory is that most people do not remember childhood in random access terms — rather they seem to have a way into the scene. Once in, they seem to be able to visualize-imagine in apparently different ways or pictures. Similarly, many colleagues report that they visually imagine (potential) audiences as they write, prepare, or review lectures.

In some cases, friends have reported difficulty in transferring images from one mode or locale to another. A fellow student in a linguistics course many years ago who spoke German natively only at home had no "accessible" German in the classroom. Some musicians I have asked find it difficult to talk ABOUT their instruments unless they have them in hand. The carry-over of images from one context to another is clearly not a simple matter.

Yet, as pointed out earlier, we are extremely good at remembering faces, dynamic expressions of those we know well. I occasionally feel that I am still learning, at least comprehending more deeply, what some of my teachers said fifteen or more years ago. How is this possible?

It suggests to me that a lot of what is called memory is not exactly

---

[10] Although consciousness has been attributed to the individual (mind), this is a useful way of thinking about it in interactional terms.
Consciousness is "the ability and willingness of an individual to cue-in on a shared, multi-person picture of the world when it is situationally appropriate."
This concept would imply, among other things, a broadening of current views of psychopathology and the rational possibility of handling popular notions such as levels of consciousness, parapsychology, and extrasensory perception.

in one's "head" or "mind." Perhaps it can be said to be located in interactional contexts, that in some, possibly deep sense, an individual really does not "know" or remember; what he carries (words seem to be less than adequate here) is access to the interactional scene. Possibly this is followed (in imagistic time?) by a personification of how we would act in that context. An example: I have asked a number of people how they (literally) place money in a salesclerk's hand when paying for a purchase. All have claimed not to know! But I have observed very few confusions or ambiguities occurring in such scenes. They must KNOW, but where, then, can that knowledge be said to be located? In the two minds? In the interactions? Actually, most of my informants could easily visualize themselves in such a scene and could (kinesthetically) FEEL the proper hand-arm position. Is the "memory" in their bodies, then?

A number of people who regularly do very concentrated work — e.g. musicians, teachers who speak without notes, the mnemonist — report that such work is physically (as well as mentally) exhausting. Why? Does it take a great amount of (bodily) energy to utilize the brain? Or is the ability to do such work consistently (also) a bodily exercise? Perhaps all the necessary images are not stored (only) in the brain.

L. Close your eyes — it is often much easier to visualize images this way. Is this somehow paradoxical, or is it easier simply because so much (real) visual input is eliminated?

Perhaps there is more to it, because imaging with eyes closed appears to be much more active than one might suppose. What seems to happen is that the closed eyelid actually presses inward upon the eye (stimulating it?), helping to create one's sense of visual image.

If true, this suggests to me that our ability to create our own images in this active physical sense may be much more complete and subtle than we have thought possible. It also suggests that blinking is more than an eye-moistening device. I have observed, for example, that shifting eye focus is almost always accompanied by a blink; if not, there is a sense of eye strain. It is very difficult to maintain focus without blinking. Why? I know of no satisfactory answer to these questions.

Within the body framework, one might postulate that eyelids act somehow as a locus of access information. One keeps or stores a lot of information-images of the sort, for example, that enables one to "remember to remember." Perhaps we keep our attention-tenders in particular bodily locations. Rather than postulating a brain or mind that operates and tracks on multiple levels simultaneously, I propose that the brain operates PRIMARILY as an information-switching center, not as the self-caused, self-knowing being that somehow has to constantly interpret its own interpretation, multiply regressed. No wonder it is powerfully tempting to posit a homunculus!

M. What sorts of information or knowledge are possessed by one's dominant hand, different from or greater than what one has in the other hand? Having asked this question of a number of people, and having found no one who could analyze this most important (and apparently humanoid) difference, I felt forced to conclude that this sort of body-image information was so basic to one's being that it was not available for analysis (if one doesn't already know ...); perhaps, however, it is simply a lack of vocabulary.

This problem leads one to an "end around" approach. Many musicians, for example, have fairly direct access to what they do — much violin pedagogy (there is a large written literature extending back several centuries) is the teacher's analysis of what he himself does, demonstrating how to do it, and how to image it usefully (perhaps metaphorically). At any rate, violinists have two quite knowledgeable hands, but each operates successfully in extremely different domains.

A series of problems shows up immediately in this context. One is coordination — the right (bowing) hand must just follow (in time) the left finger placement. In asking a few people about this, I found that one of the "perceptual" difficulties is that the musicians have the problem in the "wrong hand." One tends, for example, to think of a problem as one of the left hand, when the difficulty might lie in the right. This is also true of the dynamics (relative loudness and softness) — it is very difficult to keep one's left hand from pressing more firmly when the eyes see "forte." But to play well, the left hand must be freed of this belief.

One has to assign different techniques to various body parts. There are seven string and double-string combinations for violin bowing. One has to know where they are without looking, and with the right hand up to three feet away from the point where the bow actually contacts the string. In order to play well, one must feel in his arm where the movement primarily takes place and must assign the various string bowings to arm locations. Most bowing assignations are actually located at various positions on the right upper arm and shoulder. It seems to me that a lot of practice-makes-perfect is in reminding oneself about one's own (metaphorical) bodily organization.[11]

---

[11] The notion of TALENT is interesting here, because many violinists reach a series

This all suggests that in attempting to achieve any very deep understanding of human movement, in or out of interactional settings, we will be forced to learn much more about how we organize and know our own and others' bodies.

N. Can there be said to be image centers in the body? A case was made for the eyelid being such a center or device. I suggest that all protruding body surfaces are possible loci for imaging.

Contemplate the tongue! Any dentist will affirm that tongues clearly have a "mind" of their own. Whatever else "orality" may be, it is certainly a cognitive investigation of the universe by the tongue. The ability to articulate speech is the smallest function of the tongue. In addition, the tongue distributes the proper kind of saliva and must manage it properly to permit speech. Management of saliva and speech are in some senses coterminous (Sarles 1973b).

The tongue is no more a passive member in face-to-face interaction than are the muscles of articulation. The English-speaking tongue is in virtually continuous contact with the upper teeth or alveolar ridge; more important, it is delicately tensioned, pushing. In fact, this observation first arose in an oral biology seminar when the orthodontists pointed out that most malocclusion is effectively caused by "tongue thrusting."

One might suggest that the tongue is actively tracking during interaction and might contribute to or be part of the mentation processes. In a paper read to the Dental Research Association (Sarles 1972c), I suggested that the interactional miming discussed earlier is modeled "incorrectly" by faces that are unable to copy another's face (e.g. in individuals with Down's syndrome).

The Down's/Mongoloid child, who appears to have nonoperant external facial muscles and who will predictably be retarded, may merely be unable to use his tongue as others do. Professionals who work with such persons report that almost all of them speak similarly to one another. If the tongue has something to do with mentation, it is not surprising that they appear to be mentally "defective." But this form of so-called defect may not be mental in the sense of an abnormal brain. Rather, the apparent mental-mind defect may be seen as a problem in bodily interaction.

O. This conceptualization of (some) mental "defectiveness" as a

---

of plateaus where increased practice does not make for much improvement. Talent, I suggest, is in large measure a good analytic sense of one's body, trusting one's own self-analysis, and remembering one's body scheme.

problem in interaction leads to a reconsideration of the informative function of the face. Again, the Down's syndrome children who are visually diagnosable at birth provide a provocative example.

Apparently, a great deal of information that parents seem to seek and use is missing on Down's faces. Because there is so little facial movement or accompanying color and tissue changes, the affective information that parents interpret as representing the actual state of the infant is absent or severely reduced.

In interactional perspective, the effects of this are to make the infant's face appear to be less reliable and probably much less interesting than that of the normal infant. This seems to reduce the level of parentally induced interaction and to lead parents to assume that the child is less (internally) responsive to them.[12]

By spending less time, and quite probably by attempting to mimic adult faces without the full use of all the external facial muscles, the Down's child will not be able to become "normal." In fact, these children form the case paradigm caricature of facial stupidity that most of us seem to use as rough mental evaluators: mouth open, tongue down and exposed. This means directly that WE interpret and judge the mental attributes as indicated on faces — as if faces directly represented mental powers. But the actual mental states of such people might be quite different in a variety of senses!

It seems useful to consider the possibility that Down's children and many others whom we label as "retarded" look as they do because in some senses they believe that they look "normal." They attempt to "get in tune" with their parents as much as any child — the aberrant result is caused by their muscular/bodily inability to mimic properly. This in turn reduces and/or alters their parental interactions in a way that effectively confirms their beliefs and causes their faces to become (or remain) abnormal in the judgment of the community. Operating from false assumptions, such children tend to misread, but in ways which they adjust to and find comfortable.

Actually, a number of subadult and adult Down's persons do appear to look more like the general population. Many seem to have quite large brow ridges. I interpret this as their attempt to use or substitute

---

[12] In a study now being conducted by the University of Minnesota, Department of Special Education, a number of volunteer parents of such children are in a program of sustained, intensive face-to-face interaction with their Down's children — the hope being that their children's faces will come to resemble those of the family more than they do the typical Down's face, that the supportive feelings in familial interaction will increase and that the children will be better socialized.

head muscles (parietal, occipital, etc.) for their missing facial muscles. Some of them seem to be able to do this rather successfully. In the more successful cases, one feels that the sustained familial interactional effort with these people must have been enormous (Hunt 1966).

P. About comfort: my Southern Mexican Tzotzil informant and close friend, Bal, having spent a great deal of time studying gringos speaking English, commented several times that we must hold our tongues at the "top of our heads. How fatiguing that must be!" (Sarles 1966). He tried holding his bilingual Tzotzil-Spanish tongue up to the alveolar ridge and reported vague distress feelings after about ten seconds. His usual interactional, listening tongue placement was on his mouth bottom, with the tongue tip tensioned against the soft tissue protruding outward below the bottom teeth.

But this vague feeling of discomfort arises in many other contexts as well. There are a variety of bodily positions whose shift or changes will provoke a sense of fatigue in a few seconds. This is clear to would-be musicians in small muscle movements — holding the violin is, for example, a ridiculous arm position. To be able to maintain it for two or three hours is amazing. But it can be "worked up to" gradually.

There are also male-female body-holding or body-set differences that have been established very gradually during development. The typical adult female pelvis thrust feels, on imitation, very "peculiar" to a male. Holding a cigarette "like a woman," with the wrist held backward, is also strange to a man.

Trying to "feel" Slavic or French or Indian requires an American to reconstitute his mouth-holding muscles and to literally alter his appearance. And it causes discomfort.

The point of this is, I believe, that it demonstrates that we have organized our bodies in ways that become increasingly comfortable and "natural" to us. How did we come to that particular body organization which when changed causes us to feel uncomfortable? How do we (or did we as we grew up) maintain this essentially (body) ESTHETIC view, and what is its distribution by feature and population?

If, in Mead's view of interaction, we relate our faces (and bodies) to one another, are there mechanisms and limits to how we do this, which tie in the notion of discomfort suggested above? Does the sense or direction of mutual facial adjustment, for example, place more constraints on the depth or quality of message interchange, or is there some intermediate or neutral mutual adjustment area that shapes the interaction?

If the old anecdote of married couples growing to look more alike contains any germ of truth, what are its structural dynamics?

Students report that some (usually "effective") professors appear different in different settings. If we assume this to be at least partially true, what might it mean? Does the person one appears to be represent the teacher's adjustment to that particular scene, or are we dealing with some sort of illusion?

Q. In a body theory of interaction and being, there must be included an esthetic sense. The notion of body alteration being somehow uncomfortable must imply a sense of our ability and willingness to judge alterations of our body (parts) as being relatively pleasureful or not (Cabanac 1971).

Mind theories simply postulate a pleasure-pain differentiation center, as well as a primary set of emotions. The body, in mind theories, is hardly more than a locus for the end organs that are sensately responsive to stimuli, which are thence passed to the central nervous system-mind loci for interpretation.

Although I know of no well worked-out counter theories to that innate-mind presumption, it is probably worth suggesting how some alternative theories might be conceptualized. Two sorts of ideas may be considered. (1) The "body" may tend to regard as pleasurable those stimuli transmitted primarily ALONG (the fewest number of) surfaces; stimuli that may be said to cause pain are those that move ACROSS effective surface boundaries. The effective amplitude of the stimulus and its temporal dimension must also be important here. Tickling, for example, is an INTERACTIONAL event that is usually interpreted as pleasurable until it begins to involve "deeper tissues," and begins to be perceived as hurting, and (2) the external body surfaces (such as the face and eyes), being (we assume) in a continuous tensioned dynamic, may somehow be sensitive to external stimuli in such a way that they form some sorts of representation of the external world — what we call perception would then be our (second order?) reading and interpretation of our bodies' representational configurations.

One could imagine, for example, that the human eye is itself effectively a many-layered organ. Perhaps the eye forms a three-dimensional representation of the external world by choosing certain of these layers for primary focus. Very likely one chooses these foci as one chooses to speak as one does (which might help to account for why myopia has its peculiar distributions). Seeing would then be a second-order reading, not of the external world per se but of our eyes' representation of it. This notion might also help to account for why one-eyed people can operate as if they see depth and why staring is so difficult; it might enhance the reasonableness of reopening questions about why we blink.[13]

R. If the emotions are capable of being conceptualized in a body theory, they must be susceptible of shaping and structuring in the context of interaction.

How can we be said to read (correctly) tension or fear in another's body? We could be responding to his facial expression, somehow matching some mosaic in our minds with what we believe we are seeing. Or, in body theory, our bodies could be said to be attempting, in the interaction, "to get in tune" with the interactant. We then interpret our own body's attempted representation of another's mood or emotional state. This theory begins to account for the special sensitivity of some people (I do not think one can account for this in a mind theory) and the lesser sensitivity of others, and for why we often seem to read badly or misinterpret across all kinds of human boundaries (age, language, sex, etc.). It may even begin to account for why we seem to change through EXPERIENCE; hopefully it may also lend understanding to why we are RESISTANT to experiential change in many circumstances.[14]

To extrapolate even further, a body theory of being might even be used to understand some of the dynamics of speciation; it may be, for example, that our bodies find it difficult to respond to bodies that are, in whatever senses, quite different from ours. It seems very easy for most of us to empathize, e.g. sexually and parentally, with other species, but it seems to be extremely difficult to "feel" like any four-legged creature in terms of maintaining balance or running.

S. What "feels good"? Vanity, power, success.... Olympic gold medalists all report that winning "feels" great. In what senses are these feelings so important that people will devote all their energies to their enhancement? Is this any different from any other addiction?

What feels bad? Depression, fear, horror.... But some people find horror movies and stories titillating. Why do most children like ghost stories?

Of those states of being that feel good, many have a high degree of interactional input — they involve others, bringing positive attention to oneself. Famous people "walk famous." Spencer Tracy is reported to

---

[13] Most, possibly all, of the research work on monocular vision seems to have been done with binocular people who hold one eye closed. Truly monocular people have few of the problems one might predict for them in operating in the real world; e.g. driving, playing sports such as squash, and ski jumping are not difficult for one-eyed people.

[14] The nature of CONSERVATISM remains completely problematic.

have been able to demonstrate this.

Sickness feels bad; hurts hurt; pain is pain. But these are all said to be individual, private.

Assuming all of these human feelings to be bodily in some sense, how might we formulate some ways of thinking about them that might lend some insight into their nature? In mind theories, it appears, these states of being are not deeply explicable except possibly in a descriptive sense.

Most long-term, committed joggers report that jogging also makes them feel good. Here, at least, some observations can be offered. Sheer movement becomes a joy to joggers; their energy level (if they do not overdo jogging) rises; their bodies become and remain "tight." I think they feel their total bodies much more completely, and mainly they feel good. Thus the feelings have something to do with maintaining certain degrees of TENSION in various body parts, of having command. My guess is that this also somehow enhances one's ability to control whatever it is that feels good. And, I suspect, much of it has to do with being able to avoid what feels bad.

Talking about these feelings is obviously difficult. But that should not stop us from continuing to study and describe the (apparent) bodily changes with the variety of reported feelings. Much of this is in the arena of body image, and good and bad feelings must be, in some sense, a derivation of or deviation from an expected-desired set of feelings. It might be, for example, that obese people have difficulty in lower weight maintenance because they retain the essential feelings of themselves as fat people instead of retraining themselves to "think thin," which includes a necessary feeling of discomfort upon eating too much.

Tension seems to mean truly that the body is tenser than usual — who can tell if minds direct or cause bodies to become tense, or if a tenser body is interpreted by one's mind as a headache or an arthritic pain. How do people constitute their bodies to enhance good feelings, to avoid damaging them?

T. Congruence and context. A major difficulty in describing bodily or vocal variation with situation or context, as INSIDERS, is that we apparently are contextually appropriate observers. What we tend to note is unexpected, incongruent, or unusual facial expressions. This places us in an observational position in which we seem likely to confirm our own normalcy, rather than to note variation. Natural history recording movements, no matter how carefully done, can do little more than to make us better observers; it can yield little new insight or lead us to observe the range of possibilities that do NOT occur (but might) in any situation.

A first attempt to become better observers is to break context, e.g. to take a tape of a half-hour interview and to cut and splice in a variety of orders, then listen to the same voice as it ranges over a variety of topics, mood shifts, and interactional changes (Sarles 1973a). There is much more variation, and more different kinds of variation, than one ever hears just listening straight through. So we must be contextually tied observers.

Another corrective in trying to become a better observer is to keep in mind how other species or non-native speakers of our language hearing it for the first time might hear us, or of how it would sound through a closed door (Sarles 1971a). If it seems rhythmic, for example, in any sense analogous to music, it would be useful to study the mechanics of musical production.[15]

At any rate, I believe that there is much more in the voice stream, especially in interaction, than linguistic theory has begun to suggest. It appears to be investigable if we can learn to become much better observers. In contrast to current linguistic theory, I believe that the sound stream can and does convey MEANING about the situation, relationship, continuity, context, and a multitude of social and temporal variables. The obstruction to reconceptualization has been in linguistics' claims that a phonemic description of language has been EXHAUSTIVE. A careful reading of modern linguistic theory will reveal, I believe, that sound is as incidental to language as bodies are to minds.

REFERENCES

BENJAMIN, GAIL R.
    1969 "The non-linguistic content of speech." Unpublished Master's thesis, University of Minnesota.
BRONOWSKI, J.
    1965 *The identity of man.* London: Penguin.

---

[15] With practice, one can learn to hear (on purpose) the subtle differences between marcato and staccato in terms of how they fill their temporal slots: both end well before the next sound is about to begin; marcato has an amplitude change (rise and fall) that is relatively large from beginning to end; staccato is much steadier in amplitude, just stopping quickly. Counting, saying the alphabet, or listing items are very much like marcato, and this seems to be a favorite thing for children, especially, to do, both linguistically and musically. (Marches are very exciting for most of us, and are very difficult to "get out of one's head," but this may be a culture-bound observation.)

BUSNEL, RENÉ F.
1963 "On certain aspects of animal acoustic signals," in *Acoustic behaviour of animals*. Edited by R. F. Busnel. Amsterdam: Elsevier.

CABANAC, MICHAEL
1971 Physiological role of pleasure. *Science* 173:1103–1107.

CASSIRER, ERNST
1946 *Language and myth*. Translated by Susanne K. Langer. New York: Dover.

CHOMSKY, N.
1966 *Cartesian linguistics*. New York: Harper and Row.
1968 *Language and mind*. New York: Harcourt, Brace and World.

DARLING, F. F.
1952 Social behavior and survival. *Auk* 69:183–191.

DARWIN, CHARLES
1872 *The expression of the emotions in man and animals*. London: J. Murray.

EIBL-EIBESFELDT, I.
1970 *Ethology: the biology of behavior*. Translated by E. Klinghammer. New York: Holt, Rinehart and Winston.

EKMAN, P.
1972 *Emotion in the human face*. New York: Pergamon Press.

EKMAN, P., E. R. SORENSON, W. V. FRIESEN
1969 Pan-cultural elements in facial displays of emotion. *Science* 64.

ENLOW, DONALD H.
1968 *The human face*. New York: Harper and Row.

FLANAGAN, J. L.
1965 *Speech analysis, synthesis, and perception*. New York: Academic Press.

GIBSON, J. J.
1966 *The senses considered as perceptual systems*. Boston: Houghton Mifflin.

GOSS, C. M., editor
1954 *"Anatomy of the human body" by Henry Gray*. Philadelphia: Lea and Febiger.

HELMHOLTZ, H.
1954 *On the sensations of tone*. New York: Dover.

HUNT, NIGEL
1966 *The world of Nigel Hunt: the diary of a Mongoloid youth*. Beaconsfield, England: Darwin Finlayson.

LANCASTER, JANE B.
1965 "Language and communication," in *The origin of man*. Edited by Paul L. DeVore, 71-78. New York: Wenner-Gren Foundation for Anthropological Research.

LORENZ, K.
1965 "Preface," in *The expression of the emotions in man and animals*. By C. Darwin. Chicago: University of Chicago Press.

LURIA, A. R.
1968 *The mind of a mnemonist*. New York: Basic Books.

MAYR, ERNST
  1963   *Animal species and evolution.* Cambridge: Harvard University Press.
MEAD, G. H.
  1934   *Mind, self, and society.* Edited by C. W. Morris. Chicago: University of Chicago Press.
POLLACK, I., S. M. PICKETT
  1964   Intelligibility of excerpts from fluent speech: auditory vs. structure context. *Journal of Verbal Learning and Verbal Behavior* 3:79–84.
RYLE, GILBERT
  1949   *The concept of mind.* New York: Barnes and Noble.
SARLES, H. B.
  1966   "A descriptive grammar of the Tzotzil language." Unpublished manuscript.
  1967   The study of intelligibility. *Linguistics* 34:55–64.
  1969   The study of language and communication across species. *Current Anthropology* 10(2–3):211–221.
  1971a "Could a non-h? (could a non-human possibly discover that humans have language?)" Unpublished manuscript.
  1971b "Communicating across disciplines: with special reference to the behavioral sciences." Unpublished manuscript.
  1972a "The search for comparative variables in human speech." Symposium paper at the Animal Behavior Society Annual Meeting, Reno, Nevada: "Animal communication versus human speech: a discontinuity in approach or in evolution?"
  1972b "A sense for language in the context of human ethology." Paper read at the Symposium on Language Origins, American Anthropological Association Annual Meeting, Toronto, Ontario.
  1972c "The dynamics of facial expression." Symposium paper read at the Annual Meeting of the International Association for Dental Research, Las Vegas, Nevada.
  1973a "Behavioral linguistics." Unpublished manuscript.
  1973b "The self-perceived functions of saliva." Unpublished manuscript.
  1974   "Facial expression and body movement," in *Linguistics and adjacent arts and sciences*, volume one. Edited by Thomas A. Sebeok, 297–310. Current Trends in Linguistics 12. The Hague: Mouton.
SIMPSON, G. G.
  1970   Reply to Sarles, 1969. *Current Anthropology* 11(1).
SPICKER, STUART F.
  1970   *The philosophy of the body.* Chicago: Quadrangle Books.
SPITZ, R. A., K. M. WOLF
  1946   The smiling response: a contribution to the ontogenesis of social relations. *General Psychology Monograph* 34:57–125.
STEBBINS, G. LEDYARD
  1965   Pitfalls and guideposts in comparing organic and social evolution. *Pacific Sociological Review* 8 (Spring):3–10.
VESEY, G. N. A.
  1965   *The embodied mind.* London: George Allen and Unwin.

Human Linguistics and Face-to-Face Interaction

VICTOR H. YNGVE

The small but growing group of people working on the phenomena of face-to-face interaction is confronted with a critical lack of an adequate theoretical framework. Research is impeded because we lack the understanding and insight that a satisfactory theory would give and the guidance it would provide for observational and experimental programs. Lacking an appropriate theoretical structure, we find it difficult to state results and more difficult to relate them with one another. I think I can assume a consensus both for the intrinsic interest and importance of the phenomena studied, and the desperate need for an appropriate framework. The situation has reached the proportions of a crisis.

Ten or fifteen years ago I lived through a similar confrontation. The lack of adequate theory was seriously impeding the development of mechanical translation. The computer was not giving us any trouble, the problem was that we had no adequate theory of translation on which to build workable translating programs. In the early days we had pinned our hopes on linguistics. The expectation seemed reasonable that structural linguistics could provide us with relevant theory, but we encountered serious difficulties. Later we became enthusiastic about the promise of transformational-generative grammar, but we were soon disillusioned and disappointed again, for that framework did not provide what we needed either.

Today, a similar disappointment and disillusionment is sweeping through linguistics itself. The realization is growing that the transformational-generative framework is also inadequate for the very discipline for which it was designed. We are thus faced with a crisis in linguistics as well. It is interesting to note the similarities between these three crisis situations. I believe that the similarities are not just coincidental: the three crises are related, and in fact are merely three aspects of the same common crisis.

THE SCOPE OF THE TASK

Those working in the field of face-to-face interaction probably realize more clearly than others the broad range of phenomena that seem to be interconnected and need to be related to one another by some appropriate theoretical structure or framework for examining the organization of social interaction from cultural, social, and psychological perspectives through discussions of the interrelationships between speech and gesture, facial expressions, and posture and spacing.

Starting with an interest in face-to-face interaction we have been led to consider a number of diverse disciplines and a great breadth of relevant observational phenomena. In seeking an integrated framework we can start first by surveying the scope of observational phenomena that seem to be interrelated in spite of the diversity of the disciplines and theoretical frameworks through which these observations have traditionally been approached. Then, after taking this observational inventory, we can turn and consider the task of finding an integrated framework capable of embracing that full range of phenomena.

To aid in thinking about the problem it is convenient to conceive of a single observationally defined discipline that encompasses the full range of phenomena. I have been calling this field BROAD LINGUISTICS. After defining the scope of broad linguistics we will then want to search for a proper theoretical framework for it. Those who are concerned with the observations of broad linguistics will be called linguists, in the broad sense, whether they have been recruited into this field from traditional linguistics, anthropology, sociology, psychiatry, or wherever else.

First of all, broad linguistics includes the types of observations typically made by traditional linguists when studying particular languages: such data as texts, recordings, and informant responses, together with distinctions of same or different, acceptable or not acceptable, paraphrase relations, rough translational equivalences, notes on typical situations of use, and so on. These materials have traditionally gone into the production of grammars and lexicons of different languages, comparative studies, and the like. Broad linguistics also includes the materials used by historical linguists, and the observations of dialectologists on the geographical and social distribution of various linguistic items.

On the border with sociology, data on the correlation of linguistic and social variables are of interest, particularly in relation to social class, role, and relative status. There is an interest in bilingualism and the phenomena of languages in contact, and in data on pidgins and creoles and how they change with time. Broad linguistics, of course, includes considerations of how people enter conversations, maintain them, and adjourn them. It is concerned with the variables of space and distance as studied in proxemics. It does not ignore gestures and postural variables as studied in kinesics, and it includes paralinguistic phenomena.

Broad linguistics includes the linguistic data obtained by the anthropologist in his field work. This involves considerations of kinship terminology, folk taxonomy, special ritual use of language, how language and communication serve the various functions of the society, and many other related considerations. Linguists are concerned with the instrumental use of language in accomplishing certain tasks, and attention is given to the situations of use of language and how they affect communicative behavior.

On the border with psychology, broad linguistics is concerned with the results of psychological studies directed toward the capacities and limitations of speaker and hearer, since they may be very relevant to an understanding of certain basic questions. There is interest in data on the relations of language to psychological variables in perception, conceptualization, and problem solving. Linguists want to be able to handle data on language acquisition by the child as well as by the adult.

Linguists also study data related to stylistics, poetics, and the artistic use of language in general. In short, the field of broad linguistics is very broad indeed, but it is fairly clear what the scope of it is in terms of the concerns of the investigators in a number of related fields.

It is difficult to characterize broad linguistics in any more precise way than as the range of interests of a particular diverse group of investigators, yet broad linguistics does include within its scope the phenomena that seem to present themselves naturally as being somehow interconnected and inviting explanation and unification by means of a proper theory. Such is the nature of broad linguistics; it is an observationally defined discipline in search of an appropriate theoretical structure.

THE INADEQUACY OF A LINGUISTIC APPROACH

It is perhaps obvious that no presently existing discipline offers an appropriate theoretical structure capable of covering broad linguistics. Instead, we have a number of diverse disciplines, each covering some part of that observational scope, and each being unable to cover the rest. The reason for this seems to be that each discipline has its central thrust directed somewhat outside the general area of broad linguistics, or else its central thrust is too narrowly conceived to cover more than a limited portion of the area of broad linguistics. We could show this by going through the various disciplines one by one but will limit ourselves to a discussion of the current discipline of linguistics. Linguistics today enjoys the reputation of having the most comprehensive and systematic unifying structure in the general area, a structure that many have turned to for guidance. But it is easy to see that linguistics, as presently conceived, is completely inadequate for our purposes.

Linguistics is usually defined as the scientific study of language. Language is defined as the relation between sound and meaning. This relation is expressed in terms of grammar and lexicon, which lay out the rules of the language, and implicitly or explicitly specify what expressions belong in the language and what expressions fall outside it. In linguistics, grammar and lexicon play the role of a unifying theory that serves to relate the phenomena to one another and explain them.

Although this view of the conceptual structure of linguistics is almost universally accepted today, it is not new. It is a traditional conceptual structure carried down almost unchanged in its most basic elements from the Greek thought of 300 to 150 B.C. It was developed in that era by the Stoic philosophers and by the Alexandrian literary scholars. For the Stoics, it served as an integral part of a theory of knowledge. The Alexandrians were interested in preserving a great literary heritage in the face of evident language change and dialectal variation in Greek. The combined grammatical tradition that grew up was preserved and elaborated by the later Greeks and the Romans, and it reaches us today through an unbroken line. This conceptual structure was very relevant to the interests of the Greeks, but today it is largely irrelevant to the needs of broad linguistics, as we shall presently see.

Nevertheless, there has been a tendency to turn to linguistics for guidance in theory construction, for the system of rules found there seems eminently suited, with perhaps some modification, to our task.

But such attempts are doomed to failure if they are deemed to be anything more than exploratory attempts to organize some limited area of data, for the basic concepts are inappropriate.

Furthermore, linguistics, even within its own house, does not enjoy an enviable position, for there has been continual revision of theory over the last 2,000 years within the general limits of the traditional framework, and the current transformational-generative theory has been admitted by many of its main advocates to be in great trouble (Dingwall 1971).

THE UBIQUITY OF TRADITIONAL LINGUISTIC CONCEPTS

Even if we do not consciously follow the lead of the grammatical tradition in our search for a unifying framework, we are apt to fall prey to its basic conceptual structure. This is because our everyday language incorporates this conceptual structure in the very structure of its vocabulary. It is very difficult to think about much of the phenomena of broad linguistics without thinking in terms of traditional grammatical concepts. This can cause great difficulty if these concepts are in fact inadequate or irrelevant, as I believe they are.

First of all, let us examine the word LANGUAGE. The Greeks distinguished between Greek and barbarian (foreign) languages, and for Greek, they distinguished between Good Greek and corrupt or deviant Greek, filled with foreignisms and errors. Their object of study was Good Greek, and they defined this in terms of the literary traditions of earlier centuries. They were little interested in the languages of the uncultured (non-Greek) peoples, and little interested in informal discourse or conversation. Their concept of language, therefore, was normative and prescriptive in its emphasis on Good Greek, and it carried an implication of uniformity. Indeed, the observed linguistic diversity was rejected and condemned as being incorrect or uncultured. In spite of the efforts of recent generations of linguists, the normative and prescriptive implications have not disappeared, and the implication of uniformity is as universally evident as is the observational evidence against it: no two people speak the same. The Greeks discussed facial expressions and gestures in rhetoric but treated only the formal style of the orator. This tradition and the tradition of gestures in the theater were not unified with grammatical thought. Their concept of language did not include nonverbal components, but only what was expressed in alphabetic writing. These several serious limitations remain today in our concept of what a language is.

But there is more. In the very influential Stoic philosophical tradition, language was treated as a part of dialectic, the study of arguments true and false, the part of philosophy that investigated how we know the truth and how we express it. Long before Saussure, the Stoic theory of the sign distinguished the signifier, the signified, and the referent. Under the signifier, they treated sound in terms of the grammatical levels of voice, diction, and speech. Under the signified, they treated meaning in terms of the logical levels of the proposition, notion, presentation, perception, and sensation, by means of which we come to know the truth.

Language is still considered a relation between sound and meaning in spite of the fact that this static view, adapted to a theory of knowledge, offers no concepts appropriate to much of the study of conversation. If we are not careful, our theories will be similarly limited to propositional speech and the expression of meanings that are little nuggets of knowledge. Much of conversation falls outside these narrow bounds — for example, greeting behavior. The concept of language as a relation between sound and meaning survives in spite of the fact that philosophers have long ago abandoned the Stoic theory of knowledge; and in linguistics, only the treatment of the signifier has survived. Grammar has developed for 2,000 years with no explicit connection to a theory of knowledge. Linguists think they know what sound is: it can be observed; but for 2,000 years they have lacked a theory of meaning. Language as a relation between sound and meaning stands with only one leg on the solid ground of an observable phenomenon. Yet even such an astute linguist as Chomsky would like to assume that both legs stand solidly (1970:52). Such is the strength of the grammatical tradition, and a traditional but indefensible notion of meaning survives to haunt us in our everyday language.

Next, notice the popular conception of the communicative act. We have what might be called the transportation metaphor. Words are considered as vehicles that carry our meanings or convey our thoughts from one mind to another. We send a message as we would send a messenger, and we understand the burden of the message. This whole way of speaking can befog the mind and lead us into the traditional pitfalls. Not only is the concept of meaning that is involved here very misleading; we tend to forget that it is not by words alone that we communicate.

There are many illustrations of the confusions that this whole traditional conceptual apparatus has led us into. Let me mention just one. Much of the literature since Charles Darwin on facial "expressions" has operated under the assumption that there was a repertory of expressions, each conveying a particular emotional meaning. Typical experimental designs would consist of listing various emotions that were thought to be involved, such as pleasure, hate, fright, anger, and so on, and then asking a subject to express these emotions by means of facial expressions, which would be photographed. Then the procedure was to see if other subjects could correctly identify the emotions expressed. The several confusions embedded in this experimental paradigm are perhaps obvious.

THE QUESTION OF AN APPROPRIATE GOAL

If there is no appropriate unifying framework for the observational concerns of broad linguistics, and if traditional linguistics cannot be looked on except with distrust as a source of concepts and methods, what are we to do? There seems to be a need for a reassessment of the various traditionally defined disciplines that relate to portions of the phenomena studied in broad linguistics. Is it possible to build a theoretical framework capable of covering all of the concerns of broad linguistics in a unified way? If so, how would a discipline so constituted relate to existing disciplines?

In seeking an adequate framework, it is appropriate that we start with a consideration of what would be the unifying goal of such a discipline. The traditional goal of linguistics, which we have rejected, is to achieve a scientific understanding of language. Each of the other relevant disciplines has a traditional goal, and none is adequate for the whole of broad linguistics. It would seem difficult to constitute a discipline by somehow combining these diverse goals. It would be better if we could find a single goal with the desired coverage.

I should like to suggest that our goal be TO ACHIEVE A SCIENTIFIC UNDERSTANDING OF HOW PEOPLE COMMUNICATE. Such a goal, I believe, does have the coverage appropriate to the scope of broad linguistics.

It is the nature of a goal that it directs our choice of paths in trying to reach it. It is therefore important to consider carefully the exact wording of the goal. We would do well to avoid the use of terms that appear to prejudge the approach or limit the means for finding the answer. As an example of the danger, a previous wording of a goal to cover the scope of broad linguistics (Yngve 1969) was to achieve a scientific understanding of how people use language to communicate. Despite expressed intentions to the contrary, this formulation has the same problem that the current goal of linguistics has (to achieve a scientific understanding of language). The use of the term "language" appears to presume part of the answer in that it implies close ties to the grammatical tradition. As another example, the organization of behavior in face-to-face interaction is inadequate as a goal for several reasons. In the first place, it prejudges the task by focusing on the organization of BEHAVIOR, and may mean to some a behavioristic approach. Secondly, the restriction to face-to-face interaction may be too constraining — for example, it might be conceived as ruling out an interest in interactions by telephone, as well as written interaction. These might well be considered as derivative, but we would not want to rule out their consideration by the wording of our goal. Another inappropriate suggestion would be to achieve a scientific understanding of communication. This would bring the presumption that there is some abstract entity called communication that is appropriate as an object of study, but then we would be left with the task of defining communication, and this could lead to confusions as great as with the presumption of an abstract entity called language.

Our chosen wording, "to achieve a scientific understanding of how people communicate," does not seem to suffer from any of these defects. There should be no problem with the phrase "achieve a scientific understanding," for a limitation to a scientific approach seems appropriate. The term "people" can be taken in its ordinary meaning in English. Its use merely carries the reasonable presumption that there are people. The only possible problem is with the verb "communicate"; we did have a problem before with "communication." But, whereas the nominalization is vague, even ambiguous, presuming some kind of entity or abstraction, the verb does not share this problem. The only presumption is that people communicate. But, again, taking the ordinary meaning of the word, we know from observation that people do communicate. This statement of the goal thus simply points to an interesting observable phenomenon, that people communicate, and proposes to achieve a scientific understanding of it. The scope of this goal should be approximately, if not exactly, the same as the observational scope of broad linguistics.

I have called the discipline answering to this goal HUMAN LINGUISTICS. This is to eliminate any confusion with the traditional linguistics of language but at the same time to recognize that the interests of linguists today probably come closer to this goal than the interests of any other current sizable group of scholars, and, furthermore, linguistics has probably already given us more insights into this area than any other discipline.

THE BASIC CONCEPTS OF HUMAN LINGUISTICS

It is a great advantage of our new goal that we can start with people. An appropriate scientific concept of people for the purposes of human linguistics should not be difficult to formulate, for people are objects that are given in advance and that can be considered from different viewpoints: there are several other sciences that study people. Since a person is a real physical object that can be known from points of view other than human linguistics, the concept of person does not suffer from the difficulties associated with the concept of language or the concept of communication.

Of course, we are not interested in studying every aspect of people, but only those aspects that are related to how they communicate. It is thus appropriate that we set up as our first concept in human linguistics an abstraction that includes just those properties of people that are of interest. We define the COMMUNICATING INDIVIDUAL as an abstraction in linguistics that includes just those properties of the person that are required to account for his communicative behavior. In defining the communicating individual in terms of properties of interest in human linguistics, we simply exclude from consideration that which is irrelevant while at the same time maintaining the flexibility required to accommodate new observations about people that can be related to their communicative behavior.

The communicating individual, as thus defined, becomes the central concept in human linguistics and represents its major object of study. This being the case, it is clear from the very beginning that human linguistics is a part of psychology. The relationship of the traditional linguistics of language to psychology has been far from clear and has caused no end of confusion in the literature.

Communication is a group or social phenomenon, and it would seem that we would need in human linguistics at least one concept related to groups of individuals. But what kind of a concept should this be? One such concept that has been used extensively in linguistics is the concept of the speech-community. This concept is usually defined in such a way that the members of a speech-community are those people who speak the same language. The concept has given much trouble and has been discussed extensively in the literature. For our purposes it is inadequate because it is related to a concept of language which we have rejected as a basic concept in human linguistics.

We have defined the communicating individual on the basis of observable phenomena — that there are people and that they communicate. For setting up a concept of groups of individuals in human linguistics, we look again to observable phenomena for guidance. We observe that there are many people in the world but that no two are exactly alike in their communicative behavior. Yet we do observe groups within which the individuals can easily communicate with each other. We must somehow take into account both the similarity and the diversity of individuals. With a focus on people instead of on language, we are in a much better position to do this. Being free of the tyranny of the concept of language, we no longer have any reason to conceive of an individual as a language-speaker. We are then not led to an unrealistic assumption of homogeneous communities of language-speakers. We can define our groups in ways that properly reflect the facts of communication.

An individual obviously belongs to many different groups at the same time. We can accommodate the observed diversity of communicative behavior by taking these different groups into account and thus solve a number of problems that concepts of speech-community have raised. We define a COLINGUAL COMMUNITY as a group of individuals who can communicate with each other in certain ways characteristic of the group. An individual is normally a member of many different and partly overlapping colingual communities. Each colingual community is characterized by one or more linguistic features or items that serve to define the community and to set it apart from the others. The concept of colingual community is not related to the totality of communicative potentialities of the individual but only to those that are characteristic of that community and serve to distinguish it from other colingual communities.

When individuals engage in communicative activity, they will be expected to make use of linguistic features belonging to several of the colingual communities to which they both belong. Thus, a member of a profession would belong to a colingual community distinguished by certain communicative forms such as vocabulary items. When he communicates with other members of this community, he may make use of these forms. But he will also make use of linguistic features characteristic of other colingual communities. These will, of course, include larger communities with a geographic base, as well as smaller or overlapping ones related to such special interests as hobbies, sports, religion, fraternal organizations — and even to intimate family groups.

Colingual communities are thus defined in terms of people and their observable behavioral properties related to communication. It would seem that all of the phenomena previously associated with the similarities and differences of languages, dialects, jargons, technical languages, and the like can be analyzed, described, and understood in terms of colingual communities and the communicative features used to define the communities and to identify individuals as members of them.

We have defined the communicating individual as an abstraction in linguistics that includes just those properties of the person that are required to account for his communicative behavior. We may call these properties LINGUISTIC PROPERTIES and note that by definition they account for all the properties of the communicating individual, these being a subset of the properties of the person. An investigation of linguistic properties will be a major concern of human linguistics, since the communicating individual is its central concept.

There are various ways in which linguistic properties may be classified. One way is to divide them into INNATE PROPERTIES and ACQUIRED PROPERTIES. This method of classification runs into the well-known problem that a mature individual is a product of both heredity and environment, and for any given observable property there may be both hereditary and environmental contributing factors. For example, the characteristics of the voice of an opera singer could probably be traced to both genetic factors and training, and it may be impossible to separate these two essential components in the observed singing voice. Nevertheless, the classification into innate properties and acquired properties does have some merit since their methods of study are somewhat different. For studying innate properties we have, for example, methods worked out in genetics, and for studying acquired properties we have, for example, methods worked out in developmental and educational psychology.

It would seem far off the mark to approach the innate properties of the communicating individual through linguistic universals. Grammar is not a property of a person but a construct of the grammarian that purports to show the relation between sound and meaning given by some language. The idea of universal grammar as including just what is common to the grammars of all languages is an interesting abstraction in the linguistics of language, but to represent this as being an innate property of the individual characteristic of the species is to make a category mistake of the most glaring kind.

Care must also be exercised, when studying the innate properties of the individual, not to assume that just because an observed property is thought to be universal (that is, possessed by all individuals), it is therefore shown to be innate. It is quite possible that there are universal communicative requirements that would be realized in all communicating individuals through acquired properties. For example, one might expect all individuals to have a means of communicating assent or dissent, or for selectively addressing another individual in a group. Such properties might well be universal, yet acquired.

Another way of classifying linguistic properties is according to their apparent function in communication. A full understanding of the communicative function of various linguistic properties will, of course, have to await the results of a considerable amount of research. We can, however, suggest a tripartite classification that is based on some initial observational evidence. Linguistic properties can be classified as BASIC PROPERTIES, which represent the physical properties that the individual uses in communication; COLINGUAL PROPERTIES, which represent those properties by virtue of which the individual is a member of various colingual communities; and SITUATIONAL PROPERTIES, which represent the individual's changing internal accommodation to the communicative situation.

The BASIC PROPERTIES of the communicating individual are probably largely innate, but there may be a non-negligible acquired component. They represent the physical mechanism, the basic equipment, that the individual uses in communicating. Examples include the so-called organs of speech, the equipment for hearing, arms and hands to gesture with, facial features, and a nervous system and brain. In human linguistics we consider these basic properties from the point of view of their communicative function. Included among the basic properties are a large permanent memory and a small temporary memory capable of holding about seven items (Yngve 1960). It is not the task of human linguistics to discover the physiological mechanisms of nerve conduction, but eventually all the basic linguistic properties may be understood also at a lower biological level in terms of anatomy and physiology, and then ultimately understood by scientific reduction in terms of biochemistry and physics. This possibility of reduction to levels of explanation in the biological and physical sciences is one of the advantages of human linguistics over the linguistics of language. Reductions of this sort strengthen both the higher level science and the lower level science.

The COLINGUAL PROPERTIES of the communicating individual are those acquired linguistic properties by virtue of which the individual is a member of various colingual communities. Such properties are the basis for generalizations about communicative behavior because they represent aspects of communicative behavior characteristic of groups of individuals. Thus, we have a wider observational base than the single individual for the study of colingual properties, yet they are properties of the single individual. The colingual properties include a knowledge of the communicative relevance of various roles that are recognized in certain colingual communities, and how to act and react appropriately according to these roles. They are those acquired properties by which the individual knows what to do or say or what to understand in various communicative situations. Thus, under the colingual properties of the individual we understand much of what would be covered under language, or under various cultural or social concepts, but from a quite different point of view that allows us to have an integrated framework.

The SITUATIONAL PROPERTIES of the communicating individual are those acquired and changing properties by which he accommodates to the changing communicatively relevant situations in which he finds himself. Of course, the external physical environment may have communicative relevance, but it is more appropriate to take this into account only through information residing in the individual about the external physical environment. The superiority of this view can be easily shown: when the individual has a misapprehension of what the situation really is, it is his misapprehension and not the reality of the environment that controls or governs his communicative behavior. Under situational properties we include not only a knowledge of the physical situation, objects and persons in the vicinity, their names, roles, characteristics, and so on, but also more abstract situational factors such as the topic of conversation, knowledge of common experiences, attitudes, wishes, hopes and aspirations, knowledge of events — current and historical — and many other pieces of knowledge that have communicative relevance. Both colingual and situational properties, though acquired and perhaps temporary, have their basis in real biochemical differences in the individual, and at the psychological level, an individual who knows something of communicative relevance is demonstrably different from a person who does not, or who knows something different.

The basic, colingual, and situational properties of the communicating individual are exhaustive, and together they can completely account for the communicative behavior of the individual. The basic properties cover the mainly inherited mechanisms operative in the individual for communication; the colingual properties cover the knowledge that the individual has of what to do or understand in various communicative situations; and the situational properties provide the individual with a knowledge of the operative situations. Human linguistics can thus proceed with the study and elaboration of four structures: the structures of the basic, colingual, and situational properties, and the structure of their interrelation. These are structures of real physical properties of the individual considered from their communicative function. Since we are studying in human linguistics an aspect of physical reality, we can ask meaningful questions that can be approached through observational and experimental methods.

AN EXAMPLE

Perhaps a concrete example would help to clarify these basic concepts. Suppose I meet my friend John on the street, invite him to my house for the evening, and he accepts. Much is known about interactions such as this from the work of a number of perceptive observers. How would this bit of face-to-face behavior be approached from the point of view of human linguistics?

As I walk along the street, I am aware of a figure approaching and set my course so as to avoid a collision. Now the behavior involved in foot navigation and the avoidance of obstacles shades into noncommunicative behavior. But the fact that I am a person who passes on the right is a colingual property. But I can adapt in cities where they pass on the left, so my knowledge of which is currently appropriate is a situational property. I note that he has also moved so as to pass on the right. Thus, I am aware of being in an impending right-passing situation, and my situational properties change. I become a person who is about to execute right-passing behavior, and if the oncoming person should change his course I may be caught off-guard.

I also know I am in a neighborhood where I may meet a friend — a situational property — and I know how to handle head position and direction of gaze up to the point of recognition — a colingual property. When recognition takes place, the situation has changed and I behave appropriately. I will do this even in the case of mistaken recognition, until I realize my mistake. The situational properties now are that I recognize my friend, I remember that his name is John, and I have available certain relevant information about our relationship. It is also a situational property that I choose to stop and speak with him rather than execute the minimal appropriate greeting and pass on.

I know how to do this: how to indicate that I wish him to stop, how to engage him in conversation, and he knows how to react appropriately to my behavioral cues. These are colingual properties. I know how to ask him over for the evening. I know that to do this I must be in conversation with him and must have the conversational turn. I do all this, and the situation has changed. He becomes a person who is in conversation with his friend, has just been asked over to the friend's house for the evening, and now has the conversational turn. These are his relevant situational properties, together with other situational properties that will determine whether he accepts or not.

He knows what the options are as part of his colingual properties. He decides to accept and knows how to do that. He does so. He is now a different person. His situational properties have changed again. He is a person who has been invited over for the evening and has accepted. I can predict with some degree of certainty that he will show up on my doorstep. And I am a different person, too. My situational properties are different. I now expect him to show up.

MUCH REMAINS TO BE DONE

Needless to say we are very far from a complete understanding of the structure of the communicating individual in terms of his basic, colingual, and situational properties, and in this brief discussion I have not been able to treat fully what is already known. Many questions have been raised that can be decided only by observation and experiment, and much needs to be done to work out the details of these structures.

It would seem premature at this point to try to specify more exactly the abstract or formal nature of these properties of the individual: we do not yet have enough observational evidence. There is a danger in the premature adoption of a formalism: we may get overly committed to an inadequate framework that would constrain further research. Witness the problems that the grammatical tradition has caused in the study of communicative phenomena.

Nevertheless, there are indications that some kind of a state theory of the individual would be appropriate (Yngve 1969). There are many formal state theories available, but I feel we do not yet have enough observational evidence to choose among them. I have several pieces of research that tend to make me favor a state theory of the individual. The first is the work done on the depth hypothesis (Yngve 1960). Although this work was strongly influenced by concepts from the linguistics of language, with its emphasis on the sentence, it did succeed in relating a basic and undoubtedly innate property of the individual, that of a limited temporary memory, to observed syntactic structures in language and to language change. Whatever success this work has can be traced in large part to the type of state theory postulated for the individual as a producer of sentences. The astute reader will be able to recognize in that model the precursors of the basic, colingual, and situational properties of human linguistics. The other relevant pieces of research are more recent. One (Yngve 1970) reported work on conversational turn and was entirely motivated by considerations of a state theory. The other reports further work on the relation of temporary memory to conversational behavior (Yngve 1973). It has opened up a line of observation and experiment that may be crucial in deciding on the appropriate, more detailed structure of human linguistics.

REFERENCES

DINGWALL, W. O.
  1971 *A survey of linguistic science.* College Park: Linguistics Program, University of Maryland.

CHOMSKY, A. N.
  1970 "Deep structure, surface structure, and semantic interpretation," in *Studies in general and oriental linguistics, presented to Shiro Hattori on the occasion of his sixtieth birthday.* Edited by R. Jakobson, et al. Tokyo: TEC Company.

YNGVE, V. H.
  1960 A model and an hypothesis for language structure. *Proceedings of the American Philosophical Society* 104:444–66.
  1969 "On achieving agreement in linguistics," in *Papers from the fifth regional meeting, Chicago Linguistic Society.* Edited by R. I. Binnick, et al. Chicago: Department of Linguistics, University of Chicago.
  1970 "On getting a word in edgewise," in *Papers from the sixth regional meeting, Chicago Linguistic Society.* Edited by M. A. Campbell, et al. Chicago: Department of Linguistics, University of Chicago.
  1973 "I forget what I was going to say," in *Papers from the ninth regional meeting, Chicago Linguistic Society.* Edited by C. Corum, et al. Chicago: Chicago Linguistic Society.
  f.c. *An introduction to human linguistics.*

Models and Epistemologies in the Study of Interaction

ALBERT E. SCHEFLEN

In reading the current literature on interaction one is impressed with progress in the last decade toward a greater consensus and a more holistic view of the phenomena. I think this change reflects the increasing adoption of a post-Einstein, or systems epistemology. But I also notice how much we are still omitting from our view of interaction and how many loose ends we have. So I think we are still very shaky in our new conceptual base and we have only begun to exploit it. This is what this article is about.

I will proceed as follows: I first will try to classify the old box-and-line models of communication and then try to describe the epistemology on which they are based. Perhaps this step will help to get these splinter concepts out of our hair. Then I will try to characterize the format and signal model which is now rather popular. Then I will say something about the newer epistemology upon which the model rests. Last, I will try to point out the difficulties we still are facing in achieving a broad view of communicational behavior.

CLASSICAL SPLINTER MODELS AND TRADITIONAL EPISTEMOLOGY

A decade ago a conference on communication used always to end up as an argument among three points of view. The psychological theorists advocated an expression theory; the social-psychological people advanced an interactional approach which was then a stimulus-response or an action-reaction concept. And the culturally oriented participants advanced concepts of codes, linguistic or kinesic. Then the members of each of these fronts would fall to arguing with each other. The expression theorist would disagree about what was being expressed: traits, drives, emotions, values, and so on. The interactionalists would argue about aspects of information theory and almost everyone argued that verbal was more important than nonverbal, or vice versa. Still other points of view could have been argued if political scientists, economists, architects, environmentalists, and others had attended panels of communication in those days. In short, there were models of communication in each of the classical disciplines and it seemed important to determine WHICH was true.

These arguments always reminded me of others I had been in all of my life even when the subject matter was not communication. I can remember hearing adults argue when I was a kid about why so and so turned out badly. Some said it was bad seed or his own doing. Others held that he got in with the wrong crowd. My father's Presbyterian friend used to say it was simply the unfolding of a script written in Heaven. And we used to disagree about whether the great star, the team play, or the clever play won the football game and about whether great men or trends determined the course of history. So these cross-disciplinary positions were not unique to the study of communication but were rooted in common culture.

I recall the first time I gained an idea about what these different points of view were about. A group of us had been to a concert and were discussing the experience with considerable animation. One woman insisted on telling us about her brother who had played in the orchestra. One of the men wanted to talk about counterpoint and the relations of one section of the orchestra to another, for these reminded him of teams in a competitive sport. Some of the rest of us wanted to talk about Beethoven and what he was trying to say in the score of the concert. To be sure, we were arguing, but I suddenly realized we were not arguing about what had happened. We were arguing for the floor and trying to gain attention to the particular *einstellung* from which each of us had viewed the concert. We were talking past each other as far as that is concerned. We were the blind men EXAMINING DIFFERENT PARTS OF THE ELEPHANT.

Traditional Models and Determinisms

In retrospect we can classify these foci of observation.

THE ORGANISMIC FOCUS is classical in medicine, biology, and psychology, for example. In this view the focus is upon one person at any time. One looks at the behavior of this person as either an expression of traits or organismic events, as a response to external stimuli or both of these together. And this view of person and behavior can be reversed so to speak; the quality or behavior can be used to make inferences about the person who is behaving.

In this case the behavior of a participant is related to a classification of kinds of behavior and kinds of people. When a next subject is observed his behavior, too, is related to an Aristotelian class, and thus the subjects become members of a set of cases in a series.

THE INTERACTION FOCUS involves looking at one person and then another and relating the behavior of the first to the behavior of the second, and vice versa. The behavior of one participant was often viewed as a stimulus to the other, who then responded. His behavior in turn became a stimulus for the first fellow, and so forth. This action-reaction model used to be dressed up in the lingo of statistical information theory.

This early concept of interaction had a series of shortcomings. It ignored determinants in the behavior of the participants other than the behavior of each other. It was not observed, for instance, that the participants were taking turns according to a format. And the notion of alternate response did not take account of the fact that each participant's contribution could be determined by what he knew would come next as well as by what had just happened before.

IN NETWORK THEORIES a more sociological view of communication was employed. A group of interrelated people or institutions were studied and the lines of communication or the channels of connection were identified.

Notice that all of these approaches feature an initial focus upon the people as communication and then ask what they do.

In early structural studies of language or kinesic behavior the focus was on the customary communicative behavior of a particular tradition. The focus was upon which elements of sound appear in sequence in a sentence and how these are patterned or else upon what elements of movement appear in gesticulation and what is their syntax.

In the 1950's each of these particular foci had been taken up by one of the classical disciplines and the point of view thus employed was advanced as the theory or explanation of communicational events. When the diciplines came together the question was which view was true or useful. There was as yet no well-developed idea of an *einstellung* which could include all of them.

Each of the practical explanations gave rise to a school of determinism. Thus overtly or implicitly it was held that drives, instincts, social or other environmental events or cultural traditions "caused" communicational activity. These classical disciplinary notions were useful in bringing about the illusion of understanding complex phenomena by reducing them to a unicausal explanation, and upholding one of them over the others was useful in maintaining the relative status of a discipline. In fact, in the 1950's we went through three explanatory eras in rapid succession. There was a psychodynamic era, a social science era, and then a behavioral science era.

But these provincialisms of explanation were not confined to the various classical disciplines of the sciences of man. Actually, each of them was, and long had been, held by a particular social class and ethnic grouping. They had been used for centuries to justify or rationalize the behavior of that status and conversely to scapegoat and blame some other category of people. For example, a belief in the overriding importance of language is characteristic not of psychologists but of middle-class intellectual peoples. The belief in bad-seed versions of genetic determinism is characteristic of rural America. Blaming the traits of the proletariat is an upper-middle-class and "Establishment" version of psychological determinism, while the working class and the political left in America find causation in the Establishment and thus use a mixture of psychological and environmental determinism in their explanatory principles. So the concepts of particular disciplines represent traditional systems of belief and involve huge segments of the population. The values of classes and cultural traditions thus are handed to a discipline which refines them, "proves" them with statistics and other strategies, and then loans them back to a status or region for doctrinal and political usage.

Traditional Propositions About Man

So, the paradigms of the various sciences and those of common culture are quite the same. In fact, science obtains its paradigms from the conventional wisdom, dresses them up with explications and "proof," and hands them back to be disseminated again with the sanctions of status. They then can be put back to work in the business of rationalism.

Consider the relation of these models to various time-honored propositions of logic and grammar. For example:
1. There is a person or organism IN WHICH certain forces or processes are contained. These emerge, or are emoted, or expressed, or

evoked in the form of behavior.

2. There are forces in the larger world which impinge upon the person or organism and cause him (or it) to do thus and so.

Thus a person or organism is the subject of, or the object of, certain actions. This seems natural enough to a Western speaker, for his language is ordered this way (Whorf 1956). There are nouns which represent things or people and verbs which represent actions or forces. In grammar the relation of things and forces sequentially is ordered in either direction. Subjects take action or are acted upon.

Even in the ancient Western grammars these fragments of syntax have been combined. Thus a transitive form occurs in which ONE SUBJECT TAKES ACTION UPON ANOTHER. These syntactic units, in turn, have been sequenced to describe larger patterns of order. We thus can say that one subject takes action on another, and then the object reacts and takes action on the subject. These simple propositions have been articulated as the logic of experience since the time of ancient Mediterranean civilizations. They have been applied to physical phenomena for centuries. Thus, in Newtonian physics we hold that the first billiard ball hits the second, which then hits a third, and so on. And in Newtonian astronomy we have an articulation of simultaneous action in each direction. Thus the moon acts upon the earth AND the earth acts upon the moon.

We ordinarily represent these two classes of phenomena with boxes and arrows. Thus, the noun, the subject and object, is boxed, and the verb is represented with a line. And then since ancient times these forms have been qualified. The boxes are big or little. The arrows go INTO or OUT OF the boxes. The boxes are open or closed. The forces move rapidly or slowly.

Boxes can be so big that they contain galaxies, solar systems, and suns. They can be medium-sized and thus hold "society," "culture," or "the establishment." They can be small and thus hold an animal or a person, microsized, to hold an adrenal gland or a cell, or miniscule enough that they will hold only a molecule, an atom or an electron. But each can be acted upon and can act, and accordingly arrows can be long enough to cross an astronomic unit or a continent, or small enough to cross a room or occur between two clasped palms.

You will observe that all of these simplistic propositions have been formalized in the sciences of man as well as in the physical sciences. A kind of pre-Copernican, geocentric model is extrapolated to human behavior as psychological expression theories. The environment-action arc is formalized in stimulus-response theories. The DOUBLE TRANSITIVE

ACTION PROPOSITION OF NEWTONIAN PHYSICS APPEARS IN CONTEMPORARY INTERACTION THEORY. John smiles at Mary; Mary responds with a salutation. And the box-sized series is captured in scientist terms by corrupting Bertalanffy's systems theory (Bertalanffy 1950, 1960) to a view of things at levels from electron, atom, molecule, cell, or an organism and group (Miller 1965).

Notice too, that we almost can date the period of maximum popularity of these models in the recent history of the human sciences. We experienced a psychodynamic era just after World War II, a social science or interactional era in the early 1950's and a behavioral science era in the late 1950's. This later era was essentially Skinnerian at first, featuring action-and-response models. It was not until the late 1950's that a structural view of behavioral science emerged into popular usage.

BUT NOW TURN TO CONSIDER THE COMMONALITIES OF EACH OF THESE MODELS, FOR ALL OF THEM TAKE THE GIVENS FOR GRANTED: They make an absolute and dichotomous distinction between things and actions. This difference is formalized as the difference between form and substance in Aristotelian philosophy. Phenomena of relatively high density and stability beyond the short intervals of human observation are considered to be things, or living subjects; and phenomena which change or move in short periods of observational time are termed actions, or behaviors, or forces. Another assumption automatically is made about actions in this epistemology. They are assumed to be linear and to move from a past in clock time to a present and then to a future.

In Western epistemology a number of assumptions also are made automatically about the relation of things and forces. It is assumed that all things have an inside, a boundary, and an outside. It also is assumed that forces enter things from the outside, and/or reside within things, and/or emerge from things. Linear causes and effects then are located in this geography of insides and outsides. Forces and actions thus are conceived of being carried "within" a person, who either conceals or lets them out. Or forces reside "outside" of people and hence come to penetrate or not penetrate the skin. These simplistic notions, of course, can be combined in all sorts of intriguing but ambiguous ways. God or love can be inside or outside, or both, Descartes tells us. The origin of the force that emanates from genes is problematical. It comes from outside but resides within, so one can take responsibility for good genes and disavow those which come from bad genes. Other people and foreigners can be either blamed or forgiven on this basis.

The assumption of contained and emergent forces is so taken for

granted in Western epistemology that WHEN NO FORCES CAN BE OB-
SERVED THEY ARE POSTULATED ANYWAY. Thus, if the movement of
planets somehow is related then a force must emerge from each and
be transmitted to the other. This heuristic force must be named to give
it an actuality. Furthermore, if someone questions how the force can be
transported through empty space a medium must be postulated. A substance is imagined between the planets. It is named "ether" in this his-
toric case. Its properties then are described even though the substance
is nonobservable. Then on this basis an Aristotelian classification is
made of "types of ether." So whole generations grew up learning about
chemical, thermodynamic, magnetic, and some six other kinds of ether.
When some novitiates asked about the emperor's new clothes, they were
exiled, but the questions did lead to a series of experiments which were
to prove the existence of ether. The failure of these experiments later
proved to be the undoing of the ether theory. We did get rid of ether
but we still grow up learning to "know" gravity.

If bodies send or transmit forces to each other it seems logical to
postulate that these forces are contained within them. Maybe the forces
move at large or are all-pervasive within an organism, but it seems more
real to locate forces within a small thing within the larger whole. So,
for centuries we debated whether soul was in the heart or the mind, and
then whether mind was in the heart or in the brain, and so on. When
a thing like the gene is discovered it is a sheer bonanza for the genetic
determinists for now they have a tangible and perceivable means by
which to demonstrate a geography of instincts.

The debates which occurred about these matters in previous centuries always seem absurd to a contemporary discipline of scientists, but
the differences are often purely a matter of metaphor. Aristotle's explanation of acceleration said in effect that falling bodies speed up as
they approach the earth because they cannot wait to get home. But we
unashamedly explain human behavior by simple recourse to postulated
needs. During the 1940's and 1950's I heard many arguments about
the location of the id and ego. It was generally agreed that the id was
housed in the hypothalamus and the ego in the cerebral cortex, though
as early as 1945 there were heretics who insisted that Brodmann's areas
were not located in discrete places which housed separate neurological
and behavioral functions. Message, information, negentropy, meaning,
motivation, emotion, and all kinds of other substances and forces then
were changed into the conceptions of interaction which were then fashionable. These forces were divided into bits, message units, and the
like, which were counted, measured, studied statistically, and so on.

But a conceptual loop is placed on thing and force concepts which pins them down in reality, so to speak. The forces are reified conceptually in due time and hence regarded as things in themselves. These "things" are then said to CAUSE the phenomena they were fabricated to explain. As a consequence, conceptual operations, seen as things, "cause" behaviors, which are regarded as unseen forces, and these relate and connect things. A logical problem of the greatest magnitude now assails us. We have mixed up the conceptual events, or human observers with their motor behavior and have confused these in turn with individual organismic events of genetic-cultural systems.

Aristotelian Truth

One further assumption is almost invariable in an Aristotelian system of assumptions and conceptions. If multiple connections, forces, behaviors, and things seem to be interrelated, there is no adequate way to fit these into simple two-body and linear paradigms, so a choice is made. One thing-and-force relation is singled out and awarded the status of THE cause or essence of the phenomena. From this selective focus elaborate conceptual systems evolved about the rules, purposes, and meaning of unicausal links and single-body or dyadic-body relations. If alternatives are observed or postulated in dialectic by outsiders to the dogma, alternate or dichotomous theories are placed in antithesis, and one must judge and decide which is true. In partial deference to other possibilities we have conceptions of the "main cause," the essence, the prime mover, the originator of action (hero or villain), the real truth, and so on. Thus, if someone provides us with multiple-behavior displays we try to decide what he "really" means.

I have oversimplistically called this system of assumptions an Aristotelian or Western epistemology. To be sure, Aristotle did argue for real truths which only philosophers had time to learn, and he did distinguish between form and substance. But this way of thinking must have begun its evolution long before the Greek philosophers, and it has continued to be used, elaborated, and spelled out by philosophers ever since. It is also characteristic of Western civilizations but not limited to them.

Whatever issues of origin we raise about this system of epistemology, we at least can be fairly clear about its properties. It is a SYSTEM OF PROPOSITIONS which fit together and are self-confirming in retroactive loops. To anyone raised within its formulations the givens seem logical enough but we rarely even become conscious of these. So the system is maintained as a relation of ideas which thus has a kind of equilibrium. It is transmitted from generation to generation and thus has a kind of life of its own, for each member of the society becomes an acculturated person by learning it, and once he has learned it he uses it, teaches it, maintains it, and passes it along.

All of us think this way. If we pull out of these familiar patterns of thought for a while we quickly lapse back into them. When we have transient grasp of another mode of thought we lack a nonlinear, nonthing and force language to talk about it. When some genius comes along and explicates another way of thinking about nature his followers help to "explain him." They recast what he has said in the popular Aristotelian mode. The new thought is re-Aristotelianized, so to speak. And the innovator always helps out. Otherwise he cannot sell his books, be followed at conventions, and so on. Yet, somehow, alternative epistemologies can persist. This has been happening since the turn of the century.

SYSTEMS APPROACHES TO COMMUNICATION

In the last generation a new order of thinking has been applied to the study of human behavior and communication. Programmatic, spatial and cognitive models of behavior have emerged in this thought. I plan to describe some examples of these models and then characterize the epistemology from which they derive.

Programmatic Models of Human Communication

In a programmatic model of human communication the focus is upon interaction but it is perceived that the interaction is governed by a convention or format. So communication is no longer seen as in simple expression or response terms. In addition, these approaches take heed of cues or signals which regulate the process. These approaches recognize that the behavior of interaction can be determined by what is expected to happen as well as by what HAS happened. So these programmatic models include certain cybernetic or systems concepts and are not, therefore, simply Aristotelian.

FORMAT AND SIGNAL MODELS The most simplistic of this new order of models describes a convention for taking turns and identifying certain cues or signals which guide the speaking order. I will call these "format and signal models."

In the more structural and descriptive versions of this approach the behavioral contributions of one, then another, participant are described and the rules for speaking order are abstracted. Many workers in this version have had training in structural linguistics so they describe the juncture behaviors of language and the role of these in segmenting the stream of behavior. These researchers also make note of facial, postural, proxemic, and other cues by which participants indicate that they are taking or relinquishing the floor. In the more cognitively oriented versions cognizance is taken of a participant's knowledge of what has gone before, of the arrival of his turn, and of the likely shape of what is to come.

In their present usage these format and signal models are not adequate from a cultural point of view. They do not take cognizance of the relation of the format to institutional and cultural contexts. Thus the notion can persist that the formats of an interactional event spring de novo from the minds of the participants or else are universal for *homo sapiens*. Furthermore, most social-psychological ideas about communicational formats are derived from the paradigms of didactic interaction or else those of psychotherapy. As a consequence many authors describe interaction as a relationship between two people or between a person and a group of people in dyadic interaction. In these institutional interactions the roles are usually asymmetrical, so the formats call for one member of the dyad to do most of the talking. As a result, interaction is pictured as a long monologue to which rather short responses are occasionally made. More recently, the seminar has come to be used as the paradigmatic format for interaction. In this case the participants are said to take turns in speaking. In either case the emphasis usually is upon the speech behavior of transaction whenever academic paradigms form the basis of communicational analysis and other forms of communicative behavior are relegated to positions labeled "subverbal," "nonverbal," or "coverbal."

There is one other difficulty with using academic activities or psychotherapy as a paradigm for human interaction. In didactic relations the participants are often relative strangers. Their strongest affiliations are therefore with people who are not present at the interactions which are studied. Courtship and other important nonlanguage sequences usually are interdicted in academic scenes and in psychotherapy, and certain of the political and economic contexts of everyday interaction are missing from these scenes.

When the academic and clinical researcher turns to the examination of activities in everyday life he finds very different forms of communicational relations. Third, fourth, and other parties are often assembled around a central axis of individual or dyadic activity, and the locus of conversation shifts from axis to axis and from place to place. In informal interactions no one person usually is permitted to hold forth in long monologues. The taking of turns, which characterizes the formal institutional procedure in cultures of British derivation, is replaced by a competition for floor rights or a simultaneous and overlapping pattern of speaking order. And speech may not be the official activity. On the contrary, conjoint physical tasks, grooming, courtship, servicing procedures, and dominance exchanges are much more frequent, and speech takes but one role in these conjoint behaviors. These lexical interactions are likely to be extremely short. When they do occur they rarely involve the exchange of novel information but deal instead with task requirements, economic issues, and the politics of control and manipulation in the relationship.

All in all, then, the use of lexical interaction is one shape of communicational behavior which characterizes academic and other institutional meetings. We academics have been so devoted to the study of this kind of human activity that sometimes we have failed even to include task and nonlanguage activities in our definition of communication. And we have spoken as though communication has, of necessity, an interactional form. Now, obviously, I am not denying the right of academic workers to study such scenes nor do I wish to denigrate their importance in human affairs, but I am saying that WE MUST NOT USE THESE SPECIAL TYPES OF COMMUNICATIONAL STRUCTURE AS PARADIGMS FOR HUMAN COMMUNICATION IN GENERAL. We must also avoid another simplistic idea about human communication. We cannot afford to fall into a dichotomy which holds that the language behavior of a communicational event is interactional or communicational and the nonlanguage behavior is simply a means of cueing who is to speak or signaling what is supposed to happen.

COMMUNICATIONAL PROGRAMS AND METACOMMUNICATIONAL MODELS OF PROGRAMS To meet these insufficiencies some researchers have developed an idea of more complex programs of communicational behavior. In these the interactional sequence is viewed as but one of many kinds of format for behaving in concert. In these approaches the concept of signals has been developed, too, to embrace a great many kinds of activity which are termed "metacommunicational."

To gain an idea of programs we should first make explicit the definition of interaction which has come into common usage. In the interactional event the behavior of one participant influences the next behavior of at least one other participant, and this influence in turn is discernible in whatever action comes next. So the construct of interaction defines an interdependency in participant action which is manifest through time.

In fact, however, this behavioral interdependence is highly relative in degree and implication. At one extreme, two participants can become so involved with each other that they disregard the actions of others, ignore the setting and violate the customary agenda. In some cases the behavior of a first speaker does nothing more than tell a second when he can begin to speak. In still other situations participants try to shout each other down in order to state positions which they came prepared to advance. Thus their behavior shows no discernible influence of one on another. In still other situations a person shows courtship behavior or argumentative behavior even though no one else interacts with this behavior in any discernible way. In cases such as this where a group member pays little attention to the behavior of others or to the format, Miller, Galanter, and Pribram (1960) might hold that a participant is merely "executing a prepared plan." Bateson (1971) speaks of acting "TRANScontextually."

In still other communicational events two or more participants do show a marked degree of interdependence of behavior, but they do not respond to each other sequentially. Instead, they carry out separate parts in a conjoint task and do so at the same time. Or they speak together in agreement. Or one states a position to which others nod assent. So in these cases we must describe a format of coaction. In short, a variety of kinds of formats, interactional and otherwise, may be programmed by tradition to form the usual agenda of a communicational event. The degree to which a given communicational event is interactive therefore is not a simple matter of style or deviation. Some communicational programs feature interaction and others do not.

But even the official or called-for interactions of a transaction are by no means equivalent in their significance for the overall form and outcome of that event. At one extreme of significance the interaction may negotiate the program itself and the outcome of this interaction will govern all that subsequently occurs. In other cases a given student or listener learns something that is new TO HIM, but old hat to thousands of students who went before him. In some programs a sequence of interaction merely determines who wins, but this selection does not alter the overall structure of the transaction itself or the rules of its procedure. Similarly, an interaction may determine who speaks or what order of speaking shall occur, but despite this detail of order a usual spectrum of views is aired, and an administrative decision is made elsewhere as a closing step in the program. Furthermore, there are interactional sequences in the play or concert which are already scripted or scored. They are thus staged as phases in a longer program of performance whose outcome is already determined. And finally, an interaction may be held simply, while some other kind of programmatic activity is in progress. Thus, two workers may talk about a movie they saw the night before as they perform conjointly in the customary program of a physical task. Their interaction is not supposed to influence their transactional behavior.

The format and signal model has been supplemented by a description of signals which indicate the completion of one utterance and thus signal the permissibility of a next one. These same instructional behaviors have been studied by those who favor a more complicated model of coactional and interactional programs, but a much wider range of regulatory behavior also has been described. This kind of behavior can be linguistic, paralinguistic, tactile (Trager and Smith 1956; Birdwhistell 1961); kinesic (Bateson 1956; Birdwhistell 1952, 1970); postural (Scheflen 1964, 1972, 1973a, 1973b); tactile (Scheflen 1972); and/or proxemic (Hall 1963; Scheflen 1972; Erickson, this volume). It also can be built into the shape and decor of the setting and into the dress and movement styles or parakinesic qualities of movement (Birdwhistell 1963). The class of behavior serves to clarify ambiguities in the meaning of statements or acts, qualify what is being said or done, designate roles and speaking order, direct timing and coordination, and so on. Thus behaviors of this class have a regulatory or cybernetic function to the performances of a communicational program. They have been distinguished, therefore, from the offical communicational activities, but using a special suffix. Bateson called them "metacommunicational" (1955). Note that the prefix "meta-" describes a relation of behaviors. It describes a relation of regulatory behavior to customary format activity.

In the simplest case a participant simply adds a metacommunicative act to his performance. For example, a speaker drops his pitch, eyes and head, sits back and folds his arms as he finishes speaking and thus relinquishes the floor (Z. Harris 1952; Birdwhistell 1966; Scheflen 1966a, 1972). He shrugs his shoulders as he declares that he is not sure about what to do. He turns and gazes at the others, raises his pitch and his eyebrows (Birdwhistell 1966) and thus signals that someone else is to speak in response. But one participant can behave metacommunicationally AS SOMEONE ELSE SPEAKS OR ACTS. He raises his eyebrows, for instance, or imitates the stereotyped look of disgust with his face.

But sometimes these metacommunicative acts are carried out in concert. ALL listeners raise their brows, for instance, or several of them object to what has just been said. And metacommunicative activity may not be directed to the actions of a single other, but instead, to the nature of a relationship within the group. Thus frowns or other behaviors of censure may be directed at two people who are sitting too close together. Or a metacommunicative objection may be directed at a dominance battle. So THE METACOMMUNICATIVE PROCESS CAN BE DIRECTED TO AN INTERACTION. In fact a process of kinesic and lexical monitoring is ordinarily carried out at all phases of a communicational activity, and in this case the metabehavior may serve to maintain the customary sequencing of the total program.

Furthermore, the metacommunicational activity itself may be interactional. Participants may exchange a sequence of courting behavior to recruit attention and thus gain the floor. They may engage in a long exchange of dominance behavior to the same end. And sometimes a metacommunicative censure is not taken lightly or simply complied with. It is followed, instead, by an argument about the rightness of an opinion or the propriety of a way of behaving. In fact, all participants may suspend their communicational activity and engage in a long discussion of procedure. They even may negotiate another kind of agenda.

All in all, communicative and metacommunicative sequences are likely to be much more complicated than an act-and-signal sequence. A participant in the program may receive a metacommunicative signal about what he has done, change his action accordingly and then be treated to yet another critique. He then may pause in his performance, search the faces of the others and be cued by kinesic acts or statements about what is expected next. But at this point someone else may fill the gap of silence with an utterance which is then disallowed by the others, and so on. In short, a continuous process of regulation goes on which we can formulate in the cybernetic terms, "feedback" and "feedforward."

We should make explicit note of one other kind of metacommunicative situation, though all of us know it from experience. Paracommunicative style or quality is also monitored by members of an institution or cultural traditon (Scheflen 1972). Instructions or censure may be directed at HOW one speaks or acts. A given staging of a customary program may be carried out too frivolously or too solemnly to suit the ethos of a particular cultural group and a metacommunicative interchange will occur on this score too. On the other hand, the metacommunicative relation itself can be carried in paralinguistic or parakinesic modes. The vocal qualities of sarcasm are an example. The painfully slow movement of protested compliance is another. In fact, an entire enactment may be carried out in the exaggerated vocal and parakinesic forms of caricature and burlesque. Psychologically speaking, we must make certain deductions when we observe these complicated relations of audible and visible behavior. The members of an institution and a culture must carry rather detailed cognitive images of the programs, formats, parts, and styles of their tradition. They must also have a system of values and beliefs about these matters. And they must have learned a repertoire of tactics for showing these and for manipulating each other's enactments.

But we now have carried Bateson's concept of metacommunication far beyond the initial idea of signals that distinguish the interactions of play from those of battle (Bateson 1956). We also are far beyond a simple notion of cues and signals. So I think we should separate orders of metacommunicational activity. To do so we can follow a distinction of progressively more complex types of learning which Bateson himself has developed (Bateson 1972). Tentatively I would distinguish five successively more complicated orders of metacommunicational behavior. These could represent stages in the evolution of more and more complicated ways of using behavioral forms.

This ordering can be outlined briefly as follows:

1. Metabehavior 0 consists of the simple terminal and juncture behavior which is used between each of the units in a format of action. This behavior is suprasegemental in language but also kinesic (Birdwhistell 1970) and postural (Scheflen 1964).
2. Metabehavior 1 consists of simple vocal or kinesic cues, which indicate who is to act and when one is to begin.
3. Metabehavior 2 is procedural and judgmental. It consists of monitors or warnings of deviation (Scheflen 1972), instructions to hold enactment to the usual format, and judgments, criticism, and evaluations in accordance with the standards of a culture or institution. Lexically and consciously this class of metabehavior has been elaborated as a body of prescriptions for activity and etiquette, a set of values and rationales for the activities in progress and, in fact, the models of and theories about a particular kind of experience.
4. Metabehavior 3 consists of a set of tactics which are employed

wittingly or by custom to alter the performance of a format, change the relationships of participants, and manipulate the outcome. Common examples are the use of courtship behavior, dominance, or lexical persuasion.

5. Metabehavior 4 consists of procedures for inventing, modifying, or innovating formats themselves. This complicated level of communicative behavior corresponds to the one Miller, Galanter, and Pribram (1960) called "plans for making plans."

I hope the reader will not be too quick to protest that this scheme is too complicated. Chances are it will prove much too simple to define the multiple relations of human communication. It is a fundamental tenet of systems approaches that our models must be complex enough to encompass the phenomena that we have observed to occur. So those who hope to make the study of communication "scientific" by collecting a large sample of analyzed cases had better assure themselves a considerable longevity or else join their effort to those of their colleagues. The only alternative is to stick to reductionistic models and report on the "essence" of communicational experience.

THE STRUCTURAL VIEW OF MODEL UNITS So far we have allowed ourselves to see the elements of communication as the contributions of various people. Unfortunately, however, people do not usually act as organismic wholes in communication, and the program is not seen profitably as a sequence of individual actions. The fact is that there are many modalities of behavior, and each participant can enact all of these at the same time. One can speak AND form paralinguistic sounds. One can simultaneously gesture AND smile, WHILE he holds or shifts posture and interpersonal distance. He can at the same time touch, fiddle with objects, stroke his own leg AND beat time with his foot. And his whole performance may be qualified by his skin color, state of obesity, hairdo, dress, and location in the room. And to make matters more complicated, A PARTICIPANT DOES NOT CARRY OUT THESE SIMULTANEOUS ACTS IN UNIFIED CONCERT TO FORM A SINGLE MESSAGE OF REDUNDANT PARTS. At one and the same time a single interactant employs some of these modalities in communicational and some in metacommunicational business. He uses some of them in customary compliance with the requirements of the program while he uses others to manipulate what is going on. And he uses still others to carry on unofficial tasks or induce relationships which are unofficial or even illicit by the explicit definition of the situation.

Needless to say, activity in any of these modalities may be coactional or interactional. So multiple interactions occur in various modalities at the same time. In fact, each participant may deploy one or more modalities to one relationship and others to another. In a group of four people, for instance, a lexical-gestural relation may be going on in one dyad, while each member of this pair maintains tactile interaction with a side partner. A third kind of kinesic and proxemic interaction may occur among the nonspeaking, side partners, while each of them interacts kinesically and posturally with each speaker. Even when only two people are related in communicational activity each of them can be seen to direct all sorts of behavioral sequences to unseen others, empty places and to themselves. And WHILE they do this they are speaking, gesturing, and moving in relation to each other. So any time we hear a researcher speaking about "the" interaction we can guess that he has either observed an incredibly involved or stereotyped pair of subjects or else that he has seen only a fragment of what was going on.

It IS the case, however, that a customary program of communicational activity will prescribe SOME OFFICIAL MEDIUM of communicational behavior. Thus, in didactic transactions it is demanded that people speak. They may use gesture to supplement this modality of interaction and use still other modalities in a metacommunicational way. In games physical task behaviors may be featured and language is used for regulatory purposes. And in programs for love making the featured modalities are at first kinesic and then tactile, but language is used in both a supplemental and a metacommunicative manner. So we can speak of THE interaction if we are referring only to the featured or official modality of interchange for that program.

Participants may stick to this official behavior and put their whole bodies into it as they do in very sacred rituals or in games or tasks which require a consummate skill. And some programs constrain each participant to perform only a particular part in a particular modality. IF AND WHEN THESE CONDITIONS PREVAIL WE CAN HOLD THAT THE ELEMENTAL UNITS OF AN INTERACTION CORRESPOND TO THE BEHAVIORS OF SEPARATE AND PARTICULAR PARTICIPANTS.

But ordinarily this is simply not the case, and a very confusing or very reductionistic account of the interaction results from saying what he did and then saying what she did, and so on. So, in viewing a program of interaction we need to make a conceptual shift which takes us all of the way out of an epistemology of "people who." WE WILL SAY THAT THE COMPONENT FORMATS OF A CUSTOMARY PROGRAM CALL FOR

SEQUENCES OF BEHAVIOR IN A PARTICULAR MODALITY. BUT MULTIPLE SUCH FORMATS ARE INTEGRATED SIMULTANEOUSLY AND SEQUENTIALLY, IN THE COMPOSITION OF THE PROGRAM ITSELF. Some of these units occur briefly and do not recur. Others recur again and again as if to hold the definition of the situation. Others are continued throughout the whole transaction. Still others persist beyond any one transaction and thus run through many of them.

We also can assign the units of these various modalities some sort of function in reference to the official activities. The featured units are enacted at one, then another, place in the grouping again and again, just as the melodic theme of a symphony appears now in the violin section and later among the trumpets. Interlaced with this recurrence of official units are reappearances here and there and again and again of metacommunicational units. Other units support the physical setting of the event or the attention and substance of the participants. Still other units violate the rules and appear as transcontextual acts. This is how we describe the programming of a transaction in structural terms. ONLY WHEN WE HAVE IDENTIFIED THIS COMPLEX "ORCHESTRATION" DO WE ASK WHICH PARTS OF WHOSE BODY ARE RESPONSIBLE FOR GIVEN UNIT ELEMENTS AT A PARTICULAR TIME. We can then follow this question by asking which relationship carries certain themes at given times.

Spatial, Network, and Territorial Models

I think that these elaborations of a format and cue approach provide us with a rather sophisticated model of the temporal relations of behavior in a communicational event, but all models of this class have some serious shortcoming by the standards of a systems science. One of these is a neglect of the spatial dimension of communicational events. To be sure, a few interactionalists have commented upon the proxemics of face-to-face interaction (Hall 1963, 1966). And two of us at least have said that a change in proximity can serve as a signal about the interaction (Scheflen 1972; Erickson, this volume). But there is much more to the matter than this.

The fact that the interactionalists have not bothered much with space is not to be explained by a lack of adequate constructs. A number of these have been evolving, and some communication theorists have begun to incorporate time into their work. Kendon (f.c.) has described the spatial organization of interactional events, and our research project in Bronx soon will report on the territoriality of face-to-face groupings (Scheflen and Ashcraft i.p.). Kendon and Ferber (1973) and this author (Scheflen 1972) also have described some of the postural-orientational frames of small-group communication and included the spatial dimensions of the assembly.

In ethology the concept of territoriality now is very well developed. This concept has become increasingly useful for the study of communication, for it is now cast in behavioral terms. More recent ethological accounts, for instance, tell us about behavioral connections of animals in a territory (Lorenz 1966; McBride 1964, this volume).

Neuropsychological Models

An analogous development has occurred in the study of intraorganismic processes. In neurophysiology the emphasis is no longer upon the separate cortical areas or brain centers, but upon the connections of neuronal systems. All psychological theorists no longer are preoccupied with observing behavior in order to abstract individual traits or infer intrapsychic forces. Instead, PATTERNS of BEHAVIOR observed nowadays are in communicational context. And patterns of COGNITIVE BEHAVIOR are deduced on this basis. When structural and process models like this are employed the old differences between neurophysiological and psychological approaches tend to disappear. Pribram (1954) thus calls his approach "neuropsychological."

Miller, Galanter, and Pribram (1960) published a model of cognitive processes which represents one attempt of this kind. The principles of structural linguistics and computer science were brought together to define patterns of images and plans which, the authors claimed, must correspond to the patterns of communicative behavior which one can observe a participant to perform. These authors postulate that such patterns were modified by the perception of signals in a communicational exchange. Pribram (1963, 1971) has gone on to expand greatly this cognitive equivalent to a programmatic model. He tries to account for the fact that participants change their relationships and states from time to time in a program. He notes that markers and cues elicit an orienting reflex (Sokolov 1960). These can initiate a change in image and plan.

He postulates that physiological states are also integrated with images and percepts by means of neural connections from the cerebral ventricles. Here biased homeostats continuously monitor metabolic and physiological states (Ashby 1956). Ordinarily the homeostat maintains these states within a range by retroactive processes which are subcritical and out of awareness. But whenever changes at this level are not maintained by negative feedback, neuronal disturbances spread to subcortical and even cortical centers. Pribram postulates that information about organismic states in these is matched with images and plans and with percepts of the metacommunicative behavior of others (Pribram 1971).

A discrepancy between these subsystems is experienced subjectively as emotion though the processes involved also can be identified consciously. In this case the discrepancy also is represented by thoughts. In either event, motor activity is executed which can alter "plans" for performing in the interaction. One such execution is an enactment of metacommunicational signals about the procedure itself. Suggesting that the group take time to eat is an instance in point. In this theory emotion and some thinking are post hoc commentaries on the proceedings. They may lead, of course, to metacommunicative actions which alter what is happening, but these intraorganismic processes do not simply cause communicational behavior as we used to believe in an Aristotelian view.

Changes in an enactment may be picked up and augmented by group consensus and produce an outcome which deviates from that usually prescribed by tradition. But more often the metacommunicative behaviors of the communicational event tend to restore usual states, relationships, and transactional forms. In this case, conventional images of the program serve to maintain the enactments within a range. Thus people, too, are biased homeostats — in culturally traditional processes at the social level.

All in all, when a group is acting in concert in a usual program of communicational activity the members hold a cultural concept of the program and a set of values about how it should be carried out. Necessary behaviors are contributed by a specialization of roles. This procedure, by its completion, may maintain the stability of a family or a larger institution and thus contribute to holding the existing social order. In the process of enactment the recollections of the procedure are renewed, and novitiates get a chance to learn about this event. So each transaction can maintain and transmit a unit of culture. By the same token the transaction may sustain the cognitive, physiological, and metabolic states of each member within some particular parametric state. In such cases systems at levels from molecular to social are in dynamic equilibrium.

We can observe, however, that the outcome of a particular interaction or activity also can serve to restore an equilibrium which has been disturbed. It sometimes can disturb an equilibrium and hence be followed by another transaction which is metacommunicative to the first.

The Evolution of a Systems Epistemology

The epistemology which lies behind these developments is not Aristotelian. Nowadays it is called a "systems" view. But this view has evolved in stages, so it is not wise merely to CHARACTERIZE the systems epistemology. Instead, we should look at stages in its evolution for it is still developing.

FIELD VERSIONS AND THE EINSTEINIAN SHIFT Field concepts were evolved in physics in the nineteenth century. Einstein used these concepts to solve the Newtonian problem and develop the theory of relativity (Einstein 1920). We are not interested here in the astronomy which resulted from this ingenious application, but in the conceptual shift that Einstein employed.

In effect, Einstein held that the Newtonian problem of bodies and forces had resulted from a way of looking at the issue. He proposed instead that one focus not upon planets and stars but upon their patterns of motion and upon the relation between these patterns. Then a solar system, galaxy, and the universe itself were visualized as a field, or continuum of relations in space and time. Any given movement or any given mass could then be described and explained by reference to this context.

I do not know whether this kind of thinking was "in the air" at the turn of the century, or whether theorists in other sciences were influenced by the Einsteinian shift, but in any event a number of analogous constructs appeared at that time in a number of other sciences.

Field views emerged in physical science at levels from the structure of the atom to the relation of drifting continents. Field descriptions also emerged in the sciences of man. In physiology Cannon (1920) described steady states and homeostatic processes. Cognitive processes were described in structural terms by the gestalt theorists, among them Koffka (1935), Freud (1913), and later by Tolman (1932) and Lewin (1951). In the emerging concept of culture, patterns of behavior sometimes were described (Malinowski 1913) and somewhat later the structure of sounds in the formation of language was described (Sapir 1921;

Bloomfield 1933). The concept of territory also was formulated (Howard 1964).

Decades later, it is possible to make a critique of these field views of systems, as compared to Einstein's constructs. They did capture several features of a field approach and so I have classified them as field constructs. They focused upon behavior, i.e. upon sequences of cellular, organic, or organismic change. Thus they dealt with order from and through time. And they dealt with the relation of more local events to larger contexts. Freud's idea of psychodynamics, for example, relates events in a subject's environment to his learned patterns of behavior. So do the stimulus-response models of Pavlov (1927), Thorndike (1911), and others. And Cannon's idea of homeostasis relates the "behavioral" patterns of organ systems to the activity of the organism as a whole. Yet in other ways these field constructs fall short of their counterpart in astronomy. They employed the concept of time in a purely linear way, and they did not deal with time-space relations. On the other hand, some of them, like homeostasis, did begin to deal with the great complexities inherent in biological systems.

In the first forty years of the century a great deal of data were collected, but a process of Aristotelian reconversion was also under way. The physiologists studied intraorganismic processes in detail, but they were content to represent the environment with simple arrows. The psychological theorist acted similarly by speaking vaguely about a stimulus. Society, culture, built environments, and all other contexts simply were abstracted, named, and placed in a diagrammatic box. From this box an arrow was aimed at the individual. Responses, too, simply were represented by an arrow. Few described the behavior structure of the response. And although Freud had described the contexts in which his patients learned and lived (Freud 1930), it became more and more fashionable as the century wore on to speak of complex contexts simply as "reality." Behavioral processes came to be reified as places in the psyche from which drives or motives emerged.

In short, we ended the first forty years of the century with many of the same old box-and-arrow constructions. In each science some particular and local box was the object of study, so we had dozens of sciences of man. In fact we were further divided by the fact that the boxes of a science "contained" quite different logical types of "things." Some held organs or people. Some were made up of behavior, motor, or cognitive. And some contained inferences and theories about behavior.

CYBERNETIC AND SYSTEMS VERSIONS   In the 1940's a new interest developed in temporal relations among and across these local fields. This interest appeared in a variety of sciences. For instance, in physics the retroaction of effects upon causes was explicated as "feedback" or "retroaction." A science of nonlinear time and control known as "cybernetics" developed (McCulloch 1949; Wiener 1948). In the biological sciences levels of organization among living systems were distinguished, and relations among events at various levels were conceptualized (Bertalanffy 1950, 1960). Relations of communicational behavior among humans began to be defined as early as 1935 in a cybernetic type of model (Bateson 1958). In anthropology the emphasis began to shift from the study of artifacts and cultural beliefs to the study of PATTERNS OF BEHAVIOR in a culture (Mead 1949; Benedict 1946). Some zoologists also changed their focus of interest. They asked not about the relation of a particular animal to an Aristotelian CLASS of animals but about the RELATION OF ONE ANIMAL TO ANOTHER. Behavioral concepts about these relationships were formulated and an ethology emerged (Lorenz 1950; Tinbergen 1953).

In short a new Kuhnian cycle (Kuhn 1962) began about 1940 – forty years after the field theory cycle – but I think this new era in fact was but a stage of advancement in the epistemology of fields.

The concept of systems emerged in this second go-around. A system was defined as an interdependency of events or changes. A system was thus a sort of field. It was assumed to lie at a level of complexity in some larger field of relations which constituted its context. Change was visualized as an effect which reverberated across levels in a hierarchy of systems. These elaborations of the field model took cognizance of types of change which were much more complex than oscillation or orbiting or linear expansion. The idea of entities at a level did, however, invite a re-Aristotelianization of the construct, for it is easy to misconceive of a system as a thing. Thus, to many, the hierarchy of living systems is listed as the molecule, the cell, the organ, the organism and the group. Once a field of behavioral relations has been reified it is almost inevitable that once again forces will be postulated next to describe connections and relations. This, of course, is just what happened in the 1950's when the first version of human communication theory came down the pike. People were said to transmit information to each other as if they were telegraphic stations. And today the term "systems" in many circles means little more than electronic hardware and a set of procedures for fiscal accounting or social engineering.

BEHAVIORAL STRUCTURE AND STRUCTURAL METHODS One can insist

that the term "systems" be used to describe the interdependency of relations in space and time. The relations in a field at the social level are relations of human behavior. Thus one denies that people as such transmit anything. They simply behave in audible, visible, and "feelable" ways. When these behaviors take on recognizable form and come to have shared meaning in the course of cultural evolution they are communicative in that particular tradition. Thus, a way of describing behavioral relations in time and space had to evolve in order to identify a system of behavioral relations. This methodology did develop in a number of sciences during the behavioral science era of the late 1950's and the 1960's. It was implemented with cybernetic and cultural explanations. This methodology is often called a "behavioral-structural" approach.

The linguistic modalities of behavior had been described as early as 1921 (Sapir 1921). Other modalities of visible behavior were described in the 1950's and 1960's (Efron 1941; Birdwhistell 1952, 1959, 1961, 1966, 1970; McQuown et al. 1971; Hall 1963; Kendon 1967, 1970, 1972; Condon and Ogston 1966, 1967; Scheflen 1963, 1964, 1965, 1966a, 1972, 1973a, 1973b); and many others. Descriptions of paralinguistic features also emerged (Trager and Smith 1956; Pittenger and Smith 1957; Pittenger et al. 1960; Duncan et al. 1968; Markel 1965). Lomax and his coworkers have described the cultural forms of singing and dance behavior (Lomax 1968, this volume). Concepts of formats and programs were developed by Pike 1954; Bateson 1972; Z. Harris 1951; M. Harris 1964; Miller et al. 1960; Birdwhistell 1970; Scheflen 1968; Duncan, this volume; Beels et al. i.p.; Kendon and A. Ferber 1973, and many others. The ethologists also have developed structural methods (Lorenz 1950; Schneirla 1951; and McBride 1964). The methods themselves have been explicated by McQuown et al. 1971; Scheflen 1966a, 1966b, 1973a; and others.

Prospects for a More Comprehensive Integration

We now have in hand constructs and operations with which we could make a thorough and systematic description of a communicational event in space and time. But we still have a way to go if we are to develop a comprehensive picture of human communication in the epistemology of systems.

In the past we have tended to describe relations of behavior either in spatial OR in temporal terms, and we have not yet brought these together. We can describe behavioral relations in a given event but we will not establish the dynamics of systematic change until we have compared many like events, noted many variations, and related each of these to changes in the context of the event. We have yet to integrate the emerging ideas of communicational relations in a small-group interaction with constructs about large communicative networks and long-term developments. And we have yet to put together a picture of the visible and audible events in a communicational field with the intraorganismic ones. In short we now have some analogous but separate pictures of various local fields of behavior.

If we judge by past experience it is not likely that we will make much more progress in an integrative direction — at least not for a while. In the past the integrative efforts of brilliant pioneers soon were reduced again to simple box-and-line models by their followers.

What reason do we have for supposing this will not happen again? As a matter of fact, one can argue that it is happening. Some authors speak as though the cause of one participant's behavior is the behavior of the others or is simply an enactment of format. A view like this has done nothing more than turn in a psychological reductionism for a social or a cultural one. And the temptation for us to act reductionistically is almost overwhelming. Each of us is likely to work on but one dimension of this multiply determined phenomenon, and as we do so it is easy to lose sight of the other dimensions. After all, we all grew up Aristotelian. And this tendency is reinforced strongly by disciplinary loyalties and the pressures to commit "real" science. These pressures, in turn, are augmented by the fact that reductionism pays off in the short term of quick reputations and provincial status. Rapid promotions are awarded to those who promise AN answer.

REFERENCES

ASHBY, W. R.
    1956   *An introduction to cybernetics.* New York: J. Wiley.

BATESON, G.
    1956   "The message 'This is play,' " in *Group processes*, volume 11. Edited by B. Schaffner. New York: Josiah Macy Foundation.
    1958   *Naven* (second edition). Stanford University Press. (First published 1935.)
    1971   "The natural history of an interview," chapter one. Edited by N. A. McQuown. Microfilm collection of manuscripts in cultural anthropology. Series 15, numbers 95, 96, 97, and 98. University of Chicago Library.
    1972   *Steps to an ecology of mind.* New York.

BEELS, C. C., J. S. FERBER, J. A. SCHOONBECK
   i.p.   *Context analysis of a family interview*. Demonstration movie and article.
BENEDICT, R.
   1946   *Patterns of culture*. Mentor Books. (First published 1934.)
BERTALANFFY, L. V.
   1950   An outline of general systems theory. *British Journal of Philosophical Science* 1:134.
   1960   *Problems of life*. New York: Harper Brothers.
BIRDWHISTELL, R. L.
   1952   *Introduction to kinesics*. Louisville, Kentucky: University of Louisville Press.
   1959   "Contribution of linguistic-kinesic studies to the understanding of schizophrenia," in *Schizophrenia*. Edited by A. Auerbach. New York: Ronald Press.
   1961   "Paralanguage: 25 years after Sapir," in *Lectures on experimental psychiatry*. Edited by H. Brosin. Pittsburgh: University of Pittsburgh Press.
   1963   "Body signals: normal and pathological." Address to American Psychological Association, Philadelphia, September, 1963.
   1966   "Some relation between American kinesics and spoken American English," in *Communication and culture*. Edited by A. G. Smith. New York: Holt, Rinehart, and Winston.
   1970   *Kinesics and context*. Philadelphia: University of Pennsylvania Press.
BLOOMFIELD, L.
   1933   *Language*. New York: Henry Holt.
CANNON, W. B.
   1920   *Bodily changes in pain, hunger, fear, and rage* (second edition). New York: D. Appleton.
CONDON, W. S., W. OGSTON
   1966   Sound film analyses of normal and pathological behavior pattern. *Journal of Nervous and Mental Diseases* 143:338–347.
   1967   A segmentation of behavior. *Journal of Psychological Research* 5:221–235.
DUNCAN, S., L. N. RICE, J. M. BUTLER
   1968   Therapists' paralanguage in peak and poor psychotherapy hours. *Journal of Abnormal Psychology*. 13:566–570.
EFRON, D.
   1941   *Gesture and environment*. New York: King's Crown.
EINSTEIN, A.
   1920   *Relativity: the special and general theory*. New York: Holt.
FREUD, S.
   1913   *The interpretation of dreams*. New York: Macmillan.
   1950   "Fragment of an analysis of a case of hysteria," in *Collected papers*, volume three. London: Hogarth. (First published 1905.)
HALL, E. T.
   1963   A system for the notation of proxemic behavior. *American Anthropologist* 65:1003–1026.

1966 *The hidden dimension.* New York: Doubleday.
HARRIS, M.
1964 *The nature of cultural things.* New York: Random House.
HARRIS, Z.
1951 *Methods in structural linguistics.* Chicago: University of Chicago Press.
1952 Discourse analysis. *Language* 28:1.
HOWARD, E.
1964 *Territory in bird life.* London: Murray.
KENDON, A.
1967 Some functions of gaze direction in social interaction. *Acta Psychologica* 26:22–63.
1970 Movement coordination in social interaction. *Acta Psychologica* 32:100–125.
1972 "Some relationships between body motion and speech," in *Studies in dyadic communication.* Edited by A. Seigman and B. Pope. Elmsford, New York: Pergamon Press.
f.c. Formation systems in interaction.
KENDON, A., A. FERBER
1973 "A description of some human greetings," in *Comparative ecology and behaviour of primates.* Edited by R. P. Michael and J. H. Cook. London: Academic Press.
KOFFKA, K.
1935 *Principles of gestalt psychology.* New York: Harcourt.
KUHN, A.
1962 *The structure of scientific revolutions.* Chicago: University of Chicago Press.
LEWIN, K.
1951 *Field theory in social science.* Edited by D. Cartwright. New York: Harper Brothers.
LOMAX, A.
1968 *Folk song style and culture.* AAAS Publication 88. Washington.
LORENZ, K.
1950 The comparative method in studying innate behavior patterns. *Symptoms of Social Experimental Biology* 4:221–268.
1952 *King Solomon's ring.* New York: Thomas Y. Crowell.
1966 *On aggression.* New York: Harcourt. (Translated by M. Wilson.)
MALINOWSKI, B.
1913 *The family among the Australian Aborigines.* London: University of London Press.
MARKEL, N.
1965 The reliability of coding paralanguage. *Journal of Verbal Learning and Verbal Behavior* 4(a):306–308.
MCBRIDE, G.
1964 *A general theory of social organization and behavior.* St. Lucia: University of Queensland Press.
MCCULLOCK, W. S.
1949 The brain as a computing machine. *Electronic Engineer* (June).

MCQUOWN, N. A., *et al.*
1971 "The natural history of the interview." Microfilm collection of manuscripts in cultural anthropology. Series 15, numbers 95, 96, 97, and 98. University of Chicago Library.

MEAD, M.
1949 *Coming of age in Samoa.* New York: Mentor. (First published 1928.)

MILLER, J. G.
1965 Living systems: basic concepts. *Behavioral Science* 10:193–411.

MILLER, G. A., E. GALANTER, K. H. PRIBRAM
1960 *Plans and the structure of behavior.* New York: Henry Holt.

PAVLOV, I. P.
1927 *Conditioned reflexes.* London: Oxford University Press.

PIKE, K. L.
1954 *Language. Part I.* Glendale, California: Summer Institute of Linguistics.

PITTENGER, R. E., C. F. HOCKETT, J. H. DANEHY
1960 *The first five minutes.* Ithaca, New York: Paul Martineau.

PITTENGER, R. E., H. L. SMITH, JR.
1957 A basis for some contributions of linguistics to psychiatry. *Psychiatry* 20(1):61–78.

PRIBRAM, K. H.
1954 "Toward a science of neuropsychology," in *Current trends in psychology and the behavioral sciences.* Edited by R. A. Patton. Pittsburgh: University of Pittsburgh Press.
1963 "The new neurology: memory, novelty, thought and choice," in *EEG and behavior.* Edited by G. H. Glaser. New York: Basic Books.
1971 *Languages of the brain.* Englewood Cliffs, New Jersey: Prentice-Hall.

SAPIR, E.
1921 *Language.* New York: Harcourt, Brace.

SCHEFLEN, A. E.
1963 Communication and regulation in psychotherapy. *Psychiatry* 26:126.
1964 The significance of posture in communication systems. *Psychiatry* 27:316–331.
1965 Quasi-courting behavior in psychotherapy. *Psychiatry* 28:245–257.
1966a "Natural history method in psychotherapy: communicational research," in *Methods of research in psychotherapy.* Edited by L. A. Gottschalk and A. H. Auerbach. New York: Appleton-Century-Crofts. Monograph 1, Commonwealth of Pennsylvania.
1966b *Stream and structure of communicational behavior.* Behavioral Monograph 1, Commonwealth of Pennsylvania.
1968 Human communication: behavioral programs and their integration. *Behavioral Science* 13:44–45.
1972 *Body language and the social order.* Englewood Cliffs, New Jersey: Prentice-Hall.

1973a *How behavior means.* New York: Gordon and Breach.
1973b *The stream and structure of communicational behavior* (revised edition). Bloomington, Indiana: Indiana University Press.
SCHEFLEN, A. E., N. ASHCRAFT
  i.p.   *Human territoriality.* Englewood Cliffs, N.J.: Prentice-Hall.
SCHNEIRLA, T. C.
1951 "The levels concept in the study of social organization in animals," in *Social psychology at the crossroads.* Edited by J. H. Rohner and M. Sherif. New York: Harper Brothers.
SOKOLOV, E. N.
1960 "Neuronal models and the orienting reflex," in *The central nervous system and behavior.* Edited by M. Brazier, 187–276. New York: Third Conference, Josiah Macy, Jr. Foundation.
THORNDIKE, E. L.
1911 *Animal intelligence.* New York: Macmillan.
TINBERGEN, N.
1953 *Social behavior in animals.* London: Methuen.
TOLMAN, E. C.
1932 *Purposive behavior in animals and men.* New York: Century.
TRAGER, G. L., H. L. SMITH, JR.
1956 "An outline of English structure," in *Studies in linguistics.* Edited by W. M. Austin. Occasional Papers 3.
WHORF, B. L.
1956 "Language, mind and reality," in *Language, thought, and reality. Selected writings of Benjamin Lee Whorf.* Edited by J. B. Carroll, 246–270. New York: John Wiley.
WIENER, N.
1948 *Cybernetics.* New York: John Wiley.

PART TWO

Methodological Studies

When Infant and Adult Communicate How Do They Synchronize Their Behaviors?

M. BULLOWA

Let me state the problem: the neonate lives in his own time domain while his caretakers live in theirs (Holubář 1969).[1] In order for an infant to survive and to come into communication with caretaking adults, infant and adult must somehow come to synchronize their behaviors so that communication and interaction between them can occur and can develop. So far as I know, the question as to how it comes about has not yet been investigated.

The data base was collected under NIMH research grant MH-04300 (1960–1964). Recent work and this paper originate from the laboratory of the Speech Communication Group of the Research Laboratory of Electronics, Massachusetts Institute of Technology, Professor Kenneth N. Stevens, director, under grant NB 04332 from the National Institutes of Health. I wish to thank Jeanne Chall, Allan Kessler, Raymond Stefanski, and Roger Wales who have read the manuscript and made valuable suggestions, some of which I have adopted. I would also like to thank Mrs. Hedy Kodish who typed the manuscript.

[1] Holubář says, "The relationship of the sense of time to age of the individual studied is a significant one. Two different dependencies are apparent. In the first place, the sense of time develops in ontogenesis, so that in humans its inception can be observed only at approximately 4 years of age, the degree of perfection of adulthood being attained at 13 to 14 years (Binet and Simon 1916). In the main, it is correlated with the development of general intelligence. Secondly, the sensation of the constantly accelerating passage of time with increasing age is universally known; it is the psychological basis of the concept of biological time (together with the retardation of biological processes with age and the irreversible changes in all tissues in the course of aging) — see, for example, Carrel 1931, 1939. This phenomenon is sometimes stated as the law of Janet: for a constant duration of stimulus, the length of the subjective duration of the sensation is inversely proportional to the length of life already lived (Janet 1928). I believe that over and above the various psychological interpretations this dependence of the sense of time on age is one of the most important pieces of evidence for a metabolic basis for biological clocks ..." (1969: 19).

The aspect with which I want to begin is the segmentation of the behaviors which enter into communication. In adult/adult communication, as I will explain below, participants become temporarily entrained in each other's communicative rhythms. The infant has a rudimentary capacity to do this, but a great deal more development along these lines takes place before the language process begins. I suspect that this aspect of development is a necessary precursor to "language acquisition" because the patterning of speech (a neuromuscular activity) has to fit into the ongoing patterning of the rest of the body's motor activity in a very precise way (described below in the section on linkage of speech and body movement). The infant must develop something like the adult pattern of hierarchically nested segmentation of his behavior at a number of levels.

Let us consider the contrast between the behavior of a newborn infant and of an infant seven to ten months later at the age when current wisdom says he is taking his first steps toward language acquisition: the emergence of "suprasegmental" aspects of speech. Recent studies on the neonate have produced a description of an organism actuated by endogenous impulses to perform a small repertory of recognizable, organized, mainly rhythmical behaviors: notably crying and sucking (Wolff 1967) and characterized by spontaneous cycling between what were formerly called "states of arousal" (Prechtl and Beintema 1964).

Close observation has sorted out many regularities in what not so long ago was thought to be random activity. When I am watching an isolated newborn infant from the point of view of segmentation, I find these changes in state and bursts of activity almost all there is to describe. We see this newborn organism as mainly passive because he is incapable of locomotion and does not give clear signals which we can interpret with more specificity than global distress or comfort. And yet he can be shown capable of rudimentary social interaction (Brazelton i.p.) in his ability to orient to, and conform posturally (cuddle) to, an adult.

By eight months (in our culture)[2] an infant typically sits alone and takes steps when held in position to walk, although he cannot yet balance his entire weight. He usually creeps or crawls. But more interesting, in the context here, is that he is actively cooperative with his caretakers.

In one of my films (MO59) of an infant at eight months, Mackie's mother is taking his clothes off to bathe him. Just after she has taken his right arm out of its sleeve, and before her hands have moved over to his left, Mackie raises his left arm (which had been at his side) as if

[2] It has been reported (Geber 1956) that children in tribal Africa are walking independently by this age.

to have it taken out of its sleeve. Later, with his clothes all unfastened, mother holds him upright and he steps out of them. Thus, without being capable of speech, Mackie is entering into a complex social interaction which involves intermeshing his gross body movements with those of his mother.

Moreover, in the same film, when he is seated "alone" on the floor surrounded by toys, he shows signs of spontaneous organization of his behavior as he manipulates objects. He initiates interaction with his mother, who has been seated on a chair nearby, by looking to her after he has been struggling to get a top out of a box full of toys. She bends over and gets it out and attempts to spin it for him.

I don't think anyone watching this eight-month-old or film of his activity would doubt that his behavior showed evidence of organization beyond the neonatal level or that two-way communication was going on without benefit of speech. Concurrently, there have been many other advances in the motor area: at the current limit of his capacity, Mackie is able to pick up and release objects. On developmental testing he almost succeeds in opposing his thumb to pick up a small pellet.

The newborn can get caught up in his caretaker's hierarchically organized behavior and so interaction between them is possible at a very rudimentary level. By eight months, still lacking speech, the infant not only can participate in multilayered activities with much greater variety than just after birth, but on his own he can show more structured activity and even initiate interaction with an adult.

Findings from a number of disciplines are relevant to this issue. The organization of adult individual behavior and communicative behavior in man are relevant because this is the target system toward which the infant must strive. And because there are continuities as well as differences between man and other animals, the organization of behavior and communication in animals, especially in primates, has to be considered. Because language, and its physical manifestation, speech, are so prominent in human communication, it is necessary to know how speech is coordinated with other ("nonverbal") manifestations of communication. It is also necessary to look to the human infant for capacities on which to build to make communication with adults possible and increasingly adult-like. In addition it is necessary to know a lot about methods and techniques. As in any other scientific enterprise, this one involves a wide range of concerns. They range from the point of view from which to approach it to the most mundane of practical technological details. This account does not attempt to be exhaustive on any of these issues but will touch on some essentials of each of them.

POINT OF VIEW

Before plunging into the details of subject matter, I want to state the "philosophical" stance from which this investigation is approached. I will not argue its merits, but I will try to make it explicit. There are certainly other possible approaches, and many will be needed before we can hope to know what is going on in the development of communicative capacity.

The approach may be considered essentially that of field ethology, characterized by observation of naturally occurring behavior and interaction, aided by taped and filmed records. The use of empirical description falls within ethological tradition. Blurton-Jones (1972: 14) states:

> There is a hidden assumption in ethology that observations should take precedence over theories, not only to the extent that the results of an experiment determine which of two hypotheses is discarded, but also that theories should be formed after a large collection of observations have been made.... This assumption is part of the reason for the ethologist's stress on the descriptive phase of science and for the insistence that theories or even any remark about behaviour should immediately allow one to answer the perennial but essential question: "How do you tell if that is so or not?" This is the meaning of "operationalism" as used by ethologists.

In the classic literature of ethology, motivation is always either ascribed or implied (as "instinct" through the labeling of behavior as sexual, aggressive, etc.) The same is true of Freudian drive theory which, as Kortlandt (1955) pointed out, shared this feature with early ethological theory. The subjective trend is carried even further in the psychological-philosophical school known variously as phenomenology, existentialism, etc. But we really know very little of the motivation of others, be they animals, infants, or other adults, unless we question or manipulate them. It is possible to strive for "objective description" of what organisms are observed to do: HOW they move rather than WHY they move. There is a trend in this direction in current ethology (Smith 1968; Golani and Mendelssohn 1971).

An example of how the structure arising in data manipulation can lead to a presumption of motivation occurs in a paper by Marshall (1965), a psycholinguist. He took data obtained and published by ethologists on the distribution of precopulatory behavior of male pigeons. He applied the tree structure of a phrase structure grammar from the field of linguistics,[3] using the observed items of behavior of the pigeons as terminal sequences, i.e. bowing+driving+attacking+displacement preening

---

[3] The theme of grammatical models applied to ethology is further developed by Vowles (1970).

+billing+mounting+copulation. The statistics on the frequency with which one behavior item followed another indicated whether a sequence was obligatory, optional or virtually impossible.

It was the data structure which led to grouping driving + attacking at the next higher level above the terminal sequences as "aggressive behavior" rather than a preconceived notion that aggression was included in expression of the "reproductive instinct." In fact, in describing this paired sequence of behaviors (which happen to be optional in the total sequence) a nonmotivational label would have been equally serviceable, but common usage probably dictated the choice. This example illustrates how it is possible to ascribe motivational concepts even when one doesn't start with them.

Because I don't feel that I can meaningfully attribute instincts or motives to infants and that calling a mother's behavior an expression of maternal instinct doesn't help us understand the behavior, I want to use motivational terms as sparingly as possible and to confine their use to the level of everyday usage. Thus, an observed sequence during which mother feeds the infant can be described as "feeding activity" rather than "engaging in nurturant behavior." Any motivational implication is at the level of the superficial intent of getting the food into the infant. Feeding activity may consist of a sequence of included activities as terminal sequences, like those of the male pigeons, but there is no "deep" implication as to what motive is being served. Thus I would bypass the issue of whether it is or is not "good social science" to attribute motivation as from the supposed viewpoint of the subject (Wright 1967) or as if the observer were carrying out the activity (Lewin 1951) or, as Kaplan (1964: 142) puts it, "I understand the act when I see it as though it were the outer form of my own corresponding action." This is less of an issue in animal ethology, where it is easier to keep from identifying with the observed animal.

While the study of the communication relationship is my objective, it is impossible to escape from speaking of individual behavior. Like Scheflen (1965; see below in the section on linkage of speech and body movement), I want to describe the individual contribution of each participant to the interaction between them, recognizing that this leads to something different than the sum of the behaviors. One might focus (as in the Midwest Study[4]) on one of the participants and consider the other

---

[4] The Midwest Study, referred to in this paper, was reported most completely by Roger G. Barker and Herbert F. Wright (1955). Material from chapters dealing with the methodology for the Midwest Study was published in Wright (1967), the source of references and quotations herein.

participants as context or environment. This "ecological" method leads to finding the influence of environment on individual behavior but not to what characterizes communication.

I am not arguing that this is the best way to approach the problem. I am simply trying to make explicit what I am doing at the start. In the sections that follow I will cite some of my methodological models and some of the studies in relevant areas which have contributed to this approach. This is not an attempt at exhaustive review of any of these fields nor does it mention all the people and literature who have influenced me. I hope it will make the method and sample data sheets presented in the final section easier to understand.

NATURALISTIC DESCRIPTION OF HUMAN BEHAVIOR

Sometimes it is thought that naturalistic description belongs more to literature than to science. Certainly there are examples in literature which present both the specifics and the generalizations about "human nature" in accurate and recognizable form. A major difference between the literary and the scientific approach to human behavior lies in the scientist's attempt to find recurrence and regularity in the events described. He is trying to get from the particular instance to universal laws. This distinction is not absolute. Great literature, such as the classical works of Homer and the Greek drama, while presenting named characters, say things about them and through them which are still recognized as very general statements about aspects of human nature. And Darwin (1877) describing his infant son's development was presenting only one instance of development. When some form of behavior recurred it was already different because time had elapsed in a developmental sequence. Is Darwin's account art or science?

To get back to the scientist's recurrence and regularity: recurrence implies units of some sort which can be recognized when they recur. In the laboratory units of behavior are under the control of the experimenter. In field studies the observer must determine appropriate units for recording his observations. Preserving field observations on tape or film (which abstracts from the natural scene only the visual and auditory elements) only postpones the problem of unitizing. Anticipation of and working to find regularity implies the scientist's belief that the phenomena he is observing and studying are not random and that, if he orders them in an appropriate way, he will be able to find generalizations about how the units are related. As Menzel (1969: 90–91) puts it, manipulate only as much as is necessary to answer your questions clearly, and otherwise leave things alone, for there is order even in what seems to you to be the worst confusion, and you might well introduce worse confusion if you use your hands before you use your eyes.

A special sort of regularity is expressed in the concept of hierarchical ordering. This is a form of relationship of wide application which considers units at one level to be built up of units of a lower level and which can be in turn aggregated into units at a higher level. This concept has wide application in science. Cosmogonies have been based on it. Syntheses of knowledge, such as Thomson's *Outline of science* (1922), express it. General systems theory is the current form. A major result of systems thinking is the recognition that the whole may be greater than the sum of its parts, i.e. the properties of a unit at one level are not directly derivable from the properties of the units of which it is composed.

There are various ways of expressing hierarchical relations among units. One of the most familiar is in tree structures. In the application of tree structure in generative grammar, for instance, the terminal arborizations are the observed or devised "terminal strings" of "surface structure", i.e. the data. Which terminal strings are utilized depends on what level is in focus in a particular discussion. In a discussion of syntax the terminal strings will be words; in discussions of phonology they will be distinctive feature matrices. Both are outputs of sets of rules operating on abstract entities such as: sentence, noun phrase, verb phrase, and consonantal, vocalic, and nasal (Chomsky and Halle 1968).

I am going into this because what I will be dealing with is terminal strings of data units (mostly not linguistic ones). It is necessary to make a decision about the level of unit on which to focus attention in order to "unitize" the observations. To some extent this depends on the "resolving power" of the recording instrument[5] and how it is used. The "how it is used" is important because one may not always want to use the full resolving power available, just as a linguist does not always pay attention to distinctive feature matrices.

This brings me to the discussion of what in the social science literature are sometimes referred to as "molar" and "molecular" units in a hierarchy. Molar units are those which have meaning when viewed independently, but this must be qualified because the distinction depends on level of focus. The movement of a limb is a molecular unit. Taking a step is a molar unit if only one or two steps are taken, but a molecular

---

[5] Film taken at two frames per second for the data discussed in the final section.

unit if a step is part of the molar unit: walking. That is, the boundary between molar and molecular units is itself subject to shift depending on magnification or viewpoint. In general, for human action, molecular units tend to be at what would usually be considered a physiological level. Molar units, on the other hand, are at a social level, i.e. understood as separate actions by the actor and other people, including scientific observers. As Menzel (1969: 107) points out, "Precision is INFORMATION rather than minutiae; it is that which eliminates our uncertainty about behavior, or reduces it to a given degree."

For the purpose of this investigation I am concerned with molar units at several levels. I have described elsewhere a method for dealing with the molecular units in filmed data by a method appropriate to that level and its purpose: the study of approach and withdrawal movements in the course of interaction between mother and infant (Bullowa and Putney 1973).

HOW SPEECH AND BODY MOVEMENT ARE LINKED

That speech may be viewed as part of behavior seems obvious enough, but the intimate connection between speech and how the body moves apparently is not.[6] There has been a tendency to look on gesture as a more primitive system than speech, one which may be used instead of language (see Kendon 1972: 205-6 for a discussion of this), perhaps because it is shared to some extent with other primates. The idea that speech and body movement could be part and parcel of the same system of interpersonal communication seems to be of recent origin.

Representatives of several disciplines have investigated how verbal and nonverbal signaling systems are related as they are used in behavior and communication, much as primatologists have looked into the relation between signaling with sound in relation to the behavior which accompanies it (Altmann 1967; Andrew 1962). Although the work I am citing has dealt mainly with adults, the fact that investigation along these lines has been done is basic to what I am proposing. It is necessary to know the details of this fully developed system in order to explore its development, just as it is necessary to know a language in order to investigate its acquisition.

---

[6] In this section I am not dealing with all that is known of nonverbal communication nor even with all of that which accompanies speech, but only with those aspects related to the segmentation of discourse. A comprehensive categorization of nonverbal behaviors and their usage is given by Ekman and Friesen (1969).

Linguists have a professional interest in segmentation and the hierarchical relations among segments, e.g. from Halliday (1961: 250): "Language is patterned activity. At the formal level, the patterns are patterns of meaningful organization: certain regularities are exhibited over certain stretches of language activity." He says further that "the units of grammar form a hierarchy that is a taxonomy" (1961: 251). Linguists find phonological segments and higher-order units like syllables, words, phrases, sentences, paragraphs and discourse[7] (even though there are still details of definition which remain controversial). Most of these units, beyond perhaps the phonological ones, are also meaningful to nonspecialists as is the notion that paragraphs consist of sentences and sentences of words and words of letters (if not of phones or phonemes). Thus, segmentation and hierarchical order in language are popular as well as technical notions.

At this point I will refer briefly to the work of Pike (1967), a linguist. He was interested in the similarity between the details of language structure and larger aspects of the organization of human social behavior. Like Marshall (1965), referred to in the first section, Pike applies methods and concepts from linguistics (in his case a form of structural linguistics) to a nonlinguistic realm of behavior. He, too, applies hierarchical structure based on a linguistic model, but the behavior to which he applies it consists of large-scale units with many participants, e.g. family breakfast, a church service, a football game. I cite Pike's 700-page treatise, *Language in relation to a unified theory of the structure of human behavior,* as an example of a linguist's view of behavior without detailing the level of complexity with which he deals.

A linguistic concept which he uses and applies extensively is the distinction which I discussed in the first section as objectivity versus subjectivity. For these concepts he coined the terms *etic* and *emic* on linguistic analogies (e.g. phonetic versus phonemic). "The etic viewpoint," he writes, "studies behavior as from outside a particular system, and as an essential initial approach to an alien system" (1967: 37). Thus, in approaching an unknown language, a linguist, like any other scientist approaching an area of behavior, must first make an etic inventory. In ethology this would be called an "ethogram" (Hess 1962). Contrastive analysis, a method used extensively in linguistics, is required to establish the emic units.

Several nonlinguists have been successful in demonstrating the relation between language (or at least its physical manifestation in speech) and nonverbal behavior. They have worked with sound film and so can

[7] I am avoiding terms which have only technical meaning.

look at small units and can review the primary data repeatedly. One of the most successful pieces of work on the relation between speech and body movement has been done by Condon, a philosopher (Condon and Ogston 1967). He has worked with the smallest speech units available: the phonological segments. Using sound film taken at speeds up to forty-eight frames per second, he has shown for speakers that grossly observable movement of body parts (onset or change in direction) coincides (i.e., falls on the same film frame) with the onset of phonological segments. (In ordinary speech there are ten to twenty of these change points per second.) This is the phenomenon of "self-synchrony."

In this "microanalysis" neither the linguistic nor bodily units can be identified as perceptual wholes. And yet these phonological segments must have some sort of "reality" for the listener, for Condon and Ogston went on to discover "interactional synchrony": the synchronizing of body movement of the listener with the segmentation of speech to which he is attending. This does not imply that speaker and listener make similar movements but that the onset or change in direction of whatever movements occur coincide with onset or change in phonation. Like the body movements, phonation is a product of neuromuscular activity. The change in neuromuscular activity in the vocal tract of the speaker is perceived by the auditory apparatus of the listener, whereas in self-synchrony synchronization could be accomplished within the speaker's own nervous system.

Kendon (1972), a social psychologist, has investigated self-synchrony at higher levels of organization than Condon, on whose work he builds. Because his analysis is centered on speech, he uses terminology which reflects this. His lowest order unit is the "prosodic phrase" (probably Lieberman's "breath group" [1967], "the smallest grouping of syllables over which a completed intonation tune occurs" (Kendon 1972: 184). Phrases combine into "locutions," which tend to "correspond to a complete sentence." Within the locution he recognizes "phrase clusters." At higher levels he recognizes "locution groups" and "locution clusters." The locution clusters are the paragraphs of discourse. His analysis of the sound track is based on what linguists would consider "paralinguistic" features. He presents

data to show that associated with each unit of speech ... there is a configuration of movement that is distinctive or contrasting with the movement configuration associated with the speech unit that preceded it at the same level of analysis (1972: 188).

Kendon's units are not presented as units of communication, but it is not hard to see how they fit into an analytic scheme for communication such as Scheflen's (1965), as will be seen below. The analyzed data presented in detail by Kendon consist of three successive locution clusters (paragraphs) from filmed one-to-many discourse of a man in a London pub.

Kendon concludes with five "hypotheses about how speech and movement are related" which I summarize:
1. There exist related hierarchically ordered sets of units for speech and body motion.
2. "Each speech unit is distinguished by a pattern of movement and of body-part involvement in movement."
3. "Prior to each speech unit there is a change in position of one or more body parts" ("speech-preparatory" movement).
4. Time between speech-preparatory movement and onset of speech is related to the size of the speech unit: earlier and more extensive for larger units.
5. (a) Confirmation of Condon and Ogston's self-synchrony, and (b) that when the form of a movement matches the lexical content of speech, the movement begins before the lexical item it marks but ends when the lexical item ends. He comments on this last point:

> It seems that speech-accompanying movement is produced along with the speech, as if the speech production process is manifested in two forms of activity simultaneously: in the vocal organs and also in bodily movement, particularly in movements of the hands and arms (1972: 205).

I call attention to Gruber's (1967) finding based on my data that the child's early "performative sentences" are accompanied by performative gestures which carry the same message. As the child gets older and produces more complicated sentences through embedding "reportative sentences" (Gruber's term) into performatives, the meaning content of the gestures may diminish or disappear. From Kendon's work it would seem likely that gestures remain attached to the sentence residues as they are strung out sequentially in surface structure.

It would be an interesting experiment to see what happens to the gestures that accompany simple sentences when such sentences are used as building blocks in transformationally complex sentence structures. It is possible that the form taken by gestural residues might have some relation to the depth of embedding in terms of generative grammar. Lieberman (1967) found a relation between simple sentences and the physiology of breathing during phonation (the "breath group"). Such a study might find an additional way in which speech is tied to body activity at a higher level of organization than Stetson's (1945) "chest pulse."

Scheflen, a psychiatrist, using data recorded on sound film during psychotherapy sessions, developed a method (context analysis) which, like Pike's, uses methods developed in structural linguistics. In essence, contrastive analysis is used to test for structural units. "Context analysis" was worked out cooperatively with Birdwhistell, an anthropologist and expert in the analysis of human body movement (kinesics in his terminology). (See Scheflen 1965 for the most comprehensive description of the system.) One of the most important contributions of Scheflen's work is the recognition that the person is NOT the unit of communication:

We can, by confining our observations to one participant, tease out a complex of his behaviors which are HIS contribution to a structural unit of communication.... For the purposes of understanding COMMUNICATION at the cultural level, it must be seen that the individual cannot survive as a full human being apart from a socially evolved system. If we are to find the units of human communication, therefore, we will have to examine how the individual performances are put together and organized in the system (1965: 65–66).

This book permits the reader to see something of the process of dealing with the data according to the requirements specified by its author. The complete typescript of the thirty-one-minute session and a detailed analysis of the film are presented. For the first six minutes the two streams of data are shown merged together. Many artist's sketches from the film frames illustrate significant configurations. Scheflen shows in the course of the book how units at each level are detected and tested and how the entire complex interaction among the four individuals involved in this encounter is structured. Both repetition (stability) and change are considered. This work takes us from individual behavior to communication and from etic to emic description. Meaning is ascribed, as Kaplan (1964) would wish (see the first section above), in terms of the perception of the scientific observers rather than of the observed.

In a paper on posture in communication systems (1964), Scheflen focuses on "postural indicators of units." The account is substantially the same as in the book, but segregates these definitions from other material. Three hierarchical levels are defined, from lowest to highest: the point, position, and presentation. The point, marked by a shift in the position of the head and eyes, "marks the end of a structural unit at the next level higher than the syntactic sentence . . . The maintenance of head position indicates the duration of the point" (1964: 320). A sequence of points marked by a "gross postural shift involving at least half of the body" (1964: 321) is called a position. Positions generally last from about half a minute to five or six minutes but may be held by both speaker and listener in the psychotherapy sessions from which the data were derived for up to twenty minutes. The presentation coincides with the physical presence of a person in an interaction. Scheflen suggests that a reentrant usually assumes a different role or engages in a new type of interaction. He considers these markers "natural divisions in a behavioral stream. They advise the observer to search the stream for the divisions of some interval, for some shift in activity. They do not as yet, however, indicate what the behavior or shift is" (1964: 324). To complete Scheflen's system as described in his 1964 paper, he deals with "postural indicators of the steps in a program." In his illustration, a course of psychotherapy is a program.

For speech used in the process of communication the combined speech and body movement units described by Condon, Kendon, and Scheflen provide a (partially overlapping) hierarchy of levels of communicative activity associated with language use in adults. So far, small and specialized data samples have been used. But as data from additional situations are studied (e.g. Kendon and Ferber 1973, on greeting behavior), and yield consistent findings, there is no reason to doubt that the phenomena described are examples of universal phenomena.

Moreover, other data analyzed for different purposes, as for the Midwest Study, support the belief that human behavior (individual and shared interaction) can always be viewed as structured in this hierarchical way, whether or not it is accompanied by speech. Well beyond the age range on which I am focusing attention, the Midwest investigators found a developmental sequence from many short "episodes" of behavior at two years to fewer and longer ones at ten years (Wright 1967).[8] In addition, more levels of structure are detectable as the child

---

[8] Wright further states, "Thus, the younger children did more things in a day and their action units generally were shorter than those of the older children. In other words, the number of units, both episodes and linkages, was negatively correlated with age, and the average duration of units was positively correlated with age.

Further, the older children as compared with the younger showed more episodes in each linkage; more overlapping episodes; more instances of three or more simultaneously overlapping episodes; more instances of five or more sequentially overlapping episodes; more episodes that ended by merging into the subsequent behavior units; more episodes between the segments of discontinuous episodes; and more complete episodes.

These findings are mutually supporting. They indicate marked differences between the younger and older children in structural characteristics of behavior. The younger tended to do things sequentially, one at a time, to shift frequently from one action to another, and to persevere in a given activity a relatively short time, whereas the older tended to engage in actions of longer duration, to pursue more than one action at a given time, and to carry to completion a higher proportion of their episodes" (1967: 127).

goes through this development, just as the syntax of his language makes use of an increasing number of hierarchical levels as he gets older. It is the earliest part of this developmental sequence which I feel needs to be brought into focus.

COMMUNICATION BETWEEN INFANT AND ADULT

The child, in order to communicate, must learn to comprehend and enunciate a complex hierarchy of systems which makes up the language (Birdwhistell 1959).

The problem of how mutual tuning between infant and adult takes place is fundamental to the development of interpersonal communication and its eventual blossoming in speech and language. Such tuning (or mutual sensitivity) makes possible the exchange of the more detailed and specific messages which are encoded in speech. In the human individual the onset of speech has a long prehistory (Bullowa 1970) stretching back, no doubt, into the womb.

So far as I can ascertain, that phase has not yet been subjected to detailed study, although modern instrumentation would make it possible to monitor simultaneously, for instance, maternal and fetal heartbeat and to study phase relations between them. There is interest in the possibility that the fetus in utero is exposed to the sound of maternal voice (propagated through the body). The recent finding that the neonate synchronizes his gross body movements to the segmental features of adult voices (Condon and Sander, unpublished material) suggests that some pretuning has already occurred before birth. It would be interesting to know about this phenomenon in premature infants.

During the first hours and days after birth, the neonate, left to himself, has been found to shift from one "state of arousal" to another for apparently autonomous reasons (Prechtl 1969). But the infant cannot be left alone all the time. In the process of meeting his needs (except for sleep) his caretakers interact with him in intimate bodily ways. Through these caretaking activities the infant begins to interact with adults who willy-nilly exhibit all the structured behavior of the human species and its modifications by cultural, familial, and individual influences.

In the previous section the way in which speech is related to body movement was considered. When children old enough to have speech have been studied in this regard, they appear to show fully structured communicative behavior with verbal and "nonverbal" components fully integrated.⁹ It is my impression, based on repeated review of synchronized tapes and films of infants with their caretakers taken weekly from birth, that the sharing of interactional rhythms between infant and adult begins and develops very early and provides the frames into which language eventually will fit.

Bateson (1971), working with my tapes and films, demonstrated and studied the time relations of "protoconversation" from around two months of age. In this shared activity infant and mother, while facing each other at close range, vocalize alternately in what resembles an adult conversational mode. Brief exchanges of this kind occur even earlier in our material. But, in addition to vocal and mimetic interactions of this type, there are many opportunities in the course of the ordinary caretaking and recreational activities shared by mother and infant for the infant to experience and acquire the hierarchically ordered organization of behavior of his caretakers.

The use of the term *acquire* suggests that I am considering the segmentation of behavior simply as a skill to be learned. Actually, what I have in mind is more in the nature of a process to participate in. I have recently been observing an infant from birth with the issue of segmentation in mind. She is four months old as of this writing. What I have been watching is her increasingly active participation in communication with family members. To me the most striking feature at present is the contrast between this infant's behavior "alone" and during interaction. I have watched the mother pat the infant's open mouth rhythmically and heard the infant vocalize, producing between them an undulating sound. The infant's vocalization starts and stops with the mother's patting. The infant is equally cooperative in feeding, bathing, etc. She is able to go along with her mother in complicated interactional sequences. But, when put in her crib, she has a small repertoire. She can raise her head and chest in prone. She can turn from prone to supine, but not the reverse. She can watch and reach for objects. She can go to sleep. These activities follow one another like beads on a string. Naked-eye observation does not detect any embedded units, although repeated study of film of such behavior conceivably might. One might propose that during communicative activity she is participating in some aspects of her mother's hierarchically structured behavior.

An aspect of infant behavior of concern to most parents is the newborn's disregard for time of day. I have been interested in the maneuvers

---

⁹ For instance, Condon (personal communication), and Kendon and Ferber (1973).

used by mothers to try to get the baby to sleep through more of the night.

Gesell (1945) reports observations of the sleep-wake cycle of an infant during the first sixty weeks after birth and the follow-up to four years of age. Based on these data he published a series of dial graphs, each representing twenty-four hours, showing periods of sleep and wakefulness. At the beginning there are many short periods asleep and awake which show no relation to time of day. Diagrams for successive ages show fewer and longer periods of each and a tendency for sleep to predominate during night hours and wakefulness during the daytime.

Gesell, with his maturational bias, interprets this thus:

Consolidation is essentially an embryological phenomenon. This does not mean that the infant has been altogether immune from the acculturation, but it does mean that the culture has to wait until the infant achieves a capacity to consolidate his sleep sequences into lengthening stretches. The conditioning culture does not create this capacity (1945: 156).

My impression is that, while maturation sets limits, as it always does, there is more flexibility than Gesell implies. My own impressions from the small number of infants whose development I have observed from birth and the much more extensive developmental studies of Brazelton (1969) suggest that there is a great deal of individual difference between infants in this area as in most others.[10]

Wolff, a research child psychiatrist, has spent a great deal of time observing infants in their own homes during their early months. He combines naturalistic observation with ad hoc experimentation and augments his data from other sources. He did not use film extensively in his pioneering studies. He presents data (1967: 197) to "... show that even apparently simple motor patterns are organized in complex time sequences," i.e. there are bouts of rhythmic activity. He writes:

---

[10] Since preparing the manuscript I have come across a more recent and more sophisticated literature on the ontogeny of human sleep-wake patterns, well represented by Sterman and Hoppenbrouwers (1971). Common-sense definitions of sleep and wakefulness come into question as sleep-wake cycles are studied simultaneously with activity, cardiac, respiratory, and electro-encephalographic tracings. However, the general pattern of consolidation reported by Gesell is borne out: "The findings of numerous investigators indicate, at least with regard to sleep, that the fragmented physiological and behavioral criteria of this state coalesce gradually throughout the first few months of life. Thus, a pattern which conforms to the definition developed for the adult can be identified at 3 months of age. Other evidence suggests that the temporal characteristics of sleep follow a similar course of development, achieving sustained duration and nocturnal distribution at this time" (Sterman and Hoppenbrouwers 1971: 224–225).

... Lashley's persuasive demonstration that there is a functional continuum from spontaneous rhythmical motor movements instigated by an isolated nervous system to the simple motor reflexes of human infants, to the violinist's rapid finger movements in playing an arpeggio, to the syntax of spoken language; and that whenever human behavior is arranged in temporal sequences of high frequency, central regulatory mechanisms come into play which cannot be reduced to experience alone, but must originate in intrinsic regulators of serial order (1967: 199).

The reference is, of course, to Lashley's (1951) celebrated Hixon Symposium paper. The examples Wolff discusses in detail are neonatal crying and sucking. In each case he found evidence that the activity was under central nervous system control and insensitive to interference from sensory input, and that each was " ... organized in remarkably stable, high frequency rhythms...."

After reviewing evidence from studies of rhythmic automatisms, Wolff concludes:

Motor development may then be viewed as the transformation of simple rhythmical repetition or "circular reaction" into integrated actions (Piaget, Jean: *The origins of intelligence of children*. New York, International Universities, 1952) whose rhythmical origins are no longer apparent exactly because the component motor parts have been integrated and the associated rhythms have been submerged in complex phase sequences. In keeping with Lashley's thesis, but unprejudiced by fact, I have assumed that the simple rhythms of neonatal behavior are not REPLACED by qualitatively different regulations of serial order, but that the endogenous rhythms are dissociated from their manifest reflex patterns, and enter into complex phase relations with other dissociated rhythms which can then control the sequence of internalized actions and thought patterns. Empirical support for these assertions is hard to come by from the study of humans alone. One would not expect the resultant complex rhythms in behavior to be obvious to direct observations, but with refined instrumentation designed to detect subtle phase interactions, and by developmental studies focussing on the transformation of simple rhythms, it should be possible to investigate the problem empirically (1967: 215).

I find this encouraging and suggestive.

The infant may not be able to alter his rhythm but a sensitive adult may be able to tune in on what an infant is doing and, through interacting appropriately, lead the infant into new activity with more complex rhythmic structure. Something like this must have happened to make it possible for the mother and infant I was observing to produce undulating vocal sounds together.

Tuning means to match rhythms. In considering mutual tuning between infant and adult we need to find the rhythms available for tuning.

The obvious place to start is with the most highly structured "biological rhythms."

This small sample of writings on endogenous rhythms early in life and the possibility of their entrainment in other more complicated rhythms gives some notion of the complexity of the problem of how an infant takes on the very intricate patterns of his more mature caretakers. I am not suggesting that this is on the verge of solution but only that these issues are related to the problem of how the infant gets into interactional synchrony as Condon and Sander have demonstrated and how social interaction can develop so rapidly.

STUDY OF THE DEVELOPMENT OF SEGMENTATION

Introduction

I have outlined the problem and reviewed some of what seem to me to be relevant issues. I start, then, with the conviction that communicative behavior, like all behavior, is segmented and hierarchically ordered (second section above); that speech is integrated into the hierarchy of behavior and, when speech is used communicatively, the rhythm of speech is shared by speaker and hearer (third section); and that the task involved in an infant's becoming a participant in communication is to find a way for infant and adult to enter into rhythmic alliance (fourth section).

I will now suggest a way to begin such an investigation. I am starting as a field ethologist might on a descriptive level.

A preliminary survey of this development will be based on five longitudinal series of weekly half-hour observations of normally developing infants in their own homes collected for the purpose of studying first language acquisition.[11] The field data are preserved on audiotape and on film taken at two frames per second. The portion of the data to be explored for this purpose is from the first year for three infants and the first eight months for two others.

[11] A technical description of the "data base" obtained in the course of an NIMH funded project (MH-04300) "Development from Vocal to Verbal Behavior in Children" conducted at the Massachusetts Mental Health Center (1961–1964) follows:
A field technique was devised for taking film at two frames per second with a robot camera which could be synchronized with tapes taken with a stereophonic tape-recorder. The two tracks were used independently to record (1) environmental sounds including the vocalization of the subjects and (2) a simultaneous field description whispered into a shielded microphone.

The task is to find etic units in the data. The largest behavioral-interactional etic unit which can be studied from these half-hour records is the activity organized around carrying out a task. Even had longer observation periods been recorded, this would still probably have been the largest unit. The adult's day is taken up with sequential (and sometimes overlapping) activities of this kind. Meals are prepared, the house is cleaned, the baby is bathed, dressed, fed, etc.

Of course, the mother's activities are not necessarily confined to the house, but, during our observations around eight or nine o'clock in the morning, the activities we had the opportunity to record took place at home and often in the kitchen. For descriptive purposes and to use a neutral designation, I will call units at this level "major activity units" or "activity segments" in this article. As the superstructure of these major activity units one would probably have to consider the activity of an entire day. While not all types of major activity unit are represented, some of the principal ones shared with the infant were observed repeatedly. Such material could yield clues as to how the infant begins to behave differentially in different situations and could contribute to understand-

---

These films were taken weekly during half-hour observation periods in the subjects' homes, usually in the morning. They deal mainly with ordinary routines: feeding, bathing, dressing, play, etc. The infants were all first born to white middle-class non-intellectual families already enrolled in the Longitudinal Study on Perinatal Factors (NIND and B). Our field team consisted of an observer (the Principal Investigator) and an audiovisual technician. (Young men, undergraduate psychology majors at a cooperative college, filled this position.) On each visit we carried in and set up field equipment which was monitored by the technician from a fixed position. The observer could move around within the room but tried to remain minimally interactive with the subjects during observations.

The file for each observation contains:
1. Technician's record on the conditions obtaining during recording: times of arrival, audiovisual recording, and departure, people present, weather and room temperature, lighting, equipment used and technical problems.
2. Field notes: Narrative descriptions of the observation written independently by the observer and the technician on returning from the field.
3. Audio index: Charting of all sounds on the audio track (track a) for each five-second segment on the tape (marked off by a beep pattern placed on the tape in the field), i.e. vocalizations by person and environmental noises. This index was prepared by the technician.
4. Audio transcript (track a): Secretarial typescript of adult speech with same segmentation as audio index.
5. "Hushaphone" transcript (track b): Secretarial typescript of observer's simultaneous field description segmented as above. "Hushaphone" refers to the trade name of a device for shielding a telephone which we adapted to our field need for dictating in the presence of our subjects. There is no leakage of whispered voice when this device is used, so that the observer feels no constraint in describing all activities seen.

ing of how the infant comes to organize his day more and more on the adult pattern as he gets older.

Major activity units can be found to consist of component units and these in turn of THEIR components and so on down to the limit of the resolving power of the instrument (camera), in this case the single frame taken every half second. This is according to the same principle of organization as Kendon's five hierarchical levels and Scheflen's three.

It is possible to enter the hierarchy at any level and explore levels above or below. It seems practical and desirable to start at the level I am provisionally calling major activity units: the tasks the caretaking mother performs, to explore their component units in terms of component tasks, and to stop before describing specific movements of body parts (Condon's level). Bathing has a preparatory phase (preparation of baby and of bath water and things to be used), washing, drying (powdering, oiling, etc., which are optional) and cleanup (which may be postponed). Dressing, which frequently follows, is a major activity in its own right because it may be done independently and (in very hot weather) may be omitted after bathing. Each component activity may be further segmented.

In the study of an hierarchically organized structure there is always a problem of when to stop looking at smaller- and smaller-sized units. The decision must be based on the issues being considered and the data available or obtainable. As a first approach in terms of the problem I have posed and the available longitudinal records, I suggest starting with a broad survey of all films and associated material taken during the first year (about 200) at relatively superficial levels in order to sketch out the course of development during that period. This usually involves three levels: the major activities, their principal components, as illustrated above, and, in many cases, subcomponents. Thus, in the major activity, bottle feeding (highest level) there are preparatory, feeding proper, and cleanup activity units (middle level), and, within feeding proper, for instance, testing temperatures, checking level in bottle, giving bottle, burping, etc. (lowest level charted).

The order of units at each level may or may not be invariant. Undressing always comes before bathing for a tub bath, but may be interspersed with bathing during a sponge bath. Some units may be optional for the same mother-infant pair or between pairs. (And certainly differences among units and their order differ between cultures, and yet we can recognize major activities across cultures; compare Bateson and Mead 1954.) Some units repeat cyclically within an activity sequence, e.g. feeding and burping may alternate several times during a bottle feeding.

Several phenomena disturb the neat diagrammatic scheme of hierarchical structure of activity. Some overlapping is likely to occur, especially around change points at various levels. The extent of this remains to be determined. Activities from a different category may be intercalated in an ongoing activity, e.g. a mother may stop and talk to her infant or hand him a toy if he fusses in the midst of dressing. If she did this without stopping her ongoing activity, it would be considered overlapping activity. Then, too, there may be interruptions from outside, e.g. the telephone or doorbell may ring and cause the mother to stop what she is doing, someone may enter the room and interact, and, in our field observations, the observer may hold a brief conversation with the mother.

While the mother is imposing her structured activity on the young infant, the infant is engaged in activity of his own. Sometimes it may not be possible to characterize this more precisely than in terms of intensity of activity, e.g. quiet, mildly active, moderately active, etc. This may be an outgrowth of the neonate's "states." At other times very clearcut activities can be specified: the infant orients, cuddles, takes the nipple, refuses it, etc. As he develops, more and more of his activities become specifiable.

We assume that the adult does not alter her customary level of organization in carrying out caretaking activities with an infant, although when addressing an infant, adult speech and gestures tend to become stylized and "simplified." On the other hand, the organization of the infant's behavior is rapidly increasing in specificity and complexity. But we don't know how older infant behavior is segmented nor the time table on which this segmentation develops. What we expect to learn from the study of these series of observations is the outline of this process during the first year.

Activities of individual persons as seen on film can be charted against time. In some ways, this resembles the "specimen records" of Barker and Wright's Midwest Study (Wright 1967). But while the focus of that study was on the way in which change of environment changes what people do, the focus of attention in this study is on segmentation and hierarchical organization of the activities themselves and how this affects the organization of behavior for the participating infant. During an observation some activities are interactive and some individual. The charting is continuous and shows shifts in and out of interaction (joint activity). To quote Scheflen (1965: 65), "We can, by confining our observations to one participant, tease out a complex of his behaviors which are HIS contribution to a structural unit of communication."

Methodology

The method for study of the already recorded data consists in aligning information from all available sources for each field observation and assigning segmentation at the levels discussed above. The record for each field observation covers approximately thirty minutes. A time grid dividing an observation (O) into five-second portions was imposed as a pattern of beeps on the tape at the time of recording. This O-segmentation has been used in transcribing the tapes which accompany the film. O-segmentation is indicated on the film by a pattern of lights in the margin of every tenth frame. It takes ten data sheets, ruled to accommodate three minutes of observation each, five seconds to the line, to display the data from each half-hour field observation. Before reviewing a film for activity charting, information transcribed in O-segmented form — occurrence of vocalization, "Hushaphone" field description and adult speech — is transferred to the data sheets.

A number of preparatory steps are necessary before activity charting of the film:
1. The film is scanned for major camera shifts.
2. A list of persons present in the room during the observation is copied from the "technician's sheet" and, if they are not all present at the start or if anyone has left, the time when he came in or left is determined and entered.
3. The film is scanned for persons on screen and all changes are noted. Since the audiovisual technician was instructed to keep the infant on camera if possible, it is other participants who are likely to appear and disappear from view.
4. Major posture changes of the persons on screen are coded.
5. A description of events in the household between our arrival and the start of field recording is abstracted from the record and placed at the top of the first data sheet for the observation.
6. The scene on the first frame is described at the top of the first sheet.

More detail about these steps is given in the following subsection.

Scanning the film for changes in activity is done, using rapid viewing (six to eight frames per second). Then we go back over change points and sections difficult to decipher at slower speed as needed. The object is to locate beginnings of new major activities and their components, overlappings, intercalated activities, interruptions, etc., within the ten-frame O-segment rather than to assign them to specific frames. For young infants, change in intensity of activity is noted as well as specifiable actions such as orienting, sucking, etc. Activities of adults other than the mother, the observer included, are noted except when the observer is holding the Hushaphone to her mouth and attending the observed.

Activity is specified in terms of person, location, and artifact. The times of onset, duration, and sequencing are taken care of by the structure of the data sheet. The location of activity and artifacts utilized are noted in special places on the data sheet in order that changes of location within the room and beginning and duration of the use of each article will stand out. The limits of these items frequently give clues to segmentation. The remainder of the activity information is given in activity sentences. Each entry is a simple present-tense, subject-verb-object declarative sentence with whatever modifiers may be needed to insure specificity. Persons are represented by symbols: o for infant, ♀ for mother, E for observer, etc. These symbols will be used hereafter in the text. Artifacts (also noted separately) when used in activity sentences may be represented by symbol, with subscripts if needed, to distinguish between several of the same kind, e.g. b_r and b_b for red ball and blue ball.

Verbs are not restricted; although, if several with indistinguishable meanings occur, the most common form is preferred. Compound subjects are used when several persons engage in symmetrical coextensive joint activity, e.g. o and ♀ engage in mutual gaze. Compound predicates are not used because they are subject to confusion about duration of activities. Instead, if the same person initiates and terminates two or more activities simultaneously, the sentences are bracketed:

{ ♀ orients to E
{ ♀ talks to E

or enclosed in parentheses: (♀ orients to E, ♀ talks to E). If ♀ went on talking to E after, for instance, orienting back to o, the sentences would not be bracketed. Only one sentence is necessary if one person is object (direct or indirect) of another's activity, i.e. ♀ dresses o or o orients to ♀.

Most of the activities charted are those of members of the observed family. The observing team is assumed to be carrying out observer activities: T (the audio-visual technician) monitoring tape and keeping the camera directed toward o, E watching and describing behavior and interaction into the Hushaphone. Their activity is included on the data sheet only when it differs from these expectations or when the observed's activities are directed toward them. Activity sentences, together with information elsewhere on the data sheet, make it possible to consider and evaluate observer participation in the interaction. The technician is behind the camera, but his participation in interaction (rare) is usually determinable. Orientation of the observed toward him or the equipment is usually apparent.

Some action and interaction not totally visible on screen can be inferred from the film by taking into account information from earlier or later frames. For instance, the mother goes off screen in the direction of the sink, and sounds of water being poured can be heard on the sound track. The inference that she is discarding the bath water she was seen using earlier can be made. The sentence "♀ discards bath water in sink" would be tagged *i* for inferred. Whether the observer is watching the infant from standing or sitting level can sometimes be inferred from the height of the Hushaphone cable when she is off screen.

After the activities are coded it is possible to undertake "analysis," the vertical bracketing of activity or BEHAVIOR segments — B-segments — and their subunits. Each bracket is tagged for type of segment and symbols for the participants. All data on the sheet are taken into consideration in assigning segmentation.

The Data Sheet

The data sheet (see sample, Table 1, following page 126) is ruled horizontally and vertically. Space is left at the top for identifying information and for, on the first page of an observation, a description of events just before the start of the record and of the scene on the first frame of film. Each horizontal line is to contain information from five seconds of observation (one O-segment). Numbers at each end give film frame numbers, final digits omitted.

The vertical columns are of varied width. From left to right they are: Person R (in room), Person S (on screen), Activity, Location, Artifact, Posture o, Posture ♀, Posture x (other). Vocalization o, Vocalization ♀, Vocalization x, Hushaphone Notes, Additional Notes and Analysis. (The sample data sheet is shorter than those actually used.) As noted earlier, most of the sheet is filled out from written sources and quick film scans before activity charting is done. A few special conventions should be mentioned.

Camera shifts are indicated by directional arrows (eight radial directions) in the left margin for O-segments in which gross movement occurs. (Slight camera wobble is overlooked.)

In person columns a new list is made whenever any change occurs.

An activity sentence is placed in the space for the O-segment in which it begins. Certains verbs, such as "glance," imply short duration, whereas "orients to o" implies that action continues until a new action supercedes. On the other hand, the location and artifact notations, which refer to activities, do have ways of indicating duration. Activity being described is understood to continue at the same location until a new location is noted. If an activity other than of ♀ or o, such as that of E, is mentioned in an activity sentence, the location for it is bracketed and tagged for person. The employment of an artifact in more than one successive O-segment is indicated by an arrow to the final segment in which it is in use. Note that the same object may appear as either a location or an artifact depending on the activity in which it is involved. A chair is a location when sat on, an artifact when moved.

Indication of posture (including position for o) is coded in a simple diagrammatic code and, like person codes and location notations, remains applicable until a change occurs. Only major changes are coded. Inferences are tagged with i. If a person makes more than one CHANGE of posture in an O-segment, the postures are coded in succession from left to right and the right hand one then applies until changed. For persons off screen, when posture cannot be inferred, it is coded O.

In vocalization columns a v indicates that the voice of the person indicated at the top of the column was heard at least once during that O-segment, but does not indicate the nature or amount of vocalization. The information is from the audio index described in Note 11.

Hushaphone transcripts are edited and condensed. The restrictions on sentence form used for activity charting need not apply. When it seems relevant to preserve the flavor of the original field dictation, the words quoted are in quotation marks. A Hushaphone sentence is placed in the O-segment in which it began on the tape and, if it continued beyond that segment, a downward arrow indicates the segment in which it ended. There is only an approximate fit with events on screen because there could be a lag in starting a description in the field.

Adult speech from the tape is entered in the additional notes space. The words of each speaker are on the line representing their occurrence on the tape if possible, preceded by speaker code and a colon. Material which cannot be transcribed is indicated in parentheses, characterized when possible, e.g. "(baby-talk voice)". A dash indicates an unfinished sentence. Usually there is room to place transcribed speech where it occurs on the tape, but occasionally this is impossible. Then the vocalization columns show when it actually occurred. The same area on the data sheet accommodates any other pertinent material from any recorded source. The source is identified by code. If a note clearly applies to a specific episode, it is placed as near the episode as possible.

In the Analysis space, brackets for the major segments are to the right and nested segments successively to the left. Exceptions are intercalated activities and interruptions which are indicated as cutting across ongoing activities. A segment which is not wholly contained on a data sheet is indicated by upward arrow if carried from the previous sheet or by downward arrow if to be carried forward to the next sheet. Labels on brackets indicate kind of activity segment and participant codes.

On the first line of each data sheet, information in columns in which a notation applies until changed are carried over, i.e. person R and S, location, artifact (if continued by arrow), posture, Hushaphone downward arrows and continued segmentation brackets and labels in the analysis space.

Sample Data

The sample data presented are from the first home visit to a normal, full-term, firstborn boy and his mother. He was twelve days of age. Previous observations of this mother and infant were of bottle feeding in the hospital. Because this was the first time we recorded the mother caring for her baby in her own home, I interrupted my dictation of field observation into the Hushaphone-shielded microphone to talk with her more frequently than usual. In my field notes I wrote that I did this to put her at ease. The data sheet begins at the start of the twentieth minute of recorded observation and covers the subsequent two and one-quarter minutes.

There is a change in major activity in the first O-segment (Frame 228). Dressing ends and feeding begins. The end of the dressing segment is signaled by the closing of the box of cotton and the beginning of the feeding by the mother looking to the stove. Between these activities, she repositions the baby on the table. This repositioning of the baby is not functional as she picks up the infant after looking to the stove. I, as observer, apparently reacted to the end of a major segment by sitting up straight. This happened before the mother picked up the infant and went to the stove. My straightening also presages my speaking to the mother. I went through the same sequence at the end of the bathing segment.

There is some overlap between the bathing segment (which had preceded dressing) and the feeding segment which shows up on the data sheet. In Frames 245 and 248, the mother picks up and puts aside blankets used during sponge bathing and earlier from a chair near the table, preparing it to sit on while feeding the baby. This interpenetration between preparatory and cleanup phases of adjacent, and even separated, activities does not appear to interfere with major segmentation.

All of the rest of the activity shown on this sheet belongs to the preparation for feeding. In this case about five minutes elapse between starting to heat the bottle and the feeding proper, when the mother offers the bottle to the baby around Frame 290. The mother picks up the baby in Frame 229. This shows in the posture code as well as in an activity sentence and in the Hushaphone Notes. The camera tracks mother and baby to the stove so that the observer is left off camera. The observer interrupts by asking a question to which the mother replies in a voice which trails off. By Frame 232 the mother has turned her attention to the baby who had been fussing and by Frame 236 she is rocking him in her arms to soothe him and using a "baby-talk voice." In Frames 238 and 240 she pays attention to the heating of the bottle (f ♀). These are small intercalated activities superimposed on the ongoing soothing (s o♀) interaction.

In Frame 241 she returns to the table, tracked by the camera, and puts the baby down. She keeps her hand on the baby as she arranges a place for herself to sit (overlap of f ♀ and s o♀). The baby's limbs do not move. I interrupt again in Frame 244 and this time the conversation between observer and mother continues to alternate for some time, but the mother, after initial orientation to the observer, goes back to arranging her own place to sit while continuing the conversation. Nor does she disregard the baby for long; she puts a hand on him again as she resumes preparing her place, thus restoring the same concurrent activities as before. All through this the baby lies quietly. With her place arranged, the mother walks to stove and back to the table without the bottle. The camera does not track the mother this time because the baby is left on the table. She sits and orients to the baby. The mother and baby quickly establish contact and begin a sequence of interaction which has the pattern of a conversation (c o♀). The vocal component does not occur on the tape until Frame 256 beyond this data sheet.

The vertical bracketing of activity units (B-segments) is done in the right-hand columns. The sample data show the end of one major activity and the beginning of another in the first O-segment, Frame 228. Dressing (D on the bracket) ended with the closing of the box of cotton. (Actually some of the cleanup activity was postponed until later, overlapping and becoming part of the preparatory activity for feeding.) The repositioning of the infant and the glance toward the stove mark the initiation of feeding (F). Although the content of the rest of the data sheet is considered "feeding," all that shows here is preparatory activity

(P). The feeding proper will not start until Frame 290 about five minutes later. At the bottom of the sheet downward arrowheads indicate that feeding and the preparatory phase continue. Within the preparatory phase the main activities are heating the food (f ♀) and preparing the place and the infant (p ♀). The chair is cleared of blankets left over from the sponge bath and repositioned in front of the table. A cloth is placed over the infant's body. Some activities may be considered intercalated in relation to the major activity: feeding. Interactions with the infant occur while waiting for the milk to heat: soothing (s o♀) and the beginning of a conversation (c o♀). Finally, there are interruptions initiated from without, in this case conversations with the mother initiated by the observer (I ♀E).

Comment

The sample submitted here comes from within the first two weeks of postnatal life. There is already evidence of mutual adjustment in interaction as in the last B-segment (v o♀) on the data sheet. In looking at samples of data at four, eight and twelve months, I have been impressed, on the one hand, with the speed with which the infant becomes able to mesh his activity with more and more complex aspects of his mother's, and, on the other hand, with the relatively slower pace at which he develops segmentation of his behavior when on his own. This makes it look as if the mother is leading the infant into more complexly structured behavior through entraining him in her adult patterns.

The five infant/mother pairs in the "data base," while showing individual differences, are probably all in the usual range for American middle-class families with firstborn infants in respect to amount of adult/infant interaction. One would have to compare infants with much and little opportunity for interaction with adults to approach the learning versus maturation aspects of this development.

There is clearly a wide gap between the survey of about 200 half-hour observations I am contemplating and the elegant and much more detailed analyses of shorter samples of sound film by Condon, Kendon and Scheflen. Both Kendon and Scheflen were able to take the step from etic to emic analysis. I am, at this stage, closer to the ethological tradition than to the linguistic. I have set out to produce a special kind of ethogram (inventory of behavioral units) with activity units at several hierarchical levels in the context of developmental sequences. This should yield data about length of units, frequency of units, sequencing of units, individual and joint participation in units, etc. all in developmental sequence. This could permit a first approximation to emic units and the possibility of structural analysis. I am sure the first results will be quite crude, but I feel it is worthwhile to open up this area to investigation.

REFERENCES

ALTMANN, STUART A.
1967 "The structure of primate social communication," in *Social communication among primates*. Edited by Stuart A. Altmann, 325–362. Chicago: University of Chicago Press.

ANDREW, R. J.
1962 The situations that evoke vocalization in primates. *Annals of the New York Academy of Sciences* 102(2):296–315.

BARKER, ROGER G., HERBERT F. WRIGHT
1955 *Midwest and its children: the psychological ecology of an American town*. New York: Harper and Row.

BATESON, GREGORY, MARGARET MEAD
1954 Film: *Bathing Babies in Three Cultures* (revised version). New York: New York University.

BATESON, MARY C.
1971 *The interpersonal context of infant vocalization*. Quarterly Progress Report 100, pages 170–176. Cambridge: Research Laboratory of Electronics, MIT.

BIRDWHISTELL, RAY L.
1959 "The frames in the communication process." Paper presented at the American Society of Clinical Hypnosis Annual Scientific Assembly.

BLURTON-JONES, N., editor
1972 *Ethological studies of child behaviour*. London: Cambridge University Press.

BRAZELTON, T. BERRY
1969 *Infants and mothers: differences in development*. New York: Delacorte Press.
i.p. *Neonatal behavioral assessment scale*. London: Spastics International.

BULLOWA, M.
1970 "The start of the language process," in *Actes du Xe Congrès International des Linguistes III*, pages 191–200. Bucarest: Editions de l'Académie de la Republique Socialiste de Roumanie.

BULLOWA, M., E. PUTNEY
1973 "A method for analyzing communicative behavior between infant and adult from film." Prepared for 1973 biennial meeting of the International Society for the Study of Behavioral Development, August 21–25. Mimeograph.

CALDWELL, BETTYE M.
1968 "A new 'approach' to behavioral ecology," in *Minnesota symposia*

on child psychology, volume two. Edited by J. P. Hill, 74–109. Minneapolis: University of Minnesota Press.

CHOMSKY, NOAM, MORRIS HALLE
1968   *The sound pattern of English.* New York: Harper and Row.

CONDON, W. S., W. D. OGSTON
1967   A segmentation of behavior. *Journal of Psychiatric Research* 5: 221–235.

DARWIN, CHARLES
1877   A biographical sketch of an infant. *Mind* 2:285–294.

EKMAN, PAUL, WALLACE V. FRIESEN
1969   The repertoire of nonverbal behavior: categories, origins, usage and coding. *Semiotica* 1:49–98.

GEBER, MARCELLE
1956   Développement psycho-moteur de l'enfant Africain. *Courrier* 6: 17–29.

GESELL, ARNOLD
1945   *The embryology of behavior.* New York: Harper.

GOLANI, I., H. MENDELSSOHN
1971   Sequences of precopulatory behavior of the jackal (*canis aureus* L.). *Behaviour* 38:169–192.

GRUBER, JEFFREY S.
1967   "Correlations between the syntactic constructions of the child and of the adult." Paper presented at the Society for Research in Child Development. Unpublished mimeograph.

HALLIDAY, M. A. K.
1961   Categories of the theory of grammar. *Word* 17:241–292.

HESS, ECKHARD H.
1962   "Ethology: an approach toward the complete analysis of behavior," in *New directions in psychology.* Edited by Roger Brown, et al. New York: Holt, Rinehart and Winston.

HOLUBÁŘ, JOSEF
1969   *The sense of time* (original edition 1961). Cambridge: MIT Press. Translated from the Czech by John S. Barlow.

KAPLAN, ABRAHAM
1964   *The conduct of inquiry.* San Francisco: Chandler.

KENDON, ADAM
1972   "Some relationships between body motion and speech," in *Studies in dyadic communication.* Edited by Seigman and Pope, 177–210. Elmsford, New York: Pergamon.

KENDON, ADAM, ANDREW FERBER
1973   "A description of some human greetings," in *Comparative ecology and behavior of primates.* Edited by R. P. Michael and J. H. Crook. London: Academic Press.

KORTLANDT, A.
1955   *Aspects and prospects of the concept of instinct (vicissitudes of the hierarchy theory).* Leiden: E. J. Brill.

LASHLEY, K. S.
1951 "The problem of serial order in behavior," in *Cerebral mechanisms in behavior*. Edited by Lloyd A. Jeffress, 112–136. New York: John Wiley.

LEWIN, KURT
1951 *Field theory in social science: selected theoretical papers*. Edited by Dorwin Cartwright. New York: Harper and Row.

LIEBERMAN, PHILIP
1967 *Intonation, perception, and language*. Cambridge: MIT Press.

MARSHALL, JOHN C.
1965 "The syntax of reproductive behaviour in the male pigeon." Oxford: Psycholinguistics Unit, Institute of Experimental Psychology. Unpublished mimeograph.

MENZEL, EMIL W., JR.
1969 "Naturalistic and experimental approaches to primate behavior," in *Naturalistic viewpoints in psychological research*. Edited by Edwin P. Willems and Harold L. Rausch, 78–121. New York: Holt, Rinehart and Winston.

PIKE, KENNETH L.
1967 *Language in relation to a unified theory of the structure of human behavior*. The Hague: Mouton.

PRECHTL, H. F. R.
1969 "Brain and behavioural mechanisms in the human newborn infant," in *Brain and early behaviour*. Edited by R. J. Robinson, 115–131. London: Academic Press.

PRECHTL, HEINZ, DAVID BEINTEMA
1964 *The neurological examination of the full term newborn infant*. Clinics in Developmental Medicine 12. London: Spastics International and William Heinemann.

SCHEFLEN, ALBERT E.
1964 The significance of posture in communication systems. *Psychiatry* 27:316–331.
1965 *Stream and structure of communicational behavior* (revised edition 1972). Behavioral Studies Monograph 1. Eastern Pennsylvania Psychiatric Instiute. Philadelphia: Commonwealth of Pennsylvania.

SMITH, W. JOHN
1968 "Message-meaning analyses," in *Animal communications*. Edited by Thomas A. Sebeok, 44–60. Bloomington: Indiana University Press.

STERMAN, M. B., TOKE HOPPENBROUWERS
1971 "The development of sleep-waking and rest-activity patterns from fetus to adult in man," in *Brain development and behavior*. Edited by M. B. Sterman, D. J. McGinty and A. M. Adinolfi, 203–227. London: Academic Press.

STETSON, R. H.
1945 *Bases of phonology*. Oberlin, Ohio: Oberlin College.

THOMSON, SIR JOHN ARTHUR
1922 *Outline of science*, four volumes. London: G. P. Putnam's Sons.

VOWLES, D. M.
1970 "Neuroethology, evolution, and grammar," in *Development and evolution of behavior: essays in memory of T. C. Schneirla.* Edited by Lester R. Aronson, Ethel Tobach, Daniel S. Lehrman, and Jay S. Rosenblatt, 194–215. San Francisco: W. H. Freeman.
WOLFF, PETER H.
1967 The role of biological rhythms in early psychological development. Bulletin of the Menninger Clinic 31:197–218.
WRIGHT, HERBERT F.
1967 *Recording and analyzing child behavior.* New York: Harper and Row.

ADDENDUM

This postscript constitutes a caveat to any who would attempt to apply the method described — or for that matter any method — to coding film of ongoing human interaction. When we who work with film and video present "data" we do not usually tell of the hours of struggle we have gone through before finding some sort of order in the passing scene. Once we have found it, there is a Eureka feeling and it all seems so self-evident. It's hard for us to understand why others don't see it too. We work from a conviction that there is no such thing as truly random activity in human (or animal) behavior. To find this order we have to be very precise in specifying our criteria for the categories we use. We want our work to be incontrovertible and reproducible. We still are a very small band and widely scattered. We tend to approach our practical coding problems as if we are charting new territory for the first time and we tend to develop idiosyncratic terminology. This is true whether we attend to a limited set of specific acts or to the "stream of behavior."

I am going to say something about the practical difficulties because I think this needs saying, and I am saying it in personal anecdotal terms. When I prepared the sample data for this paper I had been working for several months with various forms of continuous (stream of behavior) coding of observations of very young infants (mostly during the first month of life) and their parents. At this age and at 2 frames per second there are relatively few kinds of observations which can be made of the infant. He moves his limbs at varying rates with varying force. From this we estimate his "activity" as quiet, mildly active, moderately active, or extremely active. He orients. This is usually judged from the turning of his head, since the films were not always taken in a way to visualize the eyes, and the sparse sampling rate does not in any case permit an unequivocal judgment of whether his eyes are open or what he is looking at. In a feeding situation he may reject or accept the nipple and suck. There isn't much more to detect of very young infant behavior from this sort of film. Sometimes the concurrent description adds details not visible on film, but the reporting is spotty. (This is one reason why so many studies are based on reporting at fixed intervals on a limited standard set of behavioral items.) Therefore, for these very young subjects, the record consists in large measure of an account of the caretaker's activity *vis-à-vis* the infant or the observer or her autonomous activity. This is relatively easy to do, although it is not without coding problems.

But in the time between submitting the paper and attending the conference, more thorny problems showed up. I attempted continuous coding of observations from older infants using films which I had scanned earlier to check field impressions. I found that, as the infant became more organized in his activity, it was no longer possible to chart mother's activity toward a quiet or active infant who was oriented either toward or away from her face. Baby and mother may be doing quite different things which are still clearly related. I think of a dressing sequence in which the baby on mother's lap looks to and reaches toward his own feet while mother is reaching for and preparing socks and shoes. The relationship between their activities is more conceptual than physical, even though the physical relationship of baby sitting on mother's lap with his back toward her makes his reach and gaze toward his own feet possible. Somehow the obvious actor/recipient-of-action model of the first month or so is no longer appropriate. A new element has come into play, or perhaps one that always existed has escalated, and this must be taken into account if the description is to do justice to what is observable on the film. It is at this point that I turn to the ethologists, especially those who study ongoing human and primate behavior, for practical guidance, hoping that they have already faced and solved the problems I have encountered.

The moral of this is a warning not to take my methodology too literally. It is suggestive and, I believe, tends in an appropriate direction. But actually refining a large amount of useable detailed information from naturalistic observation (in the field or preserved for playback) presents many unsolved problems which I, for one, intend to labor to resolve.

Table 1. Sample data sheet

Obs No L028
August 7, 1962
Age: 12 days
Film: 278
Tape: 418CD

Prior to observation: Recording began 9:30 A.M. This data sheet starts at beginning of 20th minute. ♀ had undressed o, bathed o (about 14 minutes), dressed o (about 4 minutes). Dressing ends in 228 as this data sheet starts. o had been fussy. o quieted in 226.

Initial: (frame 2280) o supine on towel on kitchen table, feet toward ♀ (seen from right side), ♀ stands at table facing o, o feet touch ♀ body. ♀ reaching over o to box of cotton. ♀ gaze to box. E sits near table (at left edge of screen) leaning toward ♀ and o, hushaphone to mouth.

Frame	Person R	S	Activity	Location	Artifact	Posture o	Posture ♀	Posture x	Vocalization o	Vocalization ♀	Vocalization x	Hushaphone notes	Additional notes	Analysis	Frame
228	o♀ ET	o♀ E	o quiet (limbs not moving) ♀ closes box ♀ repositions o ♀ glances to stove E straightens back	kitchen table	box of cotton	♂	—	⊼						D F p	228
229			o activates mildly ♀ picks up o			♂	⌒			v		♀ picks o up and holds o		f♀	229
230	o♀	o♀	glances to stove ♀ glances to E_i ♀ cradles o in rt arm ♀ walks to stove ♀ glances to E_i	betw table and stove			—	O		v			E: Where do you want to go? ♀: I'm just, I think —	I ♀E	230
231			♀ touches pot handle c lt hand ♀ turns on burner c lt hand	at stove	pot knob					v		♀ cradles o in rt arm as she turns on flame under pan	♀: his milk and his —	I	231
232			o orients to ♀ ♀ orients to o ♀ glances to stove							v			♀: (murmur)	s o♀ f	232
233			o quiets ♀ reorients to o ♀ removes lint (?) from o							v			♀: (murmur)		233
234			♀ smoothes (+ removes lint from?) o hair							v		♀ looking at o	♀: (baby talk voice)		234
235			♀ puts lt arm around o ♀ puts lt hand over baby body									♀ smoothed o hair, ♀ talks to o	EFN — I interrupted this observation several times to chat with her, feeling it important to put her at ease about the observation.		235
236			o activates mildly ♀ puts lt hand under o ♀ rocks o (by pelvic rotation)									♀ rocks o			236
237														f	237

#											
239								v			
240		♀ touches ♀ face c rt hand ♀ glances to stove ♀ turns to table				♀ smiles "and seems more relaxed with him"					f ♀
241	↓	(o orientation indeterminate; head concealed) ♀ walks to table ♀ orient'n shifts to table	betw stove and table		↓	o yawns					
242	↘	o ♀+ E	[♀ orients to o ♀ puts o on tbl (supine f+ to ♀+ cam)] o quiets ♀ places lt hand on o ♀ rearranges chair	kitchen table	chair →		⊣	q			p ♀
243						♀ arranges chair for self					s
244			♀ orients to E ♀ straightens ♀ takes hand from o ♀ glances to chair? E straightens E removes Hushaphone			E: Where would you want to sit if I wasn't here? Because I can move. ♀: I was sitting right here in the kitchen. E: Not from that side anyway or would you want this side? ♀: Well you see I can sit facing this way. That's all right. E: You see, I'm very mobile. I can move anyplace. So you go where you would go and I'll adjust myself. ♀: (laughs) Yeh, it's usually from the right in the kitchen. E: Sure. ♀: Nice and easy. E: You let me know what you want to do and I can move around anyplace. ♀: Well I usually sit facing this way but I can sit facing that way.	⊓		v		I ♀ E
245			♀ picks up and discards blanket [♀ orients to E ♀ gesticulates to E] E gesticulates to ♀	blanket₁					v		p
246			♀ touches ♀ face ♀ orients E E stands up E backs away	(E near table)			⊿|		v	no Hushaphone	
247		o ♀ c	♀ brushes back ♀ hair ♀ orients to chair				⊢	⌐	v		
248			[♀ puts lt hand on o ♀ clears chair of blanket]		blanket₂ →				v	conversation with ♀	s o ♀+ p ♀+
249			♀ picks up cloth ♀ glances to E;		cloth →		≡		v		s
250			♀ places cloth over o ♀ moves chair around table (nearer to camera)		chair →				v		p I
251		o ♀	♀ orients to stove ♀ walks to stove	betw table and stove			O	∧			f ♀
252			♀ orients to o ♀ walks to chair ♀ sits down at table	kitchen table						o "very quiet", o eyes open	o ♀
253		o ♀ c	o activates mildly ♀ puts lt hand on o				⊢			o moves "a little", o orients to ♀ "when she sits beside him"	
254			♀ glances to E ♀ orients to o ♀ handles o							♀ handles o hand, o faces away from ♀	p F

Tonic Aspects of Behavior in Interaction

SIEGFRIED FREY

THEORETICAL OUTLINE

Recently, Schleidt (i.p.) has proposed a new theoretical model for interaction processes termed "tonic communication." This model considers it highly relevant to raise the question about the time span within which a communicative behavioral event remains effective. Schleidt starts with the assumption that the occurrence of a communicative behavioral event exerts an influence on the receiving communicant which lasts for a certain period of time. He defines the time span within which the behavioral event remains effective as the "tonic effect" of a behavior.

Most of the current experimental strategies try to investigate the communicative value of behaviors by relating a behavioral event shown by the communicator to a behavioral event shown by the communicant. This approach works with the implicit assumption that behavior of individuals in interaction is organized in a quasi-digital way: the behavior of the communicator exerts an internal effect on the communicant. The response of the communicant then assumes the function of a new communicative stimulus which, in turn, elicits a response from the other participant, and so on.

Part of the research underlying this paper was made possible by a fellowship awarded to the author by the Foundations' Fund for Research in Psychiatry. The author gratefully acknowledges the generous support received from the FFRP. The author also wishes to thank Dr. Paul Ekman and Dr. Wallace Friesen of the University of California, San Francisco, for their constant help and encouragement in the development of our Movement Analysis Technique (MAT), and for their permission to test the accuracy and efficiency of MAT on their own material.

Schleidt feels that this approach reflects an inadequate view of interaction processes. He argues that we cannot adequately understand interaction processes if we assume that the occurrence of a behavioral event exerts an influence like a switch "in a railroad switchyard, [where cars are] running from one point of decision to the next" (Schleidt i.p.). Rather than assuming that behaviors show a "once-for-all-effect," he claims that each behavior shown by an individual modulates the communicative value of other behaviors shown by the same individual. The degree to which a behavior can modify the communicative value of other behaviors depends — according to Schleidt — largely on the degree of tonic effect of a behavior. As to the dynamics of interactive behavior, Schleidt expects that:

... whenever the time constant of decay of such an effect is long compared with the interval between successive [behavioral events] their effect will be cumulative, since the effect of any new [behavioral event] will add to the decaying residue of previous effects (Schleidt i.p.).

Of course, the expectation about such a cumulative effect applies only to stimuli that exert the same kind of effect on the receiving individual. An overlap of the tonic effects of stimuli of different communicative meanings should result in mutual weakening of their communicative effects. Generally speaking, this means that the communicative value of a behavioral event can vary widely, depending in each case on what has happened before the event occurred. Additionally, the meaning of the behavioral event may change retroactively, depending on the events that follow.

As can be seen now, the tonic communication model has important implications for a theoretical view of communication processes. If we follow Schleidt's reasoning that behavior receives its meaning from its role in the context of other behaviors shown by the same individual, we should expect that a certain behavior emitted by a person is in large part a consequence of a complex behavioral program rather than a consequence of a stimulus perceived right before the behavior occurred. On the other hand, we should expect that there is also a program inside the recipient which helps him to evaluate whole series of behavioral events in terms of a context within which a certain behavioral event has only a modulating effect.

While Schleidt seems to see his model as being mainly speculative, it appears that the model does not contradict common experience. A great part of the behavior shown in everyday life consists of ritualized forms of behavior with little informative content. This behavior can be seen as being pre-programmed to serve the function of setting a certain communicative state.

Quite a few questions asked by a four-year-old child, by a devout pupil, by a loving friend are not intended to provoke a specific and informative answer, but mainly to reassure or to elicit assurance, in short, to maintain contact. Exchanges of greeting phrases in passing by [How are you?/Fine: how are you?] constitute a condensed and ritualized form of conversation, which conveys only that the status quo is continued (Schleidt i.p.).

In cases in which we want to convey important information, we make considerable effort to present the critical information in a context that makes sure that the information will not be misunderstood. Thus, if we have to transmit bad news, the critical information is frequently embedded in a context of friendly behavior, designed to convince the person that we feel extremely sorry about the state of things. In any case, the behavioral context within which we present the critical information will be different, depending on whether we want the person to take the critical information as being important or not important.

Of course, those efforts can only make sense if the person we talk to takes the context into account in evaluating the critical information. This actually can be confirmed in everyday experience. In any case, it would be strange indeed if the response of a person would take into account just a small part of what was said and not the whole context in which a certain piece of information was presented. It would be interesting to raise the question about the strange impression we often get from the interactive behavior of psychotics. It might well be that the psychotic's way of organizing information violates the rules of interactive exchange, insofar as the emphasis is put on a specific event while the context is disregarded.

METHODOLOGICAL PROBLEMS

Of course, anecdotal evidence from everyday life does not help very much if we try to investigate interactive processes systematically. However, a certain plausibility of the tonic communication concept is most welcome in order to justify the big efforts necessary to test Schleidt's hypotheses systematically. Clearly, his model complicates research in the field of interaction because it calls for the development of new methodological approaches that can provide data about the full repertoire of behaviors occurring in interaction.

In past literature we find many attempts to systematize behavior on a descriptive level in order to provide information about the repertoire of behaviors occurring in interaction. All those attempts suffer much from the fact that a very large number of discriminable behaviors has to be classified on the basis of a relatively small scale of alternatives. Depending upon the description system used, the units employed to distinguish between behaviors vary widely with respect to their complexity: we find descriptions which are as specific as "head turn left," "head erect," "right hand to the lap," "right hand to the knee" (Fretz 1966), or as complex as "agitated" (McReynolds 1965), 'bizarre' (Framo and Adlerstein 1961), "extravagant" (Spoerri 1967), "nervous" (Burdock et al. 1964). The use of complex units has been severely criticized (e.g. by Webb, et al. 1966) because of the low degree to which such units fulfill methodological requirements for reliability. Attempts to employ specific units were not very successful for another reason. If we were to try to establish a system to describe the full scope of behavioral differences, we might run out of labels or would soon be confused by an enormous body of data that is hardly clearer than the process described by such detailed analysis. Consequently, most investigators who described behavior via specific units restricted their analysis to the investigation of just a few behavioral details. We are not surprised, therefore, if Kendon (1973) concludes that "we do not have even the beginnings of the behavioral repertoire of man, except in the case of language."

A NEW TECHNIQUE FOR THE ANALYSIS OF BODY MOVEMENT

In order to obtain information about the repertoire of human movement behavior, a new technique for the measurement and multidimensional analysis of body movement — "movement analysis technique" (MAT) — has been designed by us at the Max Planck Institut für Psychiatrie. The MAT consists of two component approaches:
1. A validated, operationalized classification method for the assessment of movements and postures occurring in situations where people are communicating while sitting in a chair, and
2. A formalized system for a quantitative multidimensional analysis of body–movement data.

In its current form the MAT works as follows:

RECORDING OF BEHAVIOR Videotape records are taken of a subject

 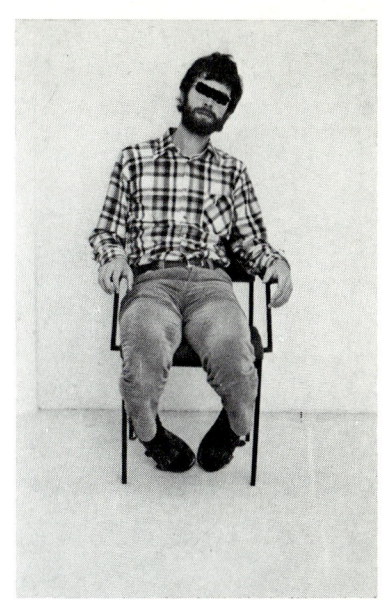

Plate 1. Top: Positions of original subjects,
  Bottom: Corresponding positions of model, read back from the codings.

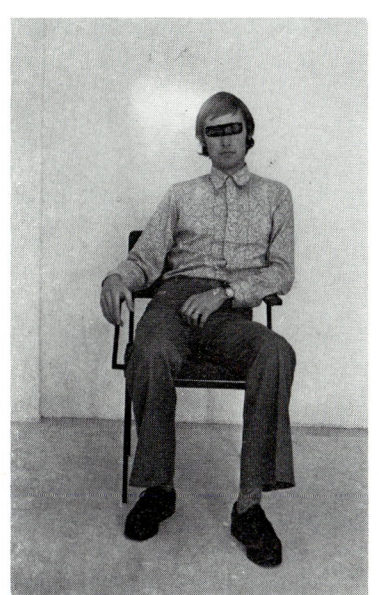 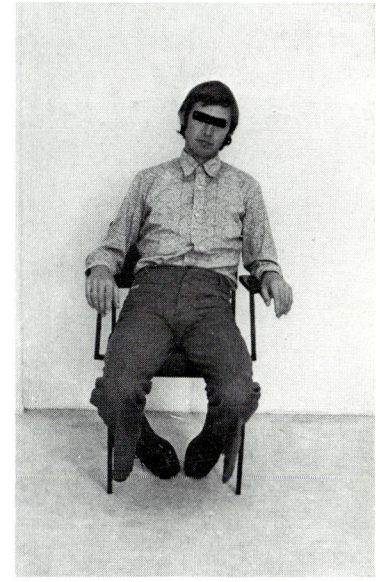

 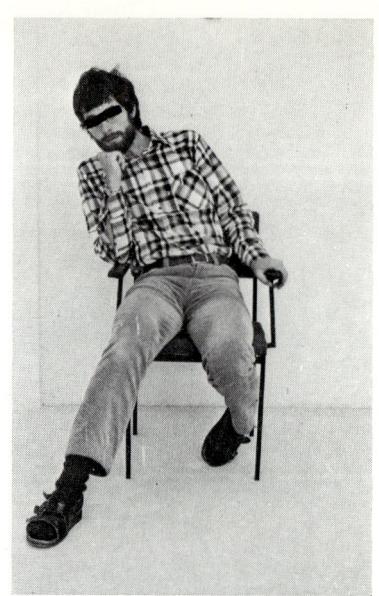

Plate 1 (cont.)

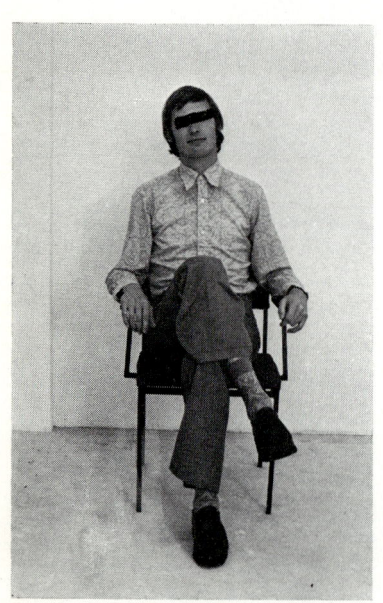 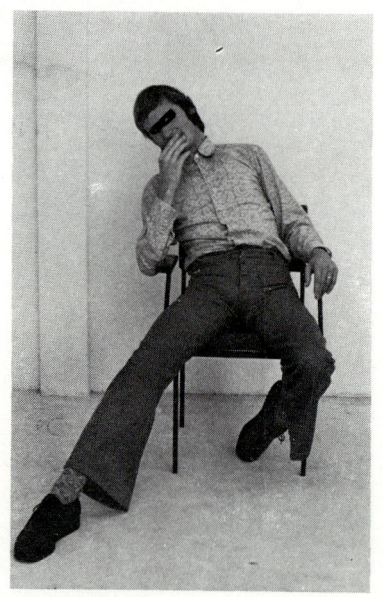

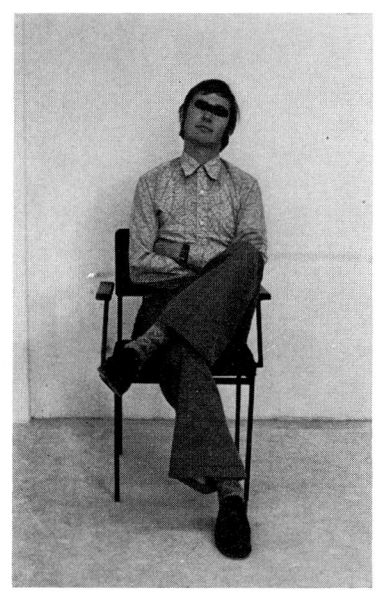 

Plate 1 (cont.)

 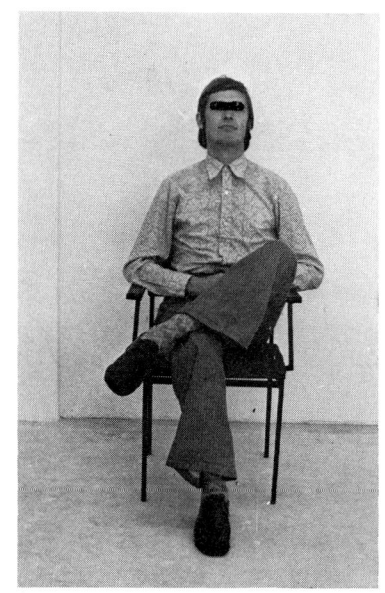

Plate 1 (cont.)

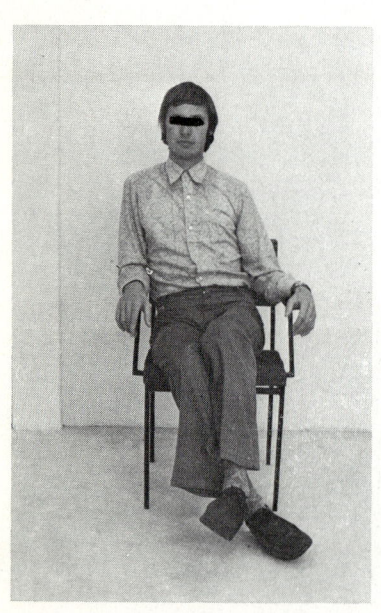
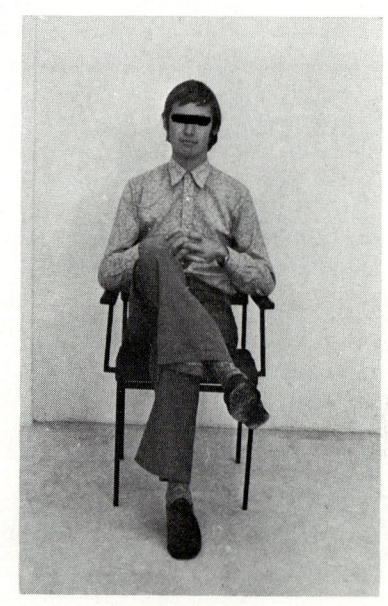

 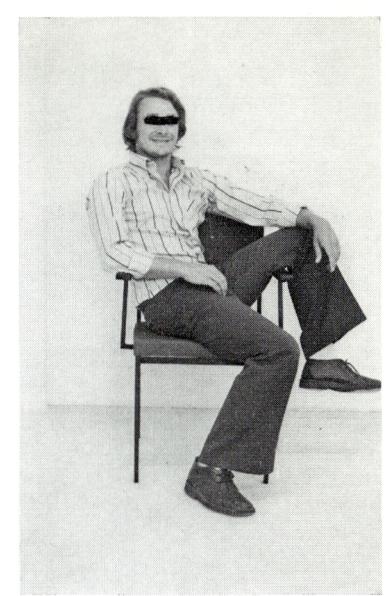

Plate 1 (cont.)

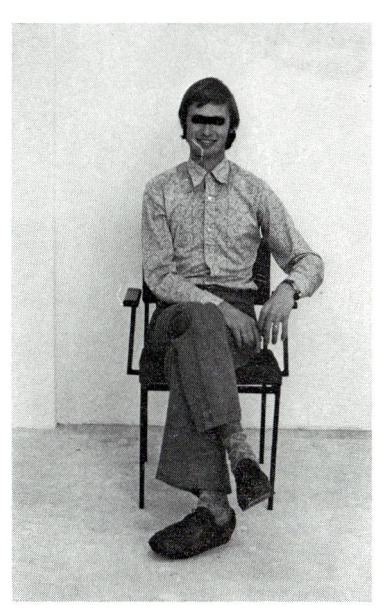 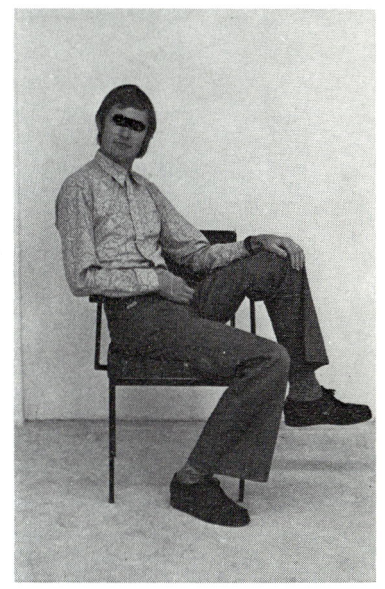

 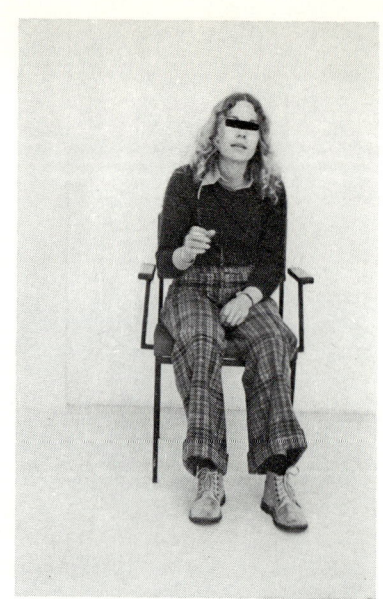

Plate 1 (cont.)

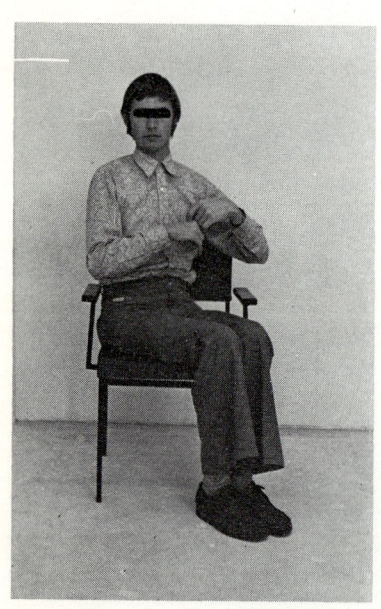 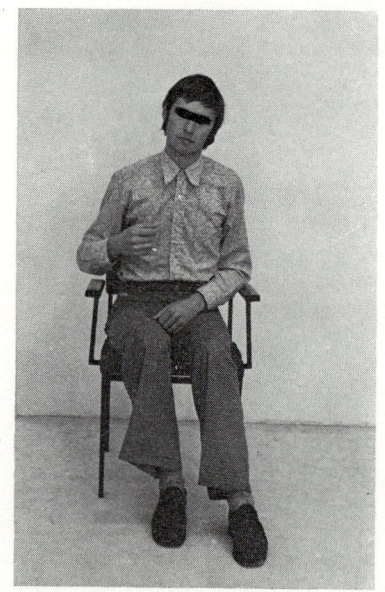

sitting in a chair in front of a hidden camera. A second camera films a digital clock and the picture of the clock is inserted in the picture taken of the subject.

COLLECTION OF RAW DATA The raw data for our analysis of behavior are positions assumed by the subject at different points in time. According to our current procedure, we register one set of positions at one-second intervals. Our coding system allows us to assess at one time a set of eight separate positions, which refer to the following parts of the body: head, trunk, right hand, left hand, right thigh, left thigh, right foot, left foot.

The positions of the head and the trunk are defined in relation to a three-dimensional orthogonal system of reference based on the main spatial axes. Our system of reference permits the assessment of position differences on the basis of sagittal, rotational, and lateral flexions. The "upright body position" shows neither sagittal, nor rotational, nor lateral flexions. Deviations from this standard position in each dimension are distinguished according to the direction of deviation. Thus in each case three locations can be distinguished:

Location 1 The object of observation does not show a deviation from the standard location in the studied dimension.
Location 2 The object of observation does show a deviation from the standard location in this dimension.
Location 3 The object of observation does show a deviation from the standard location in this dimension, but opposite to location 2.

In the sagittal dimension the classification scheme for head and trunk thus distinguishes the following positions: (1) standard position (the head/trunk is tilted neither forward nor backward); (2) deviation from standard position (the head/trunk is tilted forward); (3) deviation from standard position in the opposite sense to Location 2 (the head/trunk is tilted backwards). The locations in the rotation dimension (degree of turning from standard position) and in the lateral dimension (degree of sideways tilting from the standard position) are assessed likewise.

The positions for each of the body parts studied result from the combination of locations in the three dimensions, and every position is considered different if it differs in at least one dimension. Because, according to this simple classification, three locations can be distinguished in each of the three independent dimensions; the classification system for head and trunk thus allows the distinction of $3 \times 3 \times 3 = 27$ positions each.

The positions of the hands and the thighs are assessed by means of a system that permits locational determination in the vertical and in the horizontal dimensions. For the hands we distinguish between twelve vertical and five horizontal locations. For the thighs our distinction is between three locations in the vertical dimension and three locations in the horizontal dimension.

The positions of the feet are classified by means of a three-dimensional reference system. We distinguish between six locations in the vertical, three locations in the horizontal and three locations in the depth dimension.

Studies on retest and intercoder reliability brought satisfactory results. Percentages of agreement on the assessment of positions varied from 83 to 97. The modal value of agreement for both retest and intercoder reliability is 94 percent. In order to test the validity of positional codings, we performed a study in which we tried to reconstruct original positions of subjects from our raw data. For this purpose, the head, trunk, hands, thighs, and feet of a human model were placed in positions, read back from the codings obtained with the original subjects. Pictures taken of this model were then compared with pictures showing the subject's original position. In this way the degree of accuracy to which the codings represented the subject's actual positions could be assessed.

As shown in Plate 1, the results this study yielded must be considered very satisfactory in regard to the power of accurate discrimination between different positions which our coding system provided.

ANALYSIS OF THE RAW DATA The raw data gathered by means of our coding system represent specific positions at specific points in time. Depending upon which behavioral parameter we wish to characterize, it will be necessary to reorganize the information given in our raw data. In this way we can select and evaluate the information relevant for statements about the particular parameter. If we decide to investigate a large number of behavioral properties, we will have to reorganize our data in a multitude of ways. Principally, we can say, however, that as long as the characterization of behavioral parameters requires solely information about positions in time, we should always be able to provide an answer on the basis of our data, no matter how complex these parameters are defined as being.

In order to demonstrate the principles of such a reorganization, we might think of a question that requires us to discriminate among movements and postures. We employ the term "movement" to indicate that during the observation time t_1 to t_n the subject observed was seen at more than one spatial location. We speak of "posture" if the location of the subject observed was being maintained over successive points in time. Clearly, on the basis of this definition we can discriminate (via computerized analysis) not only between movements and postures, but also among movements and among postures if data about positions at successive points in time are available. Furthermore, if we define differences in movements as differences in the sequence of spatial locations and/or differences in length of time interval across which positions are being varied, we can easily establish an empirical repertoire of movements. Likewise, we can easily give a repertoire of postures if we define differences in postures as differences in spatial locations.

However, identification and discrimination of movements and postures is not the main purpose of our technique. Our methodology was developed mainly to achieve reliable quantitative data on a great number of complex behavioral properties such as "symmetry," "expansion," "openness" of behavior in hands and feet, and "temporal and spatial concordance" of the behavior of the hands, "amounts of displacement," and "rate of displacement," "uprightness," "right–left-orientation," "up–down-orientation," "lateral flexion," and "taxis" of the head, "body movement variability," and so on. (An example demonstrating prescriptions used for the quantification of parameters of hand behavior is given in the Appendix.)

It might be worthwhile to note that in characterizing such aspects of behavior we do not describe behavior but evaluate descriptions of behavior with regard to theoretically defined parameters. Depending upon the definition of behavioral parameters, the same behavioral event might have to be evaluated in different ways, or different behavioral events might have to be evaluated in the same way. Of course, we have to make sure that the operations by which we arrive at quantitative statements about a behavioral parameter refer strictly to the definition we give for this parameter. Therefore, the definition of a parameter must contain prescriptions that specify in each case (1) which single behavioral events ought to be assessed and (2) which evaluative procedure should be applied to them.

It appears that in most studies on nonverbal behavior descriptive and evaluative activities of the experimenter are confounded in the statements about behavioral parameters. This is especially true in those studies in which the assessment of data follows the methodological principle termed "reductive coding" by Campbell (1958). In these procedures the observer decides during actual observation whether and to what degree the behavior of the object of observation presents the characteristics in question. Because the data thus result from the processing of an unknown number of indicators which have been evaluated in a subjective weighing process, we have good reasons to be skeptical about the reliability and validity of such data. It might well be that the broad use of reductive coding techniques in behavioral research is mainly responsible for our confusion about the role of behavioral parameters in communication.

FIRST RESULTS FROM THE APPLICATION OF MAT IN STUDIES ON TONIC ASPECTS OF BEHAVIOR IN INTERACTION.

Schleidt's tonic communication model postulates that the behaviors shown by an individual in interactive conditions are most likely related to factors that exert a long–term influence. Such factors could be internal conditions such as "emotional state," "personality traits," general intentions such as the "intention to convince or to deceive somebody," "to keep in touch," and "to maintain the status quo." Such factors could also arise from external conditions, e.g. from the status of a communicant, from the behaviors displayed by the interaction partner, or from the special situational conditions in which an interaction takes place.

According to Schleidt's concept, such factors should lead to a frequent occurrence of certain behavioral events supposed to serve the general factor relevant in interaction. In contradistinction, other behavioral events should occur infrequently, assuming the function of exerting only a slightly modulating effect on the behaviors frequently occurring. If general factors are being varied, we should expect that other behavioral events become predominant within the behavioral display. If several factors are effective at the same time, it will depend on their relative weight as to which one of those factors determines the predominating behaviors.

Experiments testing such hypotheses are in fact now available. In our studies on behavior in interactive conditions, we used the above–mentioned novel measuring technique (MAT) to examine Schleidt's hypotheses on the basis of our data on head behavior. The following three behavior parameters (out of twenty–eight which we are currently investigating) seemed to be relevant for this examination: (1) "nominal differentiation of head positions" (n.D.), (2) "frequential differentiation of head positions" (f.D.), and (3) "taxis of head movements." Nominal, frequential, and sequential differentiation are the three dimensions which in our studies constitute the "variability of movement behavior" (VaM). The definition of these parameters as well as the procedure employed for their quantitative assessment has been extensively reported elsewhere (Frey 1971; Frey and von Cranach 1973). We shall therefore limit ourselves to the presentation of the essentials of the definition of nominal and frequential differentiation of head positions: The nominal differentiation of head positions (n.D.) refers to the number of the positional categories occurring during the observation time t_1 to t_n. n.D. is considered maximal, when all twenty-seven possible positions which are discriminable by our coding system occur during the observation time — n.D. is considered minimal, when only one out of twenty-seven possible position categories occur during the observation time. The parameter of frequential differentiation of head positions (f.D). refers to the frequencies of different position categories in the sample of observations — f.D. is considered maximal when the position categories are observed equally often; f.D. is considered minimal, when all observations are allocated to one particular category.

In the definition of the variable taxis of head movements we chose to preserve the biological meaning of "taxis" denoting directional orientation achieved by a movement. More specifically, in the context of our technique, we defined taxis of head movement as the still position in which a head movement comes to rest for a predetermined minimum amount of time. In the experiments to be reported here, the minimum duration of still position was one second.

Head movement always leads to a displacement of the two main sensory organs, i.e. of the eye and the ear. As to the ear, we can expect that due to its sensory characteristics a head movement will not affect to a large extent the efficiency of the auditory channel. For the visual input, however, movement of the head can be very important because the specific localization of the head determines the area within which the eyes can possibly (and easily) focus on a stimulus source. Because under normal conditions a subject can move and orient his head in any direction he desires, we would expect that if the surrounding stimuli differ with respect to their importance to the subject, head orientation will show a preference for the more important stimuli, while those stimuli which are of less importance to the subject are being neglected. Prominence in such stimulus selection would thus constitute the effectiveness of a predominating factor. Because Schleidt expects a predominating factor to elicit a frequent emission of behavior serving this factor, we should expect, in our case, that an empirical relation obtains between the visually predominant factor and our parameters of head behavior, such that n.D., f.D., and taxis are as follows:

A. If in the area surrounding the subject there is a stimulus of such extremely high prominence that other possible stimuli sources become irrelevant, we should expect that the subject's head is exclusively oriented toward that highly prominent stimulus. With respect to our parameters, we would expect that n.D. and f.D values both approach or are equal to zero, and that taxis will be toward the stimulus source.

B. If the relative prominence of a certain stimulus decreases, the corresponding response increase in relation to other stimuli should lead to a less exclusive, i.e. more variable head orientation. More specifically, we should expect that as n.D. and f.D. increase, the range of taxis relating to a number of stimuli will increase too.

C. If an originally prominent stimulus becomes less prominent, while an originally less prominent stimulus becomes prominent, we would expect that head orientations reflect these reversals. In the context of our technique, we would expect taxis to be mainly oriented to the newly prominent stimulus, and n.D. and f.D. to decrease with increasing prominence of the stimulus.

EXPERIMENT 1

In order to test Hypothesis A we presented to twelve individuals (n-12) a two–minute movie. By this simple procedure we were able to manipulate the visual environment of the subject in a way in which our stimulus source became extremely prominent. Because the movie was projected on a wall facing the subject frontally, the position most adequate for eye orientation toward the screen was in the frontal straight–forward direction of the head. In the context of our coding sytem this position is equivalent to the "upright–standard" position, showing neither sagittal nor rotational nor lateral flexions. The results of this experiment support Hypothesis A. The mean value of n.D. of twelve subjects was n.D.$\bar{x}$ = 0.034 for the duration of two minutes with s = 0.042. Thus, during the observation period, our subjects kept their heads in only one position almost all the time. This fact contributed, of course, logically to the confirmation of the second prediction of Hypothesis A, namely, the finding of a low value of the f.D parameter. Aside from this however, even in those cases in which subjects assumed positions different from the predominant one, the frequential occurrences of these other positions were minimal (f.D.$\bar{x}$ = 0.055; s = 0.108).

From the results in n.D. and f.D. it is apparent that almost no head movements occurred. Consequently there were only very few values that referred to taxis of head movement directly. However, in cases in which taxis, i.e. movement–orientation, is absent, position–orientation yields information equivalent to the taxis parameter. Therefore we are able to test on the basis of position-orientation data that part of our hypothesis which concerns the taxis parameter. The data on position orientation are presented in Figure 1.

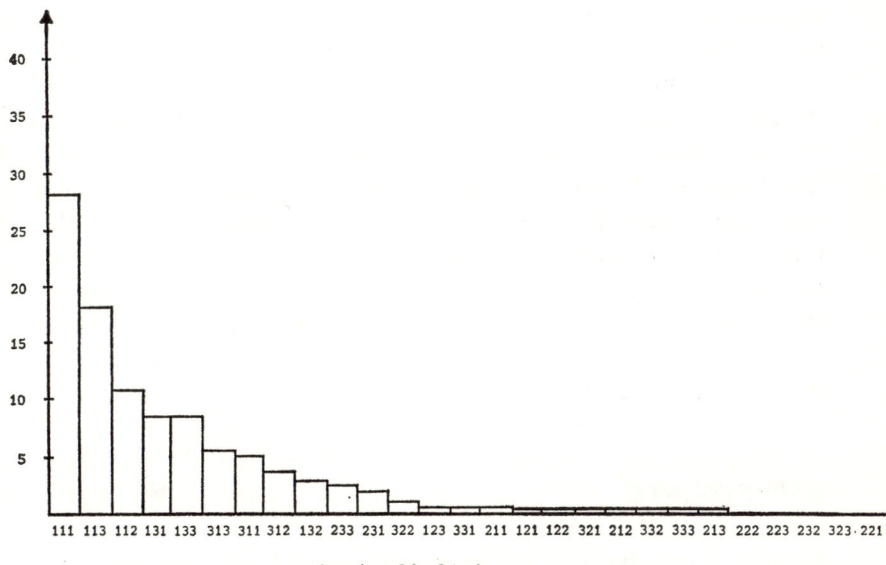

Figure 1. Percentages of occurrence of different head positions as discriminated by MAT in the situation "movie presentation." The head position categories are ordered with respect to their relative frequencies of occurrence, for a total of 1,426 position registrations (approximately 120 observations of each of the twelve subjects).

The numbers on the abscissa refer to the twenty–seven position categories discriminable by MAT. The code used for identification of position categories consists of a set of three numbers which are to be interpreted as follows: the first number of a set (to be read from left to right) refers to the sagittal dimension, the second number refers to the rotation dimension, and the third number to the lateral dimension. In the SAGITTAL DIMENSION Code 1 indicates that the head is tilted neither forward nor backward, Code 2 indicates that the head is tilted forward, and Code 3 indicates that the head is tilted backwards. In the ROTATION DIMENSION Code 1 indicates that the head is turned neither to the right nor to the left, Code 2 indicates that the head is turned to the subject's left side, and Code 3 indicates that the head is turned to the subject's right side. In the LATERAL DIMENSION Code 1 indicates that the head is tilted neither to the left nor to the right, Code 2 indicates that the head is tilted to the subject's left side, and Code 3 indicates that the head is tilted to the subject's right side.

Inspection of Figure 1 provides the empirical confirmation for our expectation about head orientation, formulated in Hypothesis A. The upright–standard position is, as expected, the most frequently occurring position. Furthermore, deviations from this position occur only in the sagittal and lateral dimensions, but not in the rotational dimension. This result strengthens our prediction, as head movements occurring in the rotation dimension would lead to a situation where the stimulus source is out of view, while movements in the lateral dimension do not affect the field of vision to any significant extent. The same reasoning explains the phenomenon that in the sagittal dimension, deviations from the standard position are only in the backwards direction, for tilt–forward head movements quickly lead to a displacement of the stimulus source, such that it would be out of view. Tilt-backwards head movements have, of course, fewer consequences for the visibility of the stimulus source.

EXPERIMENT 2

In order to test Hypothesis B we assessed the n.D., f.D., and taxis values of an experiment in which eighteen subjects communicated with an interviewer in a lighted room for about two and a half minutes. Because this experiment took place in a room with very little noise, one can safely assume that the interviewer constituted a predominating stimulus source to the subject. However, because in contrast to our first experiment (where a movie had been presented), the room was not darkened, we expect the interviewer to constitute a stimulus source of less prominence than the stimulus source "movie" in Experiment 1. Consequently, while head positions should be oriented mainly toward the interviewer (our main stimulus source), changes in head orientation should occur in the form of fairly regular movements, which could serve the function of screening the subject's environment. Nevertheless, with comparatively little noise present in the experimental room, taxis of these movements should be predominantly oriented toward the interviewer.

The results of this experiment bear out these predictions and thus confirm Hypothesis B. In Experiment 2, n.D. values (n.D.$\bar{x}$ = 0.418, s = 0.092) as well as f.D values (f.D.$\bar{x}$ = 0.597, s = 0.95) were found to be significantly higher than the corresponding values in experiment 1 ($p < 0.1$ percent, Mann–Whitney U Test). This means that, compared to Experiment 1, the subject's head showed significantly more orientational alterations. However, the median magnitude of the f.D. values indicates that a predominance for a particular orientation still exists.

As to the data on taxis, our expectations are met, too. In Experiment 2 the subject was seated facing a wall in the frontal position. The interviewer, however, was located to the right of the subject at a distance of 1.5 meters, such that the angle formed by the lines subject-to-wall and subject-to-interviewer, amounted to about thirty-five degrees. Thus in order to be able to focus on the interviewer, the subject had to rotate his head to the right.

Figure 2 gives evidence that taxis of the head was predominantly oriented toward the interviewer. But Figure 2 also confirms our expectation concerning an increase of taxis events NOT directed toward the predominant stimulus source. As in Experiment 1 we note once more, that lateral and sagittal deviations from the position of "best view" are more likely to occur than deviations in the rotation dimension. These results certainly deserve continued attention in further studies.

EXPERIMENT 3

In order to test Hypothesis C we used data of an experiment designed and carried out by Ekman and Friesen (1971) and analyzed by the author, using MAT. In one of their experimental conditions, Ekman and Friesen arranged a situation in which subjects watched a movie while at the same time they communicated with an interviewer.[1] Because in our studies reported above the movie as well as the interview-

---

[1] Ekman and Friesen's experiment was designed to investigate the influence of "deception" and of "emotional stress" on nonverbal behavior. Within their experiment they had, in fact, four situations in which a subject communicated with an interviewer while watching a movie. Two of these four situations constitute the sample analyzed here. Each of the two situations was about one minute in duration. They differed with respect to the stress exerted by the movie, as well as with respect to the deception involved in the communication. However, since in the context of the questions discussed here we cannot refer to stress and deception variables, we shall not describe the details of their experimental design.

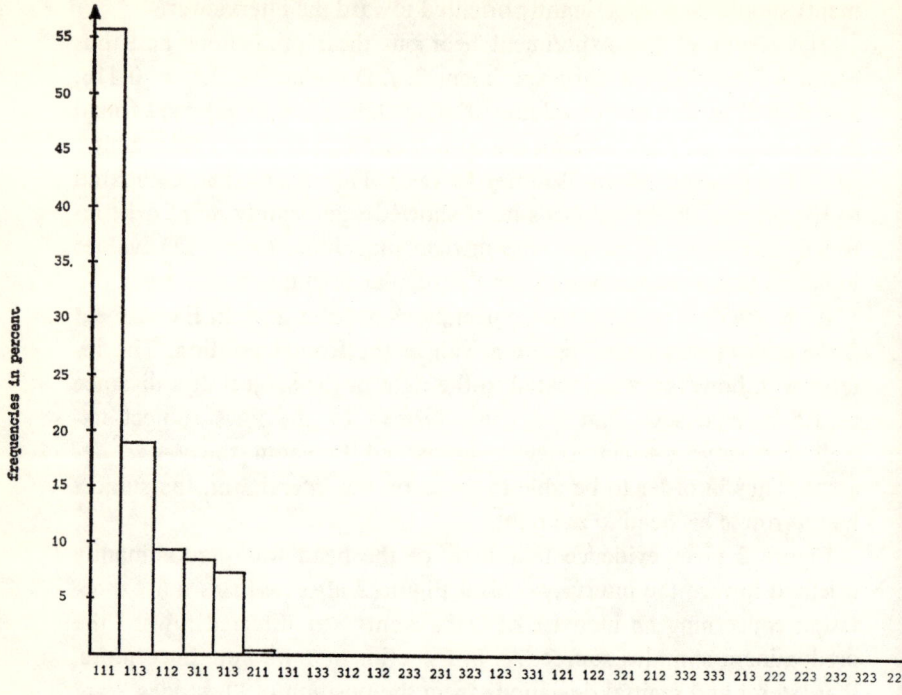

Figure 2. Relative frequencies (in percent) of taxis of head movements as measured by MAT in the situation "interview". The taxis categories are ordered with respect to their relative frequencies for a total of 493 movements, assessed in the data of eighteen subjects.

er had been shown to be stimuli of high relevance for the variance of head orientation data, we were interested in the analysis of a situation in which both prominent stimuli were effective at the same time. As in Experiment 1, the movie was projected on a wall facing the subject. The spatial relations between interviewer and subject were almost identical to the conditions obtaining in Experiment 2.

Comparison of the results of this study with those of Experiment 2 confirms Hypothesis 3. Figure 3 shows that the stimulus-source interviewer yielded a value of head taxis that is considerably lower than the measure of the same parameter in Experiment 2 (this difference was significant at a level of $p < 0.1$ percent, as tested by the Mann–Whitney U Test). Also, with respect to taxis of head movement the stimulus-source movie clearly predominated the stimulus-source interviewer. However, a comparison between Figures 2 and 3 shows that taxis predominance for the stimulus movie in Experiment 3 was considerably

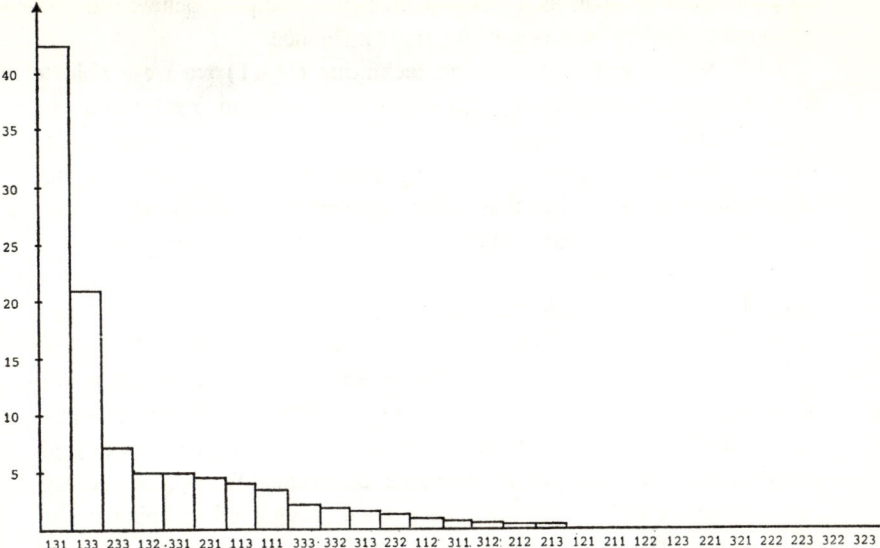

Figure 3. Relative frequencies (in percent) of taxis of the head as measured by MAT in the situation "movie+interview". The taxis categories are ordered with respect to the magnitude of their frequencies. The analysis is based on a total of 231 taxis events, obtained from sixteen subjects. Observation time for each subject is approximately two minutes.

weaker than taxis predominance for the stimulus interviewer in Experiment 2. This result is of particular interest to us, because it suggests that, in principle, MAT can provide access to the dynamics of different communicational contexts.

CONCLUSIONS

The results of the studies reported above attest to the relevancy of Schleidt's tonic communication model for the analysis of interaction processes. Thus, in conditions where the relation between head orientation and visually prominent stimuli were investigated, the variance of the behavioral variables could be explained by factors exerting a tonic influence as defined in Schleidt's model. By systematic variation of the tonic predominance of visual stimuli, we could even trigger systematic shifts in our dependent variables n.D., f.D., and taxis. The data therefore allow us to conclude that particular orienting movements of the head cannot be understood as a consequence of particular stimuli perceived by the subject immediately before a behavioral event occurred, but must be seen as a consequence of a complex behavioral program controlled by factors exerting tonic influence.

While with our new measuring technique (MAT) we were able to lend strong experimental support to the tonic communication concept, much further work remains to be done in order to strengthen and to extend Schleidt's concept. It will be necessary to relate variables of possible tonic influence other than those selected in this study with behavioral parameters not investigated here. Because Schleidt's concept is formulated in rather general terms, the testing and clarification of the scope of its empirical adequacy seems to be one of the most important steps to be taken next. And it is in this context that our novel technique (MAT), designed to be a tool for the measurement and multidimensional analysis of body movement, gains its significance. MAT seems to provide a methodology for thorough empirical testing of concepts of high complexity at a point when the usual experimental approaches, e.g. the reductive coding techniques, have been recognized as being inadequate. And it is precisely the empirical access which constitutes one of the basic preconditions for the further meaningful development of theoretical concepts that can elucidate the dynamics of the organization of interactive behavior.

APPENDIX: Log of instructions for the quantification of several parameters of hand behavior.

The classification system enables us to determine the hand's localization in the vertical and in the horizontal dimension. The size of the units in the vertical and in the horizontal dimension is defined with respect to anatomic properties of the subject. In doing so we hope to eliminate somewhat those positional differences that are due to anatomic differences between subjects. The vertical and the horizontal units are defined as follows:

Vertical dimension

1. Head
2. Head and neck
3. Neck and trunk
4. Upper part of trunk
5. Upper and lower part of trunk
6. Lower part of trunk
7. Trunk and thigh
8. Thigh
9. Thigh and lower leg
10. Lower leg

Horizontal dimension

1. Hand is located outside the body, left side
2. Hand is located inside the body, left side
3. Hand is located inside the body, left and right side
4. Hand is located inside the body, right side
5. Hand is located outside the body, right side

11. Lower leg and foot
12. Foot

Openness

Openness means the degree to which the hands' localization forms a barrier in front of the subject's body. Openness reaches a maximum if the right hand is located horizontally at Position 5 and the left hand at Position 1. Openness is considered minimum if the right hand is located at Position 1 while the left hand is located at Position 5.

Openness is assessed from our raw data according to the following equation:

$$O = \frac{\sum_{i=1}^{n}(O_{i\ \text{right hand}} + O_{i\ \text{left hand}})}{4n}$$

O stands for the degree of openness of the hands during the time of observation.
O_i stands for the openness score of a specific positional observation.

For the right hand, the following openness scores are attributed to the five localizations we can distinguish in the horizontal dimension.

Position (1) $O_i = -2$
Position (2) $O_i = -1$
Position (3) $O_i = 0$
Position (4) $O_i = +1$
Position (5) $O_i = +2$

For the left hand we have:

Position (1) $O_i = +2$
Position (2) $O_i = +1$
Position (3) $O_i = 0$
Position (4) $O_i = -1$
Position (5) $O_i = -2$

n stands for the number of specific positions (observations).
The score for openness therefore varies between -1 and $+1$.

Modification of Openness

This score is supposed to tell us how often the openness of the hands was changed. If a sample of n openness assessments is obtained, successively occurring assessments can show the same or different O_i scores. The degree to which modification of openness (MO) occurred during the observation time is calculated according to the following equation:

$$MO = \frac{OC}{n-1}$$

MO stands for the degree to which openness was modified during the time of observation.

OC stands for change in openness between two successively occurring positions of the hands.
n stands for the number of observations.

Effect of Modification of Openness

From any given openness score a change in openness is possible within the range $4 + |O_i|$. The score for the effect of modification of openness tells us to what degree openness was changed by the OC events. This score is calculated according to the following equation:

$$\text{EMO} = \frac{\sum |(O_{i\,r.h._{p2}} - O_{i\,r.h._{p1}}) + (O_{i\,l.h._{p2}} - O_{i\,l.h._{p1}})|}{4 \sum \text{OC} + \sum |(O_{i\,r.h._{p1}} + O_{i\,l.h._{p1}})|}$$

EMO stands for the degree to which openness was changed by the OC events.

$O_i\,r.h._{p2}$ stands for the openness score of the right hand at the second one of the two subsequently occurring positions for which the openness difference is calculated.

$O_i\,r.h._{p1}$ stands for the openness score of the right hand at the first one of the two subsequently occurring positions for which the openness difference is calculated.

$O_i\,l.h._{p2}$ stands for the openness score of the left hand, second position.

$O_i\,l.h._{p2}$ stands for the openness score, left hand, first position.

Symmetry

As the axis in regard to which symmetry is assessed we take that vertical axis of the body to which the anatomy of the person is symmetrically arranged. The degree to which the hands were located symmetrically with respect to this axis during the observation time is assessed according to the following equation:

$$S = \frac{4n - \sum_{i=1}^{n} \text{DNS}_i}{4n} = \frac{4n - \sum_{i=1}^{n} |(O_{i\,r.h.} - O_{i\,l.h.})|}{4n}$$

S stands for the degree to which the hands were located symmetrically to the vertical axis of the body during the observation time.

DNS_i stands for the minimum displacement necessary in order to achieve symmetry to the vertical axis of the body. The amount of displacement necessary to achieve symmetry is assessed on the basis of the definitions given for the transformation of positions to openness scores.

Temporal Concordance of the Activity of the Hands

Since our raw data refer to positional events, we cannot tell from looking at a single raw datum whether the hand was "moved" at the instant of the assessment of the position. However, we are able to make safe inferences about "movement" if we compare the positional codes of successively occurring positional events. Of course, if successively occurring positional events show different positional codes, we conclude that the hand was moved within the 1-second interval between codings. Likewise we would assess "still position" if the codings of successive positions show no difference.

Temporal concordance of the activity of the hands is supposed to tell us the degree to which during the observation time the hands were either both in rest or both in movement during the 1-second interval between codings. The degree of concordance of the Activity of the hands during the observation time is calculated according to the following equation:

$$TCA = \frac{\sum MM + \sum RR}{n-1}$$

TCA stands for the degree of Temporal Concordance of the hands' activity during the observation time.
MM stands for the occurrence of movement within the one-second-interval between two successively occurring positions, for both right and left hand.
RR stands for "no movement" within the one-second-interval between two successively occurring positions, for both right and left hand.

Temporal Concordance of the Occurrence of Movement

The degree to which movement occurs simultaneously in both hands is assessed according to the following equation:

$$TCM = \frac{\sum MM}{n-1-\sum RR}$$

MM and RR are defined above.

Temporal Concordance of the Occurrence of No-movement (Still Positions)

$$TCR = \frac{\sum RR}{n-1-\sum MM}$$

TCR stands for the degree to which still positions occurred simultaneously in both hands.
MM and RR are defined above.

So far we were looking at both hands at once. The following measures are supposed to characterize behavioral properties for each hand separately.

Two terms will frequently occur in the definition of these behavioral properties: "expansion" and "displacement". "Expansion" refers to a static quality of behavior: it is an attribute of one position at one time. "Displacement" refers to a dynamic quality of behavior. It is an attribute of a date obtained by comparing two positions at two successive points in time. Therefore, if we talk about "expansion" we deal with "positions" that are static by definition; if we talk about "displacement" we deal with events that constitute movement.

Outward Expansion of the Hand

The degree to which the hand is expanded outward is calculated according to the following equation:

$$OE = \frac{\sum_{i=1}^{n} oE_i}{2n}$$

OE stands for the degree of outward expansion in horizontal direction averaged over the total observation time.

oE_i stands for the outward expansion of a specific positional observation. For the right hand, the following outward expansion scores are attributed to the localizations we can distinguish in the horizontal dimension:

Position (1) : oE = 0
Position (2) : oE = 0
Position (3) : oE = 0
Position (4) : oE = 1
Position (5) : oE = 2

For the left hand we have:

Position (1) : oE = 2
Position (2) : oE = 1
Position (3) : oE = 0
Position (4) : oE = 0
Position (5) : oE = 0

n stands for the number of observations.

Vertical Expansion of the Hand

The degree to which the hand is expanded in the vertical direction is calculated according to the following equation:

$$VE = \frac{\sum_{i=1}^{n} vE_i}{4n}$$

VE stands for the degree of vertical expansion of the hand from a zero point. The latter is defined as lying in the trunk-thigh area.

vE_i stands for vertical expansion score of a specific positional observation. For the right hand as well as for the left hand the following outward expansion scores are attributed to 12 localizations we can distinguish in the vertical dimension:

Position (1) : vE = 4
Position (2) : vE = 3
Position (3) : vE = 3
Position (4) : vE = 2
Position (5) : vE = 1
Position (6) : vE = 1
Position (7) : vE = 0
Position (8) : vE = 1
Position (9) : vE = 1
Position (10) : vE = 2

Position (11) : vE = 3
Position (12) : vE = 4

Expansion of the Hand

This behavioral property is supposed to account for the horizontal as well as for the vertical degree of expansion. In this case the zero point from which the expansion is calculated is chosen as Position 7 on the vertical dimension and Position 3 on the horizontal dimension. The expansion values that are attributed to the distinguishable positions in vertical and horizontal dimension are defined in such a way that (1) horizontally distinguishable positions can contribute the same quantity of expansion to the final score as the vertically distinguishable positions; (2) the direction of the deviations of the position of the hand from the zero point gets ignored in both vertical and horizontal dimensions; and (3) the intervals in horizontal and vertical dimension are defined in a way, such that they are approximately equal in size.

The degree to which the hand is expanded from the zeropoint is calculated according to the following equation:

$$E = \frac{\sum_{i=1}^{n} hoE_i + \sum_{i=1}^{n} veE_i}{4n}$$

E stands for the degree to which, in horizontal as well as in vertical direction, the hand is expanded from a zero point located in the middle of the body, i.e. at 'thigh/trunk" height.

hoE_i stands for the horizontal expansion score of a specific positional observation. For the right hand as well as for the left hand the following hoE-scores are attributed to the five distinguishable localizations in the horizontal dimension:

Position (1) : hoE = 2
Position (2) : hoE = 1
Position (3) : hoE = 0
Position (4) : hoE = 1
Position (5) : hoE = 2

veE_i stands for the vertical expansion score of a specific positional observation. For the right hand as well as for the left hand, the following veE-scores are attributed to the twelve distinguishable localizations in the vertical dimension:

Position (1) : vE = 2
Position (2) : vE = 2
Position (3) : vE = 2
Position (4) : vE = 1
Position (5) : vE = 1
Position (6) : vE = 1
Position (7) : vE = 0
Position (8) : vE = 1
Position (9) : vE = 1
Position (10) : vE = 2

Position (11) : veE = 2
Position (12) : veE = 2
n stands for the number of observations.

Rate of Displacement of the Hand

The rate of displacement of the hand is calculated according to the following equation:

$$RD = \frac{\sum M_i}{n - 1}$$

RD stands for the relative frequency of movement events during the observation time.

M_i stands for the difference in the positional codings of two successively occurring positions.

n stands for the number of observations.

Amount of Displacement in Horizontal Directions

The amount of dispacement in the horizontal direction is calculated according to the following equation:

$$ADh = \frac{\sum |(O_{i\ p1} - O_{i\ p2})|}{\sum (2 + |O_{i\ p1}|)}$$

ADh stands for the relative amount of displacement in the horizontal direction.

$O_{i\ p1}$ stands for the position of the hand at the first one of two subsequently occurring positions. The nominal value of the positional score is given by definitions appearing on the first page of the Appendix.

$O_{i\ p2}$ stands for the position of the hand at the second one of the two subsequently occurring positions. The nominal value of the positional score is given by definitions appearing on the first page of the Appendix.

Amount of Displacement in Vertical Direction

The amount of displacement in the vertical direction is calculated according to the following equation:

$$ADv = \frac{\sum |(vp_i - vp_2)|}{\sum (4 + |vp_1|)}$$

ADv stands for the amount of displacement in the vertical direction,

vp stands for the distance of the hand from the zero point on the vertical axis (trunk/thigh, position 7; see first page of Appendix). These distances are defined as follows:

Position (1) : vp = +4
Position (2) : vp = +3
Position (3) : vp = +3
Position (4) : vp = +2
Position (5) : vp = +1
Position (6) : vp = +1
Position (7) : vp = 0

Position (8) : $vp = 1$
Position (9) : $vp = 1$
Position (10) : $vp = 2$
Position (11) : $vp = 3$
Position (12) : $vp = 4$
vp_1 stands for the vp-score of the first one of two subsequently occurring positions.
vp_2 stands for the second one of two subsequently occurring positions.

REFERENCES

BURDOCK, E. I., G. HAKEREM, A. S. HARDESTY, J. ZUBIN, Y. M. BECK
1964   *Verhaltensinventar für die Krankenstation.* Biometric Research Unit, Columbia University and New York State Department of Mental Hygiene.
CAMPBELL, D. T.
1958   Systematic error on the part of human links in communication systems. *Information and Control* 1:334–369.
EKMAN, P., W. FRIESEN
1971   "Progress report." Department of Health, Education and Welfare, Washington, D.C. (Unpublished).
FRAMO, J. L., A. M. ADLERSTEIN
1961   A behavioral disturbance index for psychiatric patients and ward disturbance. *Journal of Clinical Psychology* 17:260–264.
FRETZ, B. R.
1966   Postural movements in a counseling dyad. *Journal of Counseling Psychology* 13.
FREY, S.
1971   "Eine Methode zur quantitativen Bestimmung der Variabilität des Bewegungsverhaltens." Unpublished doctoral dissertation, Universität Regensburg.
FREY, S., M. VON CRANACH
1973   "A method for the assessment of body movement variability," in *Social communication and movement: studies of interaction and expression in man and chimpanzee.* Edited by M. von Cranach and I. Vine. London: Academic Press.
KENDON, A.
1973   "The role of visible behaviour in the organization of social interaction," in: *Social communication and movement: studies of interaction and expression in man and chimpanzee.* Edited by M. von Cranach and I. Vine. London: Academic Press.
MCREYNOLDS, P.
1965   On the assessment of anxiety: I. by a behavioral checklist. *Psychol. Rep.* 805–808.
SCHLEIDT, W.
i.p.   Tonic communication: continual effects of discrete signs in animal communication systems. *Journal of Theoretical Biology.*

SPOERRI, T.
1967 Motorische Schablonen und Stereotpien bei schizophrenen Endzuständen. *Psychiatrica Neurologica* 15:81–127.

WEBB, E. J., D. T. CAMPBELL, R. D. SCHWARZ, L. SECHREST
1966 *Unobtrusive measures: nonrelative research in the social sciences.* Chicago: Rand McNally.

Facial Expression Dialect: An Example

HENRY W. SEAFORD, JR.

Both my maternal and paternal kinsmen are Southerners. As far as I can remember, I always enjoyed the ease with which I could establish rapport with them and their neighbors. Even the way they looked at me, I later reflected, seemed different. In the midst of my professionalization in anthropology these pleasant memories began to suggest a topic for investigation. Could it be that just as my Virginian and Carolinian relatives possessed an obvious linguistic dialect, they also manifested a "dialect" of facial expression?

Although I had noted in the literature references to cultural differences in facial expression these usually pertained to different conditions under which, for example, people smiled in one culture or the other. Moreover, I came across no detailed study of the way culture affects facial expression. Partly as a result of Andrew's (1963: 1041) suggestion that anthropologists should make cross-cultural studies to delineate the cultural component of facial expressions, I began to collect high school and college yearbooks in the mid-sixties with the idea that if I looked at enough faces I just might be able to notice some describable regional differences. After inspecting some 10,000 photographs, I did. Statistically significant at greater than the .01 level were differences between faces from the Confederate States and all others. In a paper delivered in 1966 at the Pennsylvania Sociological Society I labeled this phenomenon the "Southern syndrome." Its primary components were the high frequencies of contractions of the *orbicularis oris*, the *triangularis* and the *depressor labii inferioris*. In spite of the obvious

This research was supported by NSF Grant GS-2338, and grants from the Faculty Research Fund at Dickinson College.

difficulties with using small photographs for analysis, the yearbook survey suggested that actual fieldwork would probably be fruitful.

During the summer of 1968 I toured the four Southern states which, according to the school annual survey, had the highest frequencies of the Southern syndrome — beginning with Georgia, followed by South Carolina, Virginia and finally, with the lowest frequency of these four, North Carolina. Fortunately, their proximity to my laboratory in Pennsylvania was appealing — Virginians seemed to manifest the Southern syndrome as frequently as any other southerners. Professor Coughlin, Chairman of the Department of Sociology and Anthropology at the University of Virginia, facilitated my getting office space and being named a research associate at the University. My business thus being completely adapted to the local scene, I began advertising for informants. Over sixty responded and were interviewed for fifteen minutes while I snapped photographs of them. A Leica M-3 with a ninety millimeter lens was held vertically so that my right eye could maintain contact with the informant as we conversed about things of mutual interest. In addition, each informant read a composition calculated to reveal linguistic dialect provenience. A data card eliciting background information was filled out. By taping the interview the sounds of the camera shutter could be correlated with the film exposure to discern, upon subsequent analysis, whether or not the expression was an artifact of pronunciation. Pennsylvanians provided the control sample.

The earlier, yearbook study was confirmed, but a more sophisticated taxonomy of patterns emerged. Contractions of the *orbicularis oris* sometimes assisted by *m. mentalis* results in the Orbicular Clamp. When this is accentuated by contractions of the *modiolus*, a Purse-Clamp is produced. A Pursed Smile (with or without visibility of teeth) is a frequent contraction pattern of the Southern syndrome. Quite often this is elaborated by the arrangement of the lower lip across the lower teeth by the *quadratus labii inferioris*, the Inferior Press Smile. Angle Depression, the action of the *triangulares*, also characteristically accompanies smiling in Virginia. Virginians discretely protrude the tongue — the apex spread by the *verticalis* as it passes through the lips — often after they have made a verbal statement. This "turn" signal was called Tongue Display Type A to distinguish it from another behavior involving the curling of the tongue behind the teeth — Type B. The latter most frequently occurs during smiling and was designated Tongue Smile. Mandibular Thrust can accompany speech or silence in contexts which could not possibly be interpreted as "pugnacious" or any related attitude. Two other expressions involving either the rolling in of the lower lip between the teeth (Inferior Inversion) or both lips (Double Inversion) occurred quite often in both samples but were more significant (1.0 and .01 respectively) in Pennsylvania.

Each sample consisted of sixty-two informants, both male and female, approaching a fifty-fifty distribution. Significant at greater than the .01 level in the Virginia sample were Orbicular Clamps, Purse-Clamps, Pursed Smiles, Inferior Presses and Angle Depressions. Tongue Display Type A would have been highly significant, as recorded in my photographs, if I had not made a procedural *faux pas* collecting the data. Type B occurred twenty-five times in the Virginia sample and three in the Pennsylvania. An informant whose parents were Virginian was responsible for one of the three times it occurred in Pennsylvania. The same informant effected one Tongue Smile, making a total of five for the Pennsylvania sample and fifteen for the Virginia. Women are more likely to effect most of the expressions. A chi-square test of the differences between the samples exceeded $P = .01$.

Preparation to describe muscular activity consisted of perusing the literature, dissecting a chimpanzee face, observing facial muscle preparations of a few dozen human cadavers, inserting electromyograph electrodes in my face on one occasion, and palpating the muscular contractions thereof on another. Although one is never sure he is precisely determining all the muscles taking part in a given contraction pattern, contractions of the *orbicularis oris*, the *triangularis*, the *mentalis*, the *quadratus labii inferioris* and *superioris* (not necessarily the individual heads thereof) and the *zygomaticus* seemed evident enough. Reference to specific contractions makes it easier to describe the various patterns and permit replicability. Therefore the advantages of such procedure, in my opinion, outweigh its disadvantages.

In searching for an explanation of the Southern syndrome, two possibilities obtrude. The orbicular contraction may represent the cultural diffusion of a kinesic behavior during colonial times. Perhaps it was proper to emulate certain British facial expressions, many of which from my casual observance and acquaintance with the traditional "stiff upper lip," involve this muscle. Observation of colonial portraiture did in fact reveal a few Orbicular Clamps, but I am not at all sure whether one could say that particular way of contracting the *orbicular oris* was or is customary in English culture. Observation of Londoners this summer (1973) did reveal various kinds of orbicular contractions, but a more systematic study would be necessary to make any definitive statements about the resemblances between Englishmen and Virginians.

Another possible explanation for some of the patterns appeals to the ethological data. In spite of a provocative study by Smith, Chase, and Lieblich (1974) suggesting that tongue showing in general — not only the maximally protruded tongue — is a signal for rejecting social interaction,[1] my interpretation of the literature is that lip smacking, involving the display of the tongue, is positively associated with friendly intent. The slow lip smacking of grooming chimpanzees as described by van Lawick-Goodall (1965) suggests that this behavior does not have to be done frenetically, as in the case of some macaques in the same context, to indicate friendliness. Why could we not wildly speculate, then, that when humans discretely extend their tongues (apart from moistening dry lips) the signal is a kind of approach-generating device? If a subculture is characterized by a value system emphasizing friendliness — as Southern culture certainly does — why not expect that its members would show high frequencies of tongue display? Chevalier-Skolnikoff (1973) has most recently called attention not only to the tongue showing of lip smacking (for *Macaca arctoides*), but to pursing ("puckered lips") as well, being signals of friendliness. One can hardly overlook data like these, suggesting explanations of why many persons from a particular subculture show their tongues and purse their lips.

There is, of course, the possibility that Southern facial muscle contractions are related to the articulations of the speech dialects of that region. Muscles used often in speech might have a propensity for contracting frequently. Some effort was made to explore this by observing blind or deaf Southerners. One might anticipate that blind people might manifest some of the same facial muscle contractions as the seeing, if the phenomenon were related to language. If not, then maybe the facial expressions are transmitted by visual imitation, something which could be checked by observing congenitally deaf Southerners, who well might contract their facial muscles similarly to their hearing counterparts while not being able to speak the dialect. Limited observations of a few blind and about a half dozen deaf netted no typically Southern facial expressions, except in the case of a former school teacher who had lost her sight in her adulthood. Preteenage children do not seem

---

[1] These investigators call attention to tongue showing after reprimand or upon discovery while involved in some proscribed activity. In this light I find interesting a statement by Price-Williams (1968: 309) that "sticking out the tongue" in Chinese culture signals embarrassment. If the degree and configuration of the protrusion were specified, these data would be much more useful. However, if some kind of tongue showing indicates embarrassment in some (all?) cultures, we have the antithesis to aggressive behavior – the quest for social rapport.

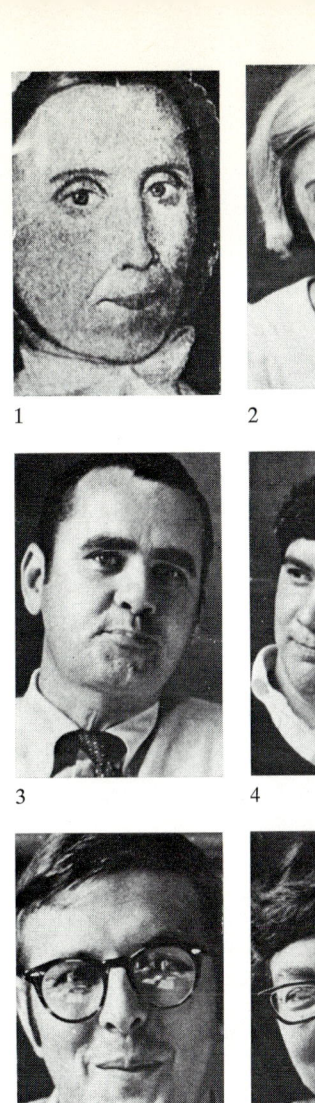
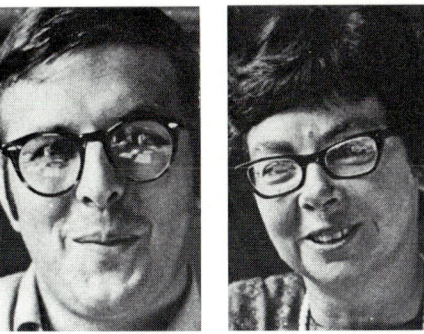

Plate 1. Examples of facial expressions
1. Painting of eighteenth-century Virginian (Weddell 1930) showing at least tonus, if not slight clamping and perhaps mesial contraction, of *m. orbicularis oris*.
2. Modern Virginian with apparently similar contractions to 1.
3. Orbicular Clamp.
4. Purse-Clamp with *mentalis* assist. (Note pitting of chin.)
5. Pursed Smile.
6. Pursed Smile
7. Inferior press resulting from arrangement of lower lip by *m. quadratus labii inferioris*.
8. Inferior press resulting from arrangement of lower lip by *m. quadratus labii inferioris*.

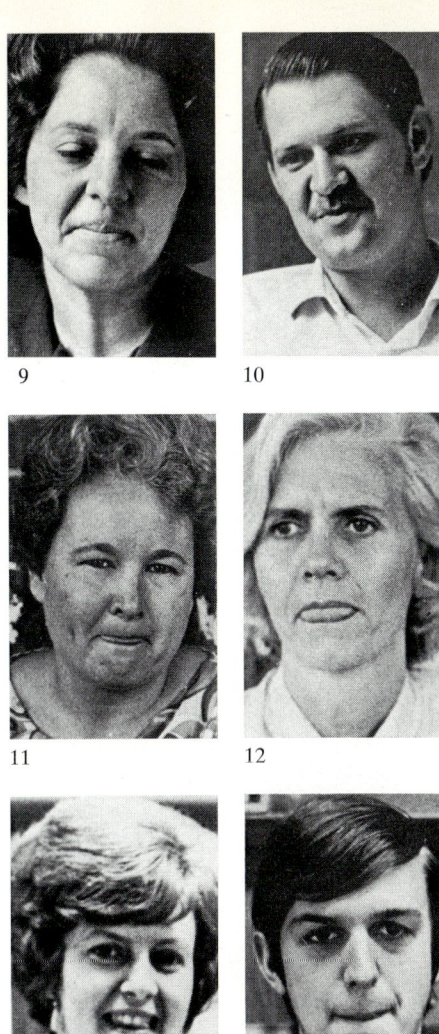

Plate 1. Examples of facial expressions (cont.)
9. Angle Depression Smile.
10. Angle Depression Smile.
11. Type A Tongue Display.
12. Type A Tongue Display.
13. Type B Tongue Display by Pennsylvanian whose parents are Virginian.
14. Mandibular Thrust
15. Inferior Inversion by Pennsylvanian.
16. Double Inversion by Pennsylvanian.

to show the patterns except in a few cases I have observed when the child seemed socially sophisticated.

Even though the foregoing speculations may ultimately prove ill-conceived, we have been able to give respectable documentation to a case of facial expression "dialect," which seems to be related to culture in one way or another. If there are doubters that the Southern syndrome exists, I suggest a trip through the South and extended face-to-face interaction with hospitable Southerners of the middle and upper classes. I am sure you will find it as charming as I did.

REFERENCES

ANDREW, R. J.
1963 Evolution of facial expression. *Science* 142:1034–1041.
CHEVALIER-SKOLNIKOFF, SUZANNE
1973 Visual and tactile communication in *Macaca arctoides* and its ontogenetic development. *American Journal of Physical Anthropology* 38:515–518.
PRICE-WILLIAMS, D. R.
1968 "Ethnopyschology II: comparative personality processes," in *Introduction to cultural anthropology*. Edited by J. A. Clifton. Boston: Houghton Mifflin.
SMITH, W. JOHN, JULIA CHASE, ANNA K. LIEBLICH
1974 Tongue showing: a facial display of humans and other primate species. *Semiotica* 11(3):201–246.
VAN LAWICK-GOODALL, J.
1965 "Chimpanzees of the Gombe Stream Reserve," in *Primate behavior*. Edited by Irven DeVore. New York: Holt, Rinehart and Winston
WEDDELL, A. W., *editor*
1930 *A memorial volume of Virginia historical portraiture*. Richmond: William Byrd Press.

PART THREE

Organization of Behavior in Social Encounters

Micro-Territories in Human Interaction

ALBERT E. SCHEFLEN

We can define a territory as an area of space which is bounded for a time in some discernible way and used by an animal or a group of animals — human animals included. A territorial border is ordinarily respected by other members of the same species. When it is not, its users or owners are likely to defend it by certain kinds of behavior.

Ordinarily we imply a space of considerable magnitude when we speak of a territory — an area at least the size of a room and more often the size of a property, a colony, or a range. But there is no reason that we cannot construe the term more broadly. We could say that ANY increment of space for any duration is territory so long as it is discernibly bounded, respected, and defended. So a territory could be as small as one's palm or thorax and as durable as a touch or as a display of chests in an interchange of dominance.

What I will describe here are some territories of small magnitude. They range from a few inches in diameter to a few square yards, but they have a wide range of durations. Spatially, these mini-territories are organized by levels. A number of very small ones are assembled in particular and conventional ways to form a slightly larger one, and these larger ones are in turn put together to form a territory that is larger still, and so on. These levels will be described integratively, starting with a very small one I call the "spot." Then we will take

This research has been carried out over a period of five years in continuous association with Dr. Adam Kendon and there would be no way of saying at this point how many of the ideas of this paper were contributed by Kendon or mutually developed. The research in human territoriality was supported by the NIMH grant #MH15977; by Jewish Family Service of New York and by the Bronx State Hospital.

up the cubit, the "k" space, the "location," the "module," and the nucleus.

Each cultural tradition has its own micro-territorial sizes and arrangements so we do not want to go off half-cocked with any assumptions about universals. In the main I shall limit myself to the descriptions of the micro-territories of British-American peoples, for most of the people we have studied have grown up in this tradition or tended to adopt it. But I will talk about the micro-territories of other kinds of Americans whenever I can.

SPOTS

A person may arrive in a place and put down one or more of his or her possessions. A purse may be placed on a seat or table, for instance, or a robe, towel, and camera may be put on the ground at a public beach or a picnic ground. By convention this placement establishes a claim to that spot and its immediate surroundings. Under conditions of medium or low density other members of that community and culture will respect this claim. They will not move the possessions or take places immediately around them. In fact, in traditional America one could leave his drink, cigarettes, and money on the bar of a tap room or tavern, absent himself for many minutes or even an hour, and return to find that his claim was undisturbed.

One can also claim a spot next to where one is sitting or standing by placing a possession in that spot or by putting a body part there. When two seats are side by side, for instance, a common elbow rest may be placed between them. One person may claim this by placing his arm on the spot but in this case a single spot belongs ambiguously to each seat, so each claim may be disputed. The issue may be decided by sharing or taking turns or else one person's claim may prevail on the basis of dominance or of status granted to age, gender, prior claims, and so on.

Many spots are conventionally allocated to a seat. At the dinner table, for example, each seated participant is awarded table space which is subdivided into spots for forks, plate, glass, and so forth in a traditional system of usage which is formalized as etiquette.

In territories which are owned by a group, spots may be allocated on a more permanent basis. There is a spot in which fathers keep pipes, another for shoes, as under the bed, one in which mothers place note pads and pencils, and so on. In fact, each resident or worker at a place is ordinarily assigned A SET OF spots: so many bureau drawers and desk drawers, a part of a closet, and so on. Even the hospitalized mental patient is allocated a small set of spots.

The spots we have so far mentioned are located on the physical surfaces of floors or furniture. Another type of spots is located on the human body itself. These can or cannot be gazed at. They can or cannot be touched, contingent upon the situation and the relationship of the actor to the spot in question and the cultural tradition. In British and British-American culture men and women can look at each other's faces and shoulders but not into each other's eyes unless they are in courting relationship. But men cannot stare at women's breasts and neither party is to look at genital regions. In Black-American and Black-Caribbean, however, much less face-to-face looking is permitted and participants in an interaction ordinarily look at imaginary spots above and beyond each other.

In classical British culture the touching of any body spots is taboo in public. In the old British-American tradition, however, the palms were touchable spots in greeting and very transient cheek spots were touchable for embracing among kin and close affiliates. Black American adults have followed similar rules about bodily spots. But in recent years middle mainstream Americans of many backgrounds have taken to public touching and embracing almost to the point of ritual. Eastern European Jewish Americans have employed touching of the elbows, shoulders and upper chest in conversation. Touching of a woman's palm, wrist, and antecubital fossa by a male seems to be widely prohibited in public in many cultures (Birdwhistell, personal communication, 1962).

Traditional constraints about public touching and gazing in British culture are accompanied by a rather larger proxemic (Hall 1963) or interpersonal spacing pattern. In fact, the British and the British-Americans not only tend to stand farther apart, but they also place seats at greater distance than do Mediterranean peoples. So the size and distribution of spots is interdependent with the nature of larger territorial organizations. Thus in high density the participants each have smaller "personal" spaces (Sommer 1969) and the spots too are smaller and more limited in number. At all levels of territorial organization this interdependency can, of course, be found.

As far as I can tell the spot does not have a standard size in British-American tradition. It is usually of a magnitude conveniently measured in inches. This size increment also does not have a name in our culture. In Egyptian and Greek civilizations a small spot, known as the palm, was used. The Egyptian palm was seven dactyles in size; the Greek four. Because the number of dactyles to a cubit varied in the measuring systems of these peoples, we cannot say exactly what size the palm was until we know about the cubit. But we can guess that it was about twelve square inches in Greek culture, somewhat larger in Egyptian.

THE CUBIT AND THE "K" SPACE

Although a set of spots is deployed on and around a person he cannot himself occupy so small a territory. He bases his body instead in a somewhat larger space which is more standard in size and more exactly defined than the spot. For this element of space I will use the ancient term "cubit." The English cubit is eighteen English inches, squared. We should note that the cubits of the ancient world tended to be slightly larger than this — often about twenty or twenty-four square English inches.

The term "cubit" ordinarily refers to the elbow and this linear measure is said to be the distance from the elbow to the end of the middle finger. But this unit of measure is also equal to the distance from ELBOW TO ELBOW and therefore represents the approximate width of the body in the case of the average-sized, asthenic, Nordic body. So the cubit width will contain the torso and forearms of a rather slender adult. More accurately, it was probably the space required for the arms of an Englishman at work in Elizabethan or Colonial times, when people were smaller than they are now.

The English cubit also measures other things which are important in human affairs. The adult human body approximates a fathom, two yards or four cubits in length, and is divided into four communicationally active regions — the lower leg, the thigh, the pelvic-abdominal region, and the area of the shoulder-girdle and head. Each of these regions is about a cubit in size. Many appliances and small domestic spaces are a square cubit in magnitude. The seat of the traditional British straight-back chair is exactly a cubit wide and a cubit high. Finally, larger areas of space which I have not yet described are exact increments of the cubit. Thus the human body can be stood or sat in about a cubit of chair or floor space, but the body as a whole cannot be contained in a cubit. It is contained rather in four cubits (when lying or standing). So the minimal space allocation for a person in stationary posture is four cubits. I will call this unit a "k" space. In high density, standing crowds each participant can hold but a single "k"-space, as I will describe later, but ordinarily he or she uses more space than this.

In lying and sitting positions the cubit becomes rectangular in shape as do most English-American and Western-European spaces (at least this is so with spaces which are less than the magnitude of a neighborhood). In its rectangular form the cubit usually becomes twenty-four inches in width, although twenty-one and twenty-seven inch sizes do appear in Anglo-American furniture. The depth of the cubit in seating arrangements may remain eighteen inches, but is often reduced to fifteen inches. In the traditional British-American double bed, for example, each user is allocated a space of twenty-four by seventy-two inches, although a space of twenty-seven by seventy-six and even of thirty by eighty-two is provided by the contemporary American queen-sized and king-sized beds. Analogously twenty-one or twenty-four inches by seventy-two inches of space are provided by benches and sofas when these are used for lying down.

The seats at a table for eating or meeting are also eighteen inches wide in this culture but three inches are usually provided for elbow room on each side. The allocation of personal spots on the table classically provided a total space of twenty-four inches in width. Three inches of the cubit are off the edge of the table. This spot is for elbows, in accordance with usual British-American etiquette. Three inches at the center of the table are surrendered from each table cubit for locating centerpieces, common serving dishes, microphones, and so on.

The surrender of a strip of territory at the interface of facing seats in the case of the table exemplifies a characteristic which we can see at all levels of territorial organization. The two strips at this interface are used as an intersect. In the case of properties along a street, for example, we can discover that each has surrendered a strip of land to the public domain for the construction of streets and sidewalks.

In any event the table cubit is a theoretical twenty-four by eighteen inch space, but its forward strip of three inches has been taken over as common property and its rear three inches have been located off of the table and added to the next, or seating, cubit. It is thus a twelve by eighteen inch cubit. Underneath it another cubit space is provided for knees and feet.

This two-layer cubit is actually at the front of an array of three cubits which will characterize the place any one person occupies at the table. In this case the cubits are oriented in a queue or file. The next one from the table provides a place to sit down. The chair seat is eighteen inches wide by twenty-one inches deep in the classical British-American dining room or meeting room. Notice that the forward three-inch strip of the chair lies beneath the back strip of the forward cubit — the one which lies off the table and gives room to the elbows in eating. The middle cubit may be wider than the seat width of eighteen inches. It may have side room strips of about three inches on each side and thus be as large as eighteen by twenty-four inches. The rear cubit lies behind the chair if its occupant is seated forward. This cubit allows space to move back in for after-dinner conversation or to sit back in at a meeting when one is NOT the speaker. It is also used to enter and leave the chair and sometimes for servicing the chair's occupant. Its size may be eighteen to twenty-four inches wide and may be twelve to eighteen inches deep. We can code each of these cubits positions at the table. The front one I will call "o," the middle or seat cubit "p," and the rear one "q." We will see later that these correspond to three successive concentric zones in the nucleus of area when we examine the relative positions of each member of a face-to-face in an interaction.

In the case of living room types of seats (as on a sofa or a soft chair), the forward cubit provides leg room and sometimes space for a coffee table or hassock. The thighs are placed in the middle cubit in sitting back or the middle cubit can be used to sit forward as one does in taking the floor. The rear cubit holds the back and head in sitting back (and the back of the overstuffed chair or sofa). In this case, too, a strip of room may be allowed along each side of each cubit.

Thus the array of three cubits may allow an occupant to sit forward or backward and thus decrease or increase the proximity of interpersonal distance from his vis-à-vis. He can also, of course, decrease or increase his distance from the objects of a physical task which are located at some spots in his forward or "o" zone cubit.

Notice, too, that the forward cubits of facing seats in a living room are much farther apart than they are across the table. In fact the open area of a living room is traditionally six cubits wide in the British-American living room and a court for passage, play, or standing conversation is allowed.

These work and seating spaces are of cubit magnitude, but they are larger than the eighteen-by eighteen-inch English cubit we started to discuss. Furniture cubits nowadays are likely to be twenty-four by twenty-four in middle class America. In fact, a lateral space of eighteen or twenty-one inches has become quite uncomfortable for the full-sized adults of this century. As a case in point consider the discomfort one experiences on public conveyances where a seat space of eighteen inches is provided but only one lateral or elbow-room spot is available for the common usage of two seats. I assume that the increasing size of British and American peoples has resulted in the cultural evolution of a somewhat larger cubit space — one that is more in keeping with the size of the ancient Mediterranean cubits. (The Hebrew cubit was about 20.15 English inches; the Egyptian cubit about twenty-five. The classical English cubit does, however, still appear in high density situations and small furniture measurements. For example, children use but a cubit of lateral space.

Suppose we come back now to the idea of a "k" space. So far I have described it as an array of four vertical cubits in standing. In seating postures it is an array of three focus-oriented cubits, though the forward is duplicated above and below the table. But we can also use the idea of an array or strip of cubit locations in another way. Four table cubits along the side of a table could also be a "k" space. This arrangement appears along an institutional table which seats four people at minimal distances along each side. But in most dining and meeting arrangements a head and foot have been established, so cubit locations appear at each end of the table and only twenty-four inch cubits appear on the surface at each side.

The cubit-sized space is not only used to stand in, sit in or eat in. It also confines elements of communicational behavior. Consider, as an example, the space for gesticulation. In the case of British and British-American people, who often gesture from the wrist, the gesticulation space may be only spot sized. But French, Eastern-European-Jewish, Black Americans and Spanish-Americans tend to use at least a cubit in gesticulation. Italian-Americans, who gesture from the shoulders, use a much larger range — a range which sometimes approaches four cubits (Efron 1941).

We can also describe touch in terms of cubit-sized elements. Two lovers in side-by-side relation at close interpersonal distance occupy adjacent cubit-sized locations. They may make tactile contact in one or more of their bodily regions and thus the tactile connection employs two, four, or even six adjoining cubits. On the other hand peoples like the British who do not touch in public may leave a cubit of space between them in side-by-side relations and two to six cubits between them in face to face. So they are not then in tactile range.

By the same token gaze-holding involves a relation of two faces at some distance or other. So this communicational activity employs a CHANNEL OR "K"-SPACE OF CUBITS. The same thing can be said of mutual orientations of the thorax or pelvis or mutual orientations of feet and leg stance. I have described these relations in detail elsewhere (Scheflen 1972, 1973a, 1973b).

Notice that participants in communication do not usually act as organismic wholes. Instead, THEY USE BODILY REGIONS DIFFERENTIALLY. A single person may be simultaneously engaged at one point in time in orientational relations to one side of him, in tactile relations to the other side, and in gaze and vocal relations across the group. Thus each person uses his bodily regions differentially and multiple simultaneous communicational relations obtain among bodily regions at any point in time. These differential activities employ spaces which are channellike in form and "k"-sized. Their territorial elements are measurable in cubit increments. These spaces are treated as territories. They are defended from intrusion and respected by others who look away or otherwise make private their space of occurrence. In short, I think the cubit-sized space provides a basis for comprehending and measuring activities and relations of activities.

THE LOCATION

The location is that increment of space which is ordinarily occupied by one person for some finite interval of time. Territorially speaking, the location is an integration of "k"-space cubit and spot subterritories.

At high density, as I already said, a person may have but four cubits of vertical room, but ordinarily he is allotted four such "k"-spaces in standing activities. He has space to move around in, so the standing location is ordinarily four "k"-spaces or sixteen cubits in size. The seated location is three cubit "k"-spaces with lateral spots, and the seated location is also three or four cubits high. So it too is twelve to sixteen cubits in size.

In British-American situations the standing location of two by two cubits covers an area of space equal to about a yard or meter. This space is equivalent to three by three English feet, or thirty-six by thirty-six square inches. Vertically, the location is equal to four square yards or sixteen square cubits.

In seated locations the three English cubits plus the elbow space provide an area of twenty-four inches wide, fifty-four inches deep and maybe seventy-two inches high. This sixteen-cubit area is also four square yards in size AND THUS EQUAL IN AREA TO THE STANDING LOCATION. These two variants of the location are diagrammed in Figure 1.

I shall not go extensively into structural methods here, but I must say a word about how these measurements are made. The task is easy in the case of seated locations. One merely goes around measuring people, chairs, sofas, chair-table clusters, and kitchen spaces with a tape measure. He finds so high a degree of regularity that he soon neglects to compute means and standard deviations.

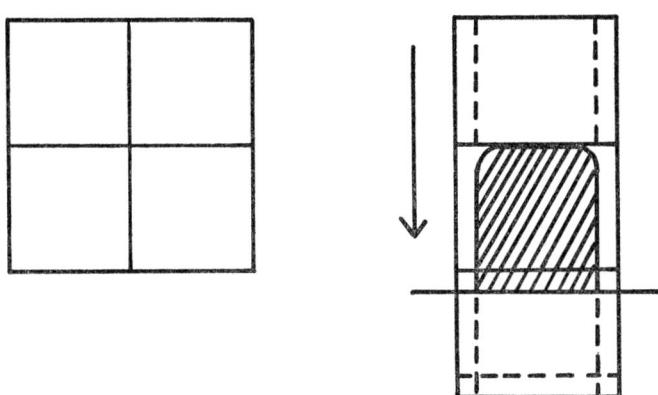

Figure 1. The standing and the seating location

But determining the size of the standing location in physically unstructured space is a more difficult matter. One must watch hours of motion pictures or videotapes of standing groups and ascertain just how much area the average participant takes and is allowed to take. Furthermore, the standing location is highly fluid since it is not concretized into built objects and it is thus susceptible to considerable expansion and decrease under a variety of contextual conditions. So I must specify that THE FIGURE OF ONE SQUARE YARD IS REAL ONLY WITH MEDIUM OR LOW DENSITY, AMONG PEOPLE WHO ARE OF NEITHER ESPECIALLY HIGH STATUS AT THAT PARTICULAR MOMENT, NOR HIGHLY AFFILIATIVE WITH ANYONE ELSE.

This is a rather negative way of stating that location size does vary with density, status, affiliation, and other parameters. We shall consider some of these systems relations. In very high density as many as four adults may pack together and orient in common. Each thus uses "k"-space and all four are packed into one standard location. Two adults who are strongly affiliated may maintain and show this affiliation by standing very close together and thus share a single location. In doing so they demonstrate what Goffman (1963) calls "withness." In private the "with" pair may face each other in embrace and thus form a "vis-à-vis" relation. In public they usually take side-by-side positions facing other people in common, and thus hold a "unit" relation. In either case they may also touch faces, arms, pelvises, or thighs and/or feet. They may also gaze and exchange utterances. Sometimes the close "with" also embraces an infant who is held by one of the adults. In seating location the "close with" of adults requires a very special form of sitting on one "cheek" or else a queue formation in which one member sits on another's lap. If small children and one adult are involved several may sit on one lap and others can drape themselves from chair arms and knees so a tiny army can be accommodated in a space just over a location in size. In lying down the members of a couple can hold a "u" relation and thus adjacent locations or they can form a "v" relation and thus occupy one location in common.

There are, of course, still other ways in which a single location can be employed for multiple purposes. For example, a person and a baby, a pet, or a package can be easily held in this increment of territorial space.

But in those cases in which the location is not filled with bodies and props, it holds but a single person and three empty "k" spaces. In these cases one can change his position in the location in order to meet a variety of contextual conditions. He can, for instance, stand at the back of a standing location or sit back in his seated location. He thus leaves his forward cubits open, maximizes interpersonal distance, and in all probability he thus cools his involvement. If he is standing in a location next to one occupied by a stranger he can move to the far side of his location. He thus maximizes the side-by-side distance by leaving an open cubit, showing that he and the stranger are not to be regarded as a "with."

There are contexts in which a participant receives more than one location. An obvious case in point is a situation of movement. A walking person or "with" uses a transit of successive locations. A player moves through a circuit of them. A pass receiver in football can use a zig-zag path of thirty or forty locations in seconds. A set of dancers may move through a row of locations, then another, and so on. But even the stationary location may be larger than a square yard. A figure of dominance, such as the special guest, the lecturer, or the head of house, may take the location at the head of a table. In this case he is awarded vacant locations at each side. The housewife and worker may move from one location at a counter to another as they take up one then another phase of a programmatic task. And the household member or the occupant of an office may claim and equip a set of side locations around his favorite chair. The desk and credenza arrangement of the executive provides him with five or six immediately contiguous locations.

If we observe Black Americans of any social class we can observe that they employ locations just about as I have described except in some small ghetto apartments where there is no room. What data we have indicate that this order of spacing is used in Jamaica and in Nigeria as well. We simply do not know if this similarity between black and British spacing is a coincidence or the result of a long association between these cultures in Africa, in the West Indies, and in the United States.

But we observe the use of small locations in Jewish-American, French-American and Italian-American subcultures. The Italian-American gestures in wide sweeps and uses a good deal of lateral space, so he will fall silent if cramped into a space much less than a yard. Then he may move about somewhat frantically until he makes elbow room. But the Puerto Rican and Cuban people do not behave this way. Two parents and several children will sit side by side in tactile contact and watch television for hours, stroking each other during the show sequences and conversing during the commercials. Two or three Puerto Rican children will sit in a single armchair and watch television for hours. Or one child will sit on the floor and hold a younger sibling between his legs. Across from him at close range another sibling sits, talks, or plays. We have seen Cuban men stand with their faces just one cubit apart for conversation even though there was plenty of available space. Needless to say Black Americans and British Americans will back off from the use of such distances. In interactions a chase or an oscillation in spacing then occurs if the participants are from different cultures.

THE MODULE

We call a row or a queue of locations a "module." A row module can be of almost any length. So can a queue. In fact a module may consist of rows and columns of "k"-spaces or locations, as in the case of a crowd of spectators. For example, people in side-by-side relation employ a module of locations if they are not holding or exhibiting "withness."

If there is plenty of room an array of people will space themselves in accordance with their relationships and thus mark off locations. If two strangers happen to be standing side by side, for example, and there is plenty of space, they will probably leave full location between them and thus form a module three locations in size. If strangers are crowded on seats of a bus, train, or plane, they may be forced to occupy adjacent "k"-spaces. In this case they will probably demonstrate strangerhood by turning away from each other a bit, by placing arms between themselves, and by avoiding gaze and conversation. In British-American culture if people are queued in ample space they will ordinarily leave a cubit between them and thus each will hold place in the center of a separate location. But in long lines in limited space they will queue closely and almost reach tactile contact. In this case they are likely to fold their arms or clasp their hands in front of them. But the head of the line will usually be allowed a full location in which to transact his business.

Notice that in these instances the closing of legs and arms is, in a sense, allomorphic or equivalent to leaving a cubit of space. Communicational systems are replete with examples of this sort of alternative. One can look down and away, OR turn away, OR step back, OR cover the front of his body in indicating nonengagement. One can touch OR gaze OR stand closer in showing or establishing an affiliation.

The side-by-side module is often equipped with or built into an item of furniture. The example of modular counters has already been mentioned. The dining or meeting table also provides "k"-strips of table and chair cubits to form a module at each of its sides. Chairs can also be arrayed in rows for conversation across a central open space. The bench and sofa are modules of furniture which have evolved specifically for side-by-side deployment. The sofa, one should notice, is classically two locations, four cubits or six feet in length IN INSIDE DIMENSIONS. It thus has a capacity of one "v" level conversation; three side-by-side adult locations, or four child locations. But all adults are familiar with the difficulty of sitting in the central location of this sofa module. For one thing he must sit back if those at his sides interact and he must in this case keep moving his head like one who watches a tennis match.

The occurrence of vis-à-vis interaction within a single location has already been mentioned. But even small interpersonal space peoples leave at least a cubit if conversation is held. Jewish-American conversational partners use a distance of about thirty inches, which places the participants within easy tactile range. In British-American culture a full location is left between conversants if they are standing. A three-location face-to-face "x" module is thus formed with an open location in the middle. One or both of the conversants may have a side-by-side affiliate who shares his location. So an adult foursome can occupy a module of this size.

In full face-to-face seated conversations, British, British-Americans, and Black Americans leave more than open locations between themselves. In the classical British-American living room, as I have said, the facing seats are placed three locations apart. Contemporary middle-class Americans of many extractions seem to favor less distance, however, so seats are often placed about two locations apart.

There is another very common type of module, in which the locations are placed at right angles to each other. The occupants are thus oriented at an angle of about ninety degrees, but they may turn their heads to interact in face-to-face relation. Temporary or transitory conversations usually occur in this relation or those in which third parties are awaited. The common modular forms I have described here are diagrammed in Figure 2.

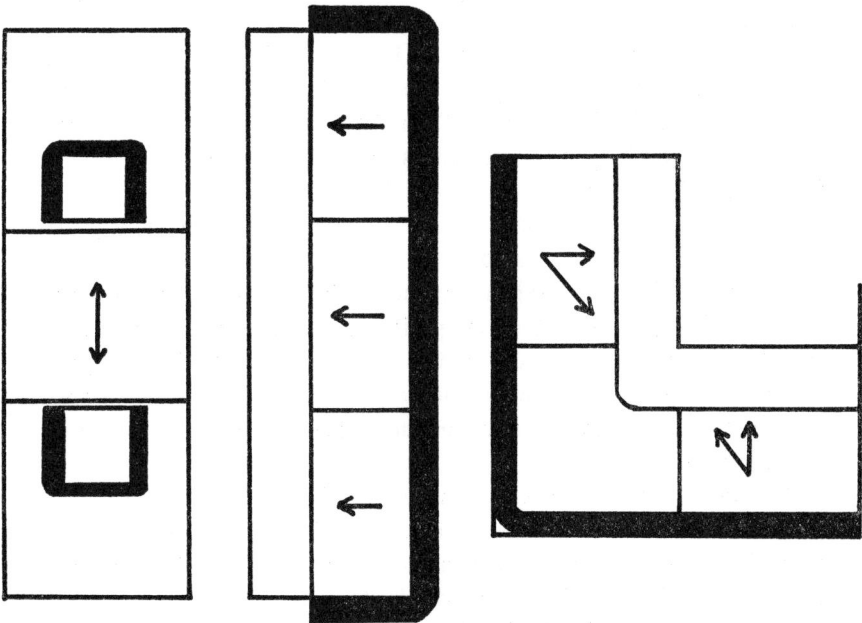

Figure 2. Common types of modular arrangement

THE NUCLEUS

So far, the micro-territories I have described are arrays or queues which at the most are one by five yards in size. They hold two or two close pairs of interactional participants in vis-à-vis relation or side-by-side array. But often people form small triangles, squares, or circles. Two arrays face each other across a space or table. In these cases more than a single module of space is required.

In the dining room, for example, two side locations of chairs face each other across a two-location table. And at the head and foot positions locations appear. So this cluster occupies a space three by four locations, or about nine by twelve English feet in size. It is surrounded by another zone (or locations) on all sides which is used for passage and the storage of serving tables, buffets, and unused chairs. The total size is thus five by six locations, or about fifteen by eighteen feet; thirty locations appear in this space.

We call the central area of table and seats "the nucleus" of the total area. We call the location strip around this the "region."

In the living room the nucleus is left open as a court (see above). Sometimes coffee tables are placed in this court, but the seats and other furniture are placed in the region. In the classical British-American living room this court has been a three by four nucleus and the total room size has been five by six locations, or thirty square yards. Thus these two rooms are traditionally the same size. In fact this size is called "the square rod" in the British system of measures. Actually the rod is 30.25 square yards or 16.5 by 16.5 English feet if it is square. When made rectangular as it is in these traditional rooms, the rod area is five by six yards or locations, or fifteen by eighteen feet, ten by twelve cubits in area.

This room-sized area appears in the English home and great house as far back as the late Medieval period. In fact, an excavated Saxon house from the ninth century is also a rod in area. And the bays of the Gothic, Carolinian, and Romanesque cathedrals are a rod in area. And so are the rooms of many Roman, Greek, and Egyptian buildings (Scheflen 1974).

This need not surprise us for we are studying an unbroken line of Western tradition. But it does shock us to find these magnitudes of space in Mayan and pre-Aztec civilizations, too. Maybe Mediterranean people did sail to Mexico, or maybe both civilizations had a common ancestor or maybe this is the size of space which is necessary for a primate gathering of eight or ten animals.

REFERENCES

EFRON, D.
    1941   *Gesture and environment.* New York: King's Crown.

GOFFMAN, E.
    1963   *Behavior in public places: notes on the social organization of gatherings.* New York: The Free Press.

HALL, E. T.
    1963   A system for the notation of proxemic behavior. *American Anthropologist* 65:1003–1026.

SCHEFLEN, A. E.
    1972   *Body language and the social order.* Englewood Cliffs, New Jersey: Prentice-Hall.
    1973a *The stream and structure of communicational behavior* (revised edition). Bloomington: Indiana University Press.
    1973b *How behavior means.* New York: Gordon and Breach.
    1975   "Some urban territories in the United States," in *The mutual interaction of people and their built environment: a cross-cultural perspective.* Edited by A. Rapaport. World Anthropology. The Hague: Mouton.

SCHEFLEN, A. E., N. ASHCRAFT
    i.p.   *Human territoriality.* Englewood Cliffs, New Jersey: Prentice-Hall.

SOMMER, R.
    1969   *Personal space.* Englewood Cliffs, New Jersey: Prentice-Hall.

One Function of Proxemic Shifts in Face-to-Face Interaction

FREDERICK ERICKSON

INTRODUCTION

"Proxemics," a general term coined by Hall (1963, 1968) for the study of cultural patterns in the use of space, has been used by him and by others in a more specific sense to refer to the study of patterns of interpersonal distance in face-to-face encounters. A number of researchers, including Scheflen (1973), Kendon (1972), Porter, Argyle, and Salter (1970), Lott, Clark, and Altman (1969), Sommer (1965), Cowan (n.d.), and Hall himself, have investigated proxemic features of interaction, with approaches that are quite various. The investigation of proxemics reported here was part of a larger study of verbal and nonverbal aspects of interaction between American, black, Latin, and white ethnic school counselors and job interviewers and their interviewees. This research is reported more comprehensively in a final report, *Talking to the Man: a microethnography of interethnic relations in gatekeeping encounters* (i.p.).

PROXEMIC SHIFTS AND SITUATIONAL SHIFTS

Scientific researchers, artists (writers, theatrical directors, choreographers), and specialists in sacred and secular ritual have noted impres-

This study was sponsored by the Center for Studies of Metropolitan Problems, NIMH (MH18230 and MH 21460) and also supported by the Ford Foundation. The support of both is gratefully acknowledged. The author is also indebted to Carolyn Leonard-Dolan and Jeffrey Shultz for their collaboration in the research project, and to Edward T. Hall for editorial advice.

sionistically that (at least in Europe and the United States, and perhaps universally) changes in interpersonal distance during interaction ("proxemic shifts" which may also involve changes in body orientation of speakers) seem to accompany changes in the topic or in the social relationship between speakers.[1]

Blom and Gumperz (1972: 424–425) in their discussion of the social meaning of linguistic style among speakers in a Norwegian village, identify posture changes and changes in the spatial relationship between two speakers as indicators of what they term "situational shifts" — momentary changes in the mutual rights and obligations between speakers accompanied by shifts in language style. Because Blom and Gumperz's behavioral data were collected on audiotape, their reports of proxemic behavior are limited in that they depend on evidence derived from observation alone.

Scheflen (1973), working from sound film, has noted an analogous function of proxemic shifts in his analysis of a group therapy interview. Units of postural configuration and proxemic relationship he terms "positions" are used by him as indicators of major segments within an interview. He advocates beginning the analysis of interaction at this middle level of integration of communicative behavior (1973: 18). Positions reappear throughout his analysis as a leading theme, a key indicator of interactional structure. Kendon (1972) has employed a similar approach in his analysis of interaction at a garden party.

As of this writing I am not unaware of an empirical study of the relationship between proxemic shifts and other features of interaction that has been done on a fairly large number of films of analogous encounters. It is reasonable to assume, as Scheflen and others seem to have done, that proxemic shifts indicate situational shifts, but this relationship is not self evident. In my own work on eighty-three five- and ten-minute films of different gatekeeping encounters I have collected empirical evidence that speaks to this question.

The results reported here are derived from a subsample of twenty-six ten-minute films of junior college counseling interviews (four counselors, twenty-two students). Two of the counselors were white (Irish-American and Italian-American) and two were black. The students were Polish-American, Italian-American, black, and Mexican-American.

From watching videotapes of gatekeeping interviews in viewing sessions with informants I got the impression that proxemic shifts were occurring at situational shifts within the encounters. It also seemed to me

[1] I assume, with Cicourel (1972), that the social relationship between speakers is continuously negotiated during the course of an encounter.

that the points in the videotape about which informants made comments during the viewing session were points at which the proxemic relationship between speakers was changing or had just changed.

My co-worker Leonard-Dolan also found that proxemic shifts occurred with topic shifts in three films she analyzed of conversations between university students who were strangers. Further, there was much more proxemic stability (and ability to begin a topic and stay with it) in the two intraethnic encounters (black/black, Polish-American/Polish-American) than in the interethnic encounter (black/Polish-American). In the interethnic encounter a number of conversational false starts occurred. The relative proxemic/topic stability in the three encounters is illustrated in Figure 1 (Leonard-Dolan 1972).

I wanted to test the relationship between proxemic shifts and other aspects of interaction more systematically. If it could be demonstrated that proxemic shifts were reliable indicators of situational shifts, then a good deal of research time could be saved by myself and by other researchers because coding for proxemic shifts was relatively simple. Before conducting fine-grained analysis on a large sample of films I wanted a means of eliminating most of my materials so that I could concentrate on a manageable amount of film footage. I wanted a means of defining segments of a whole encounter that had special salience within it: segments that could be considered analogous to similar segments in films of other encounters. These abstracted segments could then be analyzed in detail. The remainder of each film could be examined for contextual information, but with finite staff resources available I would not be committed to analyzing each complete film at every level of behavioral integration.

Accordingly, my co-workers and I devised a code for gross features of proxemic shifts and a set of codes for gross features of other aspects of verbal and nonverbal behavior. Information from these various codes, when combined together, provided a synoptic view of interactional structure. On the basis of this picture of the whole, relationships among parts could be inferred. All the codes are briefly described below, after which a more elaborated description of the proxemic code follows.

1. Speech behavior
a. Two codes for paralinguistic phenomena, one for voice pitch, one for voice intensity and rhythm
b. Three codes for dealing with linguistic phenomena, one for the "referential functions" of speech (explicit semantic content manifested in lexicon and syntax), one for "social functions" of speech (implicit

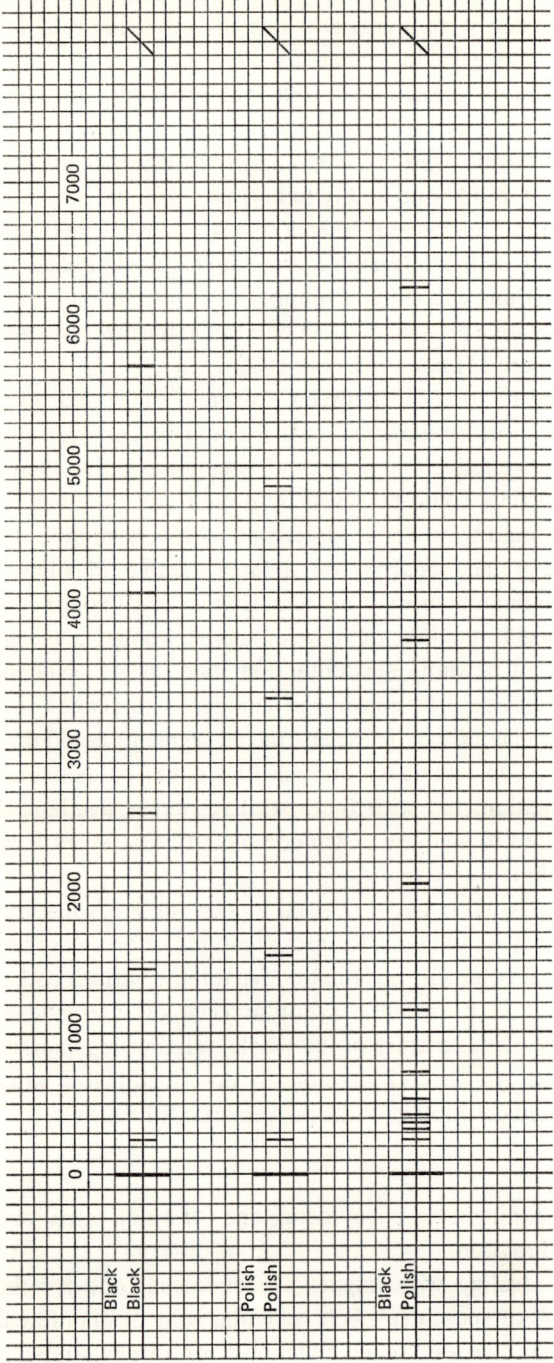

Figure 1. Phases in five-minute encounters as indicated by topic shift and proxemic shift

semantic content) and one for (symmetric) verbal overlapping or (asymmetric) verbal interruptions of one another by the two speaker/listeners

2. Non-verbal behavior.
a. One code for gaze direction and involvement, indicating when speakers looked at or away from each other
b. One code for proxemic phenomena, indicating when speakers moved closer to or farther away from each other
c. A notation system for describing kinesic rhythm — the timing (not the quality or specific content) of body motion and gesticulation — at micro-second intervals[2]

3. Hierarchical ordering of natural units (segments) of speaking/listening behavior.
a. "Etic" codes for segmentation (in which units are defined from the "outsider" perspective of the research staff — analogous to phonetic analysis in linguistics)
i. A code for overall behavior asymmetry, identifying sections during which the smooth flow of interaction broke down between speakers — an "asymmetry sections code"
ii. A procedure for identifying segments within the sections of behavioral asymmetry — an "asymmetry segments" code
iii. A procedure for identifying microsegments within the asymmetry segments
b. "Emic" codes for segmentation (in which units, demarcated as whole events, are identified impressionistically by the encounter participants themselves from an "insider" perspective or by naive judges from a "quasi-insider" perspective)
i. The emic codes for the overall impressions of the encounter participants themselves, one indicating the location of a viewing session comment in relation to the flow of interaction in the original encounter, another code indicating the content of viewing session comments
ii. A group of "quasi-emic" codes for overall impressions of interaction process administered as a questionnaire to naive judges who

---

[2] This is the microanalysis procedure used with the abstracted segments described in the section above. Kinesic rhythm is identified through manual coding at 24 frames per second, and speech rhythm is identified through a polygraph print-out of the film sound track segmented into 24 frames per second, the print-out of the time unit being synchronized with the cinema projector. This procedure locates voice intensity patterns in synchrony with body-motion patterns. The kinesic code is a simplified version of the one developed by Prost (1967). The whole procedure follows the orientation of Byers (1972).

viewed videotapes of the original encounters and scored a questionnaire for each encounter.

The methodological principle behind all this was to gather independent evidence for the hierarchical integration of interactional phenomena. Independence was maintained by having different individuals code for different behavioral phenomena, and by controlling for different combinations of sensory media through which the behavioral phenomena could be apprehended by an individual coder (see Table 1).

Table 1. Sources and kinds of coded data

Code	"Data source"		"Data kind"
(Behavioral phenomenon)	(Sensory modality)	(Information medium)	
Proxemic	Visual	Cinema (silent)	Etic
Eye contact	Visual	Cinema (silent)	Etic
Kinesic/asymmetry — segments	Visual	Cinema (silent)	Etic
Kinesic/asymmetry — microsegments	Visual (first) Auditory (second)	Cinema (silent) Cinema (sound)	Etic
Paralinguistic (pitch)	Auditory	Audiotape	Etic
Paralinguistic (intensity accents)	"Auditory" (machine print-out)	Cinema sound track	Etic
Kinesic/asymmetry — sections	Auditory — visual	Cinema (sound)	Emic (encounter participants and judges)
Overlap/interruption	Auditory — visual	Cinema (sound)	"Quasi-emic" (judges)
Interaction process	Auditory — visual	Video	"Quasi-emic" (judges)
Viewing session	Auditory — visual	Video	Emic (encounter participants)
Topic (referential function of speech)	Visual	Transcript	Etic
Time reference (referential function of speech)	Visual	Transcript	Etic

PROXEMIC CODE PROCEDURES AND CONTENT

Visual information alone was available to the two proxemics coders. They watched each film on a silent editor/viewer (a Zeiss Moviscop). The films were frame-numbered, using the Van Vlack B–Roll. For the first viewing the coders speeded up the moving image "faster than life" (i.e. faster than 24 frames per second), advancing the film with hand-operated rewinds. (At faster-than-life speed the kinesic behavior of the speakers, viewed without sound, takes on the jerkey character of a Keystone Cops chase sequence, visually accentuating the proxemic shifts that occur.) The approximate location of the most gross shifts was noted. Then the coder rewound the film, watching for the gross shifts as they occurred backwards and checking the notes on their approximate location.

Starting a second time at the head end of the film the coder would advance it at regular speed until the first gross shift appeared, then would work back and forth in slow motion to identify the precise frame numbers for the beginning and end of the shift, noting this and a code for the content of the shift (moving closer/moving away) on a data chart with a time line graduated in 200–frame units from 0–16,000 frames (at 24 frames per second). Figure 2 is a schematic version of the chart. The level of grossness of the shift is indicated by vertical location on the chart (Levels A–D). "Grossness" was operationalized as:

Level A Both individuals move both of their bodies as a whole in the proxemic shift.

Level B Both individuals move upper or lower half of their bodies ("upper half" is the head, torso, and arms, "lower half" is the legs and feet).

Level C One or both individuals move a few body parts forward or back a moderately large distance (more than one foot).

Level D One or both individuals moves a few body parts or a single body part forward or back a small distance (less than one foot).

The content of the proxemics code is presented in Table 2. A few examples of the code are located in Figure 2.

Table 2. Proxemic shift content code

	Interviewer	Student	Proxemic behavior
Moves Forward (toward other)	0	0	Neither person moves
	1	0	Interviewer moves forward (student does not move)
	0	1	Student moves forward
	1	1	Both move forward
Moves Back (away from other)	2	0	Interviewer moves back (student does not move)
	0	2	Student moves back
			Both move back
	1	2	Interviewer moves forward, student moves back
	2	1	Student moves forward, interviewer moves back

Figure 2. Proxemics code data chart

	0	4000	8000	12000	16000
Level A	200/11				16000/22
Level B			5933–5962/22		
Level C		2507–30/21,12			
Level D		2571–80/10			

INTER–CODER RELIABILITY

Two coders were used. Despite our attempts at thorough operationalization and training there was considerable disagreement of a special kind between coders. This made computing inter–rater reliability by traditional methods inappropriate.

The differences were stylistic rather than substantive. The raters differed not in identifying the general location of the shift, but in more specific distinctions — one coder nesting subshifts within what the other coder designated a whole shift, or one coder disagreeing with the other in placing an instance in either hierarchical levels C or D. Both coders were consistent with themselves, one coder tending to discriminate according to much subtler features than the other. This is illustrated by data from an actual case shown in Table 3.

Table 3. Inter-coder disagreement

	Coder 1 Location	Coder 2 Location	Disagreement
Example 1	2406–2440	2387–2462	Coder 1's shift is contained within coder 2's shift
Example 2	4719–4735 4817–4835 4829–4844	4708–4857	Coder 1's three shifts are all contained within coder 2's single shift

Upon examination, most of the "disagreements" turned out to be of this kind. We resolved the remaining few by eliminating the instances coded at Level D, except for those instances in which both coders agreed on location.

SUMMARIZING EVIDENCE FROM THE VARIOUS CODES

We had transcripts of the original counseling interviews and transcripts of the comments made by participants in viewing sessions.[3] It was a

---

[3] The location of a viewing session comment was indicated on the audio-tape by the point at which the audio track of the videotape being viewed by the informant went "off" and the voice of the informant commenting on that point went "on."

simple clerical task to key the viewing session comments to points in the encounter transcript being referred to by comments. Once this was done, and once shifts in referential content of talk and other nonverbal aspects of interaction that had been coded (shifts in proxemics, paralanguage, and eye contact) were cross-referenced to utterance numbers, it was possible to prepare a summary table which indicated the presence or absence of change along the various coded dimensions and showed the location of changes relative to one another across dimensions (see Figure 3).

From these summary tables and the original code charts we could retrieve information about the relation of various verbal and nonverbal behavior classes to each other in marking situational shifts and smaller segments with the section bounded by situational shifts. For example, from the differences in texture of presence or absence of change illustrated in Figure 3, it is apparent that a change in the organization of interaction occurs at x between utterances 33 and 34–35, then a less gross change occurs at utterances 37 and 38, and another major change occurs at utterances 42 and 43. The CONTENT of the change is not indicated by the summary table but the LOCATION of change is indicated. The table combines etic evidence (such as the code for proxemics and for referential speech content) with emic evidence from the code indicating presence or absence of viewing session comments. This procedure combines evidence differing in source and in kind in the demarcation of "units," "segments," "structure points," or "micrositutional shifts" in the filmed examples of interaction.

THE FUNCTION OF PROXEMIC SHIFTS AS SEGMENT MARKERS

The summary table illustrates the integration of verbal and nonverbal behavior in a total interactional system. It also suggests the function of proxemic shifts as markers of "important" segments in the encounters.

The significance of proxemic shifts as markers can be demonstrated by comparing the occurrence of proxemic shifts to the occurrence of other markers. At segment boundaries indicated in the summary tables by co-occurence of change along THREE OR MORE OUT OF A POSSIBLE SEVEN behavior codes, proxemic shifts occurred very frequently — more frequently than any other single coded indicator. Thus a proxemic shift is the best predictor of a new segment in our data.

The finding that for all counselors, proxemic shifts occur less at segment boundaries in intraethnic encounters is interesting. At this writing

Figure 3. Illustration of a summary table

Line	Topic	Overlap/ interruption	Proxemics Coder 1	Proxemics Coder 2	Para-language Coder 1	Para-language Coder 2	Time Reference shift	Viewing Session comment	Eye contact
28	1								2
29									
30									
31	1					1			
32									
33	1				1	1			22
34		1	¹	1	11	1			2
35	11111			1	1	1			3
36					1	1			
37	11			1	1	1	1		
38	1			1	1	1	1		32
39			1		1	1			
40					1	1			24
41									
42	1					1	1		
43	111111111	1		1	11	11	111	1 (1)	4342
44									
45	111	11			1	1	1		2
46									
47	1				1		1		23
48					1	1		1	32
49	1	1			1	1	1	1	2342
50					1	1			2
51	1				1	1			2
52									
53	1111	1			1	11	11		2434
54					1	11			
55	111	1							4
56					1				

the significance of the finding is unclear. A possible explanation is that because the totals for segment markers include markers of subsections (or subtopics) within larger sections (whole topics), it may be that many of these subsection markers tend not to include a proxemic shift.[4]

[4] Many of the segments indicated in the summary tables are of short duration. At 30 percent of all utterance numbers we find the co-occurrence of three or more markers, so many of the segments are only three utterances long — time enough for a "question-answer-question" sequence.

In that case the percentages would indicate that more major topics are started upon in the interethnic encounters and not sustained as long. This would be consistent with the Leonard-Dolan findings reported above on proxemic and topic stability intraethnically and instability interethnically. A closer examination of each case will be necessary to determine this.

At the goal statement point the speech functions performed by the interviewer change from ASKING (about who the student is as a social person) to TELLING. The interviewer speaks to the student's goal, giving advice and granting or withholding permission to pass through the mobility gate. His telling functions here are the encounter's raison d'etre.

We found that uncomfortable moments, some of which were also goal–statement points,[5] were INVARIABLY in 26 out of 26 cases marked by at least one proxemic shift at the beginning or at the end of that section — usually by a shift at both ends (see Table 4).

The goal–statement points, in 22 out of 26 cases, were marked by a proxemic shift.[6] If microshifts smaller than those for which the proxemics code was designed to retrieve are included the figure changes to 25 out of 26 possible cases.

AN ADDITIONAL FINDING

In 15 out of the 19 cases for which we have both proxemic and viewing session data, viewing-session comments were being expressed by

Table 4. Proxemic shifts occurring at "segment boundaries"

Counsellor	Interethnic Encounters	Intraethnic Encounters	Number of Cases
Irish American*	100%	91%	(6)
Black American	100%	84%	(6)
Black American*	97%	91%	(6)
Italian American	77%	71%	(8)
Overall	92%	80%	26

* For these counselors some of the interviews designated "intra-ethnic" are actually intra-"pan-ethnic," a term we use for the social categories "White Ethnic" and "Third World." For the Irish-American counselor the interviews designated "intra" were with Polish-American students, Polish-Americans being members of the same "pan-ethnic" class as Irish-Americans.

[5] In the summary table example (Figure 3) the goal statement (also the most uncomfortable moment) occurs at lines 42–51.

[6] In all 18 of the 18 cases for which we have complete data on other verbal and nonverbal phenomena, the goal statement point is demarcated not only by a proxemic shift, but by an average of 4.6 other segment markers, out of an average of 5.7 segment markers that could possibly have occurred.

an informant at the moment a proxemic shift was occurring or had just occurred in the original encounter. The sensitivity to proxemic shifts by the encounter participants themselves (who represented a variety of Old World cultural backgrounds) is paralleled by the reactions of our research assistants, who identified uncomfortable-moments sections as invariably bounded by a proxemic shift. One of the two uncomfortable-moments coders was Scandinavian-American, the other was Egyptian.

CONCLUSION

In our data, proxemic shifts occur very frequently at the beginning and ending of segments of interaction that can also be identified by changes of speech content and style, and by changes in the interaction process. This suggest that proxemic shifts may function as indicators of situational shifts and topic changes in an interaction.

Ultimately we must confront the problem of truth value of statements of function. We have demonstrated high correlation between proxemic shifts and other aspects of interaction. We have not demonstrated cause. For this experimental conditions are necessary.

The additional finding, uniformity of results in the emic, impressionistic responses to proxemic shifts by our informants and coders despite wide cultural diversity among them, is interesting. It suggests that emic segmentation of interaction according to proxemic cues may be a human universal. Further research, under controlled conditions with a broad cross-cultural sample, could shed light on this question.

REFERENCES

BLOM, JAN-PETER, JOHN J. GUMPERZ
   1972   "Social meaning in linguistic structure: code switching in Norway" in *Directions in sociolinguistics: the ethnography of communication*. Edited by John J. Gumperz and Dell Hymes. New York: Holt, Rinehart and Winston.

BYERS, PAUL E.
   1972   "From biological rhythm to cultural patterns: a study of minimal units." Unpublished dissertation, Columbia University, New York. (University Microfilms 73-9004).

CICOUREL, AARON
   1972   "Basic and normative rules in the negotiation of status and role," in *Studies in social interaction*. Edited by David Sudnow. New York: The Free Press.

COWAN, RICHARD A.
n.d. *Invisible walls.* Film illustrating proxemic features of interaction. University of California at Berkeley, Extension Media Center.
ERICKSON, FREDERICK
i.p. *Talking to the man: a microethnography of inter-ethnic relations in gatekeeping encounters.*
HALL, ERWARD T.
1963 A system for the notation of proxemic behavior. *American Anthropologist* 65(5):1003–1026.
1968 Proxemics. *Current Anthropology* 9:83–95.
KENDON, ADAM
1972 "The greeting as an interactional event." Address delivered at Annual Meeting of American Anthropological Association, Toronto, Canada, December 3, 1972.
LEONARD-DOLAN, CAROLYN
1972 "A method for film analysis of communication style." Paper presented at the Annual Meeting of the Society for Applied Anthropology, Montreal, Canada, April 8, 1972.
LOTT, E. E., W. CLARK, I. ALTMAN
1969 *A propositional inventory of research on interpersonal space.* United States Naval Medical Research Institute Report.
PORTER, EVAN, MICHAEL ARGYLE, VERONICA SALTER
1970 What is signalled by proximity? *Perceptual and Motor Skills* 30: 39–42.
PROST, JACK
1967 Bipedalism of man and gibbon compared using estimates of joint motion. *American Journal of Physical Anthropology* 26:135–148.
SCHEFLEN, ALBERT E.
1973 *Communicational structure: analysis of a psychotherapy transaction.* Bloomington: Indiana University Press.
SOMMER, ROBERT
1965 Further studies of small group ecology. *Sociometry* 28:337–348.

Coverbal Behavior Associated with Conversation Turns

NORMAN N. MARKEL

TURN: The time for action or proceeding which comes in due rotation or order to each of a number of persons *(American College Dictionary)*.
CONVERSATION: Informal interchange of thoughts by spoken words *(American College Dictionary)*.
VERBAL: Of or pertaining to words *(American College Dictionary)*.
COVERBAL: The behavior of interlocutors which occurs in association with or accompanying words, but which is not essential for the articulation or grammatical functioning of those words (author's definition).

TURN

A number of students of human behavior have recognized that the alternation of action and inaction (such as having the floor or not having the floor) is the basic fact of conversational interaction. Jaffe and Feldstein (1970), Matarazzo and Wiens (1967), Sears (1951), and Watzlawick, Beavin, and Jackson (1967), are just a few of the authors who have recognized, in one way or another, that the rotation of performance among individuals in a group was the most salient feature of group dynamics. However, the most recent, and perhaps most seminal, use of the conversation turn as the unit of analysis appeared in articles by Duncan (1972) and Schegloff (1968). Both authors focus on the turn

I would like to thank those who read and commented on a preliminary draft of this paper: Louise Damen, Karen Evans, Cindy Gallois, Martha Hardman, Betty Knickerbocker, Layne Prebor, and the participants in the Spring 1972 Gainesville Group for the Study of Nonverbal Behavior.

as the unit of behavior; Duncan studied the paralinguistic and kinesic behavior associated with turn taking, and Schegloff studied the rules governing the sequencing of turns in conversational openings.

The important feature that makes the turn so vital to the study of conversational interaction is its ability to simply and reliably segment the behavioral stream of conversational interaction. In my own research I have adopted the following operational definition of the turn: A SPEAKING TURN BEGINS WHEN ONE INTERLOCUTOR STARTS SOLO TALKING AND ENDS WHEN A DIFFERENT INTERLOCUTOR STARTS SOLO TALKING. For every speaking turn there is a concurrent listening turn, which is the behavior of one or more nontalking interlocutors present. One important feature of this definition is that when one interlocutor breaks into the turn of the other, producing SIMULTANEOUS SPEECH, it does not end the turn of the first interlocutor. It is only when the second interlocutor starts solo talking that his speaking turn begins. Another feature of this definition of the turn is that "switching pauses" are assigned to the preceding turn. A switching pause is the period of silence from the end of one interlocutor's solo talking to the beginning of his partner's solo talking (Jaffe and Feldstein 1970). This period of silence has, in other studies, been referred to as "reaction time" and "latency" (Gallois 1973).

Also to be noted are two types of simultaneous speech. In one the speaker does not give up his turn and continues his solo talking; in the other the speaker gives up the floor and simultaneous speech ends as his partner begins solo talking. I refer to the former instance of simultaneous speech as "overtalk" (Prebor 1972) and the latter instance of simultaneous speech as "switching overtalk." The terms overtalk and switching overtalk are used to avoid predisposing in a particular direction the interpretation of the social or psychological significance of these behaviors (e.g. as referring to them as "interruptions" would do). In some instances overtalk may be the listener's positive reinforcement to the speaker indicating that the listener is in tune with the speaker and is encouraging him to continue. Or, in some cultures switching overtalk may be the accepted means of obtaining a speaking turn.

The turn appears to be the etic unit on the sociolinguistic level of analysis of conversational interaction. Because the turn is the ubiquitous aspect of conversational interaction that can be unambiguously defined and reliably identified, it is analogous to the phone employed in phonological analysis. Following Pike, the phone is defined as a point in the stream of articulation where maximum closure or maximum openness occurs. The phonetician then describes that phone in terms of the position or activity of the lips, tongue, and larynx occurring at that point of maximum closure or maximum openness. Variations in articulation features occurring with phones are attributed to either allophonic variation of one phoneme or distinctive features of different and mutually exclusive phoneme classes (Markel 1969: Chapter 5).

Similarly, once the stream of conversation has been segmented into turns, and the body movements occurring with these turns have been described, i.e. etic analysis, then the principles of nondistinctive variation, complementary distribution and contrast, i.e. emic analysis, can be employed. Using these emic principles it is possible to discover whether different body movements occurring with different turns are behavioral variations of one type of turn, or if these body movements are distinctive features that mark a different type of turn. Differential body movements associated with differential function are the objective basis for establishing mutually exclusive classes of turns. I propose that these contrasting classes of turns be labeled *turnemes*.

CONVERSATION

Conversation is by definition a social-psychological phenomenon. "Interchange" is the social aspect and "thought" is the psychological aspect of a conversation. I am interpreting "thought" here as a cover term for any and all mediating processes that occur in the heads of speakers. This would include attitude, or predisposition to respond, mind, personality, emotional state, cognition, self concept, and so on. The definition indicates that "spoken words" (which I take as being synonymous with "verbal behavior") are the overt behavioral manifestation of the mediating processes going on in the head of the speaker. However, in this instance the dictionary definition is inadequate, for we are all now aware of the fact that the body movements and gestures that are displayed either concurrent with spoken words or without any accompanying spoken words, serve as well as spoken words to indicate the thoughts of the speaker. Because both spoken words and body movements can serve the same function (i.e. manifest thought) the difference between them is more appropriately described in terms of structure rather than function. In this regard I believe that Mehrabian (1972) is on the wrong track in referring to the difference between verbal and nonverbal behavior as the difference between behavior which the culture makes explicit (verbal) and that which is implicit (nonverbal), because the explicit/implicit difference is a functional difference. The structural differences between verbal and nonverbal behavior are discussed in greater detail in the next section.

INTERLOCUTOR A   INTERLOCUTOR B

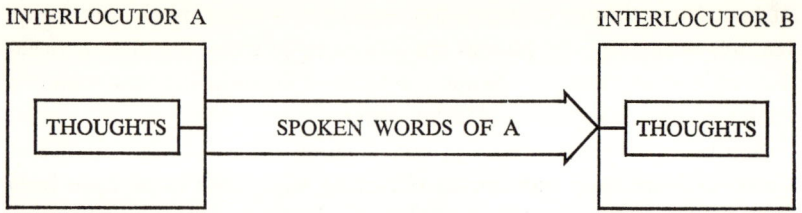

Figure 1. Schematic representation of the definition of conversation

Figure 1 is a schematic representation of the definition of conversation. This diagram of the definition of conversation will, of course, be recognized as being similar to most models of communication (e.g. Markel 1969: Chapter 1). As indicated above, this diagram is deficient in two ways, first by not indicating that thoughts are interchanged by means of the body movements/gestures that accompany speech and, second, by not indicating that thoughts are interchanged by the body movements/gestures that occur without speech. A more accurate diagram of conversation is shown in Figure 2.

INTERLOCUTOR A   INTERLOCUTOR B

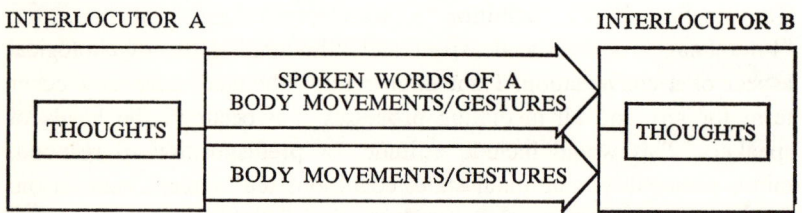

Figure 2. Schematic representation of the definition of conversation including body movements/gestures

For the sake of completeness, I should add that "body movements/ gestures" is not, in fact, an adequate description of all nonword overt behavior that occurs in conversations either concurrently with spoken words or unaccompanied by spoken words. There are, for example, conditions of and changes in the surface of the skin, static positions and postures, changes in pupil size, voice qualities, etc., that also communicate the thoughts of an interlocutor. A compendium of these behaviors can be obtained from the following sources: Argyle (1969), Hinde (1972), Knapp (1972), Markel (1969), and Mehrabian (1972).

The "informal" dimension that is built into the definition of conversation is particularly noteworthy. This definition means that a true conversation is characterized by its "naturalness," i.e. the interlocutors are behaving in a way typical of their social statuses and psychological states, given the social and physical environment in which they are placed. An attempt to obtain a high level of informality should, then, be part of every research design studying conversation interaction.

VERBAL–COVERBAL

Behavior in conversational interaction is either verbal or coverbal. Verbal behavior is that which is essential to the speaker for the articulation of words and also behavior that the speaker must employ to indicate the grammatical function intended for these words. For example, if a speaker wants to talk about a tin mine, he must very carefully and exactly place the tip of his tongue against the back of his teeth to articulate the *t* sound. At the same instant, the air stream must be COMPLETELY stopped. If the tongue is moved any amount whatsoever from its contact with the back of the teeth, thereby allowing air to escape, the speaker will produce an *s* not a *t*. A native speaker of English would respond quite differently to "sin mine" in contrast to "tin mine."

In addition to the behavior of the lips and tongue, which are essential to pronounce the sounds of "tin mine," it is an essential part of verbal behavior for the lungs to produce more air pressure on "TIN" than on "mine" so that the phrase "TIN mine" is understood as a noun phrase rather than a verb phrase. In the latter case there would be more force on "MINE" than "TIN" (e.g. "When you finish tinning yours, tin MINE").

Coverbal behavior is never essential for the articulation or grammatical functioning of words. If a speaker wants to talk about a "TIN mine," whether or not he nods, looks into the eyes of the interlocutor, smiles, or scratches his chin as he says "TIN mine," none of these behaviors will in any way change the meaning from "a place where tin is removed from the ground." This does NOT mean, however, that coverbal behavior does not carry information or meaning. On the contrary, looking into the eyes, smiling, etc., can carry so much information or meaning to an interlocutor that the words being spoken are not heard.

The verbal versus coverbal distinction has an aspect that is of special interest for those concerned with social psychology. As was indicated above, a speaker has relatively little option in either articulating the specific sounds that make up words, or in determining their distribution. To produce words the speaker is obligated to produce highly stereotyped, specific sounds, the quality of which cannot vary significantly if he intends to be understood. On the other hand, the speaker usually has a number of options in selecting types of coverbal behavior. For example, the speaker can nod his head in a number of ways, varying from an extremely large but infrequent up-down swing to an extremely small but frequent up-down swing. Similarly, the rules regulating the distribution of phonemes in words are much more rigid than the rules regulating the distribution of coverbal behavior. If I intend to articulate the word "tin" I am obligated to produce the phonemes *t, i* and *n* exactly in that order and no other. However, the rules regulating the distribution of coverbal behavior are much more flexible. For example, while there are obviously rules which regulate acceptable amounts and vigor of nodding in conversations, these rules involve a range of options, and the speaker can choose from a range of force and frequency with which to nod (this is also true of the listener). In other words, in the distribution of coverbal behavior, individual selection can play a great role because the individual has a wider range of options. It is for this reason that coverbal behavior is of more interest to the social psychologist than verbal behavior.

Perusal of the literature about nonverbal behavior/communication indicates a range of coverbal behavior from the microscopic such as Birdwhistell's (1970) "stress kineme" to the macroscopic such as Scheflen's (1965) "postural cue." My personal experience in recording the microscopic details of verbal behavior suggests that it is inefficient to use a microscopic analysis of behavior for the purpose of understanding social interaction. On one research project I spent many hours of listening to an initial psychiatric interview to come to the conclusion that the linguistic and paralinguistic microdetails in the opening statement of the patient indicated that the word "walls" was very important. My report to the psychiatrists on the project pointed this out and the significance of "walls" was, in fact, reinforced by later events in the therapy session. However, by merely observing that the word "walls" occurred three times in the first six seconds of the patient's opening remarks, the same conclusion as to the significance of "walls" could have been arrived at – with a fraction of the expenditure of time and effort. I have, therefore, come to the conclusion that research seeking to understand the social psychology of conversational interaction through manifest behavior can move ahead with greater speed and less effort by focusing on macroscopic rather than microscopic coverbal behaviors.

Specifically, I believe the coverbal behaviors that will be most fruitful in leading to an understanding of the social psychology of conversational interaction are head nodding, face looking, smiling, head touching, and speaking. These particular coverbal behaviors were selected because (1) research indicates that they reflect important social psychological dynamics of conversational interaction; (2) they are easily observable in a socially acceptable way by the participants in, or the observers of, an ongoing conversational interaction; and (3) they are easily and reliably recorded by judges viewing a videotape of the interaction which may not always be taken under studio conditions (i.e. tapes made in the field).

Important in Conversation

The most recent literature indicating the interactional importance of these particular behaviors deals with head nodding (Dittman 1972); face looking (Kendon 1967) and its dyadic correlate eye contact (Russo 1970; Argyle and Dean 1965); smiling (Van Hoof 1972); head touching (Freedman 1972); and speaking and its conversational correlate, simultaneous speech (Jaffe and Feldstein 1970).

Observable in Ongoing Interaction

Everyday experience indicates that when engaged in a conversation, if you are going to look at your partner, you have to look in the direction of the face. Looking away is all right, but looking at any other part of the body is not acceptable, and is likely to disrupt the flow of conversation. One research study reports that when an interlocutor's gaze deviates beyond his partner's ear, the partner will turn to look in that direction (Ellsworth and Carlsmith 1968).

Readily Recordable From Videotape

My experience with recording behavior from videotapes indicates that certain behaviors occurring in the face region cannot be easily or reliably recorded from videotapes of a conversational interaction. For example, it has been shown that pupil size is an important nonverbal behavior relating to the psychological state of the individual (Hess 1968). However, pupil size cannot be easily seen on a videotape and, therefore, I propose that it not be included as a coverbal behavior to be studied in research on conversational interaction.

REFERENCES

ARGYLE, M.
1969 Social interaction. New York: Atherton Press.

ARGYLE, M., J. DEAN
1965 Eye contact, distance, and affiliation. Sociometry 28:289–304.

BIRDWHISTELL, R. L.
1970 Kinesics and context. Philadelphia: University of Pennsylvania Press.

DITTMAN, A. T.
1972 Developmental factors in conversational behavior. Journal of Communication 22(4):404–423.

DUNCAN, S.
1972 Some signals and rules for speaking turns in conversations. Journal of Personality and Social Psychology 23(2):283–292.

ELLSWORTH, P. E., J. M. CARLSMITH
1968 Effects of eye contact and verbal content on affective response to a dyadic interaction. Journal of Personality and Social Psychology 10:15–20.

FREEDMAN, N.
1972 "The analysis of movement behavior during the clinical interview," in Studies in dyadic communication. Edited by A. W. Siegman and B. Pope. New York: Pergamon Press.

GALLOIS, C.
1973 "Temporal aspects of the conversational style of bilinguals." Unpublished masters thesis, University of Florida.

HESS, E. H.
1968 "Pupilometric assessment," in Research in psychotherapy. Edited by J. M. Shlien, 573–583. Washington, D.C.: American Psychological Association.

HINDE, R. A., editor
1972 Nonverbal communication. Cambridge: University Press.

JAFFE, J., S. FELDSTEIN
1970 Rhythms of dialogue. Academic Press: New York.

KENDON, A.
1967 Some functions of gaze direction in social interaction. Acta Psychologica 26:27–63.

KNAPP, M. L.
1972 Nonverbal communication in human interaction. New York: Holt, Rinehart and Winston.

MARKEL, N. N., editor
1969 Psycholinguistics: an introduction to the study of speech and personality. Homewood, Illinois: Dorsey Press.

MATARAZZO, J. D., A. H. WIENS
1967 Interviewer influence on durations of interviewee silence. Journal of Experimental Research in Personality 2:56–59.

MEHRABIAN, A.
1972 Nonverbal communication. Chicago: Aldine-Atherton.

PREBOR, L. D.
1972 "The natural history of a conversation." Unpublished doctoral dissertation, University of Florida.
RUSSO, N. F.
1970 "Eye contact and distance relations in children." Unpublished doctoral dissertation, Cornell University. University Microfilms, Ann Arbor, Michigan.
SCHEFLEN, A. E.
1965 Quasi-courtship behavior in psychotherapy. *Psychiatry* 28:245–257.
SCHEGLOFF, E. A.
1968 Sequencing in conversational openings. *American Anthropologist* 70:1075–1095.
SEARS, R. R.
1951 "Social behavior and personality development," in *Toward a general theory of action*. Edited by T. Parsons and E. A. Shils, 465–478. Cambridge: Harvard University Press.
VAN HOOF, J. A. R. A. M.
1972 "A comparative approach to the phylogeny of laughter and smiling," in *Nonverbal communication*. Edited by R. A. Hinde, 209–241. Cambridge: Cambridge University Press.
WATZLAWICK, P., JANET H. BEAVIN, D. D. JACKSON
1967 *Pragmatics of human communication*. W. W. Norton.

Interaction Units during Speaking Turns in Dyadic, Face-to-Face Conversations

STARKEY DUNCAN, Jr.

The problem of segmentation lies at the heart of structural research on social interaction. It is necessary to discover and to document basic structural units, having, in Scheflen's words, "(1) a given set of component parts; (2) a definite organization; and (3) specific location in a larger system" (1966: 271). As Scheflen (1966) further points out, this larger system is likely to be arranged hierarchically. A model of such a system and its constituent units would be that of phonological and syntactic units operating within a hierarchical language system.

The linguist's approach to structural units is to focus, insofar as possible, on the language behaviors (as that term is traditionally construed) of single individuals: his informants. But sociolinguists (e.g. Hymes 1969; Gumperz and Hymes 1972) have emphasized that language is typically used in a broader communication context. This broader context includes, among other things, both (a) one or more other persons with whom the language user is interacting, and (b) other behaviors, such as those in paralanguage (Trager 1958) and body motion, that are displayed conjointly with language.

The notion of units for social interaction may take into account this broader communication context. Within a given speech situation (Hymes 1972), behaviors in paralanguage and/or body motion may

This study was supported in part by Grants MH-16,210 and MH-17,756 from the National Institute of Mental Health, and by Grant GS-3033 from the Division of Social Sciences of the National Science Foundation. Susan Beekman, Jeanine Carlson, Mark Cary, Diane Martin, George Niederehe, Ray O'Cain, Thomas Shanks, Cathy Stepanek, Tichina Stubblefield, and Andrew Szasz contributed to the transcriptions and data analysis. I am indebted to Dick Jenny, Wayne Anderson, and the client, who generously consented to serve as participants in this study.

function, in an integrated fashion with those in language, to mark units. Further, it is possible that, in addition to units marked solely by the actions of an individual interactant, there may be other units that can be properly marked only through the coordinated actions of more than one interactant. It has been proposed (Duncan i.p.a.) that units of this second sort be termed "units of interaction."

Here I will discuss some findings leading to the hypothesis of units of interaction operating in dyadic, face-to-face conversations to segment speaking turns, thereby creating units on the next lower hierarchical level.

METHOD

The interviews and the methods of transcription used for this study have been detailed elsewhere (Duncan 1972). Briefly, detailed transcriptions of intonation, paralanguage, and body motion were made of both participants in two dyadic, face-to-face conversations, as recorded on videotape. The first nineteen minutes of each conversation were used.

One of the conversations was between a male of about forty years and a female of about twenty, who were previously unacquainted. The second conversation was between the male in the first conversation and a second male, also about forty. These two interactants had been good friends for a number of years. Both conversations were intrinsically motivated; that is, both would have taken place, regardless of whether or not they had been videotaped.

Coordination of Body Motion and Speech Transcriptions

Speech syllables were used to locate all transcribed events. Thus, the movements of both participants in a conversation were located with respect to the syllables emitted by the participant who happened to be speaking at the time or to the pause between two syllables.

Unit of Analysis

A unit of analysis was selected that lay in size between the phonemic clause (Trager and Smith 1957) and the speaking turn. The unit was defined in terms of behaviors displayed by the participants. Boundaries of the unit were defined as being at the ends of phonemic clauses (though not necessarily those with rising or falling terminal junctures), which additionally were marked by the display of one or more of the following behaviors: (a) an unfilled pause; (b) the turning of the speaker's head toward the auditor; (c) a drop in paralinguistic pitch and/or loudness in conjunction with a phonemic clause, either across the entire clause, or across its final syllable or syllables; (d) a relaxation of the foot or feet of the speaker from a marked dorsal flexion; (e) an audible inhalation; (f) the use of any pitch level–terminal juncture combination other than 2 2| at the end of a phonemic clause; (g) a paralinguistic drawl on the final syllable or on the stressed syllable of a clause; (h) the termination of any hand gesticulation used by the speaker, or the relaxation of a tensed hand position (e.g. a fist) by the speaker; (i) the use by the speaker of one of a set of stereotyped expressions, such as "but uh," "or something," or "you know," termed sociocentric sequences by Bernstein (1962); (j) a drop in paralinguistic pitch and/or intensity, in conjunction with a sociocentric sequence; and (k) the completion of a grammatical clause, involving a subject-predicate combination. More detailed definitions for these behaviors are given in Duncan (1972).

SPEAKING-TURN INTERACTION UNITS

The notion of "interaction units" was conceived as a result of findings on certain behaviors regularly associated with the exchange of speaking turns in dyadic, face-to-face conversations. To account for these observed regularities, a "speaking-turn system" (Duncan i.p.a, i.p.b) was hypothesized. A brief outline of the main elements of this system may provide a useful context for understanding the proposed interaction units during speaking turns.

In general, the speaking-turn system, as presently developed, is conceptualized as consisting entirely of discrete elements, arranged hierarchically.

Turn-System States

Two mutually exclusive discrete states are posited for each participant in a dyadic conversation: speaker and auditor. A "speaker" is defined as a participant who claims the speaking turn at any given moment. An auditor (Kendon 1967) is a participant who does not claim the speaking turn at any given moment.

The turn system was largely designed to explain the means by which the two participants coordinated their respective actions, so as to accomplish smooth exchanges of the speaking turn. In contrast to such smooth exchanges, both participants may simultaneously claim the speaking turn. This situation represents a breakdown of the turn system for the duration of the situation.

On the basis of research findings, a series of discrete signals and accompanying rules has been proposed (Duncan 1972; Duncan and Niederehe 1973) with respect to the exchange of speaking turns. Each of these signals is made up of a set of behavioral cues, also considered to be discrete. These signals, their constituent cues, and accompanying rules regarding the appropriate display of and response to these signals will be briefly described.

Speaker-Turn Signal

The auditor may claim the turn when the speaker displays a turn signal. In proper operation of the system, if the auditor so claims the turn in response to the signal, the speaker is obliged to relinquish immediately his claim to the turn. When the speaker is not displaying the turn signal, however, auditor claims of the turn are inappropriate, leading to simultaneous turns.

The turn signal is permissive, not coercive. The auditor is not obliged to claim the speaking turn in response to the display of the signal by the speaker. The auditor may alternatively communicate in the back channel, or remain silent.

The turn signal is composed of a set of six behavioral cues, found variously in intonation, content, syntax, paralanguage, and body motion. These cues were mentioned above as behaviors f, g, h, i, j, k, used in the definition of units of analysis.

The display of any single cue was sufficient to constitute a display of the signal. However, the probability of an auditor turn-claiming response to a signal display was found to be a linear function ($r = .96$) of the number of cues displayed, without regard to the specific cues comprising the display.

Speaker-Gesticulation Signal

The display of this signal appears to negate any turn signal concurrently being displayed. It was found that display of the gesticulation signal virtually eliminates claims to the turn by the auditor. The gesticulation signal is composed of a single, discrete cue: the hands being engaged in a gesticulation, as opposed to being engaged in a self-adaptor (Ekman and Friesen 1969), or to being at rest.

Speaker-State Signal

This signal is hypothesized to mark a participant's shift from the auditor to the speaker state. The speaker-state signal is defined as the display of at least one of a set of two discrete cues: (a) a shift in head direction, away from one pointing directly toward the vis-à-vis; and (b) initiation of a gesticulation. This gesticulation is the same behavior that had the effect of suppressing turn claims of the vis-à-vis, as mentioned above.

The cues comprising the speaker-state signal were observed, not only at the beginnings of speaking turns but also during the course of speaking turns. These cues, displayed during turns, will be further considered below.

Speaking Turns as Interaction Units

It is clear that a smooth exchange of the speaking turn requires the appropriate, coordinated action of both participants. This smooth exchange involves the following ordered sequence of three events: (a) the speaker displays a turn signal (and does not conjointly display a gesticulation signal); (b) the auditor switches to the speaker state, displaying a speaker-state signal; and (c) the previous speaker switches to the auditor state, relinquishing the turn. Omission of any one of these three steps, or violation of their order, results in no exchange of the speaking turn and/or the simultaneous claiming of the turn by both participants.

This ordered sequence of actions of both participants may be said to move the conversation ahead on one hierarchical level: that of speaking turns. The exchange of the turn has therefore been hypothesized to constitute an interaction unit on that hierarchical level.

The concern of this study is with units on the next lower hierarchical level than that of the speaking turn. These lower-level units would be used to segment the speaking turn. Like the speaking turn, they will be interaction units requiring the action of both participants in dyadic, face-to-face conversations. For lack of a better term, they will be called "within-turn units."

SPEAKER-AUDITOR INTERACTION DURING SPEAKING TURNS

The most obvious behaviors observed during speaking turns are the head nods and vocalizations, such as "m-hm," "yeah," displayed by the auditor. These and related behaviors will be termed "back-channel behaviors," or more simply "back channels," after Yngve (1970).

An initial inventory was made of potential back-channel behaviors and their respective locations in our corpus. Classification of behaviors as potentially in the back channel was aided by the astute observations and research results of Dittmann and Llewellyn (1967, 1968), Fries (1952), Kendon (1967), and Yngve (1970).

While back-channel behaviors by both speaker and auditor were observed in the corpus, the results to be described are based on analysis of auditor back channels exclusively. There was a total of 355 separate auditor back channels and seventy-one separate speaker back channels.

Auditor Back-Channel Signal

The following behaviors were observed in our corpus and, on the basis of the results reported below, were considered to be various forms the auditor back-channel signal took in the corpus. In the examples that follow, "S" stands for "speaker" and "A" for "auditor."

A. M-HM. This expression is used to stand for a group of readily identified, verbalized signals. Included in the group are such expressions as "m-hm," "yeah," "right," and the like, and Kendon's (1967) examples of "yes quite," "surely," "I see," and "that's true." Most of the "m-hm" signals may be used singly or in repeated groups, as in "yeah, yeah."

B. SENTENCE COMPLETIONS. Not infrequently in our materials an auditor would complete a sentence that a speaker had begun. In such a case he would not continue beyond the brief completion; the original speaker would continue with his turn as if uninterrupted. Sentence completions have been independently reported by Yngve (1970).

Example: S: "... eventually, it will come down to more concrete issues ...." A: "As she gets more comfortable." S: "and I felt that ...."

C. REQUEST FOR CLARIFICATION. Contrasting with sentence completions are brief requests for clarifications. Such requests were usually accomplished in a few words or a phrase. Example: S: "... somehow

they're better able to cope with it." A: "You mean these anxieties, concerned with it?" S: "Possible that other people have...."
D. BRIEF RESTATEMENT. This back-channel behavior is similar to the sentence completion, except that it restates in a few words an immediately preceding thought expressed by the speaker. Example: S: "... having to pick up the pieces." A: "the broken dishes, yeah." S: "but then a very...."
E. HEAD NODS AND SHAKES. Head nods and shakes may be used alone or in company with the verbalized back-channel signals. Head nods may vary in duration from a single nod to a rather protracted, continuous series of nods.

Auditor Back Channels and Claimings of the Turn

Within the turn system as it is presently formulated, there are two apparently different types of actions an auditor may take: he may (a) communicate in the back channel, or (b) shift to the speaker state, claiming the turn. The investigators cited immediately above were unanimous in their judgments that back-channel behaviors do not constitute a speaking turn. It was possible to lend further documentation to these judgments by exploring the differences in distribution of these two types of behavior in our corpus.

Data analysis yielded results suggesting that the various subsets of auditor back channels were similar to each other and different from claimings of the turn in four respects.
A. Auditor back channels did not tend to be marked by the speaker-state signal, whereas claimings of the turn did. Duncan and Niederehe (1973) reported that a two-by-two contingency table in which columns represented display versus nondisplay of the speaker-state signal, and rows represented auditor back channels versus beginnings of speaking turns, yielded chi-square values of 27.80, $df = 1$, $p = .00001$, for one interview, and 47.09, $p < .00001$, for the other interview.
B. Auditor back channels had a less orderly distribution than turn claims, with regard to the unit of analysis. Auditor back channels were located more frequently than expected during, and appreciably after, the units. Turn claims were predominately located immediately after such units. The chi-square associated with these distributions was 29.44, $df = 3$, $p = .00002$.
C. The auditor's display of back channels was unaffected by the speaker's display of the gesticulation signal, while turn claims were

almost entirely suppressed by that signal. For the two-by-two contingency table in which columns represented display versus nondisplay of the gesticulation signal and rows represented back channels versus turn beginnings, chi-square = 43.35, $df = 1$, $p > .00001$.

D. Turn claims and certain auditor back channels were related to two different sets of speaker cues. In Duncan (1972), turn claims were shown to be systematically related to the prior display of a set of six cues, comprising the speaker turn signal. In contrast, auditor back channels were found to be related to a set of two cues, comprising the speaker within-turn signal. This signal will be discussed in the next section.

Taken as a whole, the evidence points to multiple distinctions between auditor back channels and speaking turns. The findings in this respect are in full agreement with the observations of other investigators cited above.

Speaker Within-Turn Signal

It was found that a subset of auditor back channels was systematically related to the prior display of two speaker cues, typically occurring close to the end of units of analysis: (a) completion of a grammatical clause, and (b) turning of the speaker's head toward the auditor. The display of either one of these two cues was sufficient to constitute the signal. The grammatical-completion cue is identical to that mentioned as a speaker turn cue. Thus, this cue is common to the two signals. The head-turning cue was not included in the speaker turn signal, because it failed to differentiate smooth exchanges of the speaking turn from instances of simultaneous claimings of the turn by the two participants.

Auditor back channels that occurred immediately after the end of a unit of analysis, or at the beginnings of the next unit (that is, slightly delayed), were related to the two speaker cues. Auditor back channels that occurred prior to the end of units of analysis were not so related. It is believed that this subset of "early" back channels was not related to the speaker cues, because these back channels too often occurred before the speaker cues were displayed.

Considering the between-unit and late auditor back channels, 88.8 percent occurred following the display of one or both of the speaker within-turn cues. A chi-square, applied to a two-by-two contingency table in which the columns represent the speaker's display versus nondisplay of the within-turn signal and the rows represent auditor's subsequent display versus nondisplay of a back channel, yielded a value of 39.31, $df = 1$, $p < .00001$. A correlation of .99 was found between the number of speaker within-turn cues displayed (0, 1, or 2), and the probability of an auditor back channel.

Under certain circumstances, the display of the speaker within-turn signal was related to the subsequent display of a speaker continuation signal, discussed immediately below.

Speaker Continuation Signal

The speaker continuation signal was related to the preceding display of both (a) the speaker within-turn signal, and (b) the auditor back-channel signal, in a manner to be described below. The speaker continuation signal was composed of one of the cues of the speaker-state signal: shift away in head direction.

When no auditor back channel intervened between the end of one unit of analysis and the beginning of the next, a relationship was found between the speaker's display of within-turn cues at the end of one unit and his display of the continuation signal at the beginning of the next. It was found that 84 percent of the displays of the speaker-state signal followed the display of one or both of the speaker within-turn cues. A chi-square, applied to a two-by-two contingency table in which the columns represented the speaker's display versus nondisplay of the within-turn signal and the rows represented the speaker's subsequent display versus nondisplay of the continuation signal, yielded a value of 20.48, $df = 1$, $p = .00005$. A correlation of .96 was found between the number of speaker within-turn cues displayed (0, 1, or 2) and the probability of a subsequent speaker continuation signal.

When an auditor back channel occurred before the end of a unit of analysis, the probability of a subsequent speaker continuation signal significantly increased. This increase was observed, regardless of whether or not speaker within-turn cues preceded the back channel. The chi-square was calculated from a contingency table in which the columns represented display versus nondisplay of an early auditor back channel and the rows represented display versus nondisplay of the speaker continuation signal. In the case in which no speaker within-turn cues preceded the early back channel, the chi-square was 20.95, $df = 1$, $p = .00005$. In the case in which one or both speaker within-turn cues preceded the early back channel, chi-square $= 38.10$, $df = 1$, $p < .00001$.

In contrast, when an auditor back channel was located not before the end of the unit of analysis, but rather between units, there was no accompanying increase in the probability of a subsequent speaker continuation signal. Table 1 summarizes the findings on speaker and auditor signals hypothesized to play a part in within-turn interaction units.

Table 1. Speaker and auditor signals hypothesized for within-turn interaction units

Name of signal	Constituent cues	Related to subsequent display of:
Speaker within-turn	1. Completion of a grammatical clause 2. Turning of head towards auditor	1. Between-unit auditor back channel 2. Speaker continuation signal
Between-unit auditor back channel	(5 different types, both audible and visible, observed)	
Early auditor back channel	(same as between-unit auditor back channel)	1. Speaker continuation signal
Speaker continuation signal	1. Turning of head away from auditor	

DISCUSSION

The findings, briefly described above, led to the hypothesis of units of interaction serving to segment speaking turns into smaller units. These within-turn interaction units parallel speaking-turn interaction units in their structural characteristics: (a) both require the appropriate, coordinated action of both participants, and (b) both involve ordered sequences of action.

The beginning of a within-turn interaction unit appears to be marked by a speaker continuation signal, analogous to the marking of a turn beginning by a speaker-state signal. This beginning of a new within-turn unit appears to be associated primarily with either one of two preceding events: (a) a speaker within-turn signal, regardless of whether or not a between-unit auditor back channel intervened, or (b) an early auditor back channel, regardless of whether or not a speaker within-turn signal preceded it.

In view of these findings, and of the requirement that an interaction unit involve the actions of both participants, it may be hypothesized that within-turn interaction units may be marked in either one of two alternative ways.

One of these alternative ways would involve an ordered sequence of three events: (a) a speaker within-turn signal, (b) a between-unit auditor back channel, and (c) a speaker continuation signal. In this sequence, the initial speaker within-turn signal is required, not only because of its relationship to the following continuation signal, but also because of the finding in our corpus that between-unit auditor back channels, not preceded by a within-turn signal, were never followed by a continuation signal.

The second way of marking a within-turn interaction unit would involve an ordered sequence of only two events: (a) an early auditor back channel, and (b) a speaker continuation signal. In this sequence the initial speaker within-turn signal is not required, because, when an early auditor back channel occurred, the display of a within-turn signal was found to have no appreciable effect on the probability of a subsequent display of either (a) the early back channel, or (b) a speaker continuation signal. The primary relationship was between the early back channel and the subsequent speaker continuation signal.

The within-turn interaction unit appears to provide the participants with a means by which to pace a speaking turn at a rate that takes both speaker and auditor into account. Through the back channel, the auditor may indicate his present condition with respect to what the speaker is saying. The auditor might, for example, use a request for clarification at those points at which he is not adequately following the speaker. On the other hand, the results suggest that an early back channel serves to indicate not only that the auditor is adequately following the speaker's message but also that the auditor is actually ahead of it. Accordingly, it would be appropriate for the speaker to proceed directly to the next unit, regardless of whether or not he had previously displayed a within-turn signal. This "skipping ahead" action by the speaker is not, however, automatic. It depends, apparently, both upon the auditor's early back channel and upon the speaker's assessment of the situation.

In contrast, a between-unit auditor back channel would indicate that the auditor is following the speaker's message as it is developing. Therefore, it would not affect, either positively or negatively, the probability of an ensuing continuation signal.

By the same logic, a late auditor back channel would indicate not only some auditor acknowledgement but also that the auditor is not quite following the speaker's message. No analyses were brought to bear on this possibility because late auditor back channels occupy the same position at which continuation signals are typically displayed. It was not possible, therefore, to test the probability of ensuing speaker-state signals.

An hypothesized interaction unit on a given hierarchical level has been discussed here. The next higher level — that of the speaking turn — has been considered elsewhere (Duncan i.p.a, i.p.b). It is hoped that continuing research will shed further light both upon units at these two hierarchical levels and upon possible units at higher and lower levels. Scheflen (1965) has proposed a higher level unit, termed the "position", that may be marked by behaviors related to posture shifts.

If research now in progress continues to confirm the findings presented here, then it would appear that interaction units may constitute an element of the structure of social interactions, at least in face-to-face dyadic conversations.

APPENDIX 1

Figure 1 presents a logical model of the turn system, as it is presently understood. No claim is made that the diagram represents a model of the actual perceptual and decision processes employed by the interactants.

Drawn to be read like a computer flow chart, the figure is designed to show graphically the hypothesized organization of signals and rules, in terms of the development of a single speaking turn. Each diamond represents a decision as to whether or not the indicated discrete signal is being displayed. As a result of that binary decision, a path is chosen leading from the diamond. Paths crossing vertical boundaries (shown as double lines), drawn to separate the actions of the respective participants, connect signal displays that must occur in the indicated ordered sequence. Paths not crossing such boundaries carry no implication of ordered sequences.

The starting point, shown on the left, assumes that one of the participants (A) holds the speaking turn, uncontested. The outcomes shown at the right are based on those phenomena that actually have been observed in the interviews subjected to analysis.

Interaction Units during Speaking Turns

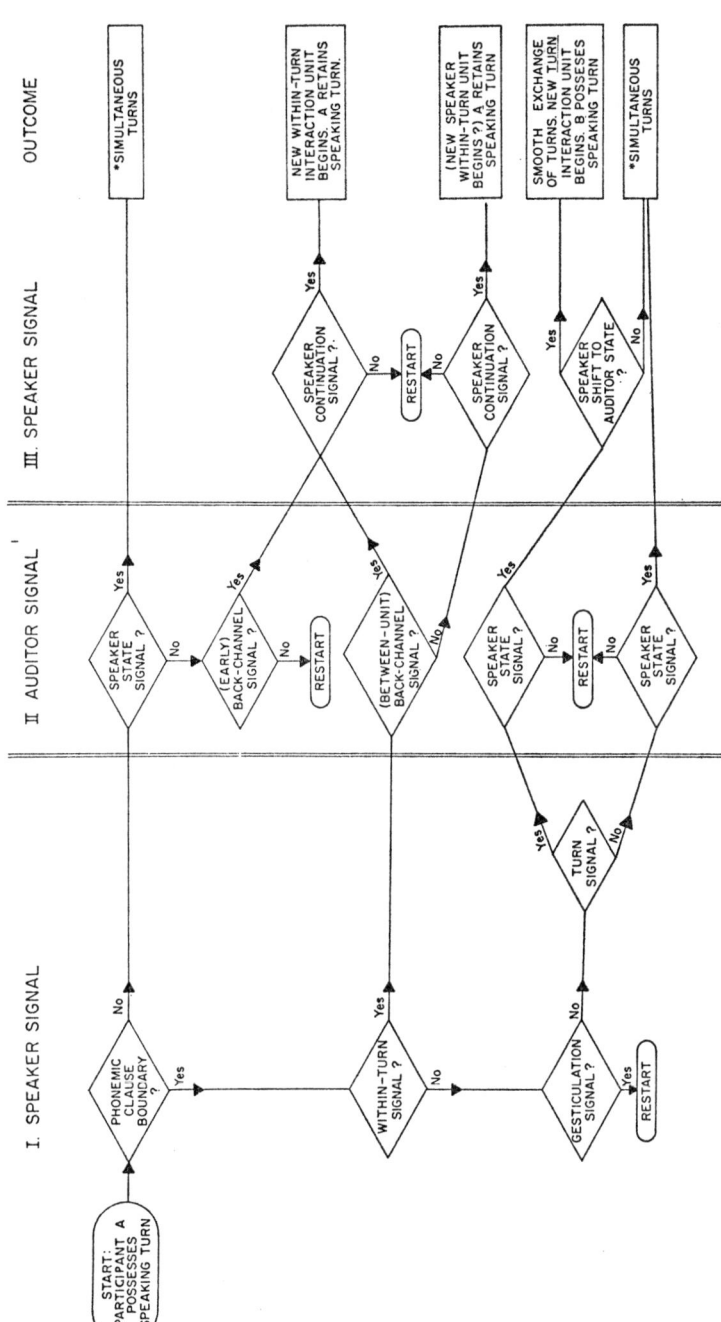

Figure 1. The turn system.

REFERENCES

BERNSTEIN, B.
1962 Social class, linguistic codes, and grammatical elements. *Language and Speech* 5:221–240.

DITTMANN, A. T., L. G. LLEWELLYN
1967 The phonemic clause as a unit of speech decoding. *Journal of Personality and Social Psychology* 6:341–349.
1968 Relationship between vocalizations and head nods as listener responses. *Journal of Personality and Social Psychology* 9:79–84.

DUNCAN, S. D., JR.
1972 Some signals and rules for taking speaking turns in conversations. *Journal of Personality and Social Psychology* 23:283–292.
i.p.a Toward a grammar for dyadic conversations. *Semiotica*.
i.p.b "Language, paralanguage, and body motion in the structure of conversations," in *Language and thought*. Edited by W. C. McCormack and S. A. Wurm. The Hague: Mouton.

DUNCAN, S. D., JR., G. NIEDEREHE
1973 "A speaker-state signal within the turn system." Unpublished manuscript, University of Chicago.

FRIES, C. C.
1952 *The structure of English*. New York: Harcourt, Brace.

EKMAN, P., W. V. FRIESEN
1969 The repertoire of nonverbal behavior: categories, origins, usage, and coding. *Semiotica* 1:49–98.

GUMPERZ, J. J., D. HYMES, editors
1972 *Directions in sociolinguistics*. New York: Holt, Rinehart and Winston.

HYMES, D.
1969 "Linguistics — the field," in *International encyclopedia of the social sciences*, volume 9, 351–371. New York: Crowell, Collier and Macmillan.
1972 "Models of the interaction of language and social life," in *Directions in sociolinguistics*. Edited by J. J. Gumperz and D. Hymes, 38–71. New York: Holt, Rinehart and Winston.

KENDON, A.
1967 Some functions of gaze-direction in social interaction. *Acta Psychologica* 26:22–63.

SCHEFLEN, A. E.
1973 *Communication structure: analysis of a psychotherapy transaction*. Bloomington: Indiana University Press.
1966 "Natural history method in psychotherapy: communicational research," in *Methods of research in psychotherapy*. Edited by L. A. Gottschalk and A. H. Auerbach, 263–289. New York: Appleton-Century-Crofts.

TRAGER, G. L.
1958 Paralanguage: a first approximation. *Studies in Linguistics* 13:1–12.

TRAGER, G. L., H. L. SMITH, JR.
 1957 *An outline of English structure.* Washington, D.C.: American Council of Learned Societies.
YNGVE, V. H.
 1970 "On getting a word in edgewise." *Papers from the sixth regional meeting Chicago Linguistic Society*, 567–577. Chicago: Chicago Linguistic Society.

Communicative Functions of Phatic Communion

JOHN LAVER

INTRODUCTION

The term "phatic communion" is widely accepted in Malinowski's original definition as "a type of speech in which ties of union are created by a mere exchange of words" (Ogden and Richards 1923: 315). When Malinowski invented the term, he crystallized a conceptual area that had been previously amorphous, and the analysis of the different functions of language took a step further forward. However, as often happens when a label and a definition are first supplied for a new conceptual area, the very act of identification has seemed to inhibit further enquiry. Malinowski's view on the function of phatic communion has been echoed by almost all writers who have touched on the subject since 1923. A typical formulation is that of Lyons, who says that phatic communion "serves to establish and maintain a feeling of social solidarity and well-being" (Lyons 1968: 417).

This inhibition of the investigation into the functions and phenomena of phatic communion may also have been reinforced by the historical accident of the development of linguistics as a subject: in its struggle for existence as a legitimately autonomous discipline, linguistics perhaps overemphasized the study of the form of language, during the period between the 1930's and the 1960's, at the expense of the study of the functions of language (Lyons 1970: 8). Now that linguistics feels more at ease as an independent discipline, scholars from a linguistic background seem to find journeys into neighboring territory more congenial, as

Copyright © by John Laver. This article also published in 1974 in *Semiotic aspects of spoken communication* by John Laver (London: Edward Arnold).

witnessed by the vigorous growth in the last fifteen years or so of bridge-disciplines such as sociolinguistics and psycholinguistics. With the consequent renewal of interest in the functions of language, the investigation of such topics as phatic communion is of increasing relevance.

The point of departure for this article is the notion that phatic communion is not a simple phenomenon, and that its function of creating ties of union, if that is indeed its principal function, is achieved by subtle and intricate means whose complexity does not deserve to be minimized by the use of such phrases as "a mere exchange of words."

The specific questions addressed by the research reported here are: What are the actual phenomena of phatic communion? When do these phenomena occur within the span of a given interaction, and in what type of interaction? With what other types of behavioral phenomena is phatic comunion associated? What are the social functions of phatic communion, and finally, what is the functional significance of a speaker's choice of indulging in one type of phatic communion rather than another?

The data used in the research come solely from English-speaking cultures. It has to be conceded from the outset that the methodology used was not stringent, consisting of informal observation of everyday social encounters, and relying for functional conclusions, at least in part, on the intuitions of the observers as native participants in such encounters. My personal observation of behavior in the opening and closing stages of encounters was supported by over a hundred student projects, in Britain and America, mostly observing the closing stage of encounters in a wide variety of different types of interactions. The reasonably wide measure of agreement about the behavioral phenomena involved, particularly in the closing stage, encourages me to believe in the typicality of the observations, but it nevertheless has to be emphasized that work in this area is still exploratory, and more controlled experimental approaches are needed to confirm or refute the representativeness of the observed data and the validity of the conclusions. At present, conclusions about social function are inevitably mostly speculative, particularly when appeal is made to the conscious intuitive interpretations of participant observers. This article is thus intended to encourage exploratory inquiry, rather than to offer definitive conclusions.

Phatic communion of course has the literal meaning of "communion achieved through speech." A pervasive attitude in recent research into face-to-face interaction has been that speech is only one among the many strands of communication, and that the communicative function of any one strand is better understood in the context of the operation of the other strands than in isolation. All the different communicative strands, speech, gesture, posture, body movements, orientation, proximity, eye contact and facial expressions, should be thought of as woven together to form the fabric of conversation, and we can understand the particular texture of an interaction only by seeing the relationship of the different strands (Laver and Hutcheson 1972: 11).

I shall try to show that the social function of the linguistic code used in phatic communion is not different in principle from the function of the paralinguistic, kinesic, proxemic, and visual codes manipulated in the behavior that characteristically accompanies phatic communion. The position I would like to reach at the end of the article is that the fundamental social function of the multistranded communicative behavior that accompanies and includes phatic communion is the detailed management of interpersonal relationships during the psychologically crucial margins of interaction.

In examining the phenomena involved in phatic communion, and in trying to reach functional conclusions, I have had to have recourse to the descriptive language of a number of disciplines, not only that of linguistics and phonetics, but also of psychology, anthropology, and sociology. In one sense, however, all these disciplines fall under the aegis of a superordinate discipline, that of semiotics, the general theory of communicative signs (Morris 1938: 80; Sebeok et al. 1964: 5). In this article, three particular semiotic notions will be used, adopted from C. S. Peirce, the nineteenth-century pragmaticist philosopher: the SYMBOL, the INDEX, and the ICON.

The concept of the symbol will be used in the common linguistic usage of linguistic elements (of varying size) being used as symbols of their referents. The concept of the index will be used NOT in the sense adopted by many philosophers, where "index" is used to mean a deictic device (Lyons 1968: 275), but in the sense advocated by Abercrombie (1967: 6), where he defines an index, following one of the interpretations suggested by Peirce, as a sign which "reveals personal characteristics of the ... speaker." The concept of the icon will be used in the sense directly proposed by Peirce, of one event acting as the sign of another through similarity of structure between the two events (Feibleman 1946: 91). From the point of view here, the most important of these concepts is that of the index because a major position to be stated is that the prime function of phatic communion is the communication of indexical facts about the speakers' identities, attributes, and attitudes, and that these indexical facts constrain the nature of the particular interaction.

It is convenient to divide the temporal structure of interactions into three major phases, the opening phase, the medial phase, and the closing phase. As a preliminary comment, we might say that the function of the behavioral activity that characterizes the opening phase is to lubricate the transition from noninteraction to interaction, and to ease the potentially awkward tension of the early moments of the encounter, "breaking the ice," so to speak, before the main business of the encounter is embarked upon in the medial phase. The closing phase is once again a transitional phase, easing the transition from full interaction to departure.

Strictly, all three phases are normally characterized by phatic communion in the narrow sense of involving the participants interacting through speech. But phatic communion as normally understood, applying to choices from a limited set of stereotyped phrases of greeting, parting, commonplace remarks about the weather, and small talk, strongly characterizes the marginal phases of interaction only, and it is these marginal phases that will be the focus of attention here.

The structure of the article will be to look first at characteristics of the opening phase, then of the closing phase, and then to offer some general conclusions about similarities of function of phatic communion and associated behavior in the two margins of interaction. The concluding section will view the area from an anthropological standpoint, offering an analysis of behavior in the margins of interaction in terms of different types of rites of passage.

THE OPENING PHASE OF INTERACTION

Within English-speaking cultures (and perhaps all cultures) phatic communion seems to be an almost universal habit indulged in during the opening phase of interactions. Nevertheless there are some situations in our culture where we normally avoid phatic communion during the opening phase as being inappropriate to that particular type of situation. An obvious case is where the interactants have already met that day, or at least within the last six or seven hours, and have already indulged in extended phatic communion in their first meeting. Another case is where the roles of the interactants are already very clearly defined, as in situations such as a university lecture, buying a railway ticket, or talking to a telephone operator. In all these situations, the role structure of the encounter is known to the interactants in advance.

The conclusion this leads to is that when the interactants DO indulge in phatic communion, they do not already know the precise details of the roles they are about to play in the oncoming interaction, and that the process of phatic communion allows them the opportunity to explore, in a tentative way, the social identity and momentary state of mind of the other participant, in order to be able to define and construct an appropriate role for themselves in the rest of the interaction. In other words, I am suggesting that an important function of phatic communion is to help the participants to reach what Goffman (1959) has called the "working consensus" of the interaction, about some aspects of their respective roles in those situations where the role structure is not previously obvious to the participants.

How this working consensus is arrived at may be illuminated by a brief analysis of the typical sequence of behavioral events on the various channels of communication during the opening phase, together with a more detailed examination of the linguistic and phonetic components of phatic communion.

In the following account of the sequence of events in a typical opening phase of an interaction, the notion of "sequence" is to some extent artificial and conveniently analytic: some of the different stages, in different channels, can obviously overlap in time, and some, on different occasions, may be omitted.

The first stage in any encounter, as many writers have pointed out, is for the participants to make mutual eye contact. We recognize the necessity of eye contact as the first stage, in ordinary language about encounters, when we speak of "trying to catch someone's eye" before being prepared to start talking — in a restaurant situation with a waiter, for example. To accept eye contact is the first signal of acknowledgment that one accepts the other participant's invitation to engage in an encounter.

The second stage in the opening phase is the exchange of "distant" gestures of greeting or acknowledgment. These, exchanged between acquaintances, are much more understated in our culture than our distant gestures of parting, involving only slight movements of the hand and arm, or head.

The third stage is for the participants to assume an appropriate, conventional facial expression of cordiality, or polite attention, or merely of attention, depending on the previously established or anticipated relationship between the two participants.

The fourth stage is for the participants to reach the appropriate proximity for the remainder of the opening phase of their interaction. This is one area in face-to-face interactions that has been more studied than most (Hall 1959, 1963, 1964, 1966; Sommer 1969).

The fifth stage is the exchange of conventional contact gestures of greeting, as appropriate to the relationship between the participants.

The sixth stage is for the participants to take up their mutual bodily orientation, in postures appropriate to their relationship (Scheflen 1964; Argyle and Kendon 1967).

The seventh stage is the exchange of stereotyped linguistic symbols used as tokens in the transactions of phatic communion. The analysis of this stage of the opening phase is the main object of this section, and I shall return to its discussion in a moment.

The eighth and last stage of the opening phase is the indication by the participants that they would like to initiate the main business of the interaction, by the use of various signals of transition. These include such actions as an abrupt head movement, moving the head slightly upwards so as to allow the establishment of eye contact on a level gaze; a slight shift in posture, commented on by Scheflen (1964) as a "marker of a position," where he uses "position" as a technical term for a unit of temporal structure of interaction of slightly smaller extent than my unit of a "phase;" sometimes an adjustment of proximity, often slightly increasing the distance between the participants, iconically adumbrating, as it were, the diminution in the need for overtly expressed cordiality now that the "ice-breaking" opening phase is coming to an end; and sometimes the use of a linguistic marker such as "Well . . . ," or more overtly transitional comments such as "What I came to see you about was . . . ," or "Well, what can I do for you?"

Before coming on to the detailed analysis of the linguistic tokens used in phatic communion, I would like to offer some brief preliminary comments on posited functions of the use of phatic communion in the opening phase. Firstly, it would seem to have an important propitiatory function in defusing the potential hostility of silence in situations where speech is conventionally anticipated. Malinowski comments on this:

> . . . speech is the intimate correlate of (man's gregarious nature), for, to a natural man, another man's silence is not a reassuring factor, but, on the contrary, something alarming and dangerous . . . . The breaking of silence, the communion of words is the first act to establish links of fellowship . . . . The modern English phrase "Nice day today" or the Melanesian phrase, "Whence comest thou?" are needed to get over the strange and unpleasant tension which men feel when facing other in silence (Ogden and Richards 1923: 314).

Hayakawa (1952: 70) says something similar ". . . it is possible to state, as a general principle, that the prevention of silence is itself an important function of speech, and that it is completely impossible for us in society to talk only when we 'have something to say'."

Secondly, as suggested earlier, phatic communion has an exploratory function, in that it allows the participants to feel their way towards the working consensus of their interaction. Their perception of such factors as their relative social status can be controlled by aspects of their linguistic behavior during phatic communion, and this will be discussed in more detail below; but the phonetic behavior of the participants is important also. When a person speaks, he reveals often very detailed indexical information about his personal characteristics of regional origin, social status, personality, age, sex, state of health, mood, and a good deal more (Abercombie 1967: 7–9; Laver 1968; Laver and Hutcheson 1972: 11–14).

As listeners, we infer this information from phonetic features such as voice quality, voice-dynamic features such as control of pitch, loudness and tempo, and from accent, as well as to some extent from features of linguistic choices made by the speaker. So that, just the fact of speaking and of allowing the other participant to hear the sound of one's voice, regardless of the actual linguistic content of the utterance, provides the listener with some of the information he needs to reach some initial conclusions about the psychosocial structuring of the interaction. Between participants who are already acquainted, the exploratory function mentioned here serves to reconfirm previous information, and between strangers serves as an initial identification.

Thirdly, as will be evident from earlier comments, phatic communion has an initiatory function, in that it allows the participants to cooperate in getting the interaction comfortably under way, using emotionally uncontroversial communicative material, and demonstrating by signals of cordiality and tentative social solidarity their mutual acceptance of the possibility of an interaction taking place.

The linguistic tokens used in phatic communion are highly conventional, and as listeners we can therefore nearly always tell when a speaker is engaging in phatic communion. Many writers have maintained that not only are the linguistic tokens selected from a finite, small set of possible utterances, but also that the referential content of the particular utterance is irrelevant to the nature of the interaction. Abercombie (1956: 3), for example, writes that: "The actual sense of the words used in phatic communion matters little," and goes on to recount the story of Dorothy Parker,

alone and rather bored at a party [who was] asked "How are you? What have you been doing?" by a succession of distant acquaintances. To each she replied "I've just killed my husband with an axe, and I feel fine." Her intonation and expression were appropriate to party small-talk, and with a smile and a nod each acquaintance, unastonished, drifted on.

Malinowski made the same point: "Are words in phatic communion used primarily to convey meaning, the meaning which is symbolically theirs? Certainly not! They fulfill a social function, and that is their principal aim...." (Ogden and Richards 1923: 315). Nonetheless, I would wish to take the position that the semantic meaning of the tokens selected in phatic communion is indeed relevant to the nature of the interaction, firstly by constraining the semantic theme within which the participants must make their choices of tokens in a particular occasion of phatic communion, and secondly, and more importantly, by providing the participants with a subtle means of communicating to each other their views about such indexical aspects of their momentary relationship as their relative social status.

To deal with the first point: Lyons (1968: 417) writes about the use of a phrase such as "It's another beautiful day," as the opening utterance in a conversation between a customer and a shopkeeper. He says:

Quite clearly, this utterance is not intended to "convey" to the shopkeeper some information about the weather, it is an instance of "phatic communion." At the same time, it does have a meaning, different from the meaning of innumerable other utterances that might have occurred in the same context ... and the next "move" in the conversation will generally be related to the particular utterance on the basis of this meaning.

Thus part of any individual's expertise in the (often quite extended) interchanges of phatic communion is his ability to sustain a particular semantic theme, once one of the participants has embarked upon that theme. So the semantic sense of the linguistic tokens is not entirely irrelevant, in at least this limited aspect.

The second point is both more important and more speculative than the first. Its rationale is that the type of linguistic token chosen by a speaker may reflect his view of the social structuring of the interaction. In reaching this conclusion (and I shall discuss the data involved immediately below), I have to concede that I rely on the social intuitions of native participants in the sharply stratified society of British English culture.

If we take into account the literal reference of the linguistic tokens used in phatic communion, one striking general principle emerges: in a rather broad sense, all the tokens have deictic reference. Apart from formulaic greetings, the tokens refer either to factors narrowly specific to the time and place of the utterance or, more widely, to factors in the context of situation in which the utterance occurs which are personal to the speaker or the listener.

In the narrow sense of deictic reference, we could call the tokens involved NEUTRAL tokens: their reference in English is very frequently to a description or a prediction of the weather. Characteristic examples would be, (typically with an abbreviated syntactic structure):
1. PAST REFERENCE: "Terrible night last night," "Nasty smog yesterday"
2. PRESENT REFERENCE: (adjective+noun): "Nice day," "Beautiful morning"
3. FUTURE REFERENCE: "Going to clear up," "Snow's coming," "Frost tonight"

Other neutral tokens of narrowly local reference are ones which, like comments on the weather, have relevance to factors affecting both participants equally. Examples would be: "Nice party" (to a fellow guest); "Great view" (to a fellow tourist); or "About time the trains were cleaned" (to a fellow passenger).

In the broader sense of deictic reference, it is useful to distinguish between tokens that comment on factors personal to the speaker and those personal to the listener. We might call these SELF-ORIENTED and OTHER-ORIENTED tokens respectively.

Self-oriented tokens usually take the form of declarative statements, and examples would be: "Hot work, this," or "My legs weren't made for these hills" (to a fellow country-walker).

Other-oriented tokens are very often in question form, as in: "How's life (business/things/the family/the wife/etc.)?" or "How do you like the sunshine, then?" or "Do you come here often?" Occasionally there are other forms of comment, such as "That looks like hard work."

In offering this typology of the different categories of linguistic tokens, I am preparing the ground for the speculative proposition that the choice of token category made by a speaker on a particular occasion is indexically significant for staking claims about solidarity and relative social status. The proposition arises from the observation that there seem to be some interesting constraints, in British English at least, on the options of choice of category conventionally open to the speaker initiating phatic communion. If we take the three different types of status relationships in an interaction, with a superior talking to an inferior, an inferior talking to a superior, and an equal talking to an equal, then if the relationship between the two participants is solidary, the opening speaker, regardless of his relative social status, has a free choice of category for his opening remark. But if the speakers do NOT share a solidary relationship, the conventional options of category-choice are rather different.

The NEUTRAL category remains available to a speaker of any relative social status, but the conventional choice between the SELF-ORIENTED and the OTHER-ORIENTED category is normally governed by the status differential between the two speakers. In an "upwards" interaction, where a nonsolidary inferior speaks first to an acknowledged superior, he may choose the self-oriented category, but not the other-oriented category. In a "downwards" interaction, where a nonsolidary superior speaks first to an acknowledged inferior, he may choose the other-oriented category, but not the self-oriented category. In "level" interactions between nonsolidary acknowledged equals, neither the self-oriented nor the other-oriented categories may be chosen. This is not to say that the "forbidden" categories are not frequently chosen, but it does imply that when the conventions about "permitted" categories are broken, such contraventions have special social significance for indexical attitudes about the status relationship between the two speakers, and sometimes about the solidarity factor of their relationship.

Let us consider first the "permitted" choices in nonsolidary interactions, and their indexical implications for the attitudes of the participants. Firstly, speakers of whatever relative social status are on safe, uncontroversial, unassertive ground when they select the neutral category of token. This may partly explain why the neutral category is by far the most frequently chosen. It has the indexical effect of offering momentary solidarity. Secondly, in nonsolidary interactions where there is a status differential, convention seems to support a position where the superior is prepared to "invade" the psychological world of the inferior, as it were, but does not expect the inferior to intrude upon his, while the inferior is not prepared to invade the psychological world of the superior, although conceding him the right to invade the inferior's world. In both cases, where the superior exploits his conventional right of invasion, by the use of an other-oriented comment such as "That looks like hard work," or where the inferior concedes the superior's conventional right of invasion, by the use of a self-oriented comment such as, "Hard work, this," the effect is to reassert and reinforce the status differential.

The analysis of the indexical effect of making conventionally forbidden choices of category is more complex. Where a nonsolidary superior opens a conversation with an inferior with a self-oriented remark such as, "I do like a breath of fresh air" (as he might during an encounter on a walk in the country), the indexical effect is to invite the listener to a momentary solidarity in which the (perhaps visually establishable) status differential is tacitly acknowledged as irrelevant. Where a nonsolidary inferior opens a conversation with an obvious superior with an other-oriented remark such as, "Out for a breath of fresh air, are you?" then the indexical effect is to invade the psychological world of the superior without prior invitation, and tacitly to assert that the status differential between the two participants is irrelevant to the momentary relationship. At the least, the nonsolidary inferior behaves in a way more conventionally appropriate to a solidary relationship.

In the case of interactions between nonsolidary equals, the use of a self-oriented remark extends an implicit invitation to a momentary solidarity, while the use of an other-oriented remark seems to have a slightly more intrusive air, of tacitly demanding entry to momentary solidarity. In both such cases, the initiating participant runs the risk that his overture or demand will be declined by the other participant, but such rejection during phatic communion between equals seems rare.

The indexical function of choosing a forbidden category of token in nonsolidary interactions thus seems generally to be an attempt to facilitate momentary solidarity, and to minimize the relevance of the status differential that in fact exists. It seems paradoxical that the conventionally permitted choices of token category in nonsolidary interactions should have the function of reinforcing status differentials, while the use of conventionally forbidden token categories, and of the neutral category, should minimize status differentials and maximize momentary solidarity.

A somewhat similar paradox can be seen in another indexical function of phatic communion, still to do with the different categories of token discussed above, in the management of "psychological distance." If we set up a scale of psychological distance, extending from "intimate" through "cordial, uncommitted, distant" to "hostile," the use of neutral tokens, such as comments about the weather, count as "uncommitted." Because they constitute emotionally unassertive ground, the use of these tokens seems to serve to allay both undue hostility and undue curiosity on the part of the other participant. They thus facilitate comfortable social relations with other speakers, and fulfill social obligations of pacific, cooperative behavior, but they also significantly protect the psychological privacy of the speaker from uncomfortable invasion. If such comment has any validity, it is interesting that this very common exploitation of the resources of phatic communion has a very delicately balanced double function, asserting "ties of union" of social solidarity, but simultaneously limiting their strength.

The last aspect of phatic communion in the opening phase of interactions that I would like to discuss is once again directly concerned with the indexical management of interpersonal relations between the two participants, and has an ethological bias, to do with considerations of territoriality.

When one participant is static in space, and the other is moving towards him, in whatever type of physical locale, then, unless there are overriding special reasons, there seems to be a strong tendency, both in Britain and America, for the "incomer" to initiate the exchange of phatic communion. A number of conclusions spring from this, all deriving from the general notion that by breaking the silence first, the speaker defines some aspects of the role he is prepared to play in the oncoming interaction.

Firstly, the speaker recognizes that in some sense the static listener is in a closer psychological relationship with the immediate territory than he is, and that in a way the listener can be regarded as the owner of the territory.

Secondly, he acknowledges his own awareness of the fact of his invasion of the listener's territory.

Thirdly, he declares in effect that his intentions are pacific, and offers a propitiatory token. The phatic communion token is propitiatory not only in the sense mentioned earlier of defusing the potential hostility of silence, but also in that, by conceding the initiative to the listener to accept or reject the token (by replying or declining to reply), the speaker puts himself momentarily in the power of the listener. To pursue this ethological analogy for a moment, the behavior of a speaker initiating phatic communion is somewhat comparable to the submission-surrender behavior of a dog beaten in a fight, where the dog rolls on his back and proffers his unguarded throat, apparently inviting complete destruction by the victor, but in fact secure in the social knowledge that such invitations to destruction are effective in inhibiting the aggressive impulses of the dominant participant. An analogy closer to home is the propitiatory appeasement offered to irate traffic police by ethologically-sophisticated traffic offenders.

Fourthly, merely by speaking, and implicitly inviting the listener to participate in a linguistic interaction with him, the speaker asserts a claim to sociolinguistic solidarity with the listener. If the listener accepts the invitation to a spoken interaction, then by implication he gives the speaker a safe-conduct to enter his territory without making him suffer a counterdisplay of hostility. A suggestive analogue here would be the military control of territory, where passwords and countersigns are overt signals of mutual solidarity.

As a summary comment on the functions of phatic communion during the opening phase of interaction, it would seem from the discussion above that the most important functions are the following: to provide the participants with acceptable means of stating the outlines of the roles they are prepared to play in the oncoming interaction, at least in terms of status, psychological distance and territoriality; to extend and accept invitations to sociolinguistic solidarity; and to facilitate the comfortable initiation, free from tension and hostility, of the interaction.

THE CLOSING PHASE OF INTERACTION

Once again, it seems to be an almost universal habit, certainly within English-speaking cultures, to indulge in phatic communion during the closing phase of interaction. But, as with the opening phase, there are some situations where we avoid phatic communion, and not surprisingly, they are very similar to those in which it is avoided in the opening phase. One such situation is where the participants can make a reasonable assumption that they will meet again within the space of a few hours at the most. Another case is where the situation itself defines the roles of the interactants, as in a university lecture, buying a railway ticket, talking to a telephone operator, and so forth. One concludes that the parallelism of the avoidance of phatic communion in both the opening phase and the closing phase justifies a parallel conclusion — namely, that phatic communion in the closing phase is relevant to the participants' need to establish a continuing consensus for future encounters.

If one function of phatic communion in the parting phase is to contribute to a continuing consensus which can stand as a tentative pre-structuring of the participants' next encounter, a supporting function is to consolidate the relationship experienced in the current interaction. How this consolidation is achieved, and how the closing phase is organized, may be illuminated by a brief analysis of the typical sequence of behavioral events on the various channels of communication during the phase, together with a more detailed examination of the linguistic component. In general, the sequence of the stages is the mirror image of the stages of the opening phase.

The first stage is for the initiator of the closing phase to perform appropriate signals of transition, indicating his desire for the onset of the closing phase and the end of the medial business phase. One channel characteristically exploited for the exchange of such transition signals is the visual channel. In a private, two-person interaction, a sudden prolongation of the typical duration of eye contact seems to function as one transitional signal; in nonprivate encounters between two interactants, such as the party situation, or social meeting at conferences, avoidance of eye contact for a longer period than conventional during the medial phase, often coupled with "roaming" gaze, seems to have the same function. Another transition signal is a greater shift of orientation or of posture than typically occurs in the medial phase. Other signals include an overt glance at one's watch, or a facial expression such as a slight smile coupled with a raising of one's eyebrows, where the momentary interactional state of the medial phase makes no call for such an indication of apparent cordial, attentive agreement. Linguistic signals of transition from the medial phase include the same sort of vague, curtailed utterances as are used in the transition from the opening phase to the medial phase, such as "Well . . ." More specific signals of incipient termination of the medial "business" phase are also possible, where one participant will briefly summarize the points of agreement reached during the medial phase in a "position statement," as it were (in those interactions where the purpose of the interaction was mainly to reach such "positions").

It is somewhat artificial to separate the second stage from the first, but one might consider that the second stage begins when the transition from the medial to the closing phase is complete, in the view at least of the initiator of the closing phase, and that behavior in this second stage has the function of adumbrating in an iconic way the incipient departure of one of the participants. Finality is often initially adumbrated by gestures such as the ostentatious finishing of a drink, a cup of coffee, or a cigarette, or clipping a pen into a pocket, taking off, folding up and putting away spectacles, and so forth. Proximity can also be manipulated, in an interesting way. The initiator of the closing phase often backs off slightly, increasing the distance between the two participants, iconically adumbrating the increasing distance of parting. What is interesting here is that this change in proximity is in a sense a gambit offered to the noninitiator, together with other signals of termination, and that the gambit is quite often not accepted by the other participant. When this happens, the initiator usually resumes the degree of proximity he has just moved away from, and then, slightly later, tries again.

Once again, it may be that the gambit offered is not taken up, and a striking characteristic of many interactions is the resultant oscillation of proximity. The general property of oscillation on many different communicative channels seems to characterize this stage of the closing phase, but proximity can be taken as a paradigm example. A revealing conclusion springs from this observation of oscillation, namely that conversations can be terminated amicably only by mutual consent. The initiator of the closing phase has to obtain the consent of the noninitiator through the process of offering gambits on various communicative channels, and the closing phase can be developed further only when the gambit has been seen to be accepted. In other words, the social process of parting normally has an essential feedback component. Only when the appropriate feedback has been received can parting progress, otherwise continual reentry to earlier stages of the interaction is necessary. The everyday phrase "to take one's leave" is therefore strictly a misnomer: "leave" cannot normally be "taken" unilaterally; it has to have the consent of the person left. Conventional parting is thus a cooperative achievement obeying rather strict constraints.

Other adumbrative signals of departure are changes in orientation, in street interactions, for example, where the participants move aside from each other's anticipated line of departure, and stand facing each other at right angles to their eventual exit direction. In this situation, gaze direction often also adumbrates the exit direction, with frequent glances towards the anticipated direction of departure. On some communicative channels, iconic adumbration is accompanied by an exaggeration of the signals. For instance, BEFORE AN INCREASE IN THE DISTANCE BETWEEN PARTICIPANTS ACTUALLY BEGINS, there may be an increase in the vigor of facial expressions, such as would be necessary to make them visible at a greater distance, and an increase phonetically in both pitch height and loudness, such as would be similarly necessary for audibility at a greater distance.

The third stage is the exchange of tokens of phatic communion, whose functional characteristics will be examined in more detail in a moment.

The fourth and fifth stages, which are usually simultaneous, are the exchange of conventional contact gestures of parting and the adoption of conventional facial expressions, where and as appropriate to the relationship.

In the sixth stage, the distance between the participants begins to increase, and the seventh stage is the exchange, at an appropriate distance, of conventional distant gestures of parting. The seventh and last stage, terminating the encounter, is the breaking of mutual eye contact.

If we return now to the analysis of the linguistic tokens used in phatic communion in the closing phase, it is interesting that the tokens mostly make explicit reference to psychological and social aspects of the relationship between the two participants, with very much less reliance on topics of neutral value such as the weather. Apart from the formulaic forms of farewell, nearly all the tokens are self-oriented or other-oriented. However, the typology of tokens that will be discussed in this section will rather be directly concerned with their posited indexical function, in terms of the various aspects of the management of the interpersonal relationship between the participants.

The first aspect I wish to comment on is the use of phatic communion to mitigate the potential sense of rejection that a participant might feel when his fellow participant initiates the closing phase. Such mitigation is one of the factors that secures cooperation and consent in terminating the encounter comfortably. In this class of tokens, an expressed need to terminate the encounter is justified by explicit appeal to a compulsion external to the speaker. The reasons given for the parting may be real or invented, but this appeal to an external authority seems to figure quite frequently in closing comments. Examples would be: "I'm sorry, I have to go, I'm about to give a lecture"; "I'm afraid I must be off, I've a million things to do"; "I wish I could stay longer, but I have to get back to relieve the babysitter." A particularly interesting subcategory of this type of token is where deference is expressed to the needs of the listener himself, as the compelling external authority. Instances are: "Musn't keep you"; "I guess you have to get on, I'll be going." The utility of this device is aptly described in the following quotation: "What better way to assuage the displeasure of the departure than to set its reason in the welfare of the other participant?" (Tiemann, personal communication).

This function of assuaging the noninitiating participant is also achieved, to a lesser degree, by the second major aspect of the use of phatic communion in the closing phase, that of consolidating the relationship between the two interactants.

Consolidation is managed in a variety of ways, reflected in the use of different types of phatic communion tokens. The first comments on the quality of the current encounter, now drawing to a close. Such tokens very often carry implications of esteem for the other participant, as in phrases like "It was nice seeing you," "I do enjoy our little chats," and "Talking with you always cheers me up." Consolidatory caring for the the other participant is also reflected in tokens commenting on his future welfare, such as "Hope your cold gets better soon," benevolent admonitions like "Take care, now," and "Watch how you go," and occasionally benedictions such as "God bless."

The second type of consolidatory token makes explicit reference to the continuation of the relationship, as in phrases like "See you next week," "Let's not leave it so long this time," "Be seeing you," "Let's meet again soon," "See you at the match on Saturday," and many similar phrases. It is interesting that the formulaic phrases of farewell in English, unlike those in many other European languages, contain no such promise of continuation of the relationship. The French *au revoir*,

German *auf Wiedersehen,* Italian *arrivederci* and Spanish *hasta la vista* all literally anticipate a repeated encounter, but the English "good bye" contains no such implication. One has to go to less formulaic idioms in English to find the equivalent promise of continuation, such as "See you," and "Be seeing you."

An important subcategory of the type of phatic communion token promising continuation of the relationship is the type which reminds the listener that he is bound in a web of social solidarity with the speaker by the ties of common acquaintance. The tokens usually anticipate that the listener will meet the common acquaintance before the speaker, in phrases like "Remember me to Tom," or "Say hello to Jeanie for me," or "Tell Jeanie I was asking after her." These tokens not only bind the two present participants together by an announcement of one aspect of their solidary relationship, but also allow the speaker to use the listener as an agent to reinforce his social bonds in the network of his acquaintances. The reverse situation, where the speaker offers to perform the same service for the listener, seems much less common. This may be because such phrases as "I'll remember you to old Fred, shall I?" seem to smack rather of a reminder of neglected social duty on the part of the listener in his having omitted to include the request in his closing phatic communion comments.

Lastly, terms of direct address seem to be used more frequently in the marginal phases of interaction than in the medial, business phase. The type of address term chosen in the closing phase acts as an index of the speaker's view of such factors as the level of intimacy which he thinks will characterize future encounters between the two participants.

As a summary statement of the functions of phatic communion in the closing phase of interactions, one could say that two principal functions are served. Firstly, it allows the participants to achieve a cooperative parting, in which any feelings of rejection by the person being left can be assuaged by appropriate reassurance from the person leaving. Secondly, it serves to consolidate the relationship between the two participants, by means of behavior which emphasizes the enjoyable quality of the encounter, the mutual esteem in which the participants hold each other, the promise of a continuation of the relationship, the assertion of mutual solidarity, and the announcement of a continuing consensus for the shape of encounters in the future.

GENERAL CONCLUSIONS ABOUT PHATIC COMMUNION IN MARGINAL PHASES OF INTERACTION

It may have become clear from the discussion above of phatic communion and associated behavior in the two margins of interactions that two broad functions are being served. One is the establishment and consolidation of the interpersonal relationship between the two participants. The other is the comfortable management of the transition from noninteraction to full interaction, and the transition from interaction back to noninteraction. General conclusions about the purpose of phatic communion can be focused on these two areas separately.

PHATIC COMMUNION AND INTERACTIONAL CONSENSUS

The most important thing to be said about the establishment and consolidation of the interpersonal relationship between the two participants is that it is achieved by indexical communication. That is, the claims being staked by the speaker, and the conclusions being drawn by the listener, are all concerned with the communication of the identity and attributes of the interactants, and with their psychosocial relationship. A second important comment is that the behavioral acts used to stake the claims and as evidence in drawing the conclusions consist not only of linguistic behavior (although this has been the primary focus of this paper) and of nonlinguistic aspects of speech, but consist also of nonvocal behavior such as posture, body orientation, gesture, facial expression and eye contacts. So phatic communion, in Malinowski's narrow sense of a "mere exchange of words" plays only a part, though perhaps a large part, in a communicative function served by many different aspects of behavior, not just by one's use of spoken language alone.

In considering the indexical processes of establishing and consolidating the interpersonal relationship between the two participants, many striking parallels emerge from a comparison of the functions of phatic communion in the opening and the closing phases of the interaction. Where the opening phase explores indexical characteristics of the relationship, the closing phase consolidates them by restatement. Where the opening phase serves to propitiate potential hostility, the closing phase assuages potential feelings of rejection. Where the opening phase establishes solidarity, the closing phase consolidates and promises continuance of solidarity. As an overall comment, where the principal function of the opening phase seems to be the attempt to reach a working consensus for the remainder of the interaction, the chief function of the closing phase seems to be to announce a continuing provisional consensus for future interactions. If this is a valid comment, then it makes phatic communion and associated behavior a most important social and psychological instrument, in that the cumulative consensus about a relationship reached as the result of repeated encounters between the two participants constitutes the essence of that relationship. Skill in managing the behavioral resources of phatic communion thus becomes not the triviality dismissively referred to as small talk, but a very basic skill essential to a major part of the psychosocial transactions that make up daily life.

Finally, to comment on an area that will be relevant also to the discussion of the transitional functions of phatic communion, it is interesting to note the functional differences between the opening and closing phases, as opposed to their similarities. In some aspects of the behavior characteristic of the marginal phases, there is a sense in which the two phases look in different directions, so to speak. To some degree, the opening phase looks inwards to the oncoming interaction, while the closing phase looks outwards, as it were, to the resumption of social life outside the momentary relationship of the encounter. It is as if the encounter constitutes a transitory microcosm with an ephemeral existence within the macrocosm of the wider social experience of the two participants. This is certainly appropriate in a limited way, but of course each participant brings aspects of his wider "macrocosmic" social identity to the momentary encounter; and some aspects of the closing phase, in its consolidatory function, are partly retrospective, and reiterative of the recent "microcosmic" shared experience.

PHATIC COMMUNION AND RITES OF PASSAGE

It has been stated above that phatic communion occurs primarily at the initial and final margins of social interactions, and that one of the chief functions it serves is the facilitation of psychologically comfortable transition from silence to interaction, and then from interaction to silence again. The point has also been made that phatic communion is achieved through stereotyped patterns of behavior, and that indulgence in such behavior is almost universal in a very wide range of different types of daily interactions. It seems reasonable to call such obligatory stereotyped behavior CEREMONIAL, or RITUAL, behavior. The study of ritual behavior has been the province of anthropology, and in this final section I should like to look briefly at the characteristics of the rituals of phatic communion from an anthropological perspective, concentrating on the observation that phatic communion is essentially a ceremony involved with transitions from one social state to another.

Van Gennep's concept of rites of passage remains influential to the present day (e.g. Gluckman 1962). He was primarily concerned with major transitions of social identity:

... a man's life comes to be made up of a succession of stages with similar ends and beginnings: birth, social puberty, marriage, fatherhood, advancement to a higher class, occupational specialisation, and death. For every one of these events there are ceremonies whose essential purpose is to enable the individual to pass from one defined position to another which is equally well defined (Van Gennep 1960: 3).

He divided rites of passage into rites of transition, separation or incorporation, and saw them as relevant to "sacred" and "profane" states. I wish to make no explicit appeal here to the notion of social encounters as "sacred" events, entry into and exit from which need to be ceremonially ritualized, but I would like to adopt his concept of a rite of passage, and apply it to the much smaller-scale ceremonies of everyday conversational interaction, as distinct from the life crisis situations to which the concept is customarily applied. I wish merely to suggest that phatic communion can be usefully described as a ceremony functioning as a rite of passage, easing and signaling the transitions to and from conversational interactions. The rationale for such ritual ceremonies will be passed over here without comment.

To think of phatic communion as ritual behavior, and to discard the metaphor of the "sacred" as not useful in this area is to follow Firth (1972: 3).

If by ritual is meant symbolic action relating to the sacred, the term is inappropriate for the formal behaviour of greeting and parting. But in the broader sense of formal procedures of a communicative but arbitrary kind, having the effect of controlling or regularising a social situation, the term is relevant.

He further justifies the notion of such behavior as being "ritual" in a passage broadly sympathetic to many of the attitudes expressed in this article:

Greeting and parting is often treated as if it were the spontaneous emotional reaction to the coming together or separation of people, carrying overtly its own social message. But sociological observation suggests ... that for the most part it is highly conventionalised .... In a broad sense greeting and parting behaviour may be termed RITUAL since it follows PATTERNED

ROUTINES; it is a system of SIGNS that convey other than overt messages; ... and it has ADAPTIVE VALUE in facilitating social relations (1972: 29-30). In the terms of this article, the "signs" involve both linguistic and non-linguistic acts, and the "other than overt" messages carried by the signs are the indexical messages which manage and control the interpersonal relationship between the participants.

Inspired by Parsons (1916: 41), Firth coined the term TELECTIC rites "from the Greek concept of putting off the old and putting on the new, for such behaviour for greeting and parting, where the major stimulation is provided by the arrival or departure of a person from the social scene" (1972: 3). This seems an apt term for the ceremonial transition from the broader social macrocosm to the momentary microcosm of the encounter, and also for the ceremonial transition from the recent shared microcosm to the readopted macrocosm, if one sees the transitions as being essentially from a preceding state to a succeeding state. But if one views the closing phase as functioning partly to restore the participants to their own independent social worlds outside the immediacy of the encounter, then this transition would be better characterized as "putting off the new and taking up the old again." We might therefore suggest that many of the transitional ceremonies of the opening phase could be called PROLEPTIC rites, to emphasize the taking on of a momentary identity specific to the current encounter, and that many of the transitional ceremonies of the closing phase could be called ANALEPTIC rites, to emphasize the resumption of identities appropriate to the broader social macrocosm outside and largely independent of the encounter and its events.

A characteristic proleptic rite would be the use, between strangers, of an opening phatic communion token of the type which stakes particular indexical claims about the participant's view of his social status relative to the other participant. A characteristic analeptic rite would be the use by a participant of a phatic communion token of the type "Tell Jeanie I was asking after her," where the use of the past tense implies that the speaker is in effect anticipating the termination of the encounter, looking back on it from the future, as it were, and "re-placing" himself and the other participant in the broader web of social relationships that contribute to the definition of their macrocosmic identities. Another analeptic rite would be the use of the type of phatic communion token that justifies termination of the encounter by appeal to an authority external to the speaker's control and springing from obligations in the macrocosmic background to the encounter. An example of this would be "I must go off and finish my shopping."

One final point needs to be made about phatic communion as a rite of passage, and that is that a given act of phatic communion may often serve many ritual functions simultaneously. Thus the token just mentioned, "Tell Jeanie I was asking after her," can be seen as acting not only as an analeptic rite, but also as one or more of the following: a rite of transition, marking incipient termination of the encounter; a rite of separation, as a ceremonial of parting; and as a rite of incorporation, ceremonially reiterating the fact of solidarity through a reminder of shared acquaintance with absent members of some acknowledged group.

CONCLUSION

Two general conclusions have emerged about the function of phatic communion. The first is that it serves to establish and consolidate the interpersonal relationship between the two participants. The other is that it eases the transitions to and from interaction. The single most important detailed conclusion is that phatic communion is a complex part of a ritual, highly skilled mosaic of communicative behavior whose function is to facilitate the management of interpersonal relationships.

The information exchanged between the participants in this communicative process is not primarily referential information, but rather is indexical information about aspects of the participants' social identity relevant to structuring the interactional consensus of the present and future encounters. The function of phatic communion thus goes beyond the creation, in Malinowski's phrase, of "ties of union": it certainly does serve to establish such broad ties in that the tokens of phatic communion are tokens exchanged in the ritual transactions of psychosocial acceptance, but it also provides the participants with a subtle tool for use in staking indexical claims which shape and constrain their detailed relationship in the crucial marginal phases of encounters when their psychological comfort is most at risk.

REFERENCES

ABERCROMBIE, D.
  1956 *Problems and principles.* London: Longmans.
  1967 *Elements of general phonetics.* Edinburgh: Edinburgh University Press.
ARGYLE, M., A. KENDON
  1967 "The experimental analysis of social performance," in *Advances in experimental social psychology.* Edited by L. Berkowitz, 55–98. New York: Academic Press.

FEIBLEMAN, J. K.
1946 *An introduction to Peirce's philosophy.* New York: Harper and Brothers.

FIRTH, R.
1972 "Verbal and bodily rituals of greeting and parting," in *The interpretation of ritual.* Edited by J. S. La Fontaine, 1–38. London: Tavistock Publications.

GLUCKMAN, M., editor
1962 *Essays on the ritual of social relations.* Manchester: Manchester University Press.

GOFFMAN, E.
1959 *The presentation of self in everyday life.* New York: Doubleday.

HALL, E. T.
1959 *The silent language.* New York: Doubleday.
1963 A system for the notation of proxemic behavior. *American Anthropologist* 65:1003–1026.
1964 "Silent assumptions in social communication," in *Disorders of communication.* Edited by D. McK. Rioch and E. A. Weinstein, 41–55. Baltimore: Association for Research in Nervous and Mental Diseases.
1966 *The hidden dimension.* New York: Doubleday.

HAYAKAWA, S. I.
1952 *Language in thought and action.* New York: Harcourt, Brace and World.

LAVER, J.
1968 Voice quality and indexical information. *British Journal of Disorders of Communication* 3:43–54.

LAVER, J., S. HUTCHESON, editors
1972 *Communication in face to face interaction.* Harmondsworth: Penguin.

LYONS, J.
1968 *Introduction to theoretical linguistics.* London: Cambridge University Press.
1970 *New horizons in linguistics.* Harmondsworth: Penguin.

MORRIS, C. W.
1938 "Foundations of the theory of signs," in *Foundations of the unity of science.* Edited by O. Neurath, R. Carnap and C. W. Morris, 1:77–138. Chicago: University of Chicago Press.

OGDEN, C. K., I. A. RICHARDS
1923 *The meaning of meaning.* London: Routledge and Kegan Paul.

PARSONS, E. C.
1916 Holding back in crisis ceremonialism. *American Anthropologist* 18:41–52.

SCHEFLEN, A. E.
1964 The significance of posture in communication systems. *Psychiatry* 27:316–331.

SEBEOK, T. S., A. S. HAYES, M. C. BATESON, editors
1964 *Approaches to semiotics.* The Hague: Mouton.

SOMMER, R.
1969 *Personal space.* New York: Prentice-Hall.
VAN GENNEP, A.
1960 *The rites of passage.* Translated by M. K. Vizedom and G. L. Caffee. London: Routledge and Kegan Paul. Original edition 1909.

PART FOUR

Behavior in Interaction and Linguistic Theory

The Correlation of Gestures and Verbalizations in First Language Acquisition

WALBURGA VON RAFFLER ENGEL

Before the "Chomskyan revolution" the language development of children was explored painstakingly and patiently, accompanied by explanations of context and situation. It was also customary to take into account the interpersonal relationship in which it occurred. A number of learning theories were formulated even though none of them proved fully satisfactory. Nor was there posited a sure unique way to explain the balance between what is innate and what is acquired in cognition, perception, and language within the child's maturational curve.

Given the complexity of the task, research in first language acquisition moved ahead tentatively and at a slow pace. No linguist claimed to have fully discovered how language developed. Slow, dedicated research efforts are not glamorous and were not to the taste of the flamboyant generation of the sixties. At that time graduate students followed the flashy road of "writing grammars" out of a few fragments of children's speech. To simplify matters, the researchers chose as a point of departure the period when the child's utterances already began resembling actual words of adult language. These first words were equated with the full or partial meaning of their adult equivalents. That a child's "word" could have a totally different meaning from the corresponding value in the speech of adults was not even considered. The inclusion of situational clues was not part of the methodology. Natural language was treated as if it were mathematics. Whatever did not fit the scheme was discarded as "marginal data."

The worship of elegance and neatness on a + and — chart did not allow for real life occurrences, such as the one told to me by the mother of a second-grader. The school teacher wanted to know from the child what she was afraid of and the child replied "of it." "What is 'it'?" the teacher asked and the child answered that, indeed, the real terror of "it" was that she could not figure out what "it" was. "It" was either a punishment or a disease, but most likely a dangerous monster which would "get her" if she misbehaved. She had wondered many a night what this "it" was that "she would get." It turned out that when the child did something wrong, her mother used to yell at her, "You'll get it!" In the English language "it" is a pronoun and "you'll get it" is an idiom.

Another family lived in a section of town where an airplane usually flew over their house at dinner time. The child would become greatly excited and poke her mother, trying to direct her attention to the sky. This mother liked sedate dinners and would try to calm the child by telling her, "It's nothing, nothing." Finally, when one day the family went to the airport, the child pointed to all those planes and exclaimed: "Mother, so many nothings."

The technical term for the children's use of "it" and "nothing" is "anecdotal references." The "serious" linguistic journals in the United States have no room of such "anecdotes" and many linguists are openly skeptical of the value of data that have not beeen gathered by some "scientific method." The linguist, seemingly, is now allowed to observe a natural situation in order to extrapolate the objectives on which he wants to concentrate. That, after all, is what Piaget did in Geneva. Rather than look out for what he wants to test subsequently, the "modern" linguist must delineate his objectives right from the outset. And in the recent past, he was even supposed to apply one and only one "rigorous" method to his testing procedure.

Once the goals are defined and the method is applied, things do change. The researcher then has the greatest freedom. The refinement of the methodology becomes an end rather than a means. Perfecting one's method, of course, is an excellent thing. But it cannot be done at the expense of one's research objectives — unless the method, not the investigation of facts, is the objective of one's research. If such is the purpose of a work, this ought to be stated in advance.

The naturalness, and even the veracity, of the testing situation have been discounted or, at best, relegated to a mere surface manifestation; while, on the other hand, it is considered scholarly to invent rules for the sole purpose of dealing with imaginary difficulties. The above "it" out of its context, and "nothing," out of its situation, could not be correctly interpreted. Meaning is not interpretative. To say that it is generative holds little that is new to the non-transformationalist.

The generative–transformational fad of disambiguating sentences *in vacuo* originated in the attempt to create "deep structures" in adult language and was carried over into the analysis of child language. Nobody denies that language has rules, just as there are behavioral laws which govern all other aspects of human interface. To establish rules for the development of human language without consideration of its communicative function is like describing the behavior of fish outside of water. To formulate rules for the analysis of language outside the span of human memory and the workings of the human brain is not describing human language at all. Somehow the early transformationalists equated the child's brain with a computer.

And somehow the monologue and the statement are still taken as basic even though the greatest amount of verbalization occurs in dialogue. Surely, the child's earliest verbal manifestations occur in a social interaction which is visual as well as verbal. Telephone conversations and story writing come much later. If the visual mode were not part of language acquisition, the blind would talk as early as normal children. I am referring not only to the visibility of referents but also to the fact that body language accompanies verbal language. In the works by the generativist school, cognition and language were also sloppily equated. The learning process was not under scrutiny because language was assumed to be innate. Nativism was a convenient cover term, left fairly vague and never scientifically documented. As no learning theory was capable of fully explaining the process of language acquisition, Chomsky jumped to the conclusion that language was simply not learned at all. The generative–transformationalist linguist fought the straw assertion by all the linguists of earlier schools that nothing in man's *faculté de langage* was inborn. In this manner this school created the absurd dichotomy between "empiricists" and "rationalists." Nobody bothered to read Descartes or to distinguish him from Kant and Plato.

Nor did transformational grammar make any clear distinction between langage acquisition and speech programming. Competence was one more term used to lump together two basically different processes as well as the differences among individuals, adults and children alike.

Discussing whether language in its overt form derives from syntax or from semantics touches upon only a minor part of the central problem of language acquisition. It seems to me that the latter cannot be understood without keeping in mind the integrated fashion in which verbal and kinetic behavior manifest themselves in the speech act. Most universals are trivial and this may be one of them. It may have been its triviality that kept it from being researched for so long. The obvious is taken for granted.

Greenberg had looked for universals since the early fifties; and language, rather than languages, has been the goal of linguistics since its beginnings. The past ten years of sweeping deductions from an all–encompassing theory have produced little of lasting usefulness. In order to induce the general laws of language acquisition finally, we are now back to experimental research.

In this paper I shall limit my small contribution to a series of considerations on the relationship of language and gestures in children. Given my limited sample, my results are not conclusive and are principally intended to indicate some additional facets of the new approach to some of the problems in the study of developmental psycholinguistics.

All children seem to share the ability to develop language in the midst of a large amount of non-verbal communication. This applies both to the acquisition of passive language (understanding) and active language (verbalization).

Wundt believed that in the infant gestures precede verbalization. In my opinion these two factors appear together. Not only do they originate at the same time; they are probably complementary. Infants three to nine months old will point with their finger while uttering their carrier-sound.

I shall not enter here into a discussion of Bernsteinian theory, as this is beyond the scope of the present paper. Participatory observations conducted in 1968 by a student of mine in a racially mixed day-care center have revealed, however, that consistently the children who were more vocal were also the ones most active in gesturing. It does not seem, nevertheless, that the complementarity of verbal and kinetic behavior should preclude that a compensatory value might be attributed to one or the other of these complementary aspects by emphasizing the one to the detriment of the other. Normal babies of deaf mute parentage will eventually stop the vocal part of crying and intensify tears and jerkings.

It is controversial to establish when language, or even pre-language, can be said to commence. I shall here mention only briefly that obstetricians are well aware that they can calm an infant with a kindly stroke of their hand even immediately after birth, and they rarely do this without talking to the infant.

Babies will cry louder and kick more vigorously when their need for food is late in being met. To classify such behavior as instinctive reflex does not exclude its being a universal phonokinetic mode of communication. Zazzo has demonstrated that a two-week old infant may be capable of conscious imitation. It is possible that the customary disassociation of gestures and sound in the analysis of infant vocalization has led us to underestimate the communicative power of the human newborn.

The period when children produce words that have a clearly defineable counterpart in the corresponding language of adults is less controversial. It also lends itself very easily to examples in support of my theory of the synchrony of phono-kinetics in language acquisition.

First I shall cite the instances reported in the literature where bye-bye is listed among the first words of children between one and two years of age. These are American children, and in the American culture, as in most other cultures as well, adults may say bye-bye to each other without waving their hand. But rarely, if at all, do they when talking to small children, or do older siblings when talking to their younger brothers, omit the gesture.

My own son whose communicative behavior I recorded very carefully during his first year of life, said ča (for ciao, the Italian equivalent of "bye-bye") with a faint gesture of the hand when he was seven months old. No other language-specific word was produced by him before he was nine months old.

What is striking beyond the early and cross–culturally frequent occurrence of "bye-bye" in children is the fact that adults and older children do not omit the kinetic component of the speech act when interfacing with small children. That "mothers' language" is following certain instinctive patterns has been demonstrated beyond doubt. I want to suggest that we also study the pattern of "mothers' kinesics."

Another feature that needs investigating is the onset of lying in children. Infants understand neither lies, sarcasm, nor facetious jokes. My son acquired one of these notions when he was two-and-a-half years old. With an ironic grin on my face, I sometimes used to hide an object, telling him that I was not going to give it to him, and then give it to him right away. At the outset he did not consider this much of a joke and was perturbed. Later on, the child consistently grimaced when saying the opposite of what he meant. He seemed to deduce that a certain type of facial mimicry was the equivalent of a certain form of negation.

At two years of age my son was capable of imitating discourse intonation but could not yet repeat all the verbal components of an utterance. When I became somehow impatient I used to sing the little ditty "Bisogna, bisogna aver pazienza!" When the child felt that he had overtaxed my patience, he would hum the melody of the ditty with exactly the same shrug of the shoulders and slight widening of the arms which accompanied my own sing-song.

One American child whose language development we followed, carefully taking notes of the necessary situational annotations, was the son of a student of mine in Nashville, Tennessee. His parents used to stretch out their right hand and say to him as well as to other children: "How big you are! That big." From ten months on, the child would stretch out his hand in the same manner and say, keeping the intonational contour of the whole model statement: "How big! Big."

Most illustrative is the behavior of the three-year-old son of a colleague of mine at the University of Florence, Italy. The child distinguished two homophones entirely by facial mimicry. He had one word *kappa* for both Italian *scarpa* [shoe] and *schiaffo* [slap]. *Kappa* in the meaning of "slap" was consistently accompanied by the same stern facial expression his father displayed when telling the child that he was preparing to administer this kind of punishment.

The intimacy of the acquisition of language tied in with the acquisition of gestures is shown by the case of a multi-retarded child also having poor eyesight. The child's caretaker occasionally adds "hm" at the end of her utterances with a slight sidewise bend of the head and an upwards movement of the shoulders. The child does exactly the same thing, with the identical intonation and facial mimicry.

This anecdote demonstrates very neatly the correspondence between verbalization and kinesics. Much more research needs to be done in this area if we wish to distinguish paralinguistic gestures from instinctive gestures and if we want to divide the former into word gestures and discourse gestures, not to mention discovering the universals of paralinguistics, or rather the extent to which such gestures can be termed culture-free.

Somewhat more attention has been given in the literature to the kinetic behavior at the beginning and end periods of the speech act. Very little, however, is known about this in children, and nothing at all about its developmental sequence has been studied. One student at Hebrew University in Jerusalem has observed that her eleven-month-old child would look at her mother's face and would keep quiet when she found that face unresponsive. When her mother was smiling the child would start vocalizing "aba," "mama," "dada," "ada."

A good insight into the relationship of verbalization and kinesics should be gained by observing bilingual children. The problem, nevertheless, is greatly complicated by the fact that gestures seem to be more part of culture than of language. Language acquisition, in any case, cannot be studied outside of culture.

The data presented in this paper are not sufficiently conclusive to support a theory of the complementarity and the synchronous acquisition of language and kinesics. I do hope, however, that they are sufficient to suggest that an investigation of the question is warranted.

ADDENDUM[1]

The issue of what is inborn and what is learned is indeed central to research in child development, including the acquisition of language and kinesics. Chomsky has the merit of having drawn attention to the controversy of nature versus nurture beyond the boundaries of educators and psychologists. Where I disagree with him is in his approach to this old problem. He created a whole system of linguistic analysis and postulated that his particular theory of syntax corresponded to an innate schema, a view which has not been supported by empirical evidence. Focusing entirely on language, Chomsky failed to correlate language and cognition and to look at language as a form of communicative behavior which, therefore, had to be correlated with kinesics. I believe that the data support the Piagetian view that cognition precedes language and that language develops in a close tie with other forms of communication. The auditory and oral channels work together with the visual mode in the child's attempt to gain understanding and, consequently, to express himself.

One two-year-old boy whom I studied several years ago used both "upstairs" and "downstairs" with the meaning of "on the other side of the stairs." When he eventually became aware that the two words were not synonymous, he would act out the situation and watch his mother's reaction to his saying the one word or the other until he was sure that he understood and used each word correctly. The child manifested an innate desire to learn and was actively involved in that task.

The process of language acquisition is one of listening and observing on the receptive side. On the productive side it consists of trial and error in speaking and acting out. Chomsky has listed WHAT is acquired and, given that there is a certain regularity in the sequence of acquisition of a number of linguistic features, he has concluded that these features are innate. He has constructed a hypothetical network to connect some of these features and asserts that the human brain comes equipped with this network in a way similar to a computer input.

[1] This addendum is in response to the comments and questions on the original paper given at the Congress session.

I am inclined to believe that what is inborn is cognition. Cognition determines the child's approach to learning in general and to language in particular. To find out what syntactic and other linguistic features are acquired at certain maturational periods I have been looking for HOW they are acquired. It is not the WHAT that explains the HOW but the HOW that explains the WHAT. In conclusion, it seems to me that the way language is acquired is inborn. In addition, the way language is used seems to be hereditary. I made a statement in 1964 (to which I still hold) that degree of loquatiousness and other styles of verbalization are transmitted from parent to child. A presentation by Karen Fischer at the International Symposium on First Language Acquisition in Florence, Italy, in 1972 has produced excellent documentation on the issue through her research with fraternal and identical twins. Grammar, lexicon, phonology, and meaning are not universal and are neither inborn nor hereditary.

In my opinion the same holds true for kinesic behavior, but nobody has yet undertaken conclusive research in that area. As I see it, a formulation of the basic problems in the acquisition of kinesics (excluding purely instinctive gestures from that field of study) involves the following, which do parallel the acquisition of verbal language:

1. The use of gestural means for communication is universal and innate. It remains to see if it is species-specific to man. It is possible that in man the kinetic use of specific parts of the human body (such as the head, the trunk, the hands, etc.) corresponds to the three main divisions of Osgood's semantic differential.

2. The amount and expanse of kinetic movement may be hereditary by race. In most instances the same is reinforced by culture.

3. The specific direction of each kinetic movement is culture-bound and transmitted through learning. The learning process takes place by imitation and through teaching. The proportion of these two means varies by culture and by class and socioeconomic group.

The above three points can be illustrated by an example:

1. All people count with the help of their fingers. Right-handed persons count on their right hand and left-handed individuals make use of their left hand. This distinction holds true in most cases I have observed, but it is complicated by the fact that some persons use both hands, touching the outstretched fingers with the index of the other hand.

2. The speed of the movement of the fingers and the possible involvement of the lower part of the hand in some kind of motion seems to differ among racial groups. My observations on wrist movement in counting are not conclusive.

3. Some cultures start counting by stretching out the index finger while others begin with the thumb. It is most confusing to Europeans when Americans indicate the number two by means of the index and the middle finger. Because they expect to see the thumb and the index finger for the number two, they sometimes interpret this sign as the number three.

Given that kinesics and language can be viewed as essentially similar in what is innate and what is acquired in each of these divisions of human communicative behavior, the next question then is how do they interact during the developmental stages. This will be the concern of my comments here. (The description of the interlocking usage of kinesics and verbal behavior has been dealt with by the other papers in this volume and I have learned very much from them).

Language can be analyzed in its levels of phonology, lexicon, sentence and discourse syntax, and semantics. I disagree with Chomsky who does not accord priority of development to any of these levels. In a sketchy theory I outlined in Prague in 1970 I suggested that language develops by levels of abstraction. Children combine interpretative semantics (e.g. word order) and generative semantics (contextual meaning clues) in their attempt to understand what they hear. A theory of development by levels of abstraction facilitates the formulation of an explanatory theory of the verbal-kinetic interaction in the child.

Transformational-generative theory has much oversimplified the whole issue of communicative development. Sociolinguistics and psycholinguistics have been too neatly separated; and within psycholinguistics the visual mode has been severed from speech perception. In the expressive domain it has become increasingly clear that the oral mode ties in closely with kinesics. Small children say "thank you" when receiving and when giving an object. For them the meaning of "thank you" is associated with the transaction of an object.

By the end of the third month of life in the human infant a profound physiological change is taking place in the vocal organs. The change is approximately completed at nine months of age. At exactly these same dates in the baby's life one also notices definite changes in gestural behavior.

The same developmental parallelism holds in respect to brain lateralization. At birth it seems that vocalization and kinesics are kinesthetically linked together. It is not conceivable that a baby will cry harder and kick less when he signals hunger or boredom. An exhausted infant may still cry in pain but this is not a positive act of communication. Only after lateralization sets in are we able to observe vocal and gestural behavior as units to be analyzed separately. After the process of lateralization is complete at about two years of age, children can be seen talking with only a minimum of body motion. I realize that talking of lateralization is an oversimplification and that neurologists are still far from the truth. Neurolinguists also have not done much research into kinesics as opposed to grasping motions.

In the verbal-kinetic development of children, the separation of speech-preparatory and speech-accompanying gestures emerges only gradually. In the earliest stages speech and gesture seem to begin together. This is another area where research is much needed. A grant application I made not too long ago was promptly turned down.

To conclude my remarks, permit me to say once more that generative-transformational grammar has contributed very little to our understanding of the communicative development of the human infant. A totally different approach is called for.

Paralanguage, Communication, and Cognition

RICHARD M. HARRIS and DAVID RUBINSTEIN

According to a well-known axiom of modern linguistics, speech is the primary "embodiment" of language, and writing is a secondary medium derived from it. By this deliberate reversal of the valued priorities of the traditional grammarians, structural linguists of the twentieth century sought to put linguistic "reality" in its proper perspective.[1] The "classical" fallacy" (Lyons 1968: 9), in a tradition that goes back to the ancient Greeks, had been to ascribe an absolute measure of importance to the written language (as reflected in the highest forms of literature) to the dereliction of spoken vernaculars.

While linguists had convincingly cast off writing's traditional mantle of supremacy, most of them had failed to perceive a more subtle bias which the earlier philosophy had also embodied: the assumption that words (more particularly, morphemes) and their patterned combinations are always, *a priori*, the PRIMARY bearers of meaningful concepts. Generations of linguists have accepted this notion unquestioningly, and have been governed by its apparent logic. Today, with but few exceptions, we witness further extensions of this basic line of approach.[2] This

We wish here to acknowledge a debt of gratitude to Mrs. Susan Gould whose research assistance and cooperation in preparing this manuscript made it suitable for publication.

[1] After all, so the argument goes, in the course of human history man was a speaker long before he mastered the art of writing. Most societies, even today, make do without written conventions, while there is no social group of men which does not communicate effectively through the medium of sound. Even the child first masters the forms and patterns of his spoken language, and only later learns a written representation based on his previous knowledge of his language.
[2] Only relatively recently have linguists begun to go beyond the grammatical analysis of isolated utterances to explore, among other things, the extensive covariation between

overemphasis on the importance of the VERBAL character of spoken utterances underestimates the importance of vocal effects, as well as other systems of human signaling. This could be called the MODERN FALLACY.

In reality, man lives in a world conceptualized not only by language, but by all "socially organized channels for transceiving information," as Goffman (1969, Preface: ix) has phrased it. These include — in addition to words — facial and body modes, tones of voice, space regulation, tactile, and (as yet unstudied) olfactory systems, as well. Each one of these "knowledge processes" is, from a cultural point of view, an internalized system of symbolic representation, exhibiting a high degree of internal organization, and representing largely a product of social learning. Not only are these various modalities shaped by cultural convention, but they are further subject to social and psychological requirements. Taken together, they provide the "normal" individual with the ability to make his way smoothly in the complex flow of social life.

In any conversational encounter, often the flashpoint is the WAY things are said, not the things THEMSELVES. So much of social interaction is wrapped up in things FELT, rather than in things REASONED. These familiar facts have prompted much discussion among philosophers of language concerning whether "emotive" speech is, in fact, cognitive as such, or in the same way as, verbal speech. With the central focus usually on words, tone of voice and body motion appear only marginally important, as qualifying the "central" message. Words are deemed "cognition," while "expressive" behaviors are "affect." It will be argued that both types of systems contribute direct and significant information, but of essentially different kinds.

From a developmental standpoint, the child's emerging knowledge of his world is a function not only of linguistically mediated experience, but is the product of many "inputs" and cognitions. The role of VOICE in cognitive growth, particularly, has scarcely been studied, but represents a crucial, although neglected, aspect of child development in general, and first-language acquisition in particular.

In this article we will first try to examine the limitations of the older approach to communication, and go on to discuss some of the sources

---

social stratification and linguistic differences (a notable example of the upsurge of academic interest in this area is the recent launching of a new journal with the title, *Language in Society*). But even so, the emphasis remains restricted to matters of grammar and lexicon. The time must not be far off when the systematics of socially motivated variation of a paralinguistic, kinesic, and proxemic nature will be part of a FULL description of a communicative event.

that vitalize the new, broader perspective incorporating VARIETIES of human signaling competence. Then we will focus on the dimensions of speech sound — language and paralanguage — comparing the character of their symbolism and the experiential domains served by each, respectively. Finally, we will argue for the cognitive status of paralinguistic functioning and outline some of the implications that this capacity seems to have for the growing child's acquisition of intelligence.

THE DIMENSIONALITY OF HUMAN COMMUNICATION

Man's increasing awareness of himself and his environment is surely one of the characteristic traits of this century. Perhaps never before in human history has man's social life — the culturally patterned ways in which he initiates, sustains, and regulates his relations with others — been the object of such intense, widespread interest and systematic investigation. Nor is there any precedent in history for the level of technological sophistication enjoyed by our age. Riding the wave of a continuing revolution in technology, social and behavioral scientists are coming to depend more and more on newly available extensions of the ear and eye in their study of human behavior. With the aid of modern film projectors and videotape recorders — now deemed indispensable research tools — it is possible today to capture and record many of the unconscious, fleeting movements we make with our eyes, head, face, and body, which give form and significant purpose to social interaction.

This instrumentation gives us a more permanent record of the visible aspects of human transactions, which can be set aside and reviewed at the analyst's leisure, slowed down for more detailed viewing, or stopped (as in "stills") for gross or microanalysis. Similarly, researchers are using improved quality of audiotape and equipment to record and analyze the subtle nuances of tone of voice by which we manage the impressions we give off to others and thereby structure our interpersonal relationships. These and other mechanical innovations have provided a whole new set of self-perceptions from which students of man hope to gain increased understanding of the nature and interdependence of social, cultural, and psychological factors in human RELATEDNESS.

The earlier traditional psycholinguistic model of man portrayed him as "the good talker," whose willful verbalizations were for the purpose of providing or obtaining NEW information, and constituted the "heart" of the communication act. His observed modulations of voice and movements of face and body were viewed as mere "side effects" or "noise," whose role was to modify the central verbal message. As long as this linear, unidimensional conception of man was dominant, we saw little beyond the gross topography of human communicative behavior. Man's deeper dimensions remained hidden from sight. He appeared as something of a cardboard character who communicates TO (but is not engaged in communication WITH) his fellows in intermittent, stop/start fashion by way of a series of stimulus/response chains. This outlook construed silence (lack of vocalization) as the absence of any message. This earlier "point of view" is discussed more fully in contrast to the newer "integrative" approach to human communication, by Birdwhistell (1970, Chapter 11).

During the last two decades, a major shift has taken place. The static "new information" model has largely given way to a broader, more dynamic perspective — the "integrative model" which gives theoretical recognition to the full range and complexity of human signaling behavior. We now can directly observe that, although not in full consciousness, man DOES communicate accurate and consistent information through all channels available to him. The pioneering work of Birdwhistell (1966) on body motion, Hall (1966) on "interpersonal" space, and McQuown (1957) on voice modulation has shown the learned, shared, and symbolic nature of these codes. Their findings have generated a new body of observations of "nonverbal"[3] behavior requiring a broader conception of "communication," and a greater appreciation of its richness. We apparently CONCEPTUALIZE emotional states, motivation, and other "felt" aspects of a relationship from the way people vocalize and move. Because these behavior systems vary in their perception and use from society to society, they represent significant cross-cultural variables, which are of great interest to anthropologists (see Watson 1970).

Dynamically conceived, social interaction brings into play a complex coordination of all such instrumentalities; and communication is thus a continuous, multi-channel process. Goffman, in a series of essays (1959, 1963, 1972), has brought to attention and illustrated a number of our "ritualistic" requirements of conduct in social encounters. While a speaker may "keep close tabs" on his words, he is less able consciously to control his other signaling behaviors. This is why in face-to-face encounters, we re-establish eye contact with the listener at periodic intervals in order to check up on how we are "coming across," whether we are being perceived as we wish to be, or whether certain adjustments

---

[3] This unhappy term enjoys increasing currency in the literature, for lack of a better one. We have tried to use it sparingly in our discussion, and have striven for a gain in clarity by usually coupling it with "nonsegmental." Some improvement in terminology is certainly desirable here. Until such time, "nonverbal" is to be placed in quotes because indicating what it is NOT does not yet tell us what it IS.

in our self-presentation are in order. All this points to the fact that in our casual interpersonal life, language is but one of an array of implementation systems, all finely coordinated so that, at any moment, at least one is in continuous operation. We may, for example, stop talking, but we continue to indicate, by our posture (Scheflen 1964), gaze-direction (Kendon 1967), and physiognomy (Ekman et al. 1972), that we are still participants in the immediate transaction at hand.

The continuous nature of the interactive process serves the purpose of continually providing the answers to three fundamentally important existential questions: "Who am I?" "Where am I?" and "Where will I go?" By the systematically patterned ways in which he handles his voice, body, and microspace, a speaker (or major actor) is continuously sending out a signal which identifies the culture of which he is a member, the subculture with which he is affiliated, and the social "class" to which he belongs. In much the same way, these patterned behaviors act as psychosocial indicators of how one is experiencing a relationship. In similar fashion, these shared behavior displays tend to disclose the interpersonal expectancies of participants in an interaction. Thus, man has built up, through cultural evolution, a complex network of co-systems or subassemblies within the symbolic process which enable him to engage predictably in patterned relationships, to be able to "read" his partner and be "read" by him.

Condon (1970) has shown that the research orientation in this growing field has increasingly involved microsegmentation of sound films of human behavior and necessitated microtranscription of body motion, voice modulation, and space conduct. As awareness has grown that the "flow" of information is "differentiated" along various "channels," some investigators have begun to explore the interrelations between channels and the nature of their messages. Key (1972), for example, is concerned with the interrelations of verbal and vocal structures. Ekman and Friesen (1969) have studied relationships between gesture and speech. Condon (1967) and Condon and Ogston (1966) have studied how body motion is organized and patterned in relation to speech. Similarly, Kendon (1972) has analyzed certain relationships between visual and auditory behavior. He has also provided valuable information on the functions of gaze-direction in social interaction (1967). On more than one occasion as well, Birdwhistell has commented that the most successful work in kinesics has derived from attempts to study linguistic/kinesic relations.

The vital question of how paralinguistic effects are integrated with the rest of linguistic and nonlinguistic structure raises an important consideration. In any continuous, multilevel communications system, other things are operative while a particular behavior is going on. This opens up the possibility of "cross-channel conflict" or "meta-incongruity" between messages transmitted by the various sense modalities. Instead of mutual reinforcement, there is an essential MISMATCH between, say, the emotional tone of voice and the verbal message one is trying to convey. A normal adult listener, inspecting a speaker's paralanguage, goes back and recognizes contradiction at that level, while a child may be seriously disturbed and confused by such complex behavior. This phenomenon — and it is a frequent one in daily life — is of considerable interest to clinicians, and continues to receive attention in the literature (see, most recently, Bugental, Kaswan, and Love 1970; Bugental et al. 1971).

Another important aspect of interactive behavior is the phenomenon of interactional synchrony, first described by Condon and Ogston (1966), in which it is found that there are "rhythmic relations" between the flow of movement in the listener and flow of speech in the speaker. Kendon's work shows further support of this, and also gives evidence that the way in which individuals may be in synchrony with one another can vary, with these variations being related to their respective role in the interaction (1967). Evidence of VOCAL SYNCHRONY, as well, has been found in our own study of dyadic communication.[4] This will be detailed in a later section.

SUBDIVIDING THE SPEECH PROCESS

There is, after all, a difference between a word and its oral expression. "Tone of voice" is a real notion because the vocal features to which it refers are real phenomena.[5]

---

[4] Words apart, we find that vocal participation in conversation entails mutual monitoring of voices. This will be discussed fully, along with some related observations, in our forthcoming paper on "Strategies of voice management in dyadic interaction."

[5] Numerous examples from literature can be found to illustrate popular awareness of this phenomenon. Here is a particularly relevant series of examples taken from Walker's *Voices from the bottom of the world: a policeman's journal* (1969) that are representative:

"...But when he finally spoke his voice was strong, sharp, and edged with anger as he barked 'ATTENTION'" (6).
"My tone dismissed her completely and she stood up" (53).
"'That's an ORDER,' I said sharply when the bartender refused to move, and his eyebrows darted up suddenly."
"'What's that? What you say, white boy?' His voice was hard, thin."
"I felt my stomach shrink again, and modified my tone" (77).
"My voice dropped to a whisper near the end, carrying George dramatically into the mood" (14).

Because it is a fact of experience that we regularly and systematically use and respond to a much broader spectrum of speech sound than the strictly VERBAL, we can abstract a VOCAL aspect of human behavior. We rely heavily on vocal cues in gaining a proper understanding of what has been said. We manifest our emotions, indicate our rough location along a scale or social categories (age, sex, status, occupation), as Crystal (1971) has shown, and otherwise inform about how we are experiencing an interpersonal relationship through graded changes in tonality, volume, rate of speech, and a great many more subtle modifications in the management of our voice.

As children we learn not only new labels for objects in our experience and patterns for combining them in utterances, we also learn HOW to say them. Eskimo children, for example, exhibit noticeably louder speech behavior than we are accustomed to. However, upon growing older, they adopt a softer speaking voice as an identification symbol of preferred adult behavior (Sol Katz, personal communication). It is, indeed, quite impossible to VERBALIZE without VOCALIZING, without investing our words with some concomitant measure of speed, some degree of loudness, a modicum of tonality. Parents unknowingly instruct their children in the vocal ways of their culture in every act of speech, while holding, changing, bathing, or dressing them.

We learn to discipline our voices in unconscious conformity to the norms of our culture, and to make further accommodations in accordance with the vocal expectations of situation and social group. For example, many languages provide their speakers with a special style for communicating with infants, whose features change with the age of the child. A cross-linguistic comparison is found in Ferguson (1964). Familiar examples in English include higher pitch the younger the infant, and the use of a sing-song, wide-ranging intonation.

We see, then, that the human speaking voice is, in fact, a rich ADMIXTURE of "segmental" and "nonsegmental" features of sound. Typically, the segmental elements or articulated sounds in utterances are made up of consonants and vowels — "discrete," "digital" units, either present or absent, distinctly separable from one another, and occurring in linear sequence in the speech flow. These elements have been studied extensively by linguists. NONSEGMENTAL characteristics of utterance (modulated sound-qualities), or what we are here calling PARALANGUAGE, are less well explored and rather poorly understood by language investigators. While less susceptible to clear-cut internal divisions, the sound material in this sector is capable of being subcategorized into a number of distinct parameters. These include, among others, PITCH

RANGE, PITCH REGISTER, OVERALL LOUDNESS, TEMPO, and DURATION. Here by contrast, one has to do with the structure of continua or "analogue" features of sound which occur concomitantly, and are present in varying degrees in utterances.

Parameters of Nonsegmental Phonation

PITCH RANGE   Every language spoken in the world makes use of tone, although in highly idiosyncratic ways. That is, in all languages, each utterance follows some melodic line, with some portions spoken at a higher or lower tone level than others. In "intonation" languages, such as English, the functionally distinctive pitch levels (usually from three to five in most languages) combine throughout the full sentence to produce a CONTOUR. These pitch levels are RELATIVE in that they are defined in relation to each other, and not some absolute musical scale. Pitch-range control refers to the practice, within a selected band of frequencies, of widening or narrowing the intervals between one "note" and another. "Narrow" range produces the familiar "flat" tone or "monotone" effect in speakers, while "widening" the register serves to introduce more "interest" or "warmth" into one's speech.

PITCH REGISTER   While speaking, we often modulate our voices upwards or downwards to a different TONAL RANGE in which the same number of pitch levels are contrastively used. This amounts to a "register-shift," somewhat comparable to a "change of key" in music. It is not uncommon to move among three or more pitch registers in daily vocal interaction.

OVERALL LOUDNESS   Something else we do when speaking is to modulate the loudness of our voice as it affects portions of utterance larger than the syllable. Our dynamic range in English is usually from considerably OVERSOFT through considerably OVERLOUD, although this may vary from culture to culture. Often, for example, we tone down the loudness at some point prior to the end of our sentence, which produces the intuitive impression of a shift towards greater intimacy.

TEMPO   This refers to the velocity of vocalization or speed of utterance. We may slow down or speed up midway through a sentence, giving evidence of hesitation or sometimes our attempt to prevent another's intrusion into the conversation. One may accelerate one's speech in order to more quickly arrive at more "neutral" or favorable "ground," or to "put distance" between oneself and some embarrassing or emotion-laden subject just broached.

DURATION   At various times when speaking, our syllables may attenuate or become clipped. Drawling syllables, for example, is one way of signaling emphasis in English, thus drawing attention to a particular thought or word. As has been suggested, the flow of communication between two people interacting together is at once extremely complex and regularly patterned. What has not been sufficiently emphasized, however, is that the rich variety of resources residing in our voices enables us to engage others in systematic relationship even at this level, and is a fundamental facet of our "auditory" PRESENTATION OF SELF in everyday life. Two highly structured aspects of voice relationships are (1) vocal interaction patterns and (2) "premonitory" cues.[6] Quite striking is the extent to which and the ways in which the voices of interacting parties are "keyed" to each other and enter into an INTERLOCKING NETWORK OF RELATIONS. The voices of all participants are "orchestrated" together (as so many musical instruments) into an organized whole, with no single voice going its separate way uninfluenced by the others. Especially in interactions involving only two or three speakers, one frequently hears voices "tracing" predictable and highly repetitive patterns in relation to others. The PREMONITORY aspect of this behavior has to do with the use of paralinguistic effects to "foreshadow" either the arrival of emotional content material, the accompanying "style of delivery," or both. We need not pause here to examine these properties, for we shall do so in some detail later.

TYPES OF SEMANTIC INFORMATION

We are concerned here with three issues: (1) the scope of semantics implied by total human communication; (2) a systematic comparison of the functions of language and paralanguage; and (3) as part of the second point, the need to distinguish between two quite different dimensions — sociological and social-psychological — of interpersonal relations.

A fundamental facet of every fluent speaker's mastery of his language is his ability to give an appropriate semantic interpretation or "reading" to every grammatical utterance. But what is this a function of? More

---

[6] A separate discussion of premonitory cues in paralanguage is in preparation, and will soon be forthcoming.

precisely, we must ask: WHERE IS MEANING TO BE FOUND? INSIDE words? INSIDE sentences? Linguists, traditionally accustomed to looking to isolated grammatical utterances as the observation base of their theories, have thought this to be the case, or at least have pretended that this is so. Katz and Fodor (1963), for example, in their search for an explanatory model of a speaker's interpretive ability, conceive this ability very narrowly in terms of certain syntactic and semantic skills relative to grammatical utterances. The empirical and methodological constraints imposed upon their semantic theory are, in our view, overly restrictive. If, as they insist, a semantic theory is a theory of the speaker's ability to interpret the sentences of his language, HOW CAN VOCALIZATION PATTERNS BE SET ASIDE?

One facet of the speaker's competence that a semantic theory will have to reconstruct is his ability to read off "additional meaning" from the voice, which may supersede the significance of the words in the sense of spelling out their true intention. No semantic theory that fails to account for the way vocalization patterns determine how an utterance is understood can be considered to be adequate. In order to justify the limited scope of their theory we are told (Katz and Fodor 1963:178): "Since, then, the readings that a speaker gives a sentence in a setting are a selection from those which it has in isolation, a THEORY OF SEMANTIC INTERPRETATION IS LOGICALLY PRIOR TO A THEORY OF THE SELECTIVE EFFECT OF SETTING" (our emphasis). However one may feel about this, it would seem to follow from this argument that a theory of semantic interpretation is also logically prior to a theory of the selective effect of VOICE PATTERN, and for this there seems little justification. Verbal language is, after all, deeply embedded within the total fabric of human sound making. Any separation of the two in the framework of a linguistic theory of semantics seems most abritrary, and is the product of the same type of thinking that evinces a predilection towards words alone, rather than words and vocal effects.

Students of language are not alone in their narrow understanding of the term *semantic*. In Goffman's writings we read, for example (1969:9): "... and in face-to-face communication this 'framing' information typically derives from paralinguistic cues such as intonation, facial gestures, and the like — cues that have an expressive, NOT SEMANTIC character" (our emphasis). Or, again, a little later in the same work (1969: 13):

Thus when the subject employs verbal means to convey information about his intended course of action, the observer — if he is properly to judge the significance of these communications — will have to attend to the expressive aspects of the transmission as a check upon SEMANTIC CONTENT (our emphasis).

A more revealing question might be: How is meaning conveyed? If, as we have indicated, communication is a "multi-channeled display," then we get meaning from all sense modalities, the full message being a function of the total behavioral setting within a given set of spatio-temporal coordinates. As Langer has written (1942:83), "Language is by no means our only articulate product." Or again:

Wherever a symbol operates, there is a meaning; and conversely, different classes of experience — say, reason, intuition, appreciation — correspond to different types of symbolic mediation. No symbol is exempt from the office of logical formulation, of CONCEPTUALIZATION of what it conveys; however simple its import, or however great, this import is a MEANING, and therefore an element for understanding (1942:90).

The problem of how the meaning of an utterance is determined involves paying attention to CONTEXT. There are at least three senses in which the notion "context" may be fruitfully employed: First, there is INTRA CHANNEL CONTEXT, e.g. units, say, morphemes, occurring relative to similar units of the same level of abstraction. Secondly, there is a STRUCTURAL CONTEXT OF IMPLEMENTATION in which each channel or "mode" occurs relative to others. A third sense of "context" is the more familiar one of social situation, or CIRCUMSTANTIAL CONTEXT OF USE. In this connection, Condon and Ogston (1966: 221) write:

Language, in its natural occurrence as speech, is never disembodied but is always manifested through behavior. For example, what does the lowering of the voice, "while" the eyes widen, "while" the brows raise, "while" an arm and fingers move, "while" the head lowers, "while" a leg and foot shift, "while" the face flushes, have to do with what was said or left unsaid? How is this modified by the equally complex configurations of change which immediately precede and follow? And how are all of the above changes, in turn, related to the similarly involved behavior of the other person or persons in the interaction?

Semantic concerns lead naturally enough to considerations of knowl edge, intelligence, and the learning process. One encounters the term "cognition" today with increasing frequency in much of the social and behavioral science literature. In an important early paper, for example, Lenneberg (1953) describes cognition as the relations that obtain between a code (usually understood to be human verbal language) and such behaviors as are indicative of learning, perception, problem solving, concept formation, memory, and the like. The reference, whether stated or implied, is usually to the logical, rational aspect of man's experience. This traditional emphasis on intellectual, conceptualized experience has coincided with a scholarly preoccupation with man's capacity for VERBAL behavior, and stresses IDEATIONAL information exchange. Such a characterization of the human cognitive process gives a distorted and incomplete picture of COMMUNICATING man. An equally basic dimension of human cognition has to do with the signalling of AFFECTIVE-EVALUATIVE information.

The essential differences between these two cognitive dimensions can be made clear by comparing the functions performed by LANGUAGE and PARALANGUAGE. Language enables us to refer to objects (chair, sky, car, dog), name events (days of the week, freedom, war, love), and make propositions (let x stand for all the ...). This is language's referential and primary function (the "integrative" function of marking social identities and the "expressive" function which includes forms of linguistic play and speech virtuosity lie outside the present discussion). From a symbolic point of view, language achieves its primary purpose admirably well because the pairing of conceptualized experience and sound is done on an arbitrary basis: for example, the sounds that symbolize the familiar four-legged, canine companion of man may be represented as *dog* in English; *chien*, in French; *kuttaa*, in Hindi; *sobaka*, in Russian; *kelev*, in Hebrew; and so on. In general terms, there is no necessary, intrinsic connection between a linguistic sign and the designated reality to which it refers. It is principally through PARALANGUAGE, however, that we are able to adapt ourselves psychologically and socially to changing interpersonal relationships. In symbolic terms, the associative "tie" between a given "set" of voice features and a particular "affect state" or "style of speaking" is more ICONIC in nature. That is, as a photograph more directly depicts what it stands for, paralinguistic cues, as signs, bear a closer relationship to the variety of experience they purport to represent. As speakers of English, for example, we associate a LOUDER voice with some degree of "anger" or disturbance"; or a SOFT, LOW tone with "intimacy" or "confidentiality." Whereas, whether we shout or whisper, "This is no time for that!" the meaning of the words remains unchanged.

If human communication consisted only in reporting information and exchanging ideas through the use of WORDS, it would not only be a drab affair, but wastefully ineffectual. Man is more than an intelligent "computer" programmed to send out meaningfully coherent strings of words according to the grammatical dictates of a particular language. This is a necessary but insufficient condition for human communication. What is also required is some means of keeping tabs on the emotional state, perceived role and locus in the ongoing relationship, and intended meaning of the words of one's conversational partner. Every culture, through its paralinguistic system, provides its followers with this built-in monitoring device.

Paralanguage affects deeply everyone who knows the code. Few of us realize the extent to which we are indeed aware of and utilize nonverbal vocal cues in making inferences about others. We are concerned here with the intrapersonal and interpersonal components of the social relationship. More specifically, when viewed in a functional framework, the paralinguistic code accomplishes the important task of signalling three basic types of information: EMOTIONAL, RELATIONAL, and INTERPRETIVE.

EMOTIONAL   Our voice is an unusually sensitive barometer of how we feel, the particular "mood" we are in at the moment of speaking. Most of us are familiar with the "cracking, squeaking voice of a nervous speaker; the dull monotone of a depressed, passive patient; the rapid rush of slurred sounds of an excited young child; the sighs of an anxiously guilt-ridden neurotic" (Sampson 1971:70). It may be difficult for us to sort the factors out, but the different voice styles are certainly not lost on us. They are manifestations of the person that serve as cues to our perceptions of him. We may successfully MASK our true, innermost feelings behind a verbal "shield," but our voice behavior will usually give us away. We learn to exude expression of this kind and to perceive it in the speech of others according to a set of shared expectations prescribed by our culture.[7] The basis of most of our intuitive impressions of this kind often turns out to be some conventional combination of the use of pitch, loudness, tempo, and duration. Why should this code orient speakers to a high level of inference? Because of its iconic, scalar character paralanguage is particularly well adapted to registering continuously variable levels of human emotion. Language cannot match such precision.

RELATIONAL   When people come together and interact, they not only transmit their personal emotions vocally, they also convey a sense of how they are related in these terms. In this latter sense, it is important to distinguish two distinct and profoundly different dimensions of our interpersonal relations: SOCIOLOGICAL and SOCIAL-PSYCHOLOGICAL. In the former, the focus is upon the person's stratificational position (as defined

---

[7] Of considerable interest here is the nature and extent of the contribution of our inherited human potential to the production of paralanguage. Further studies of animal signaling systems should more clearly delineate what biological continuities may exist between human and nonhuman primate vocalizations.

by age, sex, occupation, and socioeconomic rank) in society at large; in the latter, upon the person as an individual rather than upon his formal status. As Brown (1965:55) has suggested, "If status is the vertical of social relationship, solidarity is the horizontal."

The fundamental distinction expressed here — between positions and roles — is a contrast between the more constant, enduring elements of relationship and its shorter-lived, momentary features. Having allowed for the overall influence of culture in shaping voice behavior, we may further distinguish vocal behavior ranges determined by the traditional social categories. These sociologically derived vocal repertoires, in turn, allow considerable latitude in the range of paralinguistic alternatives corresponding to particular, culturally defined roles in a society. Thus, for example, a psychotherapist (position) is, throughout an interview, a therapist. Within this capacity, however, he discharges his responsibility in the form of a variety of roles: that of "healer," confidant, judge, father figure, and the like. Each of these roles calls forth a shared, learned selection of voice features whose covariation patterns are conventionally understood and expected by his listener(s).

In a similar connection, Bernstein (1972:474) has recently written:

Individuals come to learn their social roles through the process of communication. A social role from this point of view is a constellation of shared, learned meanings through which individuals are able to enter stable, consistent, and publicly recognized forms of interaction with others. A SOCIAL ROLE CAN THEN BE CONSIDERED AS A COMPLEX CODING ACTIVITY CONTROLLING BOTH THE CREATION AND ORGANIZATION OF SPECIFIC MEANING AND THE CONDITIONS FOR THEIR TRANSMISSION AND RECEPTION. Now if the communication system which defines a given role is essentially that of speech, it should be possible to distinguish critical social roles in terms of the speech forms they regulate.

This possibility seems plausible, *a fortiori*, for paralinguistic effects.

In strictly sociological terms, we may think of persons as social "entities," belonging to and displaying behaviors characteristic of particular groups of classes within society. We continually demonstrate our social affiliations through the use of our voices. In an informal way, we are all familiar with the "tone-of-voice" correlates of such social categories as SEX, AGE, STATUS, OCCUPATION, and "GENRES OF SPEAKING."

SEX It is probable that most languages use paralinguistic features to signal differences between the sexes, although this has been little studied. Intuitive impressions of effeminacy in English, for example, largely reduce to the use of a wider pitch range than normal (for men), with slurred effects between stressed syllables, the use of breathiness and huskiness in the voice, switching to a higher (falsetto) register from time to time, and the like. (An interesting contrast is found in Mohave, where a man imitating a woman uses his normal voice, and rather imitates verbal and segmental effects. See Devereux [1949] cited by Crystal [1971]).

AGE References to nonsegmental correlates of age are found only sporadically in the literature. Yet, one has a quite clear intuitive familiarity with "old" and "young" voices. No doubt, more specific age groups are also discriminated by "tone of voice" features (and not only by grammar and vocabulary, as is usually assumed).

STATUS Paralinguistic voice features are often used to signal the social identity of a speaker along some scale (such as "class" or "caste dialect"). In Cayuvava, a rapidly disappearing language in Bolivia, for example, an individual of lower social or economic status addresses one of higher rank in an "honorific" style which gives a prominence of nasalization to all vowels in the utterance (according to H. Key 1967; cited by Crystal 1971). One also thinks of speed of utterance as distinguishing "formal" from "informal" speech in English.

OCCUPATION In English, we are all familiar with the "tone of voice" stereotype that is generally attributed to people in different walks of life, such as doctor, lawyer, or clergyman. The "clinical voice" of medical professionals is well known, and would be interpreted (e.g. in an attempted imitation) as referring to a vocal effect in which pitch-range movements were narrowed, there was frequent use of monotone, rhythm was regular, with tempo fairly slow, and overall pitch height and resonance were increased. There are many occupations that can be recognized on the basis of the nonverbal speech features involved: the preacher, radio and television news announcer, street vendor, disc-jockey, telephone operator, and many others.

GENRES OF SPEAKING Particular speech functions or modalities are usually marked by nonsegmental vocal effect. Stylistic devices to effect transitions from scene to scene or act to act in the context of oral literature might be expected to draw upon vocal resources of this kind. Similarly, "tones of voices" may serve as conventionalized indicators of character impersonations in native story-telling.

The other side of the "relational" coin is SOCIAL-PSYCHOLOGICAL in nature: the center of attention is the person QUA person, involved in a more intimate, personal, individual relationship. Popular phrases such as "warm," "supportive," "remote," and "hostile" are conventional understandings of certain aspects of dyadic, triadic, and small-group interaction.

Paraphrasing Bernstein (1972:479), inasmuch as segmental phonation appears essentially position- rather than person-oriented, then it is a relatively more stable system. By contrast, nonsegmental sound making is continuously in the process of assimilating and accommodating the different feeling states, interpersonal purposes, and expectations of the communicants. More subject to the vicissitudes of an interpersonal relationship, it is subtly altered to suit the needs of the moment. This can perhaps best be illustrated with an example.

The illustrative material that follows is part of a transcription of a recorded initial interview between a psychiatrist and a new patient, and is taken from a textbook on psychiatric practice (Gill, Newman, and Redlich 1954). The particular segment we have selected occurs well toward the end of the interview, after the patient has disclosed the ULTIMATE intimacy. The "secret" is out now, and we are moving quickly to the climax of the episode. Having attained this closest degree of shared intimacy and understanding with the patient, the therapist NOW SOMEHOW must disengage himself from the relationship, while reassuring her that she deserves and will get psychiatric help (T. refers to therapist; P. refers to patient; numbers refer to sequential ordering of the utterances of both).

T. 150: Mmm. How come it took you so long to tell me that?
P. 150: It's hard for me to talk about.
T. 151: Sure it is. I know. I'm very glad you did tell me. Got a lot of things on your chest you think you need to get off? (Short pause) Yes. I think you should be talking to somebody. Ah... I don't know if they explained to you that we have this initial interview, and then there's a .... an intake conference where we consider the suitability of the person for psychotherapy. And I'm sure that you can benefit with psychotherapy. It's just a question of how soon we can take you. And I'll try to see that you get in as soon as you can.

Our perception of "concerned feeling" on the part of the therapist in "How come it took you so long to tell me that?" derives largely from a combination of a fairly narrow pitch range throughout, considerable DRAWL AND GLISSANDO effect on "long" with less drawl on "tell", and the onset of "slight oversoft" degree of loudness coinciding with "you" and continuing to the end of the sentence. In "synchronous" fashion, the patient answers by drawling "talk," and using approximately the same tempo as did the therapist. In T. 151, consider the nonverbal effects of "Yes. I think you should be talking to somebody." These clearly anticipate what follows immediately, and prefigure its accompanying "style of presentation." The "composite" of features includes a much-reduced pitch range (essentially monotone), increasingly softer rendition toward the end, very even rhythm, and relatively undifferentiated stress pattern on syllables throughout.

The awkward portion that follows is marked by a series of sudden "breaks" (pauses, shown by "/") in the flow of speech that reflect the therapist's inner struggle to ease himself out of a difficult position, while retaining a semblance of outward control: "I don't know if they explained to you that/ we have this initial interview, and then there's a/an intake conference/ where we/consider the suitability of the/person for psychotherapy...."

The noticeable increase in tempo during the utterance of "psychotherapy" anticipates the accelerated speed with which the following words are said (that is, up to "And I'll try to see..."). Tempo, here, is a "premonitory" cue that also serves to join together two otherwise separate sentences "in a single breath," as it were.

In terms of "phrasing," the last portion of this segment is broken into two parts, and is spoken in a lowered pitch register with a reduced level of loudness: "And I'll try/to see that you get in as soon as you can." The "kindness" suggested by these vocal effects causes regression in the patient, and she weeps.

INTERPRETIVE Paralanguage also serves the META communicational function of signaling the speaker's intention. It is a "message" about a message, a "set of instructions" informing the hearer as to how the speaker's words are meant: at face value, in a joking, playful manner, ironically, and so on. By such paralinguistic intimations of intention we may disclaim or hold off intimacy without having to be verbally explicit. In this function, nonsegmental characteristics of utterance serve to CROSS-REFERENCE words to intelligibility. Of course, as we have indicated earlier, adults know that the paralinguistic signals carry the true import of speech wherever they conflict with the import of the words. Children, however, are often caught in the "double bind" of meta-incongruence. It is also interesting to note here that sarcasm is "wasted" on the young, as well as on the foreigner — both of whom lack sufficient experience with native voice practices to comprehend these subtle innuendoes.

We began this section with a discussion of the proper scope of semantics. It has been customary in most discussions of meaning by linguists and others interested in the question to distinguish between denotative behavior, conveyed by words, and emotive behavior, conveyed by voice tone and body stance (an alternative formulation is in terms of "semantic" and "expressive." These distinctions are related to another classic dichotomy: COGNITION and AFFECT. Such differentiations are, in our view, unfortunate concessions to limited thinking. Some may prefer restricted definitions of *semantic*, but it would appear that as we come to know more about the message-import and functional role of paralanguage (and other pathways through which information is fed and processed), we will be forced to recognize a broader range of human mental activity to which the term *semantic* may be appropriately applied.

COGNITIVE CODING AND CONCEPTUAL SYSTEMS

We have seen that human social interaction draws upon all channels; and that within the auditory band, more specifically, the sound material comprises two broad categories of acoustic attributes: segmental and non-segmental. These two sound processes, though inextricably interwoven, are conceptually separable, and represent systematic, but differently organized, symbolic signaling systems. To paraphrase and enlarge upon Crystal (1969:5), we may say that the paralinguistic portion of phonation is a set of mutually defining phonological features whose relationship to the words selected is essentially variable, as opposed to that sound portion (namely, the segmental phonemes) whose relationship to such words is direct and identifying in nature.

We have further shown, and Burling (1970:55) has also noted, that "... too exclusive attention to lexical choices can lead one to ignore the possibility that meaningful choices might be made at the syntactic or other levels of language" and through other modes of handling information. In particular, voice turns out to be a subtle, but significant measure of interpersonal strivings, attitudes, and expectations. Yet, the edifice of human cognition, as usually conceived, is built upon a VERBAL (and sensory-motor) foundation and shaped by verbal design. It is this long-standing conception that gave rise to and still perpetuates the sharp disjunction of "affect" and "cognition" as two essentially unlike components of mental life. In this view, language is the representative, par excellence, of intellectual activity; paralanguage, typically cast as "emotive" or "expressive" communication, somehow stands OUTSIDE cognition. We suggested earlier and will here attempt to show that a more balanced (and more accurate) view would see the coding of the

IDEATIONAL and AFFECTIVE-EVALUATIVE dimensions of experience as two aspects of cognition — integrated, rather than polarized as competitors for scholarly attention.

A practice made fashionable by the generative tradition in linguistics is to ask "What does a speaker-hearer know when he knows his language?" By such a query it is meant to reveal that language is a manifestation of the distinctive features of human cognition. By reasonable extrapolation, we may apply the same question to PARALANGUAGE. In both cases, we are concerned with forms of KNOWLEDGE: its acquisition and use. Cognition has to do with the NATURE OF KNOWING. Any growing human being whose behavior would be predictable is likely to learn paralanguage as part of his psychosocial maturation.[8] In daily conversations, paralanguage serves to make the audible behavior of interactants more intelligible to one another. In the hearing we give to most spoken utterances, we tend to allocate most of our conscious attention to the message-import of words, while RESPONDING TO other voiced informational cues that reach us subconsciously, awakening new and different understandings. Everyone in command of the voice system of his language has this intuitive skill. Part of our knowledge of our paralanguage involves "knowing" what "selective" voice style variants may be appropriately used WITH WHOM, IN WHAT CIRCUMSTANCES, TO WHAT PURPOSE, WITH WHAT EFFECT, and WITH WHAT VERBAL AND KINESIC STRUCTURES. Presumably, in knowing ones paralanguage, one also "knows" certain deeply ingrained paralinguistic universals, as well as the particular learned modulatory voice practices and associated semantic conventions of his culture. This critical ability to gauge others' feelings, evaluate their intentions, and enter into emotional rapport via vocal signals strongly suggests conceptualization and cognitive capacity. In natural language, vocal relations, too, are relations between symbols.

Together with other assimilative processes, paralanguage thus qualifies as one of Bruner's (1966:56) "amplifiers of human ratiocinative capacities" which involve "symbol systems governed by rules that, for effective use, must be shared." As characteristic of human coding systems, generally, as Neisser (1962:61) has noted, "Information is taken in, reorganized, filtered, preserved, and perhaps distorted before it is used." The paralinguistic message, mapped by a speaker-hearer for transmission in terms of a conventionalized auditory symbolism, is perceived

---

[8] Failing this, at any stage of his communicative development, the individual may display marked deficiencies in psychosocial adaptation, appearing socially "gauche" in comparison with others of his age-group. The important implications of "arrested" development or underdeveloped competence of this kind have not yet been explored.

by another, similarly "calibrated" human being and decoded to comprehension.

The pivotal importance of paralinguistic competence in social interaction forces recognition of the need to RETHINK certain generally accepted notions such as "concept," "thinking," and "problem solving." To the traditional mind, the novelty of trying to think about thinking in other than lexical and grammatical terms may prove unsettling at first. But, so long as we regard only sensorimotor and verbal (logical) thought as really cognitive of the world, our picture of human mental life must remain a puzzling and inaccurate distortion. Langer (1942:82) has put the matter well:

And so long as we admit only discursive symbolism as a bearer of ideas, "thought" in this restricted sense must be regarded as our only intellectual activity. It begins and ends with language; without the elements, at least, of scientific grammar, conception must be impossible.

We are concerned, then, with the place that paralanguage must occupy in any broader view of cognition. One of our main contentions is that paralanguage may be rewardingly studied in its own right, as a vehicle of conception and instrument of thought, to ascertain its role in intellectual growth. Of the more general symbolist position, of which this view is a part, Langer (1942:84-85) has also written:

This psychological insight... has far-reaching philosophical consequences, if we take it seriously; for it carries rationality into processes that are usually deemed pre-rational, and points to the existence of forms, i.e. of POSSIBLE SYMBOLIC MATERIAL, at a level where symbolic activity has certainly never been looked for by an epistemologist. The eye and the ear make their own abstractions, and consequently dictate their own peculiar forms of conception.

The "modern fallacy," of which we have spoken, turns out to be an error in epistemology which cuts off all interest in the developments of which nonverbal conception is capable, and the intellectual uses to which it might be put. The cogency of this argument is strengthened when we turn to developmental aspects of communicative competence.

To an almost exclusive degree, the main thrust of language acquisition studies has been the investigation of facets of verbal structure (phonology, morphosyntax, and semantics). This has been in keeping with the lexicographical and grammatical orientation of the modern linguistic tradition. In a recent, comprehensive overview of language acquisition theories (Vetter and Howell 1971), not much more than a single full page (1971:36-37) is devoted to nonsegmental features of utterance in infant vocalization, out of a total of more than sixty-one pages! The authors, however, remark (1971:37), concerning intonation: "This would seem to be a fruitful area for exploitation by learning theorists, but it appears to have been neglected by most students of child language." A small beginning has been made along this and related lines (see Ostwald, Freedman, and Kurtz 1962; Lane and Sheppard 1966; Lenneberg 1967; Crystal 1970; Weeks 1971).

A major gap in our understanding of language ontogenesis concerns the range and acquisition of paralinguistic features at various stages of learning, and the modes of integration of paralinguistic and linguistic structures in generating acceptable utterances. Given proper experimental and observational contexts, it should be possible to demonstrate a competence/performance difference in the development of nonsegmental phonology.

The literature on cognition and cognitive growth is embarrassingly silent on the question of the role of voice behavior in the acquisition of intelligence. And yet, if we understand "cognitive growth" to mean INCREASING MASTERY IN ACHIEVING AND USING KNOWLEDGE, then voice behavior is a particular manifestation of cognitive growth, a technique of representing certain varieties of experience through nonverbal/nonsegmental auditory imagery. Cognitive and developmental psychologists have hardly made a beginning at considering the consequences of voice behavior in child development. Such would go far beyond the intent of this paper. We wish here only to indicate some of the implications stemming from such considerations.

Children start their vocal life from birth, and one readily observes the emergence and progressive development of vocalization in the first few months of life. Whining and differentiated crying in infants may be early reflections of personality dynamics and/or organic symptomatology. OUR PERSONALITY MATURES AND DEVELOPS THROUGH PARA-LANGUAGE AND BY OUR USE OF IT.

Very early in life, the child is engaged in monitoring his immediate environment, especially the behavioral aspects of other human beings who come into his "micro-ecological orbit," to use Goffman's term for the immediate social environment. Prior to the advent of intelligible words, the child already is aware of and responding to paralinguistic effects in the speech of family members about him. Even the manner in which an infant's name is intoned provides him significant indication of his tutor's emotional state, interpersonal purpose, and expectation. As he grows older, he learns to detect in the voices of others the degree of intimacy they feel toward him and, in similar fashion, to express his own measure of interpersonal involvement.

The child displays a capacity for discrimination and intricate organization of external stimuli. He hears a voice style repeated many times until the difference between it and one almost like it can finally be abstracted from the settings in which it occurred. Anyone who has ever used sarcasm with a child and failed to be understood can hardly doubt that he has not yet achieved the requisite level of mastery of his paralanguage. Paralinguistic competence involves the capacity to synthesize a simultaneity of nonsegmental voice features, to abstract such overall patterns from their original contexts of occurrence, and to normalize them across speakers. This implies a highly complex process of experience and analysis.

The difference between speech and writing has a further implication for coding and cognition which may be noted here. Whereas WORDS are the implicit units of WRITTEN sentences, it is not at all clear that the child apprehends SPOKEN utterances in these terms. What seems more likely is that he perceives integrated sounds as units of UTTERANCES, rather than individualistic sounds as comprising, in the first instance, words. This integration is apparently in terms of larger, higher-level units of utterance, incorporating not only segmental sound articulations, but also nonsegmental sound modulations. As the baby develops into a child and the child into an adult, he hears TOTAL SOUND PATTERNS. Even in the preverbal vocalization stage, the infant is presumably already babbling segments of utterance. In the auditory band, paralinguistic patterns seem to "chain together" smaller, separable grammatical units at a lower level. In terms of the larger behavioral context of an utterance, it seems necessary to conceive of much larger "units" of significant behavior as being encoded and decoded with increasing mastery by the growing child.

In Piagetian terms, the various sense modalities are so many information-handling processes. Each is an apparatus which is CHANGED IN, AND BY, THE VERY ACT OF PROCESSING INFORMATION. This change is called ACCOMMODATION by Piaget. Accommodation is the change in the organism resulting from processed input; its effect in reshaping the input is called ASSIMILATION. Piaget thus accounts for the growth of intelligence in terms of two reciprocal processes: assimilation of reality and accommodation to it.

The structures which are accommodated and do the assimilating are termed SCHEMATA by Piaget. Auditory voice perception is one of the schemata with which adults assimilate reality. We assimilate emotions, intentions, and expectations — our own and others' — to a schema. In all these areas, the child must accommodate to reality. Paralanguage is thus a second mode of assimilation — part of the cognitive process, existing side by side with language. Taken together, language and paralanguage represent a dual mental functioning with respect to the auditory perceptual field.

An intrinsic part of the socialization process is the internalization of voice patterns. The paralinguistic code, itself an object to be learned, is also a crucial factor affecting the EFFICIENCY of learning. From this we may expect to derive direct, pragmatic implications for use in the home, in the classroom, or in any learning situation. The fact, too, that we not only "know" constellations of concomitant voice features and the contrasting meanings which they expound, but also STORE them, points up the reality of paralanguage as a mental structure. Because remembering is part of the cognitive process, Neisser (1962:60) reminds us: "Only in areas of life which are culturally or personally important do schemata become articulate enough for detailed memory."

Paralanguage has clear implications for a theory of intellectual development, which have never been made explicit. The very use of paralanguage presupposes certain underlying cognitive processes required for its use. Therefore, we must recognize the need to include this representational system in the adequate study of first-language acquisition as part of human mental growth. One best explores these processes by examining the behavior of young children. This is justification enough for doing research on intellectual development in children.

It is to be hoped that developmental and cognitive psychologists, linguists, anthropologists, and other students of man increasingly will come to avail themselves of the paralinguistic component of human behavior to add realistic, new dimensions to our understanding of cognition and cognitive growth.

REFERENCES

BERNSTEIN, B.
    1972   "A sociolinguistic approach to socialization: with some reference to educability," in *Directions in sociolinguistics*. Edited by J. J. Gumperz and D. H. Hymes, 472–497. New York: Holt, Rinehart and Winston.
BIRDWHISTELL, R. L.
    1966   *Encyclopédie des Sciences de l'homme*, volume five: "Communication without words," in *L'aventure humaine*. Edited by D. Alexandre 157–166. Paris: De La Grange Bateliere S. A.
    1970   *Kinesics and context*. Philadelphia: University of Pennsylvania Press.

BROWN, R.
1965 *Social psychology.* New York: The Free Press.
BRUNER, J. S. , R. R. OLIVER, P. M. GREENFIELD
1966 *Studies in cognitive growth.* New York: John Wiley and Sons.
BUGENTAL, D. E., J. W. KASWAN, L. R. LOVE
1970 Perception of contradictory meanings conveyed by verbal and nonverbal channels. *Journal of Personality and Social Psychology* 16: 647–655.
BUGENTAL, D. E., L. R. LOVE, J. W. KASWAN, C. APRIL
1971 Verbal-nonverbal conflict in parental messages to normal and disturbed children. *Journal of Abnormal Psychology* 77: 6–10.
BULLOWA, M., C. G. JONES, A. R. DUCKERT
1964 The acquisition of a word. *Language and Speech* 7: 107–11.
BURLING, R.
1970 *Man's many voices.* New York: Holt, Rinehart and Winston.
CONDON, W. S.
1967 A segmentation of behavior. *Journal of Psychiatric Research* 5: 221-235.
1970 Method of microanalysis of sound films of behavior. *Behavioral Research Methods and Instrumentation* 2: 51-54.
CONDON, W. S., W. D. OGSTON
1966 Sound film analysis of normal and pathological behavior patterns. *Journal of Nervous and Mental Diseases* 143: 338-347.
CRYSTAL, D.
1969 *Prosodic systems and intonation in English.* Cambridge: Cambridge University Press.
1970 "Prosodic systems and language acquisition," in *Prosodic feature analysis,* 78-90. Paris: Marcel Didier.
1971 "Prosodic and paralinguistic correlates of social categories," in *Social anthropology and language.* Edited by E. Ardener, 185–206. London: Tavistock Press.
DEVEREUX, G.
1949 Mohave voice and speech mannerisms. *Word* 5: 268–272.
EKMAN, P., W. V. FRIESEN
1969 The repertoire of nonverbal behavior: categories, origins, usage, and coding. *Semiotica* 1: 49–98.
EKMAN, P., W. V. FRIESEN, P. ELSWORTH
1972 *Emotion in the human face: guidelines for research and an integration of findings.* Elmsford, New York: Pergamon Press.
FERGUSON, C.
1964 "Baby talk in six languages," in *The ethnography of communication.* Edited by J.J. Gumperz and D. Hymes. *American Anthropologist* 66: 103–114.
GILL, M., R. NEWMAN, F. C. REDLICH
1954 *The initial interview in psychiatric practice.* New York: International Universities Press.
GOFFMAN, E.
1959 *The presentation of self in everyday life.* Garden City: Doubleday Anchor Books, Doubleday.

1963 *Behavior in public places: notes on the social organization of gatherings.* New York: The Free Press.
1969 *Strategic interaction.* Philadelphia: University of Pennsylvania Press.
1972 *Relations in public.* New York: Basic Books.
HALL, E. T.
1966 *The hidden dimension.* Garden City: Doubleday Anchor Books, Doubleday.
KATZ, J. J., J. A. FODOR
1963 The structure of a semantic theory. *Language* 39: 170–210.
KENDON, A.
1967 Some functions of gaze-direction in social interaction. *Acta Psychologica* 26: 22–63.
1972 "Some relationship between body motion and speech," in *Studies in dyadic communication.* Edited by A. Seigman and B. Pope. Elmsford, New York: Pergamon Press.
KEY, H.
1967 *Morphology of Cayuvava.* The Hague: Mouton.
KEY, M. R.
1972 "The relationship of verbal and nonverbal communication." Paper read at the Eleventh International Congress of Linguists, Bologna, August, 1972.
LANE, H., W. SHEPPARD
1966 Development of the prosodic features of infants' vocalizing. *Studies in Language and Language Behavior* 3:13. Ann Arbor, Michigan: Center for Research on Language and Language Behavior.
LANGER, S.
1942 *Philosophy in a new key.* New York: Mentor Books.
LENNEBERG, E.
1953 Cognition in ethnolinguistics. *Language* 29: 463–471.
1967 "Prelanguage development," in *Biological foundations of language,* 276–280. New York: John Wiley.
LYONS, J.
1968 *Introduction to theoretical linguistics.* Cambridge: Cambridge University Press.
MCQUOWN, N.
1957 Linguistic transcription and specification of psychiatric interview material. *Psychiatry* 20: 79–86.
NEISSER, U.
1962 "Cultural and cognitive discontinuity," in *Anthropology of human behavior.* Edited by T. Gladwin and W. C. Sturtevant, 54–71. Washington: The Anthropological Society of Washington.
OSTWALD, P., D. FREEDMAN, J. KURTZ
1962 Vocalization of infant twins. *Folia Phoniatrica* 44: 37–50.
SAMPSON, E.
191 *Social psychology and contemporary society. New York:* John Wiley.
SCHEFLEN, A.
1964 The significance of posture in communication systems. *Psychiatry* 27: 316–331.

VETTER, H., R. HOWELL
1971 Theories of language acquisition. *Journal of Psycholinguistic Research* 1: 31–64.
WALKER, T. M.
1969 *Voices from the bottom of the world: a policeman's journal.* New York: Grove Press
WATSON, O. M.
1970 *Proxemic behavior: a cross-cultural study.* The Hague: Mouton.
WEEKS, T.
1971 Speech registers in young children. *Child Development* 42: 1119–1131.

Linguistic and Paralinguistic Interchange

PHILIP LIEBERMAN

Current linguistic theory rigidly compartmentalizes the "linguistic" and "paralinguistic" aspects of human communication. Linguistic communication has been equated to the transmission of cognitive, referential information. Paralinguistic communication is considered as relating to the transmission of "emotive" states. Implicit in this distinction is the notion that human language is the medium that allows modern man to think that, in essence, language IS the basis of cognitive ability. Hence the clearly unique aspects of human language, the ability of modern man to form words, phrases, etc., are considered linguistic. In contrast, the prosodic aspects of human language, that is, the modulations of pitch, amplitude, and temporal pattern, which clearly play a part in the communications of other living species besides *Homo sapiens*, are considered paralinguistic.

This distinction between the supposedly paralinguistic and linguistic aspects of communication is misleading. While all animals do make use of innately determined cries to signal certain basic states of their autonomic vegetative systems, no clear distinction can be demonstrated that distinguishes many of the "paralinguistic" phenomena from the "linguistic" in human, or for that matter in nonhuman, communication. The gasp of a drowning man is an example of an innately determined cry, as is the cry of a rabbit or dog or a man in extreme pain. Darwin (1872), in *The expression of emotion in man and animals*, clearly differentiated these basic cries, which he noted were independent of habit or training, from the "emotive" information that linguists often classify as "paralinguistic." Linguists in general tend to classify the transmission of information as paralinguistic when they lack adequate notational systems. If a speaker, for example, told his friend, "The train is due at 8 A.M., but I don't believe it," the information would be treated as a linguistic communication that made use of the speaker's and the listener's cognitive abilities. If the speaker instead had said, "The train is due at 8 A.M.," using a "tone of voice" that conveyed his disbelief, the semantic construct of "disbelief" would be treated as a paralinguistic phenomenon. Linguists lack adequate transcription systems for the prosodic aspects of language so they solve the problem by treating the information that they cannot describe with their present theoretical and notational apparatus as nonlinguistic. The situation is ludicrous. It is as though physicists decided that subatomic physics was not part of physics because the present theory could not readily account for the observed phenomena.

We can avoid painting ourselves into this intellectual corner if we consider what we really mean by the term "language." No good analytic definition of language exists. This is an unintended consequence of the search for linguistic "universals." Linguists have, for the most part, attempted to define language in terms of the universal properties that structure all human languages. This is an impossible task. We simply do not know what these universals are. If we did, we would have "solved" the problem of language and would know everything that there is to know about language. The traditional approach towards formulating the definition of language is also anthropocentric in that the definition is necessarily based on the language of present-day *Homo sapiens*, that is, HUMAN language. I think that the following definition of language avoids these problems. I will define a language to be a communications system that is capable of transmitting new information. In other words, I am operationally defining language as a communications system that places no restriction on the nature or the quality of the information transferred.

It is obvious that this definition does not require that all languages have all of the properties of human language. It is also obvious that the "phonetic" elements of human language need not be restricted to the segmental phonetic elements that traditional orthography conveys, nor even to the speech signal. Prosodic contours and gestures can have a role even as they do in the languages of other species, living and extinct.

In connection with this last point, it is probable that an advanced hominid species like classic Neanderthal man (Lieberman 1972), who lacked many of the segmental phonetic elements that characterize human speech, would probably have consistently expressed a semantic construct like disbelief by means of the "tone of his voice" or a gesture or grimace. The cultural remains of specimens of classic Neanderthal man, *Homo sapiens neanderthalensis*, demonstrate that some form of language must have been present. Fairly abstract cognitive ability must have been present in these extinct hominids because ritual burials involving the symbolic use of flowers, the use of advanced tools, and the use of fire are all part of the classic Neanderthal culture (Solecki 1972; Boule and Vallois 1957; Bordes 1968). Present-day *Homo sapiens* has a great segmental phonetic inventory, and the semantic construct of disbelief can be expressed either by means of "tone of voice" or through the use of some additional words.

There clearly is no rigid dichotomy wherein certain semantic constructs are "paralinguistic" and others are "linguistic." The rigid dichotomy is an artifice. Any semantic construct that can be paraphrased in terms of a string of words is obviously "linguistic." The use of a phonetic element that cannot be transcribed using the International Phonetic Alphabet symbol inventory does not make the semantic construct "paralinguistic." There is no clear line of demarcation at the semantic level.

No rigid dichotomy exists at the phonetic level with respect to "paralinguistic" and "linguistic" phonetic units. A phonetic element is really a signaling unit (Lieberman 1970). Linguists have been accustomed to manipulate the segmental phonetic elements that are, for the most part, the consequence of the articulatory maneuvers of the supralaryngeal vocal tract in *Homo sapiens*. Sound contrasts like the vowels [a] and [i], for example, are the result of articulatory maneuvers involving only the supralaryngeal vocal tract (Fant 1960). Many of the phonetic distinctions that differentiate the segmental phonetic elements are, however, the consequence of laryngeal maneuvers, for example, the distinction between the sounds [b] and [p] (Lisker and Abramson 1964). The distinction between these two sounds rests in the timing between the start of phonation and the release of the primary occlusion of the supralaryngeal vocal tract. Many languages make use of differences in the dynamic pattern of the fundamental frequency of phonation to signal lexical differences. The various dialects of Chinese, for example, make use of variations in fundamental frequency (which are perceived as pitch variations) to differentiate various words. A speaker of American English does not make use of these distinctions to differentiate the lexical entries of his linguistic "dictionary of words." The speaker of American English is thus free to use these pitch variations, i.e. "tone" features, to transmit simultaneously the semantic construct of DISBELIEF when he utters the words, "The train is due at 8 A.M." He might also have shrugged his shoulders or used a facial expression that conveys disbelief. The semantic content is nonetheless the same as if he had also added the words, "but I don't believe it."

The speaker thus can make use of phonetic signals that are not intimately associated with the lexical entries in his internal dictionary to convey semantic information that is considered "paralinguistic" by linguists fixed to the segmental framework of a particular language. In the present company, the particular language in question is English, which many linguists appear to take implicitly as the "universal" language.

There is no clear dichotomy at the phonetic level. Prosodic features that have an exclusive "paralinguistic" function in one language may have a "linguistic," lexical function in another language. High fundamental frequency, rising fundamental frequency, breathy voice, etc., cannot therefore be exclusively viewed as "paralinguistic" phonetic features. Nor can we even view gestures or facial expressions as exclusively paralinguistic phonetic features. The lexical entries, i.e. "words" of the sign language of the deaf, for example, make use of a wide variety of manual gestures in concert with articulatory maneuvers of the facial musculature. The language of hominids who lived until comparatively recent times (20,000 - 50,000 years ago), like the people of Shanidar and La Chapelle-aux-Saints, also probably made use of these manual and facial gestures to communicate "words." Present-day chimpanzees have, for that matter, been taught to communicate lexical information by means of gestures (Gardner and Gardner 1969). Chimpanzees exhibit cognitive and linguistic abilities that are remarkably similar, although more limited, than adult modern *Homo sapiens* (Gardner and Gardner 1969; Premack 1972). It is probable that the particular phonetic form of HUMAN language is a comparatively recent development in hominid evolution (Lieberman 1974). Cognitive ability, which can take many forms of phonetic expression, must have antedated the appearance of human language.

I do not want to leave the impression that only prosodic and gestural phonetic elements can interchange between conveying "linguistic" and "paralinguistic" information. Much of the discussion on the phonetic level of "paralinguistic" communication is based either on inadequate or incorrect phonetic and acoustic analyses. One often encounters, for example, the assertion that high fundamental frequency conveys some sort of increased "emotion" on the part of the speaker. Psychoacoustic experiments that transposed the fundamental frequency contour of a synthesized utterance from a "normal" to either a "high" or a "low" pitch range failed to show this result (Lieberman and Michaels 1962).

The same psychoacoustic experiments demonstrated that the expansion or the compression of a speaker's pitch range also failed to transmit any "emotional" nuances. These results are in accord with recent acoustic and electromyographic investigation that show great variability with respect to these parameters, both between different speakers and the same speaker, when completely "unemotional" test sentences are spoken (Atkinson 1973). The traditional statements concerning the role of pitch, which have been constantly repeated and reprinted for at least fifty years, are wrong. We simply do not know what is happening.

I must stress that this does NOT mean that prosodic features do not convey paralinguistic information. The fine structure of fundamental frequency, that is, the variations in periodicity that occur from one opening and closing cycle of the vocal cords to the next, appear to have a "paralinguistic" function in English (Lieberman 1961; Lieberman and Michaels 1962). Dynamic patterns varying from the "normal" prosodic pattern also appear to be relevant. The segmental features also can convey "paralinguistic" information in English. One of the "paralinguistic" parameters that speakers normally communicate is their intended sex. (This is not always equivalent to biologically determined sex.) It is obvious that prosodic features convey the speaker's intended sex (Brend 1971). The segmental phonetic elements also convey the speaker's intended sex. This is obvious in languages that make use of different lexical entries for men and women (Haas 1964). It is also true in languages, like English, in which speakers use articulatory maneuvers that result in formant frequency differences that differentiate the segmental phonetic elements of men and women (Mattingly 1966; Schwartz 1968; Schwartz and Rine 1968; Sachs et al. 1972). In effect, men and women have slightly different dialects that involve acoustically and perceptually different vowels and consonants. It also appears that these distinctions are the result of acculturation, that they are learned by children as they learn other aspects of their particular dialect (Sachs et al. 1972). These distinctions in vowel quality, in languages other than American English, can be used to differentiate words. There is, therefore, a "paralinguistic-linguistic" interchange. Note, however, that the "paralinguistic" versus "linguistic" interchange is again really arbitrary. The speaker's sex can, if the culture permits, be signaled either through the use of a different word or different set of syntactic or morphophonemic rules or through the use of a different set of phonetic features. The semantic, cognitive information being transferred is the same; only the means change.

We need not limit our data to the communication of humans or even of primates. The bases of cognitive ability and communication can be seen in the behavior of many species. A dog will signal that he wants water by pushing his water bowl. This is no less an example of cognitive, referential information being communicated than a human requesting a glass of water. We cannot even claim that all of the symbols used by a dog are iconographic. Dogs have been "trained" to ring bells when they want water. They could not do this unless they had the ability to associate an abstract symbol, the bell, with water. Calling the process "conditioning" does not disguise the cognitive aspects of the problem. Studies of the communications of animals at the neuroelectric level, furthermore, show the presence of "feature" detectors that are tuned to the communicative signals that these animals employ (Capranica 1965; Wollberg and Newman 1972). The basic principles that structure human communication may be found with the aid of comparative studies of communication in other species. Human language is the result of a long evolutionary process, and it involves factors that are important in many aspects of human and animal behavior besides communication (Lieberman 1974). It is immaterial whether the communications are labeled "paralinguistic" or "linguistic." There is no sharp dividing line because, as Darwin (1967: 95) noted: "Natural selection can act only by the preservation and accumulation of infinitesimally small inherited modifications..." *Homo sapiens*' linguistic abilities only appear to be unique today because the intermediate hominids are extinct. The natural communications of animals like the chimpanzee (Goodall 1971), therefore, are relevant to the study of the basic parameters that underly human language. The paralinguistic-linguistic distinction is again arbitrary.

In conclusion, I think that we should be concerned with the general question of how information is transferred. Whether it is labeled paralinguistic or linguistic is of no concern except to those linguists who want to limit arbitrarily the universe of discourse so that they may claim to have found a "universal" linguistic theory that accounts for all aspects of language.

The test of a scientific theory is not that it accounts for everything, but that it relates a number of phenomena that were seemingly unrelated before the theory was proposed. Newton's Laws of Motion never accounted for frictional phenomena. They nonetheless proved "correct" insofar as they accounted for a diverse range of phenomena that had appeared to be unrelated. To effectively analyze the problem of language as I have defined language, we have to investigate carefully the acoustic, perceptual, and physiologic parameters that structure language. We have to reexamine many of the premises that are based on either superficial or inadequate analyses, and we cannot arbitrarily limit the data sample. We may not be able to account for all of the phenomena that we observe, but we will be in a position to assess both the generality and the limitations of our theories. Only then can we progress.

REFERENCES

ATKINSON, J. R.
1973 "Aspects of intonation in speech: implications from an experimental study of fundamental frequency." Unpublished doctoral dissertation, University of Connecticut.
BORDES, F.
1968   *The old Stone Age*. New York: McGraw-Hill.
BOULE, M., H. V. VALLOIS
1957   *Fossil men*. New York: Dryden.
BREND, R.
1971 "Male-female differences in American English intonation." Paper presented at the Seventh International Congress of Phonetic Sciences, 1971.
CAPRANICA, R. R.
1965   *The evoked vocal response of the bullfrog*. Cambridge: MIT.
DARWIN, C.
1967   *On the origin of species*. New York: Atheneum. Facsimile of first edition 1859.
1872   *The expression of emotion in man and animals*. London: J. Murray.
FANT, G.
1960   *Acoustic theory of speech production*. The Hague: Mouton.
GARDNER, R. A., B. T. GARDNER
1969   Teaching sign language to a chimpanzee. *Science* 165:664–672.
HAAS, M.
1964 "Men's and women's speech in Koasati," in *Language in culture and society*. Edited by D. Hymes. New York: Harper and Row.
LIEBERMAN, P.
1961   Perturbations in vocal pitch. *Journal of the Acoustical Society of America* 33:597–603.
1970   Towards a unified phonetic theory. *Linguistic Inquiry* 1:307–322.
1972   *The speech of primates*. The Hague: Mouton.
1974 "On the evolution of language: a unified view," in *Antecedents of man and after*, volume one: *Primates: functional morphology and evolution*. Edited by Russell Tuttle. World Anthropology. The Hague: Mouton.
LIEBERMAN, P., S. B. MICHAELS
1962   Some aspects of fundamental frequency and envelope amplitude

as related to the emotional content of speech. *Journal of the Acoustical Society of America* 34:922–927.

LISKER, L., A. S. ABRAMSON
1964 A cross-language study of voicing in initial stops: acoustical measurements. *Word* 20:384–422.

MATTINGLY, I. G.
1966 Speaker variation and vocal tract size. *Journal of the Acoustical Society of America* 39:1219(A).

PREMACK, D.
1972 Language in chimpanzee? *Science* 172:808–822.

SACHS, J., P. LIEBERMAN, D. ERICKSON
1972 "Anatomical and cultural determinants of male and female speech," in *Language attitudes: current trends and prospects.* Georgetown University Monograph Series in Language and Linguistics 25. Washington, D.C.: Georgetown University.

SCHWARTZ, M. F.
1968 Identification of speaker sex from isolated, voiceless fricatives. *Journal of the Acoustical Society of America* 43:1178–1179.

SCHWARTZ, M. F., H. RINE
1968 Identification of speaker sex from isolated, whispered vowels. *Journal of the Acoustical Society of America* 44:1736–1737.

SOLECKI, R. S.
1972 *Shanidar — the first flower people.* New York: A. Knopf.

VAN LAWICK-GOODALL, J.
1971 *In the shadow of man.* New York: Dell.

WOLLBERG, Z., J. D. NEWMAN
1972 Auditory cortex of squirrel monkey: response patterns of single cells to species-specific vocalizations. *Science* 175:212–214.

Cross-Cultural Study of Paralinguistic "Alternants" in Face-to-Face Interaction

FERNANDO POYATOS

In the interdisciplinary and complex stage in which studies of nonverbal communication find themselves today it has become quite difficult to deal with any communicative modality, or even one aspect of that modality or system, in isolation. Most of us no longer accept as scientific or realistic an investigation that disregards other systems of communication occurring simultaneously, following, or preceding the one under analysis. Many different systems regulate the truly continuous flow of personal, multi-channel expression and interpersonal relationships.

The desirable, realistic, and exhaustive approach that we seek leads us, however, into a sort of impasse, as when I have tried to relate what I term paralinguistic "alternants"[1] to other communicative acts close to, or far from, the purely linguistic structure of face-to-face interaction. But before attempting to analyze nonverbal communication, the investigator ought to state clearly his position with respect to the concepts "verbal-nonverbal" and "vocal-nonvocal."

For the study of this and related areas I have been generously supported by grants from the University of New Brunswick, by grants from the Canada Council, and currently by Leave Fellowship W73-0323 from The Canada Council.

[1] Cf. Smith's (1953) vocal identifiers, Pittinger and Smith's (1957) vocal identifiers, Pittinger's (1957) vocal segregates, Trager's (1958) vocal segregates, Crystal and Quirk's (1964) voice qualities, Austin's (1965) vocal segregates, Vetter's (1969) vocal segregates, and Duncan's (1969) vocal segregates (critical of Trager's unevenly developed system). Smith (1969) uses vocal segregates, but carefully explains that they are "in fact, a series of noises very similar to phones and pattern not only terms of oppositions, but also packages which, over-all, are quite similar to words." There has been a great discrepancy as to terminology.

1. VERBAL — NONVERBAL; VOCAL — NONVOCAL

1.1. While Ekman and Friesen (1969) limit nonverbal behavior to "any movement or position of the face and/or the body," thus not differentiating between nonverbal and nonvocal, Duncan (1969) includes: paralanguage (another term subject to discussion; see Abercrombie 1968; Lieberman 1974), kinesics, proxemics, olfaction, skin sensitivity to touch and temperature, and even the use of artifacts such as Ekman and Friesen's "object-adaptors." In body motion or kinesic behavior, Duncan includes facial expression, eye movements, and postures.

Lyons (1972) first distinguishes vocal from nonvocal signals "according to whether the signals are transmitted in the vocal-auditory 'channel' or not" (also implying by the use of this term the two end-points: sender and receiver), and then considers language as made up of verbal (strictly lexical) and nonverbal (prosodic) components, the latter, of course, being still vocal. He is inclined, with Abercrombie, to apply the controversial term "paralinguistics" to features playing a supporting role, such as gestures and eye movements, and to include both prosodic and paralinguistic phenomena within nonsegmental (linguistic, therefore, subsuming verbal and prosodic).

Argyle (1972) comes closest to the classification I shall propose by calling kinesics and proxemics nonverbal, along with what he refers to as nonverbal aspects of speech, or paralanguage.

Laver and Hutcheson, in the introduction to a volume of readings on face-to-face interaction (1972), identify VERBAL with actual words and NONVERBAL with vocal or nonvocal conversational behavior (for them paralanguage) apart from words. They distinguish the following four categories: vocal-verbal (words), vocal-nonverbal (intonation and paralanguage), nonvocal-verbal (written or printed language), and nonvocal-nonverbal (kinesics, i.e., facial expression, gesture, and posture). These four means of communicating subsume three types of features — linguistic, which is "relatively uncontroversial"; paralinguistic, which, for Laver and Hutcheson, includes nonlinguistic, nonverbal phenomena that may either be vocal (tone of voice) or nonvocal (kinesics, proxemics, etc.); and extralinguistic, which is "by definition non-verbal, non-linguistic and non-paralinguistic", and may be either vocal (biologically, psychologically, and socially-based voice quality) or nonvocal (style of dress).

Laver and Hutcheson's definitions of verbal, nonverbal-vocal, and nonverbal-nonvocal coincide with the classification I have been using lately, although in the case of nonverbal-nonvocal I have included the rest of the communication systems that I place in the category of "Total

Body Communication," wherein "alternants" also have their place. Before outlining this total body-based complex of communicative activities, I offer the following definitions:

1.2. VERBAL-VOCAL COMMUNICATION is the acoustic, nonautonomous vocal system formed by segmental lexical structures and their essential suprasegmental patterns of stress, pitch, and juncture.

1.3. NONVERBAL-VOCAL COMMUNICATION is the acoustic, nonautonomous system, whether respiratory or not, formed by the extreme variations of the suprasegmental patterns of stress, pitch, and juncture, and the series of phenomena generally studied as paralinguistic (see section 5 below, where I distinguish primary qualities, modifiers, and alternants). Many of these are marginal and nonspeech sounds which go beyond traditional phonemic norms, but pauses may be added to these sounds, even as encoded and decoded semantic components of paralanguage.

1.4. NONVERBAL-NONVOCAL COMMUNICATION includes acoustic, visual, olfactory, and tactile means of conveying cognitive (language-replaceable) and indexical (speaker-identifying; see Abercrombie 1967) information, and of eliciting interaction. The conveying of information and the eliciting of interaction can be complementary.

1.5. All these ways of communicating (or conveying information, if we take communicating as intentional only) fall within total body communication; that is, they take place without the help of any external agents, except in the case of object-adaptors, which include also the body. But before further exploration of this fact, I would like to refer again to Lyon's vocal-auditory channel between sender and receiver. Within auditory, in nonverbal-nonvocal communication, I include what I have termed acoustic kinesics and, for the sake of exhaustiveness, even certain intestinal sounds and bone sounds. For this reason I prefer to differentiate acoustic from nonacoustic within total body communication because I use a classification based on sensory perception. On the other hand, I incorporate within the nonverbal-vocal category any sounds that may run through the vocal-auditory channel, whether produced normally as physiological reflexes (e.g. Crystal's [1969] "vocal reflexes"), or abnormally for the purpose of communication, as when we clear our throat to warn someone. I incorporate, in fact, all paralinguistic categories, as vocal reflexes are alternants when isolated from words.

2. FUNCTIONS OF NONVERBAL COMMUNICATION IN FACE-TO-FACE INTERACTION

2.1. Ekman and Friesen (1969) and others agree that a nonverbal act can repeat, augment, illustrate, accent, or contradict the accompanying words, and that it can anticipate, coincide with, substitute for, or follow verbal behavior. Thus, this part of communicative activity, which is not autonomous, is considered the unquestionable core of human intellectual exchange and the truly anthroposemiotic signaling system. However, verbal behavior is not the only activity to which nonverbal behavior is related in the actual communication situation; all nonverbal acts can relate mutually to each other. By way of examples I suggest the following instances:

A. PARALANGUAGE TO KINESICS: An apico-alveolar click [tz'] plus a double headshake, repeats negation; a loud and drawled "Well!" anticipates a firm handshake; an ironic "Sure!" plus a headshake contradicts the verbal affirmation.

B. PARALANGUAGE TO PROXEMICS: A whispery, breathy voice increases as intimate distance turns into erotic play; a very open voice (pharyngeal control), high volume, and tense articulation is used at public distance in oratory.

C. PARALANGUAGE TO CHRONEMICS: The pause and its structure (subject to duration, the two audible respiratory phases, kinesic markers, situational context, etc.) is a valid example of this type of relationship; another example is the type of laughter and its duration, interestingly enough, according to upbringing, social status, and situational context.

D. KINESICS TO PROXEMICS: Two Spanish male friends anticipate their embrace while still at great personal, or even social, distance; an actor's distance from the audience makes him overemphasize his gestural behavior.

E. PROXEMICS TO CHRONEMICS: The duration of a visit, whether formal, familiar, or highly regulated by protocol, is directly related to the distance kept among participants (the more informal, the longer the visit may last, and vice versa), unless unusual circumstances affect both the spatial and chronemic behaviors. At an informal party distances of flirtation, of sexual overtures, or simply of mutual interest in conversation, shorten as time goes by, conditioned by drinking and other factors.

These relationships, which can act as both modifiers and context, and which require careful investigation, take place within our own repertoire of verbal and nonverbal behavior, as well as in interaction between speakers and auditors, whether in a dyad or in groups. In other words, the kinesics of a subject can influence not only his own language, paralanguage, proxemics, and chronemics, but also the language, paralanguage, proxemics, and chronemics of the other interactors. This prompts me to distinguish between "self-regulatory function" and "interactional function."

2.2. Of those two functions, the self-regulatory one plays, in my opinion, the most important role in the series of relationships I have pointed out because by regulating one's own multirepertoire, it conditions, in turn, the receiver's response. My earlier belief that the self-regulatory function did not need an interactant is false; I have found that the presence of the other subject — even a mere awareness of him — conditions, consciously or unconsciously, our sender's behavior.

3. INTERACTIONAL SYNCHRONY, FEEDBACK, AND INTERACTIONAL TURNS

Since both the self-regulatory function and the interactional one apply to each and all of the nonverbal behaviors, I will comment, in passing at least on interactional synchrony and feedback (both internal and external), as the two concepts are intimately related to the roles played by alternants and to the self-regulatory function. However, when referring to interaction in the total communication complex, I prefer to speak of sender and receiver rather than of speaker and auditor, or listener, simply because I am thinking of all communicative activities as being interrelated in such interaction. By the same token, I refer to INTERACTIONAL TURNS, and not just to speaking turns, for, as in the functions of nonverbal communication, such turns are just as claiming, yielding, taking, and suppressing in proxemics, kinesics, and chronemics as they are in language and paralanguage (see Duncan 1973 for these last two), producing also simultaneous turns and mirroring behavior in any of these categories. In addition, interactional turns may act as back-channel activities (Argyle's [1972] feedback, and Dittmann's [1972] listener responses), which range from "uh-huh" and headnods to withdrawing two steps in surprise. Back-channel activities, in turn, can be within-turn signals or responses to such signals (Duncan 1973) by the speaker-actor. Naturally, there is also internal feedback, or awareness, whether or not the speaker intentionally attempted to communicate (Ekman and Friesen 1969).

Furthermore, what later are called self-regulatory functions, in referring to alternants, can also be called SELF-INTERACTION in the sender's behavior; that is, interaction within each system (i.e., the various kinesic, paralinguistic, or proxemic alternatives within the speaker's own repertoire) that requires a certain equilibrium. From this interaction is derived the actual sender-receiver's interactional synchrony between common or different verbal and nonverbal systems, whether in a dyadic encounter or in a group.

In this regard I hope that someone eventually does a critical analysis of what I call the "invisible dyad," which occurs, for example, in telephone conversations. Also to be analyzed are the use and perception of paralinguistic alternants at different distances, mainly personal and intimate, among blind interactants.

If by way of introduction I have mentioned certain concepts and functions related to personal interaction, it is because I intend to single out paralinguistic alternants from the context of total body communication.

4. TOTAL BODY COMMUNICATION

4.1. I suggest that most of the semantic content of face-to-face interaction is conveyed by the human body through its various channels, the rest being just complementary information or intentional communication, facilitated, apart from the extensions of our organism (Hall 1966), by the physical environment in a sensory way and by the cultural context, as understood by the receiver in the case of acculturation. The communicative behaviors themselves are always subject to the biopsychological and socioeconomic background by which each subject is conditioned, both individually and culturally (Poyatos 1972a).

If we consider body communication as common to both humans and animals, then cultural context in the human sense would be lacking in the animal world. But we can certainly refer to the social organization and signaling systems of communities such as those of bees and chimpanzees. Following Sebeok (1969), we can distinguish, on the one hand, ZOOSEMIOTIC means of communication, such as paralanguage (taken only as vocal-nonverbal phenomena), kinesics, proxemics, and tactile and olfactory perception (at least for essential functions like mating, defense of territory, etc.); and on the other hand, ANTHROPOSEMIOTIC systems, including the ones just mentioned, plus language and a much wider paralinguistic repertoire, for it is conditioned by a more elaborated articulatory system and by the human intellect.

4.2. I believe that, excluding linguistic expression, the essential communicative difference between man and members of other animal species is that man's communicative behavior, of whatever nature, is more affected by other modalities (proxemics, kinesics, eye contact, etc.). These act in two capacities, as MODIFIERS and as CONTEXT, and it is the nature of these two elements that differentiate man from the other more advanced species. The modifiers can be of a paralinguistic, kinesic, proxemic, or intellectual nature, while the context is provided by the very cultural principles and modes perceived, learned, and accepted in society.

4.3. In light of the above observations I offer Table 1, which is an exhaustive and interrelated classification of all communicative-informative elements constituting TOTAL BODY COMMUNICATION. By this term I automatically exclude any mechanical media and external agents, except handwriting (as reflecting a psychosomatic and personality condition), object-adapters (a pipe, a paper clip etc.), and body-adaptors (clothing, jewelry, etc.).

5. PARALANGUAGE

I define paralanguage as the nonverbal voice qualities, modifiers, and sounds produced or conditioned in the areas covered by the supraglottal cavities (from the lips and the nares to the glottis) and the infraglottal cavities, down to the abdominal muscles, which are, consciously or unconsciously, used by man simultaneously to support or contradict the linguistic or kinesic message. Within paralanguage I differentiate four categories:

5.1. PRIMARY QUALITIES are elements that, while being first considered as indispensable constituents of verbal language, may also modify it or alternate with it as paralinguistic phenomena. They are TIMBRE, or voice register, which is differentiated, because of the size of the vocal cords, not only by sex and age, but also geographically; PITCH LEVEL or tone in which a certain portion of speech may be conducted; PITCH REGISTERS, which become a very interesting paralinguistic feature when, for instance, the North American speaker applies his four registers to the three of Spanish; PITCH INTERVAL, which can be spread or compressed; INTONATION RANGE, extending from melodious to monotonous; VOLUME of the voice, which is also important in cross-cultural studies; SYLLABIC DURATION, which extends from clipped to drawled, the latter typically used by the North American speaker; OVERALL TEMPO of speech, which is dependent

Table 1. Total body communication

```
                              ┌ Language and prosodic features  Verbal-vocal
                              │                        ┌ Primary qualities
              ┌ Respiratory ┤ Vocal                    │ Modifiers ┌ Qualifiers
              │             │        Paralanguage      │           │ Differentiators
              │             │                          └ ALTERNANTS Nonverbal-vocal
              │             │                                      Nonverbal-nonvocal
              │             │   ┌ Intestinal sounds
Acoustic ┤    │ Non-        ┤   │ Bone sounds      ┌ Free gestures (finger snapping)
    *         │ respiratory │                Gestures │ Self-adaptors (fist against
              │             │                         │   palm)
              │             │        Non-  ┌ Visual-         ┌ Acoustic manners (knuckle
              │             │        vocal │ acoustic │ Manners │ cracking)
              │             │              │ kinesics         │ Self-adaptors (thigh slapping)
              │             │                                  │ Object-adaptors (desk tapping)
              │             │                                  └ Alter-adaptors (back slapping)
              │                        ┌ Gestures ┌ Free gestures (face, headnods, hands,
              │                        │          │   eyes)
              │                        │          └ Self-adaptors (hand to chin)
              │             Visual-silent         ┌ Free manners (interlocked hands with
              │   Motor-   ┤ kinesics             │   thumbs spinning)
              │   based     │          Manners    │ Self-adaptors (slapping one's sides in
              │                        │          │   the cold)
              │                        │          │ Object-adaptors (pipe handling)
              │                        │          └ Alter-adaptors (hand shaking, arm-in-
Visual ┤      │                                       arm)
   **         │                        └ Postures (sitting, standing)
              │                 ┌ Intimate ┐
              │                 │ Personal │ close phase, far phase
              │        Proxemics┤ Social   │
              │                 │ Public   ┘
              │                 └ Distance from object-adaptors (desk, counter,
                                     railing)
                              ┌ Body-adaptors (clothes, wigs, glasses, jewelry)
                   Static     │ Body appearance (gait, grooming signs)
                   cues       │ Dermal changes (blushing, gooseflesh)
                              └ Secretions (tears, perspiration)
          Static              ┌ Grooming (perfume, shaving lotion, hair conditioner)
Olfactory ┤                   │ Body odor (lack of grooming, breath, perspiration)
    *                         │ Odor from body-adaptors (clothes, tobacco, drinking)
Tactile                       │ Alter-adaptor kinetics (lovemaking, handshake)
    *                         │ Intimate and personal proxemics (courtship, handshake)
                              │ Kinesthetic perception (lovemaking, handshake, pres-
                              │   sure)
                              └ Skin perception (lovemaking, temperature, skin texture)
```

Conditioning background		
Biopsychological	Social: horizontal	Social: vertical
Sex / Age / Hereditary, somatogenic / Physiology / Health / Psychology / Physical medium / Socioeconomic medium	Individual / Married couple / Family-Clan / Social group / Geographical	Refined / Educated / Modest employee / Pseudoeducated / Rustic

on the biopsychological and social background; and GENERAL RHYTHM
OF SPEECH.

5.2. MODIFIERS, the second paralinguistic category, can be arranged as
they appear before the observer, that is, in contrastive sets. The terms
of these polar pairs can differ by as many degrees as we need for our
analysis, from a middle point I prefer to call medium, rather than normal.
I distinguish two groups of modifiers: qualifiers and differentiators.

5.2.1. QUALIFIERS are modifications of the voice caused not only by
changes in the area between the thoracic cavity and the mouth and nose,
but also by facial anatomy. These may cover from isolated syllables to
long stretches of speech. The qualifiers are GLOTTALIC CONTROL: breath or
respiration — whispering — phonation; VELAR CONTROL: voice oral —
medium — nasal — very nasal; ARTICULATORY TENSION: produced in the
larynx; ARTICULATORY CONTROL: voice clear — medium — slurred;
PHARYNGEAL CONTROL: very open voice — medium — rasp — hoarse;
LARYNGEAL CONTROL: aspiration — glottalization (tension); LABIAL
CONTROL: lips distended upwards or downwards — puckered or protruding — receded inward; MAXILLARY CONTROL: lower jaw thrust
forward or backward; and RESPIRATORY CONTROL: ingression — egression.

5.2.2 DIFFERENTIATORS can also be alternants, although alternants do not
modify the linguistic structure proper, while differentiators, such as
laughter, may cover whole stretches of speech (combined with primary
qualities and qualifiers), distorting it. They differentiate certain psychological and even physiological states in several cultures, and they are not
always universal (Spanish "¡Ay!" English "Ouch!"). The most typical
differentiators can be grouped according to their basic characteristic
(especially when one, like laughing, forms a whole class with different
nuances and cultural and subcultural varieties) and then by degrees.
Among the more common differentiators are: WHISPERING — mumbling,
whispering, muttering, murmuring; LOUD VOICE — screaming, yelling,
crying out (open, muffled, hoarse), screeching, squealing (oral, nasal),
shrieking, howling, roaring; CRYING — trembling voice, tremulous,
quavering voice, breaking voice, sighing, panting, sobbing, crying,
weeping, whimpering; LAUGHING — snickering, tittering, giggling,
chuckling, open laughter, guffawing, convulsive laughter (all with varying
vowel sound and nasalization); COMPLAINING — grumbling, muttering,
whining, moaning, groaning, growling, grumbling, murmuring; COUGHING
— (when it modifies the verbal utterance, not isolated as an alternant);
and YAWNING — not as an alternant or as a kinesic phenomenon (silent

yawn). Other modifying factors that might be taken for differentiators at first sight are actually caused by the conditioning background, such as when the voice is convulsive because of cold, or slurred while speaking with a pipe in the mouth.

5.3. ALTERNANTS, the fourth group of paralinguistic phenomena and the subject of this article, can be defined as ingressive or egressive, nonverbal, marginal and nonspeech sounds or clusters of sounds, articulated or not, produced or shaped in the areas covered by the supraglottal cavities (nares, nasal chamber, nasal pharynx, mouth, and pharynx), the laryngeal cavity (glottis friction or real voice), the infraglottal cavities, and the diaphragm and the abdominal muscles, which do not affect the verbal utterance (although they can be modified by primary qualities, qualifiers, and kinesic modifiers). Alternants occur either isolated or alternating with the verbal utterance and with the kinesic behavior.

6. THE PROBLEMS AND STATUS OF ALTERNANTS

6.1. Alternants are difficult to analyze, both from the physiological and the articulatory-acoustic points of view. Not only can they deceive the ear because of perceptual factors, but they also can depend on idiosyncratic elements which, particularly in a cross-cultural study, must be recognized as such. Traditionally, rather than being considered as part of the nonverbal-vocal repertoire (as is anthropophonemically possible and is, in fact, actually the case in some lesser-known languages), alternants have been shunted aside as "abnormal," when they actually belong within the acoustic body-communication system, in close interrelationship with other nonverbal modalities, and convey as much specific meaning as lexical constructs. In fact, alternants should incite "nonverbal communicationalists" to elaborate a realistic phonemic chart of a culture, or subculture, beyond what is provided by the International Phonetic Alphabet (IPA). All of the articulatory possibilities of man, as suggested in Catford (1968) should be studied, first according to specific cultures and subcultures or groups, and then according to the normal but idiosyncratic variations, and even through the psychiatric patient, if necessary. As Pike (1943:39) said, "When such nonspeech sounds occur in connected speech they sometimes carry important social connotations, and need symbols if complete representation is to be given."[2]

[2] Much could be said about the mistaken criteria and statements cited in Pike's *Phonetics* with regard to the treatment by other authors of speech and nonspeech sounds, and the limitations of phonetic alphabets.

6.2. After conversing at a recent session on paralinguistics (Northeast Modern Language Association, Boston, 1973) with Philip Lieberman and Richard M. Harris, I felt a strange mixture of joy and dismay when my doubts about the very uncertain boundaries between "linguistic" and "paralinguistic" were confirmed (Lieberman 1975). Personally, I am inclined to look for the conceptual, and even lexical, value of many of the sounds and clusters of sounds I have called alternants because they possess the distinctive, sometimes irreplaceable, semantic value that words have. Moreover, if alternants were consistently represented by the existing orthographic symbols (necessarily complemented by some additional ones) they could perfectly well appear as entries in a dictionary and be used by the letter-writing layman as well as by the professional novelist or playwright (Poyatos 1972b). It seems absurd to me that without any satisfactory etymology new words have been introduced into dictionaries, simply because usage has forced them into the English lexicon, yet many of the alternants outlined below have not been granted the same privilege.

Each language, or rather each culture, contains a great number of paralinguistic (?) alternants that are perfectly coded and decoded by interactants in countless everyday situations, both in face-to-face encounters and in the invisible dyad, their variations in form and meaning often depending on the context (e.g. a sigh), just as words do ("Well..."). Therefore, why should not a novelist be able to resort to that repertoire of alternants that exists in his mind when he is at work, that he has learned to use in proper context, but that only because of traditional and restricting spelling and "linguistic" taboos, he cannot represent vividly as part of his stylistic and technical devices? From this point of view, among others, I consider the situation quite abnormal, and I wholeheartedly agree with Lieberman (1974) that "phonetic" elements of human language need not be restricted to the accepted segmental elements conveyed by traditional orthography.

6.3. Just as Lieberman (1972) suspects that an advanced hominid species like classic Neanderthal man, while lacking many of today's segmental phonetic elements, probably used "tone of voice" for different semantic constructs, I believe that an exhaustive classification and analysis of paralinguistic alternants and a systematic orthographic representation would enrich not only our "linguistic inventory," but "literary possibilities" for writers. That the pretended "rigid dichotomy" between "linguistic" and "paralinguistic" is an artifice (paralinguistic is sometimes an automatic classification for sounds which cannot be transcribed with

IPA symbols) cannot be more true than in the case of alternants, and I suggest that very similar phonetic-semantic constructs may have preceded the appearance of human language.

7. ALTERNANTS WITHIN THE TRIPLE STRUCTURE

7.1. Considering the combination of phonemes and morphemes, even if acoustically perceived — that is, disregarding writing as a very secondary symbolic system — a sentence appears quite lifeless if we attach to it only stress, pitch, and juncture. Under normal circumstances, any stretch of speech carries some nonverbal elements, even above those suprasegmental ones that constitute paralanguage; and, if visually perceived, that sentence will probably be, even if imperceptibly (as in the invisible dyad situation or in a critically ill patient), accompanied by certain kinesic acts closely related to the linguistic and the paralinguistic structures. These three levels, linguistic (verbal-vocal or lexical), paralinguistic (nonverbal-vocal), and kinesic (nonverbal-nonvocal), form what I have termed "the basic triple structure of human communicative behavior" (Poyatos 1971), the first and main communicative complex to be considered within total body communication.

Within this triple set of more or less simultaneous communicative activities, alternants play essential roles as regulators between language and kinesics, and, with respect to each one of the three levels separately, by claiming, suppressing, or yielding the linguistic or kinesic turn or by serving as back-channel feedback in personal interaction. However, simply within the flow of the triple activity of one speaker, without considering the other interactant, the importance of alternants can be observed by using a transcription of a stretch of that activity. Such a transcription would go beyond the model by which it was inspired (Pittinger et al. 1960), because it would show the kinesic behavior, and it would be represented on the levels indicated in Table 2.

Table 2.   Levels of transcription

Phonemic transcription		PT_____	
Paralinguistic transcription	Primary qualities	PQ_____	
	Qualifiers	Q_____	
	Differentiators	D_____	
	Alternants	A_____	
Transcript		T_____	
Kinegraphic transcription	Head	H_____	
	Arms and hands	A&H_____	
	Trunk and legs	T&L_____	

8. NATURE AND CODING OF ALTERNANTS

8.1. Following the classification that Ekman and Friesen (1969) used for nonverbal (motor-based) communication acts, we can place alternants in four of their five categories in this order of frequency: affect displays, regulators, illustrators, and emblems.

AFFECT DISPLAYS repeat, qualify, or contradict a lexically stated affect, either accompanying it or replacing it, and may convey not only the primary affects suggested by Ekman and Friesen (happiness, surprise, fear, sadness, anger, disgust, and interest), but may also convey what they have called AFFECT BLENDS, or multiple emotions shown by certain alternants. These are mainly alternants produced outside of awareness. For instance, an apicoalveolar click linked to a sigh may reveal a complex and conflicting mixture of affects which, in fact (as shown by the self-regulatory function, that is, within one's own repertoire), is duplicated by the facial expression. Affect blends are one of the four variables observed by Ekman and Friesen. The others include the EVOKING STIMULI that elicit the affect (a very important factor in a cross-cultural study, as varying affect displays can be brought about by the same affect-evoker, just as different evoking stimuli may produce the same emotional reaction); the DISPLAY RULES of those affects, socially learned according to certain techniques (to conceal the clues to a given affect, to overdo it, to look affectless, or to dissimulate it with another affect), and the BEHAVIORAL CONSEQUENCES of the affective display, again related to the self-regulatory function (as its effect on one's own verbal or kinesic behavior) and to the interactive function (modifying other people's behavior).

REGULATORS are the elements responsible for the smooth or irregular flow of the interactive exchange, and they may act as turn signals (e.g. a short pharyngeal ingression to indicate claiming of the turn), or as feedback, whether intentionally ("Mm-hm") or out of awareness (e.g. a nareal ingression of amusement). Many of them have kinesic (visual) equivalents (a headnod is like "Mm-hm") and play both self-regulatory functions and interactive ones.

ILLUSTRATORS are also represented by alternants (in which case I prefer to call them ECHOIC), and both affect displays and echoic alternants may have been an important part of the expressive behavior of *Homo sapiens* (when, although lacking more refined lexical constructs, he had already developed a definite cognitive ability) accompanying the kinesic affect displays. Ekman and Friesen (1969) offer several theories, including their own, for the origin and development of these displays.

EMBLEMS, which Efrón (1941) and Ekman and Friesen (1969) applied to gestures (specifying that they have a direct verbal translation and that they may repeat, substitute for, or contradict verbal behavior), can also be applied to those intentional and symbolic communicative alternants that have a shared decoded meaning, either within a group, a culture, or across cultures.

Just as affect displays can be emblems (e.g. the apicoalveolar click of regret or disappointment) if they have a very specific and agreed-upon meaning, they can also be regulators in the interaction, while some echoic alternants may have an emotive content, and even, at a given moment, back-channel feedback.

8.2. As for the relationship between alternants and their meaning, the coding can be ARBITRARY, as it is in most of them, or ECHOIC. In this case I use echoic as representing the acoustic equivalent of the iconic or visual sign. Echoic coding can be onomatopoeic, i.e., resembling its significant (a hiss to signify a flat tire) or intrinsic, being its significant (a "human" growl meant as such).

The meaning itself can be SHARED by several individuals (at least two), by a whole community, by a whole culture, or even by several cultures; or it can be purely IDIOSYNCRATIC, whether recurrent or not. This is extremely important in interaction because both participants need to have an encoding phase followed by decoding in order for the communicative act between sender and receiver to take place. There are alternants with shared encoded meaning and shared decoded meaning as well, and they constitute the accepted repertoire which typifies a group or a culture. On the other hand, some alternants are idiosyncratically encoded by a single individual and may have no effect on the other interactant(s), or may produce the wrong effect. They may have an idiosyncratic decoded meaning too, as happens between lovers, relatives, close friends, etc. The degree of idiosyncrasy or mutuality can vary considerably, and it is clear that the ideally effective alternant is the one shared by as many individuals as possible. Pan-cultural alternants must be differentiated from cultural ones, because ignoring this differentiation may result in a cultural clash and in a failure to communicate.

9. CLASSIFICATION AND ANALYSIS OF ALTERNANTS

9.1. Although from the strict phonetic standpoint alternants show, as in Table 3, a manner of articulation (or production) and a point of articulation (or production), I prefer to arrange the inventory I have been studying according to certain dominant characteristics, paying more attention to their actual phonemic values among the speakers, to the roles they play in personal interaction, and to their function and meaning from the semiotic point of view. These criteria seem to justify some of the groups suggested, such as those of clicks or whistling alternants, in

Table 3. Alternants: articulated and inarticulated

Point or area of articulation or production Manner of articulation or production	Bilabial	Labiodental	Dental	Interdental	Apico-alveolar	Dorso-palatal	Velar	Velic (velopharyngeal)	Pharyngeal	Naso-pharyngeal	Nareal	Glottal	Esophageal
Stop													
Explosive													
Fricative													
Frictional													
Affricate													
Click													
Labialized													
Whistling													
Vibrant													
Trilled													
Spasmodic													
Lateral													
Retrolateral													
Nasal													
Nareal													
Ingressive													
Unvoiced													
Drawled													
Clipped													
Closed lips													

Vocalic
- Open lips
- Closed lips

Front Central Back
- High
- Mid
- Low

- Single
- Gliding
- Double

spite of individual articulatory differences, while the rest adhere more to a phonetic classification.

I divide alternants between articulated and inarticulated, which does not at all mean that I am perfectly happy with the second term. I could have followed those who, like Catford (1968), made an effort to demonstrate articulatory possibilities from an "anthropophonemic" point of view (referring to the actual stricture types among the infinite variety of what "is pronounceable"). Instead, I have termed "inarticulated" those semantic constructs formed by pharyngeal, nasopharyngeal, and nareal friction, precisely because, even though they have been discarded until now as nonphonemic articulations, I am trying to stress their enormous significance in personal interaction. To these two groups I add "pausal alternants," mainly unfilled pauses (but still modified by, and communicating through, a definite structure shaped by duration, paralinguistic, kinesic and proxemic modifiers, and situational context).

9.2. The problems posed by alternants are obvious. Most of them defy a systematic analysis into contrastive sets, and their qualities are difficult to measure, except for some, like phonation versus voicelessness, closed lips versus open lips, tenseness versus laxness; or when we refer to paralinguistic and kinesic modifiers (or their absence), which do not always modify meaning, as in the case of nasalization, low brows versus high brows, etc., in a number of alternants that are not affected by them. Another problem is labeling, as there are a great number of alternants for which we lack a noun and a verb, just as we have "to hiss" and "hiss," "to gasp" and "gasp." In other words, we need to name those significant sounds when referring to them, because, although it is possible to paraphrase when speaking of semantically different types of hissing (beckoning-hissing, sexual-hissing, hushing-hissing, etc.), to call the bilabial stop+ apico-alveolar fricative ([ps]) "hissing," would not be correct. Thus we must necessarily coin something like "to pist" and "pist." But how to speak of, or write, a cynical tense nasopharyngeal egression, or a closed-lip nareal one that signals contempt? For one thing, we should take more seriously the cartoon system for transcribing a good number of vocally produced sounds, and even noises produced by objects, a system that could be adapted to standard use with some refinements and additions.

Finally, another problem is that of phonetic transcription. Some symbols not yet used in conventional notations need to be devised. Table 4 gives the symbols used in this article, which are meant to be as uncomplicated as possible. Some of them are susceptible to certain additions when different features concur.

Table 4. Phonetic symbols

[·] unvoiced
[ʰ] explosive
[¹] click
[¹¹] tense click
[ʷ] labialized
[˂] vibrant
[ʔ] glottal trill
[⌣] spasmodic
[Lx] latero-velar
[Lrx] retrolatero-velar
[˜] nasal, nasalized
[Y] nareal
[Ÿ] tense nareal
[/] unilateral
[˃] ingressive

[͈] drawled
[͈͈] overdrawled
[^] clipped
[͈̂] overclipped
[x] closed-lips
[ʕ] pharyngeal
[ɫ] tense pharyngeal
[ʇ] velic
[ə̰] [ɜ̰] vowels with pharyngeal friction
[ə̃] [ɜ̃] vowels with nasopharyngeal friction
[ᶇ] velopharyngeal
[ʕ] glottalized
[-] abrupt transition, if alone
[͜] smooth transition

9.3. At any rate, the analysis of any individual alternant should be carried out according to the factors listed in Table 5. In addition, the following working symbols are used: ( ) encloses linguistic, paralinguistic, kinesic or proxemic activities that may or may not accompany the one under discussion; / is used between alternatives; w/o means "with or without"; + means "followed by"; — means "preceded by."

What follows, then, is a partial inventory of paralinguistic alternants classified and analyzed according to the norms suggested above. Some

Table 5. Factors for the analysis of alternates

Art articulation or production
Tr phonetic transcription
Lab labeling
W writing
Mod modifiers:
    Pg paralanguage
    K kinesics
    Px proxemics
Srf self-regulatory function:
    Lg language
    Pg paralanguage
    K kinesics
    Px proxemics
    Chr chronemics
N nature
M meaning:
    E encoded
    D decoded
    S sherad
    I idiosyncratic
CB conditioning background
Cc cross-cultural similarities/differences

of the factors mentioned in the preceding list may be lacking in some instances, which is due simply to the absence of a satisfactory solution.

10. ARTICULATED ALTERNANTS

10.1. CONSONANTAL ALTERNANTS combine two articulations, but when one of the two is a vowel, thus having a syllabic quality, it is still the consonantal sound that distinguishes it from other alternants and provides a specific meaning. Although I do not specify whether this consonant is voiced or voiceless (it depends on individual and subcultural variations that do not alter the meaning), I record different degrees of velar control, of shifts within the area of articulation, of pitches, etc., and refer to "unvoiced" when voicing or phonation is lacking, and to "spasmodic" for truly pseudo-spasmodic sounds that occur intentionally and not as physiological reflexes.

10.1.1. BILABIAL ALTERNANTS
1. *Art* Drawled unvoiced explosive bilabial. *Tr* [.pʰ]. *Mod:* K Protruding lips. *Srf(a): Lg* ("What a job!"), *K* Eyes closed/wide-open. *Srf(b): Lg* ("What legs!"), *K* Gazing with wide-open eyes/looking away. *If* Feedback. *N* Emblem and affect-display. *M* SED as unpleasant expectation, surprise, sexual attraction. *Cc* Also Latin.
2. *Art* Glottalized (spasmodic) explosive bilabial. *Tr* [ʔpʰ]/[ʔp̱ʰ]. *Mod:* *K* Slightly protruding lips. *Srf: Lg* ("Who knows!"), *Pg* (high pitch), *K* Half-closed/open eyes (slight head-jerk/slight shoulder-shrug/both). *If* Feedback. *N* Emblem. *M* SED as disbelief, skepticism. *Cc* Also Latin.
3. *Art* Drawled vibrant bilabial. *Tr* [Ḇ]. *Lab* To shiver, shiver. *W* Brrr! *Srf: Lg* ("It's cold!"/"It must be cold out!"), *K* Self-embrace and patting on the sides (half-closed eyes, frowning/wide-open eyes). *N* Emblem and self-adaptor. *M* SED as real, expected, or imaginary cold. *Cc* Latins rub both hands (palms, or palms and backs) together.

10.1.2. LABIODENTAL ALTERNANTS
1. *Art* High-back vowel+(drawled) labiodental fricative. *Tr* [uf]/[uf̱]. *Mod: Pg* Varying drawling (drawled pharyngeal ingression [↑]—), *K* Open/half-open/closed eyes. *Srf(a): Lg* ("I'm beat!" "It's so hot!" "It'll be hot!"), *K* (Wiping out real or imaginary perspiration), half-closing eyes, dropping head a few inches. *Srf(b): Lg* ("She's beautiful!" "She's really sexy!"), *K* Half-closed/open eyes, raised brows, slight diagonal head-jerk.

2. *Art* Drawled ingressive labiodental fricative. *Tr* [ˑf̣]. *W* Ff! *Mod:* *Pg* Varying drawling, *K* Distended lips. *Srf: Lg* ("Oh, it hurts!" "It must hurt!"), *K* Shaking one's hand/other movements conditioned by actual pain. *N* Emblem.
3. *Art* Clipped ingressive labiodental fricative+bilabial stop. *Tr* [ˑfp]. *W* Fp!. *Mod: Pg* Clipping, *K* Slightly distended, pressed lips. *Srf: Lg* ("Oh, it hurts!" "It must hurt!")
4. *Art* Drawled spasmodic glottalized labiodental fricative. *Tr* [ʔf̣]. *Mod: Pg* Varying glottalization and drawling, *K* Unilateral lip and cheek raising. *Srf: Lg* ("Who knows!"), *K* Gesture of disbelief, shoulder-shrug. *If* Feedback. *N* Affect-display, emblem. *M* SED as disbelief, skepticism.
5. *Art* Nasalized glottal trill+spasmodic labiodental fricative. *Tr* [ʔ̃f̣]. *Mod: Pg* Tense articulation, *K* (Puckered upper lip). *Srf: Lg* ("I can't stand it!"), *Pg* High pitch, *K* Puckered upper lip and nose, frowning, half-closed eyes/lips distended slightly downwards. *N* Emblem, affect-display.

10.1.3. WHISTLING ALTERNANTS

Because of their many functional and semantic affinities, I have grouped under "whistling alternants" a series of egressive or ingressive articulations that seem to share a hissing (or actual whistling) quality, composed of certain fricatives, like sibilants([s], [z]) and sibilants ([ʃ], [ʒ]), certain affricates ([tʃ], [pf], [ts]), and some consonantal clusters ([pst], [st]), besides the different varieties of labial whistling. According to Pike (1943) whistling is "a kind of double vocoid in which the front labial partial stricture is of a special type that gives WHISTLE TIMBRE while the lingual structure controls the pitch," that is, high with front-tongue position, and low with back-tongue position; and dental whistles with "both labial and lingual vocoidal modifications for pitch." Apart from actual whistling (which at a public show or game indicates approval in North America, but disapproval in Spain), these are some other varieties:

1. *Art* Voiceless bilabial stop+apico-alveolar fricative. *Tr* [ps]. *Mod: Pg* Tends to clipping. *Srf(a): Lg* ("I don't care!" "So what!"), *K* Gesture of indifference. *Srf(b): Lg* ("Hey, you!" "Hey!"), *K* Gesture of beckoning. *N* Emblem, affect-display. *M* SED as indifference, but unacceptable in North America as beckoning. *Cc* Typical in Latin countries.
2. *Art* Apico-alveolar fricative. *Tr* [s]. *Lab* To hiss, hiss. *W* Ss!. *Mod: Pg* Varying duration, *K* Neutral/slightly distended lips. *Srf: Lg* ("Waiter!"), *K* Gesture of beckoning. *N* Emblem. *Cc* and *CB* Typical in Latin countries with a hand gesture and raised brows (head-nod), but

only in a popular café. Also for calling a woman's attention in the street.
3. *Art* Apico-alveolar fricative+dental stop. *Tr* [st]. *Mod: K* Distended lips raises pitch. *Srf(a): Lg* ("Quiet!"), *K* (Frowning). *Srf(b)*: Spanish, *Lg* ("¡Hola, guapa!" "Hi, baby!"), *K* (Wink). *Srf(c):* Spanish, *K* Gesture of beckoning. *If* Turn-suppressing as hushing. *N* All emblems. *M* All SED. *Cc b* and *c* common among Spaniards. *CB c* only at a popular café.
4. *Art* Apico-alveolar affricate. *Tr* [t͡s]/[t͡s]. *Lab* To tiss, tiss. *W* Ts!, Tss!. *Mod, Srf, If,* as in 3.
5. *Art* Double apico-alveolar affricate. *Tr* [t͡s -/ t͡s]. *Lab* To double-tiss, double tiss. *Mod, Srf, If,* as in 3. *Cc* Common among Spanish males to call a woman's attention in the street as a sexual overture.
6. *Art* Like 1, but double. Also sexual overture among Spaniards.

Several interesting varieties of "paralinguistic sexual overtures" can be observed among Spaniards, the degrees of eroticism (and upbringing) usually revealed by the degree of lip-protruding.

10.1.4. CLICKS Clicks, which are reported as being phonologically utilized only in some African languages (Pike 1943; Catford 1968; above all, Stopa 1972), are actually a rich part of the paralinguistic repertoire of the best known Western cultures. They do not require respiration, but suction, and are produced by a double occlusion: a front one (bilabial, apico-alveolar, lateral, vibrant retrolateral) and a dorso-velar one, the air going in when the front occlusion opens abruptly, accompanied or not by nasal phonation.
1. *Art* Unilateral bilabial click. *Tr* [B'/]. *Lab* Regret click. *Mod: Pg* Varying articulatory tension, *K* Unilateral lip-distension affects lateralization. *Srf: Lg* ("Oh, well!"), *K* (Shoulder-shrug). *If* Feedback. *N* Affect-display and emblem. *M* SED as regret or disappointment. *Cc* More common among English speakers.
2. *Art* Bilabial click. *Tr* [B']. *Lab* To kiss, kiss. *Mod: Pg* Varying articulatory tension, *K* The shape of the lips conditions the acoustic qualities of the click. *Srf* Either as a greeting or as an expression of love and/or sexual desire, the kiss regulates the kinesic and proxemic behaviors of the interactant in many ways. *M* SED. *Cc* and *CB* Numerous factors can be analyzed, such as interesting cross-cultural varieties depending upon exact placement of the kiss; the type of sound produced, the degree of loudness or the lack of it, the accompanying kinesic behavior, and the setting in which it takes place; all these factors varying according, not only to culture, but to sex, social status, and personality characteristics.
3. *Art* Tense nasalized bilabial click. *Tr* [B'']. *Lab* To smack the lips

in gusto, gusto smack. *Mod: Pg* Varying velar control, *K* Protruding lips accent explosion. *Srf: Lg* (+Delicious!/+Beautiful!), *Pg* Emphasis accents lip pressure and retains nasalization longer, *K* Bunched fingers of one hand touch lips, then open abruptly (or slowly if indicating sheer delicacy) from mouth. *M* SED as physical or intellectual, real or imaginary enjoyment. *Cc* Latin gesture now quite common in North America.

4. *Art* Dorso-palatal click+drawled pharyngeal ingression. *Tr* [tz'↑]. *Lab* To smack one's palat, palatal smack. *Mod: Pg* Varying pharyngeal friction, *K* Often wide-open mouth after release of click. *Srf: Lg*(+"Good wine!"), *Pg* Emphasis enhances pharyngeal egressive friction, *K* Half-/wide open mouth (+open/closed eyes). *N* Emblem. *M* SED as enjoyment of good food or drink. *CB* Standard among pseudo-educated and rustics in several cultures.

5. *Art* Apico-alveolar click+clipped pharyngeal ingression. *Tr* [tz'↑]. *Lab* Pre-speech click. *Mod: Pg* Varying ingression. *Srf: Lg* ("Wait" "Well..." "You musn't say that"), *K* (Lip-moistening/lip-moistening+ [tz'↑], such as is done by President Nixon during a speech), *Px* Unconsciously, regardless of distance, even on the phone. *If* Feedback/turn-claiming/turn-suppressing. *N* Regulator. *M* IE/IED/SED, as intention to speak, or to stop someone from saying something.

6. *Art* Apico-alveolar click. *Tr* [tz']. *Lab* Transitional click. *Srf: K* (+lip-moistening-). *Srf: Lg* ("That is" "In other words"). *If* Internal feedback, turn-holding (claiming) signal.

7. *Art* Apico-alveolar click. *Tr* [tz'] *Lab* Hesitation click. *Mod: K* Neutral/distended lips (+slight shoulder-shrug)/slight shoulder-shrug. *Srf Lg* ("I don't know what to do"), *Pg* Falling/raising pitch. *If* Feedback. *N* Affect-display. *M* SED as hesitation.

8. *Art* Single/double apico-alveolar click. *Tr* [tz']/[tz'-tz']. *Lab* Disapproval click. *Mod: K* (Unilateral tense lip-distension). *Srf: Lg* ("Naughty boy" "How could you?" "Wrong"), *K* Double headshake (frowning/raised brows)/fixed gaze, almost no K signs/shaking index finger at someone. *If* Can be turn-suppressing. *N* Emblem, affect-display/affect-blend (disapproval-disappointment). *M* SED as criticism, scolding, etc.

9. *Art* Apico-alveolar click. *Tr* [tz']. *Lab* Negation click. *Mod: K* Slight unilateral lip-distension raises pitch, protruding lips lower it. *Srf: Lg* (Verbal negation), *Pg* (+single/double negation vowel, or its closed-lip variant, [ə]/[əˣ]), *K* (Unilateral/bilateral headshake, raised/lowered brows, w/o raised index finger/slight finger shake at someone). *If* Feedback/turn-claiming/turn-suppressing. *N* Emblem. *M* SED as negation.

10. *Art* Double apico-alveolar click. *Tr* [tz'-tz']. *Lab* Double negation click. *Srf: Pg* (+single negation vowel or its closed-lip variant), *K* Same as 9.

11. *Art* Apico-alveolar click. *Tr* [tz']. *Lab* Discontent click. *Srf: Lg* ("What a pity!" "Oh well!"), *K* Unilaterally distended lips. *If* Feedback. *N* Emblem, affect-display/affect-blend. *M* SEM/SED depending on context.

12. *Art* Apico-alveolar click. *Tr* [tz']. *Lab* Resignation click. *Srf: Lg* ("Oh, well!"),*Pg* (+pharyngeal ingression), *K* Unilateral lip distension (raised brows). *M* SED as resignation.

13. *Art* Apico-alveolar click. *Tr* [tz']. *Lab* Sympathy click. *Srf: Lg* ("What a pity!" "How awful" "What a bad luck"), *K* (One or two headshakes, unilateral lip-distension). *Cc* Spaniards and other Latins use one or two head nods.

14. *Art* Apico-alveolar click. *Tr* [tz']. *Srf: Lg* ("Well, come on!" "It's getting late" "About time!"), *Pg* (+drawled tense nareal friction/drawled tense nareal friction-), *K* +tense lateral mouth distension/tense lateral mouth distension-, (closed eyes/raised gaze), (foot-tapping/finger-rapping, hastening hand gesture). *M* SED/IE/ID as impatience, contempt, irritation.

15. *Art* Apico-alveolar click, ingressive nareal friction. *Tr* [tz' ›Y]. *Lab* Annoyance ingressive click. *Mod: Pg* Medium/clipped ingression, *K* Neutral/slight unilateral lip distension raises pitch. *Srf: Lg* ("What a nuisance!" "Are you coming or not?!"), *Pg* Affect emphasis increases articulatory tension and drawling of ingression, *K* Same as 14. *If* Feedback, perhaps turn-suppressing. *N* Affect-display/affect-blend. *M* SED/IE/ID.

16. *Art* Apico-alveolar click. *Tr* [tz']. *Lab* Flirtation click. *Srf: K* Slight unilateral mouth distension and eye-wink. *If* Interactional turn-offering. *N* Emblem, affect display. *M* SED feminine flirtatious advance.

17. *Art* Double apico-alveolar click. *Tr* [tz'-tz']. *Lab* Masculine sexual click. *Mod: Pg* Varying degrees of labialization, and higher or lower pitch, with distended or protruding lips. *Srf: Lg* (+/verbal sexual overture), *K* Eye wink and bending slightly over towards woman, *Px* Public or far-phase personal distance. *If* Woman usually ignores it in America, but smiles/snaps back/ignores it in a Latin country. *N* Emblem, affect-display. *M* In Western cultures, SED.

18. *Art* Latero-velar click. *Tr* [lx']. *Srf(a): Lg* (+/Gee up!). *Srf(b):* Spanish, *Lg* (+"¡Fuera!" "Out!," to throw out, or chase away, a dog; or, mostly, jokingly, a person). *Srf(c):* Spanish, *Lg* ("¡Se acabó!" "And that's it!"). *Srf(d):* Spanish, *Lg* ("¡Qué fresco!" "The nerve," or the like). *Srf(e):* Afghanistan, *Lg* (meaning "Damn it!," or the like). *Srf(f):* Afghanistan, Kenya, to express disgust. *Srf(g):* Kenya, *K* Shaking head abruptly to express anger. *N* Emblem, affect-display. *M* SED. *Cc and*

CB b, c, and d, not common among the educated, but most common among Castilian small-town people in Spain.
19. *Art* Retrolateral-velar vibrant click. *Tr* [lrx']. *Cc* In Spain, also to urge a horse.
10.1.5. VELAR ALTERNANTS
1. *Art* Nasalized fricative velar+mid-back vowel. *Tr* [xɔ]. *Lab* Spanish euphemistic velar. *Mod: Pg* Varying tension and duration. *Srf: Lg* ("¡Joder!," "Fuck it!"), *K* (Unilateral bending of the head, raised/lowered brows. *M* In Spain, SED as superlative connotation of surprise, disappointment and some other affect displays. *CB* Masculine.
2. *Art* Lower high-front to mid-central nasalized gliding vowel+tense velo-pharyngeal fricative. *Tr* [ĩə̃h̃]. *Mod: Pg* Varying velar control and vowel location, and articulatory tension, *K* Distended mouth (raised nose, frowning). *Srf: Lg* ("Oh, I can't stand the sight of it!"), *K* (Pincing one's nose if something smells badly/gesture of dismissal). *N* Emblem; affect display if not physical reaction. *M* SED as repugnance.
10.2. VOCALIC ALTERNANTS are mainly glottalized (voiced) central vowel-like sounds (mostly [ə] and [ɔ]) with up to five pitch levels and varying nasalization, each of which has a closed-lip variant with identical or almost identical meaning, sometimes appearing in abruptly or smoothly linked pairs, the second element with pharyngeal friction ([ə]/[ə]); some appear as gliding vowels. I refer to "closed-lip variants" (CLV) because one tends to articulate the vowel with the lips closed.
1. *Art* Overdrawled mid-central glottalized vowel/CLV, pitch 1. *Tr* [ʔə̰¹]/[ʔə̰x¹]. *Lab* Hesitation vowel. *Srf: Pg* (+apico-alveolar click [tz']/ drawled pharyngeal ingression [ʔ ↑]-), *K* Neutral face/lowered or raised brows/biting lower lip, frowning or lowering one eyelid; in CLV, protruding/receding lips. *If* Hesitating turn-taking/turn-claiming. *N* Emblem/affect display. *Cc* Typically Anglo-American, but European borrowing through TV, live interviews, etc., can be observed. In Spain, for instance, "lexical" hesitation is more common.
2. *Art* Glottalized gliding mid-to-higher-back vowel/CLV, pitches 2-3. *Tr* [ʔɔ̰ɔ̰]/[ʔɔ̰ɔ̰]/[ʔɔ̰x̰]. *Lab* Interrogation vowel. *Mod: Pg* Varying velar control (nasalization) and pitch. *Srf: Lg* ("Is that so?/Tell me about it"), *K* Lowered/raised brows (half-nod [postural shift to listen]), *Px* (Shortening distance to speaker). *If* Feedback, turn-offering. *N* Emblem. *M* SED as interest.
3. *Art* Overdrawled labialized higher mid-back vowel/CLV, pitch 3. *Tr* [o̰↛]/[o̰↛]. *Lab* Estimation vowel. *W* Oooh.../Ooow... *Mod: Pg* Varying drawling and pitch (3 to 1). *Srf: Lg* (About), *Pg* The "wilder" the guess (or the more emphasis), the higher the pitch, as a rule, *K*

Protruding/receding lips. *Cc* While in English one says "We were, oooh...thirty people," in other languages, like Spanish, the tendency may be to using "estimating" words.

4. *Art* Double mid-central vowel/CLV, pitches 2-3. *Tr* [ə̰-ə̰]/[ə̰-ə̰x]. *Lab* Affirmation vowel. *Mod: Pg* Varying velar control, duration, and pitch (also 2-2); it may vary to [ə]. *Srf: Lg* (Verbal affirmation), *Pg* (Pharyngeal ingression [›↑]-), *K* (Single/double head-nod/single nod, eye wink); no *K* may reveal doubt. *If* Necessary as alternating or simultaneous feedback for smooth flow; also in the invisible dyad. *N* Emblem, variations can be affect displays; both may act as regulators. *M* SED as affirmation. *CB* Mostly by adults and "mature" children, as this type of feedback is not common in children. *Cc* While it is Anglo-American standard, and much borrowed in other cultures, it is never heard, for instance, among Spanish rustics (but I know farmers around tourist resorts who use it).

5. Double drawled+pharyngealized clipped mid-central vowel/CLV, pitch 2-3. *Tr* [ə̰-ə̰]/[ə̰-ə̰x]. *Lab* Emphatic affirmation vowel. *W* Ah-ha. *Mod: Pg* Same as in 4. *Srf: Lg* (Emphatic affirmation), *K* Emphatic nod (wink); no *K* may reveal doubt, fear. *If* Feedback, but perhaps more turn-claiming to corroborate the speaker's statement. *N* Affect-display. *M* SED as affirmation. *Cc* Spaniards use an emphatic voiceless fricative velar [x]; commonly [a-xa-xá].

6. *Art* Drawled glottalized mid-central nasalized gliding vowel/CLV, pitches 4-2. *Tr* [ʔə̃³]/[ʔə̃²]. *Lab* Agreement vowel. *Mod: Pg* Pitch height depends on emphasis. *Cc* Many Anglo-American speakers use the closed-lip variant to agree with expressions like "Nice day," "Too expensive."

7. *Art* Double glottalized mid-central vowel/CLV, pitches 2-2/3-2. *Tr* [ʔə̰-ʔə̰]/[ʔə̰-ʔə̰]/[ʔə̰x-ə̰x]. *Lab* Negation vowel. *W* Ah-ah, Uh-uh. *Mod: Pg* Varying velar control, can be very nasal; 3-2 emphasizes; it may change to [ə]. *Srf: Lg* (Verbal negation), *Pg* ([tz']-), *K* Unilateral/bilateral/double headshake (frowning). *If* Turn-claiming/turn-taking, after pre-speech [tz' ›↑]. *N* Emblem, affect display/affect-blend. *CB* The more informal, the more emphatic (as with children).

8. *Art* Double (clipped+drawled) glottalized mid-central vowel/CLV, pitches 3-1/3-2. *Tr* [ʔə̰-ʔə̰]/[ʔə̰x-ʔə̰x]. *Lab* Emphatic negation vowel. *Srf: K* (Tense unilateral/bilateral/double headshake tense frowning/raised brows). *Cc* Both affirmation and negation vowels are more typical of Anglo-American speakers, but they have been transmitted to other cultures through movies and visitors.

9. *Art* Glottalized gliding mid-to-higher-back vowel/CLV, pitches 3-2. *Tr* [ʔɔ⁰]/[ʔɔ̃]/ British [ʔɔ⁰]. *Lab* Surprise vowel. *Mod: Pg* Varying velar control, emphatic by raising pitch and by drawling. *Srf: Lg* ("I see!"

"Is that so?!"), *K* Slight head-lift, raised brows. *If* Feedback. *M* SD, but not always SD without context.
10. *Art* Overdrawled trilled glottalized gliding mid-central to back vowel CLV, pitches 2-1. *Tr* [ʔɔ̃'] [ʔɔ̃ɔ̃]. *Lab* Displeasure moan. *Mod: Pg* Varying drawling and vowel quality, varying articulatory tension in direct proportion to displeasure. *Srf: K* (Facial signs of disgust, irritation, because subject may be waking up, or tired, or unwilling to do something, even serious thinking). *If* Feedback/turn-suppressing. *M* SED/IE only ("Oooh, let me sleep," "Oooh, not now," "I'm beat!").
11. *Art* Drawled glottalized gliding mid-to-higher-back vowel/CLV, pitches 4-2. *Tr* [ʔɔ̃']/[ʔɔ̃']. *Lab* Pleasure vowel. *Mod: Pg* Drawling and nasality increase with pleasure.
12. *Art* Overdrawled glottalized nasopharyngeal trilled gliding mid-to-higher back vowel/CLV, pitches 4-2. *Tr* [ʔɔ̃']/[ʔɔ̃ɔ̃]. *Lab* Sensual moan. *Mod. Pg* The higher the pitch and the more drawling, the more feminine, sensual, and/or erotic; trilling increases with muscular tension until released to open-glottis voicing. *Srf: Lg, Pg* Words and/or alternants heavily modified by velar, glottalic, pharyngeal, and respiratory controls, *K* From simple stretching (in real or imaginary pleasure) to "Marilyn Monroe's moan," to erotic play with closed eyes, open/closed mouth distension. *N* Affect-display, may act as stereotyped emblem, as in movie actresses.

11. INARTICULATED ALTERNANTS

1. *Art* Drawled pharyngeal ingression. *Tr* [↘ţ]. *Lab* Hesitation inspiration. *Srf* (Hesitation vowel), *K* As with hesitation vowel. *If* As with hesitation vowel.
2. *Art* Clipped pharyngeal/velic/nasopharyngeal ingression. *Tr* [↘ţ]/ [ʇ]/[ţ̃]. *Lab* Short prespeech inspiration. *Mod: Pg* (Almost simultaneous with the apico-alveolar click, [tz' ɔ̝ţ]). *Srf: Lg* (Verbal turn-claiming), *Pg* (Hesitation vowel/hesitation inspiration), *K* (+moistening lips/ moistening lips-, and putting tongue out and in, w/o hand forward, as for stopping someone, when turn-claiming/turn-suppressing). *If* Turn-claiming/turn-suppressing. *N* Regulator and/or affect-display. *M* SED with claiming/suppressing gesture, *IE* possible. *CB* Common in a nervous person, or under tension, as in a heated conversation.
3. *Art* Pharyngeal ingression. *Tr* [↘ţ]. *Lab* Prespeech inspiration. *Mod: K* Biting lower lip (upper is more feminine) modifies friction to a sort of labiodental. *Srf: Lg* ("Oh, no!" "No, wait!" "Well..."), *K* Raised/ lowered brows. *If* Same as in 1. *M* SED as fear of speaker's comment, desire to cut in, or correct his statement.

4. *Art* Drawled pharyngeal ingression. *Tr* [⇉↑]. *Lab* Long prespeech inspiration. *W* ("Ah—"). *Mod: Pg* Varying velar control, *K* As in 3. *Srf: Lg* (I'll tell you what" "Listen to me"), *Pg* As in 3, *K*(*a*) Brows slightly lowered, *K*(*b*) Quick blink (tongue out-in), *K*(*c*) Tongue out-in, *K*(*d*) Posture shift (combined with *a, b, c*). *If* Same as in 3. *M* SED as readiness for "important" statement, self-assurance, dominance. *CB* Movie actors' repertoire.

5. *Art* Drawled pharyngeal ingression. *Tr* [⇉↑]. *Lab* Postspeech inspiration. *Srf: Lg* (+"And that's the story of my life"), *Pg* (+nareal egression with closed lips [ɣₓ]/ initiated apico-alveolar click [tz']), *K* +pressed lips/brief kinesic pause-/+posture shift. *If* Can be turn-yielding. *N* Regulator. *M* SED as end of statement or speech.

6. *Art* Ingressive closed-lip nareal friction. *Tr* [⇉ɣₓ]. *Lab* Resignation sniff. *Srf: Lg* ("Oh, well"), *Pg* (Resignation click [tz']), *K* Slightly raised brows, unilateral lip-distension (typical of actress Giulietta Masina). *N* Affect-display, but also affect-blend. *M* SED as resignation, naive pride, depending on situational context.

7. *Art* Drawled tense closed-lip nareal friction. *Tr* [ɣₓ]. *Lab* Aggressive nasal expiration. *Srf: Lg* (Words of impatience, rage, contempt), *Pg* Preceded by short ingression to take air in (with a long one it would be a sigh)/(Apico-alveolar aggressive click [tz']-), *K* (Pressed jaws and lips, w/o lateral/unilateral distension, clenched fists/arms akimbo) *N* Affect-display/affect-blend. *M* SED/IE/ID. *Cc* Latins adopt the arms akimbo posture more often, specially rustics and the less educated, and mostly women.

8. *Art* Tense spasmodic glottalized nasopharyngeal friction. *Tr* [⁀ɟ]. *Mod: Pg* Varying pitch with slight semantic change. *Srf: K* Neutral face/pressed lips and unilateral mouth-distension, abdominal and head jerk. *M* SED/IE/ID as skepticism, amusement, contempt, cynicism.

9. *Art* Spasmodic closed-lip nareal friction with glottal trill. *Tr* [ᵗɣₓ]. *Mod: Pg* Same as in 8. *Srf* and *M* Same as in 8.

10. *Art* Ingressive closed-lip nareal friction. *Tr* [⇉ɣₓ]. *Lab* Masculine sniff. *Mod: K* Pinching one's nose produces explosion. *Srf: Lg* ("I'm ready" "There I go!" "Boy, I'd like to get her!"), *K* Unilateral mouth and nose distension (pinching the nose with thumb and side of index finger and then releasing it). *N* Emblem, affect-display. *M* SED as readiness, decision/ ID as nervous tic. *CB* Besides being mostly masculine, tension and *K* modifier increase with poor upbringing and sensitiveness.

11. *Art* Drawled pharyngeal ingression+drawled nasopharyngeal/ nareal egression (CLV). *Tr* [⇉↑-ɟ]/[⇉↑-ɣ]/[⇉↑ₓ-ɣₓ]. *Lab* Sigh. *Mod: Pg* Narealization produced by K modifier, that is, by closed lips. *Srf: Lg*

(Different verbal expressions of affect); eggression modifies simultaneous verbal utterance (whispered or voiced), *K* Raised brows+lowered brows (bilateral/unilateral lip-distension). *If* (Feedback) *N* Affect-display. *M* SED/IE/ID as distress, indifference, relief. *CB* More feminine than masculine, more in old age. *Cc* Typical among women in church in a Latin country, alone or modifying their praying or expressions like Spanish "¡Ay, Dios mio!."
12. *Art* Overdrawled tense pharyngeal ingression (CLV). *Tr* [>†]/[>†x]. *Lab* Pleasure inspiration. *Mod: Pg* Varying nasalization. *Srf: Lg* (+"Aaah!"), *K* Wide-open eyes. *N* Affect-display. *M* SED as real, imagined or anticipated physical or intellectual pleasure. *CB* Intensity and range of kinesic modifiers increase in direct proportion to poor upbringing, or in exceptional circumstances.

12. PAUSAL ALTERNANTS

Certain pausal phenomena have been discussed already: hesitation, prespeech and postspeech clicks, vowels, and various types of ingressive and egressive frictions. More than prespeech, however, I prefer the term "preaction," since an apico-alveolar click [tz'] may occur during a pause preceding kinesic or proxemic activity. Whether the click is a speech pause, a kinesic one, or a proxemic one is not always clear, as the click may precede a combination of all three. I would like to suggest the term PAUSAL ALTERNANTS to include this category of paralinguistic phenomena, but excluding filled pauses such as consonantal, vocalic, or inarticulated alternants.

A pause in itself, whether in speech, in kinesics, or in proxemics, may occur accompanied by noticeable variations of the two respiratory phases (AUDIBLE PAUSE), due perhaps to physical exhaustion, an emotional state, etc., thus not lacking a semantic content. But even when there is a complete gap from the point of view of audible activity (SILENT PAUSE), that portion of silence has a definite structure marked by duration, kinesic and proxemic indicators, and situational context.

While some authors like Boomer and Dittmann (1962) distinguish between juncture pauses (syntactically regular) and hesitation pauses (syntactically irregular), I would like to suggest the following types of unfilled pauses within paralinguistic (but applicable to other activities) pausal alternants:

A. TRANSITIONAL PAUSE. This occurs at turning points in conversation or interaction, whether passing from one topic to another or from one part of "the story" to the next. It may be prompted also by postural shifts, proxemic shifts, and situational shifts (standing up to leave, on seeing someone approaching, etc.).

B. INITIATORY PAUSE. This does not indicate hesitancy. Once a topic, or an action for that matter, has been decided upon, there may be, and usually is, a brief moment of mental "organization," of taking an initial impulse that will develop and maintain the activity. I might add that it is possible to distinguish this pause from the one immediately preceding it, which could be a termination pause, the transition between both marked by blinking, lip-moistening, postural shifts, etc.

C. HESITATION PAUSE. While hesitancy offers several audibly filled pauses (just as the first two types do), it is shown also by means of the gaze vaguely fixed on the floor, on the ceiling, or on a point in infinity (as if looking for a cue there), by visually perceptible inspiration, by blinking, insecure smile, pinching both eyebrows with thumb and index finger, etc.

D. FEEDBACK-SEEKING PAUSE. This one is shown mainly by staring at the other interactant(s), lips parted perhaps, perhaps smiling, or frowning at suspected failure, putting the tongue out and in once, etc.. A more showy version is displayed, as part of his repertoire, by a comedian, who does all these things more consciously — both hands on his chest, or arms akimbo, loosely hanging over the sides or open as in a "come on" gesture.

E. TERMINATION PAUSE. Besides using a post-speech click or a pharyngeal ingression, the speaker may indicate the conclusion of his activity by unconsciously taking breath in, shutting his mouth tight, shifting his posture, etc., or consciously clasping both hands, smiling, opening his arms as in a "that's all" gesture, etc.

Much could be elaborated on the various types of pausal alternants and their structural relationships with pausal phenomena in other communicative activities. My purpose here, however, was to outline this and other categories of what I have proposed as paralinguistic alternants, a proposal that can be greatly improved through the suggestions made by fellow researchers in nonverbal communication.

REFERENCES

ABERCROMBIE, D.
    1967 *Elements of general phonetics*. Edinburgh: Edinburgh University Press.

1968 Paralanguage. *British Journal of Disorders in Communication* 3:55–59; reprinted 1972 in *Communication in face-to-face interaction*. Edited by J. Laver and S. Hutcheson. New York, London: Penguin.
ARGYLE, MICHAEL
1972 "Non-verbal communication in human social interaction," in *Nonverbal communication*. Edited by R. A. Hinde, chapter nine. Cambridge: Cambridge University Press.
AUSTIN, WILLIAM M.
1965 Some social aspects of paralanguage. *The Canadian Journal of Linguistics* 11 (1).
BOOMER, DONALD, ALLEN T. DITTMANN
1962 Hesitation pauses and juncture pauses in speech. *Language and Speech* 5:215–220.
CATFORD, J. C.
1968 "The articulatory possibilities of man," in *Manual of phonetics*. Edited by B. Malmberg, chapter ten. Amsterdam: North-Holland Publishing.
CRYSTAL, DAVID
1969 *Prosodic systems and intonation in English*. London, New York: Cambridge University Press.
CRYSTAL, DAVID, RANDOLPH QUIRK
1964 *Systems of prosodic and paralinguistic features in English*. The Hague: Mouton.
DITTMANN, ALLEN T.
1972 Development factors in conversational behaviors. *Journal of Communication* 22:4.
DUNCAN, STARKEY, JR.
1969 Nonverbal communication. *Psychological Bulletin* 72(2):118–137.
1973 Toward a grammar for dyadic conversation. *Semiotica*.
EFRÓN, DAVID
1941 *Gesture and environment*. New York: King's Crown. Reprinted 1972 as *Gesture, race and culture*. The Hague: Mouton.
EKMAN, PAUL, WALLACE V. FRIESEN
1969 The repertoire of nonverbal behavior: categories, origins, usage, and coding. *Semiotica* 1:49–98.
HALL, EDWARD T.
1966 *The silent language*. Garden City: Doubleday.
LAVER, JOHN, SANDY HUTCHESON
1972 *Communication in face-to-face interaction*. New York, London: Penguin.
LIEBERMAN, PHILIP
1972 *The speech of primates*. The Hague: Mouton.
1975 "Linguistic and paralinguistic interchange," in *Organization of behavior in face-to-face interaction*. Edited by Adam Kendon, Richard M. Harris, and Mary R. Key. World Anthropology. The Hague: Mouton.
LYONS, JOHN
1972 "Human language," in *Non-verbal communication*. Edited by R. A. Linde, Part A, 3. Cambridge: Cambridge University Press.

PIKE, KENNETH
1943   *Phonetics*. Ann Arbor: The University of Michigan Press.
PITTINGER, ROBERT E., HENRY L. SMITH, JR.
1957   A basis for some contributions of linguistics to psychiatry. *Psychiatry* 20:61-78.
PITTINGER, ROBERT E., CHARLES F. HOCKETT, JOHN DANEHY
1960   *The first five minutes: a sample of microscopic interview analysis*. Ithaca: Paul Martineau.
POYATOS, FERNANDO
1970   Lección de paralenguage. *Filologia Moderna* 39:265-300.
1971   "The basic triple structure of human communicative behavior." Paper presented at Annual Meeting of the Northeast Modern Language Association, Philadelphia.
1972a The communication system of the speaker-actor and his culture: a preliminary investigation. *Linguistics* 83:64-86.
1972b Paralenguage y kinésica del personaje novelesco: nueva perspectiva en el análisis de la narración. *Revista de Occidente* 113-114:148-170.
1975   "Analysis of a culture through its culturemes: theory and method," in *The mutual interaction of people and their built environment*. Edited by Amos Rapoport. World Anthropology. The Hague: Mouton.
SMITH, HENRY L., JR.
1953   *The communication situation*. Washington: Foreign Service Institute.
1969   "Language and the total system of communication," in *Linguistics today*. Edited by A. A. Hill. New York: Basic Books.
SEBEOK, THOMAS
1969   *Approaches to animal communication*. The Hague: Mouton.
STOPA, ROMAN
1972   *Structure of Bushman and its traces in Indo-European* Warsaw: Polska Akademia Nauk-Oddzia W Krakowie.
TRAGER, GEORGE L.
1958   Paralanguage: a first approximation. *Studies in linguistics* 13:1-12.
VETTER, HAROLD J.
1969   "Language, speech, and paralanguage," in *Language, behavior, and psychopathology*. Chicago: Rand McNally.

Face-to-Face Interaction:
Signs to Language

WILLIAM C. STOKOE, JR.

INTRODUCTION

Under a few easily specified conditions the face-to-face interaction of deaf persons consists of behavior so organized that it cannot, in the present state of the art of several disciplines, be fully described. It is behavior too much like that of language to be caught in the theoretical nets of those who deal with nonverbal communication. It is physically manifested in nonvocal signs that put it out of reach of much linguistic theory — or else theoreticians choose to exclude it from their consideration. Students of nonverbal behavior whose orientation has been ethological, cultural, psychiatric, or paralinguistic have looked at what is done by the 99.9 percent of persons whose primary channel for interaction is speech. Those oriented in the disciplines of psychology and education have usually added negative characterization, beyond the basic designation of nonverbal, to the communication of deaf persons, viz. haphazard, nonlinguistic, or agrammatical.

This article is addressed directly to a special case of face-to-face interaction, asking: may the organization of behavior in the face-to-face interaction of two persons deaf from birth have the kind of structure and elements usually meant by the term LINGUISTIC? To make the strongest possible case, those persons so interacting will be understood here to have, in addition to ex natu lack of functional hearing, the experience of growing up in a family including at least one deaf parent, in the United States, France, or Israel. (Deaf persons elsewhere may and probably do

Research on which this paper is based has been supported in part by NSF grant GS-31349 and NIH grant NS-10302.

have stable and viable sign languages; but as I have observed sign language interaction firsthand only in the three countries named, this article will offer a special rather than a general or universal theory of sign language.)

The definition of linguistically organized behavior to be used here must be broad enough to transcend those theories which posit, among other components, a phonological component. Like Lenneberg (1971) I take human capacity for language, i.e. a potential for linguistic organization of behavior, to be a deep, cognitive, ultimately neurophysiological capability of the species, essentially indifferent to whether its vehicle of expression be vocal sound or visible activity. One argument against such stipulation has been that man "always" organizes his communicative behavior most completely in language mediated by speech (as animals cannot and do not organize theirs) and that consequently language behavior both utilizes and depends upon speaking and listening behavior.

The fact that human beings with functional hearing so use speech cannot be disregarded (Kavanagh and Mattingly 1972). The fact that human beings who are born deaf may not organize their language on speech has been disregarded by behaviorally oriented linguists. Bloomfield (1933) supposed that the silent languages of the deaf were derived from spoken language. Evidence adduced since 1960 has shown that such derivation is not the case, though finger spelling is of course directly coded conventional orthography, hence speech-derived, and though some influence, especially lexical borrowing, can be found in French Sign Language (FSL) and American Sign Language (ASL) from French and from English, respectively (Stokoe 1960, 1966, 1969–1970, 1970, 1972a, 1972b, i.p.; Stokoe et al. 1965).

The scope of this specific issue of language and its symbolization, like the question "What is language?" has changed much since 1933. Today one important, i.e. verifiable, question is whether the eye and brain can do what the ear and the brain do. Now, the approach can be different. Whether without the short-term recall capability of the auditory system the visual-cognitive system has similar or different organization at the physical, at the etic, and at the syntactic-semantic levels, or whether optic and auditory nerve connections are in some ways analogous or are of a different order of complexity, we may consider the matter here in terms of the organization of observed and observable behavior in face-to-face interaction.

The interaction of deaf persons will vary along many dimensions, even though the persons may have been incapable from birth of hearing speech and are native signers of American, French, or International Sign

Language. Age, sex, and status of those interacting are important variables, but perhaps more so is the polar but continuous dimension which may be called KNOWN/UNKNOWN. Are the interacting persons complete strangers? Acquaintances? Intimates? As with hearing persons who interact, certain behavior, e.g. greeting and leave taking, appears to depend much upon this variable. Moreover, because the interaction itself inevitably changes the degree of acquaintance, the relation of the dimension known/unknown to interactive behavior is complex.

It might seem possible to simplify this complexity for experimental purposes by considering one pole: let both parties to the interaction be unknown to each other. This condition may be hard to find. Before hearing persons are close enough to interact verbally and face-to-face, there is appreciable opportunity for some information to be gained visually. Each may also have overheard the other speaking. Deaf persons in similar circumstances may be thought not to experience the kind of knowing that comes from overhearing another speaking one's own language, but in fact a deaf person looking without being looked at may not only see the other signing and so learn age, sex, and other information displayed and inferable from display, but will also "listen" in the sense of seeing a portion of the other's primary interactive activity and so gather information about its system, its style, and its user. Hence, when interaction proper begins, even of strangers, considerable information may have been exchanged, and the process of choosing and setting various controls already begun.

ELICITATION OF THE DATA

Instead of pursuing further this general comparison of the interaction of deaf persons and of hearing persons, I would like to consider in detail and in the context of this comparison some recorded data. There is contrast in the data, although the informant recorded on videotape meets the specifications of ex natu deafness and native competence in ASL. What contrasts are two kinds of interactive behavior — of one informant first face-to-face with a deaf friend and second face-to-face with a hearing person specially qualified.

The short tape segments are presented below in transcription. They record only one side of each interaction. Tapes and films of dyads have been made and stored at the Linguistics Research Laboratory (Gallaudet College, Washington, D. C. 20002), but most of them lack naturalness — the participants are distracted by the camera, and there are difficulties in seeing all that needs attention. In each half-interaction reported on here, the informant faces the camera and tells a person behind the camera what he is planning to do in the summer vacation upcoming.

The informant's qualifications

Separate directions are given to the informant for each performance: First, he is told to imagine that the person behind the camera is a deaf friend from his old (residential) school (for the deaf). Second, he is told to imagine that the person behind the camera is a hearing teacher or counselor (at Gallaudet College, where these are required to have some proficiency in reading finger spelling and signs). An actual deaf or hearing person behind the camera helped the informant to interact with naturalness, and other considerations helped as well. Because the signer is used to being watched (from full front) instead of being listened to, the head-on camera is less intrusive than a camera looking in from the side on a conversation. Because a signer watches the whole appearance of the person addressed (here in nearly full view behind a small television camera), the addressee-to-signer feedback can function nearly normally. Because the informant on the tape here described is an accomplished actor, his ability to take direction and to assume and sustain roles was exceptional.

What the tapes show are discourses which may look somewhat like nonverbal behavior or gesticulation but which are in fact actions completely organized in contrasting ways. The system of organization of some of the material — that obtained from the second direction — is demonstrably that of English grammar. The material obtained from the first direction is obviously organized according to some other principle.

Data: Behavior Organized Like English

When the informant is responding to the direction to relate summer plans to a hearing teacher or counselor, the viewer of the tape, even with no special training, can lip-read some of the performance. No sound recording is made, but the informant makes speech-like facial gestures though using little or no voice. Often, too, there is simultaneous coding, the signer's facial speechlike gestures accompanying the rendering of a word by a conventional sign or by finger spelling. There is further redundancy; some signs are immediately followed by finger spelling of the

Face-to-Face Interaction: Signs to Language

word that the sign has encoded. I believe anyone knowing English could without difficulty decipher the behavior of the informant face-to-face with a hearing (i.e. English-speaking) person. All that would be needed is sufficient time and two code books, one a manual alphabet card, the other any of a dozen handbooks of glosses for conventional signs. The reason I am so confident of the decoding ability of those who may never have conversed a deaf person is not simply the redundancy and the latent lip-reading ability all speakers of a language have; it is also the fact that the message is what cryptographers call plain-text, i.e. normal English.

Data: Behavior Otherwise Organized

The other set of material, elicited by asking the informant to give the same message to a deaf friend, will not yield at all to this kind of decipherment. It requires some knowledge of a language other than English. In it, to be sure, some speechlike gestures of the face and some finger spelling occur; but the former are less frequent and the latter is performed in a manner so different from the finger spelling of the signed English messages that it is virtually invisible to layman and investigator alike until the tape is slowed or stopped and viewed frame by frame. This non-English or less English-like material differs most, however, in the signs themselves and the way that they are used and formed. Most of the signs used in the English-like taped material will be found, as aforesaid, in many word-to-sign glossaries and in the *Dictionary of American sign language* (Stokoe et al. 1965). But many of the signs used in the non-English material are either so altered as they occur in context from the citation forms as to defy recognition or are hitherto unrecorded signs. This is not to undervalue the arduous lexicography of my colleagues a decade ago but to remind ourselves that signs put down on a dictionary page may be as different from signs actually seen in live interaction as words put down on a dictionary page differ from words heard spoken by live speakers.

Data: the Transcriptions

It would be possible to give below a transcription of the sign performances on the tape exclusively in the symbols used in the 1965 *Dictionary* for sign notation. To do so would however be to burden readers unnecessarily because few will have occasion to read or use that notation again. It should also be possible to justify using English-word glosses for signs, once the dangers of doing so are duly stated. The chief danger of transcribing sign performances, English-like or not, in words is that the transcriber or reader of the transcription may come to suppose that signs are code symbols for words and just those words — the ethnocentric trap into which Bloomfield seems to have fallen. Once the danger is known and the heinousness of the fallacy is recognized the reader can be wary.

A second danger is that those not warned may take the transcript, which looks like ungrammatical English, to mean that the sign language being so transcribed has no grammar of its own and that its users have no competence in English. Related to this is the danger that sign/word pairing, even for purposes of transcription, may somehow give the impression, eventually, to some deaf persons learning English, that English words go together just as signs for them do. Again to know the danger may be to avoid it, but I would still not use English words to transcribe the tapes if there were an equivalent of the International Phonetic Alphabet (IPA) adaptable to gesture, gesticulation, and sign language, and as well known and as readily read back into performance as the IPA. As a final caution, let every reader who proceeds recall that any other language rendered lexical item by lexical item into English words will lose well-formedness in both languages.

Something more needs to be said about my editorial practice and the conventions of transcribing. First, the same sign will be shown now as "I", now as "me", partly because the informants have competence in English and often say or may be seen to be saying one or the other, and partly because this two-valued gloss makes the transcription less unnecessarily bizarre. Second, glosses will not be written with plural endings, even when context and lip-read performance suggest plural meaning, because number is indicated in ASL without the noun and because a repeated sign (Stokoe 1970) will be shown by repeated word. Third, possessive affix will be written "apostrophe-S," because in the idiolects of the informants it is signed after a noun with manual-alphabet S and a twisting motion. Table 1 gives the conventions used in transcribing the tapes. Tables 2 and 3 give the transcriptions.

Table 1. Transcription conventions

word	gloss for a sign
hyphenated word	gloss for a sign
word	gloss for initial-dez sign
word	finger-spelled word
[word]	word spoken visibly
(act)	action or paralinguistic gesture

Face-to-Face Interaction: Signs to Language 321

Table 2. "S" transcript of "summer plans told to deaf friend" *

1. tomorrow morning I group friend several-will-go to *ocean city* — 9
2. for interview [and] — 3
3. find place sleep — 3
4. leave finish — 2
5. I come-here *back next* night — 5
6. will-get *a bus* to home *pa* finish — 7
7. I will-get my mother — 4
8. bring-back me here — 3
9. get my mother — 3
10. bring-here — 1
11. see my girl friend's graduation finish — 7
12. I bring mother back to there home finish — 8
13. I will there come *back* to *w*ashington again — 8
14. and join friend — 3
15. we several-will-go to *ocean city md* — 6
16. there work maybe we work in *laundry or hotel or* restaurant — 11
17. I not know for sure — 5
18. maybe work in *laundry* (shrugs) maybe — 5
19. I not know for sure — 5
20. and may stay there *ocean city* through *labor day* — 9
21. *labor day* well that *day* I suppose I will come here again *aug* last for registration — 16
22. will-go *back* to there *ocean city* — 6
23. stay there through *labor day* — 5
24. come-back for class — 3
25. go-there commute to *labor day* — 6
26. my *job* will *be* finish — 5
27. not know for sure (shrugs) start next-week *t*uesday wednesday (shrugs) — 8

156

TEMPORAL ORGANIZATION OF THE BEHAVIOR IN SIGN (S) AND SIGNED ENGLISH (E) (TABLES 2 AND 3)

There is no generally accepted method for analyzing the kind of behavior represented in S and E. Choice of a method is further complicated by paradox: what looks like nonverbal behavior is clearly seen to intend

* The sign glossed "finish" (end of S4, 6, 11, 12) merits a paper alone. Madsen devotes fifty examples and eighty-two exercise and test items to what he calls "the 'finish' idiom" and "the 'late' idiom" (1972: 141–150). Most of these turn on use as auxiliary (cf. Stokoe et al. 1965: 221, 284), i.e., 'finish' = have + V + -en; 'late' = have + neg + V + -en. But in Table 3 the sign does not have this grammatical function; nor does it have the specific denotation which fits its English gloss, i.e., 'completed' or 'the end.' Instead, it works here across sentence boundaries. Just as *then* (E5, 6, 12) in English begins a proposition and signals that it relates as sequel to what came before, so 'finish' in ASL ends a proposition and signals that what follows is a sequel. This similarity/opposition of 'then' and 'finish' is one of the fascinations of sign-English contrasts.

Table 3. "E" transcript of "summer plans told to hearing teacher"

1.	tomorrow morning I will go to *ocean city md* with my friend	12
2.	and there purpose *of go* there *is* for interview	9
3.	and find place to sleep	5
(4)		
5.	then I will come *back* to Gallaudet	7
6.	then I [will] get *a bus* to *pa*	8
7.	get my mother	3
8.	and bring mother	3
(9, 10)		
11.	to girl friend's graduation	5
11a.	will (checks self) which will *be held* next-week *m*onday	7
12.	then I will take *her* to home again	8
13.	and again I will come back to here	8
14.	and join with my friend	5
15.	we will go to *ocean city* next-week	7
16.	maybe we will work in restaurant/*restaurant* (smiles)/or laundry *laundry* (shrugs)	10
17.	I not know for sure	
(18, 19)		
20.	I maybe we will stay there to *labor day*	9
21.	we will come back here for registration *registration*	8
22.	and we will go back *to* work for few day	10
(23)		
24.	naturally we will come *back* for class	7
(25)		
26.	and we will finish our job by *labor day* (shrugs)	9
		145

putting propositional material into word-like formulation. In this account of some ways that the behavior in S and in E may be organized, I have chosen to treat separately the temporal and the spatial arrangement of both the tenor and the vehicle, i.e. the content and the expression, in these two examples of face-to-face behavior.

S consists of twenty-seven units I am calling propositions, and E, similarly broken down, contains twenty. Other divisions of S and E can, of course, be made, but the numbered lines of S and E show the similarity of the ideas without, I hope, begging too many organizational questions. In general terms, then, the propositional content of S and E is equivalent.

Temporal Organization of Content

The general temporal organization of the content of both performances is clear and not unusual: (a) the whole account is set in future time, and (b) the order of subordinate parts, whether taken to be propositions or expected events, follows chronology, with minor exceptions. Time is prominently indicated at the beginning of both performances. "Tomorrow morning," the meaning of the first two signs in each, signals directly that what follows is in planned or imagined stage, not accomplished. Following verbs state what is expected to occur but discussion of them belongs to expression. The chronological sequence of expected events is part of content, but again what indications are given of sequencing are part of overt behavior, expression.

There are several departures from strict chronology, i.e. the general time scheme is not rigid. In S17, S19, and S27, the informant turns attention from contemplated actions to present uncertainty. There is no manual marking of the sign for "know" in these three almost identical sign sequences to distinguish it from the sign verbs in those propositions which do refer to future time, but the informant does change his facial expression and bodily set which may be the macroscopically viewed (Markel, this volume) visual cues sufficient to suspend the future time scheme which most of the content follows.

There is in E2 further information on this point. Almost at the outset in this performance, the informant disengages from future time established by "tomorrow morning" and "will". This departure is clearly marked by the operation of the semantic-syntactic rules of English. Although the whole proposition E2 does not, in word glosses, look particularly well-formed, the important elements here are "purpose ... is for interview." If the informant had spelled WILL BE instead of IS, then there might be no departure from the scheme, but an egregious error giving cause to doubt the speller's English competence or his cognitive capacity for distinguishing tomorrow from now, future from timelessness, action from purpose, and specific from general. This same informant a few minutes before signing E had produced all of S. It seems likely therefore that he has all this cognitive capacity and more. He has used "will" and "is" in proper English ways in E1 and E2. He has also in S done what is proper in ASL, though as yet we have not seen what that is.

The informant does not depart from the future time sense in S2 or S3, but these are shorter propositions than E2. When he produced E a few minutes after completing S, one supposes that the content and the expression of S were fresh in mind, and therefore one may consider E2 as an expansion of S2. One may also recall that the directions (... to a deaf friend, ... to a hearing teacher) serve to present situations, so that in S and E we may have a typical example of diglossia (Ferguson 1959), the informant using his H variety of language to an authority figure in an institutional setting and his L variety with an intimate (Stokoe 1969–1970).

Two other departures from strict time sequence in the future occur in

S, but one of these amounts only to reiteration of propositions (S18, S19). The content as much as the expression shows uncertainty, and repetition much emphasizes it. This repetition does not occur in E; his earlier formulation of plans in S may have helped the informant to proceed with less uncertainty. However, there is E11a, a detail of content not in S, a minor slip. The informant starts a proposition, "checks," and resumes with the sign "which," then follows with "will." Remember, in E he is on English rules — "graduation" in ASL may function both as object of "see" and subject of "happen," "take place"; but in signing English, "which" the relative pronoun must be used. The informant's realization that his sign expression has become inappropriate to the content, his "checking," is visible in a macroscopic visual cue but of extremely short (microscopic?) duration (cf. Markel, this volume).

There is in S9 and S10 a similar occurrence, which interrupts the content's time flow and seems to result also from a slip and recovery. Between S8 and S9 there is a pause and a check also macroscopically visible and longer than that between the first two signs of E11a. I read the cue as symptom of the familiar confusion that comes when one finds he has talked his way into a structure which has no outlet to the main artery of thought. S8 begins with the sign "bring-back," which has several semantic features: "return," "motion," and "something moved." Next is a very quick sign, split-second inward pointing, "I/me." Then the index points up as the hand remains motionless. It is possible to read this last as "her," a reference to "mother" in S7; but it is also possible to read it as the somewhat prolonged beginning of an emphatic and final "to-this-place," for the index turns over forward and points definitely down. But this has closed a pattern; the informant is briefly hemmed in; then he repeats parts of S7 and S8: "get my mother," "bring her." But this time he uses the horizontal, flat-hand "here" (Stokoe et al. 1965: 33) and can continue with "see . . ." (S11), confident that his deaf friend will understand that he is bringing his mother here for a purpose, not just bringing her here, as S7 seemed to say.

The reason for this microscopic analysis of the informant's behavior is that in the corresponding passage, E9–E10, the informant is not uncertain about time or sequence or other details of his plans but may have been momentarily misled in S by the syntactical organization he tried first.

Temporal Organization of Expression

Another kind of repetition or reiteration in E16 and E21 directly concerns the time organization of expression, because it adds nothing to content. In these two places, instead of proceeding with the expression of a proposition, the informant reencodes three lexical items, using another sytem. In E16 he touches both sides of his mouth with the manual alphabet *r* (his deaf friend had been expected to recognize this sign in S); then he smiles as his hand, still near his face, spells out the word RESTAURANT. Later, laundry and registration are similarly spelled after being signed, and the spelling is accompanied by the same smile. Macroscopically one might call it "sympathetic." But whether it compassionates with the hearing partner of the interaction for needing this double coding, or registers amusement at this check in communication flow, or presents an apology for the nontransparency of the sign, it calls attention to the most striking difference between S and E.

In S the interactive behavior expresses some doubt about what jobs will be secured and some hesitation about precise arrangements in late August, when jobs and college run concurrently. Over and above the propositional content, the pauses, repetitions, shrugs, and apologetic looks are macroscopic cues to this uncertainty. However, there is no uncertainty or self-consciousness in the expression of most of the propositions themselves. Signs are firmly and definitely made. They are economical of time and are fluently joined. Finger-spelled words in S are so fast as to be literally invisible to nondeaf viewers until the tape is played back frame by frame. The letter-denoting configurations are fleeting, and the hand as it spells is often in motion to and from other signs.

In E the uncertainty about the kind of jobs is expressed propositionally; there is a similar resolution of the overlapping of work and classes, but despite the reduction of repetitiously expressed doubt about features of the content, the general effect from viewing E is of even greater uncertainty, hesitancy, tentativeness. As it does not concern the content, then this uncertainty must be about the expression; and as the recoding of some signs in finger spelling suggests, the focus of the problem is not the informant's capacity to encode but his perception of decoding ability or performance in the hearing person he interacts with.

More microscopically considered, expression time may be observed and ultimately measured in the time of making a sign (duration), the time between signs (transition), and the time between propositions (juncture; see Covington 1973). In S, transition time is short as is duration, i.e. the informant signs rapidly to a deaf friend. But the junctures are long; between propositions he has time for getting ideas together, arranging their order, perhaps for the first time with the whole summer in mind. In E, however, he uses more time for the duration of signs, for finger-spelling configurations, more in transitions, but less relatively in junctures. Yet, in spite of this different distribution of time, the total time for the two performances of the same material is quite different.

S is signed in seventy-five seconds and E in 125 seconds, a ratio of 3 : 5 in overall length. There are 156 signs in S and 145 in E when counted as follows: each sign is counted whether it has a single or compound gloss; each finger-spelled word is also counted as a sign, as is each word visibly spoken if it is not accompanied by manual activity. The signing rate is thus 2.08 signs per second in S and 1.16 signs per second in E.

It may be well here to expand the abbreviations. S is Sign or American Sign Language (Stokoe 1970); E is signed English. Both performances use the same channel, vision, though different codes — Sign and English. (Finger spelling may be considered signing with the sign denotata reduced from lexemes to letter symbols; and visibly speaking is signing syllables, albeit ambiguously, with the face). I have elsewhere shown the two codes to be related diglossically (1969–1970). Woodward more recently (i.p.) has described them as points (or lects) on a diglossic continuum which includes varieties of signing quite like English and varieties that utilize more or fewer rules of ASL.

Time/Rate Comparison of S, E, Sign, and Speech

Bellugi and Fischer (1972) have compared rates of articulation in pairs of performances by informants using sign and speech (they also examined simultaneous performances which need not concern us here). Their informants, A, B, and C, were asked to tell "some story from their childhood or some story they knew well" (1972: 178). A, B, and C have normal hearing; informant O4 is deaf; but all did acquire ASL at home from deaf parents. Information from their experiment and from S and E is combined in Table 4.

Table 4. Total time in seconds for paired performances

	A	B	C	O4
Speaking	144.0	87.0	51.3	–
Signing	154.5	66.1	38.8	–
Organized as in S				75.0
Organized as in E				125.0

Before making a cross-channel or bimodal comparison of the rates of talking and signing, Bellugi and Fischer used a technique suggested by Goldman-Eisler (1968), who discovered that variation in rates of talking depends much on time spent in "pausing," less on time spent in actual articulation. Bellugi and Fischer decided that "we need to try to eliminate pauses from both sign and speech" (1972: 177); i.e. of course, for purposes of rate comparison and not to speed up communication.

It may be that people actually talk at a nearly constant rate, varying mainly in their pause time, so that excluding pauses can lead to close determination of human or universal speech rate. However, I doubt the wisdom of excluding pauses from sign for three reasons: (1) pauses in speaking and pauses in signing are not at all the same kind of phenomena; (2) pauses in both spoken and signed performances may be important in assessment of the performer's whole behavior; and (3) even with all the pauses left in, there is still enough temporal contrast between S and E and between them and the raw data Bellugi and Fischer use to support their conclusions and to reveal further information about signing behavior.

Taking these in order, (1) it is possible easily to identify a pause in speaking with a cessation of sound and not difficult to exclude "non-speech sounds like 'um' " (Bellugi and Fischer 1972: 180). But pauses in signing do not — nothing in signing does — coincide with a cessation of the visual input. When no manual sign is being performed, and when there is no "analogue to making a non-speech sound" (1972: 180), the whole signer remains as visible as ever. There is no change in loudness of the visual signal analogous to the power differential between sound and silence. The subtlest change in any visible aspect of the signer's body can operate communicatively. Such minimal changes, Birdwhistell's KINES, in a sign language context, however, may be not kinesically organized unconscious signals but essential, though perhaps minor, elements of a linguistic ensemble.

When (2) the whole organization of behavior in face-to-face interaction is under scrutiny, the total temporal frame and all its divisions are important, as discussion of temporal organization in the content and expression of S and E may already have shown.

The rate of signing and of speaking, including pauses (3), can be calculated from the data Bellugi and Fischer give: total times (1972: 179), rates excluding pauses (180), and percent of time pausing (182). Table 5 gives the actual rates in signs per second or spoken words per second for their three informants, A, B, and C, and for O4, the signer of S and E.

When all the time used in pausing is left in, it is no longer so true that "THE RATE OF ARTICULATION FOR WORDS IS NEARLY DOUBLE THE RATE FOR SIGNS FOR EACH OF OUR SUBJECTS" (Bellugi and Fischer 1972: 180, emphasis theirs). Doubling the sign rates yields for A 3.5, B 4.1, C 4.38, rates not achieved in the spoken performances. The two rates for informant 04 are slower, but 2.08 would not look out of place in Table 5 as a rate for articulation of words; and a rate of 1.16 signs per second might be that of some subject telling a story in signs.

Table 5. Rates compared in four paired performances

	A	B	C	04
Spoken, words/second	2.81	3.75	3.64	–
Signed, signs/second	1.75	2.05	2.19	–
Organized as in S(ign)				2.08
Organized as in E(nglish)				1.16

In comparing rates, however, it must be remembered that informant 04 was putting together, apparently for the first time in S, details of his summer travel and work schedule. The three subjects in the Bellugi-Fischer experiment were telling a "story they knew well" (1972: 178). This difference in familiarity of material can account for the slower rate of 04's signs in S than the speaking rate of the others; but he signs faster than two of the others, when they are signing familiar stories. They are native signers, too, but not deaf as he is. It would be good to have a comparison of signing rates of deaf and hearing native signers.

If the unfamiliarity of the content makes 04 sign more slowly than three speakers and one signer in S and slower than all three signers in E, it cannot, however, account for the difference in his rates of signing. As was noted earlier, the informant signing E had S as a rehearsal. It might therefore be supposed that his rate of signing in E would be faster. Instead, it is much slower.

Other factors seem to account for the difference in the rates of articulation in S and E. One is what Bellugi and Fischer suggest: "It may also be that sign language has special ways of compacting and incorporating linguistic information..." (1972: 199). This can explain why words were articulated faster than signs in the paired performances they analyzed. But informant 04 signs at two different rates, and his performance E, organized as English might be expected to resemble English speech in its articulation rate. A further explanation of the slow rate of signing E is called for.

The performer of S, despite having at his disposal various ways of "compacting and incorporating," discussed by Bellugi and Fischer (1972: 196 ff.), by Woodward (i.p.), and by this writer (1970), articulates signs, hesitation, uncertainty, repetition and all at a rate (2.08) not far below that (2.81) in the slowest of three spoken, familiar stories. Here is strong confirmation of the conclusion quoted above. I would put it thus:

a sign may carry more semantic and syntactic information than a word, but only if the whole sign expression is organized according to the system called American Sign Language.

When signs are used as code symbols for words in English structures, i.e. as in E, the rate of articulating them does not approach that for speaking words. The rate, in the case of E, falls considerably below that for "normal" (i.e. Table 5) signing. The advantage just stated, that signs do more linguistic work than words, is at once lost by coding words in signs. But the low rate of signing in E is not caused so much by simple coding and linguistic coding as by face-to-face interaction. The informant, in E, signs at the rate he is ascertaining to be the reception rate or comprehension rate or decoding rate of his partner in interaction.

If the temporal organization of behavior in S and E, followed by this complicated comparison of rates, has not convinced the reader that deaf persons may think and interact as fast as hearing persons, at least it should be clear that deaf persons interact with deaf persons, and hearing persons interact with hearing persons, more rapidly, fluently, and naturally than do deaf and hearing persons with each other. This happens because the interactive behavior of deaf persons is organized around a visual language. The elements of this visual language are neglected by those who hear, because they use such elements for other communicative purposes. The organization of this visual language is not even considered, or is denied, because those who hear tend to conceive of speech and language as identical.

SPATIAL ORGANIZATION OF BEHAVIOR IN S AND E (TABLES 2 AND 3)

If the discussion above of temporal ordering of the expression and content in two accounts of a signer's summer plans has had a familiar ring reminiscent of school grammar and rhetoric, one large difference should be reemphasized. These accounts are neither spoken nor written but performed in another mode. They are also at one more remove from occurrence than is usual in such discussions; i.e. speech acts are presented in discussions as phonetic or phonemic transcription or, as is often done now, in standard writing conventions. The accounts S and E were performed by a living, moving person. They have been recorded thanks to an advance in technology less epoch-making than the invention of writing but here more feasible. They are presented in an ad hoc and not unambiguous convention of substituting words for certain chunks of their features.

What will be attempted in this section, then, is analysis of the spatial organization of behavior in S and in E, with particular reference to the actual appearance of the activity, which is recoverable only in videotape recordings, not directly reproducible in print or voice.

What makes such reproduction or channel transposition impossible is the very issue under discussion, i.e. the way that space is used in organizing the interactive behavior called sign language. In both the language of S and (at the other end of the ASL continuum) the diglossic or creolized language of E, space is used in producing sign vehicles to denote time. Future is not simply forward of the signer but forward in an arc swept by the upraised forearm. Motion forward with other components has other significance. Past is denoted by motion back, also in the upper region of forearm mobility. Present is between these, though the sign glossed "now" places the hands a little forward of the signer and at about waist height.

These linkings of time with gestural space are not sign language universals, of course, any more than there is a universal sign language; e.g. a deaf and mute Polynesian discovered by Kuschel makes a sign by pointing forward and down, even bending the body forward to reach out farther, to denote "a long time ago" — *i gaa 'aso* in Bellonese-Rennellese (1973: 23). Convention and repeated use may make time signs seem to be natural, but they are more arbitrary and less natural than most signers and observers have thought.

Generally, the spatial aspect of the content in S and E is fairly simple. There is first a preliminary trip from Gallaudet College to Ocean City and return; then a bus trip to Pennsylvania and return; next, return to and stay in Ocean City for summer work; finally, for a few days at the end of August and beginning of September, a trip to college to register, return to work, and commuting between college and work. This series of movements in the real world, so far only imagined or contemplated, is put into expression in behavior very differently organized in E and in S.

Spatial Organization of Overt Behavior in E

Because E is organized foremost as English rules require, the expression of the planned changes in place is almost entirely accomplished by lexical and syntactic means. In the sign and finger-spelling phrase "will go to *Ocean City*" the motion of going is symbolic, i.e. the sign "go" denotes what the word "go" denotes. There is motion in this sign as in most of the signs of ASL, but obviously the hands do not go from here to Ocean

City; in fact, they remain in front of the signer in the same small space for "go" as for the rest of the signs. This space is narrowly circumscribed in E: the hands do not move laterally beyond imaginary parallel planes that touch the signer's shoulders; vertically the hands move no lower than the waist, except for junctures when they may drop relaxed to the lap of the seated signer, and no higher than the temple; the forward movement of the hands never continues until the arm is fully extended so that the back-to-front dimension of this manual signing space is smallest. Very approximately, then, it is a space about 24 inches high by 18 inches wide by 12 inches deep.

The sign "go" in E occurs four times and each time in the citation form (Stokoe et al. 1965: 69). It is performed by rolling the horizontal index fingers around each other "forward," i.e. outward at the top of the revolution, inward at the bottom. In space traversed and motion it is the exact opposite of "come," which is also used four times in E. For "come" the fingers rotate "inward"; i.e. toward the signer at the top of the revolution, outward at the bottom. The expressive form of these signs seems to confirm Jakobson's statement (1972) that semantic opposition and repetition combine to require more than simple reversal of direction. The sign for "come" may be analyzed to begin with a beckoning gesture of the right index finger. However, this is a generalized gesture, not an invitation to a particular interactive partner, but a symbol for a whole extensive class of actions, as is the word "come"; therefore, the finger is held low and pointing to the left, so that nothing is left of the beckoning action to make it specific.

It may be that to further generalize the sign the left hand joins. At any rate it is a two-hand sign, with the index fingers alternately moving in. And the actions of the hands are repeated. Here Jakobson's observation becomes pertinent. Rapid alternating in-and-out movement of the fingers would obscure intent, for if movement in means "come" and movement out means "go", horizontal in-and-out movement means neither or both. In Jakobson's example if forward inclination of the head can mean "yes" and a backward tilt mean "no," nodding must be ambiguous, and so a new set of muscles is employed, and the contrast between nodding and shaking (and not just between forward and back or left and right) is needed to express semantic opposition. In the case of "come" and "go" as expressed in E, each hand or finger making the basic movement toward or away relaxes and drops slightly in its return to initial position so that the locus of the moving fingers is a circle or cylinder.

The other verbs in E that denote motion in space are "bring" (E8) and "take" (E12). These retain some gestural or iconic relation of expression to meaning, i.e. their performance involves some side-to-side motion across the signer's front. After signing "bring" with movement from his left to right, the informant a little later signs "take" from right to left, because it is the same person who is to be brought "there" and taken back.

The places referred to in E as in S are three: Gallaudet College, Ocean City, and Pennsylvania. These are expressed respectively by a sign, a finger-spelled two-word name, and a finger-spelled abbreviation. These are also referred to by signs glossed as "here," "there," and "home." But whether names or general references are used, the designation of places in E is that of English, i.e. the specific or general lexical item is used to denote the location, just as are words spoken or written.

Spatial Organization of Overt Expressive Behavior in S

As soon as one looks back from viewing E to the performance in S, a striking change is noted; it is as if space, from being passive, had become active. This occurs even in unexpected places.

The verb meaning "go" is expressed in S by a complex sign denoting plural and future as well as motion, but spatially considered it contrasts with all the signs in E. It begins with the right hand, fingers up, palm in, upraised beside the head and ends to the signer's left and farther forward than the hands ever go in E. More than that, the signer, who is seated in a swivel chair, twists to the left, looks to the left, and maintains that orientation while completing S1, S2, S3, and S4. Then, as he swings back to full face forward, the sign "come here" also iconically describes the return with a forearm swung freely from the elbow. The other verbs denoting motion are "leave" and "bring," and they are also expressed with much more motion of hands, arms, and trunk than these verbs in E. Moreover, there is no bring/take opposition in S (these glosses in E are supported by visible signs of speaking). The verb glossed "bring" in S does reverse in direction to do double duty, i.e. it is "bring" from left to right and "take back," "return," or "bring back" (there)" from right to left. The smaller number of verbs denoting motion in space in S should not mislead the reader. There is more, much more, expressive motion in S; while in E the English-like organization of the content and expression symbolizes motion with lexical variety more than visible movement.

In S even verbs only minimally denoting motion are performed with expressive movement. "Get" in S7 and "join" in S14 are signs that put back into the meaning of these verbs some of the motion they have lost

Face-to-Face Interaction: Signs to Language   333

as words. The sign for "stay" is also expressed (S20) with large movement, a reminder that motion forward and beginning with a little downward component can denote in ASL nonmovement, i.e. motionlessness, through a period of time.

Even more striking, a use of space in S is that which designates places. One might expect, in a variety of signing that is divergent from English organization, that more motion would be used to express verb semantics; but places are stationary, or so our language impresses us. In words, location and distance of places from each other can be variously expressed, e.g. one hundred miles away, a half-day's drive, a long way. Such verbal ways of emphasizing distance are not used in E, but in S the signer and presumably his interacting partner are aware of the distances involved. To locate Ocean City the signer reaches out, turns slightly to the left, and looks at a point beyond his "there"-pointing hand. Home in Pennsylvania is also located to the signer's left, but back and up. The signer's trunk straightens, moving his head farther back, as the reference is to this place. The signer is right-handed and makes most one-hand signs with his right, but the sign "home" on the left cheek and the finger-spelled abbreviation *pa* are performed by the left hand. To "bring" his mother to college he moves both hands down across to his right as his body turns; to "bring" her back home again he moves the hands up across to the left, also with trunk movement.

In the expressive behavior of S both these remote places contrast spatially with "here." Just as designation of Ocean City and Pennsylvania are made with a shift of focus to the signer's left, so reference to "here" brings his body back to full front, his eyes forward and a little down, and, in the final sign of S8, his hand downward and to the right of center.

In the last part of the account in S, when the conflicting calendars of college and summer resort require commuting, the frequent travel contemplated is rendered with appropriately expressive movement. Because the place references have already been established in the space between the signer and his partner in interaction, the sign glossed "commute" in S25 ("going back and forth" in Stokoe et al. 1965: 3) sums up the separate trips and return trips in an effective symbol for shuttling travel.

The purpose here is to consider the expressive behavior and not to make a microlinguistic study of spatial reference (see Friedman 1973). Nevertheless, I would like to look at one more example in which the spatial organization of the signer's behavior differs sharply from the expression of a similar proposition in E, i.e. in English. Although S13 is presented as a sequence of signs, it contains an instance of simultaneous expression of lexical units: "I will there come *back* to Washington again." The first three signs, "I will there," are made by the signer's right hand; the next sign "come" is made by his left; and the right hand spells *back*. The temporal arrangement of these signs is impossible in speech or writing, but if one could speak with two voices at once like an operatic duet, it would be possible to duplicate this common ASL feat. While the first voice holds the words "from there," the second utters one word, "come"; then the two voices chime, the first intoning "back" at the same time as the second intones "here."

Taken altogether S is a remarkable performance, especially in the way its behavior differs from that usually associated with the use and expression of language. While I agree with Bellugi and Fischer (1972) that signs can do more communicative work in the same time than words, their emphasis is on syntactical differences; mine here has been on visible difference in behavior and not on signs versus words spoken so much as on signs used signwise versus signs used verbally. Hearing persons who are native signers may utter words at twice their rate of signing (excluding pausing time under the assumption that nothing visible of any import takes place while the hands pause), but a deaf signer in face-to-face interaction signs twice as fast to another deaf signer as to a hearing person who signs. And the deaf signer uses verbal organization of the "nonverbal" activity for the slower performance, but ASL organization and spatial expression for the faster. No one seeing the two as visible behavior is likely to rate the more English-like or verbal performance as more expressive.

Comparison of Spatial Features of S and E

The overall effect of seeing S and E on one who knows no sign language but studies nonverbal behavior is that they differ greatly. In S the signer is free, fluent, full, and natural in moving, but restricted, jerky, and constrained in E. The cubic space where the hands move, about one by two by one and one-half feet in E, is dimensionally enlarged by higher and more forward excursions of the hands. But it is symbolically still more enlarged because the signer's rhythmical movements of trunk and head in S displace the whole three-dimensional system that bounds the hand movements, i.e. the invisible box where the hands move is rotated to the left and back, forward and back, and slightly backward and back to original position.

The subtlety of these shifts of space and their potential for expression of semantic content is hard to overestimate, once it is realized that it is in just this way that all the human language capacity of deaf persons interacting with each other has been put into expression for at least two hundred generations. The whole case for neurophysiological foundations of sign language cannot be argued here, but it is noteworthy that the researches of Hubel (1972) show that a single cell in a cat's brain responds to the following combination of stimuli in the visual field and to nothing else: (1) a line or edge oriented 8 o'clock to 2 o'clock ± a few degrees, (2) movement upper left to lower right, (3) illumination on the edge from above. If one brain cell in the cat can make such fine discrimination of light, angle, and movement, the physiological potential for a visual language of fully linguistic complexity can hardly be doubted, especially when it is remembered that more than half the nerves terminating in the brain come from the eyes.

Seeing the difference in movement and use of space in S and in E may also impress those interested in the relation of body movements to mental health. The signer's eloquent movement and natural rhythm in S and his obvious constraint in E suggest that, while a person born deaf can quite successfully learn the rules of English and use them in conversing with hearers who take the trouble to learn two codes, while such a person may even learn to encode his meaning slowly and redundantly to follow the interactively signalled reception capability of his addressee; natural, unconstrained, and full interaction will take place with those who, like him, use signs and space and time in the same way. To forbid this kind of interactive behavior and force the more English-like behavior of E cannot be conducive to mental health (Schlesinger and Meadow 1972). But what if the deaf person must forgo his use of space, must organize his meanings as in E, and then must repress all his visible activity except moving his organs of speech?

One final conclusion from this review of the organization of behavior in two special cases: human beings deprived of the sense that makes listening and speaking natural may very well develop their capacity for language more effectively in face-to-face interaction with others like them, i.e. deaf persons may learn much better and faster than any hearing person can teach them.

REFERENCES

BELLUGI, URSULA, SUSAN FISCHER
  1972   A comparison of sign language and spoken language. *Cognition* 1:173–200.

BLOOMFIELD, LEONARD
1933 *Language.* New York: Holt, Rinehart, and Winston.
COVINGTON, VIRGINIA C.
1973 Juncture in American sign language. *Sign Language Studies* 2:29–38.
FERGUSON, CHARLES A.
1959 Diglossia. *Word* 15:325–340.
FRIEDMAN, LYNN A.
1973 "On the semantics of space, time and person reference in the American sign language." Unpublished master's thesis, University of California, Berkeley.
GOLDMAN-EISLER, F.
1968 *Spontaneous speech.* London: Academic Press.
HUBEL, DAVID H.
1972 "Specificity of responses of cells in the visual cortex," in *Recent contributions to neurophysiology.* EEG Supplement 31:171–177. Amsterdam: Elsevier.
JAKOBSON, ROMAN
1972 Motor signs for "yes" and "no." *Language in Society* 1:91–96.
KAVANAGH, J. F., I. G. MATTINGLY, editors
1972 *Language by ear and by eye.* Cambridge: MIT Press.
KUSCHEL, ROLF
1973 The silent inventor: the creation of a sign language by the only deaf-mute on a Polynesian island. *Sign Language Studies* 3.
LENNEBERG, ERIC H.
1971 Of language knowledge, apes, and brains. *Journal of Psycholinguistic Research* 1:1–29.
MADSEN, WILLARD J.
1972 *Conversational sign language II: an intermediate-advanced manual.* Washington D.C.: Gallaudet College.
SCHLESINGER, HILDE S., KATHRYN P. MEADOW
1972 *Sound and sign: childhood deafness and mental health.* Berkeley: University of California Press.
STOKOE, WILLIAM C., JR.
1960 *Sign language structure.* Studies in Linguistics Occasional Paper 8. (Available from author).
1966 The linguistic description of sign languages. Monograph series in Language and Linguistics 19:243–250.
1969 Sign language diglossia. *Studies in Linguistics* 21:27–41.
1970 *The study of sign language.* Washington: ERIC Clearinghouse for Linguistics, Center for Applied Linguistics.
1972a Semiotics and human sign language. *Approaches to semiotics* 12. The Hague: Mouton.
1972b "A classroom experiment in two languages," in *Psycholinguistics and total communication: the state of the art.* Edited by T. J. O'Rourke, 85–91. Washington: American Annals of the Deaf.
i.p. "Classification and description of sign languages," in *Current trends in linguistics* 12. Edited by T. A. Sebeok. The Hague: Mouton.

STOKOE, W. C., JR., D. C. CASTERLINE, C. G. CRONEBERG
1965 *A dictionary of American sign language on linguistic principles.* Washington: Gallaudet College Press. (Available from author).
WOODWARD, JAMES C., JR.
  i.p.   "Implicational lects on the deaf diglossic continuum." Doctoral dissertation, Georgetown University.

Problems and Methods of Psycholinguistics in Face-to-Face Communication

A. A. LEONTIEV

WHAT IS COMMUNICATION?

However we define it, the great role that communication plays in the life of a society is obvious. The formation of a personality, or the making of "a socialized man" in Marxian terms, is impossible without communication: if this meaning of it is concealed under normal circumstances, it becomes quite obvious when teaching blind and deaf mutes (Meshcheryakov 1971). At the same time, however, communication is a necessary condition of any social activity of a human being, including the activity that is individual in its external manifestations but social in its genesis and conditionality (e.g. scientific and theoretical work in general).

Irrespective of SITUATIONAL context, communication does not represent a process of establishing contacts between isolated personalities or psychological monads, but a method of inner organization and inner evolution of a society.

Communication is not so much the interrelation of people in a society, but is primarily the interaction of people AS MEMBERS of a society. Following Marx, we can define communication as a method (and at the same time a condition) of ACTUALIZING SOCIAL RELATIONS. This methodological concept defines our approach to interpersonal communication as well, setting forth the psychological (social-psychological) functions of communication in a society (such as cooperation in labor, contact, social control, group identification, opposition to a group, and so on) as one of the basic problems.

PSYCHOLOGY OF COMMUNICATION AND PSYCHOLOGY OF FACE-TO-FACE COMMUNICATION

The main concerns of the psychology of communication as a branch of general psychology fall into the following three groups: (1) the psychological functions of communication; (2) the formation and functioning of communication mechanisms and means, depending on its functions, personal traits, and other psychological factors; and (3) the interrelation of communication with other aspects of human psychological activity and personal traits. If we use Thayer's terms, the psychology of communication deals with the "intrapersonal" and the "interpersonal" levels, leaving the "communicative system" and the "organizational" level to the sociology of communication (Thayer 1968).

The following system of criteria is offered as a classification of communication types.

1. *Direction of Communication* Communication can be either group-directed or person-directed. The distinction lies in the attitude of a speaker to different types of communicative situations, which are conditioned by a number of social and situational factors, but which are not connected with them by necessary bonds (Bgazhnokov 1973). We can number among the situational factors the axial or retial nature of feedback in communication; spatial (proxemic) differences (Watson 1970); the nature of anticipation of a recipient's (or recipients') reaction (Janoušek 1968) and so forth. The psychological (social-psychological) function of communication is the main social factor. Group-directed types of communication include mass communication, oratorical speech, and advertising, while person-directed communication includes primarily dyadic communication (Borden, Gregg, and Grove 1969).

2. *Psychological Dynamics of Communication* Communication always presupposes a certain psychological background. That is, communication never starts at point zero. It involves the real or imaginary community of a communicator and a recipient (or recipients). This community may be defined by a distribution of social roles (in formal communication), or it can be primarily psychological (the knowledge of different facts about the interlocutor, the ability to model different traits of his personality, e.g. his motives, his goals, etc., or his personality as a whole, more exactly, the "trend" of a personality [Bozhovich

1968]). Changes in the psychological characteristics of a recipient (or recipients) and a communicator (because of the feedback) take place as a result of communication. These changes can occur in the field of knowledge (information, learning), in the field of habits and skills (training), in the sphere of real activity stimulated by communication (suggestion, persuasion), in the sphere of motives and needs, attitudes, orientation, and so on (persuasion) (A. N. Leontiev 1968; A. A. Leontiev 1972). In dyadic and other types of communication, described as interpersonal, these changes are extremely sharp: "the static relationship is nonexistent; relations are always growing or diminishing" (Borden, Gregg, and Grove 1969: 103-104).

3. *Semiotic Specialization of Communication* This characteristic is defined by the means used in communication. From this point of view we can distinguish material communication (Marx spoke in this sense about "the real-life language"), sign-mediated communication (mediated by meanings), and sense-mediated communication (mediated by personal meaning which arises in the recipient's mind ON THE BASIS of the perceived objective meaning but which is not equivalent to this meaning; on this category, see A. N. Leontiev 1972; A. A. Leontiev 1969a, b; on artistic communication as a typical kind of sense-mediated communication, see A. A. Leontiev 1973a). Within sign-mediated communication, in turn, one can distinguish verbal communication; communication by means of sign systems which are psychologically equivalent to language (primary sign systems, e.g. the mime language of deaf mutes), communication by means of secondary sign systems based on a language (Morse code, the flag-hoist code, etc.); communication by means of secondary sign systems of a specific nature (a map, a radio-scheme); communication by means of material objects which are situationally comprehended, thus acquiring ad hoc semiotic specialization (e.g. a present sent by mail).

4. *The Degree of Mediation* This coordinate of communication is more sociological than psychological in nature. It determines the number of transformations the initial statement undergoes on the way from a communicator to a recipient.

The "interpersonal" types of communication are characterized by the global and multilevel nature of semiotic specialization: it uses (if it is not formal) not only language but paralinguistic, kinesic and proxemic means, various kinds of suggestion methods, etc. The degree of mediation in these types of communication, as opposed to, for example, mass communication, is minimal. It should also be noted that interpersonal communication is characterized by the development and growing coordination of "social technique" employed in the communication (Argyle 1967), sense-mediated communication becoming predominant over sign-mediated.

The described criteria, in spite of a certain superficial similarity (direction of communication and degree of mediation, for example), are autonomous. Hence, communication which is interpersonal in degree of mediation and at the same time group-directed is quite possible; the purposeful spread of rumours (used as a weapon of psychological warfare) is such an activity.

If the first two criteria are correlated with the "strategic competence" of a communicator (Thayer 1968), then the other two are correlated with his "tactic competence." In the psychological conception we share (cf. A. A. Leontiev 1973b), the first two criteria determine the PRE-SPEECH ORIENTATION and the planning of communication; the last two define the PROCESS of communication and the MEANS used in this process. We will consider the orientation link problem later on.

According to the described criteria, we can define face-to-face communication as person-directed, with various psychologic dynamics. In this respect it is characterized by poly-functionalism, multileveled (meaning a hierarchical system of levels) semiotic specialization and a minimal degree of mediation.

The pre-speech (more broadly: pre-communicative) orientation is conditioned by the correlation of the act of speech with the communicative situation, the "singling out of separate elements (in the situation) used as consistent orientators, which direct and control the realization of separate operations" (Galperin 1966: 248) or the action as a whole.

In various communicative situations the kind of orientation differs. Thus, in various kinds of operations such as retelling texts (i.e. in Skinner's [1957] term, "controlled verbal behavior"), the semantic analysis and comprehension of the text are regarded as the orientation link of the communication. When describing a picture (as well as in tele-reporting), perceptual actions serve as the orientation link, etc.

In face-to-face communication, orientation includes the following basic components: (a) orientation in the goals and social-psychological functions of the communication; (b) orientation in the personal and group factors of the communication, primarily in the system of social roles; (c) orientation in the content of the communication; (d) orientation in the interlocutor; and (e) situational orientation. By the last is meant the behavior that takes into account the circumstances of the contact such as its proxemic and temporal features as well as "microsociological" relationships, i.e. observing appropriate etiquette. These criteria of orientation and psychological dynamics of communication characterize the communicative attitude of a communicator and emerge as a result of the primary processing of all this information.

PSYCHOLINGUISTIC METHODS USED IN RESEARCH ON THE PROCESS OF COMMUNICATION

The possibility of using psycholinguistic data as indicators of change in orientation factors and of communicative dynamics in general is conditioned by the above-mentioned internal connection (Galperin 1966) between the structure of pre-speech orientation activity and the structure of the communication process. The existence of this connection and dependence is itself well known in psycholinguistics. The factor of reversibility in the creation of syntactic structures proves to be either relevant or irrelevant, depending on whether the aim in orientation is verification (i.e. orientation occurs simultaneously in the situation and the text) or the simple description of a picture (Slobin 1966; Turner and Rommetveit 1968). Flores d'Arçais (1966) established a correlation between the perceptual strategies involved in viewing a picture and in the choice of a syntactic structure.

The French psychologist S. Moscovici and his colleagues were the first to undertake the study of face-to-face communication by psycholinguistic methods on a large scale, though earlier experiments in this field are also known (Back 1961). Moscovici distinguishes between "communicative systems" and "communicative channels." These terms correspond in general to Thayer's "strategic competence" and "tactical competence" and to the first and second pairs of criteria mentioned above. Moscovici uses the concepts "pressure" and "distance" to characterize differences in communicative systems: the pressure level is defined by the relationships existing between interlocutors, the distance level is determined by the attitude of each of them to the content of the communication. When communicative channels are the same, distinctions in communicative systems, as Moscovici showed, are mainly lexical (common communicative volume and diversity of vocabulary); when systems are the same, a difference in the channels provides grammatical variations in messages (percentage of different parts of speech and certain other parameters) as different channels, "side-by-side," "back-to-back," and "face-to-face" situations, and communication between interlocuters separated by a screen were chosen. In the "side-by-side" and "back-to-back" situations, as compared to the face-to-face situation, it was found that there was an increase in the percentage of nouns and link-words, and a decrease in the percentage of verbs and in the total volume of speech production (Faucheux and Moscovici 1966; Moscovici and Plon 1966; Moscovici 1967).

In reviewing the psycholinguistic research in communication which has been carried out in the Soviet Union, it is expedient to first mention V. S. Ageyev. Ageyev's experiments were based upon the results of Moscovici's research (Ageyev 1972). He studied only two situations, "side-by-side" and "face-to-face," with the following results: (1) the data obtained by Moscovici for French were confirmed by Russian material; (2) the significant factor was not the situation itself (the position), but the fact of its change, i.e. the need for a new orientation; (3) the "face-to-face" situation yielded a significantly greater number of words directly connected with the topic of conversation; (4) the number of proper names used in the conversation doubled; (5) the number of hortative phrases like "And what do you think?" was more than twice as great; (6) the number of reformulations of an interlocuter's utterances was almost three times as great; (7) the number of utterances expressing agreement doubled, while the number of contradictory utterances sharply diminished; (8) the number of interruptions sharply increased; (9) the number of rejoinders was generally greater; (10) the usage of the personal pronouns "I" and "we" became more frequent (while the overall percentage of pronouns and link words in general diminished); and (11) the number of stock phrases had almost quadrupled.

B. Kh. Bgazhnokov studied the psycholinguistic parameters of person- and group-directed communication. Two series of experiments were performed. In the first series the subjects (senior schoolchildren) were asked to explain the meanings of some psychological terms to other classmates in private; then they were to explain the same terms to the whole class. In the second series the succession of tasks was reversed: they first explained the material to the whole class, and then to a single pupil.

The experiment showed a significant difference in the psycholinguistic parameters of person- and group-directed communication, depending upon the sequence of the communicative tasks, and yielded some of the following results: in the first series, the person-directed communication resulted in twice the speech volume (three times, if we take into account not only the subjects' speech but that of their interlocutors as well); in the second series, there was a marked tendency toward approximation of group-directed communication in terms of the percentages of different parts of speech (fewer nouns and more verbs) — thus, the subjects demonstrated the rigidity of the earlier orientation. The amount of dialogue in person-directed communication was sharply reduced in the second series; there appeared a tendency to suppress the verbal activity of the interlocutor. Similar results were obtained with group-directed communication: in the first series the subjects transferred the earlier "personal" approach to group communication. It is characteristic that a change in the concrete communicative situation should prove for the subjects to be less significant by a number of parameters, than a change of orientation in communication (Bgazhnokov 1973).

Some interesting research by Kuzemenko (1972) and Sorokin (1973), dealing with orientation in the content of speech, touches upon the role of such orientation in the perception of texts. The work of the first author showed that success in textual comprehension depends on the communicative attitude. It also demonstrated that the hierarchy of orientation factors affecting comprehension differs according to which language (English, Russian, Chinese, or hieroglyphic) is being read and which group of subjects is tested. Sorokin has worked out psycholinguistic methods for the semantic scaling of texts; when these are applied, it turns out that the evaluation of texts of different types (scientific, popular-scientific, and fictional) depend from the outset on the attitude toward the content — in terms of various features. T. M. Dridze (1972), in the course of a large-scale psycholinguistic investigation of the relationship between text and recipient, succeeded in particular in clarifying the dependence of the "stereotype" concept on the recipient's attitude to the text; this attitude, in turn, is conditioned by a number of sociological factors.

V. V. Andriyevskaya (1971) showed that with a fuller orientation in the content, the effect of frequency-associative connections becomes much less. A. P. Zhuravlev (1971) and V. F. Satinova (Passov and Satinova 1971) investigated the ways in which attitudes toward content are reflected in different kinds of semantic transformations when retelling a text.

Attitudes toward the truth or falsity of the content of speech is also reflected in psycholinguistic parameters. This dependence was experimentally demonstrated in Soviet psycholinguistics by V. V. Batov: an intentionally false statement contains less frequent words, which, in the author's opinion, corresponds to a general tendency to "nontriviality" of communicative structures. (The latter, in turn, corresponds to a higher degree of motivation in choosing these structures) (Batov 1972).

S. M. Vul studied the dynamics of alternation of linguistic characteristics in intentionally false texts and determined some of its more general linguistic features (Vul 1970).

Attitudes toward various temporal conditions were studied by three authors. V. V. Andriyevskaya (1970) noted that under time pressure conditions an associative experiment yields mainly high frequency words. N. V. Vitt (1971a) investigated the same problem using foreign language material. The latter demonstrated a sharp increase in the number of errors under time restrictions.

Psycholinguistic characteristics of speech under conditions of emotional stress were studied in particular. Under these conditions the correct orientation was found to be either difficult or disrupted.

There are similar investigations in the literature, but they usually treat only isolated characteristics; they receive more or less broad consideration in only three works (Osgood and Walker 1959; Dibner 1956; Mahl 1963). The reflection of emotional tension in the psycholinguistic parameters of communication was investigated in the Soviet Union by Vitt (Vitt 1971; Vitt and Yermolayeva-Tomina 1971) and especially by Nosenko (Leontiev and Nosenko 1973).

In the latter work, the following psycholinguistic features of emotionality were demonstrated: the average length of speech fragments between hesitation pauses (shorter); the average pause duration (longer); the ratio of the sum of pause durations to the duration of phonation (greater); the number of FALSE starts; paraphrases, semantically irrelevant repetitions, grammatical disagreements; logically and grammatically incomplete sentences; nonfunctional inversions; stock phrases (greater); vacillations in loudness (more noticeable); the frequency of utterances with pronounced positive or negative connotation (much higher); the frequency words with absolute meanings, such as "always," "every," and "to the end" (higher).

Some speech characteristics of subjects of the excitable type in comparison with the inhibited type were demonstrated. The relative independence of these features from language structure was shown.

The basic work on the mechanisms and role of orientation in an interlocutor was done by A. A. Bodalev and his school and is summarized in two monographs (1965, 1970), but the psycholinguistic correlates of this orientation link have been studied insufficiently.

To conclude this section, we mention a series of works by E. F.

Tarasov (1969, 1972), who analyzes the significance for communication of orientation in the system of the social roles of communicators. A. U. Kharash in his work (1972) considered similar questions concerning public speech.

NON-VERBAL COMPONENTS OF THE PROCESS OF VERBAL COMMUNICATION

For the topic of this report the connection of paralinguistics, especially kinesics with the general psycholinguistic structure of the processes of speech formation, has a special interest.

Unfortunately, though paralinguistic and kinesic phenomena themselves have been investigated thoroughly (including some recent publications in Russian [Kolshansky 1973; Nikolayeva 1972] that are relatively little known to Western readers), their psycholinguistic aspect remains unstudied. In this connection one can point to only one investigation (Maslyko 1970) which showed how one might establish a psycholinguistic hierarchy of kinesic and paralinguistic phenomena. The hierarchy would be determined by the correlation of these phenomena with consecutive stages in the production of a verbal utterance, i.e. from the inner programming to the external phonation. (The author used our model, which was worked out together with T. V. Ryabova [A. A. Leontiev 1969a, b].)

At present, a broad research program into the national and universal pecularities of paralinguistics, kinesics, and other nonverbal components of the process of communication is being carried out at the Institute of Linguistics of the Academy of Sciences of the U.S.S.R. In this project, research has been or is being carried out with Russian, Belorussian, Lithuanian, Latvian, German, English, Estonian, Tajik, Abkhazian, Kabardin, Korean, Checheno-Ingush, Japanese, Chinese, Vietnamese and other languages.

The results of these investigations have not yet been published. It would be most desirable to expand the range of languages being investigated; and for this purpose a special questionnaire has been developed intended for ethnographers, philologists, and linguists who have no special psycholinguistic training.[1]

---

[1] The questionnaire that was worked out by A. A. Leontiev, E. F. Tarasov, and J. A. Sorokin is available from the author of this article (Group of Psycholinguistics and Theory of Communication, Institute of Linguistics, Marx-Engels Street I/14, Moscow G-19, U.S.S.R.).

CONCLUSION

This report has given in a condensed form an account of the theoretical foundations which make up the basis for the main Soviet investigations into the psycholinguistic parameters of communication, giving special attention to face-to-face communication. The most important results of these investigations have been described and references to other publications have been given, and the state of research on the non-verbal components of face-to-face communication has been outlined.

Summing up, we think that further experimental and theoretical elaboration of the psychology of face-to-face communication in the above-mentioned directions is advisable, particularly in the area of the different types and components of pre-speech orientation activity. Such elaboration has more than abstract theoretical interest; it is essential for the purpose of TEACHING face-to-face communication. Although this may appear to be paradoxical, it nonetheless becomes very important when we are dealing with the formation of the professional habits of a teacher, doctor, diplomat, journalist, investigator (Shakhrimanyan et al. 1973), actor (Sobkin 1972), not to mention the group of professions such as lecturer, advertising agent, and the like, for which the German language has the apt term *sprachintensive Berufe*. But it is especially important, for instruction in face-to-face communication can be a vital component in the ethical and aesthetic education of the individual and the social significance of this task can hardly be exaggerated.

REFERENCES

AGEYEV, V.
    1972 Situativnye variatsii parametrov rechi [Situational variations of speech parameters]. *Psikholingvistika i obuchenie inostrantsev russkomu yazyku* [Psycholinguistics and the Teaching of Russian to Foreigners]. Moscow: MGU.

ANDRIYEVSKAYA, V. V.
    1970 Vliyanie vremennogo rezhima kommunikatsii na formalnye kharakteristiki soobshcheniya [The influence of the time rate of communication on the formal features of information]. *Sotsialno-psikhologicheskie i lingvisticheskie kharakteristiki form obshcheniya i razvitiya kontaktov mezhdu lyudmi* [Social-Psychological and Linguistic Characteristics of the Forms of Communication and of the Development of Contact between People]. Leningrad: LGU.

1971 O vzaimosvyazi logicheskikh i yazykovykh determinantov pri realizatsii yazykovogo zamysla [On the interrelationship of logical and language determinants in realizing speech intentions]. *Materialy IV Vsesoyuznogo syezda Obshchestva psikhologov* [Materials of the IV Congress of The Society of Psychologists]. Tbilisi.

ARGYLE, M.
1967 *The psychology of interpersonal behavior.* London: Penguin.

BACK, K. W.
1961 "Power, influence and pattern of communication," in *Leadership and interpersonal behavior.* Edited by L. Petrullo and B. Bass. New York: Holt, Rinehart and Winston.

BATOV, V. V.
1972 Unpublished experimental investigation. A portion appears in Batov and Kochinov 1972.

BATOV, V. V., M. M. KOCHINOV
1972 Vliyanie motiva na vybor slov v alternativnykh vyskazyvaniyakh [The influence of the motive on the choice of words in alternative expressions]. *Obshchenie kak predmet teoreticheskikh i prikladnykh issledovaniy* [Communication as Tool of Theoretical and Applied Investigation]. Leningrad: LGU.

BGAZHNOKOV, B. KH.
1973 Psikhologicheskaya orientatsiya kak faktor, opredelyayushchy kharakter rechevogo obshcheniya [Psychological orientation as factor, determining the character of verbal communication]. *Obshchaya i prikladnaya psikholingvistika* [General and Applied Psycholinguistics]. Moscow.

BODALEV, A. A.
1965 *Vospriyatie cheloveka chelovekom* [The perception of a human being by a human being]. Leningrad: LGU
1970 *Formitovanie ponyatiya o drugom cheloveke kak lichnosti* [The concept-formation about the other person as a personality]. Leningrad: LGU.

BORDEN, G. A., R. B. GREGG, T. G. GROVE
1969 *Speech behavior and human interaction.* Englewood Cliffs: Prentice Hall.

BOZHOVICH, L. I.
1968 *Lichnost i ego formirovanie v detskom vozraste* [The personality and its development in a child]. Moscow: Pedagogika.

DIBNER, A. S.
1956 Cue-counting: a measure of anxiety in interviews. *J. Consult. Psychol.* 20:475.

DRIDZE, T. M.
1972 Yazyk informatsii i yazyk retsipienta kak faktory informirovannosti [The language of information and recipient as informing factors]. *Rechevoe vozdeystvie* [Verbal Influence]. Moscow: Nauka.

FAUCHEUX, C., S. MOSCOVICI
1966 Contribution à une psychosociologie du langage. *XVIII Congrès international de psychologie.* Symposium 34. Moscow.

FLORES D'ARCAIS, G.
1966 An experimental investigation on language and perception. *The Center for Cognitive Studies Sixth Annual Report, 1965-1966.* Cambridge: Harvard University.

GALPERIN, P. YA.
1966 Psikhologiya myshleniya i uchenie o poetapnom formirovanii umstvennyx deystvy [The psychology of thinking and the doctrine of stage-like formation of mental activity]. *Issledovaniya myshleniya v sovetskoy psikkologii* [Investigations of Thinking in Soviet Psychology]. Moscow: Nauka.

JANOUŠEK, J. J.
1968 *Sociální komunikace* [Social communication]. Praha: Svoboda.

KHARASH, A. U.
1972 *Lektsionnoya auditoriya: sotsialno-psikhologichesky aspekt* [The lecture audience: social-psychological aspects]. Moscow: Znanie.

KOLSHANSKY, G. V.
1973 Funktsii paralingvisticheskikh sredstv v yazykovoy kommunikatsii. [Functions of paralinguistic means in verbal communication]. *Voprosy Yazykoznaniya* [Problems of Linguistics] 1.

KUZEMENKO, O.
1972 Unpublished experimental investigation. Pedagogical Institute at Chita.

LEONTIEV, A. A.
1969a Smysl kak psikhologicheskoe ponyatie [Sense as a psychological concept]. *Psikhologicheskie i psikholingvisticheskie problemy vladeniya i ovladeniya yazykom* [Psychological and Psycholinguistic Problems of Speaking and Mastering a Language]. Moscow: MGU.
1969b *Psikholingvisticheskie edinitsy i porozhdenie rechevogo vyskazyvaniya* [Psycholinguistic units and the generation of verbal expression]. Moscow: Nauka.
1972 K psikhologii rechevogo vozdeystviya [Toward a psychology of verbal interaction]. *Materialy IV Vsesoyuznogo simpoziuma po psikholingvistike i teorii kommunikatsii* [Materials of the IVth Symposium on Psycholinguistics and the Theory of Communication]. Moscow.
1973a Iskusstvo kak forma obshcheniya [Art as form of communication]. *Psikhologicheskie issledovaniya* [Psychological Investigations]. Tbilisi: Metsniereba.
1973b Le principe heuristique dans la production et la compréhension du langage. *Bulletin de Psychologie* 26:5–9.

LEONTIEV, A. A., E. L. NOSENKO
1973 Nekotorye psikholingvisticheskie kharakteristiki spontannoy rechi v sostoyanii emotsionalnogo napryazheniya [Some psycholinguistic characteristics of spontaneous speech during emotional stress]. *Obshchaya i prikladnaya psikholingvistika* [General and Applied Psycholinguistics]. Moscow: Nauka.

LEONTIEV, A. N.
1968 Nekotorye psikhologicheskie voprosy vozdeystviya na lichnost [Some psychological problems of personality influencing]. *Problemy nauchnogo kommunizma* [Problems of Scientific Communism] vypusk 2. Moscow: Mysl.
1972 *Problemy razvitiya psikhiki* [Problems of the development of the psyche] (third edition). Moscow: MGU.

MAHL, G. F.
1963 "The lexical and linguistic levels in the expression of emotions," in *Expression of the emotions in man*. Edited by P. H. Knapp, 77–105. New York: International Universities Press.

MASLYKO, E. A.
1970 K psikholingvisticheskoy prirode paralingvisticheskikh yavleny [Toward the psycholinguistic nature of paralinguistic phenomena]. *Materialy Tretyego Vsesoyuznogo simpoziuma po psikholingvistike* [Materials of the Third Symposium on Psycholinguistics]. Moscow.

MESHCHERYAKOV, A. I.
1971 Razvitie sredstv obshcheniya u slepoglukhonemykh detey [The development of the means of communication by blind and deafmute children]. *Voprosy filosofii* [Problems of Philosophy] 8.

MOSCOVICI, S.
1967 *Communication processes and language*. Advances in Experimental Social Psychology 3. New York-Leningrad: Academic Press.

MOSCOVICI, S., M. PLON
1966 Les situations-colloques observations théorétiques et expérimentales. *Bulletin de Psychologie* 19.

NIKOLAYEVA, T. M.
1972 *Zhest i mimika v lektsii* [Gesture and mimics in lectures]. Moscow: Znanie.

OSGOOD, C. E., E. G. WALKER
1959 Motivation and language behavior: a content analysis of suicide notes. *Journal of Abnormal Social Psychology* 59(1).

PASSOV, E. I., V. F. SATINOVA
1971 Transformatsiya kak psikholingvistichesky kriteriy ponimaniya rechi [Transformations as psycholinguistic criterium of understanding speech]. *Voprosy psikholingvistiki i prepodavanie russkogo yazyka kak inostrannogo* [Problems of Psycholinguistics and the Teaching of Russian as a Foreign Language]. Moscow: MGU.

SHAKHRIMANYAN, I. K., V. A. VARLAMOV, V. V. TARAKANOV
1973 Soderzhanie rechevykh i nerechevykh komponentov v deyatelnosti sledovatelya [The content of speeech and non-speech components in the activity of the investigator]. *Obshchaya i prikladnaya psikholingvistika* [General and Applied Psycholinguistics]. Moscow.

SKINNER, B. F.
1957 *Verbal behavior*. London.

SLOBIN, D. J.
1966 Grammatical transformations and sentence comprehension in childhood and adulthood. *Journal of Verbal Learning and Verbal Behavior* 5(3).

SOBKIN, V.
1972 "Unpublished manuscript." University of Moscow.

SOROKIN, YU. A.
1973 Eksperimentalnaya proverka realnosti nekotorykh priznakov teksta [Experimental testing of the reality of some text features]. *Obshchaya i prikladnaya psikholingvistika* [General and Applied Psycholinguistics]. Moscow.

TARASOV, E. F.
1969 Sotsiologicheskie aspekty rechevogo obshcheniya [Sociological aspects of verbal communication]. *Rol i mesto stranovedeniya v praktike prepodavaniya russkogo yazyka kak inostrannogo* [The Role and Place of Geographical and Ethnological Knowledge in the Practice of Teaching Russian as a Foreign Language]. Moscow: MGU.
1972 Sotsialnoe vzaimodeystvie v rechevom obshchenii [Social interaction in verbal communication]. *Materialy IV Vsesoyuznogo simposiuma po psikholingvistike i teorii kommunikatsii* [Material of the IVth Symposium on Psycholinguistics and the Theory of Communication]. Moscow.

THAYER, L.
1968 *Communication and communication systems*. Homewood, Illinois: R. D. Irwin.

TURNER, E. A., R. ROMMETVEIT
1968 Focus of attention in recall of active and passive sentences. *Journal of Verbal Learning and Verbal Behavior* 7(2).

VITT, N. V.
1971a K voprosu o vzaimosvyazi intellektualnykh protsessov i funktsionalnogo sostoyaniya [Toward the problem of the interrelationship of intellectual processes and functional state]. *Lingvopsikhologicheskie problemy obosnovaniya metodiki prepodovaniya inostrannykh yazykov v vysshey shkole* [Linguopsychological Problems of Basing the Methodology of the Teaching of Foreign Languages in High School]. *Tezisy dokladov* [Theses of Lectures]. Moscow.
1971b Vliyanie sostoyaniya psikhocheskogo napryazheniya, vyzvannogo ogranicheniem vremeni, na kachestvo rechi [The influence of the state of psychotic stress, evoked by time pressure, on the quality of speech]. *Materialy IV Vsesoyuznogo syezda Obshchestva psikhologov* [Material of the IVth Congress of The Society of Psychologists]. Tbilisi.

VITT, N. V., L. V. YERMOLAYEVA-TOMINA
1971 K probleme svyazi rechevykh kharakteristik i svoystv pervoy

sistemy v emotsionalnom sostoyanii [On the question of the relation of speech characteristics and the properties of the first system in emotional state]. *Materialy IV Vsesoyuznogo syezda Obshchestva psikhologov* [Materials of the IVth Congress of Psychologists]. Tbilisi.

VUL, S. M.
1970 Kharakter i predely izmeneniy pismennoy rechi pri eyo prednamerennoy iskazhenii [The character and limits of written speech by deliberate distortion]. *Materialy Tretyego Vsesoyuznogo simposiuma po psikholingvistike* [Materials of the Third Symposium on Psycholinguistics]. Moscow.

WATSON, O. M.
1970 *Proxemic behavior*. The Hague: Mouton.

ZHURAVLEV, A. P.
1971 Testovoe izmerenie sposobnosti vozpriyatiya smysla predlozheniy. [Test measuring of the ability to perceive the sense of sentences]. *Voprosy psikholigvistiki i prepodavanie russkogo yazyka kak inostrannogo* [Problems of Psycholinguistics and the Teaching of Russian as a Foreign Language]. Moscow: MGU.

PART FIVE

Interaction, Social Relationships, and Social Structure

Territoriality and the Spatial Regulation of Interaction

IAN VINE

Face-to-face interaction is in many respects the most fundamental process in the functioning of social systems. Not only does it play a major role in shaping the individual's course of development (Vine 1973), but it is a key source of his satisfactions and disappointments throughout life. At the same time it is basic to the establishment, maintenance, and development of most social groups, institutions, and cultures. Yet only in recent years has the study of face-to-face interaction become a central focus of interdisciplinary cooperation among social scientists. Probably the most significant impetus to this new emphasis came from Birdwhistell (1952), who showed that the "kinesic" visual signals that accompany speech contribute at many simultaneous levels to the total communication process. The subsequent interest in what has rather inaccurately been termed "nonverbal communication" has forged new links between several disciplines.

Particular signals from a given individual must be considered in relation not only to concurrent signals in other channels but to signals emitted by others who are present, and to the physical setting of the interaction. Further understanding of the various subsystems and suprasystems of the communication process depends on additional contextual factors, such as the histories of the interactors and their past encounters, their immediate and future goals, the cultural definition of the interaction situation, and ultimately the basic biology and ecology of their species. Several recent volumes attest to the awakening of interest in these issues and to how far we still have to go in

The author wishes to acknowledge the support of the Social Science Research Council (United Kingdom) during the preparation of this article.

resolving problems of research methodology, obtaining more data, and arriving at some theoretical integration of findings (Argyle 1969; Birdwhistell 1971; Blurton-Jones 1971; Ekman, Friesen, Ellsworth 1972; Goffman 1971; Hall 1966; Hinde 1972a; McQuown 1971; Sebeok 1968; Siegman and Pope 1972; von Cranach and Vine 1973).

Contributions to a number of the questions concerning face-to-face interaction have come from outside the human social sciences, namely from animal ethology. This has been particularly true in relation to spatial factors in interaction, or what Hall (1963) called "proxemic" features. Hall (1966) subdivided spatial contexts according to three different types of spatial structuring, referring to "fixed-feature," "semifixed-feature," and "informal" spaces. These terms refer, respectively, to the layout of the fixed physical environment in which interactions occur, to the arrangement of mobile features such as chairs and tables and to the spatial arrangements of interactors with respect to each other. Sommer (e.g. 1969) and Goffman (e.g. 1971), among others, have investigated in some detail how aspects of these various types of spatial structuring can affect interaction, and how these spaces may in turn be manipulated according to the requirements of interaction itself.

The methods and theoretical concepts of proxemic research have revealed a strong debt to ethology, but unfortunately this influence has not been entirely beneficial. Much use has been made of the ethological notion of TERRITORY, which has been applied and developed extensively in describing animal spatial behavior since Howard (1920) first used it in connection with the defended breeding areas of birds. Difficulties in the interpretation of the concept, particularly because territoriality has acquired strong connotations of being "innately" linked to aggressive fighting (e.g. Ardrey 1967; Lorenz 1966), have been discussed at length elsewhere (Vine i.p.). Also, this emphasis has distracted attention from what may be more important similarities and differences between animal and human spatial behavior.

THE SPATIAL REGULATION OF INTERACTION IN ANIMALS

A critical analysis of the literature on spacing in other vertebrates reveals that several of the major concepts used, especially TERRITORY, have caused some confusion within ethology through being defined and interpreted in a wide variety of ways (Vine i.p.). One reason for this has undoubtedly been the considerable diversity of the actual patterns of space usage, and of the social behaviors associated with space, among other animals. In popularizing the territory concept, authors like Ardrey (1967) have helped to foster within the human sciences a false belief in a simple dichotomy between individual or family possession of exclusive territory and a rigidly hierarchical social group structure as the alternative forms of effective social organization of a species. In each case some genetically based aggressive competition with other territory holders or nonmembers of the group is postulated.

Such a view does violence to the known facts of animal spacing, for not only are there many intermediate forms of social structure, but in many species aggression is relatively rare except at the weakest level. In a number of cases different populations show quite different forms of spacing behavior within a single species, and there can be major changes over the course of the annual cycle. In some animals, such as the feral domestic fowl studied by McBride, Parer, Foenlander (1969), several permutations of territorial and social dominance behavior can coexist within a single population at any given time. Furthermore, what may superficially be described as territory holding can sometimes be more appropriately described in terms of other spacing concepts.

Many factors are in fact involved in determining whether an animal has a territory or not, whether the territory is shared, and if so with how many other animals, how large it is, how continuously it is occupied, what means are used to maintain it, and so on. Ecological as well as individual and social factors can have important effects. The former may include the general type of habitat, whether it hampers or facilitates detection of animals at a distance, amounts and distributions of particular resources such as food or sheltering places, or habitat size and the population density of animals within it. Among the individual factors are rapid or long-term fluctuations in internal physiological condition, sex, age, and breeding maturity, and apparently constitutional differences in aggressiveness. Variables depending on animals' social relationships can include their relative dominance ranks (which may vary according to their activities or what resources are competed over), often any previous history of encounters between the individuals, and specific features such as whether a female is accompanied by offspring.

In addition to fixed territories, mobile territories can be identified conceptually, based on animals' attempts to maintain small exclusive areas around their bodies rather than at fixed sites. In this case avoidance can be as effective as threat or attack in keeping other individuals at a distance, but the size of the area claimed can be affected by many of the factors listed above. For example, it can depend on an animal's current activity or the identity of the potential intruder.

With fixed territories, an important distinction must be made between an animal's familiarity with or attachment to an area and the nature of its motivational and behavioral responses to intrusions. It is also clear that relatively exclusive use of an area, and thus most advantages of territory holding, may be achieved without strict defense of boundaries. An animal's regular presence, coupled with maintaining interindividual separation by threat or attack rather than avoidance, may ensure that others use a region infrequently. Thus, unless a fairly clear boundary can be identified, it is difficult to know whether to call it a territory. Either means may achieve the major function of spacing out a population, but the single term may lead to the neglect of other important differences.

In view of the variety of definitions of TERRITORY and other terms used in discussions of spacing, it is necessary to adopt an explicit set of operational meanings, preferably avoiding reference to functional and motivational factors that may underlie the behaviors involved. The following definitions are based on those advocated elsewhere (Vine i.p.), and are an attempt to avoid some of the difficulties generated by the sources of variability mentioned above.

A. HOME RANGE: an area that an animal uses regularly over a relatively extended time period during the pursuit of routine activities (such as obtaining food). It may be used unevenly, and may consist of no more than a number of MOVEMENT ROUTES between discrete areas used frequently (such as feeding or sleeping places). Where such CORE AREAS can be identified, they may be MONOPOLIZED ZONES used only by the individual or group but need not necessarily be defended as territories in any strict sense.

B. TERRITORY: the term may be used loosely to describe all or part of the home range when access by other animals is controlled or prevented by the resident individual or group. However, a strictly delimited or TRUE TERRITORY is a clearly bounded, fixed area from which all but a few specifiable classes of intruders are successfully excluded in most instances. This can be achieved either by regular boundary patrol, by boundary marking, or by detecting intruders sufficiently rapidly to move to the site of the intrusion before major violations occur. These definitions specifically omit references to the means of exclusion or control of access once intruders have been confronted.

C. INDIVIDUAL SPACE: a mobile, body-centered area from which an individual attempts to exclude others, and which typically extends farther in front of the head and body than to the sides or rear. For an approach that maintains some given relative body orientation of any two individuals, the limit of the area is a measure of the INDIVIDUAL DISTANCE of the animal whose area is being specified. Where a group of animals maintains a similar area around the group as a whole, this is termed their GROUP SPACE.

D. SOCIAL SPACE: a mobile, body-centered area defined by the maximum separations, or SOCIAL DISTANCES, that an individual will tolerate from others (again depending on body orientation) before attempting to increase proximity. The group equivalent of social space has apparently been accorded little empirical or theoretical attention but may be termed a GROUP SOCIAL SPACE. (The tendency of litters of young animals to remain collectively close to a parent might be described in this way.) From the above definitions, it is clear that most interactions between individuals will occur inside the social space but outside the individual space of either one. Their typical separation distance, which will again vary with their body orientations, may be termed the EQUILIBRIUM DISTANCE. It must be emphasized, in connection with all the mobile space definitions, that the size of the area will depend especially on the particular animal approaching a given individual, and on their relationship or relative social ranks.

Few if any authors have given explicit separate definitions of the territory itself and the behavioral characteristic of TERRITORIALITY. However, the distinction is important. The latter term may best be defined as a trait whereby an individual's priority over others in obtaining, or ability to control their access to, some specifiable local resource (such as food or nest materials) over which they may compete will depend in part on how much each has previously used the location involved. Territoriality is thus a dimension along which the behavior of individuals can vary. At one extreme the individual may possess a clearly bounded territory and be able to exclude all others from it, but if adjacent territories are held in similar fashion by others, it will have no access elsewhere. Relative dominance between any pair of animals thus depends exclusively on their locations. At the other extreme, where individuals may meet on equally unfamiliar ground, their relative dominance in any resource competition will be quite unaffected by the location, and the only spatial factor of relevance will be how large their individual spaces are. This is the limiting case, or a totally nonterritorial situation.

Advantages of the definitions suggested above are that they can adequately describe all the varieties of spatial dependency of social interaction and that they recognize the intimate links between spacing and relative social ranks with respect to particular resource acquisition or activities; but they also allow that the degrees of overt aggression involved in encounters can depend substantially on other factors. The agonistic behavior involved in maintaining separation or a boundary can thus be recognized as varying from attack, through aggressive threat, neutral confrontation, and defensive threat, to avoidance or flight. Territoriality, in the sense of dominance being dependent to some degree on familiarity with the location of an encounter, may well be the norm among vertebrates. In this sense, inasmuch as the size of individual space may be similarly affected, maintenance of it may also be included within territoriality, especially if location also influences whether intrusions on individual space elicit avoidance or aggression. The definitions also acknowledge that holders of anything less than a true territory may on occasion allow even a strange individual to enter the area providing that appropriate submissive or "appeasement" rituals are followed. For holders of true territories these rituals may also be required from those (such as a mate) for whom access is regularly permitted; they may also be important in ensuring that individual space is kept small toward certain individuals or classes of individuals.

No attempt will be made here to review the literature on territoriality and mobile spacing in animals, as many assessments are available elsewhere (e.g. Brown and Orians 1970; Crook 1968; Klopfer 1969; Kummer 1971). It is apparent, however, that relatively few species have been convincingly shown to hold true individual or group territories on a long-term basis, and that relatively few show strong aggressiveness over space for long periods. Among mammals, except in some species during the breeding season, some degree of sociability is the norm; the members of groups share large, almost completely overlapping ranges, which in turn often show appreciable overlap with the ranges of other groups. Intergroup encounters are often infrequent, and mutual avoidance is more typical than are strongly aggressive displays or fighting. Except in species with well-developed mechanisms for olfactory marking, such as many carnivores, maintaining large ranges as exclusive true territories would be impossible or uneconomic. An interesting variation found especially in some members of the cat family is the use of scent marking to achieve a "time-sharing" system (Leyhausen 1965), whereby temporal avoidance and use of the same movement routes can be efficiently combined.

From the viewpoint of human spatial behavior, spacing among other primates is of most obvious comparative interest. Very few have been shown to be strongly territorial, although among the primitive prosimians there are some species in which individual males apparently continuously hold very small, fixed territories and may engage in aggressive and frequent boundary disputes (Jolly 1972). More typically, many monkeys and apes show variants of the group home-range system, and in many cases groups tend to avoid each other (e.g. Crook 1970; Eisenberg, Muckenhirn, Rudran 1972), although anthropoid age groups are typically "open" (Reynolds 1966). In at least a few monkeys, such as the dusky titi (Mason 1968), and in two ape species, the gibbon and siamang (Chivers 1972; Ellefson 1968), small family groups maintain permanent true territories. Although in some cases interindividual or intergroup aggressive displays can be very dramatic, territorial fighting and consequent injury are distinctly rare among primates.

The importance of ecological factors in influencing territoriality in primates is indicated by cases where a single species, such as the vervet monkey (Gartlan and Brain 1968) occupies a variety of habitats and shows marked variability in spatial intolerance between these. Present evidence supports the tentative conclusion that holding true territories and showing high spatial aggressiveness are associated with living arboreally in small groups and having very limited ranges, often apparently because of fairly high population densities. Typically these conditions arise in forests where food supplies are relatively concentrated and these local concentrations are reliable from year to year (for example, the preferred fruits of particular trees). More terrestrial primates need to range over large areas, often after thinly distributed or unpredictable food, and they encounter other groups relatively infrequently. Not only would they be unable to monitor boundaries thoroughly, but being nomadic and having no fixed nests or stable resource concentrations, they would gain no immediate or obvious long-term advantage from attempting to hold true territories.

With regard to mobile space, probably all vertebrates maintain some degree of individual space. The influential distinction drawn by Hediger (1950) between "distance" and "contact" species can by no means be an absolute one in view of the number of variables that can affect individual space size. In many primates individuals groom each other and may even huddle in extended physical contact, but probably none do so regularly for extended periods in a full face-to-face orientation. In other species the equilibrium distances may be substantial (e.g. Rosenblum, Kaufmann, Stynes 1964).

Frequent close-proximity encounters are almost certainly a major source of the substantially increased aggressiveness in primates living at high natural population densities, and especially in crowded captivity (Alexander and Roth 1971; Rowell 1967; Southwick 1969). A further factor influencing the nature of encounters is whether animals are familiar or are strangers, with increased aggression being shown to strange animals (Scruton and Herbert 1972). This effect might be seen as a result of the familiarity with the terrain either increasing individual space or increasing the likely bias of agonistic motivation in cases where one animal or a group is on home ground.

In summary, comparison of the forms and behaviors associated with animal spatial usage suggests that ecological factors may be more significant than sometimes recognized in determining the structuring of fixed-feature space and related social behaviors. In a number of species adjustment is possible in varying ecological situations, and the complexity of other determinants makes any attempt to identify unequivocal homologies that may exist between man and his primate relatives very hazardous, especially as no common ancestors are now surviving. Territoriality in its general sense may perhaps have the same basis in man as in other primates, but the motivational basis of the advantages of familiarity with an area remains somewhat speculative (Kummer 1971) and is very likely to involve additional complicating factors in man that arise through his creation of cultural norms. Because the holding of true territories and associated tendencies to behave more aggressively show no clear phylogenetic trend, there is no reason on the evidence considered to expect any specific innate basis for it in man.

Maintenance of the varieties of mobile spaces may also be very general among vertebrates, including other primates, but variability between individuals as well as between species can apparently also be considerable. Again, its basis has not been investigated in sufficient detail to support any strong predictions in relation to man. Unfortunately, the emphasis on territoriality has apparently led to neglect of comparative treatments of individual space or group space on a broad scale, but again there is little evidence of phylogenetic trends. Nevertheless, we may expect fixed-feature and "informal" or mobile spacing in man to be influenced by the same factors as seem general for other species with somewhat related ecologies. Thus, the ethological perspective may draw our attention to aspects of human spatial behavior that may otherwise go unnoticed or be regarded as exclusively cultural. It may thus suggest useful hypotheses concerning spatial factors which interact with our behaviors of initiating, maintaining, concluding, and often simply avoiding social encounters.

FIXED-FEATURE SPACE, SEMIFIXED-FEATURE SPACE, AND HUMAN TERRITORIALITY

There can be no doubt that in varying degrees man shows territoriality, as here defined, and that in certain contexts we attempt to maintain true territories, on an individual as well as a national scale. It must be admitted, however, that much of our evidence is anecdotal or informally descriptive (e.g. Goffman 1971; Hall 1966; Sommer 1969), and more quantitative data would be valuable. More seriously, the evidence that suggests that interactions involving territorial disputes are not infrequently aggressive in character is of an even more general kind. In addition to discovering whether territoriality is itself particularly responsible for the affective tone of an encounter, we must ultimately be concerned to ask what functions it serves, how fundamental it is to our behavior, and whether it will remain adaptive in a world where inevitably we shall be living in conditions even more crowded than at present. Far from being soluble by simple projections from animal behavior, these questions will demand precise and carefully controlled research.

Already there is a growing body of experimental or systematic observation research on human territory, but unfortunately its interpretation is hampered by terminological differences, perhaps more than is the case in animal ethology. Although some authors, like Hall and Sommer, have usually followed the most typical ethological definitions, involving defense of an area and exclusion of intruders from it, others have used quite different criteria. These have included criteria that more appropriately apply to home range, especially when strictly limited areas are used habitually (Esser et al. 1965; Sundstrom and Altman 1972), or where there is habitual selective use of semifixed features such as particular objects, beds, chairs, etc., in shared areas (Altman and Haythorn 1967; Altman, Taylor, Wheeler 1971; DeLong 1970). Other studies have recognized that some measure of overt defense of or control over an area should be involved (Becker and Mayo 1971; Eastman and Harper 1971; Sommer and Becker 1969), but such reactions to particular chairs alone have also been called territorial (Lipman 1968, 1970). Although control of relatively immobile objects like chairs and beds can without difficulty be regarded as involving territoriality, it seems inappropriate to apply the term where small mobile objects are involved, and it seems desirable to retain the distinction between home range or monopolized zones and territories.

Other authors have gone further in including not only the personalized marking of areas as a form of territoriality, even where no other evidence of control is necessarily involved (Rapoport 1968), but also the marking of objects, defense of possessions and even people, protection of personal information, one's thoughts, and one's identity (Altman 1970; Goffman 1971; Pastalan 1970). Although such examples all involve control or possession, there is no convincing evidence to justify any assumption that underlying processes and mechanisms are necessarily similar in all cases, and the restriction of the territoriality concept to cases where space is involved seems imperative. Less critically, Lyman and Scott (1967), Scheflen (1970), and others have included PERSONAL SPACE as a type of territory. (The term is equivalent to INDIVIDUAL SPACE, but as it has entered general use since being proposed by Sommer (1959), it will be used here when referring to individual space in man.) Because the distinction between fixed or semifixed and body-centered space is a significant one, maintenance of personal space will not be regarded as true territorial behavior in this study.

The case for recognizing that cognitive and experiential factors ARE involved in human responsiveness to spatial features is of course inescapable. Subjective awareness of ownership is clearly relevant to our conceptions of territory (Altman 1970; Goffman 1971), and the same is true of perceptions, motivations, expectancies, and so on. Stea (1970) has made similar points regarding home range, and Leibman (1970) has emphasized that personal space is a "psychological bubble." However, attempts to incorporate these features in definitions (e.g. Altman 1970) make their assessment in operational terms very difficult and apparently rule out any comparisons with other species. Furthermore, we have as yet very little detailed knowledge of any but the behavioral aspects of territoriality or mobile spacing in man. In exploring the importance of these subjective features, it will also be necessary to recognize another frequently ignored aspect of many human territories, namely, that ownership often includes property rights as well as control of access (Tiger and Fox 1971). They can thus be inherited, bought, or sold like other economic commodities. In other cases, we may have official and more or less permanent "jurisdiction" (Goffman 1971; Roos 1968) over an area without owning it, just as we may acquire rights merely by virtue of others coming to accept that a norm has been established through regular use.

It may well be that although individuals, groups, communities, and nations possess what can be regarded behaviorally as territories with similarities to those of animals, the effect these have on encounters with intruding individuals is based much more on individual choice or cultural norms involving property than on any constitutional similarity in underlying processes. However, the assumption that man has no physiological commonality with other species, or that adults are "entirely instinctless" (Montagu 1968: 11) is patently absurd; it is an empirical question whether or not evolutionary adaptation has given rise to inherited predispositions which, in spite of our obvious differences from other species, will help us to understand some aspects of human territoriality (Vine i.p.). In particular, it may be instructive to consider what limited evidence we have regarding our immediate ancestors and the course of human history. Apart from this, we have more voluminous data from anthropology and cross-cultural studies, and that material dealing with cultures that have until recently been relatively immune from the rapid changes in Western civilization may be particularly instructive.

Two basic evolutionary factors appear to be of major relevance in the development of territoriality. First, we know that man is the only living primate who depends for a substantial proportion of his diet on eating other species. This predatory existence is likely to have itself led to major social changes, as despite the fact that we can survive without meat, we appear to have evolved primarily as a hunting as well as a gathering species. Given our rather meager physical size, speed and strength, this imposed a major requirement for close cooperation and communication within the group, almost certainly before we developed language and a highly elaborated culture (Lee and DeVore 1969; Service 1966; Tiger and Fox 1971).

Second, in terms of the evolutionary time-scale our development of systematic agricultural practices is extremely recent, but breeding domesticated animals and cultivating crops favored and ultimately required a sedentary rather than nomadic life style. Eventually the changes in society this implied led to the growth of large, complex settlements which accentuated role and caste divisions, and may have been responsible for the large-scale shift toward an individualistic rather than communistic social emphasis (Mumford 1961).

As hunter-gatherers, the early hominids of the human evolutionary line almost certainly operated in groups composed of the males of several basic family units; thus they could not have held individual (or family) territories in any strict sense. Nevertheless, the predominant view (e.g. Tinbergen 1968) is that some form of group territory was typically maintained. If this is so, then any inherited human predisposition to generalized territoriality would be much more likely to take this form than one involving the attempt to acquire individual territories because the 10,000 years of agriculture and sedentary life that have made it possible to develop individual ownership of strictly defined space can have had relatively little effect on our basic constitution. It remains possible, of course, that our inheritance is in no way so specific and that we can adapt fairly readily to alternative systems on the basis of learned adaptations to ecological changes. In fact, territoriality, as it has been interpreted here, is in any case nonspecific and can result in a variety of spatial arrangements. Whether a given degree of territoriality results in individual or group territory holding may depend on factors unrelated to what may actually be inherited.

It may in fact be misleading to think of early man as holding group territories. Reynolds (1966) argues strongly that our hominid ancestors retained the "open group" social system of the great apes. Core areas of relatively large home ranges might be in any case more or less monopolized without being at all strictly defended, as can occur in other species. Moderate overlap of ranges could probably be tolerated quite easily without much threat to any single group's needed resources. One interesting possibility does emerge, however, if we compare man not with other primates but with other carnivores. Overlap of ranges appears normally to be tolerated only if food is very accessible or if temporal separation in range use can easily be achieved. Presumably, otherwise there might be interference in the hunt between adjacent groups. However, as man cannot achieve "time sharing" by scent marking and cannot use loud calls to signal his presence to other groups, he may have found it necessary to define more exclusive ranges with reference to natural landmarks or by using visual artifacts. This would have led to more precise spatial delineation of areas than might have been necessary or even advantageous in terms of resource conservation as such. Various other influences could then have combined to favor further developments toward strict exclusion and boundary defense, particularly if prey became scarce or the human populations expanded too rapidly. Various other sources of intergroup competition (e.g. Corning and Corning 1972; Tiger and Fox 1971) may thus have become focused around rigid boundaries, resulting in associated cultural norms of boundary confrontation that arose only indirectly from basic territorial dispositions.

Not least among extrinsic influences may have been the attribution of symbolic and religious functions to space. Although hunter-gatherers in general apparently have much more flexible notions of space ownership than agriculturalists, they can show complex perceptions of the significance of land according to its function. Rapoport (1972) describes the basic historical pattern still partially applicable to Australian aboriginal cultures, in which religious myths about and ritual uses of land have had major significance. As nomads who for the most part construct only the most temporary and inconsequential physical shelters, basic family groups roam over extensive ranges which may contain several core areas. Range boundaries are fairly precisely known to the group, but there is frequent visiting between groups, and access to resources may be freely given. Notions of ownership of land are based simply on use rights.

The composite area owned by a tribal collection of such aboriginal groups is more akin to a true territory and is regarded as permanently defined and god-given. Boundaries are still somewhat imprecise unless there are clear natural landmarks, but intrusion by outsiders is only sanctioned in specified circumstances. Some parts of the tribal region are set aside as areas of religious significance to particular clans or aggregations of groups. In these areas there is in fact more precise and exclusive definition of boundaries and sometimes they are marked with visible artifacts. Sanctions against intrusion are nevertheless largely internalized and depend on the aborigine's religious reverence for space. (The same applies to many Western churches, which are left open despite the valuable property they may contain.) When tribes periodically come together for large ritual meetings, the positioning of the shelters that comprise their camps is also governed by their symbolic interpretations of space, rather than by any obviously territorial separation between tribes. Thus, symbolic and religious considerations seem to take precedence in their spatial organization over those of more economic and obviously adaptive significance.

Rapoport indicates that there has been some variability among the aborigines themselves in their treatment of boundaries, and that they are not necessarily typical of all hunter-gatherers. His analysis does, however, give some support to the view that strong territoriality was probably not the norm throughout most of human history (Reynolds 1966), and that any underlying genetic predisposition toward territorial behavior lacks a strong association with systems that release aggression.

On the other hand, the likely basis of the strictly defined family home territory and of the group settlement marked by walls or similar physical boundaries CAN be identified in relation to agriculture, as can at least some aspects of our sometimes violent defense of these. Probably the first agriculturalists needed fences to protect their stock (as well as their children and themselves) from nocturnal predators, at least in some habitats. At about the same time, economic competition between nomadic hunter-gatherers, nomadic shepherds, and the sedentary cultivators for land itself must have begun, aggravated rapidly by the population explosions which agricultural affluence permitted (Mumford 1961; Russell and Russell 1968). The storage of surplus grain would itself invite plunder and inevitably these new sources of economic, social, and spatial imbalance in human society produced stresses and frustrations that on any psychological theory of aggression might lead to violence. Even though space itself may have been a key factor, there seems no good reason to explain the aggression simply by invoking territoriality as the basic mechanism involved.

If the above account of how strict territorial attachments and aggressive encounters at boundaries may have arisen in relatively recent times is correct, even in outline, it may not be surprising if man appears to be partially lacking in innate "appeasement" mechanisms and a readiness to flee or withdraw which prevent aggressive interactions in other species from leading typically to bloodshed (Lorenz 1966; Tinbergen 1968). Not only are we lacking the long evolutionary history as hunters which might favor innate constraints on using natural weapons, but the artificial weapons we have developed can kill at a distance, where such mechanisms of "cut-off" (Chance 1962) that can stop aggression are ineffective. Perhaps more significantly still, at our original low population densities the confrontations at close quarters that normally precede attack must have been much less frequent.

Alternative biological views of aggression which emphasize its territorial basis must have difficulty in explaining why our appeasement techniques are not more effective, especially Ardrey's view (1967) whereby boundary confrontations have always been sought out for the security, identity, and stimulation that they supposedly bring as a positive benefit. There are many sources of aggressive responsiveness, in other species as well as man (e.g. Hinde 1972b; Johnson 1972), and a variety of physiological factors may be involved (Corning and Corning 1972). But although aggression may be adaptive in particular circumstances, it can only be so if it is matched by a readiness to submit or flee. Where basic territoriality was involved, primitive man may well have shown such a readiness, having little to lose by doing so. Our modern willingness to lose even our lives rather than to acknowledge the dominance of another may be of some advantage to the group, but is not so to the individual. If ecological change and culture had not taken over from genetic evolution, our territoriality would have remained adaptive, for at least until our recent past, genetic evolution has operated at the level of individuals (Corning and Corning 1972; Hamilton 1964).

THE EFFECTS OF TERRITORIALITY ON INTERACTION

On the argument that has been advanced, the territoriality that man may be expected to show and does appear to show, at the micro-level of face-to-face encounters between individuals, could have remained basically adaptive and could be responsive to the same factors that appear to influence the nature of interactions within other species. The available evidence not only confirms this but shows that where territorial asymmetries are involved, we DO normally have ample means of dealing with associated dominance variations without recourse to agonistic behavior. Intergroup territorial relationships, especially at a national level, involve too many other factors to be interpreted simply, and these will not be discussed any further.

Some reference must nevertheless be made first to intergroup territoriality as it operates on a relatively small scale. Probably the most obvious true territories at the level of the group are the areas occupied by adolescent gangs. These groups periodically show agonistic activity during boundary confrontations, and apparently do seek these deliberately, perhaps to obtain positive satisfactions of security, identity, and stimulation (Ardrey 1967; Tiger and Fox 1971). However, it is probably significant that such gang warfare is found typically only where poverty, overcrowding, or other sources of social stress are widespread, and it thus may be difficult to satisfy these needs in other ways. In addition, the territorial control exerted by gangs is normally quite specific to their true rivals, as in other species, and they do not normally make any attempt to control access by other persons. The same is also apparently true of urban criminal gangs (Johnson 1972).

There are other obvious cases involving fairly well defined local intergroup boundaries within cities, such as boundaries between racially defined, social class-based, or religion-based enclaves. Here the boundary may be meaningful to all concerned, but those crossing the line between such areas are normally tolerated, providing only that they do not themselves attempt to assert dominance over the residents. The situation may become more overtly hostile when other factors have raised the tension between groups, as in racial ghettos, but in these cases the boundary itself is only accidentally a cause of conflict in most instances.

On the level of the individual or family territory, the control of entry to private homes is of major interest. Here man perhaps comes closest to fulfilling the conditions that favor strong territoriality in other primates, for a small, closely knit group holds a strong concentration of valuable and readily defensible resources in a small location. However, in this case man shows fairly marked cultural variability. For example, Hall (1971) describes how black Americans may be more protective than whites toward a group of neighboring homes as a whole but show less territoriality regarding individual homes among themselves. Members of the working class in at least a number of Western cultures show the same freedom as blacks in using one another's homes, and also tend to make less clear territorial divisions between their homes and their streets (Fried and Gleicher 1961).

Whatever the cultural or subcultural variations, in even the most rigidly protected homes there is clear variation of access norms. Not only the residents but frequently immediate neighbors or very close relatives and friends need do no more than announce their presence to obtain free access. The same may apply to culturally legitimated strangers, such as public officials. We are more likely, however, to ask them at least to state their purpose, and sometimes to prove their identity as well. The nature of the reason for wanting to enter and the manner in which access is requested can have a marked effect on the owner's response, both at the boundary and when entry has been allowed, in all cases involving casual acquaintances or strangers. The "access rituals" discussed at length by Goffman (1971), which involve showing deference to the resident, can be seen as means of indicating that dominance is not being claimed and of acknowledging the resident's preferential rights in the home. Of special interest is the fact that such deference behaviors may be engaged in mutually (Goffman 1956), indicating that superficially, and in order to facilitate normal involvement in the subsequent interactions, the resident is giving up dominance rights.

Milgram (1970) reports an unpublished study by Altman and others which is revealing with regard to the access allowed to strangers. Individual male or female stooges requested access to small-town or city homes, supposedly to make necessary (but not essentially urgent) telephone calls. Overall, about half the owners allowed access to these polite but unknown individuals. A major variable was the sex of the stooge, with twice as many males as females being refused (similar, but for partially different reasons, to the typical sex difference in responses to intruders among animal territory holders). The town-versus-city variable was even more dramatic in its effects. In cities only 14 percent of householders allowed males to enter, whereas 50 percent let in females. Overall, three-quarters of the city dwellers did not even open their doors, whereas in the town this applied in only a quarter of the cases. In the town almost all householders allowed females to enter. These latter differences are presumably due to reduced trustingness in city dwellers, probably associated with anticipation that strange intruders may violate the resident's rights.

The final aspect of fixed-feature territoriality to be discussed concerns behavior within homes, workplaces, or public buildings. Again, cultural and subcultural differences may be critical, but directly pertinent data are somewhat lacking (Hall 1966; Watson 1971). Several studies are available, however, for Anglo-American cultures. Goffman (1959) emphasized the clear division between "out-front" and "backstage" regions in many indoor locations, particularly in service settings like restaurants, where the servers may be distinctly deferential to customers out front but are likely to offer strong resistance if they attempt to go backstage, and in any case will there take on a dominant role. Most research has been conducted in the out-front regions of places, such as cafés, waiting rooms, and libraries, which can be classified as service or public settings. Experiments concerned more with the avoidance of interaction than with interaction itself have investigated whether seat choices in such locations are governed by attempts to claim temporary, bounded territories or simply to maintain personal space (Becker and Mayo 1971; Eastman and Harper 1971; Leibman 1970). In general, it appears that the latter consideration predominates. Other studies on the significance of fixed and semifixed spatial features on interaction and its avoidance in public settings, but mostly not concerned directly with territoriality, are discussed by Cook (1970), Sommer (1969), and others.

Few studies of work locations have provided information on territoriality, but a number of general observations are relevant. Joiner (1971) considers that in built environments in general, territorial divisions are marked in three ways: position, distance, and symbolic decoration. (Thus, in a church the area used for the priest's rituals is usually raised above the level of the pews provided for the congregation, is separated from the pews by an empty space, and may be conspicuously ornamented.) These principles are often applied in working locations too, for example, in delineating the foreman's office from the shop floor in a factory. Joiner's discussion and research have concentrated mainly on one-man offices, and he shows how furniture arrangements can often divide the office into a private (or backstage) region and a public (or out-front) region for visitors. Partly by the arrangement of semifixed features, a boundary may be defined; the occupant may resist any attempt by visitors to stray over this. Joiner shows that furniture is positioned to form a clear barrier more frequently in offices occupied by those whose social status or occupation is such that they may expect to be motivated to maintain a high degree of dominance when interacting with typical visitors. It is also interesting that "Come into MY office" usually precedes a serious reprimand, so the issue is not just one of privacy.

It must be mentioned here, however, that the relationship between dominance assertion and fixed-feature or semifixed-feature space need not be directly concerned with territories at all. Studies of seating position in relation to participation or leadership in discussion groups (e.g. DeLong 1970; Sommer 1969) have shown that intending leaders may choose particular seats, and particular seats may facilitate leadership, but the effects are explicable in terms of good visual access to the group members being a requirement for effective participation. A final example which does show the link between dominance and territory in work environments may be cited from the study by Roos (1968) on territoriality on warships. He found that, despite their obvious status superiority, officers would not normally invade the private backstage areas of other ranks. Furthermore, when a crew member was working in a space under his temporary jurisdiction, such as cleaning an allotted part of the deck, officers would typically apologize for any intrusions they made.

Research on spatial aspects of interaction in the private home remains sadly lacking, although the data obtained from questionnaires by Altman, Nelson, and Lett (1972) suggest that family norms do typically give some measure of control over one's own room. In many families the seats to be occupied during communal meals were also precisely specified. However, families did differ in the degree to which their head member had relatively absolute control throughout all home regions, and cultural variability may also be considerable. There is a clear need for direct observational data within the home; the study initiated by Scheflen (1970) using video cameras left *in situ* should eventually provide valuable normative data.[1] Another approach (Desor 1972) involved asking subjects to place toy figures in model rooms "without overcrowding them." Desor found that separations between figures depended on the room size, the imagined situation, and similar factors. Because results agreed well with those obtained in other, real-life studies, the technique might also be used to investigate variables linked to territoriality.

Studies by Altman and his co-workers on pairs of subjects confined in small rooms for up to ten days (e.g. Altman and Haythorn 1967; Altman, Taylor, Wheeler 1971) showed that a very strict division of areas and objects often developed rapidly between pair members. Interpretation of this finding is complicated by the number of variables involved, but the associated lack of privacy was not the only factor, for territorial divisions still developed, although more slowly, when subjects could retreat into separate rooms. Stress levels were high in these studies, but because isolation of single individuals for much longer periods need not be stressful (e.g. Aschoff 1965), some aspect of social interaction was probably responsible for the high percentage of subjects who refused to continue in Altman's studies.[2] In more normal home conditions, however, lack of privacy may play a more significant role in the causation of crowding stresses.[3] It appears that in Altman's research strict territoriality may have reduced stress, as the "aborters" showed less subdivision of areas and objects in the early days. Some evidence that individuals are more relaxed and secure when interacting on familiar ground is available for private homes (e.g. Coleman 1968), although quantitative data is apparently only available for infants (Castell 1970).

The final group of studies to be discussed concern behavior in communal residential environments, of which old people's homes, delinquency residences, college residence halls, and mental hospital

---

[1] Scheflen (1971) reports early findings from this study revealing that "territorial" divisions of the home do appear in black and Puerto Rican families living in the Bronx ghetto area. Individual family members may thus be partially restricted to certain rooms of the home. Similar effects probably exist to a degree among middle-class whites living in more spacious accommodation (Smith et al. 1969).

[2] Smith and Haythorn (1972), in a study of groups subjected to twenty-one day confinement and isolation, found that stress and hostility increased if space was limited severely, especially for three-person groups as compared with pairs. This result is clearly consistent with the interaction hypothesis.

[3] These possible mediating factors are considered further in Vine (i.p.) in accounting for the association between various types of stress index and both short-term and long-term crowding.

wards have been studied (e.g. Esser et al. 1965; Lipman 1968, 1970; Sommer 1969; Sundstrom and Altman 1972). In general these have indicated that at least some individuals restrict their ranges substantially and may show evidence of territorial attachments, sometimes with strongly aggressive defense (particularly in Lipman's studies of defense of seats in old people's homes). On the other hand, high status individuals tend to have free access to all areas, by virtue of their abilities to intimidate others; thus, range restriction need not give complete territorial advantage. Whether or not such individuals do use particular areas to an appreciable degree seems, on Sundstrom and Altman's evidence gathered in a residence for delinquents, to depend not only on status or ability to dominate but also on the desirability of such areas in relation to other areas and on the overall amount of conflict within a group. Unfortunately, the degree to which the behavior in this study or that of Esser et al. was actually territorial is in doubt, as control of access to areas was not one of their criteria for territoriality.

CONCLUSIONS REGARDING HUMAN TERRITORIALITY

Although the quantity, variety, and often quality of data on how interactions between individuals are affected by territorial factors leave much to be desired, it is possible to draw a number of tentative conclusions from the existing evidence. Although we often show strong attachments to areas that we use frequently, and although these core parts of our ranges may sometimes be monopolized to a moderate degree (at least at any given point in time: in urban life we in fact time-share locations to a considerable degree), we do not necessarily treat them as true territories. Familiarity with an area through frequent use can apparently be one factor enhancing our dominance if others enter it, although additional factors like owning a region or being responsible for it almost certainly operate independently to produce the same territorial effect. Although familiarity alone may be a strong influence, and can sometimes lead to overtly aggressive behaviors and attempts to claim an area as a true territory and to completely exclude others, its effects can often be weak. Thus, territoriality in the form that seems most similar to that of other species is presumably subject to considerable variability in man because of factors that are as yet very imperfectly understood. This may constitute a *prima facie* case for the importance of learning in determining its human forms and intensities.

Developmental evidence is sparse, but Castell (1970) failed to find any advantage for the child in its own home rather than a strange one when fifteen- to thirty-six-month-old infants engaged in dominance conflicts over toys. Although such an effect might have been offset by the presence of both mothers, it suggests that general territoriality may be slow in developing. On the other hand, adults may require relatively little experience of a location, in some contexts, before there are territorial effects on their interactions with intruders. Edney (1972) found that even the EXPECTATION of subsequently using a room affected the amount of space they moved around in and how close they came to a stooge (posing as a workman) who entered while they were performing a task that involved moving about. Edney interpreted his data as showing that experience or expectation of use led to a reduced tendency to avoid the intruder, as compared with that of control subjects, through an increased tendency to regard it as a territory. (One could alternatively say that subjects attempted to intimidate the workman by invading his personal space.)

Perhaps the most significant conclusion is that territoriality in man, even when reinforced by culturally legitimated ownership of space or motivation to maintain privacy, does not itself appear to depend appreciably on strongly aggressive behavior in most contexts. Not only are many classes of other individuals often allowed to cross boundaries, but any assertion of dominance is typically highly ritualized and frequently amicable, unless the intruder poses any genuine threat to the owner. This corresponds well with the behavior of most other species and has fewer aggressive aspects than in many (particularly other carnivores). For the most part we learn to avoid attempting to enter true territories, which are conveniently marked and in fact defended by physical rather than human barriers in most cases. We thus normally avoid the occasions where aggressive interactions are most likely to arise. By making use of our extensive tool-using ability, we can reinforce the powerful effect of cultural norms themselves and avoid the necessity to defend valuable resources by direct interpersonal threat. In this way we of course reduce the need for "appeasement" mechanisms which can prevent territorial conflicts from becoming too intense.

We are left now with the question of how territoriality and mobile spacing are related. There is evidence from young children that dominant individuals can command larger personal spaces (King 1966) and larger equilibrium distances from others (Hudson, McGrew, McGrew 1971). In adults the latter are greater if interactors are of unequal status (Lott and Sommer 1967). Evidence for personal space being larger on familiar ground is as yet indirect or casual, but Felipe and Sommer (1966) report much greater resistance (as opposed to avoiding or fleeing) to invasion of personal space in strongly territorial mental hospital patients. A complication arises in considering distance alone in relation to personal space and dominance because close proximity between noninteractors can either mean that their space boundaries are small or that they show high dominance by refusing to retreat. But where the intruder was clearly dominant, Felipe and Sommer found that invasion led to flight.[4]

With regard to group space, relatively little research has yet been carried out (Goffman 1963, 1971; Kendon 1973; Scheflen 1972). But unlike personal space, group space can often be maintained by concerted adjustment of the bodies involved; for example, by standing in a circle facing inward, a group can effectively exclude intruders. Where groups are oriented outward or are more separated, other persons may detour behind them or apologize if forced to pass in front or through them in constricted regions. This can again be interpreted as a submissive behavior and is not infrequently shown when an individual rather than a group is present and a close approach is unavoidable. Alternatively, "civil inattention," involving deliberate gaze-avoidance, may be accorded to such an individual or group.[5] In all these cases involving mobile space, individuals typically make the same apparent attempts to avoid offering any threat or seeming to invade others' privacy that have been suggested as typical where fixed-feature and semifixed-feature spaces are involved. The universal use of distance greeting rituals as a prelude to actually interacting, even where close friends are involved, can be seen in part as a reassurance that an approach does not involve any such threat (Eibl-Eibesfeldt 1970; Kendon and Ferber i.p.).

[4] Barasch (1973) has subsequently confirmed this effect of status difference on response to invasion in a comparison of the response of student library-users to student and faculty member intruders.

[5] Field experiments by Cheyne and Efran (1972) and by Efran and Cheyne (i.p. a) show that individuals typically avoid passing through the space commanded by a stationary pair, especially if they are clearly interacting, provided that the space between them is not greater than about four feet (the limit of the "personal distance" zone suggested by Hall 1966). This applies even if making a detour is physically difficult. Efran and Cheyne (i.p. b) found evidence that subjective discomfort is experienced if such detours are impossible and the group space has to be crossed. Film analysis revealed that visual "cut-off" (Chance 1962) and other avoidance behaviors are then shown. In addition, Knowles (1972) found that walking pairs tended to make combined detours rather than allowing another (deliberately "negligent") pedestrian to pass between them. Not infrequently they also remarked on the carelessness or impoliteness of the intruder.

It is clear that although very close approaches entailing invasion of the personal space area which one defines for a given situation and relationship with the other person involve stress and discomfort (Evans and Howard 1972; Felipe and Sommer 1966; Garfinkel 1964; McBride, King, James 1965), there are a variety of rituals and behavioral forms of avoidance that ensure that aggression is typically avoided, as also applies to territory. Even when the invasion involves a direct stare, which is a threatening signal, especially among strangers, overtly aggressive responses are unusual, although probably among strangers a stare is more likely to elicit aggression from an individual on his home ground. In general it would appear that far from being the MOST aggressive species, man is one of the LEAST physically aggressive over space, and particularly where strangers invade personal space. Even when crowded into close physical contact with others, we can tolerate such invasions for short periods, as in elevators or subway trains.

Can we then conclude that space itself has no direct relation to human aggression? The answer here must be negative, for we know that if the threat is sufficient, territorial aggression CAN occur, even at the level of face-to-face interactions between individuals. In most such disputes weapons are not used, exchanges often involve only an exchange of verbal or nonverbal signals, and even in fights little harm is done. These simple facts are often overlooked by those who postulate that we have strong and maladaptive aggressive tendencies.

There are, however, probably several ways by which our normal inhibitions about inflicting damage on another may be discarded. In one possible process space itself is strongly implicated. Social crowding increases both the frequency with which we encounter others and the number of close approaches to which we are exposed, particularly those by strangers in public places where neither individual is more at home (and where, therefore, neither has a strong dominance advantage which might more precisely specify the nature of the appropriate behaviors for each). When we are very closely crowded, such as in dense street crowds, normal personal space limits are continuously violated. It has been suggested (Vine i.p.) that we may adapt to this by a psychological cut-off process which "depersonalizes" others, so that we can then treat them just as physical obstacles rather than as real individuals.[6] Perhaps though, this can only be effective for short periods;

---

[6] Sommer (1969: 37) has referred to the way we treat others as "nonpersons" in very crowded locations, and the roots of this hypothesis date back at least to the writings of Simmel (Brindley, personal communication 1973).

in other species sustained face-to-face confrontation does lead to agonistic reactions, and we may be similar in this respect.

In territories such as homes, overcrowding is also likely to increase the frequency of inappropriately close encounters, as well as giving rise to other stresses through making privacy difficult to obtain. The more continuous nature of these invasions may well cancel out the advantage that closer interpersonal relationships make close proximity more tolerable in such settings.[7] In this case too, some measure of depersonalization of the other may in fact be called for, and may be partially successful. In either situation, if depersonalization is practiced too often it may become habitual and affect interaction in general. Such a process would presumably weaken normal restraints against behaving aggressively to others in general, just as it appears to lead to the loss of normal politeness and excuse rituals, even in contexts where spatial invasions are not involved.[8]

It may well be, therefore, that although territoriality and the maintenance of personal space are in general terms homologous with the same dispositions in other species, they have been developed culturally in man to the point where interaction rituals of various types almost completely replace agonistic interactions. It can therefore be said that human spacing mechanisms constitute "one subsystem of or modality of communication" (Scheflen 1970:36). The problem arises when, as a species, we cease to remain in balance with our environment, and there is real competition for basic resources or there are other sources of social stress. In these contexts cultural interactive rituals can break down, and nonviolent means of social adaptation and adjustment may fail, even at the level of face-to-face interaction.

REFERENCES

ALEXANDER, B. K., E. M. ROTH
    1971   The effects of acute crowding on aggressive behaviour of Japanese monkeys. *Behaviour* 39:73–90.

---

[7] Scheflen (1971) observed that overcrowded ghetto dwellers make complex behavioral adjustments to reduce the difficulties of having less than their preferred personal space during encounters within the home.

[8] Nevertheless, the ability of some cultures to tolerate extremely crowded living conditions without showing increased aggressiveness or other stress indices, as in Hong Kong (Mitchell 1971; Schmitt 1963), suggests that sufficiently strong cultural norms of "togetherness" can in some contexts inhibit this development.

ALTMAN, I.
1970 "Territorial behavior in humans: an analysis of the concept," in *Spatial behavior of older people*. Edited by L. A. Pastalan and D. H. Carson, 1–24. Ann Arbor: University of Michigan and Wayne State University Press.

ALTMAN, I., W. W. HAYTHORN
1967 The ecology of isolated groups. *Behavioral Science* 12:169–182.

ALTMAN, I., PATRICIA A. NELSON, EVELYN E. LETT
1972 The ecology of home environments. *Man-Environment Systems* 2:189–191.

ALTMAN, I., D. A. TAYLOR, L. WHEELER
1971 Ecological aspects of group behavior in social isolation. *Journal of Applied Social Psychology* 1:76-100.

ARDREY, R.
1967 *The territorial imperative: a personal enquiry into the animal origins of property and nations*. London: Collins.

ARGYLE, M.
1969 *Social interaction*. London: Methuen

ASCHOFF, J.
1965 Circadian rhythms in man. *Science* 148:1427–1432.

BARASCH, D. P.
1973 Human ethology: personal space revisited. *Environment and Behavior* 5:67–72.

BECKER, F. D., CLARA MAYO
1971 Delineating personal distance and territoriality. *Environment and Behavior* 3:375–381.

BIRDWHISTELL, R. L.
1952 *Introduction to kinesics: an annotation system for analysis of body motion and gesture*. Louisville: University of Louisville Press.
1971 *Kinesics and context: essays on body-motion communication*. London: Allen Lane, Penguin.

BLURTON-JONES, N. G., editor
1971 *Ethological studies of child behaviour*. Cambridge: Cambridge University Press.

BROWN, J. L., G. H. ORIANS
1970 Spacing patterns in mobile animals. *Annual Review of Ecology and Systematics* 1:239–262.

CASTELL, R.
1970 Effects of familiar and unfamiliar environments on proximity behaviour of young children. *Journal of Experimental Child Psychology* 9:342–347.

CHANCE, M. R. A.
1962 An interpretation of some agonistic postures: the role of "cutoff" acts and postures. *Symposium of the Zoological Society of London* 8:71–89.

CHEYNE, J. A., M. G. EFRAN
1972 The effect of spatial and interpersonal variables on the invasion of group controlled territories. *Sociometry* 35:477.

CHIVERS, D. J.
1972 "The siamang and the gibbon in the Malay peninsula," in *Gibbon and siamang*. Edited by D. Rumbaugh, 103–135. Basel: Karger.
COLEMAN, A.
1968 Territoriality in man: a comparison of behavior in home and hospital. *American Journal of Orthopsychiatry* 38:464–468.
COOK, M.
1970 Experiments on orientation and proxemics. *Human Relations* 23: 61–76.
CORNING, P. A., CONSTANCE H. CORNING
1972 Toward a general theory of violent aggression. *Social Science Information* 11:7-35.
CROOK, J. H.
1968 "The nature and function of territorial aggression," in *Man and aggression*. Edited by M. F. A. Montagu, 141–178. New York: Oxford University Press.
1970 "The socio-ecology of primates," in *Social behaviour in birds and mammals*. Edited by J. H. Crook. London: Academic Press.
DE LONG, A. J.
1970 Dominance-territorial relations in a small group. *Environment and Behavior* 2:170–191.
DESOR, J. A.
1972 Towards a psychological theory of crowding. *Journal of Personality and Social Psychology* 21:79–83.
EASTMAN, C. M., J. HARPER
1971 A study of proxemic behavior: toward a predictive model. *Environment and Behavior* 3:418–438.
EDNEY, J. J.
1972 Place and space: the effects of experience with a physical locale. *Journal of Experimental Social Psychology* 8:124–135.
EFRAN, M. G., J. A. CHEYNE
i.p.a Shared space: the cooperative control of spatial areas by two interacting individuals. *Canadian Journal of Behavioral Psychology*.
i.p.b Affective concomitants of the invasion of shared space: behavioral, physiological, and verbal indicators. *Journal of Personality and Social Psychology*.
EIBL-EIBESFELDT, I.
1970 *Ethology, the biology of behavior*. New York: Holt, Rinehart and Winston.
EISENBERG, J. F., N. A. MUCKENHIRN, R. RUDRAN
1972 The relation between ecology and social structure in primates. *Science* 176:863–874.
EKMAN, P., W. V. FRIESEN, PHOEBE ELLSWORTH
1972 *The face and emotion: guidelines for research and an integration of findings*. New York: Pergamon Press.
ELLEFSON, J. O.
1968 "Territorial behavior in the common white-handed gibbon, *Hylobates lar* Linn," in *Primates: studies in adaptation and variability*. Edited by Phyllis C. Jay, 180–199. New York: Holt, Rinehart, Winston.

ESSER, A. H., A. S. CHAMBERLAIN, E. D. CHAPPLE, N. S. KLINE
 1965 "Territoriality of patients on a research ward," in *Recent advances in biological psychiatry*, volume seven. Edited by J. Wortis, 36–44. New York: Plenum Press.

EVANS, G W., R. B. HOWARD
 1972 "A methodological investigation of personal space," in *Environmental design: research and practice*, volume one. Edited by W. J. Mitchell, 2-2-1 to 2-2-8. Los Angeles: University of California Press.

FELIPE, NANCY J., R. SOMMER
 1966 Invasions of personal space. *Social Problems* 14:206–214.

FRIED, M., PEGGY GLEICHER
 1961 Some sources of residential satisfaction in an urban slum. *Journal of the American Institute of Planners* 27:305–315.

GARTLAN, J. S., C. K. BRAIN
 1968 "Ecology and social variability in *Cercopithecus aethiops* and *C. mitis*," in *Primates: studies in adaptation and variability*. Edited by Phyllis Jay, 253–292. New York: Holt, Rinehart and Winston.

GARFINKEL, H.
 1964 Studies of the routine grounds of everyday activities. *Social Problems* 11:225–250.

GOFFMAN, E.
 1956 The nature of deference and demeanor. *American Anthropologist* 58:473–502.
 1959 *The presentation of self in everyday life*. Garden City, New York: Doubleday Anchor.
 1963 *Behavior in public places: notes on the social organization of gatherings*. New York: Free Press.
 1971 *Relations in public: microstudies of the public order*. London: Allen Lane, Penguin.

HALL, E. T.
 1963 A system for the notation of proxemic behavior. *American Anthropologist* 65:1003–1026.
 1966 *The hidden dimension*. Garden City, New York: Doubleday Anchor.
 1971 "Environmental communication," in *Behavior and environment: the use of space by animals and men*. Edited by A. H. Esser, 247–256. New York: Plenum Press.

HAMILTON, W. D.
 1964 The genetical evolution of social behavior. *Journal of Theoretical Biology* 7:1–52.

HEDIGER, H.
 1950 *Wild animals in captivity: an outline of the biology of zoological gardens*. London: Butterworths.

HINDE, R. A., editor
 1972a *Nonverbal communication*. Cambridge: Cambridge University Press.
 1972b "Aggression," in *Biology and the human sciences*. Edited by J. W. S. Pringle, 1–24. Oxford: Clarendon Press.

HOWARD, E.
1920 Territory in bird life. London: Murray.

HUDSON, P. T. W., W. C. MC GREW, PENNY L. MC GREW
1971 "Attention structures in a group of preschool infants," in *Architectural psychology 1970*. Edited by B. Honikman. London: Royal Institute of British Architects Publications and Kingston Polytechnic.

JOHNSON, R. N.
1972 *Aggression in man and animals*. Philadelphia: Saunders.

JOINER, D.
1971 Social ritual and architectural space. *Journal of Architectural Research and Teaching* 1:11–22.

JOLLY, ALISON
1972 *The evolution of primate behavior*. New York: Macmillan.

KENDON, A.
1973 "The role of visible behaviour in the organization of social interaction," in *Social communication and movement: studies of interaction and expression in man and chimpanzee*. Edited by M. von Cranach and I. Vine, 29–74. London and New York: Academic Press.

KENDON, A., A. FERBER
i.p. "A description of some human greetings," in *Comparative ethology and behaviour of primates*. Edited by R. P. Michael and J. H. Crook. London: Academic Press.

KING, M. G.
1966 Interpersonal relations in preschool children and average approach distance. *Journal of Genetic Psychology* 109:109–116.

KLOPFER, P. H.
1969 *Habitats and territories: a study of the use of space by animals*. New York: Basic Books.

KNOWLES, E. S.
1972 Boundaries around social space: dyadic responses to an invader. *Environment and Behavior* 4:437–445.

KUMMER, H.
1971 "Spacing mechanisms in social behavior," in *Man and beast: comparative social behavior*. Edited by J. F. Eisenberg and W. S. Dillon, 220–234. Washington, D.C.: Smithsonian Institution.

LEE, R. B., I. DE VORE, editors
1969 *Man the hunter*. Chicago: Aldine.

LEIBMAN, MIRIAM
1970 The effects of sex and race norms on personal space. *Environment and Behavior* 2:208–246.

LEYHAUSEN, P.
1965 The communal organization of solitary mammals. *Symposium of the Zoological Society of London* 14:249–263.

LIPMAN, A.
1968 Building design and social interaction. *Architects Journal* 147:23–30.

1970 Territoriality: a useful concept? *Royal Institute of British Architects Journal* 77:68–70.

LORENZ, K. Z.
1966 *On aggression.* London: Methuen.

LOTT, D. F., R. SOMMER
1967 Seating arrangements and status. *Journal of Personality and Social Psychology* 7:90–95.

LYMAN, S. M., M. B. SCOTT
1967 Territoriality: a neglected sociological dimension. *Social Problems* 15:236–249.

MASON, W. A.
1968 "The use of space by *Callicebus* groups," in *Primates: studies in adaptation and variability.* Edited by Phyllis C. Jay, 200–216. New York: Holt, Rinehart, Winston.

MC BRIDE, G., M. G. KING, J. W. JAMES
1965 Social proximity effects on galvanic skin responsiveness in adult humans. *Journal of Psychology* 61:153–157.

MC BRIDE, G., I. P. PARER, F. FOENLANDER
1969 The social organization and behavior of the feral domestic fowl. *Animal Behavior Monograph* 2:127–181.

MC QUOWN, N., editor
1971 *The natural history of an interview.* New York: Grune and Stratton.

MILGRAM, S.
1970 The experience of living in cities. *Science* 167:1461–1468.

MITCHELL, R.
1971 Some social implications of high density housing. *American Sociological Review* 36:18–29.

MONTAGU, M. F. A.
1968 "The new litany of 'innate depravity,' or original sin revisited," in *Man and aggression.* Edited by M. F. A. Montagu, 3–17. New York: Oxford University Press.

MUMFORD, L.
1961 *The city in history: its origins, its transformations, and its prospects.* London: Secker and Warburg.

PASTALAN, L. A.
1970 "Privacy as an expression of human territoriality," in *Spatial behavior of older people.* Edited by L. A. Pastalan and D. H. Carson, 88–101. Ann Arbor: University of Michigan and Wayne State University Press.

RAPOPORT, A.
1968 The personal element in housing: an argument for open-ended design. *Royal Institute of British Architects Journal* 75:300–305.
1972 "Australian aborigines and the definition of place," in *Environmental design: research and practice,* volume one. Edited by W. J. Mitchell, 3-3-1 to 3-3-14. Los Angeles: University of California Press.

REYNOLDS, V.
1966 Open groups in hominid evolution. *Man* 1:441–452.

ROOS, P. D.
1968   Jurisdiction: an ecological concept. *Human Relations* 21:75–84.
ROSENBLUM, L. A., I. C. KAUFMANN, A. J. STYNES
1964   Individual distance in two species of macaque. *Animal Behavior* 12:338–342.
ROWELL, THELMA E.
1967   A quantitative comparison of the behaviour of a wild and a caged baboon group. *Animal Behavior* 15:499–509.
RUSSELL, CLAIRE, W. M. S. RUSSELL
1968   *Violence, monkeys, and men.* London: Macmillan.
SCHEFLEN, A. E.
1970   Territoriality and communication. Final Report NATO Symposium on Non-Verbal Communication, 35–38.
1971   Living space in an urban ghetto. *Family Process* 10:429–450.
1972   *Body language and the social order.* Englewood Cliffs, New Jersey: Prentice-Hall.
SCHMITT, R. C.
1963   Implications of density in Hong Kong. *Journal of the American Institute of Planners* 29:210–217.
SCRUTON, DIANE M., J. HERBERT
1972   The reactions of groups of captive talapoin monkeys to the introduction of male and female strangers of the same species. *Animal Behavior* 20:463–473.
SEBEOK, T. A., *editor*
1968   *Animal communication: techniques of study and results of research.* Bloomington: Indiana University Press.
SERVICE, E. R.
1966   *The hunters.* Englewood Cliffs, New Jersey: Prentice-Hall.
SIEGMAN, A. W., B. POPE, *editors*
1972   *Studies in dyadic communication.* New York: Pergamon Press.
SMITH, RUTH H., DONNA B. DENNER, MILDRED T. LYNCH, MARY WINTER
1969   Privacy and interaction within the family as related to dwelling space. *Journal of Marriage and Family,* 559–566.
SMITH, S., W. W. HAYTHORN
1972   Effects of compatibility, crowding, group size and leadership seniority on stress, anxiety, hostility and annoyance. *Journal of Personality and Social Psychology* 22:67–79.
SOMMER, R.
1959   Studies in personal space. *Sociometry* 22:247–260.
1969   *Personal space: the behavioral basis of design.* Englewood Cliffs, New Jersey: Prentice-Hall.
SOMMER, R., F. D. BECKER
1969   Territorial defense and the good neighbour. *Journal of Personality and Social Psychology* 11:85–92.
SOUTHWICK, C. H.
1969   "Aggressive behavior of rhesus monkeys in natural and captive groups," in *Aggressive behavior.* Edited by S. Garattini and E. B. Sigg, 32–43. Amsterdam: Excerpta Medica Foundation.

STEA, D.
1970 "Home range and the use of space," in *Spatial behavior of older people*. Edited by L. A. Pastalan and D. H. Carson, 138–147. Ann Arbor: University of Michigan and Wayne State University Press.

SUNDSTROM, E., I. ALTMAN
1972 "Relationships between dominance and territorial behavior: a field study in a youth rehabilitation center." Unpublished technical report, Department of Psychology, University of Utah.

TIGER, L., R. FOX
1971 *The imperial animal*. London: Secker and Warburg.

TINBERGEN, N.
1968 On war and peace in animals and man: an ethologist's approach to the biology of aggression. *Science* 160:1411–1418.

VINE, I.
1973 "The role of facial-visual signalling in early social development," in *Social communication and movement: studies of interaction and expression in man and chimpanzee*. Edited by M. von Cranach and I. Vine, 195–298. London and New York: Academic Press.

i.p. Social spacing in animals and man. *Social Science Information*.

VON CRANACH, M., I. VINE, editors
1973 *Social communication and movement: studies of interaction and expression in man and chimpanzee*. London and New York: Academic Press.

WATSON, O. M.
1971 *Proxemic behavior: a cross-cultural study*. The Hague: Mouton.

Expressive Interaction and Social Structure: Play and an Emergent Game Form in an Israeli Social Setting

DON HANDELMAN

> What I saw at first ... was occasional flurries of horseplay so simple and unvarying in pattern and so childish in quality that they made no strong bid for attention .... But as I began to pay closer attention, as I began to develop familiarity with the communication system, the disconnected became connected, the nonsense made sense, the obscure became clear, and the silly actually funny. And ... the interaction began to reveal structure.
> DONALD ROY[1]

In an insightful study entitled "Banana time," Roy (1959–1960) described the daily antics of three middle-aged naturalized American men who were engaged in tedious, monotonous jobs through a long workday, physically isolated from the rest of the factory which employed them. These men had divided their working day into a series of "times" during which activities not specified by the official reality of the setting were engaged in. During and in between these "times" the workers engaged in a series of mock disputes, attacks, pranks, and jokes.

Two points, unspecified as such by him, emerge from Roy's account. These men were engaged in extended play throughout the working

---
Fieldwork and analysis of data were supported by the Bernstein Trust for Anthropological Research in Israel, directed by Max Gluckman. Additional support was later provided by the Canada Council. Emanuel Marx of Tel-Aviv University made valuable comments on an earlier version of this paper, while discussions about play with Wesley Sharrock and Bruce Kapferer of the University of Manchester were of great benefit. All personal and institutional names in this paper are pseudonyms.
[1] In: "Banana time," page 161.

day, and their play activities were predicated upon an overall daily balance of mutuality and reciprocity.[2] Each working day began and ended with "times" of sharing through which these men reaffirmed and cemented their bonds with one another. Therefore, each day took the form of a frame of integrative occasions within which other occasions of play (representing outcries, aggressions, self-mockery, and the absurdity of the employment situation) were permitted extensive expression and enjoyment.

The organization of the working day in this setting made as much sense as "play" as it did as work activity; and the integration of play in the local social order was integral to any understanding of how the setting functioned (see Huizinga 1970:27).

The purpose of this article is to detail the background and operation of a mode of uninstitutionalized play I term the "donkey game" (briefly described in Handelman and Kapferer 1972: 507–512) in a sheltered workshop in Jerusalem.

Factors which contribute to an understanding of the game are: aspects of the personal histories of workers, the orientation of the institution's administration, the social organization of the workshop, and other modes of play in this setting. I will argue that while modes of play were integral components of the local social order, the "donkey game" represented a more pointed distillation of commentaries upon that social order which were communicated more intermittently and haphazardly through other modes of play.

In the work setting described by Roy, play was significant not only because it contrasted with the spirit and content of expected work activity (and so permitted the release of structurally derived tensions) but also because the organization of play constituted, in Bateson's terms, a "metalanguage" through which these men could communicate their comments and criticisms of aspects of the local social order and their positions within it.

In doing so they could retain work activity within the local order (as management required, and upon which their livelihoods depended) while stressing the arbitrariness of this order, and how it might be conceived if men were not so held in check by personal, situational and cultural restraints. Douglas (1968:365) has noted that:

---

[2] The rubric "play" is here considered as the most general category of "unserious" activity, subsuming jokes, joking activity, discrepant role play, horseplay, pranks and games. Redl (in Bateson 1956: 213) notes that: "... practically any activity can be on the playfulness level, whether it is taunting or chasing, outrunning somebody, hiding or seeking, looking, trying to avoid being caught, or lying."

The joke merely affords opportunity for realizing that an accepted pattern has no necessity. Its excitement lies in the suggestion that any particular ordering of experience may be arbitrary and subjective. It is frivolous in that it produces no real alternative, only an exhilarating sense of freedom from form in general (see also Sutton-Smith 1971:300).

Here Douglas touches upon the paradox of play, but does not go far enough. Bateson (1972: 183) has pointed out: "... (a) that the messages or signals exchanged in play are in a certain sense untrue or not meant; and (b) that that which is denoted by these signals is nonexistent." The content of play exists within an "as if" framework and is not meant to be taken seriously. Therefore, in Douglas' terms, it cannot offer a "real" alternative.

Yet, by adapting forms of play to a social setting, participants are playing and experiencing alternatives which, for their duration, are integral to that social order, and in a way constitute it. It is because play does not have to be reacted to seriously that it permits messages about alternatives to be exercised and stored, to become part of the knowledge of the group. Here — in enabling cohesiveness and criticism to exist through multiple levels of communication (see Bateson 1956:197) — would appear to be a vital function of play.[3]

Understanding the messages of play forms and content (as distinct from the message: "this is play") contained within the special framework of play (see Huizinga 1970:25-32; Bateson 1956, 1972: 189; Emerson 1969; Coser 1959) in interaction which does not form part of an institutionalized pattern or subcultural tradition requires that particular attention be paid to the social settings of such activities.[4]

In such instances conceptions of social activity associated with types of settings strongly channel and control social interaction. In

[3] Cavan (1966:9) writes: "... whether defined as play or defined as ordinary life, activity becomes serious once the ensuing events are no longer inconsequential, are no longer matters about which one is or can be indifferent."

[4] For whatever reasons, social scientists have been preoccupied with unserious activity among animals and children, thereby relegating uninstitutionalized unserious activities among adults to a marginal category of interest (see Berlyne 1969: 827–828). Anthropologists, in their own right, have sought to comprehend, for example, game forms which relate directly to cultural or subcultural traditions (cf. Labov 1972; Dundes et al. 1972), or social relationships which are displayed in part through institutionalized joking (cf. Radcliffe-Brown 1961; Hammond 1964; Sharman 1969). Even where uninstitutionalized play forms have been investigated in Western social settings, the tendency has been to analyze these activities along the lines suggested by Radcliffe-Brown (cf. Bradney 1957; Sykes 1966; Lundberg 1969).

Lofland's (1971:16) terms, a social setting provides its members with "a similarity of circumstances of action" (see also Gump et al. 1963:173). Associated with types of settings are "standard patterns of performance" (Gump and Sutton-Smith 1971:97) which are "routinely expected within the setting, treated as fitting and proper for the time and place, and persistently independent of the changing populace" (Cavan 1966:3).

Yet, in the setting described by Roy, and in the one to be described here, play was not part of the "official" reality of the setting as conceived by those superordinates whose expectations set standard patterns of performance. Play was an emergent property of the adaptations of members to the social setting. Therefore the content and logic of play had to be understood in terms of the local social order from which they derived, and into which their messages fed back.[5]

Play is conspicuous by its absence from or its marginality in descriptions of work settings. Nevertheless, there are hints that play may well be integral to a wide representation of such settings. For example, Homans, in his reanalysis of the bank wiring room, writes:

A game called "binging" was played.... If, according to the rules of this game, a man walked up to another man and hit him as hard as he could on the upper arm — "binged" him — the other had the right to retaliate with another such blow, the object being to see who could hit the harder (1950:60–61).

Lupton, in his study of a garment workshop, notes almost in passing:

The tedium was broken by the usual joking and leg-pulling and the workers appreciated the wireless programmes, and sometimes joined in singing....

---

[5] The structures of organizations have been traditionally treated as programmatic constructions which define "formal" organization as distinct from "informal" organization, the assumption being that the former is the more legitimate core of social structure, while the latter exists because it solves functional problems which the program cannot meet. Bittner (1965) has explicated this false dichotomy. "Organization" or "social structure" exist only in the ways in which competent users understand them to operate and use them in different meaning contexts. As considered here, the organization of a local social setting consists of the different usages that categories of users apply to that place and time in their regular activities there. Whether a play definition or a work definition is in effect during any given time will depend upon the interpersonal resources which persons can realize in their interactions. The structure of the setting will comprise all interaction programs expressed in that location in the past, of which users are aware; and the expression of any given program, and alterations in it, will feed back to support or alter the structure of the setting. Dimensions of organization which provide interpersonal resources to express aspects of social structure will be outlined later on.

On warm summer days workers would create, in animated conversation, a fantasy world in which everyone was bound for Blackpool on pleasure bent instead of being tied to the work bench (1963:36; see also Kapferer 1972: 229; Bradney 1957; Sykes 1966; Cunnison 1966:213–215).

BACKGROUNDS OF WORKSHOP MEMBERS

All sixteen workers employed in the sheltered workshop had emigrated to Israel from other countries in the Middle East and Mediterranean area (e.g. Serbia, Turkey, Syria, Iraqi Kurdistan, Georgia, Persia, Yemen, Tunisia, and Morocco). Six had arrived prior to 1948, and the remainder after the founding of the state. The ages of the seven women ranged from sixty-six to eighty-four, while those of the nine men ranged from sixty-one to over ninety. One woman was married, while six were widowed. While two men were widowers and another a bachelor, the other six were still married, and four of them were the breadwinners of households which contained children of school age.

Prior to their employment in the workshop the men were employed in unskilled or semiskilled occupations. At various points in their occupational careers the men were unable to continue to work to support their households, and were forced to rely upon welfare aid for subsistence. The welfare department attempted to terminate such affiliations speedily, while these welfare clients were prepared to accept termination of affiliation in exchange for employment which would enable them to continue to support their families properly.

Because of their lack of skills, advancing age, and various bureaucratic factors, such employment opportunities were rarely available. While the welfare department and clients searched for ways of terminating their affiliations on terms suitable to both, welfare aid continued to be allocated to the client households. In the course of receiving increasing benefits, clients became more committed to the welfare career-line than they were to terminating their welfare affiliations in exchange for suitable employment.

The increasing costs of affiliation made the department more determined to terminate these affiliations.[6] With time, clients were

[6] Most of the welfare caseworkers with whom these men had to treat, and who pressured and at times coerced them into terminating their welfare affiliations, were women. Instead of being able to maintain their traditional behavioral superordination toward women in general (cf. Shokeid 1971: 165–205), these men were forced to approach female officials as supplicants.

stripped of their resources to resist the attempts of the department to erase them from the welfare rolls. These clients were by then too weak and/or too old to do other than accept whatever employment was offered them.

These clients were shunted to SAGE, a non-profit institution which comprised a number of sheltered workshops for the indigent elderly, thereby terminating their welfare affiliations in the main, and relieving the welfare department of the burden of support.[7] For these men the result of the process of welfare dependency was a lessening of their capacity and freedom to govern their own fates. Entering low-wage employment in SAGE was not a choice they perceived as valuable or rewarding; yet they no longer had the personal or situational resources to resist such placement in employment.

While the women also reached SAGE through the welfare department, none had previously been employed in formal positions. Moreover, prior to the loss of their husbands, they had only limited contacts with the welfare authorities. For the women, as against many of the men, SAGE represented a solution to their problems of personal upkeep, and none actively attempted to resist their placement there. In fact, this employment provided most of the women with the first independent incomes they had enjoyed; and within the workshop they were able to work and compete on an equal basis with males, again a new experience for them.

Whereas the men reached SAGE through an extended process of increased dependency, limitations on their personal capacities, and acts of supplication toward female officials, SAGE presented the women with variant, possibly exciting, opportunities to dispose of their own limited earnings. While most of the men still had to support families, the women had only to support themselves. SAGE offered a social reality which reversed traditional sex-linked roles, with the women offered an income independent of spouse, and the opportunity to compete with men, while the men were offered a limited income, the competition of women, and an overall sense of dependency and insufficiency introduced in the process of welfare affiliation and reinforced in SAGE. These sex-linked disinctions came to be expressed in modes of play, and especially in the "donkey game."

---

[7] The development of welfare career-lines in the Israeli context is analyzed in detail in Handelman (1973).

ORIENTATIONS OF THE SAGE ADMINISTRATION

SAGE occupied an interstitial niche in the social services of Jerusalem. By employing welfare clients with no other job opportunities, SAGE offered the welfare department scarce services. SAGE received extensive private donations and did not have to rely upon government subsidies. Therefore the SAGE administration was able to exercise quite independent policies. Because most of its employees were over the official retirement age it was not bound by Israeli labor legislation.

So workers were not union members, and had no recourse to any external labor body in the event of disputes over wages or over conditions of employment. SAGE was also not subject to the minimum wage laws of Israel, nor to regulations governing job tenure which made it difficult for employers to fire employees who had been employed for over six months as fulltime workers.

The administration was composed of middle-class, middle-aged women of European extraction who were ideologically committed to orienting their aged employees toward rewarding life goals. These employees were to be "rehabilitated" through work which would restore their feelings of self-worth as self-sufficient and contributing members of society;[8] and the act of work was considered to have greater significance for "rehabilitation" than the content of such activity or wages paid for it.

This major administrative orientation was at times contradicted by two others. The administration came to value production, and workers were expected not only to provide a semblance of "make-work" (Goffman 1959:109-111), but also to concentrate more on output. Sometimes the administration considered SAGE a "club" in which the aged could interact sociably while at work. The official reality of the setting expected sociable interaction to be limited to conversation interspersed in work activity in which workers did not extensively leave their own work locations.

Workers were expected to behave toward administrators as toward "patrons" to whom they owed their good fortune of employment. As Paine (1971:19) has written: Patrons "protect" their clients ... the patron chooses for the client those values in relation to which the

---

[8] At times, in describing workers to visitors, the administration would refer to them as "the scum of the earth" who were being rehabilitated. This presumed that workers had not had occupational histories of any substance before entering SAGE. While this was correct for most of the women workers, it was incorrect for the men.

patron protects the client; moreover, the patron expects the client himself to embrace these values...." So workers were expected to display gratitude toward their benefactors and to offer unquestioning obedience to administrative directives. In the main, female workers without previous occupational histories found it easier to conform to these expectations than did male workers who had been accustomed to greater independence in previous work.[9]

The female-centered SAGE administration — emphasizing patronage, deference, and obedience — continued the themes of dependence first introduced by the welfare department. In this situation men exhibited more adjustment difficulties than did women; and again these sex-linked distinctions came to be expressed in workshop play.

DIMENSIONS OF ORGANIZATION IN THE WORKSHOP

During any duration of time, behavior in a social setting derives from the positioning of members in certain dimensions of social organization which make available resources for interaction. The appearance of a setting, its social reality, is continually subjected to minor alterations as members realize resources in their activities to replicate and innovate patterns of interaction. A description of a social setting as a local social order must recognize the relevance of at least three aspects of positioning — the hierarchical dimension of authority which structures contacts of inequality, the horizontal dimension of reciprocity which guides contacts of symmetry, and the locational dimension of territoriality which permits members to occupy, utilize, and control social space.

Utilizing their positions in dimensions of organization, setting members situationally selected their presentations to effect realities congruent with their conceptions of the setting. What might be termed "expected behavior," as perceived by a category of member, was a conception of optimum behavior which could be supported by such persons. Other patterns of behavior which found expression represented different combinations of elements of organizational dimensions

[9] In the workshop women were more successful in gaining recognition from the administration. For example, wage scales were predicated upon length of employment. All workers who had been employed for eighteen months were supposed to earn a maximum wage. While all of the women so employed did earn such a wage, a number of the men so employed did not; and it was clear that the decision to raise the wages of a worker was at least as dependent upon demeanor as it was upon length of employment.

which constituted the setting for as long as they were maintained, and which signified "deviant" expressions only insofar as those present had the resources to denigrate and suppress them (see Erikson 1962: 308). Otherwise, such patterns remained alternative expressions of the potential of the setting to develop multiple social realities during different social occasions.

Within the workshop the hierarchical dimension related to the organization of production, the reciprocal dimension related to the organization of ego-centered network links among members, and the locational dimension related to territorial rights associated with the work places of members. The internal arrangement of each dimension of organization produced separate, yet interdependent, positional distributions for all workshop members which could be expressed in various combinations in interaction.

While these dimensions were analytically distinct their elements also overlapped. So the contents of network links included contacts of work, a few of which derived directly from the organization of production, while others were related to attempts to alter the organization of production through the extension of positional influence. The organization of social space, while partially dependent upon the organization of production, exerted little effect on the latter dimension, but did have a strong effect on the development of network links among shop members. In turn, these largely symmetrical links affected the perception of territorial violations.

On some occasions, the elements of a single dimension would comprise the primary resources for activity, while on others the elements of a number of dimensions would comprise such resources. Therefore, while the shop was officially a place of work, behavior there could not be assigned solely to elements of the organization of production and its derivative activities.

Depending upon presentation and audience reception, nonwork activities were not deviant and sanctionable, but played major roles in the local social order.[10] In this setting (and presumably any other) dimensions of organization provided members with a multiplicity of resources with which to fashion their activities (cf. Strauss et al. 1964).[11]

[10] For example, while arguments might begin over issues of work and production, they also began over perceived territorial intrusions, or over issues related to ties between shop members (see Handelman 1971: 498–622).
[11] The contents of dimensions of organization were established through observation of activity in the setting over a lengthy period of time. From these data recurrent elements of organization were induced. Induced dimensions of organization

The workshop consisted of two connected rooms. Three men and seven women worked in the back room, while six men worked in the front. The workshop supervisor was a young woman who represented the administration and who directed the work activities of shop members. The workshop produced mainly necklaces and earrings of ceramic beads.

Production proceeded as follows: most workers made various kinds of beads by hand. These beads were strung on nylon thread by a necklace stringer. The length of strung beads was polished by a necklace polisher. The strung thread was then cut to correct length, and fastenings were attached to complete the necklace.[12] The supervisor prepared the clay and fired the beads in the kiln. She had appointed an unofficial charge-hand, a female worker named Zohara, to set most of the necklace patterns and to oversee the activities of the necklace stringer, also a woman.

According to the administrative perspective, the organization of production required only the following nodes of interaction: (a) the supervisor to have contacts with all workers; (b) the unofficial charge-hand to supervise the work of the necklace stringer; (c) the necklace polisher to hand waxed necklaces to the charge-hand; and (d) the ring makers (who made small metal rings which were interspersed among beads in necklaces) to hand their products to the charge-hand.

All other interpersonal contacts in the setting could be regarded as emergent properties (see Blau 1964:3–4) of interpersonal arrangements among workers. Such properties constituted the dimension of ego-centered network links in the workshop.[13] The following were found to be significant repetitive contents of these links: (a) contacts of conversation between workers, (b) contacts of work (largely unrequired by the administrative perspective of production), (c)

---

then became the guidelines for analyzing particular encounters. Encounters, not discussed here, were sequences of focused interaction during short time durations, the elements of which derived from dimensions of organization but whose form and resolution were dependent upon the particular selection, allocation, and realization of organizational elements by encounter participants (see Handelman i.p.). In turn, the effects of encounters were fed back into dimensions of organization, with the potential to modify the latter.

[12] While beyond the scope of this article, the nuances of the process of production were much more subtle and complex than represented here (see Handelman 1971).

[13] The method used to describe attributes (span, density, star multiplexity) of such networks is found in Kapferer (1972: 169–173).

acts of aid and personal assistance proffered by a worker to another, and (d) joking activity among workers.[14]

All of the female workers embraced the official reality of the setting as propounded by supervisor and administrators. The women were generally linked to one another rather than to the men; and these linkages contained contents of conversation, contacts of work, and personal assistance. One exception to this pattern was the unofficial charge-hand whose network was of wide span, although of low star multiplexity.[15] While her authority was very limited, she continually attempted to extend her influence over the activities of the other workers, both men and women; and her presence was strongly felt in the setting. Of the men, three overtly embraced administrative emphasis on work, obedience and deference. One was David, an "innovator," a designer of new bead forms, who received much praise and support for his efforts from the supervisor. Another, Ezra, was a specialist, a designer and painter of ceramic tiles whose work was highly esteemed. The third was over ninety and had virtually no systematic contacts with other workers. All of these men had networks of narrow span and low star multiplexity.[16] Five of the remaining six men — Shlomo, Yihye, Mashiah, Eliahu, and Zackaria — interacted intensively with one another. Their network spans were narrow, but highly multiplex (i.e. a high proportion of their links were with one another, and most or all of these links were multiplex in content). The sixth, Shalom, was the only man to maintain extensive links with both male and female workers, and his network was of wide span and fairly high star multiplexity (the measurements of each worker's network span and multiplexity are found in Handelman 1971:258).

[14] I worked on the assumption that links based on a single content (uniplex links) would be weaker and less stable than links based on two or more contents (multiplex links). Of all linkage contents only joking activity was not found as the sole content of any link. I concluded that in this setting the presence of repetitive joking activity in a link represented the most viable interpersonal bond that came closest to what might be termed "friendship." With a few exceptions joking activity was found only in links between men, and only in links between those men who did not overtly embrace administration orientations of work, obedience, and deference.
[15] In this case, while the charge-hand's network included a large number of workers, most of her links with these persons were uniplex rather than multiplex; hence her network span was wide while star multiplexity was low.
[16] My impression was that the women, the innovator, and the specialist were most careful about guarding their private territories against incursions. One example of incursion is given in Handelman and Kapferer (1972: 486–490). Such concern with territory was most evident on the worktable of the specialist, Ezra. Aside from controlling a very large table, he had built a barrier of plywood which was attached to its borders.

Four of the five men who did not embrace the "official" reality of the setting, and who interacted intensively with one another, were still the breadwinners of large families. Because they did not meet the behavioral expectations of their superiors, all five had poor reputations as workers, and did not earn salaries commensurate with their seniority in SAGE, even though two of them — Shlomo and Yihye — ranked second and third respectively in work output in the shop (Handelman 1971:237-239). While these men strongly depended on their interpersonal bonds with one another for support in interaction, they were rarely able to realize resources which derived from the dimension of production in claiming prestige or in settling disputes in their favor.

After experiencing the humiliation of their welfare careers, these men were employed for low wages by a female administration which demanded obedience and deference. In the workshop these men were required to do simple tasks,[17] under the supervision of a young woman, and were exposed to the sallies of a female charge-hand and her female cohorts.

Taken together, the discrepancies between their previous roles, their roles outside SAGE, and their roles in the workshop were great indeed. Given their lack of recourse and their need for subsistence wages, they had no serious avenues through which to express their discontent and disaffection with the local social order. However, play provided one such mode of communication which they utilized extensively.

PLAY IN THE WORKSHOP

Modes of play, while recurrent, were spontaneous and intermittent, with variable form and content. Play with extensive verbal content and minimal physical movement away from the work locations of participants tended to be featured in interaction among the women; while play which combined utterances and extensive physical movement was limited to interaction between men. I shall briefly outline modes of play I observed and indicate how the "donkey game" was more closely related to men's, rather than women's, play in the setting:

---

[17] Where the specialist and the innovator maintained that their work required skill and ingenuity, the other men usually maintained that their work was akin to that of children, quite incommensurate with the capacities of adults.

Jokes and Humorous Stories

Short jokes and stories with a humorous bent were largely the province of women who communicated them along the lines of network links. These play forms were interspersed in serious conversations to emphasize or illustrate a point, or were reactions to events in the workshop. Since jokes and stories were related while the women remained within their work locations, such play did not disrupt work activities and was tolerated by superordinates.

Singing

This was exclusively a female activity performed from within work locations without disrupting work activity and tolerated by superordinates.

Traditional Tales

Story-telling was the province of Shalom, the necklace polisher; and his recitations were directed at everyone within earshot. While this activity would be accompanied by attentiveness and excited comments it did not disrupt the appearance of work and was tolerated.

Because these modes of play did not contradict the official reality of the setting, their display reinforced administration sentiments that the workshop could be used properly for sociable interaction, and reinforced the impression that participants were committed to work activity and correct demeanor, thus enhancing their position in the eyes of the administration.

Joking Activity

Such sequences of interaction predicated upon an extended message of "this is play" and including at least two active participants were composed of utterances and extensive physical movement, and were performed by men connected through multiplex links. In the following example, Shlomo returned to the workshop after an absence and entered the back room to greet Zackaria who was seated at his work place.

Shlomo began by calling out, "Crazy Zackaria" and "Zackaria the donkey, you're crazy!" Zackaria grinned while continuing to work. Shlomo advanced until he stood next to Zackaria, whereupon the latter picked up a pair of pliers and lunged at the former, who nimbly dodged and laughed. The following interchange then ensued:

Zackaria: "Watch out, Shlomo; this (the pliers) is a revolver. I'll shoot you into little pieces for the cats to eat."

Shlomo: "Crazy Zackaria, I'll cut you into pieces and throw you down the toilet."

Zackaria: "I'll sell you to the Arabs for steak."

Shlomo: "I'll sell your brain to Barazani the Kurd, to chew."

Zackaria: "I'll sell you piece by piece in Mahane Yehuda [market] for soup."

Shlomo: "I'll cut off your ears to put on a donkey."

Zackaria: "I'll cut off your penis for a donkey's tail."

Shlomo: "I'll cut off your eggs [testicles] to hang in the women's toilet."

(At the mention of genitalia, Zohara began to mutter, "dirty, dirty", and she and the other women nearby averted their heads from the participants.)

Zackaria then stood and embraced Shlomo, and each began to pummel the other on the back and shoulders, giggling and laughing.

The content of this sequence contained overtones of hostility and aggression which, within the context of a strong interpersonal workshop link between these men, appeared to communicate significant messages about their place in the local social order. If mature responsible men were to be mutilated and equated with animal or human sustenance, what indeed was their manhood worth in this setting? When Shlomo cried: "I'll cut off your eggs to hang in the women's toilet," he communicated (a) that Zackaria was the "castrated" victim of women, particularly the women of SAGE,[18] while (b) his testicles hanging in the women's toilet (where females rearranged their clothing and performed bodily functions) reaffirmed the proper capacity of the mature male to sexually threaten and dominate females. Whether as hunter or trophy, these sentiments could only be expressed covertly as the participants interacted surrounded by an audience of women. Again, the referents of "crazy" were to the madness of location and not to Zackaria's mental state. They then hugged and pummeled one

---

[18] An example of how the women could degrade Zackaria is found in Handelman (i.p.). During this period in his life Zackaria had come under severe pressure from his wife and the welfare department (Handelman 1973).

another. This appeared to communicate the mutual enjoyment and equality of two males in an activity which excluded female participation, and which embarrassed female onlookers who supported official reality as the local social order.[19]

External Role Play

On occasion workers would playfully enact in the setting roles relevant to the wider social environment. Initiators of such role play were always men, and usually those who did not fully embrace the official reality of the setting. Such play usually revolved around the mockery of roles of expertise and power, like social worker and doctor, upon whom these players were dependent in their life situations. For example, Mashiah, in delivering rings to the charge-hand, would sometimes begin his approach in the following way: "Here comes the social worker to help Zohara."

He would then take out a *groush* (a monetary unit equivalent to a penny) and hand it to her, stating: "Now Zohara, if you are a good girl and behave yourself properly, I'll give you another *groush* at the end of the month. Now be a good girl."[20] Other workers in the room might then take up the chorus: "Look at the social worker who comes to help. Give me a *groush* too. With only a *groush* I can be young again."

Usually the men who adopted such roles played them toward women who, within the framework of play, then became the supplicants and subordinates. On another occasion Shalom adopted the role of doctor toward a woman worker. He began in this way: "Now I'm the doctor. Beware of the gasses; all day, boom, boom; a whole night, boom, boom." He waved his forefinger at her. "You shouldn't eat so

[19] While adult Jewish women of Middle Eastern extraction do participate in serious disputes which may become violent (see Shai 1970: 56–71), my impression is that outside of their families they are generally excluded from such joking activity in contacts with adult men. If this is so, a further message of such activity in the workshop was to reaffirm the boundaries of the female role, while asserting that male activities had more prestige.

[20] Mashiah mocked the limited allocations of the welfare department as well as the criteria of allocation. Here he indicated that welfare clients had to present themselves as worthy of aid, in a moral or personal sense, in order to receive allocations. Therefore Zohara had to be a "good girl" in order to benefit, showing attributes quite removed from her age, marital status, and position in the shop. I might also note that by playing the social worker while allocating to her the role of "girl," Mashiah altered the balance of power between them, and limited the extent to which she could criticize his work on such occasions.

much. Now the gasses catch you, boom boom." He began to chuckle. "When you have to fart in the street, soon, soon, look left, look right, to see if anyone comes, lift your leg a little, and boom boom." He burst into laughter and handed the woman three olives. "Take these pills; one in the morning, one at noon, and one at night. I'm a good doctor. Here, I'll write a prescription for you." He picked up a pencil and scribbled on a scrap of paper. "No more gasses, no more boom boom." He handed her three more olives. "And here are the pills for tomorrow. I'm the doctor. If you don't feel better I'll give you an invitation (appointment) here tomorrow."

From time to time the men would also play the role of "host," entertaining their "friends" (other workshop men) or "guests from America."[21] Speedily the kiln would become an oven, plates piled with beads would become portions of chicken, kebab, and rice, shop tools would become eating utensils, and settings would be laid for the feast on worktables, as imaginary cognac was drunk from empty water glasses. In their real contexts outside SAGE such times were occasions of mutuality and conviviality among kinsmen, friends, and allies. In the workshop context the messages of this play stressed the exclusiveness of male camaraderie and the exclusion and subordination of women.

Pranks

Occasional pranks were initiated only by men, with other men as their targets. Pranks were simple in conception and were always predicated upon elements of anticipation, tension, and surprise, followed by an outburst when the victim discovered the hidden twist in what he had perceived as a usual context. A favorite prank simply entailed slipping a foreign object, such as a smooth stone, into a man's jacket pocket and then awaiting his discovery and reaction.

Other pranks were more complex. One morning, after shopping in the Old City markets before work, Mashiah had brought a white hen to the shop. When he went to the toilet, Shlomo put the hen within a cupboard in Mashiah's work table. Upon his return the latter immediately asked about his hen. One worker said he had been too

[21] Since SAGE depended upon private donations, many tourists and potential benefactors, especially from the United States and England, passed through its workshops. These visitors were treated with politeness, respect, and at times deference. Therefore playing "host" to a "guest from America" also contained elements of self-ascribed status.

Expressive Interaction and Social Structure

busy to see, another questioned the existence of the hen, while a third stated that the hen had escaped into the courtyard outside, which Mashiah then searched thoroughly. In his absence, Shlomo placed the hen under a table in the other room. Mashiah returned, suspicious, searched his work table and both rooms; but no one in either room gave the location away. Mashiah's eventual discovery of his hen was greeted by laughter which increased when Mashiah seized a length of wood and began to lightly strike Shlomo who, while pretending to cringe, laughed along with the rest.

In another instance, with Mashiah in the other room, Shlomo caught a stray cat and placed it in Mashiah's drawer. Mashiah then went to the toilet outside the workshop. All awaited his return with anticipation. But when he came he again reentered the other room. There workers steered him back to his work place, telling him to stop wasting working time. He returned, sat down, lit a cigarette, and leisurely took a few puffs. He then opened the drawer, the cat leaped out, yowling, into his lap, gripping his jacket and pants with its claws. Shocked and shouting, amidst cheers and clapping hands, Mashiah almost fell over, and then joined in the general laughter.

Where women's play was sedate, with little physical movement, and supported the official reality of the setting, the play of men was often raucous, disruptive of work activity, and critical of the local social order. Where women's play did not contribute elements to the donkey game, men's play did. Joking activity contributed the terminology of the absurd; external role play contributed conceptions of roles in play with fairly defined boundaries and associated expectations; and pranks contributed elements of stealth, anticipation, tension, and surprise. Where other modes of play and their messages were spontaneous and intermittent with variable outcomes, the game constituted a routinization of play, and consequently of routinization of critical commentaries on the local social order.

Two further points about workshop play should be mentioned here. At times the women used the idiom of "theatre" in referring to workshop events, while such references were not made by men. So the women would suggest that one should pay admission to the shop to observe play antics; or would state, "Every day another play." These references were congruent with their roles as spectators who could not actively participate when men transformed official reality through play.

References to "children" and "childhood" were common, and were directed by the supervisor and by administrators to men at play, and by men at play to one another. Such references were uttered infrequently by the women. When a superior interrupted the men at play, the following kinds of comments were often heard: "All of you are here to work; you aren't children," "Children, sit down and remain quiet," or "Stop behaving like little children."

Given the orientation of the administration, the dependence of the men, and the official reality of the setting, admonitions that only children performed such antics were themselves an absurdity for the men. When they commented, "We study here; we have a teacher. This place is like a children's school," or stated that, "When we graduate we'll go to kindergarten," the men were communicating that their position of dependence and subordination was itself akin to the position of children, and perhaps that "childish" behavior was an appropriate response.

Or perhaps they were saying that they had to be akin to children to acquiesce to and cope with such arrangements. As well, the imagery of childhood perhaps symbolized a more innocent state within which play was appropriate as players encapsulated themselves in an "as if" world from which only limited attention had to be paid to external demands.

THE DONKEY GAME

The stimulus for the donkey game occurred during a session of joking in which Shlomo, Mashiah, Yihye, Eliahu, and Zackaria participated. Shlomo reiterated an original and absurd explanation of Zackaria's parentage. He suggested that in the latter's country of origin there grew a donkey tree from which donkeys would spring fully grown under the light of a full moon. He then suggested that one night Zackaria's mother had wandered into the countryside and, tired, had lain down to rest under such a tree. When the full moon rose a donkey sprang from the tree and impregnated the woman, who later gave birth to Zackaria. The men were greatly amused by this, and the theme was extended to explain Mashiah's paternity in the Yemen where foals sprang whole from the donkey tree.[22]

[22] Some days earlier Yihye had first introduced the motif of the donkey tree, then the idea that in Zackaria's country of origin, whenever the moon shone on the tree a foal emerged, and this was how Zackaria was born. To this Shlomo added that in the Yemen there grew a "woman tree" from which a woman appeared every midnight. He explained that Mashiah's father, while drunk, had taken such a woman as his wife (Handelman 1971: 463).

Within a few days Shlomo constructed a device consisting of a length of copper wire with a large ceramic button or rag fastened to one end. The other end of the wire he bent into a hook. He then began to hang this device onto the belts, pockets, and collars of the men with whom he had multiplex links. This he accomplished with stealth and deftness so that the recipients were unaware of what he had done. When they discovered the device he would cry, "donkey, donkey."

The device came to be termed a "tail," and the men who were initially recipients began to participate in transferring and hanging the donkey's tail. Here the terminology of the absurd was consistent with that used by these men in their joking activity. The only utterance required in this activity was the cry of "donkey" when the victim discovered his tail. The cry was not necessarily limited to the players, as the audience would often join in. If superiors were present the cry was usually eliminated. Then too, the number of transfers made would be limited.

As this activity was played, "rules" were developed which became the internal organization of the game. These were not stated as rules, but if not followed the game broke down. Only one tail could be in play at any time. Two elementary roles emerged in the game, that of the transferer and that of the recipient. Since this form of play, in keeping with other modes of play among these men, took the form of balanced reciprocal interaction, it was important for the participants to keep track of who had last received the tail in order for turns to be allocated so that the last recipient became the next transferer. Each player, by being obligated to become the recipient or victim thereby earned the right to become the transferer. Introduction of a second tail would have destroyed the symmetry of turns and role allocations.

The tail had to be transferred within an unspecified period of time. This indeterminacy heightened the anticipation of players. All knew who had the right to hang the tail, but aside from the last victim none knew when this would occur or under what circumstances. The lack of a specific time period for a turn also enabled the participants to adapt the game to the official reality of the setting and its situation of the moment.

There was no specified order of transfer, and the holder of the tail had the right to choose the next victim. This again heightened anticipation and tension in play, for the transferer was not ruled out as the next recipient; and at no time could a player assume that he was temporarily excused from the game because he had just played a turn.

Transfers had to be accomplished within the workshop, i.e., the game had to be played within the setting it commented upon. To have played in another area of SAGE would be to risk disruptions by onlookers unaware of correct responses.

While the donkey game incorporated elements of modes of spontaneous men's play, it was routinized activity in which behavioral expectations were given set boundaries of expression. The tail itself was symbolic of the body of shared knowledge that constituted the game. When the tail was removed from pocket or work table, others knew that a turn was to be played and that the "rules" of the game were in effect. Because verbal elements were minimal, participants had little opportunity to elaborate or alter the content of the game; and every turn of play reinforced its routinization instead of introducing divergent elements.

Playing the game took the following form. The previous recipient of the tail, the "donkey," would, at a time of his choosing, take out the tail. His intended victim might be in either of the rooms, seated at work, standing in public territory, or interacting with another worker. With casualness or stealth the transferer would approach his victim, as he would in perpetrating a prank. He would then hook the tail onto his victim. Clearly part of the fun lay in the "donkey" being unaware of his acquired identity.

The absurdity of play messages was heightened as he would continue to behave as if involved in serious activity while already in a transformed state of which onlookers were aware.

However, they did not know when this state would be publicly revealed, and this also whetted their anticipation.[23] While at times the victim was ignorant of his state, at other times he was fully aware of this, and consciously decided when to reveal himself.

Therefore, while overt behavior communicated normality, it was intertwined with a symbol of the absurd which represented the "true" identity of the players in the setting; and the incongruency between these coexisting messages about the nature of the local social order, combined with the inability of players and audience to express these discrepancies, probably also heightened anticipation and tension. The revelation of the absurd indentity hidden within the apparent normality of the local social order signaled that others could acknowledge and reinforce this new or "true" identity by crying "donkey, donkey" accompanied by laughter.

[23] In a few instances the tail was carried about for up to an hour before being acknowledged.

MESSAGES OF THE GAME

The messages of the donkey game were not qualitatively distinct from those of other modes of men's play; but within the more complex game such messages were simplified and required a continuing demonstration of shared sentiments around a common theme. Where joking activity, external role play and pranks were spontaneous singular experiments in communication whose course was negotiable and whose outcomes were variable, the game was directed toward a particular outcome with pointed messages.

Where David the innovator and Zohara the charge-hand had sometimes participated in joking activity and external role play, they were excluded from the game.[24] The game therefore excluded all active female participation, and was limited to those men with official reputations as poor workers uncommitted to official reality. More than other modes of play, the game distinguished the disaffected from other men and all women.

During the month of the game's existence there was an overall reduction in other modes of men's play. At the risk of an overly functional explanation, it was as if the messages contained in those other modes of play had found a more coordinated, steadier channel of expression which rendered the former more superfluous.

In the game, players had to cooperate actively to accomplish anticipation, tension and release over a series of occasions. Thus the transferer, in hanging the tail, had to choose a time and context which maximized not only his own fun, but also that of the other players. By accomplishing the transfer he linked together not only himself and his target, but all the game players, and in a wider sense much of the workshop. While this might be achieved haphazardly by other modes of play, it was integral to the game played by a circumscribed number of participants before a wider audience. The target had to cooperate by behaving as if nothing extraordinary was occurring while the tail was hung, and for as long as he chose to wear it. Here as well, other players and audience had to cooperate to sustain anticipation and tension while the tail was worn in the context of normal work activity.

That the audience had to recognize coexisting yet contradictory

---

[24] While a few attempts were made to get David to take a turn, these were not efforts to recruit him as a player, but rather to expose him as someone with similar frailties to those of the game players, and therefore as one who was not as committed to official reality as he presented himself. However Shalom maintained his intermediate position as a part-time player.

definitions of work and play without expressing wholehearted support for either until the target was ready probably also heightened anticipation and tension and accentuated release when it came. Note that once a transfer was accomplished control of the game passed to the target. Although he was labeled a "donkey" in the process, other players and audience became dependent upon him for their satisfactory release. This points out the symmetry of the game. When the transferer controlled play (i.e. until he decided to hang the tail and made his preliminary moves) anticipation and tension only began to be built up.

Therefore his control during this phase was matched by the lesser dependence of other players and audience. While the tail was actually being transferred, joint coordination and finesse were required of the transferer, target, other players and audience, in order to exchange game roles and identities; and all players were equally dependent upon one another. Once the target became the "donkey" (e.g. the absurd representation of player sentiments) all became dependent upon the will of the victim for their release and fun, and this balanced his labeled state.

The interdependence of the game players was also highlighted by contexts of play. Accomplishing a transfer while superiors were in the workshop entailed greater risk because being caught in the act would result in a public dressing down. The choice of whether to play in such contexts lay with the transferer. If he decided to hang the tail, anticipation and tension would be heightened as the attendant risks were higher. Moreover, the decision of the transferer to play also obligated his target to cooperate. Where, under such conditions, joking activity could simply be stopped or a prank aborted, the routinized nature of the game obligated players to respond and to share the risks entailed. Therefore each such venture was a joint enterprise in which the risks accepted by one member of the play group were extended to at least one other member. Such play appeared to strengthen links in the sense that Huizinga (1970:31) has described:

> ...the feeling of being "apart together" in an exceptional situation, of sharing something important, of mutually withdrawing from the rest of the world and rejecting the usual norms, retains its magic beyond the duration of the individual game.

The game subverted the official reality of the setting for many workshop members. The cooperation, or at least disinterest, of the women was required so that they would not destroy the frame of play before the "donkey" was prepared to reveal himself. The women not only acquiesced but behaved as a proper audience and appeared to derive considerable enjoyment from the proceedings. Thus they indicated to the men that the latter were indeed engaged in pleasurable activity; and this, coupled with the exclusion of the women from active play, raised the value of the game for the play group. So the women not only tacitly legitimated the game, but supported it;[25] and play, while signifying disaffection and opposition, also signified an integrated social order in which the position of the male players was central rather than peripheral.

The total exclusion of active female participation, the risks taken, the heightened feeling of being "apart together," and the routinized subversion of the official reality of the local social order, suggest that the messages of the game expressed what Goffman has termed "role distance" in describing how persons can express pointed separation between the ways in which they perceive themselves and their official roles in a setting. In practicing role distance ". . . the individual is actually denying not the role but the virtual self that is implied in the role for all accepting performers" (1961:108). The players expressed distance between the kinds of roles assigned to them by superiors in SAGE and aspects of their own self-identities. Goffman has suggested that:

Situated roles that place an individual in an occupational setting he feels is beneath him are bound to give rise to much role distance . . . where a subordinate must take orders or suggestions and must go along with the situation as defined by superordinates (1961:113–114).

The players expressed distance from their roles as subordinates to a female administration and female supervisor, and from their positions as targets of the female charge-hand, against all of whom they had no consequential avenues of recourse. By playing under the very eyes of authority, and by gaining the tacit cooperation of the women while relegating them to the position of spectators, the men were able to symbolically reassert what they perceived as their rightful position in the moral order. Furthermore, because a number of men cooperated repeatedly in play, their capacity to sustain a line of "dis-

---

[25] The game may have had quite different messages for the women than it did for the players. The revelations of male identity in the game were congruent with the women's perceptions of the role of men in the workshop. Therefore, by supporting the playing of the game the women stressed the weakness of its players, and thereby supported official reality in which the players were accorded inferior positions.

dainful detachment" was strengthened, for "... persons who are 'together' seem to be able to hold off the socially defining force of the environment much more than a person alone" (1961:110).

There is a juxtaposition of messages in the game in which both ordinary life and play acquire attributes of the other, and thereby inform experience with integration, not only through contrast but also through transformation; for both ordinary life and play are serious and absurd, and the state of one informs the other. These men did not perceive themselves as responsible for being placed in the workshop. They were hapless and helpless persons subject to the demands, first of the welfare authorities, and then of superiors in SAGE; and they found these experiences to be absurd.

They did not want to be in the setting, had little say in being sent there, needed to remain there, and had almost no way to express their need to remain and their need to leave, and had almost no way to reconcile these contradictions in their life situations except through play which had the capacity to communicate discrepant messages at the same time. As their life situations were absurd, so their play was serious commentary; but as their play was by definition unserious, that they played as they did was a commentary on the seriousness of their life situations.

REFERENCES

BATESON, GREGORY
    1956   "The message 'this is play,'" in *Group processes*. Edited by B. Schaffner, 145–241. New York: Josiah Macy Foundation.
    1972   "A theory of play and fantasy," in *Steps to an ecology of mind*, 177–193. New York: Ballantine.
BERLYNE, D. E.
    1969   "Laughter, humor, and play," in *The handbook of social psychology*, volume three. Edited by Gardner Lindzey and Elliot Aronson, 795–852. Reading, Massachusetts: Addison-Wesley.
BITTNER, EGON
    1965   The concept of organization. *Social Research* 32:230–255.
BLAU, PETER M.
    1964   *Exchange and power in social life*. New York: John Wiley.
BRADNEY, PAMELA
    1957   The joking relationship in industry. *Human Relations* 10:179–187.
CAVAN, SHERRI
    1966   *Liquor license: an ethnography of bar behavior*. Chicago: Aldine.
COSER, ROSE LAUB
    1959   Some social functions of laughter: a study of humor in a hospital

setting. *Human Relations* 12:171—181.

CUNNISON, SHEILA
1966 *Wages and work allocation.* London: Tavistock.

DOUGLAS, MARY
1968 The social control of cognition: some factors in joke perception. *Man* 3:361–376.

DUNDES, ALAN, JERRY W. LEACH, BORA OZKOK
1972 "The strategy of Turkish boys' verbal duelling rhymes," in *Directions in sociolinguistics.* Edited by John J. Gumperz and Dell Hymes, 130–160. New York: Holt, Rinehart and Winston.

EMERSON, JOAN P.
1969 Negotiating the serious import of humour. *Sociometry* 32:169–181.

ERIKSON, KAI T.
1962 Notes on the sociology of deviance. *Social Problems* 9:307–314.

GOFFMAN, ERVING
1959 *The presentation of self in everyday life.* New York: Doubleday Anchor.
1961 *Encounters: two studies in the sociology of interaction.* Indianapolis: Bobbs-Merrill.

GUMP, PAUL V., PHIL SCHOGGEN, FRITZ REDL
1963 "The behavior of the same child in different milieus," in *The stream of behavior.* Edited by Roger G. Barker, 169–202. New York: Appleton-Century-Crofts.

GUMP, PAUL, BRIAN SUTTON-SMITH
1971 "Activity-setting and social interaction: a field study," in *Child's play.* Edited by R. E. Herron and Brian Sutton-Smith, 96–102. New York: John Wiley.

HAMMOND, PETER B.
1964 Mossi joking. *Ethnology* 3:259–267.

HANDELMAN, DON
1971 "Patterns of interaction in a sheltered workshop in Jerusalem." Unpublished doctoral dissertation, Department of Social Anthropology, University of Manchester.
1973 Transactions in the development of official-client relationships: a welfare career in Jerusalem. To be presented to the Decennial Conference of the Association of Social Anthropologists, Oxford.
i.p. Gossip in encounters: the transmission of information in a bounded social setting. *Man* 8.

HANDELMAN, DON, BRUCE KAPFERER
1972 Forms of joking activity: a comparative approach. *American Anthropologist* 74:484–517.

HOMANS, GEORGE C.
1950 *The human group.* New York: Harcourt, Brace.

HUIZINGA, JOHAN
1970 *Homo ludens.* London: Paladin.

KAPFERER, BRUCE
1972 *Strategy and transaction in an African factory.* Manchester: University of Manchester Press.

LABOV, WILLIAM
1972 "Rules for ritual insults," in *Studies in social interaction*. Edited by David Sudnow, 120–169. New York: The Free Press.
LOFLAND, JOHN
1971 *Analyzing social settings*. Belmont, California: Wadsworth.
LUNDBERG, CRAIG C.
1969 Person-focused joking: pattern and function. *Human Organization* 28:22–28.
LUPTON, T.
1963 *On the shop floor*. London: Pergamon.
PAINE, ROBERT
1971 "A theory of patronage and brokerage," in *Patrons and brokers in the east Arctic*. Edited by Robert Paine, 8–21. Newfoundland Social and Economic Papers 2. Memorial University of Newfoundland.
RADCLIFFE-BROWN, A. R.
1961 "On joking relationships," in *Structure and function in primitive society*, 90–104. London: Cohen and West.
ROY, DONALD F.
1959– "Banana time": job satisfaction and informal interaction. *Human*
1960 *Organization* 18:158–168.
SHAI, DONNA
1970 *Neighborhood relations in an immigrant quarter*. Jerusalem: The Henrietta Szold Institute.
SHARMAN, ANNE
1969 "Joking" in Padhola: categorical relationships, choice and social control. *Man* 4:103–117.
SHOKEID, MOSHE
1971 *The dual heritage: immigrants from the Atlas mountains in an Israeli village*. Manchester: University of Manchester Press.
STRAUSS, ANSELM, *et al.*
1964 *Psychiatric ideologies and institutions*. New York: The Free Press.
SUTTON-SMITH, BRIAN
1971 "Boundaries," in *Child's play*. Edited by R. E. Herron and Brian Sutton-Smith, 103-106. New York: John Wiley.
SYKES, A. J. M.
1966 Joking relationships in an industrial setting. *American Anthropologist* 68:188-193.

Interactions and the Control of Behavior

GLEN McBRIDE

The messages of this paper are simple ones. Animals interact with each other, in courtship, fights, allogrooming, allofeeding or care-giving. In each interaction, the behavioral unit is not two separate animals making behavior towards each other but the whole single interaction, in which the behavior of both must be treated together, as each responds to the other at all times. Yet once two animals initiate a first interaction, they start immediately to sort out appropriate and inappropriate responses in each other. This sorting out, or a summary of it, is carried forward into their next encounter with another of the same type — male, female, intruder — or with the same animal, and becomes a part of the context for future behavior, a controller of behavior.

The experience carried forward may organize perceptions, attention, the types of interactions expected, and the times and places of the interactions or meetings with individuals. The term "relationship" expresses the construct we use to describe this mutual residue of the interactive behavior. Yet there is little precision about the way we use this word. Other behavior, such as sleep or rest, or movement, does not have this effect of generating relationships, though other interactions (actonic) with objects such as places, nests, watering points, and investigations do.

Relationships arising from face-to-face interactions seem to be a feature of most animals, and it is the resulting organization of the animals in space and time, and their perceptions of each other as they monitor the activities of those around them, that fashion a number of individuals into a society. Moreover, it seems equally clear that animals are able to exert controls over ongoing streams of interactive behavior, shaping them into specific experiences which will be appropriate to the future contexts; that is, they "know" the effect of every move in a face-to-face interaction on the relationship that will emerge from the behavior.

If relationship formation is a general property of face-to-face interactions in any species of animal, what then may be said about the human conversational interaction? To answer this, it is necessary to trace something of the evolution of the human communicative system, for this history seems to show how the ancient mechanisms for building relationships may have been modified to serve human needs, based on more complex communicative behavior.

I have suggested that speech began with the linking of a social engagement with the acting out of an event, perhaps a hunting scene, in mime, by means of a play metasignal (McBride 1968, i.p.). The message carried in the mime may have been an event that happened to the actor earlier in the day, at a distant place, so that, in one step, the space and time barriers were broken, and a typical human communication occurred. The step was huge, yet only involved a new combination of existing behavior. But this was not language.

Mime requires no agreement on the units of meaning. Over time, mime gave way to signs, and later to the use of sounds. The step to signs does require agreement on units, and so sign languages were probably the first true languages. The steps to signs and sounds were probably not discrete ones, and indeed we still regularly use signs, and occasionally mime, when words fail. Throughout the whole process, there was always a double interaction, and this is still true of either signing or spoken interactions. The new message codes were used within the context of the primary or social interaction, which remained in the ancient animal form, dealing only with issues of the type "between you and me, here and now."

The modern conversation is carried out in words, occasionally reverting to signs or even mime to supplement meaning. But the primary interaction has now become completely integrated with the flow of language. There is but one communicative system in man, though the two components may normally be recognized in all conversations. The primary interaction is carried out in visible behavior, spacing, orientation, eye contact, in touch, or in the paralinguistic component of the flow of sound. Yet there is much interchange between the two; for example, it is possible to supplement and modify the content of the speech by the use of nonverbal signals. Similarly, it is possible to turn into words the expression of the relationship, such as "I love you," or the requirements of the primary interactions, as "pay attention." This intimate complementarity of the two interactions is the product of the last two or more million years of human evolution, for language evolved in conversations!

The study of language has eclipsed that of the other components of our communicative system to such an extent that the primary interaction is still virtually unknown. I shall return to the discussion of speech and its organization from time to time, where it is necessary to dissect out the components of the conversational interaction.

What seems most important now is to ask questions about the manner in which the conversation is turned into the social relationship. I shall argue that, throughout a conversation, the verbal component is arranged in such a way as to stimulate nonverbal responses which contribute to the primary interaction. These are then decoded automatically by the observer and summarized automatically. In other words, the summary system, already highly evolved in our primate ancestors, was carried forward into man, perhaps with some changes which summarize verbal behavior, but basically still operating through nonverbal behavior in the formation of human social relationships. And thus the features of the words which will contribute to the future relationship are first converted into the nods, frowns, or movements of affect which may then be summarized automatically. Thus the form of the summary is more likely to be in relationship terms than in the conceptual content of the conversation, i.e. in terms of "he's a stimulating person," rather than "the stories he told me were stimulating." Further, because the summary system affects future behavior, the longer into the future the memory is examined, the more likely is the relationship summary to appear.

Already I have discussed a variety of behavioral phenomena. It seems useful now to pause, to ask questions about the nature of behavioral phenomena, and how they differ from and are related to psychological and physiological phenomena, that is, to specify the universe of discourse.

In another context, we could be discussing magnets and magnetism. Should we choose to study magnetism, then we need not concern ourselves with how magnetic fields are generated, for we may examine the properties of fields provided only that we have some magnets. The magnet becomes a black box. If on the other hand, we are interested in magnets, then fields and their properties become irrelevant, provided that we have some device that detects their presence. Now we may concentrate on the processes by which magnetic fields are generated.

It seems to me that when we are talking about behavioral phenomena, we have similar problems and may choose to discuss behavior and its organization, or the generative processes — the mechanisms, and how they operate. These are two logical types of phenomena, quite different from each other. I suggest that it is a reasonable generalization that most human ethologists are concerned with behavioral phenomena, and that most psychologists concentrate more on mechanisms, sensory, perceptual, learning, and motivating. Physiologists interested in behavior attend also to mechanisms, trying to relate the mechanisms found by psychologists to the functioning of the neural and endocrine systems.

Within either of these areas of study, one may erect clear universes of discourse, each complementary to the others. Whatever is known of the structure and functioning of the system within one universe of discourse must be compatible with what one knows of the others and even may be used to make predictions about another type of system for study. Within each, one may erect a hierarchy, defining levels, with function organizing the units within any level, and complementarity providing the basis for the grouping of units at any one level into a unit at the next level.

Within the human conversational interaction, there appear to be two sensible universes of discourse: that concerned with the speech itself, emphasizing its semantic content, and that concerned with the behavioral organization of the primary interaction. It is the organization of behavioral phenomena that is central to this essay. Yet it is also necessary to examine the mechanisms by which behavior is generated.

I am assuming that the generative processes producing behavior are essentially similar for all behavior, be it a fight or courtship, a display or a speech. All appear to be produced with a hierarchical organization, all involve almost infinite variety, whether this be in the verbal composition of a conversation or in the movement sequences of a cockfight. I think it is possible to see what these generative processes do. To produce a well-formed sentence, a sequence of words is produced in an arrangement that will complete semantic and syntactic goals, conceptual and complementary, respectively. Each of the component words, phrases, or clauses has specified relationships with each other's parts, and ordering is arranged so that completion, which involves complementarity, is achieved while maintaining the structural relationships between the parts. The sentence constitutes one functional segment of information.

It seems that, in the evolution of behavior, functional activities were not achieved by single movements, and sequences of movements were needed. The generative mechanisms that evolved dealt with activities that could be divided up into a sequence of functional steps or operations, rather in the way that an operations researcher may divide up a complex productive task into separate human roles, and these again into smaller sequences of operations. At any level of the division, the significance and function of any subsidiary operation depend only on its meshing with the other divisions of the task. The sentence is the best known example, where clauses are the first division and are themselves built up of smaller units, defined in their relationships to each other, as subject, verb, predicate, and so on.

If the generative processes look complex when considering a completed sentence, they become more so when we look at their operation in interactive sequences. Here a sentence which started off as a statement, may change its goal from concept to argument in response to an eyebrow raised in doubt, or may trail off into a question should it meet a negating head shake. Alternately, a segment already generated may suddenly appear to give offense to the listener, making it inconsistent with the relationship existing between the interactants; here the speaker may draw the new goal of conciliation or apology from the primary interaction, so modifying the semantic goal of the speech.

There are many ways that goals may change in interactive behavior, and this seems true of the behavior of most species. In any fight, a blow may change to a parry; the eager courting male, passing on from stage to stage, may be halted many times by reluctant responses from the female — witness the many false starts of a mammalian male to a not-quite-estrous female! And so it is that generative processes are considerably more complex in interactive situations, yielding fewer completed sentences but more satisfying and effective interaction!

In a generative process, the term goal can be defined only in terms of an end point, the finish of an operational unit. At these terminating points, multiple goals may become apparent, each different in type and involved in different universes of discourse. In speech, the conventional goals are conceptual, each contributing to the flow of ideas. Yet there are also different syntactic goals, and within the primary interaction, there may be another type of goal of a sentence, that of acknowledgment — by a nod of understanding.

The flow of speech involves a steady stream of such terminating points, at any of which contributions may occur within the primary interaction. Sometimes the nods may be drawn from the listener by "don't you?" or "didn't it?" or a hundred equivalents. Moreover we often say something aimed to directly elicit some increased arousal and special response within the primary interaction. Jokes, insults, or teasing are among many verbal transformations into the primary interaction.

This feature of interchange between the message and the primary interactions seems to be important in the understanding of face-to-face interactions and the relationships that emerge from them. Clearly, there is a large variety of behavior that may appear in the primary interaction as a result of speech. Some examples illustrate this.

Nods of understanding are probably the most common primary signal, deriving directly from the semantic component. Jokes generally elicit smiles or laughs, compliments may lead to preening motions, teasing can evoke laughter, anger, or tears, or statements of helplessness may yield complementary supportive or protective expressions.

The physical appearance of a person may facilitate or hinder social intercourse, handsomeness or ugliness contributing to the ease of establishing close rapport within the primary interaction — here usually quite irrelevantly. Equally irrelevant may be the effect of a physical disability, which causes many people to increase their spacing, affecting rapport.

There are also historical features of people that may be interpreted as part of the primary interaction; these include loudness of voice, a tendency to make too much or too little eye contact, or to stand too close or too distant in the interaction. All of these behaviors contribute to the primary interaction but are not appropriately a part of the interactive sequence. Nevertheless they may certainly affect the future behavior between the interactants.

There is another whole segment of the primary interaction, related directly to speech, that is probably concerned with the process of encoding and decoding. It seems to operate as an automatic marking and grouping system for both semantic and syntactic units of speech. The studies of Kendon (1972) have helped to clarify its operation.

He analyzed the structure of speech into a hierarchy of units which he called phrases, locutions, locution groups, and locution clusters. He found that during the passage of any of these units, a speaker tended to hold some part of his body in a constant posture, so that the changes in posture of that part also marked the change in the speech unit. He found also that the larger the speech unit, the larger and more central was the part of the body that marked its passage. The phrases were grouped by the pitch of the speaker's voice. Other markers included the beginning and end of locutions by specific movements of the head.

The picture of the primary interaction is, then, one of close interdependence with speech. Yet this component has its own conventions, format, behavioral tools, and controls, as befits the social event in which speech occurs. Thus there is a greeting and farewell, usually some acknowledgment or expression of the relationship, an expression of involvement throughout, and a variety of behavior, which is often highly synchronized between the interactants. An outsider looking in could learn much about the interactants. Yet as Goffman (1971) has pointed out, a conversation is largely protected from intruding observation from without, and this buffering is an integral part of the social event. Without it, new constraints would hamper interactive behavior, and the intruder would become a part of the social event, however inappropriate.

The complexity of the primary interaction as we know it will certainly be increased by the confirmation of the findings of Clynes (1969). He has shown that a wide range of seemingly irrelevant movements, perhaps any movement, may express the moods of affect that he calls "sentic states." Moreover, the character, or essentic form given to movements by affect appears to be highly consistent (for the same sentic state) between people, even when they come from quite different cultures. While he has made no studies which look specifically at the communication of sentic information by essentic form, such regularity as he finds is characteristic of a communication system.

The primary interaction has the essential property of face-to-face communication in any species: "between you and me, here and now." Bound within these time and space barriers, two interactants adjust their behavior to each other throughout the interaction. Yet each brings to the interaction a unique set of interactive experiences gathered throughout life, and then the particular context and performance of the interaction will bring some additional specificity to the mutual experience. From this unique experience, the adjustments the participants have made to each other will be carried forward into their next meeting, if they have a second interaction of the same type. This next meeting, then, has a history that is part of its context, and the behavior observed would not be fully intelligible without some knowledge of the history.

Though the interaction is unique, all of the experience used by both parties to adjust to each other gave some course to the interaction. There was an outcome, mutually designed, which may in turn become one step along an interactive progression, along which the participants may travel until some stable and mutually acceptable relationship is reached. The goal of the interaction is not to make a complete relationship but merely to take an adequate step along the path. Just as the suitability of the interactive behavior for making that adequate step is "known" by the interactants, so also is the appropriateness of the step along the progression, toward the final goal of friendship or bond, or enmity relationship.

The recognition of final and intermediate goals, and the appropriateness of each step, small or large, toward these goals must be present. There can be no navigation without a destination! From where do these destinations derive, and how does the guidance and transport system work?

Within any species, there is a great variety of social behavior, displays in each modality, and responses to these behaviors, along with appropriate releasing situations and controls that regulate their use. Using these tools, animals build such relationships as are appropriate to their species. Each relationship has special properties, of adjustments to each other, and of divisions of labor between the two, seen in their different responses to each context.

The relationships are major controllers of the behavior of the pair. Their mutual adjustment eliminates their need to sense all of the behavior emitted by each other, leaving only the need to monitor the stream to detect deviations from the set of habituated expectations. Each relationship becomes a "channel" built by experience into the structure of their attention. All social information passes along these channels to maintain, change, and operate the society. The relationship structure is the structure of the society, built into the attention structure of all individuals. Yet there is also design, for the different relationships within any group must complement each other before the group becomes a unit that will function effectively, contributing to the preservation of the species.

It is clear that all of the design in any society must lie within the organization of the individuals of any species, males, females, juveniles, or infants. All was built by interactive behavior, using behavioral tools especially shaped by evolutionary processes. These are in the processes that generate behavior, the sensory processes that perceive and code it and summarize it, and those monitoring systems that assess its appropriateness.

Every relationship has a form, fashioned along with the behavioral tools that shape it through evolution. But there is also variability, and ontogenetic experience may modify this form. The form is also in part specific, reflecting the unique character of its history. But for man, there is also another control operating on his interactive behavior at every stage. For man has not one society, but many. Within each culture, different forms of relationships complement each other in different ways to achieve stable systems.

There is a large variety of functional relationships in man, particularly because one of man's greatest specializations is the ability to make special functional groups, with specified functional relationships within them. Different relationships demand different intermediate goals, and different interactive processes with different homeostatic adjustments during face-to-face interactions. Whether or not this variety in social relationships is real is not clear. Certainly it is clear that there is an enormous variety of functions with special interactions carried out within the social context. But how much variety is there in the social contexts for such operations?

This raises another complexity in human relationships, which I have avoided; one which is not present in any other animal. I have emphasized the summary system of affect that generates social relationships from the primary interactions in face-to-face interactions, drawing from the speech only through the primary interaction. Yet what is said, the concepts, arguments, and imagery also contribute to human interactions, as presumably do the functional interactions, usually of an actonic type. It is not my intention to avoid these; they are simply different stories.

REFERENCES

CLYNES, M.
    1969   "Toward a theory of man: precision of essentic form in living communication," in *Information processing in the nervous system*. Edited by N. Leibovic and J. C. Eccles, 177–206. Springer-Verlag.

GOFFMAN, E.
    1971   *Relations in public*. New York: Basic Books.

KENDON, A.
    1972   "Some relationships between body motion and speech," in *Studies in dyadic communication*. Edited by A. Seigman and L. B. Pope, Elmford, New York: Pergamon Press.

MCBRIDE, G.
    1968   On the evolution of human language. *Social Science Information* 7:81–85.
    i.p.   Miming, signing, and speech. *Current Anthropology*.

PART SIX

Cultural Differences in Communicational Behavior

Communicative Styles in Two Cultures: Japan and the United States

DEAN C. BARNLUND

Man and society are antecedent and consequent of each other: every person is both a creator of society and its most obvious creation. Individual acts are framed within cultural imperatives, but cultures derive their imperatives from the acts of individuals.

Perhaps for this reason there are essentially two modes of inquiry that have been used in the study of cultures. One of these views society as an integrated totality and emphasizes the interlocking premises and values which it manifests. It proceeds by seeking to determine the philosophical assumptions, political structures, ideological premises, and world view of the culture. The other treats society as the patterns of actual behaviors that people manifest in their day-to-day encounters with each other. It proceeds by seeking to discover the dialectic that governs the conduct of ordinary affairs. The risk in the former is of reifying abstractions that do not actually regulate behavior; the risk in the latter is of becoming lost in a multiplicity of irrelevant detail. Yet, when sensitively employed, both methods should wind their way back to the same reality. Individual acts are no more than social beliefs particularized, and cultural premises no more than a multitude of individual acts generalized.

Here the effort is to contribute to a better understanding of two highly industrialized societies which differ in a multitude of significant ways, by focusing upon the most commonplace of ordinary acts — the messages by which men express their own inner experience and bind

This research was supported in large part by a Visiting Scientist's grant from the Japan Society for the Promotion of Science. A full report of the investigation will be published in Japanese early in 1973 by Simul Press, Tokyo, Japan.

themselves to the community of other men. Three specific aims guided the study: to develop a theoretical framework for exploring cultural differences in the communicative styles of Japanese and Americans; to gather data on the actual content and conduct of face-to-face encounters in both cultures; to speculate on the personal and social significance of any differences in communicative patterns.

UNIVERSE OF DISCOURSE

Every culture creates for its members a "universe of discourse," a way in which men can interpret their experience and convey it to one another. Without some common system of codifying sensations, life would become meaningless, and all efforts to cooperate would be doomed to failure. This "universe of discourse," the most precious of cultural legacies, is transmitted to each generation, in part consciously and in part unconsciously. Parent and teacher give explicit instruction in it by praising and criticizing certain ways of thinking, of speaking, of gesturing, and of responding to the messages of others. But often the more significant aspects of any communicative style are conveyed implicitly, not by edict or lesson but through modeling behavior. The child is surrounded by others who through the mere consistency of their actions display what is regarded as "sensible" behavior. Since the grammar of any culture is so often assimilated unconsciously, one's own cultural assumptions and distinctive modes of address are difficult to recognize.

It is when men nurtured in sharply differing societies meet that such cultural norms interfere with their ability to comprehend each other. Occasionally the interpersonal crises that accompany intercultural encounters are sufficiently dramatic, or the communicants sufficiently sensitive, to permit recognition of the source of trouble. Where there are patience and constructive intention, these misunderstandings may be explored and clarified. But more often the outsider, without knowing it, leaves behind him a trail of confusion, anxiety, mistrust, and hatred of which he is totally unaware. Neither communicant recognizes that his difficulty is buried in the rhetoric of his own society. Each sees himself as acting in ways that are thoroughly sensible, honest, and considerate. And — given the rules governing his own universe of discourse — each is. Unfortunately there are few cultural universals, and the degree of overlap is always less than adequate. The symbolic universe each occupies is governed by codes that are unconsciously acquired and automatically employed. Yet as long as men remain blind to the sources of their meanings, they are imprisoned within them. Cultural frames of reference are no less confining because they are symbolic and cannot be seen or touched.

PUBLIC AND PRIVATE SELF IN JAPAN

The object of this study was to probe the rules of discourse in two cultures by examining in detail the communicative styles of Japanese and Americans. Earlier research led to the postulation of a basic difference between Japanese and Americans with regard to the extent to which the self is exposed in everyday encounters. It was hypothesized that the Japanese prefer an interpersonal style in which the self made accessible to others, that is, the "public self," is relatively small, while the proportion of the self that is not revealed, the "private self," is relatively large. This has been diagrammatically represented in Figure 1.

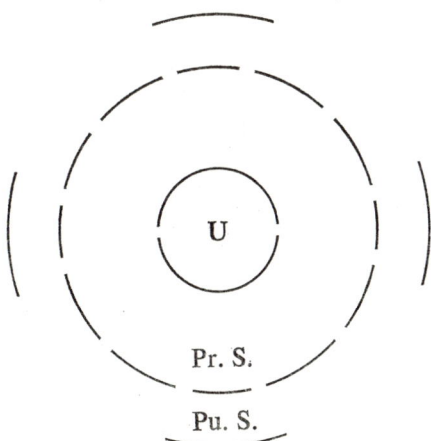

Figure 1. Japanese public and private self

At the center of the personality stand those nearly inaccessible assumptions and drives that comprise the "Unconscious." Surrounded by nearly impenetrable walls, this part of the personality is rarely exposed to communication, except in the most intimate human relationships or under professional treatment. The next area, identified as the "Private Self," marks off aspects of the person that are potentially communicable but are not often or not usually shared with others. It consists of different material for each person — past experiences, feelings about the self, latent fears or needs — that he knows and can reveal if he chooses. But this material is not ordinarily shared unless the inner need is great or unless there is considerable trust in the other person. Then these matters may become the focus of conversation. The outer area, the "Public Self," identifies those aspects of personal experience that are readily available and easily shared with others. Again the content of the public self differs with each person. It may consist of facts about one's work, personal tastes, family activities, or opinions about public issues. Information of this type is often volunteered, or willingly supplied, in reply to questions from others. Along with small talk, it comprises the most common resource for conducting conversation.

The plus and minus signs that appear in the interpersonal model (Figure 2) merely indicate that encounters within a culture may produce agreements or disagreements. But within the confines of a shared

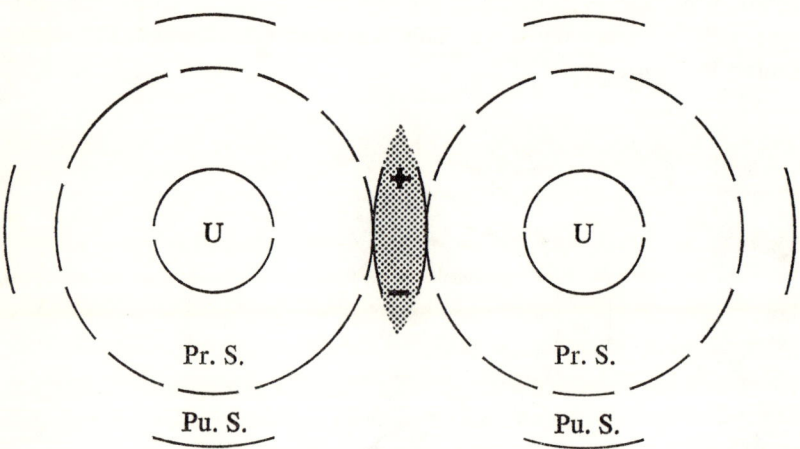

Figure 2. Japanese interpersonal communication

communicative style, the meaning of a gesture, or a word, or an inflection is more likely to be shared even if the conclusion to which it points is not. In this sense people of the same culture often do not misunderstand each other, they disagree. Conflicts may be readily recognized and may be resolved by employing a common symbolic code for exploring the grounds for disagreement.

If a dominant orientation among Japanese is to permit only a relatively small proportion of inner experience to be made accessible to others, then some of the following predictions should characterize their communication with each other:

A. THE JAPANESE SHOULD INTERACT MORE SELECTIVELY AND WITH FEWER PERSONS. Interaction with acquaintances is safer because they will know and respect limits of self-revelation. The risk of unexpected self-exposure is reduced by limited contact with strangers whose communicative styles may be unpredictable.

B. THE JAPANESE SHOULD PREFER REGULATED OVER SPONTANEOUS FORMS OF COMMUNICATION. The greater the degree of formality that surrounds interpersonal encounters, the smaller the chance of exceeding conventional limits on personal revelation.

C. THE JAPANESE SHOULD, ACROSS A VARIETY OF TOPICS, COMMUNICATE VERBALLY ON A MORE SUPERFICIAL LEVEL. Outer events will be seen as more suitable material for conversation than inner realities; private feelings and thoughts will be avoided where possible.

D. THE JAPANESE SHOULD SHOW A RELUCTANCE FOR PHYSICAL AS WELL AS VERBAL INTIMACY. Since all physical contacts are self-revealing, often more so than words, it might be expected that touching behavior and reinforcing actions might be less used. Reducing the number of channels through which information is carried reduces the likelihood of self-exposure.

E. THE JAPANESE SHOULD RESORT TO DEFENSIVE REACTIONS SOONER AND IN A GREATER NUMBER OF TOPICAL AREAS. The more of the self that is guarded the more one is vulnerable to exposure. Defensive modes tend to be consistent with prevailing interpersonal orientations, hence passive-withdrawal will be preferred to active-aggression in the face of threat.

F. THE JAPANESE, BECAUSE THEY EXPLORE INNER REACTIONS LESS OFTEN AND AT MORE SUPERFICIAL LEVELS, MAY BE LESS KNOWN TO THEMSELVES. Less communication of self may reduce the frequency and intensity of interpersonal conflict; but if disclosure to others is a major means of exposure to self, the Japanese may develop less self insight and have less accurate self perceptions.

PUBLIC AND PRIVATE SELF IN THE UNITED STATES

The same variables, the public self and the private self, may be used to describe the distinguishing features of American interpersonal behavior (Figures 3 and 4). It is postulated that Americans prefer a communicative style, in which the self made accessible to others is

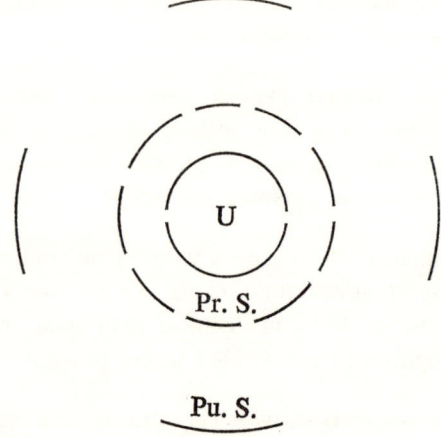

Figure 3. American public and private self

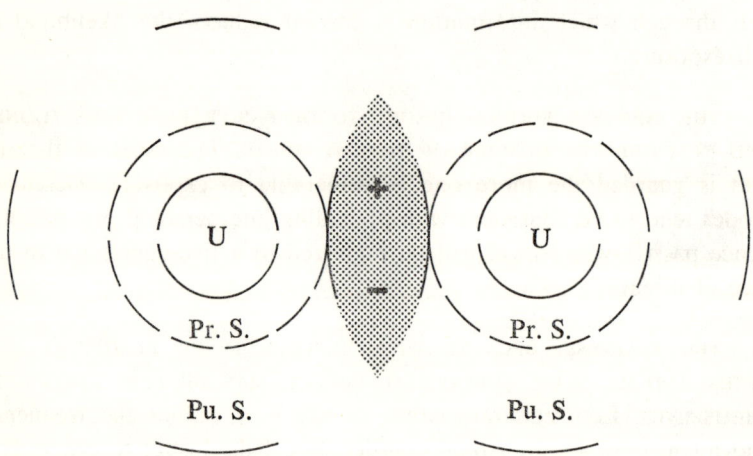

Figure 4. American interpersonal communication

relatively larger, and the proportion that remains concealed is relatively smaller. If this assumption is correct, what specific communicative behaviors should be manifest when Americans interact?

A. AMERICANS SHOULD COMMUNICATE WITH A LARGER NUMBER OF PERSONS AND LESS SELECTIVELY. They may be less discriminating about whom they talk to because there is less to be hidden, and they may be more consistent in what they talk about with a broader range of people.

B. AMERICANS SHOULD PREFER MORE SPONTANEOUS FORMS OF COMMUNICATION. Ritualized interactions, where conversation conforms to restrictive norms and rules, should occupy a smaller proportion of their social experience and, because it interferes with fuller expression, be less attractive to them.

C. AMERICANS SHOULD COMMUNICATE ON A DEEPER AND MORE PERSONAL LEVEL ACROSS A VARIETY OF TOPICS. Personal opinions and private feelings may be more highly valued as contributions to conversation than are impersonal remarks.

D. AMERICANS SHOULD SEEK PHYSICAL AS WELL AS VERBAL INTIMACY. Because they seek fuller expression of the self, they may utilize more channels of communication and engage in a greater frequency of physical contact.

E. AMERICANS SHOULD, SINCE THREAT IS PROPORTIONAL TO THE EXTENT OF SELF-CONCEALMENT, BE DEFENSIVE WITH FEWER PERSONS AND IN FEWER TOPICAL AREAS. When threatened they should favor active-aggressive over passive-withdrawal techniques as forms of defense since the former gives greater opportunity for self-expression.

F. BECAUSE THEY EXPOSE THEIR INNER EXPERIENCES MORE FREQUENTLY AND TO A WIDER VARIETY OF PERSONS AMERICANS SHOULD BE MORE FULLY KNOWN TO THEMSELVES. Greater communication of the self should provoke a higher incidence and higher intensity of interpersonal conflict but should also contribute to a deeper knowledge of the self.

What is postulated, thus, is a difference not of kind but of degree between the psychic structure and communicative behavior of Japanese and Americans, a difference that is significant rather than trivial. This difference, reflecting cultural norms and values, causes members of these two cultures to talk differently, about different topics, in different ways, to different people, with different consequences.

INTERCULTURAL COMMUNICATION

It might be useful before proceeding to speculate on some possible sources of tension or confusion that may arise in cross-cultural communication. The precise nature of such difficulties between Japanese and Americans should become clearer and more specific as our data unfold.

As the models suggest (Figures 5 and 6), such intercultural encoun-

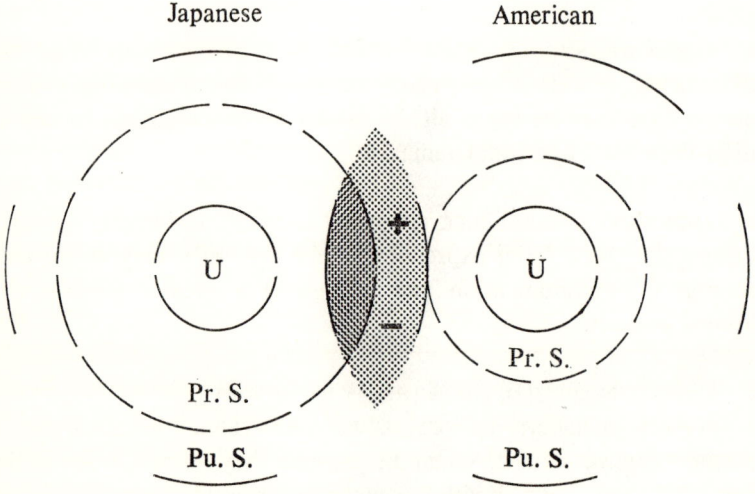

Figure 5. Intercultural communication: American style

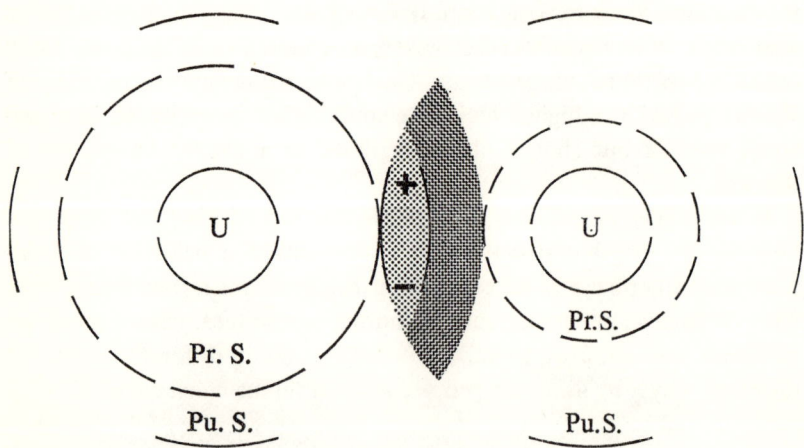

Figure 6. Intercultural communication: Japanese style

ters involve not only the normal sorts of agreement and disagreement that are probable in any conversation, but these are now compounded and aggravated by differences in communicative style as well. Each party seeks to define the relationship according to his own rhetorical tradition; each attempts to focus on topics and meanings appropriate to his own culture; each tries to prescribe a different form and script for their engagement.

In the first instance (Figure 5), the American conversational norms prevail, either because of the insistence of the American or the reluctance of the Japanese to resist them; in the second instance (Figure 6), the Japanese norms prevail, again either because of the greater influence of the Japanese or the reluctance of the American to oppose them. In most instances there is a somewhat awkward, fluctuating compromise made between interpersonal styles.

Where the Japanese may be frightened at the prospect of being communicatively invaded, the American is annoyed at the prospect of never getting beyond formalities. The Japanese is annoyed with Americans for their "flippant" attitude toward formalities, their "insensitivity" to status distinctions, their "prying" questions, their "unnatural" physical intimacy, their "hasty" decisions. In Japan these are the meanings ordinarily attached to such behaviors.

The American, talking to a Japanese associate, similarly is baffled by rituals that seem "endless," by conversations that seem "pointless," by silences that "waste" time, by humor that seems "childish," by delays that are "inexcusable," by remarks that are "evasive," and by the "distant and cold" demeanor of his foreign counterpart. What seems clear to one is patently unclear to the other. And what seems clear may actually be misunderstood.

Each society must maintain some boundary between meaning and nonsense. It does so by distinguishing between signals — cues to which the society attaches meaning — and noises — cues which the culture ignores or treats as devoid of significance. The dividing line is invisible, symbolic rather than real. When the agreement concerning the boundary between signals and noises breaks down or is breached, as it regularly is when members of different cultures interact, useful symbols dissolve into gibberish. Lacking any way of calibrating the two cultural codes, of establishing some correspondence of meaning, the members of different social systems may simply suspend efforts to reach each other. Every attempt at meaningful interaction only seems to drive them farther apart. In their confusion, they surrender to indifference or to hostility. The identification of such potentially disruptive and alienating differences in communicative styles might alert communicants from these two cultures to possible sources of misunderstanding and might suggest ways of mitigating the antagonisms they generate.

THE INVESTIGATION OF COMMUNICATIVE STYLES

The research was conducted between 1968 and 1972 with the bulk of the investigative work completed in the latter year. The subjects questioned about their communicative behavior were Japanese and American college students between the ages of eighteen and twenty-four. All but one of the samples consisted of 240 subjects equally divided between the two cultures and equally divided between males and females.

A college sample, of course, is not representative of the entire population of either country. But no limited sample would be completely satisfactory in this respect. And the college sample has certain advantages. First, the young are an important segment of society and may be more sensitive to its operation than their parents. Second, if the shape of the future is to be found, it must be sought among those who will shortly determine it. Finally, if there is likelihood of greater cultural communication between East and West, especially among the younger generation, data secured from college students will minimize rather than exaggerate any cultural differences that may be found. Thus, any conclusions drawn from these data should reflect a conservative rather than an extreme bias.

A number of instruments were used to gather information concernning the communicative behavior of Japanese and Americans. The following sections of this report summarize findings obtained from a Role Description Checklist, a Self-Disclosure Scale, a Nonverbal Inventory, and a Defensive Strategy Scale. The data reveal to whom Japanese and Americans talk, what they talk about, how much of themselves they share, what kind of physical contact they maintain with significant others, and how they defend themselves in threatening social situations.

PROFILES OF TWO CULTURES

The first question is a broad, macroscopic one: What are the GENERAL features of Japanese and American communication? In what respects are members of the two cultures alike? In what respects do they differ? And are the differences sufficient to warrant a detailed examination of the specific content and form of interaction?

A Role Description Checklist, developed originally for use in classes in interpersonal communication, provided a list of adjectives for describing the communicative attributes of people. Japanese equivalents for all the items on the scale were selected, and four additional terms, commonly used by Japanese to describe interpersonal behavior, were added. The forms were completed by Japanese and American college students who were able to speak both languages and who had opportunity for observation of the opposite culture as well as their own.[1]

The profiles obtained for each culture were highly consistent, no matter whether they originated within or outside the culture. The Japanese were seen and saw themselves as "reserved," "formal," "cautious," and "evasive." While the Japanese also added such high priority terms as "silent," "serious," and "dependent," the Americans dropped "silent" and added "cooperative." Americans were seen and saw themselves as "frank," "self-assertive," "spontaneous," "informal," and "talkative." Where Japanese respondents placed "humorous" among the high frequency adjectives, Americans substituted "impulsive."

In general, the profiles conform closely to predictions made from the theoretical models: Japanese appear to prefer more formal and regulated encounters, tend to be reserved and cautious in expressing themselves, prefer to be evasive or silent rather than open and frank. This picture is consistent with a highly contained self that is controlled or cautiously expressed, and a larger private self that is hidden or unknown. The Americans appear to be more self-expressive and self-assertive, to prefer more informal encounters, to be more spontaneous and talkative, to be more open and frank about their experience. The single adjective chosen most frequently to describe each culture, by nearly every subject in both samples, was "reserved" for Japanese and "self-assertive" for Americans.

A comparison of the composite profiles of these two cultures provides an impression of extreme contrast, even of contradiction. The qualities most frequently attributed to the Japanese — "reserved,"

---

[1] The Role Description Checklist, since it required opportunity to observe nationals of the opposite culture, consisted of 122 Japanese and 42 American students enrolled at International Christian University in Japan. Students sampled were able to communicate in both languages and had opportunity for daily face-to-face interaction with members of the other culture.

"formal," "evasive," "cautious," "silent," "serious," and "dependent" — are attributes on which Americans score zero or only slightly above zero. The qualities most frequently assigned to Americans — "self-assertive," "frank," "informal," "spontaneous," "talkative," "humorous," "independent," and "relaxed" — are those on which Japanese score close to zero.

A review of the extensive literature on both cultures by critical observers tends to validate these attributes. In the writings of Benedict (1946), Doi (1962), Halloran (1969), Moloney (1954), Maraini (1965), Nakamura (1964), Nakane (1970), and many others, one finds descriptions that are highly compatible with the terms above and that tend to validate them. It would appear, thus, that although all human beings enter the world with roughly the same sensory and nervous potentialities, each culture rapidly undertakes to cultivate a particular syndrome of interpersonal attributes. By adulthood, and usually long before, its members display sufficient distinctiveness in their interpersonal relationships to permit them to be culturally classified. Few highly industrialized cultures, however, will demonstrate such wide differences in communicative style as those that have been suggested here. And the contrast is sufficient to encourage examination of the actual mechanics of interaction within these two social systems.

VERBAL SELF DISCLOSURE: TOPICS, TARGETS, LEVELS

Perhaps there are no more basic questions to ask of a person or a culture than these: To WHOM does one speak or not speak? About WHAT does one talk or not talk? How COMPLETELY is inner experience shared or avoided? Answering these questions should provide some insight into the structure of human relationships and the norms governing interpersonal communication in Japan and the United States.

A Self-Disclosure Scale, developed by Jourard and Lasakow (1958), permits measurement of these three critical variables. Each respondent is asked to indicate his level of disclosure of thoughts and feelings on a variety of topics, with a series of significant other people in his life. The tests were administered, as were all tests used in this study, anonymously, and subjects were given unlimited time to finish.

The findings reveal that what people prefer to talk about appears to be surprisingly similar in the two cultures. The Japanese most prefer to discuss matters of interest and taste followed by opinions about public issues and attitudes toward work. The Americans order these slightly differently but the same three general topics are the most discussed in this culture too. Both cultures appear to talk least about financial matters, aspects of personality, and attitudes toward the body and sex. Males and females in neither society show any significant differences in their topical priorities.

The most thoroughly discussed of the specific questions within these broad categories are those relating to tastes in food, music, reading, television, and film, attitudes toward race, and male and female relations. The least popular specific questions are clearly those dealing with sexual adequacy, facts about sexual behavior, and feelings about appearance or personality. Thus, the evidence is overwhelming in support of similar cultural orientations among Japanese and Americans, regarding what they prefer to talk about and what they prefer to avoid talking about.

If conversational topics can be ranked according to attractiveness, is it not likely also that a hierarchy of persons exists with whom to talk? One might expect that all potential communicative partners are not equally attractive, or that they might vary in attractiveness according to the subject under discussion.

Although all potential associates score substantially higher with Americans, both cultures and both sexes appear to favor communicating with friends most, then with parents, and least with unknown or untrusted persons. Although the overall figures give a slight advantage to male over female friends, each sex appears to prefer somewhat talking with friends of the same sex rather than the opposite sex. This preference is somewhat higher among Japanese than among Americans.

With regard to parents, however, there is a sharp difference between the cultures. Mothers score proportionately higher than fathers in Japan; Japanese women rank mothers second only to friends of the same sex. As one Japanese respondent spontaneously explained, "She is my friend." Fathers, however, score significantly lower and appear to be only slightly more attractive conversational partners than are unknown and untrusted persons. In contrast, American respondents see mothers and fathers as almost equally attractive communicative partners.

Both cultures appear to regard talking with unknown people and untrusted acquaintances as unattractive, but both Japanese and Americans prefer talking to a stranger than to an untrusted aquaintance.

Choice of partner and choice of topic would not seem to be independent of each other. It might be expected that people would seek specific persons with whom to discuss certain topics. But the data from this investigation raise doubts about that conclusion. Instead, target person rankings tend to be consistent, that is, the attractiveness of a particular partner does not appear to vary but is generalized across topics. Thus, in spite of cultural differences in attitudes toward mothers and fathers, there appears again to be a striking similarity between the cultures with regard both to what is talked about and to whom communication is directed.

The most critical aspect of verbal behavior, however, is the depth of personal expression encouraged in verbal encounters. The scoring of the Self-Disclosure Scale provides a precise estimate of this level for each topic and with each partner. A score of 0.0 indicates that respondents have "told nothing about this aspect of myself," a score of 1.0 indicates that they have talked "in general terms about this aspect of myself," and a score of 2.0 indicates that they have "talked in full and complete detail about this aspect of myself."

The results indicate that the average level of self-disclosure across all topics and all target persons for the Japanese is 0.75 and for Americans is 1.12. A more representative index of personal accessibility may be obtained by omitting scores based on conversation with strangers and untrusted acquaintances. When these two categories of target persons are omitted, the average level of disclosure to trusted acquaintances (mother, father, male friend, and female friend) rises to 1.00 for the Japanese and to 1.44 for Americans. A slight sex difference appears in both samples but of such size as to be negligible.

Thus, interpersonal distance is substantially greater among Japanese than among Americans. And this holds true whether communicative partners include or exclude unknown and untrusted persons. On the whole, Japanese express themselves only in "general terms" with their closest associates. For Americans the comparable statistic lies midway between talking in "general terms" and in "full and complete detail." For them, approximately half of reported interpersonal communication with intimates appears to involve a relatively full exposure of the inner self.

It is when one examines individual questionnaires that the full impact of these results can be seen. Depersonalized averages tend to obscure the extremes and blunt the human significance of these figures. There are more than a few — especially among the Japanese sample — who, on nearly all topics and with nearly all persons, report they have told the person "nothing about themselves." As one data processor remarked while scoring the questionnaires, "Do these people ever reveal anything of themselves to anyone? Are they known to any other human being at all?"

The averages for each topical area provide a similar picture of cultural contrast (Figures 7 and 8). On all topics American respondents show a consistently higher level of self revelation. Their disclosure on the LEAST attractive conversational topic surpasses the level of disclosure of Japanese respondents on all but the MOST attractive topic. That is, Americans share as much of themselves with regard to physical and sexual adequacy as Japanese do with regard to their taste in food, music, reading, and television programs. There is also evidence of "communicative blanks." Though most subjects talk with some intimacy to some people on some topics, there are areas of private experience that are sometimes blotted out altogether. Some may avoid talking about illnesses or debts while others avoid conversations touching upon race relations or work difficulties.

The same pattern emerges from an analysis of disclosure to various communicative partners. The Japanese talk only in the most general terms even with their parents and closest friends. The average level of disclosure for Americans with all target persons, including even strangers and untrusted persons, exceeds the level of verbal disclosure of Japanese in even their most intimate relationships.

The most provocative single figure relates to verbal involvement with fathers. Although fathers tend to rank as relatively unattractive communicative partners in many cultures, this result is dramatically true of the Japanese sample but doubtful with regard to the American one. Americans apparently disclose their private thoughts and feelings as much to strangers as do Japanese to their own fathers. The data provide strong support for Benedict's (1946) characterization of Japanese fathers as "depersonalized objects" and Doi's (1962, 1972) description of Japan as a "fatherless society."

Conversation may be seen as an activity sustained by two or more persons who use their experience as a resource on which to build a human relationship. The quality of that relationship depends on their capacity to sustain a superficial or deep linkage with each other. This exploration of verbal habits suggests there is both universality and distinctiveness in the character of verbal interaction in these two cultures. In both, a similar set of priorities exists with regard to topical appropriateness. In both, there is a similar hierarchy of communicative partners. But here the similarity ends. Each culture encourages a different level of personal disclosure in interpersonal encounters. Japanese and Americans differ significantly with regard to the degree

	TOPIC	TARGET					
		Stranger	Father	Mother	Same Sex Friend	Opposite Sex Friend	Untrusted Acquaintance
Opinions	1. Religion						
	2. Communism						
	3. Integration						
	4. Sex Standards						
	5. Social Standards						
Taste & Interests	1. Food						
	2. Music						
	3. Reading						
	4. TV & Movies						
	5. Parties						
Work (Studies)	1. Handicaps						
	2. Assets						
	3. Ambitions						
	4. Career Choice						
	5. Associates						
Money	1. Income						
	2. Debts						
	3. Savings						
	4. Needs						
	5. Budget						
Personality	1. Handicaps						
	2. Self Control						
	3. Sex Life						
	4. Guilt/Shame						
	5. Pride						
Body	1. Facial Feelings						
	2. Ideal Appearance						
	3. Body Adequacy						
	4. Illnesses						
	5. Sexual Adequacy						

0 – 50 / 51 – 100 / 101 – 150 / 151 – 200 / 201 – 250

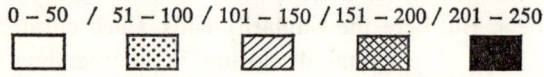

Figure 7. Summary of topic, target, and level of disclosure: Japan

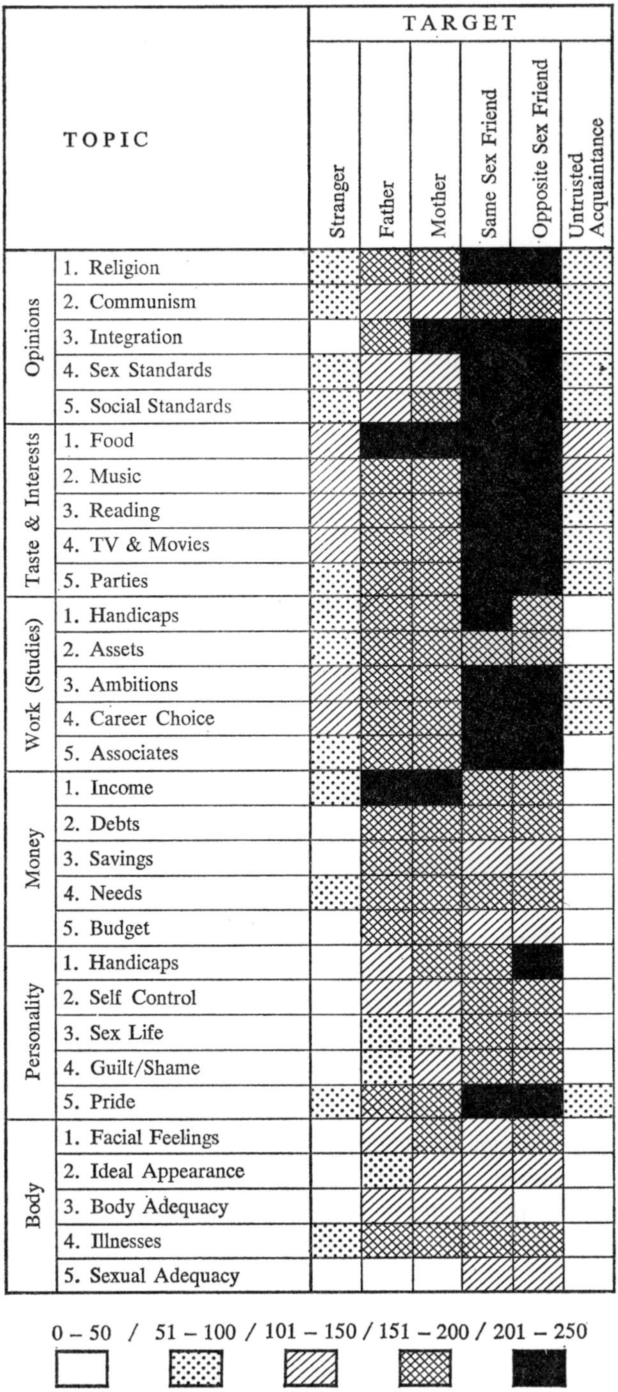

Communicative Styles in Two Cultures: Japan and the United States 443

TOPIC		TARGET					
		Stranger	Father	Mother	Same Sex Friend	Opposite Sex Friend	Untrusted Acquaintance
Opinions	1. Religion						
	2. Communism						
	3. Integration						
	4. Sex Standards						
	5. Social Standards						
Taste & Interests	1. Food						
	2. Music						
	3. Reading						
	4. TV & Movies						
	5. Parties						
Work (Studies)	1. Handicaps						
	2. Assets						
	3. Ambitions						
	4. Career Choice						
	5. Associates						
Money	1. Income						
	2. Debts						
	3. Savings						
	4. Needs						
	5. Budget						
Personality	1. Handicaps						
	2. Self Control						
	3. Sex Life						
	4. Guilt/Shame						
	5. Pride						
Body	1. Facial Feelings						
	2. Ideal Appearance						
	3. Body Adequacy						
	4. Illnesses						
	5. Sexual Adequacy						

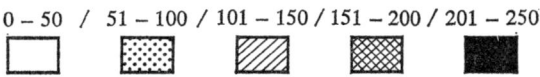

0 – 50 / 51 – 100 / 101 – 150 / 151 – 200 / 201 – 250

Figure 8. Summary of topic, target, and level of disclosure: United States

to which the self is shared in conversation: among Japanese, the "public self" appears to constitute a smaller proportion of the total self and among Americans, a larger proportion of the total self.

NONVERBAL SELF DISCLOSURE

For every human being the earliest form of communication with the world is through touch. It may well remain one of his primary means of expression and of linkage with other persons. A vast range of meaning can be conveyed through physical contact alone. The ultimate hostile act is, of course, a physical one. But so is the ultimate intimacy. Fighting and sexual intercourse represent only the extremes on a scale of expressiveness that includes an infinity of subtle feelings.

The amount of physical contact appears to be a sensitive barometer of interpersonal distance. Enemies rarely approach each other closely, and any contact is limited to destructive acts. Strangers, too, usually stand at some distance, avoiding all but ritualized forms of touching. Among acquaintances there is somewhat greater ease and spontaneity, while close friends are often visually identifiable because of their unusual physical responsiveness to each other. The more comfortable people are with each other the more one expects them to communicate by physical as well as verbal means.

Toward so potent a form of self-disclosure, cultures naturally adopt radically different attitudes. A substantial number of the most critical norms in every culture focuses on whom one can touch, when one can touch, and what one can touch. No matter how expressive a child is physically, he is soon trained to control these impulses. Casual observation alone would lead to the suspicion that people raised in Japan and the United States are exposed to different rules regarding physical contact.

The object of this research was to substitute hard fact for impressionistic description, to determine more precisely the character of nonverbal interaction in Japan and the United States. How frequently do members of these cultures touch each other? Whom do they touch or avoid touching? What areas of the body are involved in such contacts?

The Nonverbal Inventory used to collect data on patterns of interpersonal contact was adapted from Jourard's Body Accessibility Questionnaire (1966). Each person is asked to examine diagrams which reproduce front and rear views of the human body which are sectioned off into twenty-four numbered areas. Each respondent is asked to indicate whether he has "touched" or "been touched" by his father, mother, same sex friend, or opposite sex friend. By revealing areas of contact and avoidance and by indicating persons with whom the respondent has or avoids contact, the results provide profiles of physical accessibility within cultures.

There is evidence that both cultures sharply differentiate between areas of permitted and proscribed contact. There is also agreement on what specific parts of the body belong in each category. The regions of highest physical contact in both cultures include the hand, shoulder, forehead, back of neck, back of head, and forearm. Areas of avoidance include the front pelvic region, rear pelvic region, rear thigh, and leg.

In both cultures the same hierarchy of persons is involved in nonverbal contact: Japanese and Americans report their highest contact with opposite sex friend, next with mothers, next with same sex friends, and finally with fathers. However, there are some differences within this broad grouping. Where Japanese treat opposite sex friends as only somewhat more eligible than mothers or same sex friends, Americans treat opposite sex friends as considerably more attractive; where Americans treat fathers with nearly the same degree of physical intimacy they manifest with same sex friends, Japanese interact dramatically less with fathers than with other target persons. There is also remarkable consistency between "touching" and "being touched." In both Japan and the United States initiating and receiving physical contact co-varies: a higher or lower frequency of touching is accompanied by a higher or lower frequency of being touched. Males in both cultures report slightly more "touching" contact with the opposite sex, while females report a somewhat higher incidence of "being touched."

Although distinctions in nonverbal expressiveness WITHIN the cultures reveal considerable similarity between Japanese and Americans, there is a dramatic contrast between the cultures with regard to the extent of physical communication reported (Figures 9 and 10). In nearly every category the amount of physical contact reported by Americans is twice that reported by Japanese. Although Americans indicate slightly less than double the bodily contact with their mothers, they show more than triple the amount with their fathers as do Japanese. Physical contact is reported more than twice as often by Americans with the opposite sex as well.

Again reference to individual cases imparts some sense of the significance of these findings. The most striking instances are found among

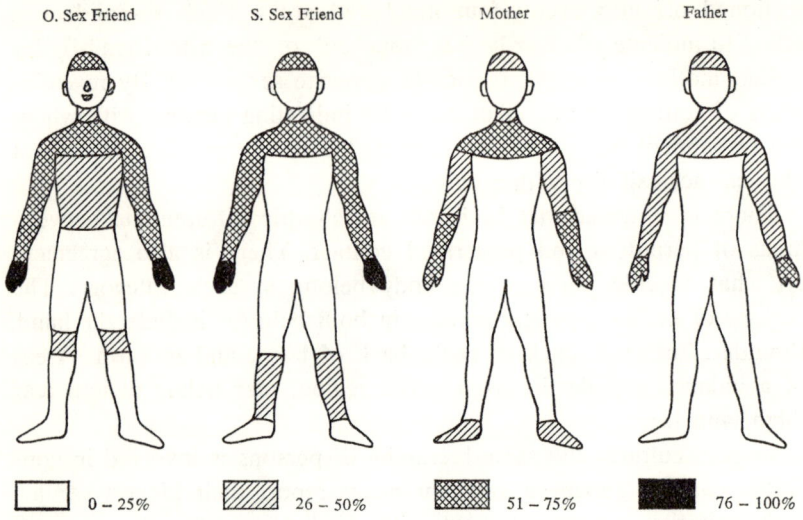

Figure 9. Physical contact: Japan

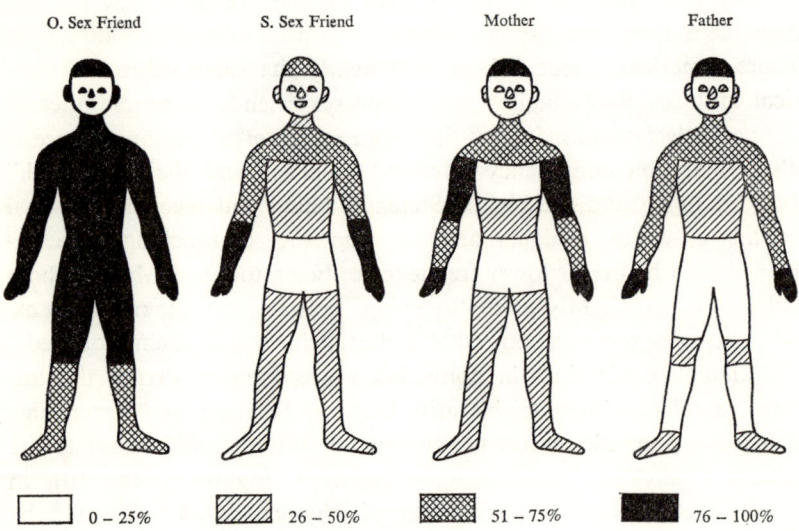

Figure 10. Physical contact: United States

the Japanese. Among the 120 persons who comprised the Japanese sample are several dozens who report very limited physical contact with any acquaintance of any kind. Among these there are a number who report no physical contact whatsoever after the age of fourteen, either with one parent or with same or opposite sex friend. Several reported they could never remember any contact with their fathers, and there are a few cases of almost total isolation even from peers. Among Americans there are no instances of this sort. All had physical contact with one or both parents and friends of one or both sexes. There were cases of relative isolation but none approaching the extremes found among Japanese. With Americans, the extreme was in the opposite direction: Most students reported physical contact with an opposite sex friend in all areas of the body, and many indicated contact in at least two-thirds of the areas with the same sex friend and with mother and/or father.

There is strong evidence here of cultures differentially enforcing norms that regulate physical communication in interpersonal relationships. Americans appear to be more physically accessible and more physically expressive to mothers, fathers, same sex friends, and opposite sex friends. The widest discrepancy exists with regard to fathers; Japanese report only a third as much touching behavior with them as do Americans. Apparently, the intense physical intimacy that characterizes infancy in both cultures takes a different course in later childhood, and by adulthood results in wide cultural differences with regard to the communication of self through physical contact.

Two quite opposite interpretations might be made of this contrast: perhaps the atrophying of this channel of communication is evidence of "growing up," of passing through no more than an infantile stage on the way to communicative maturity through words; or it may represent the curtailing of an indispensable channel that limits the capacity for empathy and intimacy. At any rate the picture of nonverbal communication obtained lends further support for the hypothesized differences in communicative style. Physically, as well as verbally, the Japanese appear to disclose less of themselves, manifesting a more limited "public self," while Americans appear to disclose more of themselves, manifesting a more extensive "public self."

DEFENSE AGAINST DISCLOSURE OF SELF

In the face of messages that challenge or threaten their private view of the world of or themselves, one might expect Japanese and Americans to favor different defensive tactics. For the Japanese it is hypothesized that the dominant communicative strategy should be one of "passive withdrawal," that though there may be variety in the content and form of their reaction, the latent psychological theme will be to avoid further exposure of their views, reduce involvement with others, and attempt to withdraw from further interaction. Americans, in the face of disturbing messages, should be predisposed to different defensive reactions. Here the underlying communicative strategy should be one of "active aggression," in which threat will be met by increasing involvement, further elaboration of beliefs, and aggressive reply to those who challenge core beliefs.

A Defensive Strategy Scale was developed that would differentiate between levels of threat, specify a wide range of possible sources of threat, and provide a spectrum of different types of defensive response. The instrument provides for reactions to low and high levels of interpersonal threat and identifies target persons who are older and younger, superior and subordinate, same and opposite sex, admired and not admired, mother and father, closest same and opposite sex friend, and stranger. The defensive messages include fourteen frequently reported reactions to threat: (1) remain silent, (2) act as if I didn't hear, (3) show nonverbally I preferred not to answer, (4) hint verbally I preferred not to answer, (5) laugh, (6) change the subject, (7) reply in abstract or ambiguous language, (8) ask others what they think, (9) say I did not want to discuss it, (10) try to talk my way out of the situation, (11) answer the remark directly, even though uncomfortable, (12) defend myself by explanation and argument, (13) use humor or sarcasm to put him in his place, and (14) tell him to mind his own business. Respondents were urged not to speculate about what they might do but to report what they had actually done in such encounters in the past.

The scale makes it possible to distinguish broadly between "passive" and "active" forms of interpersonal defense. Although the reactions that fall in the middle of the spectrum might be subject to alternative interpretations, the five that fall at either extreme would appear to be readily identified as passive or active. In the former, the person handles his anxiety by reducing involvement, disguising his reaction, or avoiding further participation. In the latter, he expresses himself more fully, extends and elaborates his position, risks deeper involvement, and may even counterattack those who threaten him.

When considerations of sex, traits of the target person, and intensity are set aside, the Japanese show considerable variety and less contrast among their defensive reactions than do Americans. They most frequently prefer to "say I did not want to discuss it," "hint verbally I preferred not to answer," and "remain silent." They rarely report "tell him to mind his own business," "use humor or sarcasm to put him in his place," or "defend myself by explanation and argument." With one exception the most favored replies are of the "passive" type, and without exception the least favored are "active." And this holds true generally for both low and high levels of threat.

A quite different pattern characterizes the reactions of Americans to the same circumstances. Here there is a sharp contrast in the defensive techniques they favor and reject. They prefer responding to threatening communications by using active forms such as "answer the remark directly, even though uncomfortable," "defend myself by explanation and argument," and "use humor and sarcasm to put him in his place." They least choose to "ask others what they think," "laugh," and "change the subject." The preference for active reaction to threat is striking with all five highest choices falling at the active end of the scale. Again the level of threat introduces no substantial difference in the response pattern.

Are there differences in the way males and females respond to threatening interpersonal situations? One would expect so. But the results do not indicate any substantial difference. Partly this is due to cultural differences overriding sexual ones. Americans distinguish so sharply between preferred and avoided defensive techniques that their scores overwhelm the less dramatic differences among the Japanese. But the expectation of large sex differences may be incorrect; to be born Japanese or American appears to be far more influential in determining communicative style than being born male or female.

Nor is there much evidence of adaptation to the source of threatening remarks. There is some tendency in that direction, especially among Japanese, but it is not a strong one. Japanese tend to favor different defenses for older and superior persons in contrast to younger and subordinate ones. They differentiate slightly between those they respect and do not respect. But essentially the same defenses are reported with mothers and fathers and with opposite and same sex friends. There is striking consistency in defensive communication among Americans. The same defensive tactics are employed with everyone, regardless of status, sex, power, or relationship.

There are, of course, individual differences. Some persons rely almost exclusively upon two or three kinds of defensive messages. In the case of the Japanese, it was often a preference for remaining silent, laughing, replying ambiguously, or preferring to talk about something else. Among Americans there were those who relied heavily upon sarcasm, talked their way out of the situation, or defended themselves by argument. Yet others reported using nearly every form of defense under some social circumstance. Some respondents differentiated little between low and high levels of threat, but others chose from an almost entirely different repertoire of messages, depending on the intensity of anxiety.

Cultural factors would appear to complicate the interpretation of the findings on defensive behavior. There are cultural differences in the concept of threat and particularly in the meaning of evasion. The American cannot understand why his Japanese associate gives such puzzling answers to such simple questions; the Japanese cannot understand how his American associate can give such glib answers to such puzzling questions.

It would appear, too, that the Japanese are among the most diligent of peoples in preventing the occurrence of embarrassing or threatening confrontations. Formalizing human relationships is a way of neutralizing differences and intercepting conflicts that might prove disturbing. Preserving harmony appears to be a cardinal virtue within Japanese society (Embree 1939; Halloran 1969; Maraini 1965). Americans, largely as a consequence of a fuller expression of inner reactions, are more likely to be exposed to threatening encounters. In short, one culture may cope with interpersonal anxiety by carefully managing conversations so that threatening situations rarely occur. The other may cultivate skill in coping with such situations because they seem inevitable or even desirable.

Finally there are linguistic and stylistic differences in speech that complicate the analysis of defensive behavior. The restricted use and availability of personal pronouns in Japanese may reduce the degree of personal involvement. The lack of number and gender, along with restrictions in tense, may make for less precise identification of referents. Greater verbal ambiguity, of course, cuts two ways communicatively: it makes assertion more dangerous because one cannot know the precise meaning assigned a remark by the receiver, and it makes every reply partly defensive by obscuring the intended meaning it contains.

Habits of language usage also may contribute to the reduction of interpersonal friction in Japan. The ubiquitous use of "ne" and "yo" may have the effect of softening or blunting the abrasive edge of bold assertions. The high frequency with which "ka" appears in conversation, transforming declarative statements into questions, may also change the temper of discussion. Conversation proceeds not by negation or contradiction as in the West, but by affirmation where the speaker seeks continual confirmation and approval from the listener. Talk becomes a means of seeking areas of consensus rather than a process of identifying differences.

Yet there remains substantial evidence of a cultural difference in defensive behavior. Regardless of the social circumstances, Americans prefer to defend themselves actively, exploring and developing the rationale for positions they have taken. When pushed, they may resort to still more aggressive forms that utilize humor, sarcasm, or denunciation. Among Japanese the reactions are more varied, but defenses tend to be more passive, permit withdrawal, and allow greater concealment. Rejected defensive modes in both cultures provide an even clearer picture. Japanese tend to avoid active and aggressive tactics in meeting threat, while Americans consistently avoid passive forms of defense. Where the Japanese may ritualize encounters to avoid the triggering of threat, Americans may find such situations an inevitable consequence of their greater expressiveness.

REFLECTIONS

At the outset, a proposition was formulated to guide inquiry into the communicative behavior of Japanese and Americans. This proposition was that the proportion of inner experience that was shared with others, the public self, and that was not shared, the private self, differ in these two nations. The first hypothesis derived from this was that the Japanese would prefer to converse with fewer people and with greater selectivity, while Americans would interact more widely and with less discrimination. This was not tested directly but there is indirect support of it in the findings. Americans, it was found, communicate at deeper levels both verbally and nonverbally with all their associates than do Japanese.

The second hypothesis was that Japanese should prefer more regulated and Americans more spontaneous forms of communication. Here, too, the evidence is indirect, but the cultural profiles suggest that such is the case. Japanese described themselves and are described as "formal," "reserved," "cautious," and "evasive," while the most common adjectives attributed to Americans are "frank," "self assertive," "informal," and "talkative." It would be difficult to identify profiles that would be more compatible with preferences for regulated or for spontaneous conversation.

With regard to level of verbal disclosure the cultures differ sharply.

Japanese rarely talk in more than "general terms" on any topic to any person, while Americans disclose on all topics and to all persons at significantly deeper levels, often approaching full and complete disclosure. The cultures differ sharply, too, on the extent to which they encourage or discourage physical expressiveness. Touching behavior is reported nearly twice as often in all categories and with all persons by Americans as by Japanese. It would appear that where one culture severely limits physical communication, the other encourages it as a legitimate form of interaction.

When interpersonal threat occurs, it appears that both cultures respond by employing forms of defense that are consistent with their prevailing communicative style. Japanese prefer to reduce involvement, to withdraw from interaction, and to withhold further disclosure of self. Americans, consistent with their more expressive style, prefer defenses that permit continued involvement and further disclosure. Thus, there is strong if not conclusive evidence of cultural divergence in coping with anxiety-arousing conversations. Practical limitations prevented any exploration of the hypothesis that these cultural differences would tend to limit the degree and accuracy of self-knowledge among Japanese and permit wider and more accurate self-knowledge among Americans.

Having come this far in identifying cultural styles, what are the further implications of these findings? In what way do such communicative patterns frustrate or enlarge human potentials? In what way do these styles promote more or less accurate communication? Toward what social pathologies do they tend when carried to extremes? Although extremely hazardous and unavoidably controversial, it is relevant to probe such questions.

What are the psychic consequences of the personality structures each culture imposes? Will the Japanese, expressing inner meanings less often and less deeply, become less known to themselves and to each other? If thoughts and feelings are continually inhibited is there risk of driving them irretrievably into the unconscious? Conversely, will repeated opportunities for fuller expression contribute to greater self-knowledge? In short, is expression of the self essential to growth of the self? Or does confining areas of expression limit psychic development?

In infancy, of course, there is no private or public self, there is only an undivided self. Whatever is experienced is announced. Yet every culture cultivates some distance, some formality, and some dishonesty in human affairs; by adulthood an inner split is accomplished and the self is compartmentalized. This division, necessary or not, is bought at a price. It takes considerable psychic energy to monitor reactions continuously, carefully segregating what must be concealed from what can be shared. This inner guardedness makes it difficult for men to experience events deeply and makes them suspicious of their own reactions. They must continually guard their own lives, sensitively forecasting reactions to each word or gesture, censoring those that may be disapproved. The result is not only to alienate men from each other but from themselves as well.

There is reason to believe that restrictions on expression may limit psychic development. A self appears to develop best through experience, the wider and deeper the better. But experiences do not acquire meaning except through symbolic transformations, and this may best be stimulated through attempts to share it with others. Some forms of mental retardation appear to result from living in environments that discourage self-expression. Gifted people — artists, poets, scientists — seem to experience both inner and outer worlds most abundantly, and this may be linked to more frequent and fuller self-expression.

Studies of human interaction from casual encounters to therapeutic ones seem to reinforce this view. Goffman (1961: p. 41) notes that "there seems to be no agent more effective than another person in bringing a world for oneself alive, or by a glance, a gesture, or a remark, shriveling up the reality in which one is lodged." It appears to be the challenge of deep verbal involvement with another person that also aids therapeutic recovery. Takeo Doi, one of Japan's leading psychiatrists, has commented on the extent to which his patients seem to possess "no self."

Yet many spokesmen of Eastern cultures would dispute this emphasis on self-expression. They would argue that men arrive at a more sensitive, more complete, and more individualistic experience of the world and of themselves through contemplation and introspection. Is silence any less effective a route into the interior of man than speech? Can externalizing every thought and feeling diminish rather than extend the dimensions of the self?

Or perhaps the two views are reconcilable: one valuing private reflection and one valuing a full sharing of inner reactions. Both seem essential and may combine in the communicatively mature person. Here there is a capacity for private reflection that is neither a defensive retreat nor a repression of response and a capacity for self-expression that is neither an aggressive confrontation nor a compulsive drive for attention.

Next, how do these communicative styles complicate or facilitate interpersonal understanding? If the cultures of the world could be placed along a disclosure gradient, neither Japan nor the United States might occupy the extreme ends, but there would be a wide gap separating them. There is evidence both of greater superficiality of contact and of greater interpersonal isolation in one culture compared to the other. How does this affect the quality of communication?

Even when men earnestly and honestly seek to understand each other, there are immense obstacles to this achievement. Each occupies a world of his own and brings to every conversation different assumptions, backgrounds, and motives. No two people perceive alike even within a single culture. And the words they employ to bridge this experiential divide are vague and diffuse in meaning. But these intrinsic difficulties are compounded when conversational partners do not even permit themselves to be known. Each presents, in part at least, a facade; what is felt is not expressed, what is believed is not reported. The messages are no longer clues to meaning but are consciously manipulated to camouflage meaning. If communication is difficult when people express themselves authentically, imagine the complications when they do not even attempt this. Concealment of self does not merely prevent understanding, it encourages misunderstanding. Even if one succeeds in grasping what has been said, it may be only a contrived public self that he understands, not the real or private self.

Yet differences in cultural styles may have still another communicative consequence. To share an experience involves not only encoding or symbolizing that experience but the decoding or the comprehension of such symbolization. The effect of encouraging such traits as "talkativeness" and "self assertion" among Americans may be the cultivation of a highly self-oriented and sensitive transmitter of meaning, while the effect of encouraging such traits as "caution" and "reserve" among Japanese may be the cultivation of a highly other-oriented and sensitive receiver of meaning. A kind of communicative specialization occurs, so that what one society does well, namely listening, the other society may do poorly; and what the other society does well, namely speaking, the former society may do less effectively.

Speculations concerning the larger social consequences of these cultural differences are the most hazardous of all. The Japanese appear to place the highest value on preserving the harmony of the group, on meeting role expectations. There is greater respect for silent introspection, less for public eloquence. Words are somewhat suspect, and the expression of feelings, particularly negative ones, is avoided. Relations appear to be more superficial and more governed by social convention. Among Americans the highest value lies in preservation of individual integrity. Conforming is a form of psychic suicide. Strength comes from the capacity to stand alone or even against the group. Actualizing oneself is the primary aim. There is less respect for private reflection and more for public eloquence. The ability to express oneself in a compelling way is highly prized.

Each of these communicative styles appears to carry its own destructive potential. The denial of selfhood, or abdication of it in favor of social harmony, can dangerously encourage conformity. A submissive self is prerequisite to a dominated self; authoritarian control might appear the ultimate destiny of a self-denying culture. Yet the opposite consequence may contain equal risk. Where priority is always granted the individual, where self-expressive acts are unrestrained by considerations of others, the outcome is not alienation from self, but from others. A society of private individuals, each preoccupied with his own self-expression, reduces to no society at all.

CONCLUSION

The "universe of discourse" in Japan and the United States — the form and content of daily interaction — appears to differ in significant respects. What people talk about and to whom they talk, what parts of the body they touch and whom they touch, seem consistent from one culture to another. But the depth of verbal disclosure and the degree of physical intimacy that is cultivated differ sharply. Patterns for coping with threatening social encounters also take different forms. Through all these symbolic activities, verbal and nonverbal, there appears a recurrent theme: individuals in one culture are encouraged to share less of their personal experience with significant other people, while individuals in the other culture are encouraged to communicate a larger portion of their private thoughts and feeling. Such differences in modes of communication carry with them serious psychic, interpersonal, and social consequences for both the individuals and the cultures.

REFERENCES

BENEDICT, R.
1946 *The chrysanthemum and the sword.* Boston: Houghton Mifflin.

DOI, L. T.
1962 "Amae: a key concept for understanding Japanese personality structure," in *Japanese culture: its development and characteristics.* Edited by R. J. Smith and R. K. Beardsley. Chicago: Aldine.
1972 Remarks to Japan Society for the Promotion of Science Seminar, Tokyo, Japan.

EMBREE, J.
1939 *Suye Mura: a Japanese village.* Chicago: University of Chicago Press.

GOFFMAN, E.
1961 *Encounters: two studies in the sociology of interaction.* Indianapolis: Bobbs-Merrill.

HALLORAN, R.
1969 *Japan: images and realities.* Tokyo: Tuttle.

JOURARD, S.
1966 An exploratory study of body-accessibility. *British Journal of Social and Clinical Psychology.* 5:221–231.

JOURARD, S., P. LASAKOW
1958 Some factors in self-disclosure. *Journal of Abnormal and Social Psychology* 56:91–98.

MOLONEY, J.
1954 *Understanding the Japanese mind.* New York: Philosophical Library.

MARAINI, F.
1965 *Meeting with Japan.* New York: Viking Press.

NAKAMURA, H.
1964 *Ways of thinking of Eastern peoples.* Honolulu: East-West Press.

NAKANE, C.
1970 *Japanese society.* Berkeley: University of California Press.

WAGATSUMA, H.
1969 Major trends in social psychology in Japan. *American Behavioral Scientist* 12:36–45.

Culture-Style Factors in Face-to-Face Interaction

ALAN LOMAX

Many of the patterns described in this account are not face-to-face interaction in the strict sense. They were first discovered in comparative studies of song and dance performance, both of which are, essentially, ways of addressing an audience at a distance. Yet when the three systems — singing, dancing and speaking — were examined cross-culturally their main structures turned out to be so similar that they seemed to be reflections of each other. The main factors found in the three systems have similar functions. They seem to co-vary across the main cultural boundaries. They are intercorrelated in strikingly similar ways, and are often correlated to the same features of social structure. All this points to the existence of a system I have termed "expressive communication style," which shapes all the particular interactional modes to a common model within a given cultural frame. Indeed, I have come to feel that it is this generalized styling model that produces the remarkable continuities anthropologists call culture. These style models underlie the patterns of timing, of interpersonal synchrony that are essential to communication. Because such patterns stand out more clearly in highly rhythmic behavior, such as song and dance, their analysis becomes extremely helpful in sorting out the less clearly redundant patterns of conversation or face-to-face interaction. Seen in this light, the qualities of speaking style, which are usually treated as idiosyncratic or transient, turn out to be stable indicators of the social and cultural attachments of language.

It is not really unreasonable that stylistic factors should turn out to be more stable than content in communication. The style of singing, moving, or speaking characterizes the steady flow of the streams of interaction into which content is set. The child learns early to respond to different patterns of action from his parents — to handling, to rhythmic games, to being fed and talked to. The tone of the parent's communication is clear before the words. In growth, the baby can coo, bounce and babble in the mode of his culture tradition long before he can handle its linguistic or kinesic grammar and its vocabulary. There seems to be little question that the child learns the basic tempi, rhythms, and synchronic baselines of its culture very early, perhaps in the womb. Moreover, it seems as if the baby must quickly acquire some principle traits of behavior STYLE in order to elicit the most favorable response from parents, and to be responded to warmly as a member of the group.

The observations now to be reported in summary form are at the macro rather than micro level. The intention was to deal with the gross, continuous signal system, learned in childhood, by means of which culture members declare their coidentity and around which they can synchronize their coaction in work, dance, or song teams. The search was at the macrokinesic, the macrolinguistic level — a realm which I believe will concern sociolinguistics increasingly, because it is here that the grosser measures of cultural and societal science can be matched by those of linguistics. It is here, therefore, that hypotheses concerning the relation of communication and social structure can most readily be framed, tested, and checked cross-culturally. It seems to me that, without a cross-cultural test frame, the general application of theories of linguistics must always remain in question, just as do many of those in psychology.

Partly because I was the first in the field, my research method was a sort of rough-and-ready natural history approach. Small samples of recorded behavior, representing the whole human range of singing, dancing, and speaking, were separately analyzed to find those criteria which both described and differentiated each corpus. These criteria were scaled and set down in teaching tapes or film loops and rating protocols. Larger sets of data were then analyzed by teams of trained coders, using the rating schemes. Interrater consensus is more than 80 percent for the speech and song systems; the movement rating consensus seems good but has not yet been formally measured. The numerical results were punched and factor analyzed. Each rating system was reduced to a small set of homogeneous factors, which were clearly analogous to each other — there were factors in each set dealing with: (1) discrimination and information rate, (2) level and kind of interpersonal coordination, (3) energy and meter, and (4) spacing.[1] Recently,

[1] Only (1) and (2) are dealt with in this paper.

Table 1. Discrimination factors

Social structure

Low economic stability	High economic stability
Low stratification and political centralization	High stratification and political centralization
Low general nutrition	High general nutrition
Roots, pigs, little fishing	Grain, large animals, fishing
Low dairying	High dairying
Permissive premarital sex sanctions	Severe premarital sex sanctions
Simple and loose work teams	Complex and tight work teams

Song performance

Low differentiation (text repeats and slurred enunciation, large intervals)	High differentiation
Low ornamentation	High ornamentation
Brief, simple melodic form	Long complex melodic form
Low energy (volume, stress)	High energy
Group performance	Solo performance
Simple and diffuse orchestral organization	Complex and integrated orchestral organization

Dance performance

Low foot, arm, hand articulation	High articulation
Low posed body parts	High posed body parts
One dimensional motion	Two–three-dimensional motion
Heavy	Light
Low fluidity	High fluidity
Simple form organization	Complex form organization
Low dynamics (strength, speed, acceleration)	High dynamics
Low multiunits	High multiunits

*Speaking style**

High repetition	Low repetition
Short speech segments	Long speech segments
High noise (harshness, nasality)	Low noise
High breathy, clipping, softening	Low breathy, clipping, softening
Stable timing	Variable timing
Low upglides	High upglides
Phonotactic*	

*Phonotactic**

Low total number of contoid types	High total number of contoid types
Low contoid discriminators (mid stops, nasals, and fricatives)	High contoid discriminators
<50 c/v proportion	>50 c/v proportion
High uvular contoids	Low uvular contoids

* For details of methods and results see Lomax 1973, i.p.

these sets of factors have been intercorrelated to determine their overlap and their intercorrelation with factors derived similarly from the Murdock *Ethnographic atlas* and representing some of the main aspects of social structure. More than 500 interesting relationships with chi squares at the more than .05 level and more than 300 at the more than .01 level have been found. The complex web of these interrelationships can only be sketched in this presentation. One convenient way is to group them under the main headings just mentioned (Table 1).

A linguist accustomed to the apparent leanness of binary analysis initially might be repelled at the seeming formlessness of the tangles of correlations herewith presented. But there are principles at work through them, which, if once viewed, will make them more attractive.

First, there is intersystem symmetry. Control, articulation, productivity, information load — these are the core patterns of all these intertwined correlations; the overall outcome is system control leading to increased productivity. Increases in productive range are accompanied by more nourishing foodstuff; populations and administrative systems increase; more words, ornaments, and intervals appear in song; more body parts are articulated and dimensions exploited in movement; more text in longer segments with a more varied delivery characterize conversation; and there seems to be more phonetic articulation in more types of consonants, especially in the frontal stops and fricatives.

The other face of this idea is increase of control of — the natural environment by technology; the social environment through regulation and centralization of authority; music through melodic elaboration, solo dominance, and complex orchestrations; dance through lightness, sustainment, and fluidity of movement along complex pathways, or through formal timed arrangements for relation of dancers; dialogue through elimination of noise and breathiness and the introduction of empathetic signals like upgliding, laughter, cooing and the like to make the long speech segments of complex economies socially and psychologically acceptable. In a gross sense all the channels in Set I (Discrimination) can be used as substitutes for one another to communicate the same things. Every culture can express its level of socioeconomic complexity in a different manner.

One other attractive aspect of these correlations is that they put us directly in touch with the social dynamics of communication, at a level we all can feel and yet at the same time reason about. The social scientist and the linguist can join forces here. For example, all the factors in Set I seem to have an evolutionary character. Their shift from low to high, from left to right, on the diagram marks an increase in human control over the environment or a symbolic reinforcement of such an achievement. Taken all together in relation to a scheme of world culture types, they show that the socioeconomy has been evolving steadily from the time of the gatherers to the present, growing steadily more productive and, at the same time, more articulated. Figures 1 and 2 illustrate this point in the parallel of the two graphs that rise steadily from left to right, from the least productive to the most productive economies. In the top graph one sees the factors of song and culture style combined. Below, only the evolution of movement style is depicted. The curved lines on each graph trace the course of parts of Set II, the integration pattern, which I will come to a little later.

Looking at all these correlations as a clump has its advantages, but it obscures the evolutionary detail that gives each feature its special significance. It's like looking down on the earth from outer space: everything, even the highest mountain, is flattened out by a perspective, in this case, of fifteen or twenty thousand years of time. Let me give you one or two of the details that I have had the time and the perspective to see.

1. Song texts and conversations grow steadily less repetitious and songs carry a heavier load of new text and finely articulated sounds. Repetition functions: to fix important items in the memory by groups with neither bards nor books; to unify groups where social bonds are light — repeats, echo, and slurring (or dropping consonants) permit easy coparticipation of those present. All these functions tend to lose their importance as society acquires specialists and mnemonic devices; individuals become socially, then legally, tied to sodalities, and reinforcement through active participation is replaced by acquisition of complex and precise messages from specialists.

2. Movement path shifts from push-pull linear, among simple producers, to curving two- or three-dimensional movement among more complex producers, reflecting the change from simple brittle-edged tools with which man had to poke or break his way straight through things to metal tools which enabled him to slash in curving paths and accommodate the direction of each stroke to the changing nature of the task. Early man used whole limbs to transmit force in a straight line and without loss to the point of impact; complex tools enabled man to fully use joint articulation in accommodating points and edges to finer and more indirect action paths.

3. In our much sketchier language studies there are two dramatic shifts along this scale: a sharp drop of vocal noise (harsh, nasal, breathy sounds) on the scale from extractive, to gardening, and then agricultural

economies; a parallel shift in the proportion of the noisier back consonants to the quieter and more finely enunciated front, and especially, mid-consonants. The background noise has dropped and at the same time finer and more numerous distinctions appear in the languaging stream. The evidence offered is less, indeed, but I feel there is an important truth here, one which needs to be proved out with more detailed phonotactic study.

Perhaps by now my fellow sociolinguists will be asking themselves what does all this talk of long-term tendencies have to do with us, with the data available from the social surroundings? Because the traits measured occur with some frequency in all culture areas and because so many of the communication styles of our species encounter each other in our multicultural land, I believe these style tendencies are relevant indeed. Let me give one or two familiar examples — with the reminder that a major cultural pattern seldom disappears unless its carriers are exterminated — combination, restatement, being more familiar.

One of the most striking features of such early black gospel singers like Sister Rosetta Tharpe back in the late thirties, was a shift away from the consonantal slurring of the older spirituals to a highly enunciated, rather finicky style in which sounds were articulated more sharply than in standard American. The same tendency was evident among the calypso singers of Trinidad, who not only outdid their ex-masters in enunciation but in the use of recondite, polysyllabic, and complexly woven texts. The sermons, songs, and conversational styles encountered at the banquet table of Father Divine showed the same tendency — increase of articulation in an urbanizing group. During the heyday of the black power movement, one of the most notable features of conversation was its underscored enunciation, accompanied by a concern to spell out in detail and verbally what every relationship consisted of socially.

The changes I chanced to observe in rock-and-roll texts further underscore this point. When young white singers first took to the genre, they sang brief, repetitious melodies, like their black models. With the entrance of the Beatles, Dylan, and other rock imitators, the texts and melodic forms suddenly became long and elaborate, as well as introspective, in true European fashion. Then there was a period that I remember with horror, when very complex texts, full of veiled references to drugs and revolt and other forbidden subjects, were so obscured by the background that only the initiated could tell what was being sung. Out of this blurring of all texts, the blacks have recently emerged as the true masters of rock — singing repetitous texts, with somewhat more sharp-edged enunciation than before, but something of the old slurring as well. At about the same time, in the cross-acculturative process, first young people and then a large segment of the society adopted black conversational mannerisms — not only vocabulary, but repeats of key words for emphasis, echoing, and a preference for interchanges in which no one holds the floor for too long. This trend seems to be waning.

I hope my readers will forgive my failure to document these observations of recent trends. I chose them to illustrate the contemporary pertinence of the general style models in our findings. What they suggest, for one thing, is cross-acculturation between the vigorously surviving African gardener, groupy, repetitious style in the black ghetto and the more articulated style prevalent in Euro-American tradition. Blacks, undergoing city influence, found finer articulations appropriate. The whites were meeting blacks half-way, but perhaps were also attracted to the integrative aspects of black style as their own collective experiences became more frequent in high schools, large offices, factories, army training, and so on. In their first period of encounter the white kids organized into gangs, clans, and communes, and "group" dependency began to replace the old West European ideal of the self-sufficient individual. My guess is that the African tradition in its Southern American incarnation then provided some of the patterns that were needed.

Perhaps another longer-term trend is indicated — the interplay of the two general tendencies I have discovered in the study of communication style. The first of these has been discussed — an increase in articulation accompanies, supports, and reinforces increasing productivity. The second general principle, which has been presented in various ways in earlier publications (Lomax 1967, 1968, 1972), is that each stage of economic development demands a different level and order of integration to reinforce the kind of teamwork most required. Shifts in the sexual division of labor and the organization of work groups are reflected and reinforced in communication style. On the whole, where women play an equal part in the main food-producing activity, where they are in a complementary work relation to males, work teams and performance teams tend to be both cohesive and multileveled. In male-dominated socioeconomies teams tend to be diffuse or regimented.

Some of these shifts are displayed in the set of intertwined correlations that follow. Here, more than in Set I, all the states are not cumulative or sequential. As a matter of fact, if the reader will refer to

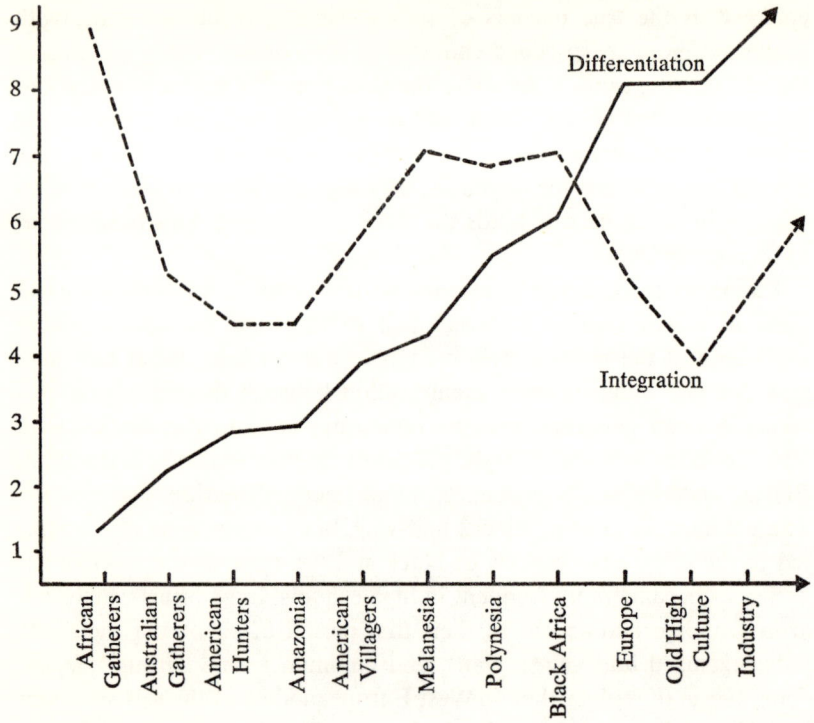

Figure 1. Evolutionary culture scale
The weighted means of the differentiative factor (solid line) and the integrative composite factor (broken line) are plotted along the evolutionary culture scale. These are the main factors from the 71 measures that were factored over the sample of 148 world cultures.
Reprinted from Lomax and Berkowitz (1972) by permission of the American Association for the Advancement of Science.

Figures 1 and 2, he will see that these changes occur in cyclic fashion. The highly complementary and integrated multileveled style of the African gatherers is succeeded by the male-dominated, unison style of the Australian gatherers (where a gerontocracy prevailed), and by a similar style heritage among the hunters and fishers and incipient producers of the Americas. As gardening, with its demand for feminine participation and for concerted group action, developed, there was a reemergence of cohesive, multileveled integration in song and dance performance. Large, horned draft animals, heavy plows, and irrigation gave the lone male again the center of the productive system, which he had held briefly during the hunting-fishing period.

A complex agricultural technology, with its accompanying lore, its dependence (particularly in riverine irrigation systems) on adherence

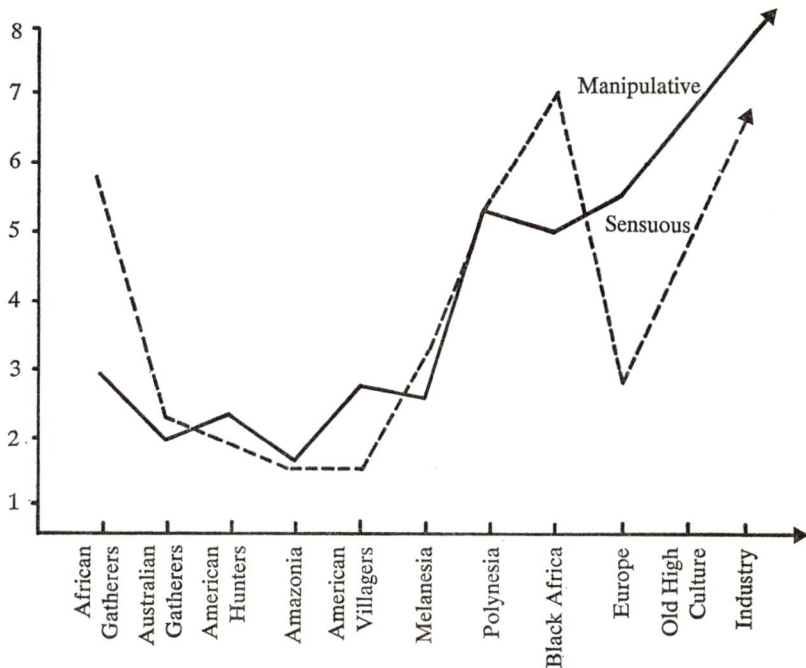

Figure 2. Evolutionary culture scale
The two main factors of the multifactor analysis of dance style are plotted along the evolutionary culture scale; 373 dance codings from 108 of the standard Murdock sample were used in this multifactor analysis.
Reprinted from Lomax and Berkowitz (1972) by permission of the American Association for the Advancement of Science.

to a calendar, increased the importance of the specialist and the centralized chain of command. All forms of expressive communication became far more highly articulated and focused on the individual. In the period of kingdoms and empires ornamentation became the mode, alongside elaborated forms of address — the language of court for example — and long, highly articulated forms such as through-composed melodies, ballets, and novels. With the coming of industry, women move back into the mainstream of production alongside the men. Figures 1 and 2 show what happens. Not only has differentiation risen along with productivity, but so have the integration factors in both systems. In music there has been a rise in the general popularity of big orchestras, choruses, and complex arrangements involving many technologists as well as musicians. Meanwhile, the whole world has adopted the erotic, pelvis-swinging model of Afro-America for social dancing. These remarks illustrate the predictive potential of the stylistic approach, though, of course, it is still in the tentative stage and subject to further testing. Table 2 shows the overall structure of the Integration Set whose effect on modern urban culture has just been discussed.

Perhaps the overarching tendency to be discerned in the left to right structure of the Integration set is the pile-up of "sociability" factors on the right. The individual in gardening societies generally lived all his life in a village, in daily, face-to-face contact with the same age-mates, work-team associates, ritual associates, and kin. The prosperity of these communities depended on the development of highly synchronous public behaviors, and one finds elaborations of such features in skills like polyphony, polyrhythms, coacceleration in verbal and dance contests, the high esteem given to communication skills of a sociable nature. The qualities are all contributory — gradual, successive, fluid, clearly marked metrically regular movement styles — wide and resonant vocalizing, gradual transitions between speakers and singers, and a generally empathetic style signaled in the body, by trunk articulation in body movement, by laughter, intoned vocal segregates, varied vocal stance, drawl in conversation, and in the phonotactic realm by lax vowels and a moderate use of consonantal discriminators.

The factors that will perhaps most interest the sociolinguist are those labeled "dominance-sharing" and "competitive." In the cross-cultural analysis of conversations, we scored (1) the frequency of interchange (or possession of the floor), (2) the frequency of brief interjected responses, (3) the frequency of murmured interjections in the background, (4) stretch dominance, i.e. the degree to which one speaker dominated. These came together in factor analysis in clusters I labeled DOMINANCE-SHARING (of the conversation space). Another cluster, which might be called the COMPETITIVE factor, was formed of scores on (1) the frequency of pauses between the two speakers, (2) the frequency of pauses within one speaker's segments, (3) the frequency of interventions (interruptions), (4) the continuousness of interchange.[2]

Conversations were thus characterized as competitive-continuous as against noncompetitive-spaced out. These two factors made it possible to characterize the interchange structure of the various traditions we studied in a very flexible and interesting way.

AFRICAN GATHERERS Highest score for sharing... interchange rate 100+ interchanges per minute, very frequent responsorial interjections,

[2] This scale runs: (1) interlocked, (2) overlapped, (3) continuous, and (4) spaced.

Table 2. Integration factors

Social structure
Low community solidarity	High community solidarity
Low complementarity	High complementarity
Low stable work teams	High stable work teams

Song style
Low choral cohesiveness	High choral cohesiveness
High noise (harsh, nasal, narrow voice)	Low noise
High irregular meters	High regular meters
High differentiation	Low differentiation
Low integration (solo, lead dominance)	Group, polyphony
Simple choral part organization	Complex part organization
Simple and diffuse orchestral organization	Complex and integrated orchestral organization

Dance style
Low articulation of trunk	High articulation of trunk
Low complex floor plan	High complex floor plan
Low dynamics pattern	High dynamics pattern
Segregation of group by age	Mixing groups by age
High foot, arm, hand articulation	Low foot, arm, hand articulation
Low foot sliding	High foot sliding
High posing	Low posing
Low act integration	High act integration
Low timing sync	High timing sync
Low fluidity	High fluidity

Dialogue
Dominance of conversation space	*Sharing of conversation space*
Low interchange frequency	High interchange frequency
Low interjected responses	High interjected responses
Low murmured interjections	High murmured interjections
Long stretches of one speaker	Short stretches of one speaker
Low competitive	*High competitive*
Many interspeaker pauses	Few interspeaker pauses
Speaker relations spaced out	Speaker relations continuous
Many intraspeaker pauses	Few intraspeaker pauses
Few interventions	Many interventions
Low gabble effect	High gabble effect
Low empathy Factor	*High empathy Factor**
Low laughter	High laughter
Low intoned vocal segregates	High intoned vocal segregates
Stable vocal role	Varied vocal role
High variation in timing	Low variation in timing
Syllables run together	Separated syllables

Phonotactic
Low mid front (ey), high back (u), labial contoids	High mid front (ey), high back (u), labial contoids
Low low central vocoid (ah)	High low central
High low front vowel (è, ae)	Low low front
Low mid back (oh)	High mid back

* The empathy factor, which is also correlated in Set I, actually seems to come into play in fairly agricultural economies such as in Africa, Polynesia, and Europe.

no murmured interjections, equal sharing of the floor with rapid, interlocked, equal speech bursts ... high competitive with absences of inter- and intraspeaker pauses, very frequent interventions, interlocking relationship and high gabble effect.

AMERICAN HUNTERS   Moderate dominance, low sharing ... fifteen or less interchanges per minute; moderately frequent responsorial interjections, absences of murmured interjections, A holds floor for long stretches with B moderately frequent ... *very low competitive,* moderately frequent interspeaker pauses, very frequent intraspeaker pauses, occasional attempted interventions, spaced-out relations between speakers, no gabble.

BLACK AFRICA   High sharing ... fifteen or more interchanges per minute, some responsorial interjections, very frequent murmured interjections, varied style of holding the floor with the sense of equal sharing in most social situations ... high level of competition with rare interspeaker pauses, some intraspeaker pauses, frequent attempted interventions; in sharing conversation space overlap is as frequent as continuousness, frequent gabble effect.

EUROPE   Moderate dominance, some sharing ... varied rate of interchange, some responsorial interjections, moderately frequent murmured interjection, main speaker frequently longer ... highly competitive, absence of interspeaker pauses, only occasional intraspeaker pauses, attempted interjections frequent; continuous relationship the rule and gabble present.

The working linguist will, of course, want much more detail than this, but not, perhaps, to convince him that style study can quickly pick out important generic tendencies which tie language to other aspects of culture. For example, there is the very high rate of social interaction discerned in Bushman and West African conversation, just at the stages along the evolutionary scale where it appeared in song and dance. There is the corresponding low score for much of Amerindian interaction. One has the feeling, listening, that the Amerindian mode we scored is highly suitable for oral briefing, for example, as a hunter carefully gives his fellows carefully spaced-out, point-to-point, maplike directions about the whereabouts of game — and they signal their understanding by grave interjections. One typical European speaking style features dominance of the floor by one speaker, with few sharp interjections, but many murmured interjections in the background, permitting the maximal dominance the specialist requires. Another, the cocktail party style, features few or no pauses, many attempted interruptions, and a continuous or overlapped relation between speakers that we scored as "gabble."

These three styles encounter each other in the United States. Their contrastive profiles in movement and conversation, drawn from the statistically distinctive numerical profiles derived by the computer, now follow.

An inspection of these highly generalized but diagnostic profiles, demonstrates again the way in which style analysis brings out the symmetry of communication systems. The basic style pattern found in speaking (and in singing) shows up as well in the movement style of the same tradition. We look forward to the day of a truly rich data coverage when we will be able to see how whole style systems respond to the pressures of varying situations and environments. Even at this crude, beginning phase, however, the dynamic aspects of this approach are clearly indicated. One might try to predict from these profiles where conflict and misapprehension might arise in interaction between carriers of these different style patterns. For example, do American Indians find whites a bit over refined and feminine, too fluid, too pushy, not sufficiently restrained, rather weak, and far too regimented for their taste? On the other hand, do blacks see whites as "square," stodgy, lacking in spontaneity, depth and warmth, as regimented and flat-voiced? Questions of this type, arising from comparison of the style profiles, can be answered and the questions checked. The predictive potential of the style analysis system can, I think, be improved with work. Its discovery on intersystem symmetry in expressive communication and of operational connections of style systems to social structures, if confirmed, opens up interesting possibilities for a communication science that could positively affect culture change.

REFERENCES

LOMAX, ALAN
    1967   The good and beautiful in folksong. *Journal of American Folklore* 80:213–235.
    1968   *Folk song style and culture.* With contributions by the cantometrics staff. American Association for the Advancement of Science Publication 88. Washington, D.C.: American Association for the Advancement of Science.
    1971   Choreometrics and ethnographic filmmaking. *Filmmakers Newsletter* 4(6).

1973 Cross cultural factors in phonological change. *Language in Society* 2:161–175. London.
i.p. Main factors in speaking style. *Language in Society*. London.

LOMAX, ALAN, NORMAN BERKOWITZ
1972 The evolutionary taxonomy of culture. *Science* 177:228–239.

MURDOCK, G. P.
1969 *Ethnographic atlas*. Pittsburgh: University of Pittsburgh Press.

UDY, STANLEY J.
1959 *Organization of work*. HRAF Press.

Culture-Style Factors in Face-to-Face Interaction   471

APPENDIX 1: MOVEMENT STYLE

	Amerindian	West Euro-American	Black Afro-American
Discrimination	*Very Low* Little or no peripheral light, three dimensional or variation much forearm, some erect	*Mid* Low peripheral, light, three-dimensional, high variation, very erect	*Low mid* Low peripheral, light, very low, three-dimensional, high variation bent posture
Square/curvy (Productivity)	*Very square* One piece central body, no successive, rigid or upright, much simultaneous, no two systems, one to five body parts, no central impulse, no curve, low fluidity, high linear, one beat, push-pull, emphatic accent, vertical steps	*Square* One piece central body, low successive, rigid or upright, marked simultaneity, no two systems, one to five body parts, absence central impulse, high curve, some fluidity, some linear, regular rhythm, low push-pull, follow-through accent, vertical and complex steps	*Curvy* Shoulder and trunk movement high successive, much twisting, low simultaneity, high two systems, eight to nine body parts, high central, high currency, very fluid, low linear, complex rhythm, low push-pull, complex stress, sliding step
Dynamics (Energy)	*Low mid* Little acceleration or speed, very strong, moderate	*Moderate* Moderate acceleration, moderate speed, moderate strength	*Very high* Very high acceleration, speed and strength
Stance (Energy)	*Nothing typical*, but 15° kneebend	*Narrow stance* Frequent 45° kneebend	*Wide open* Wide crotch, some lower some 30° kneebend
Cohesiveness (Integration)	*Very diffuse* Low coherence, timing rhythm, some adherence to formation	*Very cohesive* Very coherent, high rhythmic unity, mirror coordination of sides, marked strictness of formation	*Mid* Some coherence, unison, high rhythmic cohesion, much mirroring, low formation coherence
Touching (Spacing)	Low	Low	Some
Vertical shifts (Energy)	Little or none	Unclear	Much plunging
Orchestra (Spacing)	Somewhat independent	Related but somewhat separate	Integrated and part of

APPENDIX 2: SPEAKING STYLE

	Amerindian	West Euro-American	Black African
Repetition (Productivity)	Some repeats, some echo	Little or no repeats or echo	Some repeats little echo
Speech length	Longest burst 3-3.5 seconds	Longest burst 8 seconds	Varied
Timing, patterned and varied (Spacing)	Some varied	Some patterning	Unclear
Empathy (Integration and productivity)	*Low* Little or no humorous tone or laughter, or intoned vocal seg, stable vocal stance and role relation, abrupt transitions	*Moderate* Little humorous tone or laughter, moderately changing vocal stance and role relation, neither abrupt nor gradual transitions	*High* Humorous, some intoned vocal segments, varied vocal stance and role relation, some gradual transitions
Drawl and pitch (Integration)	Little or no drawl, little differentiated pitch	Some drawl, some differentiated use of pitch	Marked drawl, many high notes
Crowded/ spaced out	*Spaced Out* Many pauses in speech and between speakers, few interventions, little gabble	*Very Crowded* Few pauses, continuous between speakers, frequent interventions, gabble	*Crowded and Spaced Out* Integration, many pauses, between speakers, many interventions, much gabble
Dominance sharing (Integration)	Low interchange rate, main speaker longer and more frequent, supportive interjections, no murmured interjections	Occasional murmured interjections	Supportive, many murmured interjections
Noise and tension (Spacing)	*Low Tension* Marked breathiness and harshness	Excited and fast, some harshness, low nasality	Loud, slow and varied tempo, marked resonance, softened volume, frequent nasality

ADDENDUM

The detailed statistical tables supporting the correlations and factors prepared in summary table will not be included in this paper. They would require an inappropriate number of pages and their final preparation would demand staff time that is not available as I write. Therefore I've decided to reserve the statistical evidence for later, making only those scanty comments about numbers suitable to papers of general expository intent.

A number of bodies of data were interconnected in the study: (1) the scores for social and economic structure come from Murdock (1969).[3] From these standardized ethnographic data, Dr. Conrad Arensberg and I shaped a number of the Murdock measures into scalar form in order to reduce the degree of coder error normal to such a large compilation; (2) the Cantometric rating of 4000+ song performances on tape applying a grid of "natural scales" devised by Victor Grauer and the author; inter-rater consensus 80+ percent (cf. Lomax 1971); (3) Udy's (1959) ratings of work-team organization from a hundred cultures; (4) a similar analysis of dance style using the Choreometric rating system of 175+ parameters devised by the author, I. Bartenieff, and F. Pauley, by means of which patterns of body attitude, spatial use, and social choreography can be recorded from film. The material from about 400 cultures has been studied and at present sample dances from about 125 provinces of the 200 province system of Murdock are included. Consensus, which seems high, has not been formally tested (cf. Lomax 1971); (5) a rating system for paralinguistic features called Parlametrics, devised by the author, was applied to conversations from a hundred languages representing a large proportion of world language families. The consensus between the two judges was 82 percent (cf. Lomax i.p.); (6) Lomax (1973) discusses a smaller intensive study of the relative frequency of a grid of vocoids and contoids in song performances from a well-distributed sample of world cultures. The rater, a highly skilled phonologist, estimated the proportion of each type of vocoid and contoid field to the total number of sounds in the 300 songs analyzed. Thus, the trends noted and conclusions depend on a very large corpus of data. There are strong indications that the same factors of social structure that clearly affect performance style in singing and dancing also affect the relative frequency of contoid/vocoid occurrences. These results found in song performance must, of course, be checked by research in everyday speech and in many more languages. Yet, if even part of the tendencies noted are firmly established, the results will be of general interest to linguists, since for the first time a firm basis would be established between phonology and social context.

I must admit that I was astonished at the feeling which my reference to these findings aroused at the conference. My whole intention in this paper was to open up to my colleagues in interactional studies the fresh and stimulating possibilities of a new point of view and a new method. Instead of confining myself to a couple of small points, I decided that it would be far more useful to share the perspective that ten years of co-research

---

[3] This source and the ones following are listed in the References.

had engendered. While I was in the midst of explaining the outlines of this necessarily vague and new universe, I was suddenly required by members of the audience to comment on data about which I had no information and which lay far outside my professional competence. The result was a failed communication. For this, I hope a perusal of the present article will make some amends. Here my intention is to offer a framework of hypotheses based on a considerable amount of data and research which I hope will prove generally useful to some of my readers. The attempt is to base a branch of interactional and thus linguistic research on principles that directly link the results to cross-cultural studies. The aim is to offer a solution for the principal problem of sociolinguistics, which is this: the units and the measures that linguists have found useful in language description bear little or no relation to the measures used by anthropologists for the patterns described by them. For this reason a co-science up to now has proved difficult to design.

Postscripts

Postscripts

Domains of Definition in Interaction: Postscript to Expressive Interaction and Social Structure

DON HANDELMAN

As an anthropologist with an abiding interest in interaction, my admiration and curiosity have been whetted by the sophisticated analyses of co-present interaction detailed by my colleagues. However, I feel that certain organizational aspects of the context of interaction have not received sufficient attention. To a significant degree this is clearly a matter of how research problems are defined, but perhaps it would be relevant here to outline, in a very brief and rudimentary fashion, some of the linkages I perceive between domains of social organization which relate to co-presence.

It is more or less axiomatic in sociology and anthropology that in order for persons to interact in a coordinated and substantive fashion, their actions must be rooted in certain commonalities of sociocultural organization and cognition. Participants must hold at least analogous "definitions of the situation" if their interactions are to proceed in some meaningful and substantive manner. Whether a definition of the situation is perceived as a cultural given, selected as appropriate to a given occasion of co-presence, or whether it is perceived as a continuous process of negotiation among participants which proceeds until a congruent definition evolves, the definition of the situation subsumes the selective integration of aspects of domains of sociocultural organization as these domains become relevant to ongoing occasions of co-presence.[1]

---

[1] Elsewhere (Handelman i.p.), I have questioned the validity of assuming that a congruent definition of the situation must develop among participants if their focused interaction is to continue.

The idea of a definition of the situation is therefore about systems of behavioral interdependency which on any given occasion of interaction subsume elements of different domains of the social order, from the institutional to aspects of the persona of the individual participant. However, since a definition of the situation is usually treated as an often implicit given of any occasion of co-presence, the systematic linkages that compose and integrate this conception are rarely treated analytically. I would argue that a closer examination of the linkages among these domains of organization is crucial to understanding how they contribute to a definition of the situation, and to changes in such definitions that alter the meaning and course of co-presence. What follows, then, is a rudimentary attempt to specify certain domains of organization which contribute to the formation of a definition of the situation, but which tend to become obscured if the definition of the situation is simply accepted as a general given in interaction.

The general directives of a given social order, whether termed values, norms, or some other rubric, define spatio-temporal dimensions of that social order in locational terms. The territory occupied by a social order is always subdivided into locations which are named and to which are attached social meanings about the place of classes of locations in the moral order as well as the expected patterns of behavior which members should exhibit when present in a particular class of location. This perspective on the social order would see it as a configuration of classes of socially defined locations which are linked through the attribution of meaning and expected behavior given to different classes of locations, and through the enculturation of members as they learn the appropriate procedures for switching locations. Because persons are always socially located in a particular spatio-temporal configuration, it should be possible to specify general locational definitions which should guide their behavior. Therefore the location of persons in social settings is a given of any occasion of co-presence.

An examination of classes of social settings indicates that they vary along such dimensions as expected behavior patterns, the kinds of persons who are permitted access, the permeability of setting boundaries, the extent to which settings are visible or shielded from external view, and the extent to which personnel who are co-present in one class of setting are also co-present in other classes of settings. These dimensions of setting organization contribute to the definition of the social setting, and this is one domain of the definition of the situation with which students of co-presence need be concerned. It is not an exaggeration to state that when persons cross the spatio-temporal boundaries of a setting they are then expected to key their behaviors to the standardized behavior patterns expected of them in that location. Therefore the kinds of directives that operate when persons enter a setting contribute directly to the forms of co-presence which, in a statistical sense, are likely to be generated within that class of location.

Following Goffman, I have elsewhere (Handelman, 1973) considered the "encounter" as the domain of social organization that subsumes sequences of co-presence from inception to conclusion. While the form of the encounter is dependent upon the locational definition of its occurrence, the encounter is not simply a reflection of such definitions. Instead, the encounter is guided by its own dynamics of procedure, directionality, and resolution which temporarily reorder and repattern selected elements of the setting, and therefore of its accepted definition. While "rules of irrelevance," "realized resources," and "transformation rules," which compose the definition of the encounter, in part derive from the definition of the social setting of occurrence, the ways in which these derivations integrate in a configuration of co-presence provide the encounter with a potentially different initial definition of co-presence which then provides guidelines for ensuing interaction.

However, the encounter, as a process of interaction, is itself composed of "frames" which, while receiving their definitional impetus from the initial definition of the encounter, also have their own internal dynamic of transformation which permits the redefinition of the course and meaning of the overall encounter. I have suggested elsewhere that the minimal elements of this domain are (1) the extent of openness of persons present to focused activity, (2) the treatment of topics of interaction by participants, and (3) the pattern of allocation and activation of speaker-hearer roles (Handelman i.p.). A frame then describes the state of interpersonal contact between participants during a particular segment of interaction, as it is bounded by the state of the minimal elements mentioned above. These elements also describe the capacity a bounded state of contact has for developing some congruent basis for subsequent interaction during the same sequence of co-presence.[2]

To this point I have briefly mentioned four domains of organization — societal, social setting, encounter, and interaction frame — which to-

---

[2] A consideration of joking activity frames (Handelman and Kapferer 1972) distinguishes such frames in terms of whether rules of procedure in joking activity derive primarily from more general sociocultural expectations, or whether they derive from expectations which are more a product of the social setting in which they occur. Frames that are more closely linked to the social organization of the setting are termed "setting-specific" while frames that derive from more general sociocultural expectations are termed "category-routinized."

gether provide media for the transmission of meaning participants utilize to fashion their understandings of co-presence. It is most important to stress again that no domain of organization is a mere microscopic reflection of other domains, but that linkages that connect domains also specify transformations in perception and meaning as elements of different domains are permitted expression in interaction. Moreover, as each domain also functions according to its own emergent dynamic, it also generates capacities to alter the definition of that domain and perhaps to redefine and alter definitions of other domains. Therefore, as participants negotiate their related paths through a series of interaction frames, they may arrive at a definition of their activity which alters encounter guidelines about the substance and directionality of frames-to-come within the same encounter, and so alter the guiding definition of their encounter. Such a different definition of encounter may also result in the temporary alteration of the social setting in which the interaction is located. Over a series of such encounters, the definition of the setting, as either one example of a class, or the overall class, may become more permanently redefined, so that the role of this class of setting in the wider social order becomes redefined as well. I would suggest that the capacity for redefinition is most evident in the domain of frame and encounter, and less evident in the domain of social setting and the wider social order. Nevertheless, such emergent redefinitions remain a potential of all these domains. I would also stress that the transmission of definitions of the situation from the wider social order to the domain of interaction frames, and conversely the emergent redefinition of meaning in interaction which feeds back from frames to encounter, encounter to setting, and setting to the wider social order, do not occur necessarily in this sequential pattern, but are instead probably multi-directional through the same durations of time.

I would also note that at both ends of the continuum of domains of definition there are further consequences for the individual participant and for his social network. On the one hand, the ways in which interaction frames and encounters are negotiated and the effects of this on the redefinition of a setting or a class of settings, may result in the partial restructuring of individual perception and cognition, with potential consequences for the subsequent interactions a person will become involved in. On the other hand, the negotiation and emergent redefinition of frames, encounter, and social setting may well affect the social bonds which existed among participants before such interaction occurred. In turn, this may affect the organization of the wider social order.

REFERENCES

HANDELMAN, DON
- 1973 Gossip in encounters: the transmission of information in a bounded social setting. *Man,* n.s. 8:210–227.
- i.p. "Components of interaction in the negotiation of a definition of the situation," in *Language and thought.* Edited by W. C. McCormack and S. A. Wurm. The Hague: Mouton.

HANDELMAN, DON, BRUCE KAPFERER
- 1972 Forms of joking activity: a comparative approach. *American Anthropologist* 74:484–517.

Afterthoughts

FREDERICK ERICKSON

Considering the articles presented in this volume as some sort of a whole, three points seem worth raising. First, the scope of our inquiry ranged across all the classical subdisciplines of anthropology. I had not expected archaeology, for example, to be relevant to the study of face-to-face interfaction. Yet Scheflen reminded us that to study interactional proxemics it is helpful to know something about the design of Egyptian, Mayan, and medieval European dwellings and furniture. I had expected excursions beyond anthropological subdisciplines to such fields as ethology, but did not anticipate that we would deal with such information as the structure of the pharynx of the lungfish, as did Lieberman in his discussion of new research in human phonology. These diverse topics have entered our discussions not just as scholarly window dressing, but as elements of context with structural importance for the holistic study of the behaviors of face-to-face interaction. Our heuristic ontogeny literally recapitulated phylogeny.

Second, as I remember, the work of every author involved use of some kind of behavior recording medium. Here too the range was wide — from the now standard audio recording and still photography, through cinema film and videotape to X-ray cinema film. But whatever the medium employed, much of the basic data upon which we conducted our varied analyses had been collected and stored mechanically, as well as by observation.

This may have important consequences. I would not try to argue that behavior-recording media produce an "objective" record, for they have their own "sensory" biases and limitations, and as Paul Byers has observed, it is PEOPLE who point microphones and lenses and push the buttons, not the machines themselves. Even so, while the media distort they may do so with greater consistency than humans and they provide (with the exception of still photography) a fully continuous record of behavior.

As students of interactional behavior, we are forced to confront a continuous record of behavior in all its unselected detail and apparent disorder. Field notes and even shorthand transcriptions of speech inevitably schematize and oversimplify the phenomena they report. By the use of behavior recording much of the complexity of interaction comes to us in unreduced form.

Because of this I think we are better able than traditional fieldwork anthropologists or sociologists to avoid committing the "ethnographic fallacy," which results in overgeneralized and idealized accounts of everyday life. In placing undue emphasis on CENTRAL TENDENCIES in the organization of behavior, ethnographic reports usually do not take adequate account of the principles of variability that are also intrinsic to the organization of behavior.

Committing the ethnographic fallacy is embarrassing. Statements of the form "the Bonga-Bonga do 'X' " are increasingly liable to challenge. Other ethnographers doing restudies of a society may say "we went to Bonga-Bonga and they weren't doing 'X'." Members of the society, now literate, may read the ethnography and say, "Yes, we do 'X', but only some of us do it and then only under certain circumstances."

Third, most of the articles dealt with interactional behavior as SITUATED, not only in physical space but in social space. Goffman's work was presupposed in much of our discussion. Situational conditions explained much of the behavioral variability that was apparent from machine recording. We could see the SITUATION as a system of rules for interaction that mediates between the person and the sociocultural system — a context for interaction to which persons adapt themselves, within which persons reshape sociocultural rules in adaptive ways, and in spite of which persons occasionally transcend the societal and the situational rules, redefining the situation itself in the process of performing it.

Working from behavioral records and considering how definition of situation evolves continuously as persons interact face to face puts us in a good position to begin to understand more clearly the nature of order in the sociocultural rules systems that stand behind interactional behavior. Contemporary anthropology is calling into question earlier notions of that order. While there may be general prescriptive and proscriptive rules for behavior there also seem to be subsystems of optional rules. As Labov reports in his analysis of black street language, the interactional behavior governed by optional rules may seem anomalous to the observer at first glance. (It is often the "glance" — first, second, and third, that is recorded in field notes.) Through repeated "observations" permitted by the behavior record new forms of orderlines become apparent.

There may also be optional rules for drastically altering or suspending general sociocultural rules. (By this I do not mean "free variation.") This is not a new insight. Chomsky has demonstrated the creativity inherent in producing talk. During the conference Stokoe showed us the creative diversity of means employed by the deaf for doing meaning. Everyday social life might be impossible if ordinary persons were not only able to perform situational variations on socioculturally prescribed themes, but were able occasionally to take improvisation to the very "edge" of the themes and perhaps beyond them.

The notions of optional rules, suspension of rules, and of the situation as a unit of analysis, it seems to me, lie beneath what Leach called for in *Rethinking anthropology*; a new understanding of the nature of PARTIAL ORDER in systems. An analogous emphasis on intracultural variability can be found in the second edition of Wallace's *Psychological anthropology*. By studying the unreduced complexity of interactional behavior we may be able to contribute new insights into the nature of sociocultural order in everyday life; insights that will have value for anthropology as a whole.

Another way of describing the articles is that collectively they presented an emerging definition of man as more than the prisoner of his cultural instruments and extensions. In examining interactional behavior we saw men reshaping in everyday life the very cultural rules they had learned.

Biographical Notes

DEAN C. BARNLUND (1920–) received his B.S. and M.S. degrees from the University of Wisconsin, his Ph.D. from Northwestern University. Most of his academic career has been spent at Northwestern University and San Francisco State University. His interests focus on communication theory, interpersonal and intercultural communication, verbal interaction analysis, and the ecology of communication. His research papers have appeared in a variety of academic journals in the behavioral sciences; his books include *The dynamics of discussion* (1960), *Interpersonal communication: survey and studies* (1968), *Nihonjin no Hyogen Kozo* (1973), and *Public and private self in Japan and the United States* (1974).

MARGARET BULLOWA (1909–) was born in New York City. She earned an A.B. from Barnard College, an M.S. in Public Health from Columbia University, and an M.D. from New York University. She is now retired from the practice of psychiatry. Her interest in failure of communication, especially in the language sphere, led to initiating research, at first directed to language acquisition. Studies were based on weekly longitudinal recording of infant vocalization and behavior from birth to thirty months in the infants' own homes. Pilot work was started in 1959 and a research project was begun at Massachusetts Mental Health Center in 1960 and continued in the Speech Communication Group at Massachusetts Institute of Technology since 1965. A number of linguistic and social scientists have collaborated in the studies from time to time. As the thinking and writing about the data appeared to be converging with the work of ethologists working on issues of child development, she is spending a year (August 1974–August 1975) in the laboratory of N. Blurton Jones at the Institute of Child Health of the University of London.

STARKEY DUNCAN (1935–) is Associate Professor in the Committee on Cognition and Communication within the Department of Behavioral Sciences at the University of Chicago. He received his Ph.D. from the University of Chicago in 1965. His primary research interests are in the organization of language, paralanguage, and body-motion behaviors in face-to-face interaction, and in the behavioral regularities deriving from individual differences within that organization.

FREDERICK ERICKSON (1941–) is Associate Professor of Education at Harvard University. He studied historical musicology, ethnomusicology, and anthropology and education at Northwestern University, where he received his Ph.D. in 1969. His dissertation was an analysis of cultural patterns of discussion style of American urban black and suburban white young people. From 1970 to 1973 at the University of Illinois, Chicago Circle, and at Harvard he directed a film study of verbal and nonverbal behavior in job and school counseling interviews between persons of differing American ethnic backgrounds. He is currently doing video-tape and film research on the organization of behavior across a range of social occasions, including formal rituals, everyday life in families, and school classrooms, where he is studying the interactional processes by which rules for sociolinguistic and nonverbal behavior are taught and learned by teachers and children.

SIEGFRIED FREY (1940–) was born in Bad Cannstatt, Germany. He graduated from the University of Munich in 1966 and received his Ph.D. in Psychology at the University of Regensburg in 1971. From 1966 to 1971 he worked at the Max-Planck-Institut für Psychiatrie in Munich where he contributed to the development of methodology for the analysis of visible behavior. In 1971, a fellowship award of the Foundations' Fund for Research in Psychiatry enabled him to spend a year and a half at the University of California, San Francisco. There he worked with Paul Ekman and Wallace Friesen. Since 1973 he has been teaching methodology at the department of Psychology at the University of Berne, Switzerland. At present, he is also directing, under the auspices of the Swiss National Foundation, a research project for the development of a semi-automatic procedure for description and multi-dimensional analysis of visible behavior.

DON HANDELMAN (1939–) was born in Montreal. He received his B.A. from McGill University in 1960, an M.A. from McGill University in 1964, and a Ph.D. in Social Anthropology from the University of Manchester in 1971. In 1970 he was a Research Fellow of the University of Manchester. During 1971–1972 he was Lecturer in Anthropology at Tel-Aviv University, and since 1972 he has been Lecturer in Anthropology at the Hebrew University of Jerusalem. During 1973–1974 he was a Postdoctoral Fellow of the Institute of Social and Economic Research, Memorial University of Newfoundland. He has done fieldwork among West Indian migrants to Montreal, the Washo of Nevada, North African and Middle Eastern Jews in Israel, and welfare bureaucrats in Newfoundland. He has published works dealing with voluntary associations, shamanism, bureaucracy, gossip, play, and joking activity.

RICHARD M. HARRIS (1938–) received his B.A. (1959), M.A. (1961), and a Ph.D. in linguistics (1966) from Cornell University with a dissertation on regional linguistic variation in Hindi. From 1964 to 1970 he taught linguistics and Hindi at the University of Rochester where he served as Principal Investigator of the Basic Hindi Reader Project (1967–1968) and collaborated in psychiatric-linguistic research on voice communication. He then joined Temple University where he taught anthropological linguistics and continued his communicational research on voice modulation in therapist-patient interaction. Currently an Associate Social Scientist at Bronx Psychiatric Center and Assistant Clinical Professor of Psychiatry at the Albert Einstein College of Medicine, he conducts research on structural, social, and psychological aspects of vocal communication.

ADAM KENDON (1934–) studied biological sciences and experimental psychology at Cambridge University and received his Ph.D. from Oxford University for a study of face-to-face interaction using the techniques of Eliot Chapple. He was associated with Cornell University from 1959 until 1962 and was a member of the Social Skills Project at Oxford University from 1963 until 1966. After a year at Pittsburg and a year as a Visiting Assistant Professor at Cornell University, he joined Albert Scheflen at the Project on Human Communication at Bronx State Hospital, New York, where he remained until the end of 1973. He is now Senior Research Fellow in the Department of Anthropology, Institute of Advanced Studies, Australian National University, Canberra, where he is extending studies of communication behavior to various cultural areas in the Pacific region. He is the author of several scientific papers.

MARY RITCHIE KEY, Associate Professor of Linguistics at the University of California at Irvine, received her Ph.D. at the University of Texas in 1963, with graduate studies at the University of Chicago, University of Michigan, and the University of California at Los Angeles. She has done field work in Spanish and several American Indian languages in Mexico, 1946–1955, and South America, 1955–1962. Her publications include *Vocabulario Mejicano de la Sierra, Cavineña y Castellano, Vocabulario Castellano Regional, Bolivian Indian tribes, Comparative Tacanan phonology,* and *Male/female language, paralanguage and kinesics.*

JOHN LAVER (1938–   ) was born in India. He received his M.A. in French Language and Literature in 1962, and a diploma in Phonetics in 1965, from the University of Edinburgh. He was a lecturer in phonetics at the University of Ibadan (Nigeria) from 1963–1966, and has been a lecturer in phonetics at the University of Edinburgh since 1966, specializing in experimental phonetics. He held a visiting post in the Department of Linguistics at the University of California at Los Angeles in 1971. His research interests include neurolinguistics, experimental phonetics, sociolinguistics, and semiotics. Recent publications include *Communication in face-to-face interaction* (1972) and *Phonetics in linguistics* (1973).

A. A. LEONTIEV.   No biographical data available.

PHILIP LIEBERMAN (1934–   ) was born in New York. He received a B.S. and M.S. in Electrical Engineering from Massachusetts Institute of Technology in 1958 where he also received a Ph.D. in Linguistics in 1966 with a dissertation on the physiology, acoustics, and grammatical function of intonation in English. He was a member of the research staff at Air Force Cambridge Research Laboratories and Haskins Laboratories. From 1967 to 1974 he taught at the University of Connecticut and is now Professor of Linguistics at Brown University.

ALAN LOMAX (1915–   ) studied at the Universities of Texas, Harvard, and Columbia and is now Co-director of the Cantometrics Project at Columbia University. He is the author of numerous articles and books on folklore, including *Mr. Jellyroll, The rainbow sign, Folk songs of North America, Folk song style and culture,* and *3000 years of black poetry.* He is the editor of the *World library of folk and primitive music* (Columbia Records).

NORMAN MARKEL (1929–) was born in Detroit, Michigan. He received his B.A. from Wayne University in 1956 and his Ph.D. from the University of Chicago in 1960. Both degrees are in Psychology. While at Chicago he was a student of Eric P. Hamp and Norman A. McQuown. In 1961 he was awarded a Public Health Service Postdoctoral Fellowship to work with George Trager and H. L. Smith, Jr. He stayed at the State University of New York at Buffalo until 1964 as Assistant Professor of Psycholinguistics. Since 1964 he has been at the University of Florida as Professor of Speech, Anthropology, and Psychology. He teaches in the areas of speech and personality, sociolinguistic, and culture and personality. His research interest is the social psychology of nonverbal behavior.

GLENORCHY MCBRIDE (1925–) is Reader in Ethology in the Animal Behaviour Unit, Psychology Department, University of Queensland, Brisbane, Australia. He graduated in Agricultural Science (Adelaide) specializing in Genetics for his Master's (Queensland) and Ph.D. (Edinburgh) degrees. Most of his experimental and observational research has been on the behavior of chickens, both domestic and feral. Theoretical studies have examined societal structures in animals, the relationships between animals and their environments, both husbandry and physical environments, and the structure of the communicative systems in animals and man, including the evolution of the human communicative interaction. He has been a Fellow at the Center for Advanced Studies in the Behavioral Sciences at Palo Alto and a Professor of Man-Environment Relationships at Pennsylvania State University.

FERNANDO POYATOS (1933–) was born in Spain. He received his M.A. and his Ph.D. in Modern Philology from the University of Madrid. He is now Associate Professor of Romance Languages at the University of New Brunswick, Canada. He is especially interested in the interdisciplinary and integrative study of human communication forms (*Man beyond words: theory and methodology of nonverbal communication*, 1975); in the analysis of a given culture through its "culturemes" (in *The mutual interaction of people and their built environment*, edited by A. Rapoport, World Anthropology, 1975); and in the study of the paralinguistic and kinesic repertoires of the narrative character as a new perspective in the analysis of narrative technique ("Paralinguistica y kinesica del peronaje novelesco: nueva perspectiva en el analisis de la narración," 1972). His numerous articles include research published in *Linguistics, Semiotica,* and *Revista de Occidente*.

DAVID RUBINSTEIN (1927–   ) is Professor of Psychiatry at Temple University Medical School in Philadelphia. Interested in psychotherapy, he has been primarily concerned with the study of its clinical aspects and applications as well as the behavioral process of the participants. He has written on psychotherapy of schizophrenia in *Strategies for intervention in schizophrenia* (1974). He edited *Psychotherapy of schizophrenia*, a volume highlighting the latest theories in this area. He has been teaching extensively on Family Psychiatry utilizing videotaping methods for clinical and research studies. One of his recent interests has been the use of voice as a therapeutic tool in psychotherapy.

HARVEY SARLES is an Anthropologist-Linguist at the University of Minnesota. His early training was in the sciences and medicine. He worked as a mathematician/systems analyst before returning to the University of Buffalo where he received an M.A. in Anthropology and Linguistics; he received a Ph.D. in Anthropology from Chicago. He has done fieldwork in southern Mexico and in New Mexico. He approaches the notion of human nature as interactionist. Current interests include the comparative study of language and the nature of the teaching art (teacher-student interaction) as a model for ideological change.

ALBERT E. SCHEFLEN (1920–   ) was born in New Jersey. He is Professor of Psychiatry at Albert Einstein College of Medicine and Researcher at Bronx Psychiatric Center. Dr. Scheflen was trained in psychiatry and psychoanalysis in the 1950's but has since done full-time research in kinesics and communication and, for the last six years, in urban territoriality. He is the author of three books on small group communication and about sixty papers in psychiatry, communication, and territoriality.

HENRY W. SEAFORD, JR. (1922–   ) is Associate Professor of Anthropology at Dickinson College, Carlisle, Pennsylvania. After receiving his A.B. in Anthropology from Wheaton College in 1946, he continued studies at the Escuela Nacional de Antropología e Historia in Mexico where he made an ethnographic reconnaissance of the Choco region of Oaxaca (*Un breve resúmen de la economía chocha*, 1953; *Observaciones preliminares de los ritos funerários chochos*, 1955). While a graduate student at Harvard (A.M., 1964; Ph.D., 1971) he directed an anthropometric survey for the United States Air Force (*Comments on the photometric system*, 1959). His interest in the message-capacity of facial muscle contractions led to a documentation in his doctoral dissertation of regional variation in facial expression (*The southern syndrome*, 1971). Another paper is now in press ("Cultural facial expression"). Continuing interest in nonverbal communication has resulted in his most recent research — an ethnographic semantic study of deaf communication.

WILLIAM STOKOE (1919–) is Director of the Linguistics Research Lab at Gallaudet College. He received his A.B. (1942) and Ph.D. (1946) from Cornell University and studied with Smith and Trager at the then University of Buffalo. He edits *Sign Language Studies* and a monthly newsletter, *Signs for our Times*. His early work on sign includes *Sign language structure* (1960), and, with Croneberg and Casterline, *A dictionary of American sign language* (1965), which still forms a basis for scientific study of this visual-motoric transmission system of language.

IAN VINE (1942–) is a Lecturer in Social Psychology at the University of Bradford, England, teaching in an interdisciplinary department of Human Purposes and Communication since 1973. He studied and later taught psychology at the University of Bristol, where his special interests included social gazing, mother-infant interaction, and spatial aspects of behavior. During 1972–1973 he was Research Associate on a project sponsored by the Social Science Research Council investigating pedestrian behavior and aspects of crowding in public places. As well as publishing on these topics, he has edited with Mario von Cranach a volume of studies on *Social communication and movement* (1974).

WALBURGA VON RAFFLER ENGEL (1920–) has been working on the relationship of verbal and nonverbal elements in first language acquisition since the early sixties. She is presently doing research on the kinesics of bilingual children and is Chairperson of the Anniversary Film Committee of the Linguistic Society of America. Her other interests include child language (Secretary of the International Child Language Association) and sociolinguistics. Her most recent book presents a critical survey of language enrichment programs for the socially disadvantaged. She was born in Munich, Germany, and studied Classical Languages at the University of Turin, Italy, and at the Italian Institute of Archaeology (Dr. Litt., 1949, University of Turin); and then General Linguistics at Indiana University (Ph.D., 1951). She is presently teaching at Vanderbilt University and is Chairperson of the Committee on

Linguistics of the Nashville University Center, an interinstitutional program in Linguistics involving Vanderbilt University, Fisk University, Peabody College, and Scarritt College. Professor von Raffler Engel, who joined Vanderbilt in 1965, is currently President of the Tennessee Conference on Linguistics. She has taught at various American and European universities and held a visiting professorship at Ottawa University in Canada.

VICTOR H. YNGVE (1920–) was educated in Physics at Antioch College (B.S. 1943) and the University of Chicago (S.M., Ph.D., 1953). He then spent twelve years at the Massachusetts Institute of Technology, and is currently a Professor at the University of Chicago in the Departments of Linguistics and Behavioral Sciences, and the Graduate Library School. He has worked on the design of computers and programming languages, on the mechanical translation of languages, and on the syntax of English and German. His current interests embrace the relation between linguistics and psychology, the effect of memory limitations on language structure and language change, and the general question of how people communicate.

Index of Names

Abercrombie, D., 221, 286, 287
Abramson, L., 279
Ageyev, V.S., 344
Alderstein, A.M., 130
Alexander, B.K., 364
Altman, I., 365, 366, 372, 374, 375, 376
Altman, Stuart A., 102, 175
Anderson, Wayne, 199
Andrew, R.J., 102, 151
Andriyevskaya, V.V., 345, 346
Ardrey, R., 358, 359, 370, 371
Arensberg, C.M., 3, 473
Argyle, Michael, 175, 192, 195, 220, 286, 289, 342, 358
Arnold, Edward, 215
Aschoff, J., 375
Ashby, W.R., 82
Ashcraft, N., 81
Atkinson, J.R., 281
Austin, William M., 285

Back, K.W., 343
Bales, R.F., 3, 4
Barasch, D.P., 378
Barker, Roger G.: Midwest Study (with Wright), 99, 107, 115
Barnlund, Dean C., 427–455
Bartenieff, I., 473
Bateson, G., 74, 75, 77, 85, 86, 114, 390, 391
Bateson, Mary, 6, 109
Batov, V.V., 345–346
Beavin, Janet H., 189
Becker, F.D., 365, 373
Beekman, Susan, 199

Beels, C.C., 86
Beintema, David, 96
Bellugi, Ursula, 326, 327, 328, 334
Benedict, R., 85, 438, 441
Berkowitz, Norman, 464, 465
Berlyne, D.E., 391
Bernstein, B., 201, 244, 264, 266
Bertalanffy, L.V., 85
Bgazhnokoy, B.K.H., 340, 344, 345
Birdwhistell, R.L., 75, 77, 86, 106, 108, 161, 194, 254, 255, 357, 358
Bittner, Egon, 392
Blau, Peter M., 398
Blom, Jan-Peter, 176
Bloomfield, L., 84, 316
Blurton, Jones, N., 5, 98, 358
Bodalev, A.A., 346
Boomer, Donald, 311
Borden, G.A., 340, 341
Bordes, F., 279
Borgatta, R.F., 3
Boule, M., 279
Bozhovich, L.I., 340
Bradney, Pamela, 391, 393
Brazelton, T. Berry, 96, 110
Brend, R., 281
Brian, C.K., 363
Bronowski, J., 20
Brown, J.L., 362
Brown, R., 264
Bruner, J.S., 269
Bugental, D.E., 256
Bullowa, M., 95–123
Burdock, E.I., 130
Burgess, E.W., 1

Burling, R., 268
Busnel, René F., 20
Byers, Paul E., 179, 483

Cannon, W.B., 83, 84
Capranica, R.R., 282
Carlsmith, J.M., 195
Carlson, Jeanine, 199
Cary, Mark, 199
Cassirer, Ernst, 21
Castle, R., 375, 377
Catford, J.C., 294, 300, 304
Cavan, Sherri, 391, 392
Chall, Jeanne, 95
Chance, M.R.A., 370, 378
Chapple, Eliot, 2, 3
Chase, Julia, 154
Chevalier-Skolnikoff, Suzanna, 154
Cheyne, J.A., 378
Chivers, D.J., 363
Chomsky, N., 22, 52, 101, 242, 247, 249, 485
Cicourel, Aaron, 176
Clark, I., 175
Clynes, M., 421
Coleman, A., 375
Condon, W.S., 86, 104, 105, 106, 108, 109, 112, 114, 122, 255, 256, 261
Cook, M., 373
Cooley, C.H., 2
Coon, C.S., 3
Corning, Constance H., 368, 370, 371
Corning, P.A., 368, 370
Coser, L.A.: *Soziologie*, 1
Coser, Rose Laub, 391
Covington, Virginia C., 325
Cowan, Richard A., 175
Crook, J.H., 362, 363
Crystal, D., 257, 265, 268, 271, 285, 287
Cunnison, Sheila, 393

Damen, Louise, 189
D'Arcais, Flores, 343
Darling, F.F., 21
Darwin, Charles, 23, 52–53, 100, 282; *Expression of emotion in man and animals, The*, 277
Davis, Martha, 4
Dean, J., 195
DeLong, A.J., 365, 374
Descartes, René, 243
Desor, J.A., 375
Devereux, G., 265
DeVore, I., 367

Dibner, A.S., 346
Dingwall, W.O., 51
Dittman, A.T., 195, 204, 289, 311
Doi, L.T., 438, 441, 453
Donald, G., Jr., 3
Douglas, Mary, 390, 391
Dridze, T.M., 345
Duncan, Starkey, 86, 189, 190, 199–211
Dundes, Alan, 391
Dylan, Bob, 462

Eastman, C.M., 365, 373
Edney, J.J., 377
Efron, D., 86, 165, 378
Eibl-Eibesfeldt, I., 23, 378
Einstein, Albert, 83, 84
Eisenberg, J.F., 363
Ekman, Paul, 102, 127, 139, 203, 255, 286, 288, 289, 297, 298, 358
Ellefson, J.O., 363
Ellsworth, P.E., 195, 358
Embree, J., 450
Emerson, Joan P., 391
Enlow, Donald H., 21
Erickson, Frederick, 75, 80, 175–186, 483–485
Erikson, Kai T., 397
Eseer, A.H., 365, 376
Evans, G.W., 4, 379
Evans, Karen, 189
Exline, R.V., 4

Fant, G., 279
Faucheux, C., 344
Feibleman, J.K., 217
Feldstein, S., 189, 190, 195
Felipe, Nancy J., 378, 379
Ferber, A., 81, 86, 107, 378
Ferguson, C., 257, 323
Firth, R., 234, 235
Fischer, Susan, 326, 327, 328, 334
Fodor, J.A., 260
Foenlander, F., 359
Fox, R., 366, 367, 368, 371
Framo, J.L., 130
Freedman, D., 271
Freedman, N., 195
Fretz, B.R., 130
Freud, Sigmund, 83, 84
Frey, Siegfried, 127–149
Freid, M., 372
Friedman, Lynn A., 333
Fries, C.C., 204
Friesen, Wallace V., 102, 127, 139, 203,

255, 286, 288, 289, 297, 298, 358

Galanter, E., 74, 8, 81
Gallois, Cindy, 189, 190
Galperin, P.Ya., 342, 343
Gardner, B.T., 280
Gardner, R.A., 280
Garfinkel, H., 379
Gartland, J.S., 363
Geber, Marcelle, 96
Gesell, Arnold, 110
Gibson, J.J., 27
Gill, M., 266
Gleicher, Peggy, 372
Gluckman, M., 234, 389
Goffman, Erving, 6, 167, 252, 254, 260, 271, 358, 365, 366, 372, 373, 378, 395, 411, 421, 453, 479
Golani, I., 98
Goldman-Eisler, F., 326
Goss, C.M., 25
Gould, Susan, 251
Grauer, Victor, 473
Gregg, R.N., 340, 341
Grove, T.G., 340, 341
Gruber, Jeffrey S., 105
Gump, Paul V., 392
Gumperz, John J., 176, 199

Haas, M., 281
Hall, E.T., 75, 80, 86, 161, 176, 219, 254, 290, 358, 365, 372, 373, 378
Halle, Morris, 101
Halliday, M.A.K., 103
Halloran, R., 438, 450
Hamilton, W.D., 371
Hammond, Peter B., 391
Handelman, Don, 389–412, 477–480
Hardman, Martha, 189
Hare, A.P., 3
Harper, J., 365, 373
Harris, M., 86
Harris, Richard M., 5, 251–273, 295
Harris, Z., 75, 86
Hayakawa, S.I., 220
Hayes, A.S., 6
Haythorn, W.W., 365, 375
Hediger, H., 363
Helmholtz, H., 27
Herbert, J., 364
Hess, Eckhard H., 103, 195
Heyns, R.W., 3
Hinde, E.H., 192, 358, 370
Holubár, Josef, 95

Homans, George C., 392
Hopenbrouwers, Toke, 110
Howard, E., 84, 358
Howard, R.B., 4, 379
Howell, R., 270
Hubel, David H., 335
Hudson, P.T.W., 377
Huizinga, Johan, 390, 391, 410
Hunt, Nigel, 39
Hutcheson, S., 217, 221, 286–287
Hutt, Corinne, 5
Hutt, S.J., 5
Hymes, D., 199

Jackson, D.D., 189
Jaffe, J., 189, 190, 195
Jakobson, Roman, 331
James, J.W., 379
Janoušek, J.J., 340
Jenny, Dick, 199
Johnson, R.N., 370, 371
Joiner, D., 373, 374
Jolly, Alison, 363
Jourard, S., 438; Body Accessibility Questionaire, 444

Kant, Emmanuel, 243
Kapferer, Bruce, 389, 390, 393, 398, 399, 479
Kaplan, Abraham, 99, 106
Kaswan, J.W., 256
Katz, J.J., 257, 260
Kaufmann, I.C., 363
Kavanagh, J.F., 316
Kendon, Adam, 1–14, 80, 81, 86, 102, 104–105, 106, 114, 122–123, 130, 159, 175, 176, 195, 201, 204, 220, 255, 256, 378, 420
Kessler, Allan, 95
Key, H., 265
Key, M.R., 255
Kharash, A.U., 347
King, M.G., 377, 379
Klopfer, P.H., 362
Knapp, M.L., 192
Knickerbocker, Betty, 189
Knowles, E.S., 378
Kodish, Hedy, 95
Koffka, K., 83
Kortland, A., 98
Kuhn, A., 85
Kummer, H., 362, 364
Kurtz, J., 271
Kuschel, Rolf, 330

Index of Names

Kuzemenko, O., 345

Labov, William, 391, 485
Lancaster, Jane B., 20
Lane, H., 271
Langer, S., 261, 270
Lasakow, P., 438
Lashly, K.S.: Hixon Symposium paper, 111
Laver, John, 215–236, 286–287
Leach, Edmund: *Rethinking anthropology*, 485
Lee, R.B., 367
Leibman, Miriam, 366, 373
Lenneberg, E., 261, 271, 316
Leonard-Dolan, Carolyn, 175, 177, 185
Leontiev, A.A., 339–348
Leontiev, A.N., 341
Lett, Evelyn E., 374
Lewin, K., 83, 99
Leyhausen, P., 362
Lieberman, Philip, 104, 105, 277–283, 286, 295
Lieblich, Anna K., 154
Lindemann, E., 3
Lipman, A., 365, 376
Lippit, R., 3
Lisker, L., 279
Llewellyn, L.G., 204
Loftland, John, 392
Lomax, Alan, 86, 457–474
Longabough, R., 4
Lorenz, Konrad, 22, 81, 358, 370
Lott, D.F., 377
Lott, E.E., 175
Love, L.R., 256
Lundberg, Craig C., 391
Lupton, T., 392
Luria, A.R.: *Mind of a mnemonist, The*, 34
Lyman, S.M., 366
Lyons, J., 215, 217, 222, 251, 286, 287

McBride, Glen, 81, 86, 359, 379, 415–423
McCullock, W.S., 85
McGrew, W.C., 5, 377
McQuown, N.A., 19, 86, 254, 358
McReynolds, P., 130
Mahl, G.F., 346
Malinowski, Bronislaw, 83, 215, 220, 222, 236
Maraini, F., 438, 450
Markel, Norman N., 86, 189–195, 324
Marshall, John C., 98, 103

Martin, Diane, 199
Marx, Emanuel, 389
Marx, Karl, 341
Maslyko, E.A., 347
Mason, W.A., 363
Matarazzo, J.D., 3, 189
Matarazzo, Ruth G., 3
Mattingly, I.G., 281, 316
Mayo, Clara, 365, 373
Mayr, Ernst, 21
Mead, G.H., 2, 29
Mead, Margaret, 85, 114
Meadow, Kathryn P., 335
Mehrabian, A., 191, 192
Mendelssohn, H., 98
Menzel, Emil W., Jr., 100, 102
Meshcheryakov, A.I., 339
Michaels, S.B., 280, 281
Milgram, S., 372
Miller, J.G., 68, 74, 78, 81, 86
Mitchell, R., 380
Moloney, J., 438
Monroe, Marilyn, 309
Montagu, M.F.A., 367
Morris, C.W., 217
Moscovici, S., 343, 344
Muckenhirn, N.A., 363
Mumford, L., 367, 370
Murdock, G.P., 465, 473; *Ethnographic atlas*, 460

Nakamura, H., 438
Nakane, C., 438
Neisser, U., 269, 273
Nelson, Patricia A., 374
Newman, J.D., 282
Newman, R., 266
Newton, Isaac, 282
Niederehe, George, 199, 202, 205
Nixon, Richard M., 305
Nosenko, E.L., 346

O'Cain, Ray, 199
Ogden, C.K., 215, 220, 222
Ogston, W., 86, 104, 105, 255, 256, 261
Orians, G.H., 362
Osgood, C.E., 346
Ostwald, P., 271

Paine, Robert, 395
Parer, I.P., 359
Park, R.E., 1
Parker, Dorothy, 221
Parsons, E.C., 235

Index of Names

Passov, E.I., 345
Pastalan, L.A., 366
Pauly, F., 473
Pavlov, I.P., 84
Peirce, C.S., 217
Piaget, Jean, 272; *Origins of intelligence of children, The,* 111, 242
Pickett, S.M., 31
Pike, Kenneth L., 103, 106, 190, 304; *Phonetics,* 294
Pittinger, Robert E., 285, 296
Plato, 243
Plon, M., 344
Pollack, I., 31
Pope, B., 358
Porter, Evan, 175
Poyatos, Fernando, 285–313
Prebor, Layne, 189, 190
Prechtl, Heinz, 96, 108
Premack, D., 280
Pribram, K.H., 74, **78**, 81, 82
Price-Williams, D.R., 154
Prost, Jack, 179
Putney, E., 102

Quirk, Randolph, 285

Radcliffe-Brown, A.R., 391
Raffler Engel, Walburga von, 242–250
Rapoport, A., 366, 368
Redl, Fritz, 390
Redlich, F.C., 266
Reynolds, V., 363, 368, 369–370
Richards, I.A., 215, 220, 222
Rine, H., 281
Rommetveit, R., 343
Roos, P.D., 366, 374
Rosenblum, L.A., 363
Roth, E.M., 364
Rowell, Thelma E., 364
Roy, Donald F., 390, 392; "Banana time," 389
Rubinstein, David, 5, 251–273
Rudran, R., 363
Russell, Claire, 370
Russell, W.M.S., 370
Russo, N.F., 195
Ryabova, T.V., 347
Ryle, Gilbert, 21

Sachs, J., 281
Salter, Veronica, 175
Sampson, E., 263
Sapir, E., 83, 86
Sarles, Harvey B., 19–43
Satinova, V.F., 345
Scheflen, Albert E., 63–87, 99, 105, 106, 115–116, 122–123, 159–172, 175, 176, 194, 199, 210, 366, 375, 378, 380, 483
Schegloff, E.A., 189, 190
Schleidt, W., 127, 128, 129, 134, 141, 142
Schlesinger, Hilde S., 335
Schmitt, R.C., 380
Schwartz, M.F., 281
Scott, M.B., 366
Scruton, Diane M., 364
Seaford, Henry W., Jr., 151–155
Sears, R.R., 189
Sebeok, T.A., 6, 217, 290, 358
Service, E.R., 367
Shai, Donna, 403
Shakhrimanyan, I.K., 348
Shanks, Thomas, 199
Sharman, Anne, 391
Sharrock, Wesley, 389
Sheppard, W., 271
Shokeid, Moshe, 393
Shultz, Jeffrey, 175
Siegman, A.W., 358
Simmel, Georg, 1–2, 379
Simpson, G.G., 23
Skinner, B.F., 342
Slobin, D.J., 343
Smith, H.L., Jr., 19, 75, 86, 200, 285
Smith, S., 375
Smith, W. John, 98, 154
Sobkin, V., 348
Sokolov, E.N., 81
Solecki, R.S., 279
Sommer, R., 161, 175, 219, 358, 365, 366, 373, 374, 376, 377, 378, 379
Sorokin, J.A., 347
Sorokin, Yu.A., 345
Southwick, C.H., 364
Spicker, Stuart F., 20
Spitz, R.A., 25
Spoerri, T., 130
Stebbins, G. Ledyard, 22
Stefanski, Raymond, 95
Stepanek, Cathy, 199
Sterman, M.B., 110
Stetson, R.H., 105
Stevens, Kenneth N., 95
Stokoe, William C., Jr., 315–335, 485; *Dictionary of American sign language,* 319
Stopa, Roman, 304
Strauss, Anselm, 397

Index of Names

Stubblefield, Tichina, 199
Stynes, A.J., 363
Sundstrom, E., 365, 376
Sutton-Smith, Brian, 391, 392
Sykes, A.J.M., 391, 393
Szasz, Andrew, 199

Tarasov, E.F., 346–347
Taylor, D.A., 365, 375
Tharpe, Sister Rosetta, 462
Thayer, L., 340, 342, 343
Thompson, Sir John Arthur: *Outline of science*, 101
Thorndike, E.L., 84
Tiger, L., 366, 367, 368, 371
Tinbergen, N., 368, 370
Tolman, E.C., 83
Tracy, Spencer, 41
Trager, G.L., 19, 75, 86, 199, 200, 285
Turner, E.A., 343

Udy, Stanley J., 473

Vallois, H.V., 279
Van Gennep, A., 234
Van Hoof, J.A.R.A.M., 195
Van Lawick-Goodall, J., 154, 282
Vesey, G.N.A., 19, 20
Vetter, H., 270, 285

Vine, Ian, 357–380
Vitt, N.V., 346
Von Cranach, M., 4, 135, 358
Vowels, D.M., 98
Vul, S.M., 346

Wales, Roger, 95
Walker, T.M., 346; *Voices from the world: a policeman's journal*, 256
Watson, O.M., 254, 340, 373
Watzlawick, P., 189
Webb, E.J., 130
Weeks, T., 271
Weick, K.L., 3, 4
Weiner, N., 85
Wheeler, L., 365, 375
Wiens, A.H., 189
Wolf, K.M., 25
Wolff, Peter H., 96, 110, 111
Wollberg, Z., 282
Woodward, James C., Jr., 328
Wright, Herbert F.: Midwest Study (with Barker), 99, 107, 115

Yermolayeva-Tomina, L.V , 346
Yngve, Victor H., 47–62, 204

Zhuravlev, A.P., 345

Index of Subjects

Acoustic, 30–31, 268, 280–281, 282–283, 287, 294, 295, 298
Action–reaction, 65, 67–68
Activity units, 113–123
Adult, 13, 29, 30, 31, 38, 49, 57, 95–123, 164–165, 168, 170–171, 241, 243, 245, 256, 257, 267, 272, 280, 308, 377, 391, 438, 452–453. *See also* Age; Parents
Affect(ive), 23, 25–26, 32, 38, 252, 262, 268–269, 297–298, 302–311, 365, 417, 421, 423. *See also* Emotive; Expressive
Afghanistan, 306
Africa, 96, 169, 463, 464, 466, 467, 468. *See also* Names of individual countries
Age, 30, 41, 107, 160, 221, 257, 263–264, 291, 311, 317, 359, 449, 466. *See also* Adult; Child(ren); Infant
Aggressive behavior, 99, 154, 226, 310, 358–380, 390, 402, 415, 418, 419, 431, 433, 448–451, 453
Alexandrians, 50
Alternants, 285–312
American Association for the Advancement of Science, 465
Amerindians, 468, 471, 472
Amsterdam, 6
Angle Depression, 152, 153
Anglo-Americans, 163, 307, 308, 373
Animals: communication among, 19–20, 21, 97, 226, 263, 277, 278, 280, 282, 290–291, 316; interaction among, 358–365, 367, 368, 370, 376, 377, 379–380, 415–416, 419; play of, 391; space use by, 159, 172, 358–365, 367, 368, 370, 376, 377, 379–380

Approaches to Semiotics (Sebeok, Hayes, and Bateson), 6
Arabs, 402
Aristotelian epistemology, 65, 66–71, 83, 84, 85, 87
Audiotape, 78, 100, 109, 112–113, 116–122, 152, 176, 180, 182, 194–195, 253, 258, 283–287
Audiovisual records, 7, 10, 11–12, 43, 48, 98, 100, 101, 102, 103–104, 106, 109, 110, 112–122, 130–131, 151–152, 167, 176–186, 200, 253, 255, 317–319, 325, 330. 374–375 458, 483–484, 485
Australia, 369, 464

Back channels, 202, 204–211, 289, 296, 298
"Banana time" (Roy), 389
Bahavioral parameters, 132–149
Behavioral properties, 132–133, 143–149
Behavioral science, 19–24, 27, 66, 68, 253, 261, 273, 315–316, 347, 418, 483–484
Behavioral unit, 2–3, 11–12, 415
Bernsteinian theory, 244
Biopsychological, 290–293
Black Americans, 161, 165, 169, 171, 175, 176, 372, 375, 463, 471, 472
Black street language, 485
Blind, 30, 154, 243, 339
Body motion/movement, 2, 4–5, 13, 21, 25–30, 32–33, 36–39, 41–42, 96–97, 102–109, 114, 130–149, 179–181, 191–195, 199–211, 216–217, 219–220, 227–229, 232, 241–250, 252, 253, 254, 255, 286–287, 302–312, 327, 330, 332–333

Bolivia, 265
Bonga-Bonga, 484
British Americans, 160, 163, 164, 165, 166, 169, 170, 171, 172
Bronx, 81, 159, 375
Bronx State Hospital, 159
Bushman, 468

California, 127
Canada Council, 285, 389
Cantometric rating, 473
Carolinians, 151
Cartesian impasse, 19–43
Center for Studies of Metropolitan Problems, 175
Child(ren), 5, 13, 25–26, 28–31, 37–38, 49, 165, 168, 169, 241–250, 252, 253, 256, 257, 267, 270–273, 281, 308, 344, 377, 391, 428, 447, 458. *See also* Age; Infant
China, 154
"Chomskyan revolution," 241
Chronemics, 288–289
Civil inattention, 378
Classification, 3–4, 65, 69; of body movement, 129–149; of communication types, 340–343; of paralinguistic alternants, 286, 295–312
Clicks, 288, 297, 298, 299–301, 304–307, 309–311
Coaction(al), 74–76, 78–80
Code, 217, 254, 261, 263, 264, 268–273, 287, 295, 298, 316, 318–319, 320, 325–326, 329, 335, 416–417, 420, 422, 428–429, 430, 435, 454
Coding data, 116–123, 129–149, 177, 178–186, 458, 473
Cognitive phenomena, 71, 72, 77, 81–83, 84, 191, 241, 243, 247–248, 251–273, 277–282, 287, 297–298, 316, 323, 366, 477, 480
Colingual, 56–57, 58–62
Communicate/communication(al), 3, 13, 19–43, 47–62, 63–87, 95–123, 199–210, 215–236, 243, 251–273, 277–283, 285–312, 315–335, 339–348, 357, 380, 389–392, 400–406, 408–412, 415–423, 427–455, 457–458
Communicative behavior, 13, 49, 52, 54, 55–62, 63, 65–66, 71–87, 95–123, 127–142, 159–172, 176, 215–236, 241–250, 251–273, 277–283, 285–312, 315–335, 339–348, 415–423, 427–455, 457–458
Context, 30, 31, 33, 34–35, 40, 41, 42–43, 72, 81, 84, 85, 87, 99–100, 106, 128, 129, 141–152, 153, 168, 192–193, 199, 222, 241–243, 249, 261, 271, 272, 288, 290–291, 295, 300, 304, 306, 309–312, 319, 320, 339, 357–358, 365, 376, 377, 380, 392, 404, 409, 410, 415–416, 421, 422, 423, 473, 477, 483, 484. *See also* Situation
Contraction, muscular. *See* Muscular activity
Conversation, 1, 5, 8, 9–11, 49, 51, 52, 59, 60–61, 62, 72–73, 161, 164, 170–171, 177, 189–195, 199–211, 215, 236, 252, 256, 258, 269, 286, 288, 290, 311–312, 344, 398–399, 401, 416–419, 421, 430–455, 457, 460, 461, 462, 463, 466, 469, 473
Courtship, 33, 72, 73, 74, 76, 78, 161, 165, 415, 418, 419
Coverbal behavior, 72, 189–195
Cross-cultural, 10–11, 13–14, 151, 186, 245, 254, 257, 285–312, 367, 457–469, 474. *See also* Culture
Crying, 52, 96, 111, 244, 249, 271, 277, 293
Cuba, 169
Cubit, 160–161, 162–166, 168, 169, 170, 172
Culture, 21, 106, 191, 252, 364, 367, 368–380, 390–391, 477, 485; concept of, 83; as influencing behavior, 10–11, 13–14, 65, 66, 72, 74, 76–77, 82, 84, 85, 86, 87, 108, 110, 114, 151–155, 160, 161–162, 169, 170–171, 172, 175, 246, 248, 253, 254, 255, 257, 258, 262–264, 269, 273, 281, 290–293, 294, 295, 298, 357, 367, 422, 427–355, 457–469; and science, 64, 66. *See also* Cross-cultural
Cybernetics, 71, 75, 76, 85, 86

Dance, 86, 457–469, 473
Deaf, 28, 30, 154, 244, 280, 315–335, 339, 341, 485
Defensive strategy, 431, 433, 436, 447–451, 452, 453, 455
Density, 160, 161, 162–163, 165, 166, 167, 169–171, 363, 364, 365, 370, 371, 375, 379–380
Dental Research Association, 37
"Development from Vocal to Verbal Behavior in Children" project, 112
Dialect, 28, 30, 56–57, 151–155, 265, 279, 281
Dialogue marker. *See* Speech; Turn
Dickenson College, 151

Dictionary of American sign language, 319

Dimensions: in human behavior, 253–256, 259, 261–262, 263–264, 268–269, 316–317, 361, 396–400, 460, 478; in space, 131–133, 134–149

Dominance, 73, 76, 78, 160, 168, 226, 310, 361–362, 371–379, 402, 404, 460, 463–464, 466–469. *See also* Power

Down's syndrome, 26, 37–39

Duration, 2–3, 8, 95, 106–107, 110, 117, 119, 123, 128–149, 159, 166, 179, 202, 257–259, 263, 288, 291, 300, 303, 307–308, 311, 324, 325–326, 360, 391, 396, 397–398, 407, 410, 480. *See also* Time

Dyad(ic), 70, 72–73, 79, 199–211, 227–228, 256, 266, 288, 290, 295, 296, 308, 317, 340, 341, 346

Egypt, 161–162, 165, 172, 186, 483

Emic, 103, 106, 122–123, 179–180, 183, 186, 191

Emotive, 252, 256, 257, 267–269, 277, 280–281, 298. *See also* Affect(ive); Expressive

Epistemology, 50, 52, 63–87, 270

Ethnographic atlas (Murdock), 460

Ethnographic fallacy, 484

Ethological study, 2, 5, 14, 81, 85, 86, 98–100, 103, 112, 123, 153–154, 225–226, 315, 358–364, 418, 483

Etic, 103, 106, 113, 122–123, 179–180, 183, 190–191, 316

Euro-Americans, 463, 471, 472

Europe, 163, 176, 249, 395, 462, 463, 467, 468, 483

Event, 8, 29, 30, 65, 66, 70, 72, 73–74, 80–81, 82, 84, 85, 86–87, 127–129, 133, 134, 141–142, 200, 203, 208–209, 217, 219–220, 227–229, 234, 235, 391, 416, 420–421, 453

Expansion, 133, 145–147

Expression of emotion in man and animals (Darwin), 277

Expressive, 267–269, 297–298, 324–326, 331–335, 389–412, 427–455, 457–469, 477–480. *See also* Affect(ive); Emotive

Extra-linguistic, 286

Eye, 25, 26, 27, 32–33, 35, 40–41, 106, 135–136, 253, 286, 302–308, 311–312, 316, 333, 335. *See also* Eye contact; Gaze

Eye contact, 25, 32–33, 180, 183, 193, 195, 216–217, 220, 227–228, 232, 254–255, 291, 416, 420. *See also* Gaze

Face, 22–23, 25–26, 27, 28–30, 33–34, 37–39, 58, 194–195, 253, 254, 286, 293, 302–312, 326. *See also* Facial expression

Face-to-face interaction, 1–14, 19–43, 47–62, 80–81, 161, 164, 165–166, 167–168, 169, 170–172, 175–186, 199–211, 216–217, 219, 254–255, 260, 285–312, 315–335, 339–348, 357–358, 363, 371, 379–380, 415–423, 428, 457–469, 483–485. *See also* Communicate/communication(al)

Facial expression, 4–5, 7, 23, 25–26, 27, 37–39, 41, 42, 48, 51, 52–53, 72, 151–155, 216, 217, 219, 228, 229, 232, 245, 246, 252, 260, 278, 279–280, 286, 297, 300, 302–312, 318, 319, 323, 417, 419

Feedback, 75–76, 81–82, 85, 229, 289–290, 296, 297, 298, 302–312, 318, 340, 341, 392, 397–398, 480

Female, 31, 33, 39, 153, 161, 281, 304, 306, 309, 310–311, 372–373, 395, 396, 399–406, 409, 410–411, 419, 439–440, 445–447, 449, 463–465

Film, 7, 11, 98, 100, 101, 102, 103–104, 106, 109, 110, 112–122, 167, 176, 177, 179, 180–181, 183, 253, 255, 317, 378, 458, 483–484

Florence, Italy, 248

Ford Foundation, 175

Format, 63, 65, 71–80, 86, 87, 420

Foundations' Fund for Research in Psychiatry, 127

Frame, 9, 260, 327, 410–411, 457, 479–480

France, 39, 165, 315, 343

French Americans, 169

Gainesville Group for the Study of Nonverbal Behavior (1972), 189

Gallaudet College, 28, 317, 318, 332

Gaze, 1, 4, 5, 32–33, 60, 161, 165, 166, 168, 170, 179, 195, 220, 228, 255, 302, 305–306, 312, 378, 379. *See also* Eye contact

Geneva, 242

Georgia (U.S.), 152

Georgia (U.S.S.R.), 393

Gesture, 2–3, 7, 12–13, 48, 49, 51, 58, 65, 79, 102, 105, 115, 165, 169, 179, 191–192, 201, 202–203, 205–206, 211, 216–217, 219, 228, 229, 232, 241–250, 255, 260, 278, 279–280, 286, 288, 298, 302–

312, 318, 319, 320, 325, 330–334, 428, 430, 453
Great Britain, 6, 153, 161, 162, 163, 164, 165, 166, 169, 170, 171, 172, 216, 222, 404
Greece, 50, 51, 70, 100, 161–162, 172, 235, 252
Greeting, 5, 52, 107, 129, 161, 218, 219, 222, 234–235, 304, 317, 378, 420

Hand, 36, 131–133, 142–149, 201, 202–203, 219, 246, 248–249, 288, 289, 296, 302–307, 309–310, 312, 324–325, 330–334
Head, 60, 106, 131–133, 134–142, 193, 194–195, 201, 203, 204, 205, 206, 207, 219, 220, 246, 248, 253, 288, 289, 296, 297, 302, 305–310, 331, 333, 334, 417, 419, 420
Head touching, 194–195
Hebrew University, 246
Hesitation, 4–5, 258, 305, 307, 309, 311–312, 325, 328, 346. See also Juncture; Pause
Hierarchy: of behavioral systems, 96, 97, 103, 105, 106–109, 112–116, 123, 179–180, 199–201, 203, 210, 342, 345, 347, 418, 420; of conversations preferences, 438–441, 445–447; of general systems, 85, 101–102; of social status, 359, 361–362, 367, 371–379, 396–400, 411
Hieroglyphics, 345
Hong Kong, 380
Human communication theory, 19–43, 47–62, 63–87. See also Theory
Hushaphone, 116, 117, 118, 119, 120, 121

Icon, 217, 220, 228–229, 262, 263, 282, 298, 331–332
Idiosyncratic, 30, 258, 294, 298, 457
Imaging, 34–36, 37
Index, 217, 221–227, 229–236, 287
Individual space, 358–380. See also Personal space
Infant, 25–26, 28–31, 38, 95–123, 168, 257, 271–273, 375, 377, 447, 452, 458. See also Age; Child(ren)
Inferior Press Smile, 152, 153
Innate behavior, 21–25, 28–31, 40, 57–58, 59, 61–62, 241, 243, 247–249, 277, 358, 359, 364, 367–371
Institute of Linguistics of the Academy of Sciences of the U.S.S.R., 347
Interaction(al) markers, 81, 106–107, 183–186, 199–210, 220, 420. See also Turn, interactional
Interpersonal spacing, 8, 78, 161, 164–172, 175–186, 216–217, 219, 220, 228, 254, 288, 290, 306, 358–359, 365–380, 444
International Christian University, 437
International Phonetic Alphabet (IPA), 294, 296, 320
International Sign Language, 316–317
International Symposium on First Language Acquisition, 248
Intonation, 104, 200, 202, 245, 246, 252, 253, 254, 255–258, 264–268, 270–271, 278–280, 286, 291, 295. See also Pitch; Prosodic; Suprasegmental
Iraqi, 393
Irish Americans, 176, 185
Israel, 315, 394, 395
Italian Americans, 165, 169, 176
Italy, 246, 248

Jamaica, 169
Japan, 427–455
Japan Society for the Promotion of Science, 427
Jerusalem, 246, 390, 395
Jewish Americans, 161, 165, 169, 170
Jewish Family Service of New York, 159
Jews, 403
Jokes, 245, 267, 389, 390–391, 392, 398–399, 401–403, 405, 406–407, 409, 410, 419–420, 479
Jourard's Body Accessibility Questionnaire, 444
Juncture, 72, 77, 200–201, 287, 296, 311, 325–326, 331. See also Hesitation; Pause

Kenya, 306
Kinesics, 6, 13, 19, 49, 65, 75, 76, 77, 79, 106, 153, 179, 180–181, 190, 194, 217, 243–250, 252, 255, 269, 286–294, 296, 297–298, 300–312, 327, 341–342, 347, 357, 458. See also Body motion/movement; Gesture
"K" space, 160–161, 162–166, 167, 168, 169, 170
Kuhnian cycle, 85
Kurdistan, 393

La Chapelle-aux-Saints, 280
Language(s), 7, 12–13, 19–21, 22, 23, 27–32, 41, 42, 47–62, 63–64, 65–67, 72, 75,

Index of Subjects 505

77, 79, 83, 86, 95–123, 130, 154, 199, 215–217, 219, 232, 241–250, 251–273, 277–283, 285–312, 315–335, 341, 345, 346, 347, 367, 416–417, 450–451, 457, 458, 461–462, 465, 468, 474; Abkhazian, 347; African, 304; American English, 279, 281; Belorussian, 347; Cayuvava, 265; Checheno-Ingush, 347; Chinese, 279, 345, 347; English, 11, 28, 39, 54, 216, 218, 223, 227, 230, 242, 257, 258, 259, 262, 264–265, 280, 281, 283, 308, 316, 319, 320, 321, 324, 326, 328, 334, 335, 347; Estonian, 347; European, 230, 307; French, 230, 262, 341; German, 34, 231, 347, 348; Greek, 51; Hebrew, 262; Hindi, 262; Italian, 231; Japanese, 347; Kabardin, 347; Korean, 347; Latvian, 347; Lithuanian, 347; Mohave, 265; Russian, 262, 341, 345, 347; Spanish, 231, 291, 293, 304, 306, 307; Tajik, 347; Vietnamese, 347
Language acquisition, 13, 21, 28–31, 49, 96, 102, 112, 241–250, 252, 253, 270–273, 281
Language in Society (journal), 252
Lateral dimension of head movement, 131, 136–141
Latin Americans, 175, 303, 306, 311
Laugh(ter), 32, 288, 293, 420, 448–449, 460, 466
Linguistic phenomena. See Language(s)
Linguistics, 2, 12–13, 14, 19, 22, 23, 43, 47–62, 72, 103, 123, 199, 215–216, 241–250, 251–252, 259–260, 267–268, 269, 270–271, 273, 277–283, 315–316, 458, 460
Lip, 28–29, 152–154, 190–191, 193, 293, 300–312
Location: in space, 117, 118, 119, 361–362, 372, 373–374, 376, 379, 395, 396–399, 400–401, 415, 478; in study of body movement, 131–133; in systems, 199, 478, 480; as unit of space, 160–161, 166–172
London, 105, 153, 215
Longitudinal Study on Perinatal Factors, 113
Loudness, 30–31, 201, 221, 229, 257–258, 262, 263, 266–268, 277, 291–293, 304, 327, 346, 420

Male, 31, 33, 39, 161, 264–265, 281, 304, 306, 310–311, 367–368, 372–373, 395, 396, 399–409, 410–412, 419, 439–440, 445, 447, 449, 463–465
Mandibular Thrust, 152
Mann-Whitney U Test, 140
Massachusetts Institute of Technology, 95
Massachusetts Mental Health Center, 112
Max Planck Institut für Psychiatrie, 130
Maya, 172, 483
Mediterranean peoples, 172, 393
Melanesia, 220
Men. See Male
Metabehavior, 75–80, 82–83
Metacommunication(al), 73–80, 82-83, 267
Metalanguage, 390–391
Mexican Americans, 176
Mexican Tzotzil, 39
Mexico, 39
Middle East, 393, 403
Midwest Study (Baker and Wright), 99, 107, 115
Mimicry, 25–26, 28, 30, 32, 38, 109, 154, 244–246, 341, 416
Mind of a mnemonist, The (Luria), 34
Modality, 78–80, 86, 252, 256, 261, 265, 285, 291, 294, 380, 422
Models: cognitive, 71, 81–83; of communication, 254; of conversation, 192; explanatory, 63–87, 199, 260; paralinguistic, 253–254; programmatic, 71–80, 81; spatial, 71, 80–81; of tonic communication, 128–129, 134–142; of turn system, 210–211
Module, 160–161, 169–172
Molar units, 101–102
Molecular units, 101–102
Mongoloids, 24, 26
Morocco, 393
Moscow, 347
Movement of Analysis Technique (MAT), 127, 130, 134, 139, 140, 142
Muscular activity, 25–26, 27, 29–30, 37–39, 96, 97, 104, 151–155

Nashville, Tennesee, 246
National Institute of Mental Health, 199; research grants of, 95, 112, 159, 175
National Institutes of Health, 95
National Science Foundation, 199
Neanderthal, 278–279, 280, 295
Newtonian science, 67–68, 83
Newton's Laws of Motion, 282
New York, 111, 159
Nigeria, 169
Nonverbal behavior, 51, 72–73, 97, 102,

103–104, 108–109, 133–134, 139, 175–186, 189–195, 232, 235, 241–250, 254, 263, 265, 266–267, 270, 271, 285–291, 312, 315, 335, 347, 348, 357, 379, 416–417, 431, 433, 435–438, 444–447, 451–455
Nonvernal Inventory, 436
North Carolina, 152
Northeast Modern Language Association, 295
Norway, 176
Notation system. *See* Transcription
Nucleus, 160–161, 164, 172

Occasions, 2–3, 5, 8, 9, 389–390, 397, 404, 409, 477–478
Occupation, 257, 263–264, 265, 374
Olfactory, 252, 286–287, 290, 362, 368
Openness, 133, 143–144, 479
Oral response, 25–26
Orbicular Clamp, 152, 153
Organismic focus in science, 64–65, 66–70, 81–83, 84, 87
Origins of intelligence in children (Piaget), 111
Outline of science (Thomson), 101

Paralanguage, 4–5, 6, 30, 49, 75, 78, 86, 104, 177, 180, 183, 190, 194, 199–201, 202, 217, 246 251–273, 277–283, 285–312, 315, 341–342, 347, 416, 473
Parents, 25, 28–29, 38, 95–123, 169, 257, 315, 428, 439–441, 445–447, 458
Pause, 199, 200–201, 287, 288, 300, 310, 311–312, 324, 325, 326–328, 334, 346, 466–469. *See also* Hesitation; Juncture
Pennsylvania, 152, 153, 332, 333
Pennsylvania Sociological Society, 151
Performative sentences, 105
Persia, 393
Personal space, 4, 161, 162–172, 358, 366, 373, 377–380. *See also* Individual space
Phatic communion, 215–236
Phonemic clause, 200–201, 211
Phonetic, 190–191, 219, 221, 229, 278–281, 295–296, 299–312, 329, 460, 461–462
Phonotactic, 462, 466
Photograph, 151–152, 483–484
Pike's Phonetics, 294
Pitch, 201, 221, 229, 257–258, 263, 264–265, 267, 277, 279, 280–281, 287, 291, 296, 302–311, 420
Play, 389–412, 416

Polish Americans, 176, 177, 185
Polynesia, 467
Position: of body or parts of body, 39, 106–107, 131–149, 162–172, 176, 192, 210, 220, 286, 344, 416; of items in environment, 373–374; in social organization, 396–399, 401, 406, 409, 411. *See also* Posture; Status
Posture, 7, 39, 48, 49, 72, 75, 78, 79, 81, 96, 106–107, 116, 118, 119, 130, 132–133, 162–168, 171, 176, 192, 194, 210, 216–217, 220, 228, 232, 420, 473
Power, 226, 403, 449. *See also* Dominance
Prague, 249
Presbyterians, 64
Program, 73–80, 81–82, 86, 107, 128–129, 141–142, 243, 262, 347
Pronouns, 344, 450
Prosodic, 104, 277–281, 286. *See also* Intonation; Suprasegmental
Proxemics, 49, 72, 75, 79, 80, 161, 175–186, 217, 252, 286, 288–291, 300–312, 340, 341–343, 358, 483. *See also* Spacing
Psychodynamic, 66, 68
Psycholinguistics, 215–216, 244, 249, 253–254, 339–348
Psychological anthropology (Wallace), 485
Psychological distance, 225, 226–227, 343, 440, 444, 452–453
Psychotherapy, 72, 106–107, 176
Puerto Rico, 169, 375
Pupil seize, 33, 192, 195. *See also* Eye contact
Purse-Clamp, 152, 153
Pursed Smile, 152, 153

Quantitative methods, importance of, 130–134, 142

Religion, 369, 371
Rethinking anthropology (Leach), 485
Rhythm, 21, 26–29, 43, 96, 108–112, 177, 179, 256, 265, 267, 291–293, 334–335, 457–458, 466
Ritual behavior, 128–129, 161, 175–176, 218, 233–236, 254–255, 279, 362, 369, 372, 373–374, 377, 378–379, 380, 433, 435, 444, 450, 451
Role Description Checklist, 436, 437
Roles, 9, 30, 31, 49, 59, 72, 75, 82, 107, 218–219, 226–227, 256, 262, 263–264, 318, 340, 342, 346–347, 367, 373, 390, 395, 403–404, 405, 407–412, 436–438, 454, 479

Index of Subjects 507

Romans, 50, 172
Rotational dimension of head movement, 131, 136–141

SAGE, 394, 395, 396, 400, 402, 404, 408, 411, 412
Sagittal dimension of head movement, 131, 136–141
San Francisco, 127
Saxons, 172
Scandinavian Americans, 186
Segmentation, 11, 72, 96–97, 102–123, 175–186, 190–191, 199–211, 255, 257, 265, 266, 268, 272, 278–281, 287, 295, 414–420, 460, 466, 479
Self, 2, 30, 259, 411, 429–455
Self-Disclosure Scale, 436, 438, 440
Semantics, 222, 243, 249, 259–268, 269, 278–286, 287, 290, 295–296, 300, 303, 310, 311, 316, 323, 324–325, 329, 331, 333, 334–335, 342, 345, 346, 418, 419, 420
Semiotic aspects of spoken communication (Laver), 215
Semiotics, 6, 217, 288, 290, 299, 341–342
Serbia, 393
Setting: physical, 7, 8, 9, 59, 75, 80, 290, 357–358, 359, 363–364, 373–375, 379–380; social, 389–412, 477–480. *See also* Context; Situation
Sex, 5, 30, 31, 33, 39, 41, 153, 160, 221, 257, 263–265, 281, 291, 304, 306, 309, 310–311, 317, 359, 367–368, 372–373, 395, 396, 399–409, 410–412, 419, 439–440, 445–447, 448, 449, 463–465
Shanidar, 280
Sign/Signal, 10, 52, 63, 71–78, 80, 81, 82, 96, 102, 152, 202–211, 226, 227–229, 234–235, 251–255, 259, 262, 262, 269, 277–282, 286, 288, 289, 290, 315, 335, 341–342, 357, 368, 379, 391, 416, 420, 435, 458, 460, 468
Sign Language, 13, 280, 315–335, 341, 416
Silence, 30, 76, 152, 169, 190, 202, 220, 226, 233, 254, 311–312, 327, 435, 437–438, 448, 449, 453, 454–455
Sign Language, 13, 280, 315–335, 341, 416
Silence, 30, 76, 152, 169, 190, 202, 220, 226, 233, 254, 311–312, 327, 435, 437–438, 448, 449, 453, 454–455
Simultaneous speech, 10, 73, 74, 190, 195, 202, 203, 206, 211
Singing, 86, 401, 457–469, 473
Situation, 1–3, 4, 10, 13, 26, 33, 42–43, 48, 107, 199–200, 202, 229, 246, 247, 288, 339, 390, 419; definition of, 8–9, 78–79, 80, 477–480; effects of, on behavior, 1, 8–9, 26, 58, 59–62, 74, 78–79, 113–114, 134, 135–141, 209, 218–219, 222, 227, 241–243, 257, 261, 300, 310, 311, 312, 340, 342–345, 357, 375, 379–380, 396, 407, 411–412, 422, 469, 477–480
Situational shifts, 175–186, 311–312
Skin, 78, 192, 286
Smile/smiling, 25–26, 151, 152, 193, 194–195, 306, 312, 325, 420
Social Science Research Council (United Kingdom), 347
Social sciences, 1–7, 14, 48–50, 55, 57, 63–70, 71–73, 78, 81–87, 99, 100–102, 213, 253, 261, 263, 315, 340, 347, 357–358, 359, 365–367, 391, 418, 427, 458, 460, 477, 483, 484
Socioeconomic group, 248, 263–264, 265, 290
Socioeconomy, 460–461, 463–466
Sociolinguistics, 190, 199, 215–216, 226–227, 249, 251–252, 458, 462, 466, 473, 474
Song. *See* Singing
South America. *See* Names of individual countries
South Carolina, 152
Southern syndrome, 151–155
Soziologie (Coser), 1
Space, 8, 49, 80–81, 83–87, 132–133, 159–172, 226, 255, 322, 329–335, 357–380, 396, 397, 415, 416, 421, 473, 478–479, 484. *See also* Spacing
Spacing, 4, 7, 8, 48, 49, 72, 75, 78, 79, 80–81, 159–172, 175–186, 216–217, 219, 220, 228, 252, 254, 255, 286, 288–291, 300–312, 340, 341–343, 357–380, 416, 420, 444, 458–460, 483
Spain, 288, 306, 307, 308
Spanish Americans, 165
Speech, 2–3, 7, 12–13, 20, 27–32, 37, 43, 48, 51–52, 55–58, 72–79, 96–97, 102–109, 112, 115, 119–120, 152, 154–155, 175–186, 189–195, 199–211, 215–236, 241–250, 251–273, 277–283, 286–294, 296, 311–312, 315–317, 318, 319, 326–329, 332, 333–334, 335, 340–347, 357, 416–420, 428, 450–451, 453, 457–469, 473, 479, 484. *See also* Conversation; Language; Verbal behavior
Speech behavior. *See* Verbal behavior

Spot, 160, 161–162, 163, 164–165, 166
Status, 9, 49, 66, 134, 160, 167, 192, 220, 222–226, 235, 251–252, 255, 257, 263–265, 288, 304, 317, 374, 376, 377–378, 404, 435
Stimulus, 40, 65, 67, 84, 95, 127–128, 135–142, 254, 272, 297, 335
Stoics, 50, 52
Story telling, 401
Style, 3, 49, 74, 75, 76–77, 115, 176, 186, 259, 262, 263, 265–267, 269, 272, 317, 427–455, 457–469, 473
Suprasegmental, 77, 96, 287, 296. *See also* Intonation; Prosodic
Syllable, 103, 104, 200–201, 258, 259, 267, 291–293, 302, 326
Symbol(ic), 2, 217, 220, 221–227, 229–231, 233–236, 252–255, 261, 262, 268–270, 279, 282, 298, 316, 320, 326, 329, 330, 331, 332, 333, 334, 369, 373–374, 406, 408, 411, 428–429, 430, 435, 453, 454, 455, 460–461
Symmetry: in body position, 133, 144; in social relations, 396–400, 407, 410; in sociocultural systems, 460
Synchrony: of behavior, 26–27, 95–123, 179, 256, 266, 289–290, 420–421, 457–458, 466; of learning, 243–247
Syria, 393
Systems: behavioral, 5, 7, 12–13, 14, 251–256, 317, 478; category, 3–4; communicative, 102–103, 106, 108, 199, 201–211, 251–256, 264, 268–273, 278, 285–290, 294, 340, 343, 357, 362, 363, 380, 389, 416–420, 428, 457–469; conceptual, 268–273; endocrine-neyral, 418; epistemological, 70–71; general, 71–87, 101, 199, genetic-cultural, 70; material organization, 318, 325, 329; sensory, 316; social, 368, 422, 438, 460, 484; summary, 415–423; turn, 201–211

Tactile interaction, 75, 79, 161, 165, 166, 168, 169, 219, 229, 252, 287, 290, 416, 431, 433, 435, 436, 444–447, 452, 455
Talking to man (Erickson), 175
Tape. *See* Audiotape
Teeth, 152–154, 193
Telephone, 54, 243, 290, 305
Territoriality, 80–81, 166, 225–227, 357–380, 396–397, 399
Territory, 84, 159–172, 357–380, 396–397, 399, 408, 478
Theory, 19–43, 339, 458; communications, 2; communicative interaction, 3–4, 7, 13–14, 19–43, 47–62, 63–87, 127–129, 217, 277–283, 315–316, 339–348, 357–358, 428; learning, 241–250, 270–273; linguistic, 12–13, 47–62, 241–250, 259–260, 277–283, 315–316, 458; psychological, 370; systems, 2, 68, 71–87, 101
Time, 2–3, 49, 68, 74, 80, 83–87, 95, 109–111, 116, 128, 217–218, 220, 222, 321–329, 330, 333–335, 342–343, 346, 409, 415, 416, 421, 478; sharing, 10, 362, 368, 376. *See also* Duration
Times. *See* Occasions
Tokyo, 427
Tongue, 26, 29, 37, 38, 39, 152–154, 190–191, 193, 303–312
Tonic effect, 127–142
Touch. *See* Tactile interaction
Tradition in science, 19–24, 27, 43, 50–53, 61, 63–71, 83–87
Transcription, 10, 12, 23, 179, 277–278, 294–296, 300–301, 319–321, 329, 484
Tunisia, 393
Turkey, 393
Turn: conversational, 4, 9–11, 61, 62, 71–73, 152, 189–195, 199–211, 289–290, 296; interactional, 65, 289–290, 296, 297, 304–312; game, 407–408, 409

United States, 39, 66, 160, 161, 163, 164, 165, 166, 169, 170, 171, 175, 176, 216, 242, 245, 246, 249, 291–292, 305, 306, 315, 404, 427–455, 462, 468, 469. *See also* Names of individual states
Units in study of behavior, 2–4, 11–12, 67, 77, 79–80, 100–102, 103–107, 109, 113–123, 129–130, 142–143, 176, 179, 183, 189–191, 199–211, 220, 249–250, 257, 272, 279, 415, 418–420, 473, 485
University of California, San Francisco, 127
University of Florence, Italy, 246
University of Manchester, 389
University of Minnesota, 24, 38
University of New Brunswick, 285
University of Virginia, 152
USSR 345, 347, 348

Verbal behavior 20, 72–79, 102, 108–109, 166, 175–179, 183–186, 189–195, 199–211, 215–236, 241–250, 251–273, 277–283, 285–312, 316–337, 379, 400, 408, 416–420, 430–444, 447–455, 462, 466

Videotape, 7, 11, 130–131, 167, 176–177, 179–180, 182, 194–195, 200, 253, 317–319, 325, 330, 374–375, 483, 484–
Virginia, 151, 152, 153
Visual input, 25, 28–30, 35, 135–141, 317, 327, 334–335
Vocalization, 4–5, 12–13, 20, 28–31, 109, 110, 118, 119–120, 204, 245, 249–250, 254, 257, 258, 260, 263, 271, 272, 285–312, 466
Voices from the bottom of the world (Walker), 256

Washington, D.C., 317, 333
West Indies, 169
Whistling, 299–300, 303–304
Withness, 167–168, 169
Women. *See* Female
Work activity, 398–390, 395, 398–401, 405, 409, 461, 463–465

X-ray cinema film, 483

Yemen, 393, 406

DATE DUE

MAY 0 9 2005			

Demco, Inc. 38-293